GAMES NATIONS PLAY

SIXTH EDITION

GAMES NATIONS PLAY

SIXTH EDITION

John Spanier

University of Florida

PRESS

A Division of Congressional Quarterly Inc.
1414 22nd Street N.W., Washington, D.C. 20037

Excerpt on pages 435-436: From *The Great Ascent: The Struggle for Economic Development in Our Time* by Robert L. Heilbroner, 33-36. Copyright © 1963 by Robert L. Heilbroner. Reprinted by permission of Harper & Row, Publishers, Inc.

Illustration acknowledgments: Figure 2-2, reprinted with permission of *The Encyclopedia Americana*, © 1986 by Grolier Inc.; Figure 7-1, Department of State Bulletin, "World Population: The Silent Explosion," Fall 1978, 353; Figure 8-1, Center for Defense, *The Defense Monitor*, February 1979; Figure 8-2, Bureau of Public Affairs, Department of State, *Atlas of NATO*, 1985, 10; Figures 12-1 and 12-2, U.S. Arms Control and Disarmament Agency, *World Military Expenditures and Arms Transfers*, 1985, 9; Figure 12-3, Bureau of Public Affairs, Department of State, *International Terrorism*, 1985, 11; Figure 14-2, Department of State, *The Trade Debate*, inside front cover; Figure 18-1, Arms Control and Disarmament Agency, *World Military Expenditures and Arms Transfers*, 1985, 3.

Library of Congress Cataloging-in-Publication Data

Spanier, John W.
    Games nations play.

    Bibliography: p.
    Includes index.
    1. International relations.   I. Title.
JX1391.S7   1987   327   86-29167
ISBN-0-87187-400-8

Contents

Part Two

THE STATE SYSTEM

CHAPTER 7

The Ability to Play: Power and Intentions   161

Part Three

HOW TO PLAY—POLITICALLY, MILITARILY, ECONOMICALLY

CHAPTER 8

The Balance of Terror   203

CHAPTER 9

Crisis Management   240

Part Four

THE SECOND AND THIRD LEVELS

CHAPTER 13

National and Elite Styles in Foreign Policy: American and Soviet Perceptions and Behavior   385

CHAPTER 14

The Less-Developed Countries: The Primacy of Domestic Concerns   431

Part Five

FROM STATE SYSTEM
TO INTERDEPENDENCE

CHAPTER 19

Peace Through the Transformation of the State System   626

CHAPTER 20

Interdependence as a Substitute for Power Politics   651

CHAPTER 21

The Primacy of Realism   673

Glossary   I

Bibliography   XI

Index   XXIII

Figures

Tables

Preface

This sixth edition of *Games Nations Play* is new in two distinctive ways. First, it is published by CQ Press, a prestigious political science publisher. I am very happy to be one of CQ's authors and hope that this edition will be followed by many others. Second, and more important, the sixth edition has been extensively revised and rewritten. The new first chapter explains how thinking about war led to more rigorous thinking and theorizing about international politics. The final chapter is also new; it is, I believe, a persuasive argument for the realist approach as central to an understanding of world politics even in an age of interdependence. Many other new sections have been added—on order and justice, on the Strategic Defense Initiative, on the nature of the nuclear arms race, and on the failures of the Western and Soviet models of development for Third World nations. Even where subheadings are unchanged, the material has been extensively revised and updated.

Overall, this edition demonstrates more clearly than the previous five "where I'm coming from." It makes a stronger and more articulate case for realism as a key to analyzing international politics, but its purpose is still to teach the reader—primarily the college student—how to think about the subject. Most undergraduates take courses in international politics to gain some understanding of the contemporary world and, in particular, of the role their country plays. Many students are interested in learning more about particular events and issues, such as the cold war, détente, Afghanistan, Iran, OPEC, the Middle East, SALT, or terrorism. But once this information has been acquired, what will students make of it? It is my hope to provide them with the intellectual tools to analyze events for themselves and gain a deeper understanding of some of the external and internal forces that states confront and the reasons they act as they do, whether they are capitalist or Communist, highly industrialized or economically underdeveloped.

This book is fundamentally about the "games nations play," the strategies and tactics states devise to maintain their security and achieve their objectives. There are many different ways to understand this subject, and, to give students a greater insight into the complexities of international politics, I employ three levels of analysis. The first focuses on the state system and emphasizes the balance of power among nations. The second focuses on nations themselves, with emphasis on their domestic character. The third deals with the decision-making system, which derives from both the policy makers' perceptions of reality and the institutions that formulate and execute policy. This three-dimensional approach, which involves a modification of Kenneth N. Waltz's "three images" and J. David Singer's "levels of analysis," enables students to view a single policy or set of policies from three different—and often conflicting—perspectives.

The threefold scheme also reflects my own view that international events must be analyzed in the context of the state system, the environment in which they occur. This is basic. But the analyst also must pay attention to the goals of nations and their general behavior patterns as these patterns are shaped by their societies and specific policy makers. The environment has a powerful impact upon states—for example, upon their objectives and their degrees of choice among alternative policies—but their internal character and politics also exert major influences. We can paraphrase Carl von Clausewitz's remark that war is the continuation of politics by other means and say that foreign policy often is the conduct of domestic politics by other means.

The state system has endured and states have been the primary international actors for more than three hundred years. My emphasis on the nation-state, however, does not imply a neglect of nonstate actors, transnational forces, or analysis of "world order" politics. The economic, technological, and other forces of change in the contemporary world are thoroughly discussed. Nevertheless, I contend that the state-centered system has not only survived but also is in some respects stronger than ever. Many years ago Arnold Wolfers suggested that

> it is an open question which is the most striking feature of the international order—the extent and rapidity of change or the astonishing persistence of tradition. As a matter of fact, if one can criticize some recent studies it is not because they fail to take account of change but because they exaggerate its impact to the point of losing sight of the aspects of continuity and of successful resistance to change that are equally conspicuous in our day.[1]

My views on this matter will be found in Chapters 20 (on interdependence) and 21 (on the continuing relevance of the realist approach to international politics).

It should be clear, then, that this is not a book on American foreign policy or contemporary diplomatic history, but, for several reasons, a sufficient amount of historical material is interwoven. The first is to give the student a picture of the modern era. A knowledge of history, of the forces and events that have shaped the present will provide students with a better understanding of unfolding events. Second, this knowledge and perspective should assist students in assessing the importance of the changes taking place within the state system. Third, and most important, analytical frameworks and concepts do not exist in a vacuum; they are based on events that have had the most profound and far-reaching effects. Some years ago William Newman wrote that "history is useless, or even in a very real sense nonexistent, without some degree of conceptualization of what is to be looked for; at the same time the true meaning and understanding of a concept can only come from a detailed knowledge of those events that are relevant to that concept." [2]

An author is indebted to many people. I am grateful to the undergraduates at the University of Florida, who over the years have taken my introductory international politics course, have been exposed to a number of different ways of organizing the material, and have been kind and gentle in suggesting helpful improvements and criticisms. A special word of thanks is also due to Robert Wood at the U.S. Naval War College, whose critiques of the overall structure of the book over several editions have been perceptive and constructive; to Timothy Lomperis of Duke University, whose detailed criticisms of the draft of this edition were very insightful and helpful; to Joseph Nogee of the University of Houston, who has never failed to let me know what improvements I should make; to CQ Press director Joanne Daniels, who wanted this book and did everything she could to make it an even better book; and to Carolyn Goldinger, whose superb editing and hard work exceeded what any author has a right to expect. With their help I hope I have succeeded in making this sixth edition an important text on international politics.

J.S.

Gainesville, Florida
January 1987

Notes

1. Arnold Wolfers, *Discord and Collaboration* (Baltimore: Johns Hopkins University Press, 1962), xvii.
2. William J. Newman, *The Balance of Power in the Inter-War Years, 1919-1939* (New York: Random House, 1968), ix.

Part One

THE STUDY AND ANALYSIS OF INTERNATIONAL POLITICS

CHAPTER 1

War and Thinking About International Politics

Conflict and war historically have been the chief characteristics of international politics and now threaten the end of civilization. The destructiveness of war has grown so enormously as a result of nationalism, industrialization, and technological innovation, it has been observed, that the world may be living in the Indian summer of its existence, to be followed by a "nuclear winter," which will end man's history.[1] This possibility was apparent as early as World War I. When the carnage of that war ended in 1918, Winston Churchill, who was later to become Great Britain's prime minister, wrote, "Mankind has got into its hands for the first time the tools by which it can unfailingly accomplish its own extermination. . . . Death stands at attention, obedient, expectant, . . . ready, if called on, to pulverise, without hope of repair, what is left of civilisation. He awaits only the word of command. He awaits it from a frail, bewildered being, long his victim, now—for one occasion only—his Master."[2]

Although war, not surprisingly, is often regarded as somehow abnormal—at best an awful error, at worst a criminal undertaking—the fact is that the history of war is as old as human history. If it is to be regarded as a pathological deviation from the norm of harmony and peace among states, then all conflict must be similarly regarded. For war is only the kind of conflict that occurs among a particular type of social group—sovereign states.[3] "War is a clash between major interests that is resolved by bloodshed—that is the only way in which it differs from other conflicts."[4] It is this difference that in this century has greatly influenced thinking about international politics. Theories do not arise in a vacuum. They are very much related to the experiences of society. That is why we shall first look at the impact of war in this century and then at some of the principal schools of thought about

3

international conflict and war. That examination will place the discipline, as well as the approaches in this book, in perspective.

THE IMPACT OF WORLD WAR I

World War I was a cataclysmic experience for Europe. With the exception of the French Revolution, World War I was the first total war Europe had experienced since the Treaty of Westphalia (1648) ended the slaughter of the Thirty Years' War. To be sure, Europe had witnessed a number of wars during the nineteenth century, but these had been minor and of brief duration. World War I also was expected to last only a few months, and casualties were expected to be no heavier than in past wars. But, after the almost one hundred years of relative peace that followed the Congress of Vienna in 1815, which brought the war with Napoleon to a close, Europe suffered the shock of a four-year total war and a terrible bloodletting. Once Germany's initial offensive into France was halted, the war on the western front bogged down in trenches. First one side, then the other tried to break through the opponent's lines, but neither could do so. Successive lines of barbed wire protected each side's trenches. The murderous machine-gun and rapid rifle fire mowed down row after row of advancing infantry. Breakthroughs became impossible.

Yet the offensives continued. The generals had learned, after all, that the only defense was the offense—*l'attaque à l'outrance*. So headquarters continued to hurl their armies into battles. The artillery first laid down a barrage, sometimes lasting a week or longer, on the opponent's trenches. This was supposed to pulverize the enemy's position and shatter the morale of the troops. It was a simple idea that should have worked but never did. Killing became the objective. If enemy lines could not be ruptured, at least the enemy could be worn down by the various offensives. Sooner or later, these constant blows would wear down manpower reserves, and morale would collapse. World War I was not a war of mobility and maneuver, but a war of attrition—an organized, four-year-long attempt by both sides to gain victory simply by bleeding each other to death. It was an unsophisticated strategy.

The French lost 955,000 men in five months of 1914—more than 200,000 of them during the first month; in 1915, 1,430,000 men; and in 1916, 900,000 men. The losses for single battles were staggering. The German attempt to bleed the French at Verdun led to a ten-month battle costing France 535,000 casualties and Germany 427,000—almost a million men altogether. A British attempt to pierce German lines in the same year, 1916, resulted in the five-month Battle of the Somme. Although they pounded the German lines with artillery for eight days before the troops were sent into battle, the British gained only 120 square miles—at the cost of 420,000 men, or 3,500 per square mile. The Germans lost 445,000 men. Some estimates place the total Somme casualties at 1.2 million, the highest for any battle in history. At Ypres in 1917, the British bombardment lasted nineteen days; 321 trainloads of shells were fired, the equivalent of a year's production by 55,000 war workers. This time the English forces captured forty-five square miles—at the cost of 370,000 men, or 8,222 per square mile. By comparison, total British Empire casualties during the six years of World War II were almost 1.25 million, including 350,000 dead and 91,000 missing. Approximately 9 million men in uniform were killed during the four years of the Great War, as World War I was called, and the number of dead civilians totaled an additional several million.[5]

But the impact of war cannot be measured merely by citing statistics of the dead. The real impact must be understood psychologically. Losses are not just quantitative; they are qualitative as well. A nation can ill afford to lose millions of men, nor can it afford to lose almost an entire generation. Is it any wonder that the nations of Europe, which lost so many of their men—young men who would have fathered children—also lost their élan, their self-confidence, their hope for the future? For those who would have supplied this vigor and optimism—had they grown up and become the leaders of government, business, labor, and science—lay dead in Flanders Field.

For Europe, then, the Great War was the Great Divide. The nineteenth century had been one of confidence. Democracy was spreading in Europe and was expected to spread to all other continents, too, as soon as colonialism had prepared the natives of Asia and Africa for self-government. The future would belong to the common people; their rights and freedom would supplant the traditional privileges of the few. For the first time in history, people would join together across national boundaries, in a new world of mutual understanding and good will. Peace would be both inevitable and permanent. Science and technology would improve everyone's standard of living; the age-old economics of scarcity would be transformed into an economics of abundance and affluence. Poverty and misery would be ended forever. This optimism and faith in progress was aptly voiced by an American, Andrew Carnegie, in his instructions to the trustees of the Carnegie Endowment for International Peace: "When ... war is discarded as disgraceful to civilized man, the trustees will please then consider what is the next most degrading evil or evils whose banishment ... would most advance the progress, elevation and happiness of man." [6] It was just a matter of time, then, until war would be eliminated. It would have been contrary to the spirit of the age to ask whether this abolition of war could indeed be achieved.

The Great War changed this optimism to pessimism, this confidence to doubt and fear. The West's utter certainty of its own greatness and future lay shattered on the battlefields among the decaying corpses. For the first time, Western scholars talked about the "decline of the West." Europe's imperial control was weakened abroad, and at home the expected trend toward democracy was halted, if not reversed. Facism took over in Italy, Nazism gained power in Germany, and Benito Mussolini and Adolf Hitler together helped Francisco Franco seize control of Spain. In Eastern Europe, only Czechoslovakia could be considered a democratic country. The nineteenth century had believed in the supremacy of reason and its ability to make the world a safer and better place in which to live. In the interwar period, demagoguery and the manipulation of hysterical crowds, totalitarianism and its warlike spirit, seemed the wave of the future.

As the structure and hopes of the previous one hundred years began to crash all around them, the leaders of France and England became concerned above all with avoiding another war. "No more war, no more war" became their cry. And who could blame them? These leaders were concerned not merely with their personal survival. They were men of honorable intentions and decent motives, greatly concerned for the welfare of their citizens and repelled by the horror and senselessness of modern war. It is easy today to sneer at the appeasement of Hitler, but, to the survivors of World War I, another war could only mean the slaughter and seemingly wasteful sacrifices of Verdun and the Somme. They still heard the "soldiers marching, all to die." And they remembered that the strain of that war had collapsed four of Europe's great empires: Austria-Hungary, Ottoman Turkey, Imperial Russia, and Imperial Germany. They also recalled that, despite Germany's grievous losses, its European opponents had suffered twice as many losses—and their populations were smaller than Germany's. If fighting another war involved another such blood bath, surely they would be signing their nations' death warrants. Their social structures and morale could not absorb such losses for the second time in two generations. To most people who had lived through the tragic war years, peace became a supreme value. The appeasement of Hitler during the 1930s was to them not just the only policy—it was an absolute necessity. Surely it was saner to resolve differences with reason than with guns. Would it not be better to understand each other's legitimate grievances and settle differences in a spirit of good will rather than by war? Was it not preferable to make mutual concessions, thereby diminishing distrust and fear, and build the mutual confidence that could be the only basis of a firm peace? To ask these questions was to answer them for most of the survivors of World War I. Between the alternatives of appeasement and war, no one of good will and humanity had a choice.

RETHINKING MILITARY STRATEGY

Thus, Hitler was appeased because the predominant mood and policies of the political and military leaders of France and Britain were defensive. War was to be avoided at almost any cost. But if war became unavoidable, there were three concepts about how it would be fought, and each was a reaction to World War I. The French believed that the years from 1914 through 1918 had demonstrated that the defense had superiority over the offense, and, moreover, that this superiority was permanent.[7] After the losses the French had suffered, their strategists rejected offensive operations. Let the Germans launch the offensives; the French would await them in their fortified trench, the impregnable Maginot line. German assaults would be defeated with such heavy loss of life that sooner or later the Germans would desist and be exhausted. Only then would the French, together with the British and perhaps the Americans, launch an offensive to end the war. This plan in effect presupposed that the next war would be a repetition of World War I: a static trench war. Since people tend to think of the future in terms of the past—for past experience provides them with their principal guidelines—the French conception of the next war and preparation for it seemed quite logical.

The Germans also rethought their approach to war, expecting this war to be brief and therefore less costly to bear. They would achieve this by restoring the offensive and mobility to the battlefield in a *Blitzkrieg* (lightning war).[8] Mobile land forces, largely tank divisions, in combination with tactical air power would smash the enemy's lines and break through into the open and undefended areas in the rear. The infantry would advance in the wake of this one-two punch and mop up the enemy's broken and confused forces. In short, the German military leaders, unlike their French and British—and, indeed, American—counterparts, accurately comprehended the impact on military tactics of airplanes and tanks, which had appeared late in the previous war. They realized their possibilities and thought of a unique manner in which a combination of the two could restore to warfare the mobility that had been lost during the Great War at such an enormous cost of life.

Both of these reactions to World War I, different as they were, shared one fundamental assumption: that the decisive engagements of a future war would be fought on land. Another view of the conduct of warfare rejected this assumption, maintaining that the key battles would be fought in the air. Thus, the interwar years witnessed the birth of the concept of strategic air power. In a sense, this new concept of warfare was the counterpart of the French Maginot line psychology. If, as World War I had shown, the defensive forces had gained a seemingly permanent superiority over the offensive forces, then the only quick and effective way of breaking the stalemate on land and of achieving victory was to attack the enemy's home front from the air. The target would be cities, and, if these were heavily bombed, two objectives would be achieved. First, the industrial strength that sustained the troops in the field would be smashed, and second, the morale of the civilians—presumably less hardened to the rigors of war than front-line soldiers—would be broken. General Giulio Douhet, the Italian "founder" and theorist of strategic air power, described it:

> Take the center of a large city and imagine what would happen among the civilian population during a single attack by a single bombing unit. For my part, I have no doubt that its impact upon the people would be terrible. . . .
>
> What could happen to a single city in a single day could also happen to ten, twenty, fifty cities. And, since news travels fast, even without telegraph, telephone, or radio, what, I ask you, would be the effect upon civilians of other cities, not yet stricken, but equally subject to bombing attacks? What civil or military authority

could keep order, public services functioning, and production going under such a threat? And even if a semblance of order was maintained and some work done, would not the sight of a single enemy plane be enough to stampede the population into panic? In short, normal life would be impossible in this constant nightmare of imminent death and destruction. And if on the second day another ten, twenty, or fifty cities were bombed, who could keep all those lost, panic-stricken people from fleeing to the open countryside to escape this terror from the air?

A complete breakdown of the social structure cannot but take place in a country subjected to this kind of merciless pounding from the air.[9]

The role of the army and navy was to be strictly subsidiary: to perform a holding operation on the ground while the air force pulverized the enemy's urban and industrial centers and compelled the enemy to surrender. For all practical purposes airpower could win the next war all by itself.

Actually, for all their destructiveness, neither German bombers nor British and American bombers during World War II succeeded in stopping the other side's war production or in breaking civilian morale. The results of city bombing were disappointing. But late in the war, strategic air power came into its own and its impact was devastating. The targets of the Allies' air forces were transportation complexes and centers of the chemical-synthetic oil industry, both of which proved extremely vulnerable. Road, railroad, and canal transportation were brought to a virtual standstill. For a highly developed, interdependent economy, this proved fatal. How could the coal that stoked the furnaces be brought to the factories? And how could more weapons and ammunition be brought to the front? Moreover, the attacks on the oil industry reduced production drastically, and production of motor and aviation fuel was even more seriously affected. Thus, while fighter-aircraft production rose, there was less and less gasoline available for flight training or combat flying. Similarly, German tanks lacked sufficient fuel, and this shortage severely hampered their effectiveness in battle.

In the final stage of the war in Europe, strategic air power achieved the kind of impact predicted by Douhet. He provided a theory that was to guide action, but its real capabilities and limitations were not understood before World War II. Comprehension came with experience. The switch from general city bombing to selective bombing demonstrated how effective bombers could be in collapsing a modern economy and halting a military machine— provided the right targets were chosen.[10] With the atomic bomb, however, selecting the right kind of target became less critical. One bomb could destroy virtually a whole city. Hiroshima and Nagasaki proved Douhet's grim prophecy all too correct. Strategic air power had become decisive.

Bombers carrying nuclear weapons threatened those powers that might be tempted to launch a nuclear war with the possibility of committing suicide. War long had been an instrument of state policy. Whatever its costs, it had been considered a legitimate and functional institution, allowing states to defend their independence and to realize the ambitions they harbored. After 1945, the future utility of war was widely questioned. What was the point of defending one's way of life if, in the process, that way of life was utterly destroyed. Total war became irrational; the costs of such a war completely exceeded any conceivable gains. One knew that without even having to fight. Had the leaders of Europe, who went to war in 1914, been able to look into a crystal ball and foresee what the costs would be, they might have chosen a different course. Today, we have that crystal ball.[11]

THE GAMES NATIONS PLAY

The problem is that war cannot be isolated from conflict in general. To be specific, war has been the way states have transacted their business. Despite the growing costs of war in the twentieth century, the "games nations play" continue.[12] The reason why we use the games analogy is the existence of a system in which the principal players, states, reject any higher authority. Each state, like any player in a competitive game, seeks to advance its own interests in conflict with those of other states; in this pursuit of its "national interests," it will resort to the use of force if it cannot achieve or defend its goals in any other way. States play these games, of course, with different capabilities; the main players historically have been the most powerful states. The stakes or payoffs in these games are critical: survival, a degree of security, influence, and status, as well as wealth are some of the principal ones.

Because each state looks at the world from its particular perspective and must plan its moves—its strategy—to enhance its security and other objectives, the games analogy is an apt one. Each is a player, and each plays "to win" in a game in which it competes with almost 170 other nations. And although the great powers have in the past been the chief players, today other countries, such as Libya, Syria, Vietnam, Egypt, Israel, and many other less influential nations, are quite active in the game. Each must therefore concern itself with competing effectively, especially with those states that are its immediate rivals. In this context, the term *strategy* is not defined in its usual narrow military sense, referring to winning a war, but as a set of calculated moves, a set of decisions, in a competitive and conflictual situation where the outcome is not governed by pure chance.[13] In other words, we are using the idea of strategy as we would use it when we talk of playing chess or football, games that are governed by known formal rules, or politics or dating, activities governed mainly by informal rules. In international politics, as John Lovell said, each state seeks to advance its "national interests" in conflict with those of other states in a game whose rules are largely informal and unwritten, evolving mainly through the behavior of the strongest players.[14]

A state may advance its interests offensively, as, for example, the Reagan administration did in supporting insurgencies in Afghanistan, Angola, and Nicaragua against pro-Soviet regimes; it may do so defensively, as in American deterrence policy. In either case, the players must carefully weigh the alternative means of achieving their objectives and then choose the option that will maximize their gains and minimize losses, as well as their risks and costs.

Thus, there are lots of games going on, such as *adversary games*, in which two or more states are engaged in conflict, and *alignment games*, in which states seek help from other states and/or seek to attract allies away from their adversaries either in a straight de-alignment or a realignment toward themselves. Just as the alignment game is subsidiary to the adversary game, so too is the arms competition or *arms race game*, in which adversaries seek at minimum to stay even with their opponents' strengths or, at maximum, to gain superiority.[15] Another is the *economic game*, played because maintaining a state's well-being usually requires it to import goods and materials, as well as to export and, ideally, to maintain a balance between the two. The basic game, however, which historically has constituted the essence of international politics, is the great-power adversary *political-military game*. In a decentralized system of sovereign states, the lack of a superior and legitimate world government, to allocate political, military, and economic goods peacefully and manage the political and economic relations among states peacefully, ensures the survival of the state system, "the womb in which war develops."[16]

Thus, as must be clear by now, international politics refers to the relations or interactions among states, although states are not the only players. Our main concern with nongovernmental actors is their impact on the relations between states, the primary actors. Still, the field of international politics, despite the focus on states, is so broad that it has been half-jestingly suggested that none can prove its existence.[17] In any field of study it should be reasonably clear what is part of the subject matter and what is not. Yet international politics is a field invaded by historians, political scientists, economists, psychologists, mathematicians, and, lately, physicians, and the clergy, such as the American Catholic and Methodist bishops who have declared that the use of nuclear weapons, and perhaps even their possession, is immoral. Obviously, it must be an interesting, even fascinating, field to attract such a menagerie! But it is also obvious that, whether it is the bomb and the danger that it poses for all humanity, or the rise of oil prices, which in the 1970s caused such high unemployment, inflation, and economic stagnation in the Western industrial states, or in the 1980s the frequency of terrorism, whether carried out by nongovernmental groups or sponsored by certain nations seeking to affect the policies of other nations, we are talking mainly of the behavior of states. More specifically, international politics focuses on "who gets what, when, and how" (see Chapter 5).

Now that we have defined what the essence of international politics is all about, how can we understand it? The answer depends on how we study it. Let us now briefly examine some of the principal ways this has been done.

THEORIZING ABOUT INTERSTATE RELATIONS

The Historical Approach

The years before World War I were, as already noted, a time of optimism. To be sure, there were wars, but they were limited in objective and duration. The three wars of German unification of 1862, 1866, and 1870 (against Denmark, Austria-Hungary, and France, respectively) were seen as models for future wars. When the European powers went to war in August 1914, they expected the "boys" would be home by the time the leaves fell from the trees.

Before the outbreak of World War I, not much attention was given to a theory of international politics. Indeed, international politics was never a preoccupation of Western political thought, which focused primarily on domestic issues. Thinking about conflict among states was largely intermittent and fragmentary. By contrast, Western thinking about order, justice, and liberty within these states has been continuous and well developed; we find these subjects in the works of Plato and Aristotle. Before the twentieth century, however, we know of only a handful of writers whose works on interstate politics have become classics: Thucydides, who wrote about the war between Athens and Sparta in ancient Greece; Niccolò Machiavelli, who sought to advise a prince on how to unify Italy; and Thomas Hobbes, an English philosopher who speculated about the life of man in a state of nature. One could add a few names like Polybius, who wrote about the war between Rome and Carthage; David Hume, who wrote on the balance of power; and Hugo Grotius, who wrote extensively about international law.

If there was a focus at all, it was diplomatic history. In a sense, this was international politics because it recounted what had transpired between nations in the past. But in another sense, diplomatic history cannot be equated with a theory of international politics. Discovering what happened in the years immediately before 1914 can yield an enormous amount of information on specific political and military leaders, the political climate and social and economic conditions within specific countries, their planned military strategies and armaments, and how all these interacted to produce World War I. This is not to say that some of the issues, such as why the war occurred or who was most responsible for it, will ever be settled; historians in each generation tend to reinterpret earlier events. Nevertheless, diplomatic history can tell us much about such events.

That is precisely its shortcoming. Historians focus on the description of specific events, which are unique to that time and place. While they can tell us how and why a specific war happened, they do not tell us why wars occur more generally. A theory of international politics would attempt to answer this question. Such a theory would not look at each war as unique, but would analyze many wars. It would then specify from the data what specific conditions seem repeatedly to result in war. For example, if the study of half a dozen wars showed that the victors four times out of six fell out with each other, leading to a new struggle and possibly war, we could generalize and state: if, at the end of hostilities, the victors cannot agree on peace terms—or, more crudely, a division of the spoils—a new war may result. Of course, war may not break out each time this situation occurs, but, if it happened sufficiently often in the past, it is likely to recur enough times in the future. Other conditions that have led to war also can be identified. It took the trauma of World War I, however, to bring about a more sustained search for a theory of international politics. As a discipline, international politics is a product of the twentieth century and, to a large extent, a product of American scholarship.

Utopianism or Political Idealism

World War I was a shock for Europe, the worse for not having been expected. Why had it occurred? How could such a "senseless slaughter" have gone on? Alliances, arms races, and secret diplomacy frequently were cited as the causes. "Power politics" were blamed; it was alleged that all the great powers had recklessly pursued their national interests. Not surprisingly, the beginning of thinking about international politics started with utopian aspirations: there must be no recurrence of world war. Thus, the motive spurring on the initial theorizing was the passionate desire to avoid another war.[18] War was a disease infecting the body politic; it had to be cut out. But wishing prevailed over careful analysis, and the focus was on the end to be achieved. President Woodrow Wilson typified this mood. On his way to Paris to attend the postwar peace conference, Wilson was asked whether his plan for a League of Nations to keep the peace would work. He replied, "If it won't work, it must be made to work." [19]

The resulting study of international politics concentrated on three different approaches. First, there was the emphasis on the League of Nations, in which the nations of the world would be represented. This would create a forum where the negotiations and debates could be observed by the publics of all countries, making it impossible for secret diplomacy to produce another war. The assumption was that national leaders, unrestrained by public opinion, might intrigue again in the future; ordinary people, who did the fighting and dying, were believed to be peaceful and would therefore watch for and prevent agreements secretly made. Agreements or covenants were to be arrived at openly. It was hoped, therefore, that nations would cooperate within the league's framework, deemphasizing their nations' egotisms and selfish interests. Second, there were disarmament conferences that aimed to reduce, if not eliminate, the number of arms possessed by the great powers. Examples include German disarmament in the Treaty of Versailles (1919) and the Washington Naval Conference (1921-22), limiting naval rivalry in the Pacific. Third, there were legal efforts to decrease the likelihood of war. A specific American contribution was the Kellogg-Briand Pact (1928), which for the first time outlawed war as an instrument of state policy—except, of course, wars conducted in "self-defense." Collectively, the twenty years between two world wars were a time when thinking about international politics, both academically and popularly, in the English-speaking world was characterized by the almost complete neglect of power.

The search for an end to war was accompanied by a political shift in the domestic policies of most of the countries, especially Britain and France, which, until World War I, had often been belligerents. This political change was to have a profound impact on the conduct of foreign policy. Before 1914, the conduct of foreign policy had been left basically to the diplomats and soldiers. Foreign policy was not usually regarded as a matter for popular opinion and party politics, but as a matter for experts. This was as true for the democracies as for the more autocratic states like Germany or czarist Russia. But after the slaughter of World War I, the people of the Western democracies, who had suffered so much, wanted control over foreign policy as they had over domestic policy. Georges Clemenceau, France's premier, spoke a line that was to become famous: "War," he said, "was too important to be left to the generals," and foreign policy, he implied, for the diplomats. In short, foreign policy was now, like domestic politics, to be subjected to popular accountability. The result was twofold: first, a vengeful public opinion in Britain and France was a major reason for the punitive peace treaty imposed on Germany in 1919, and, second, during the 1930s a fearful public opinion was the reason for the appeasement of Hitler, and it made a policy of opposition to Germany—as well as to Italy and Japan—impossible. The public yearning for peace ironically produced the same result that the soldiers and diplomats had produced earlier.

Realism

Just as World War I was blamed on power politics, after World War II it was widely believed that war had been caused by the neglect of power. If an arms race and close alliances were thought to be responsible for the hostilities of 1914-18, the failure of the British and French to match German arms and to stand together against Hitler precipitated what Churchill was to call the "unnecessary war." [20] Realism was the reaction to interwar idealism. If war was to be prevented, more than wishful thinking was needed. The reality was that there were ambitious and warlike states that were unappeasable, that had to be opposed, and that this required, among other things, a willingness to risk war and strong military forces to support a policy of deterrence. To fear risking war left the states that most desired peace at the mercy of the more ruthless states; not to build the required strength to avoid provoking a potential aggressor left a state with no choice but to submit to an aggressor's demands and to become a victim.

Realism was to become the dominant school of thinking in postwar America, now the West's chief defender against the Soviet Union. Realism resurrected traditional ideas: that states were the primary actors in international politics; that the environment or state system in which states lived was essentially anarchical; that conflict in this system could at best be managed to reduce the likelihood of war, but war could not be abolished. The central point was that there was no final solution to the problem of war. Appeals to humanity's common interest in survival, appeals to replace the state system with some form of world government, were all in vain. The management of the system had to be rooted in every state's "national interest"; the best way of preserving peace was therefore the balance of power. The key to the conduct of foreign policy was prudence: states need to be cautious, not launch crusades against one another; they also had to be flexible and accommodating in their diplomacy. The key figures in the realist revolution were Hans Morgenthau, a German refugee scholar; George Kennan, a U.S. diplomat and historian of Russia; and Reinhold Niebuhr, a Protestant minister.

Realism, however, soon came under attack. For one thing, realism became identified with Morgenthau, whose book *Politics among Nations* had a profound influence in American academia.[21] The works of more sophisticated analysts, like Arnold Wolfers, John Herz, Kennan, and Niebuhr, were largely overlooked at first.[22] One frequent criticism of Morgenthau and, therefore, of realism in general, was that, although it claimed to describe international politics as it was and not in utopian terms, its frequent advice to policy makers on the conduct of foreign policy suggested that states did not in fact behave as the realists described. A second criticism was that, despite their common outlook, realists often disagreed with one another. For example, Morgenthau surprisingly came out early against U.S. intervention in Vietnam, but others supported that policy. Such disagreements raised questions about the value of realism as a guide to making the "correct" foreign policy. Most of all, perhaps, the realist outlook was alien to the American outlook. The emphasis on power, the acceptance of conflict and war as natural rather than abnormal and transitory, was "un-American," as we shall see in Chapter 13 and in the concluding chapter. Realism was especially offensive because it appeared at best amoral, if not downright immoral, in a country that prides itself on being a morally superior nation and that often feels guilty when its foreign policy is not—or does not appear to be—moral.

The Behavioral Method

Both idealism and realism supplied a unifying focus. What followed in the 1960s and 1970s had no such focus. Rather, what displaced realism—or attempted to do so—was a host of different approaches, some of which were called theories, and others, more cautiously, pretheories. Most were characterized by their way of investigating international politics. The word *investigating* is a clue to the alleged new approach. Utopianism had posited a purpose that had to be achieved. "The wish is father to the thought" was its origin, and its aim was to cure a "sick" international body politic. The actual behavior of states was not a matter for investigation; that behavior was all too clear and it had to be changed! Realism, by contrast, asserted that the twenty years from 1919 to 1939 demonstrated conclusively that the Western democracies' neglect of the reality of power led to the very result their behavior sought to avoid; that those states that were willing to resort to power—all antidemocratic states—threatened to become dominant; that those who believed in reason, mutual good will, and accommodation, but who were not backed by sufficient power, had to retreat and, in the final analysis, had to go to war anyway to save themselves. But the fact that realists had to advise states about how they should behave to better protect themselves suggested realism's weakness—states often acted in ways seemingly contradictory to their best interests.

This is where behaviorism entered. Rejecting both an end to be achieved and *a priori* assumptions about how states behaved, its advocates stated that their purpose was to investigate international politics without any reformist desires or biased preconceptions.[23] Their analyses would be *value free* or *empirical.* They intended to observe the many forms of state behavior, collect the necessary data, and carefully draw conclusions from their studies. In opposition to earlier researchers, who were then almost scornfully called *traditionalists,* the behaviorists claimed to be political *scientists.* Obviously, political scientists interested in international politics were part of a larger group of analysts looking at other fields, such as American and comparative politics, as well as novel areas like political methodology. Methodology was in fact the heart of the behavioral approach: how to study a particular type of human activity. And the change in the technique for studying political science was only part of a far larger movement spreading across all American social sciences.

The scientific method claimed not only an unbiased approach to research— that investigators could separate their own values from "the facts" and the manner in which they organized these facts—but also, as already suggested, it sought to generalize about the behavior of states and other political actors in the international arena. The political scientists looked for patterns of behavior such as the one mentioned earlier: when one of the victors of a war perceives that its interests are not satisfied at the postwar peace conference—or, at least, that its gains are not as great as those of some of its fellow victors—conflict results and war may occur. Or, if the defeated state harbors grievances against the victors because of the harshness of the settlement they have imposed upon it, the loser may seek to remedy this matter militarily, as well as to avenge its previous humiliation. These generalizations about the conditions under which past wars have erupted allow theorists to hypothesize that *if* the above conditions exist, *then* war results.

What especially characterized much of the behavioral inquiry during the 1950s, 1960s, and 1970s was its use of quantitative techniques, the development of formal models, the search for general "laws" of behavior, and a rather arrogant attitude toward earlier methods of research.[24] Often implicit in behaviorism's attitude was the claim that if it could not be quantified, it was not worth saying. Earlier analyses of international politics tended to be dismissed as not only traditional but impressionistic, if not poetic. Only quantitative methods, it was asserted, could be objective, free from bias, and produce accurate and verifiable empirical studies of the behavior of international actors. Despite this strong, and occasionally dogmatic, point of view, it is fair to say that even nonquantitative scholars were deeply influenced by the behavioral approach. For whatever its claims to be scientific, let alone hold the only correct approach to the truth, its essence was an emphasis on careful scholarship and analytical precision. Its goals, as two of its proponents have suggested, were to substitute verifiable knowledge for subjective belief, testable evidence for intuitive explanations, and data for appeals to "expert" or "authoritative" opinion.[25] Traditional scholars, probably feeling defensive, and also wishing to avoid being considered outside the mainstream of American political science, reacted by demonstrating greater care in their research activities.

The intensity of the battle between the traditional and scientific or empirical approaches, therefore, diminished over time. Traditional scholars showed more precision in their analyses, and at least some of the behaviorists interested in international politics were ready to admit that several charges leveled by the traditionalists were not totally unjustified. These charges included the preoccupation with what sometimes appeared to be methodology for the sake of methodology; the focus on issues to which their methods could be applied, frequently issues of a secondary or ever lesser significance, if not irrelevant; and the disregard of a world of nuclear weapons, widespread poverty, and injustice.

Even more basic, every study, no matter how carefully carried out, starts out with some assumptions. They may be implicit and the investigators may be unaware of their influence. Nevertheless, researchers' selection of facts and how the facts are organized and interpreted are hardly value free. Karl Marx, who considered himself a social scientist, began with a belief that history was the story of the class struggle between the rich and poor. He found that the voluminous statistics he collected confirmed his viewpoint. He had a picture in his mind of what reality was before he started his writing, and he organized his descriptive and analytical material accordingly.

Contemporary Approaches

Currently there are basically two schools of thought that receive much attention. Both shift the focus of analysis from politics to economics. Both are essentially nineteenth-century analyses, brought up to date and applied to contemporary conditions. One school of thought can trace its heritage to the classical liberal tradition of free trade, which was supposed to create a common interest in peace by bringing all nations a higher standard of living. War would disrupt free trade and was therefore counterproductive. In its modernized twentieth-century form, interdependence, the close linking of states to one another, also focuses on the formation of transnational economic, social, and technological bonds. Functionalism, a form of this thesis current during the 1950s, emphasized the almost automatic nature of growing ties between nations, a process that was supposed to lead to the United States of Europe.[26] In its 1970s version, the emphasis shifted from regional interdependence to global interdependence.[27] At the same time, this version of interdependence has been accompanied by two claims; one, that the economic development or modernization of states, both developed and underdeveloped, is changing the foreign policy agenda by giving priority to "low" politics, or socioeconomic issues, over "high" politics, or security and military issues; and two, that it also affects the way foreign policy is conducted—cooperative behavior rather than force.

The other perspective, somewhat alien to the other American approaches, is a contemporary version of the nineteenth-century Marxist approach, and it is called "dependency."[28] Marxism—actually, Marxism-Leninism—asserted a causal relationship between Western capitalism and imperial expansion. Dependency shares with interdependence a global outlook, but, unlike interdependence, it postulates that an international capitalist economy holds the less-developed countries (LDCs), the former colonies, in a dependency relationship as in the old colonial period. Although these nations have gained political independence, they remained economically tied to the Western industrial and capitalist states, especially the United States, for markets, capital, and technology. This relationship is an unequal one and fundamentally an exploitive one. That is why, years after achieving independence, LDCs remain economically backward. According to the theory, development will come if either capitalism is overthrown within the Western states—an unlikely prospect—or if the LDCs liberate themselves by throwing off their capitalist chains. Besides its radical approach to international politics, this school differs from interdependence in emphasizing revolution and violence to gain true "national liberation." In conclusion, this radical analysis also differs from the utopian and realist approaches by arguing that the cause of international conflict and war lies in the existence of a particular economic system; thus the struggle for power is neither the cause of war nor would its abolition be the solution for peace.

Our Approach: The Three Levels of Analysis

Theories of international politics, as we have seen, are intended to help us organize, interpret, and even predict "reality." Making any sense at all of international politics starts with learning how to cope with enormous amounts of fragmented information. Each one of us perceives reality by abstracting from the totality of experience those parts that he or she considers relevant. Our perceptions are selective. They are bound to be, for obviously no one sees every aspect of reality; the world is too complex and perplexing, so that we are forced to simplify it if we are even to begin to understand it. We all have pictures in our heads, by means of which we see the world and attempt to explain it. Our perceptions of reality are what we call *theories.* Other words, often used interchangeably with theory, are *approaches, paradigms,* or *analytical frameworks.* Whatever the words, they are a way of looking at a subject from a particular perspective—such as those described earlier. We hope they will help us organize much of that random information, select the relevant facts or data, arrange them in some intelligible order, and, as a result, assist us to interpret and understand reality or "what's going on" a bit better. If that perspective is that of the state system, with a focus on the relationships among states and the balance of power, we will see the world quite differently from those with a Marxist perspective, with its emphasis on class struggle, international capitalism, economic dominance, and dependency among states.

Each theory or approach organizes the facts differently; indeed, each is likely to pick out quite different facts. Inherent in each are certain assumptions about what features are important and what events and other factors need to be described and analyzed. Such theories may be informed and sophisticated, producing carefully formulated hypotheses as a result of precise and dispassionate observation and analysis, or they may be simple and intuitive, realizing rather crude generalizations. Indeed, some of these are based on *a priori* assumptions that the researcher assumes exist, never proves that they do, and then illustrates them with many examples. Marxism is one such approach with its doctrinaire insistence that war is the result of economic conditions, specifically the result of capitalists' search for foreign markets.

Whatever it is, a theory helps us organize and interpret the reality we call international politics. In theorizing, as we already noted, we first simplify this reality because we cannot possibly describe all aspects of international politics; we must be selective. We isolate and emphasize certain aspects of this reality and throw them into bold relief, enabling us to make a "conceptual blueprint" of the political life among states. In a sense, we act as an artist does when viewing a panorama. Artists cannot include every detail; rather, they select and highlight certain parts of the view, relegate others to the background, and omit still others. A finished picture will be the landscape as seen by an artist's eyes, from a particular physical position and mental perspective. The painting is, in this respect, a partial representation of actuality. If many intricate details are lost, that is the price we must pay for using it to help us explain and understand something else. The painting is always an "incomplete picture" emphasizing those features that someone most wanted to communicate.

We too paint a picture; indeed, to get as complete a picture of the international political landscape as possible, we view that landscape from different perspectives, or "levels of analysis." The problem is one of scope and emphasis. Our view is three dimensional, involving the state system, the nation-state, and decision making.[29] At the first level we consider the behavior of states as shaped by the international system and the rules they must respect if they are to survive and be secure. Our focus is the environment in which states live and in which their concern is with the balance of power or equilibrium. The system, it is assumed, imposes its own logic on each member state. Neglect of the balance threatens the security of states and upsets the system's equilibrium; states therefore ought to act to preserve the balance.

At the second level we explain state behavior not as the outcome of the external environment, but as a reflection of the state's nature (whether capitalist or socialist, democratic or totalitarian, developed or undeveloped). The focus here is on the individual member states rather than the system in which they all live. The concern is with the kind of economic or political system a state possesses, its degree of development, as well as factors such as its class structures, character of its elites, and "national style." The assumption is that there is a relationship between a state's domestic character and its foreign policy.

At the third level foreign policy also is explained as a product of the domestic system, but the focus is not on social, economic, political, and cultural characteristics; rather, it is on the people involved in making and executing foreign policy decisions. Similar states, for example two capitalist countries or two Communist countries, often pursue quite different policies. Therefore, it is necessary to look at the people making foreign policy, the institutions involved, and the processes of decision making to understand why specific states do what they do.

Together, these three levels give us a comprehensive picture of the "games nations play"—particularly, why they play the game, how they play it, and some of the efforts they make to regulate and moderate the game, to play it differently, or to abolish it altogether. No one level by itself presents the complete picture. The focus on individual states parallels the psychologist's concentration on the individual's personality and character. But obviously an individual's behavior can be properly understood only if it is related to the social environment—the family, peer groups, and society in general—of that individual. Rather than continue in this abstract fashion, let us take a preliminary look at examples at each level of analysis before we turn to the study of each one in greater detail.

Notes

1. Gwynne Dyer, *War* (Homewood, Ill.: Dorsey Press, 1985), xi.
2. Winston S. Churchill, *The Gathering Storm*, vol. 1 of *The Second World War* (Boston: Houghton Mifflin, 1948), 40.
3. Michael Howard, *The Causes of Wars* (Cambridge, Mass.: Harvard University Press, 1984), 11.
4. Carl von Clausewitz, *On War*, ed. and trans. Michael Howard and Peter Paret (Princeton, N.J.: Princeton University Press, 1976), 149.

5. On the slaughter of World War I, see Theodore Ropp, *War in the Modern World*, rev. ed. (New York: Collier, 1962); Hanson W. Baldwin, *World War I: An Outline History* (New York: Harper & Row, 1962); Leon Wolff, *In Flanders Field* (New York: Viking, 1958); and, particularly, Alistair Horne, *The Price of Glory: Verdun 1916* (New York: St. Martin's Press, 1962).

6. Quoted in *Political Realism and the Crisis of World Politics* by Kenneth W. Thompson (Princeton, N.J.: Princeton University Press, 1960), 18.

7. Barry R. Posen, *The Sources of Military Doctrine* (Ithaca, N.Y.: Cornell University Press, 1984), 105-178.

8. *Ibid.*, 159-219; and John J. Mearsheimer, *Conventional Deterrence* (Ithaca, N.Y.: Cornell University Press, 1983), 35-52, 99-133.

9. Quoted by Edward Warner, "Douhet, Mitchell, Seversky: Theories of Air Warfare," in *Makers of Modern Strategy*, ed. Edward Meade Early (Princeton, N.J.: Princeton University Press, 1943), 491.

10. Bernard Brodie, *Strategy in the Missile Age* (Princeton, N.J.: Princeton University Press, 1949), 107-146.

11. The Harvard Nuclear Study Group, *Living with Nuclear Weapons* (New York: Bantam Books, 1983), 43-44.

12. On games and the strategies employed, whether formal ones as in football or baseball, or informal ones as in courting, see Eric Berne, *Games People Play* (New York: Grove Press, 1964). The title of this book obviously was influenced by Berne's. Also see John P. Lovell, *Foreign Policy in Perspective* (New York: Holt, Rinehart & Winston, 1970), part 2.

13. Lovell, *Foreign Policy in Perspective*, 65.

14. Ibid.

15. Glen H. Snyder and Paul Diesing, *Conflict Among Nations* (Princeton, N.J.: Princeton University Press, 1977), 429.

16. Clausewitz, *On War*, iv.

17. Patrick M. Morgan, *Theories and Approaches to International Politics*, 2d ed. (New Brunswick, N.J.: Transaction Books, 1975), 4.

18. E. H. Carr, *The Twenty Years' Crisis, 1919-1939* (London: Macmillan, 1951), 8.

19. Ibid.

20. Churchill, *The Gathering Storm*, iv.

21. Hans J. Morgenthau, *Politics among Nations* (New York: Alfred A. Knopf, 1950).

22. Arnold Wolfers, *Discord and Collaboration* (Baltimore: Johns Hopkins University Press, 1962); and John Herz, *Political Realism and Political Idealism* (Chicago: University of Chicago Press, 1951); George F. Kennan, *American Diplomacy 1900-1950* (Chicago: University of Chicago Press, 1941); and Reinhold Niebuhr, *Moral Man and Immoral Society* (New York: Charles Scribner's Sons, 1952). Henry Kissinger was one of the younger realists. For his memoirs as the president's national security assistant and secretary of state during the years from 1969 to 1976, see *White House Years* and *Years of Upheaval* (Boston: Little, Brown & Co., 1979 and 1982, respectively).

23. Klaus Knorr and James N. Rosenau, eds., *Contending Approaches to International Politics* (Princeton, N.J.: Princeton University Press, 1969); Morton Kaplan, *Systems and Process in International Politics* (New York: John Wiley & Sons, 1957); James N. Rosenau, ed., *International Politics and Foreign Policy*, 2d ed. (New York: Free Press,

1969); and Rosenau, *The Scientific Study of Foreign Policy* (New York: Free Press, 1971).

24. Rosenau, *International Politics and Foreign Policy;* J. David Singer, ed., *Quantitative International Politics* (New York: Free Press, 1968); Dina A. Zinnes, *Contemporary Research in International Relations* (New York: Free Press, 1976); and Herbert C. Kelman, ed., *International Behavior* (New York: Holt, Rinehart & Winston, 1965).

25. Charles W. Kegley, Jr., and Eugene R. Wittkopf, *World Politics*, 2d ed. (New York: St. Martin's Press, 1985), 21.

26. Ernst B. Haas, *The Uniting of Europe* (Stanford, Calif.: Stanford University Press, 1948).

27. Seyom Brown, *New Forces in World Politics* (Washington, D.C.: The Brookings Institution, 1974); and Robert O. Keohane and Joseph S. Nye, *Power and Interdependence* (Boston: Little, Brown & Co., 1977).

28. James Caporaso, ed., "Dependence and Dependency in the Global System," *International Organization* (Winter 1978); and Howard Wiarda, ed., *New Directions in Comparative Politics* (Boulder, Colo.: Westview Press, 1985).

29. The basic organization of this book was suggested by Kenneth N. Waltz's notion of "three images," introduced in *Man, the State and War* (New York: Columbia University Press, 1959). Also see J. David Singer, "The Level-of-Analysis Problem in International Relations," *World Politics*, October 1961, 78-80. Only two changes have been introduced here: the order of the three images or levels of analysis has been reversed, and Waltz's first image (our third level), based on the traditional and behavioral analysis of man, has been replaced by emphasis on official policy makers and decision making.

CHAPTER 2

The Three Levels of Analysis: A Framework for the Study of International Politics

THE STATE-SYSTEM LEVEL

We can analyze international politics on three levels—the state-system level, the nation-state level, and the decision-making level. The term *state-system* refers to the international system that comprises all existing political units that interact with one another according to some regular and observable pattern of relations. The term *system* is used for two reasons. First, it encompasses all the sovereign states and therefore possesses the virtue of being *comprehensive.* Second, it helps us to focus on the relations or *interactions* among the component units. The behavior of each state depends upon the behavior of other states. In gamesmanship, every player's move or "strategy"—the set of moves he or she makes in the expectation of winning—is influenced by the moves of every other player.

A system, then, is simply an abstract but convenient way of defining some part of reality for purposes of analysis. We speak, for example, of a human being's circulatory system, the parts of which—the veins, arteries, organs, and cells—must all work properly if the larger system is to give peak performance or to run at all. Similarly, we speak of the cooling system, ignition system, electrical system, and exhaust system of a car. Each system, in turn, has subsystems. The electrical system includes a battery, alternator, and spark plugs. Each system, however, also may be considered a subsystem of the larger system, the car. All the parts must work together if the car is to run properly; the failure of one part affects all other parts.

In international politics, the key point is that each state is part of the system, and each is the guardian of its own security and independence. Each regards other states as potential enemies that may threaten fundamental interests. Consequently, states generally feel insecure and regard one another with a good deal of apprehension and distrust. All become very concerned about their strength, or power. To prevent an attack, a state must be as powerful as potential aggressors, for a disproportion of power may tempt another state. A "balance of power," or equilibrium, is therefore desirable to deter an assault. "Equilibrium is balanced power, and balanced power is neutralized power." [1] A balance of power is the prerequisite for each nation's security, if not for its survival, as well as for the preservation of the system itself. Any attempt by any nation to expand its power and attain dominance or hegemony, which would allow it to impose its will upon the other states, will be resisted. When the balance is disturbed, the tendency will be to take responsive action in order to return to a position of equilibrium. States are actors whose purpose is to play the roles the system has "assigned" to them in maintaining this equilibrium. If they fail in their assignment, if they disregard the operational rule that power must be counterbalanced, they place their own security in jeopardy. *The balance of power is therefore an empirical description of how states do act (or, more cautiously, how most of them, especially the great powers, act most of the time). It is also a recommendation for the way states should act.*

Three points about the state-system level of analysis should be noted briefly. First, to a very significant extent, state behavior is explained by the ever-changing distribution of power in the system. As the distribution between any two states changes, the behavior and alignment of other states also change. States thus have relatively limited ranges of choice about the kinds of foreign policy they adopt. Second, emphasis on the balance of power as the principal variable explaining a state's conduct suggests that domestic factors, such as a state's political complexion, economic organization, social structure, ideology, and public opinion, have no noticeable impact on policy. All states are viewed as monolithic units, identical to all other states in interest, motivation, and behavior. Third, although the state system does seem to explain why states act as they do in many instances, it does not explain their behavior in every case. By itself, as we shall note below, the first level of analysis can explain neither British policy in the late 1930s nor American policy during World War II. These examples will demonstrate that the systemic approach is not so much "scientific" (in the sense that it accounts for the behavior of the participating states) as it is *prescriptive*. At times it can tell us that states did behave as they should have behaved; but at other times the best it can tell us is that states did not behave as they should have done. In Inis Claude's words, "From all this there emerges a general principle of action: When any state or bloc becomes powerful, or threatens to become inordinately powerful, other states *should* recognize this as a threat to their security and respond by taking equivalent measures, individually or jointly, to enhance their power." [2] Because states frequently do not do what they should do, we must look to other levels of analysis for alternative or supplementary explanations. But first let us consider some prominent examples in which a change in the distribution of power led states to react, as well as some cases in which states did not respond to such a shift in the balance of power.

The Balance and U.S. Interventions in Two World Wars

The impact of a shift in the distribution of power is clearly apparent in the involvement of the United States in the two world wars of this century. The country's historical isolation from European "power politics" during most of the nineteenth century and the early twentieth century was the product of a balance of power on the European continent. A threat to this isolationism arose from the possibility that one state or a coalition of states might conquer most of Europe, organize its vast resources of manpower and industrial strength, and use those resources to menace the United States. Britain, to protect its own security, had long opposed any state's hegemony and thus had made it possible for the United States to maintain its isolationism. But in 1870 Prussia, during its war with France, united Germany, and the new Germany became the country with the largest population in Europe, except for Russia. Germany then launched a massive program of industrialization, and it was only a matter of time until its power overtook Britain's. Unlike previous occasions, British power, even when added to that of France and Russia, was not sufficiently great to defeat Germany. When czarist Russia collapsed in 1917, the transfer of as many as two million German soldiers from the eastern front to the western front raised the distinct possibility of a German victory. It was at that point that Germany's unrestricted submarine warfare, which included attacks on U.S. shipping, precipitated American intervention, and it was this intervention that made it possible to contain the German spring offensive of 1918 and bring about Germany's defeat.[3]

A little more than two decades later, the United States, which had retreated into isolationism again, was compelled once more to concern itself with the European balance of power. Germany's victory over France in 1940 brought the United States once again face to face with the specter of an invasion and defeat of Britain, despite the latter's large navy. President Franklin D. Roosevelt therefore undertook a number of measures to strengthen Britain to withstand any Nazi assault.[4] He sent fifty old destroyers to help defend the English Channel, and he set up the Lend-Lease program, which made the United States "the arsenal of democracy." But there was no point in "leasing" Britain the war materials it needed unless they could reach their destination. By the time of the Japanese attack on Pearl Harbor in December 1941, the United States was already engaged in an undeclared naval war with Germany in the Atlantic. American warships, escorting U.S. merchant ships to support American troops sent to Iceland by the president, allowed British merchant ships filled with war supplies to join these convoys; after Iceland, the British navy took over escort duty. American merchantmen were later permitted to sail to British harbors; the American navy even reported the positions of German submarines to British warships and shot at the submarines when they allegedly shot first. The balance of power had made this larger U.S. commit-ment to Britain necessary, even though such actions increased the risk of war with Germany. In fact, war with Germany was merely a matter of time; German submarines sooner or later would start sinking American ships in order to force Britain to surrender. The German invasion of the Soviet Union in 1941 briefly postponed the Battle for the Atlantic, and when the battle did take place, the United States was already at war. But had Adolf Hitler, before Pearl Harbor, given the order to sink all ships bound for Britain, Roosevelt, like President Woodrow Wilson before him, would have had to ask Congress for a declaration of war.

The Beginning of the U.S.-Soviet Cold War

Nowhere do the continuity of a policy and the degree to which the distribu-tion of power narrows a nation's range of choice in its foreign policy show more clearly than in the eruption of the cold war. During World War II the United States, allied to the Soviet Union, believed it had established the basis for a postwar era of harmony and peace.[5] American policy makers recognized that the Soviet rulers had reasons for being suspicious of the West: Western intervention in the civil war that broke out when the Communists seized power; the *cordon sanitaire* established by the French in the 1920s in alliance with a number of east European states and aimed at keeping the Soviets out of Europe; Western appeasement of Hitler, especially in the Munich agreement, which gave the Nazi dictator the Sudetenland in Czechoslovakia—and even-tually the rest of the country—and which the Kremlin might well have viewed as a Western attempt to "open the gates to the East." But Roosevelt believed that four years of wartime cooperation with the United States and Britain had dissolved Soviet suspicion of Western intentions and had replaced it with sufficient mutual respect and confidence to ensure that possible conflicts between the Soviets and the Western nations could be resolved amicably.

Before one of the wartime conferences between Prime Minister Winston Churchill and President Roosevelt, American intelligence analysts had con-cluded that the Soviet Union would be the dominant power in postwar Europe:

> With Germany crushed, there is no power in Europe to oppose her [the Soviet Union's] tremendous military forces.... The conclusions from the foregoing are obvious. Since Russia is the decisive factor in the war, she must be given every assistance, and every effort must be made to obtain her friendship. Likewise, since without question she will dominate Europe on the defeat of the Axis, it is even more essential to develop and maintain the most friendly relations with Russia.[6]

The significance of this forecast is clear: American policy makers apparently were unable to conceive that the Soviet Union, the acknowledged new dominant power in Europe, would replace Germany as the gravest threat to the European and global balance of power. During the war the American government therefore did not aim at reestablishing a European balance of power in order to safeguard the United States. It expected such security to result from a new era of Soviet-American good feeling.

At a conference with Soviet leader Joseph Stalin held at the Black Sea port of Yalta in February 1945, Roosevelt established what he thought were amicable relations with the Soviet Union. "Uncle Joe" made several concessions on vital postwar issues—the United Nations Organization, German occupation policy, and self-government and free elections for the countries of eastern Europe. He also promised good will for the future. No wonder that at the end of the conference, the American delegation felt "supreme exaltation." Roosevelt's closest adviser, Harry Hopkins, later recounted:

> We really believed in our hearts that this was the dawn of the new day we had all been praying for and talking about for so many years. We were absolutely certain that we had won the first great victory of the peace—and, by "we," I mean *all* of us, the whole civilized human race. The Russians had proved that they could be reasonable and farseeing, and there wasn't any doubt in the minds of the President or any of us that we could live with them peacefully for as far into the future as any of us could imagine.[7]

The American secretary of state, Cordell Hull, was even more optimistic: "There will no longer be need for spheres of influence, for alliances, balance of power, or any other of the special arrangements through which, in the unhappy past, the nations strove to safeguard their security or promote their interests."[8]

Unlike the United States, with its isolationist tradition, the Soviet Union had been a long-time player of power politics. It was therefore bound to feel fearful. If conflict was inherent in the system, it had to ensure itself of a strong position in the struggle that was certain to take place after Germany's collapse. Russia had, after all, capitulated to Germany during World War I and had come close to defeat during World War II; more than a century earlier, Napoleon had invaded and almost defeated it. In fact, Russia's experience and fear of invasion and defeat were well established, and they left that country, which had no natural frontier to protect it (like the English Channel or the Atlantic Ocean), with a double legacy. Internally, the legacy was the establishment of an authoritarian government that sought to centralize power to provide the country with a better defense and a greater degree of security; externally, the legacy was one of "defensive expansionism" to obtain "security belts" beyond its frontiers.[9]

Stalin, like earlier Russian rulers, was well aware of both balance-of-power considerations and his country's historical experience. Germany's defeat of Russia in 1917 had enabled the Bolsheviks to succeed the czar, and Hitler had almost crushed *Soviet* Russia in 1941-42. As World War II was ending, the Soviet Union could foresee that after the war it would face another Western power, whose population was almost as large as its own, whose industrial strength was far greater, and whose enormous military power had been further increased in the closing days of the war by the atomic bomb.

Thus, as the Red Army was driving the German armies backward, Soviet actions were typical of a great power, regardless of its ideology, trying to provide for its security. It imposed Soviet control over all of eastern Europe: Poland, Hungary, Bulgaria, Romania, and, after Germany's defeat, East Germany. It turned them all into satellites; Yugoslavia was already under the control of Marshal Tito, a Stalin favorite. Czechoslovakia, although under the Red Army's shadow, was not transformed into a Soviet satellite until 1948, several years later. Soviet power thus stood in the center of Europe. But this expansion also led Stalin to try to dominate Iran and to turn Turkey into another satellite in an effort to gain control of the Dardanelles and gain access to the Mediterranean. And he appeared to back Tito's support of the Communists in the civil war in Greece (see Figure 2-1).

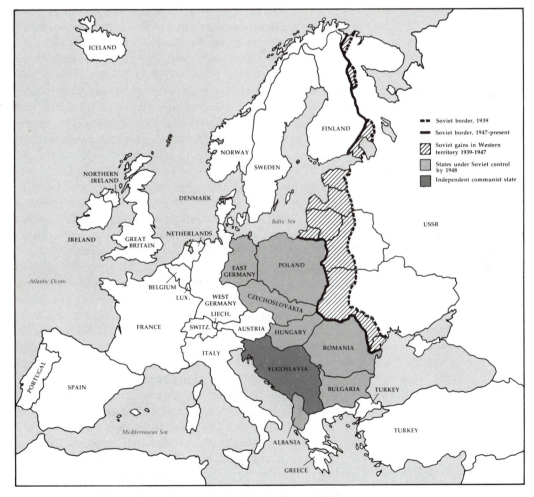

Figure 2-1 Soviet Expansion in Europe Since 1939

These actions led to the U.S. policy of containment. As weary and devastated as the Soviet Union was by the war, it emerged as a major power in the Eurasian land mass. Its armed forces were reduced—according to Nikita Khrushchev's report in 1960—from 12 million to 3 million men; Western estimates in the late 1940s were 1 million to 2 million higher, exclusive of approximately half a million security troops.[10] Still, all the other former major powers in Europe had collapsed. Germany was in ruins, France had never recovered from its defeat and occupation, and Britain foundered soon after victory. Nowhere in Europe was there any countervailing power; the only such power lay outside of Europe. The United States may have wanted to turn its back on the international scene and to concentrate once more on domestic affairs. It had demobilized psychologically and militarily. American armed forces had been reduced from just over 12 million to 1.5 million men, and the military budget had been cut from the 1945 high of $81 billion to a low of $11 billion in 1948—a full year after the announcement of the containment policy.[11] But the distribution of power in the state system left the United States no choice. It was not what the government wished to do that was to matter; it was what it *had* to do. A new balance had to be established.

The postwar falling-out among the Allies and their ensuing rivalry was reminiscent of the situation that had occurred after the coalition that had defeated Napoleon in 1815 fell apart. At the end of that lengthy war, czarist Russia, after an exhausting struggle, had soldiers in Paris and a close ally in Prussia. The czar was particularly adamant about retaining control of Poland (with boundaries quite different from those of contemporary Poland). All entreaties that he withdraw his troops behind his own frontier were in vain. (Stalin himself later controlled East Germany, of which Prussia had been a large part before World War II. When an American said to Stalin that it must be gratifying to be in Berlin after such a bloody war, Stalin curtly replied, "Czar Alexander got to Paris.")[12] It was only after Britain, Austria, and a defeated France had signed a triple alliance and were reputedly ready to go to war if the czar remained stubborn that a new balance satisfactory to all the great powers was worked out (including a part of Poland for the czar) and ratified at the Congress of Vienna in 1815.

In simple terms, the post-1945 conflict substituted Soviet Russia for czarist Russia and the United States for Britain.[13] The differences in ideology between the two Russias, or the differences in political complexion and economic systems between the two English-speaking nations, were, in the context of balance-of-power analysis, *not* the key factors in breaking up the respective wartime alliances against Napoleon and Hitler and aligning the principal powers on opposite sides. The key issue in each instance was the postwar distribution of power. In the logic of the state system, had the Soviet Union in 1945 been a capitalist state like the United States (or vice versa), the emerging bipolar balance, the division of power between the two great powers, would have brought on the cold war. The two nations became enemies because, as the only two powerful states left, each had the ability to inflict enormous damage on each other. As Paul Seabury has noted, bipolarity was "a contradiction in which two powers—America and Russia— were by historical circumstances thrown into a posture of confrontation which neither had actually 'willed, yet one from which extrication was difficult." [14] Or, as Louis Halle has pointed out, the historical circumstances of 1945 "had an ineluctable quality that left the Russians little choice but to move as they did. Moving as they did, they compelled the United States and its allies to move in response. And so the Cold War was joined." As Halle has suggested, "This is not fundamentally a case of the wicked against the virtuous. Fundamentally ... we [the observers] may properly feel sorry for both parties, caught, as they are, in a situation of irreducible dilemma." [15]

The Price of Ignoring the Balance: Britain in the 1930s

The price of failure to heed the operational rule of balancing the power of a potential opponent is a loss of security and probably war. World War II could have been prevented if Britain and France had remobilized sufficient forces and acted against Germany's various moves to upset the European balance. Germany had reintroduced conscription, its forces having been limited to 100,000 men under the Treaty of Versailles. It had reoccupied the Rhine- land—an area neutralized because Germany had twice launched its attacks on France from there. It had demanded the return of the Sudetenland—a moun- tainous area that, despite its sizable German population, had been given to the new state of Czechoslovakia so that it could better defend itself against Germany. Finally, Germany had demanded the return of land given to Poland in 1918. Each of these moves was designed to change the distribution of power in Europe in Germany's favor. Conscription would rebuild Germany's military strength. The militarization of the Rhineland would permit Germany to build the Siegfried line, hold the western front against France with minimal strength, and concentrate German power against the countries of eastern Europe in order to blackmail them into submission once they could no longer count on their French ally. And the first prize of this policy—the acquisition of the Sudetenland in 1938—dismembered Czechoslovakia, left the rest of the unhappy country prostrate for Germany to swallow a few months later, and strengthened the vise around Poland that was to pressure it into submission (see Figure 2-2). [16]

Not until after Hitler had taken over the whole of Czechoslovakia did Britain's leaders decide that he could not be allowed to go any farther. Hitler, however, believing that Britain's announced support of Poland was meaning- less and that his latest challenge would go unmet as before, attacked Poland. Britain then declared war on Germany, as did France. World War II thus began under the worst of all possible circumstances for the Western powers. These circumstances included Germany's rearmament, the building of the Siegfried line, the loss of Czechoslovakia, and the demoralization of France's other allies in eastern Europe. In short, Germany was no longer the weak

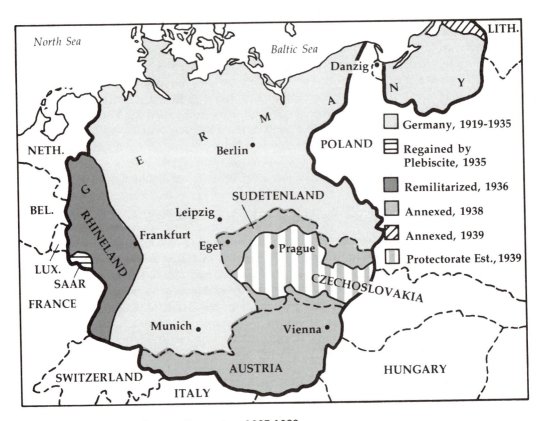

Figure 2-2 German Expansion, 1935-1939

power it had been at the time of Hitler's first expansionist moves in the mid-1930s.

The outbreak of World War II, therefore, stands as a monument to a single lesson: decent personal motives, like those of Prime Minister Neville Chamberlain, who wanted nothing more than to spare Britain the horror of another war, do not necessarily produce successful policies. At the very least, they require an understanding of the nature of the state system, its demands upon national leaders, and the rules of its operation. The American conduct of World War II was to underscore the importance of such understanding. U.S. leaders did not expect the Western coalition with the Soviet Union to collapse after Germany's defeat. They did not understand that once the common purpose had been achieved, the partners would have to concern themselves with securing their own protection in a new balance of power. They did not recognize that, even during the war, each alliance member had to take precautionary steps, in anticipation of possible future conflict and perhaps even war, to ensure itself a strong postwar position.

The Price of Ignoring the Balance:
The United States and China in the 1950s and 1960s

Even though neglect of the "rules of the game" helped account for World War II and the cold war, they have not been closely heeded or implemented since then. The most obvious case of neglect was after the collapse in 1949 of Nationalist China and the control of mainland China by a Communist government. The new Chinese People's Republic quickly formed an alliance with Russia, which in the United States was immediately referred to as the "Sino (Chinese)-Soviet bloc," as if it were a single actor.

Yet historically, China and Russia had been antagonists. As the Manchu dynasty was collapsing in China at the end of the nineteenth century and the European powers began to carve China up into spheres of influence, czarist Russia, China's neighbor to the north, became a prime carver. Russian influence expanded to northern China, especially Manchuria. (It was Russian expansion from Manchuria to Korea that provoked the Japanese to attack in 1904.) Even Stalin's Russia was hardly considered a friend of the Chinese Communists in their civil war with the Nationalist government. Stalin's advice to the Chinese Communists to cooperate with the Nationalists during the 1920s resulted in the Communists being slaughtered by the Nationalists. This was the first of several blunders and betrayals. In 1945, for instance, Stalin signed a treaty of friendship with the Nationalists, pledging support for the government the Communists were trying to overthrow. Thus, the memories of poor relations fed continuing differences between the Soviets and the Chinese Communists, both before and after they acquired power. Moreover, despite sharing a common ideology, Russia and China were also highly nationalistic countries. Stalin had reclaimed Manchuria during World War II and held on to it until his death in 1953—so much for ideological friendship! Needless to say, the new Chinese government was resentful at its treatment by a "fraternal ally." According to the balance-of-power maxim "my neighbor is my enemy, my neighbor's neighbor is my friend," the alliance of Russia and China, two large neighboring powers, soon became increasingly tense and unfriendly.

What is amazing is that the United States did not attempt to play a "divide and rule" game. As late as the early 1960s, when President John Kennedy initially intervened in Vietnam, American policy makers continued to talk of the "Sino-Soviet bloc," although differences between Russia and China had increased since 1956. The Sino-Soviet conflict was already well advanced and quite visible. But it was not until 1972 that an American president, Richard Nixon, exploited this growing split between the two Communist giants. During the 1960s and early 1970s, Soviet military power had grown enormously; in 1969 came the first of a number of border clashes. Fearing for their security, the Chinese Communists were looking for a way to deter a possible Soviet attack. Simultaneously, the United States, weary of international involvement after the Vietnamese war, was looking for help in containing the increasingly powerful Soviet Union. The Sino-American reconciliation was a natural result. Putting aside ideological differences, China and the United States acted in a way that preserved the balance of power.

But we must note one cost of this belated reconciliation. Had the reconciliation taken place earlier, the Vietnam War might not have occurred. The United States in the early 1960s thought not only that Russia and China were still close allies but also that China was the far more militant of the two, that North Vietnam was China's satellite, and that China was responsible for the strategy of guerrilla warfare in South Vietnam. Had the United States recognized the Communist government early and had diplomatic representatives in China, the United States might have known that North Vietnam was independent, that a North Vietnamese victory would not have added to Chinese power and certainly not to Sino-Soviet power, and, therefore, that it would not have affected the central balance between the United States and Russia, or Russia and China.

But more than just avoiding intervening in Vietnam, the American failure to exploit Sino-Soviet differences represented an even more profound mistake. In any conflict between major powers, prudence would suggest that no power should face more opponents than it needs to; if it faces two or more adversaries, it should concentrate on the most powerful opponent and try to isolate that power by drawing the others away from it. Why confront two strong states when it is unnecessary? This common sense and logical rule has been called the principle of the "conservation of enemies": do not face more enemies than necessary.[17] The United States ignored that rule from 1949 to 1972—and paid a heavy price.

THE NATION-STATE LEVEL

While the state-system level of analysis emphasizes the *external* determinants of state behavior, the nation-state level attributes such behavior to *internal* characteristics: the political system, historical experience, the nature of the economy, or the social structure. The emphasis is not on the likeness of states, the similarity of their motives, or the insignificant impact of domestic attributes; rather, the emphasis is on differences in motivation, attitudes, and internal composition or domestic structure among states. We therefore categorize states as democratic, revolutionary, capitalist, less-developed, and so forth. Political scientists and diplomatic historians frequently have attributed certain characteristic patterns of behavior to such categories.

For instance, it has been suggested that democracies are basically peaceful states. This hypothesis may help in part to explain the reasons for Britain's appeasement of Hitler before World War II—that is, why it did not behave as it would have done had it heeded the systemic norms related to the distribution of power. Presumably, industrialized democracies look outward only when they perceive themselves as gravely provoked by external challenges that leave them little choice but to defend themselves against aggressors. Once the challenge has been met, they will demobilize and look inward again until they can no longer avoid defending themselves against a new threat.

Similarly, it has been asserted that a total war is the only kind of war that democracies fight with a fair degree of domestic unity and moral certitude; only a high moral purpose can justify a democracy's decision to wage war. It may have been predictable that the United States would experience internal dissension and moral anguish fighting any "limited war," especially a war that had not begun with a clearly visible and overt aggression and in which the main ally was hardly a paragon of democratic rectitude. If a democracy prefers either to abstain from the use of power and concentrate on its business at home or to use its power fully in a righteous cause so that the war will end as quickly as possible and permit return to domestic affairs, then one might have foreseen, in the event of a lengthy limited war, an extreme bifurcation in public opinion. On one side would be those who say the country should never have become involved in the first place and should immediately withdraw; and on the other, those who advocate escalation of the conflict, a quick military victory, then withdrawal. Under these conditions, a president's early popular support for such a war is destined to erode, making the war very difficult to wage over a period of time.

Democracy in Peace and War

Let us go back briefly to our example of British policy during the 1930s and the principal point of our earlier analysis: that Britain did not pursue the policy it *should* have. Why? The nation-state level of analysis suggests one possible answer: Britain was a democracy in which the people expressed themselves regularly through general elections. Successive British governments therefore were sensitive to public opinion and a mood that throughout the period between the two world wars was overwhelmingly influenced by memories of World War I. There was a widespread popular demand that another bloodletting be avoided if at all possible. Those who returned from the battlefields, where they had left the corpses of their comrades in arms, were haunted by the war. In the interwar period they remained politically passive, withdrawing into their private worlds, avoiding public involvement. Erich Maria Remarque dedicted his famous novel *All Quiet on the Western Front* to this "generation of men who, even though they may have escaped its shells, were destroyed by the war." [18]

British leaders thought they had no choice. The antiwar mood was far too pervasive. In 1933 the students of the Oxford Union passed a resolution refusing "to fight for King and country." In 1935 there was a general election in which the prime minister, knowing that Britain should rearm, pledged not to do so because he felt certain that favoring rearmament would lose the election for the Conservatives. In 1938 cheering British crowds welcomed

Chamberlain back from Munich, assured that he had brought them "peace in our time." And in 1939, a few months before the outbreak of war and several months after news of Munich and Hitler's violation of the agreements reached England, the Labour party—which had been pacifist throughout the 1930s—was still opposing military conscription.[19]

Although this is only one case study of a specific democratic nation's foreign policy, it allows us to make broader generalizations about democracies' foreign policy behavior. Democracies have become welfare states, it has been suggested, because of the increasing mass participation in voting and political decision making. These social-service countries are, as a result, primarily inwardly oriented; in the absence of clearly visible threats to their security, they view the spending of large sums on arms as a waste.[20] Popular interest in foreign affairs is at best sporadic, responding to specific crises; only then will money for defensive purposes be allocated. And the aggressive and acquisitive use of force by an affluent state that is geared to public and private expenditures for personal and family well-being will be rare and, if it occurs, disapproved. Modern democratic societies have tended to emphasize values, such as health, education, and welfare, that are in conflict with the conduct of foreign policies that emphasize force, killing, or exploitation. People are not to be treated as objects of aggression or oppression.

These generalizations help to explain Britain's policies during the 1930s. Because of its nature, Britain would be an essentially inward-looking nation, and this propensity would have been intensified by the Great Depression. The need to concentrate on domestic problems and to do something about the economy—an economy that even before the depression was suffering large-scale unemployment—was bound to make foreign policy a secondary matter. Memories of the war of 1914-18 only reinforced this ordering of priorities. It was not until Hitler's immense threat to Britain's security became unambiguously clear to both the public and its leaders that foreign policy became more important than domestic policy. Then Britain took a firm stand opposing further German expansion, and the result was World War II.

The war that broke out in September 1939 was the second in twenty years to have been precipitated by Germany. It was also the twentieth century's second total war, a war fought for the total destruction and unconditional surrender of the enemy. Again, our democratic typology can be used to analyze what happened. George Kennan, American diplomat and scholar, has noted that, when democracies turn from their inward, peaceful preoccupations toward the external arena and are compelled to fight, they become ferocious.

A democracy is peace-loving. It does not like to go to war. It is slow to rise to provocation. When it has once been provoked to the point where it must grasp the sword, it does not easily forgive its adversary for having produced this situation. The fact of the provocation then becomes itself the issue. Democracy fights in anger—it fights for the very reason that it was forced to go to war. It fights to punish the power that was rash enough and hostile enough to provoke it—to teach that power a lesson it will not forget, to prevent the thing from happening again. Such a war must be carried to the bitter end.[21]

Various reasons have been adduced to support this hypothesis about the warlike nature of democracy once it is engaged in military conflict. If war and violence are considered evil—the very denial of democracy's humanitarian ideals—their use demands a moral stance; when it becomes necessary to resort to force, it must be for defensive and noble reasons. The complete destruction of the aggressor regime—particularly if its way of life is authoritarian (as was that of Germany) and therefore by democratic standards inferior, immoral, and warlike—becomes a spiritually uplifting cause. Once destroyed, the vanquished nation can be sent to democratic reform school and transformed into a peaceful state. But beyond this general need for moral justification lies the reality of war. War disturbs the scale of social priorities in an individualistic and materialistic culture. It separates families, it kills and wounds, it demands economic sacrifice, and it imposes regimentation and discipline. If a society that emphasizes personal dignity and the development of individual, family, and social welfare must go to war, the sacrifices demanded must be commensurate with some wholesome, ennobling, and morally transcending goal. Total victory, in this context, becomes the minimum aim.

Whatever the reasons for democracies to fight total wars, the consequences of such wars in the twentieth century have been dramatic. Kennan has even attributed the Communist seizure of power in Russia to the drive for total victory by the Allies in World War I.[22] After the collapse of the czarist state during that war, the February Revolution of 1917 established a provisional government composed of liberals and moderate conservatives led by Alexander Kerensky. According to Kennan, if the war had been concluded immediately, the new government might have been able to consolidate its position and Russia would then have been able to evolve in a democratic direction. But Kerensky's government felt honor-bound not to break the czar's pledge to the Western powers that Russia would not sign a separate peace treaty with Germany—which would have left the Allies to confront Germany's overwhelming power alone. Nor would the Western Allies release Russia from that pledge. They needed Russia's help to achieve total victory. Yet a conclusion of the war was a prerequisite for any possible stabilization of the domestic turmoil. The Russian people were weary of fighting. Above all else, they wanted peace. The army had already declared its desire for an end to the massacre by "voting with its feet": large numbers of soldiers had simply left the front lines and returned home.

Even more important, the provisional government could not implement a land-reform program while simultaneously trying to conduct a war. Yet this program was the key to long-term success. Ninety percent of all Russians lived on the land, and peasant land hunger had long agitated the czarist regime and eroded peasant loyalty to the autocracy. In the absence of a serious start on land redistribution, the new government was unable to rally popular support. Lenin exploited these circumstances, promising that when the Communists assumed power they would end hostilities and grant a piece of land to every peasant. In November 1917 the Communist party seized power in a second revolution. Russia's continued participation in the war had been fatal for Kerensky's provisional government. The incompatibility between Allied war aims and Russia's own domestic needs was thus resolved in the Communists' favor.

If the Western powers' predilection for total war resulted in the collapse of Russia, leaving it in the hands of a regime that was to become openly hostile to the West, it also made World War II all but inevitable.[23] For, as we now know, a second result of the exhausting experience of World War I was the grave weakening of Britain and France. A third consequence was the collapse of Austria-Hungary and the birth of a small number of unstable eastern European states that would not contribute to the Continent's equilibrium. Their independence was only temporary, lasting until Russia and Germany recovered their strength; these two great powers then shared a common interest in destroying the states between them, after which they would engage in a contest for supremacy over the entire area. A final consequence of the complete defeat of Germany was the fall of the German monarchy. The kaiser had led his country into war, but the new regime created at Weimar led it out, accepting the punitive terms imposed by the Treaty of Versailles. As a result, the German people equated the new, democratic Weimar Republic with humiliation and defeat. Amid the great social unrest that followed the runaway inflation of the early 1920s and the Great Depression of a few years later, Germany had no traditional institutions to cling to as it sought to weather the crisis. These conditions offered fertile ground for Hitler, who gained power by exploiting nationalist frustration, impoverishment, and uncertainty.

This democratic crusading style shows itself, however, not only in wartime; it can be aroused even in "peacetime," as it was during the cold war. Earlier, we cited the example of U.S. policy toward Communist China and its inability, until the Vietnam War was coming to an end, to exploit Sino-Soviet differences. The principal reason for this was American anti-Communist fervor, aroused by Soviet behavior after World War II. This crusade reached a fever pitch after the Chinese Communists defeated the pro-American Nationalist government in the Chinese civil war and then intervened militarily in the Korean War as U.S. forces were marching toward the Chinese-North Korean frontier. The United States had long considered itself to be both China's friend and benefactor. It was bad enough when the new Chinese regime began to vilify the United States in the same terms as the Russians, but it was intolerable when it began to kill American soldiers. The anti-Communist emotions, initially aroused by the Soviet Union, were now intensified and directed toward China as well. In these circumstances, recognition of China became impossible, especially because the Republican party, having accused the Democrats of having "lost China" and being "soft on Communism," made it too politically costly for the Democrats to recognize China, which the Republicans, of course, would not do. Recognition of China came only in 1979, thirty years after the Communists took over its government and seven years after Nixon had begun the process of Sino-American reconciliation.

Had the United States recognized the Chinese government after the civil war, it might have ended the Korean War sooner, avoiding many casualties. North Korea attacked South Korea in June 1950, and the United States came to the rescue of its friend. By October, the status quo had been restored. At that point, the United States decided to unify Korea. Because the United States had opposed North Korea's attempt at unification, it was not surprising that China reacted the same way and intervened with its forces. The U.S. government had known there were Chinese forces in Manchuria, but it did not know if the Chinese would intervene. The United States obviously did not think so, although the Chinese had repeatedly warned against sending American forces into North Korea. Had the United States recognized China's new government and sent diplomats to Beijing, U.S. intelligence might have been better. The American government might have taken Chinese warnings seriously and avoided a miscalculation that resulted in a war that lasted until 1953. In short, the United States might have been able to avoid hostilities with China in Korea, as well as the Vietnam War.

The Revolutionary State

Although Western behavior, according to Kennan's interpretation, helped to give birth to the Soviet Union, that country represented—in a classification coined by Henry Kissinger—a revolutionary state.[24] Whether democratic France in aristocratic Europe in the late eighteenth and early nineteenth centuries or the Soviet Union in the twentieth century, the revolutionary state presents a total challenge to the international order. It repudiates the existing order because it rejects the domestic structures of the major powers in the system. The revolutionary state's leaders pose two questions: Why do the masses live in poverty, ill health, and ignorance? Why is mankind constantly cursed by war? The revolutionaries point to the *ancien régime*. The majority of people are destitute because they are exploited by a privileged minority. Wars are fought because they pay dividends in the form of enhanced prestige, territorial acquisition, and economic gains. Although the few profit, it is the masses who are compelled to do most of the fighting and dying. People can be freed from economic exploitation, political subjugation, and international violence only by the destruction of the existing system and the overthrow of the ruling classes. In short, the revolutionary state condemns the existing order as unjust and assumes the duty of bringing *justice* to humanity.

By the very nature of its belief, the revolutionary state is thus committed to "permanent revolution"—that is, to the total defeat of the prevailing political, economic, and cultural system that has condemned humanity to eternal slavery. Only a worldwide victory of the "new order" can lead to the establishment of a universal society in which, for the first time in history, people will be truly free from oppression and need. The proclamation issued by the National Convention of the Republic after the French Revolution is characteristic of the revolutionary state as a missionary power engaged in a "just war" to establish eternal domestic social justice and international peace:

> The French Nation declares that it will treat as enemies every people who, refusing liberty and equality or renouncing them, may wish to maintain, recall, or treat with the prince and the privileged classes; on the other hand, it engages not to subscribe to any treaty and not to lay down its arms until the sovereignty and independence of the people whose territory the troops of the Republic shall have entered shall be established, and until the people shall have adopted the principles of equality and founded a free and democratic government.[25]

If this typology of the revolutionary state is valid, Stalinist Russia, in the years immediately after World War II, would have viewed the United States not as just another state trapped by the same security problem, but as a capitalist state that had to be eliminated. And, in fact, Moscow rejected the notion that national insecurity and international conflict were the result *only*—or even primarily—of the state system. Its spokesmen believed that international antagonism and hostility, as well as domestic poverty, unemployment, ill health, and ignorance, were due to the internal nature of the leading states in the system. Capitalism was viewed as the cause of all social evil. Only in a political system in which the Communist party, representing the exploited majority, the proletariat, has control and in which all the forces of production are removed from private ownership so that they may be used for the benefit of all people, instead of for the profit of the privileged few, can mankind finally live free from social injustice, deprivation, and war. As a total critique of capitalist society and a promise to deliver the masses from evil and bring them domestic justice and external peace, communism in fact constituted a secular religion of damnation and salvation. It conferred upon the Soviet Union the messianic duty of converting all people to the "true faith."

Consequently, according to this interpretation of the foreign policy behavior of a revolutionary state, the Soviet Union was engaged in a constant and irreconcilable "holy war" with all non-Communist states, seeking hegemony in the state system. Soviet hostility toward the West, it must be emphasized, predated 1945 because it was to a large degree ideological and preconceived.[26] V. I. Lenin and Stalin had felt it even before they seized power and before Western governments had adopted anti-Soviet policies. It was an enmity deduced from first principles and based not on what Western governments did but on what they were alleged to be: Western actions were almost irrelevant. Once non-Communist states were declared hostile and official declarations and policies were formulated upon that assumption, it was hardly astounding that the West became less friendly and that the Soviet leaders reaped the fruits of the policies that they had sown. Communist ideology, in short, raised the level of mutual fear and suspicion resulting from the state system and caused Stalin's Russia to undertake both "defensive expansionism" (because of its enhanced apprehension of capitalist attack) and "offensive expansionism" (because of its determination to expand the socialist world).

Any modus vivendi like the one finally worked out between czarist Russia and the monarchies of Britain, France, and Austria-Hungary in 1815 was, in the circumstances of 1945, therefore excluded. For according to the second level of analysis, the cold war would have erupted regardless of the emergence of bipolarity, because Russia had become *Soviet* Russia, and its aims and objectives extended far beyond those historically entertained by the czars.

Capitalist-Imperialist States

There is also, as noted earlier, an economic interpretation of international politics. The most prominent of these is Marxism-Leninism, which starts with the proposition that history has always been characterized by a class struggle between the rich and poor, the exploiters and exploited, those who owned society's wealth, whether it was land or factories, and those who worked for them. In a capitalist state, the workers, or proletariat, were locked in a class conflict with those who owned the means of production—the industrial middle class or bourgeoisie. The reason for conflict was that the bourgeoisie exploited the proletariat, paying them very little and skimming off large profits. According to the theory, as workers become more conscious of their lot, they become more militant; as the number of workers and their dissatisfactions grow, the day of the revolution becomes inevitable, and the bourgeoisie is overthrown. When this did not take place, however, Lenin explained that capitalism had staved off the revolution through a policy of imperialism. Unable to sell enough at home because they underpaid their workers, the capitalists sought markets overseas for their products, as well as the natural resources for manufacturing. It was this policy of colonialism or imperialism that extended European power to the Third World and earned huge profits for the capitalist states. Some of these profits trickled down to the workers, raised their living standards, "derevolutionized" them, and won their loyalty for capitalism.

This economic analysis suggested three different causes for war, all the result of capitalism. First, there was the conflict among the capitalist states dividing up the world. The two world wars are placed in this category. Second is the conflict between capitalist and socialist states. Although Russia, the United States, and Britain were allies during World War II, Stalin assumed that the latter considered him an enemy, just as he regarded the leaders of the capitalist states as enemies, and that they would try to weaken Russia while they were all trying to defeat Germany. To say the least, Stalin was skeptical about Anglo-American statements of good will and hopes for postwar peace. Did he not know better that capitalist leaders harbored only hostile intentions toward him and Soviet Russia? Anyway, capitalist hostility toward what the Soviets call socialism (different from Western democratic socialism) is the fundamental cause for war, hot or cold. The third cause of war is conflict between the capitalist states and their colonies. The former had bound the latter to them with economic chains; the colonies' raw materials and labor were used not to benefit their own people, but to enrich the capitalist states. Even after gaining their political independence, the new nations remained economic dependencies. They will remain less-developed countries (LDCs) unless they can break the economic chains that maintain their dependency status. According to Marxist-Leninist theory, genuine "national liberation" is a must; the capitalist states, of which the most powerful since 1945 is the United States, will oppose the LDCs' efforts to be free, not only politically but also economically. The capitalist system depends upon preserving the international status quo.

THE DECISION-MAKING LEVEL

Up to now we have analyzed international politics in terms of largely abstract units such as the state system. We have also personified states, but common sense tells us that "the United States" does not make decisions; certain people who occupy the official political positions responsible for making foreign policy decisions do.

It is this level of analysis that is probably most familiar to many people. At election time Americans debate the virtues of the leading candidates, their expressed and implied views, their alleged values, and groups to which they may be beholden. Citizens watch how they handle themselves on television—whether or not they have "substance," are sincere, remain "cool" under pressure. Apparently, who is president matters. It affects the priorities between domestic and foreign policies, the kinds of foreign policies that will be adopted, the extensiveness of foreign commitments, and the weapons to be produced.

We shall emphasize three aspects of decision making: the policy maker's perceptions of the world; the different kinds of decisions made and the corresponding decision-making processes; and the various types of political or decision-making systems. The central point of the decision-making approach is that it allows an observer to understand and analyze individual decisions in some detail. At the state-system level, the assumption is that state behavior is the product of an ever-changing distribution of power; at the nation-state level, the assumption is that state behavior reflects its internal character. Analysis on the decision-making level permits these assumptions to be checked out in specific circumstances and allows one to see what other objectives states had in mind that more accurately account for their behavior. This approach is particularly revealing when a state's actions do not seem consistent with first- or second-level expectations. How does one explain a state's policy that appears to ignore the balance of power? If a certain category of state—for example, revolutionary—is supposed to produce a particular type of behavior, but two states of that type act quite differently, how can we account for that? Looking at the leaders who made the decisions, their responsibilities and perspectives, and the way these decisions were arrived at is likely to reveal the answers.

Policy Makers and Their Perceptions

The first aspect of decision making, the policy makers' perceptions of the world, is very important for the obvious reason that it is the link between the external environment and policy decisions: the real world is the world perceived, whether correctly or not. This distinction between things as they *appear* and things as they *are* raises a key question: Is the objective environment as such more important—as we suggested in our analysis of the state system—or are the policy makers' subjective perceptions and definitions of that environment more important? In the terminology of Harold and Margaret Sprout, should we focus analysis on the "psycho milieu," the perceived world, or on the "operational milieu," the world that exists outside decision makers' values and beliefs?[27] Clearly, the gap between the two can range from nonexistent to very large. In the operational milieu presumably the number of feasible policies that can be implemented is limited; nevertheless, alternative policies are likely to exist, and the policy makers' perceptions will be crucial in selecting particular courses of action.

Two major events have dominated the postwar period. One is the appeasement of Hitler at Munich, which became a symbol of what not to do. Any Soviet or Soviet-bloc expansionist attempts were to be met, if necessary, by force. The lesson learned was "no more Munichs." The other major event, the war in Vietnam, was such a traumatic experience and divided the American people so deeply that the lesson became "no more Vietnams." The war seemed to have been the result of the "no more Munichs" attitude and the determination to oppose communism everywhere. But, the intervention in Vietnam soured American public opinion on this type of activism; the better part of wisdom seemed to be to stay out. At the very least, intervention should be more selective and discriminating. The question then became where, how, and with what force should one intervene. It is always easy to oppose any intervention, arguing that America's vital interests are not involved, and U.S. foreign policy since Vietnam has been haunted by the traumatic experience of the war. What is important about Munich and Vietnam is that the memory of each has influenced policy for a generation—not just a few years. And what is critical about each is that it occurred because of the perceptions held by the leading policy makers in England and the United States, respectively.

Prime Minister Chamberlain in the 1930s not only shared the general British desire to avoid another total war; he also thought his policy of appeasing Hitler's demands would achieve that end. He thought this because he saw Hitler as one of his own kind, a statesman who had been born and bred in a system founded upon nationalism. He could even cite a supporting precedent, for Otto von Bismarck, after Germany's unification in 1870, had declared that Germany was satisifed and would thereafter support the new European status quo. Hitler talked in terms of national self-determination, and why should Chamberlain not believe that the new German leader was merely a cruder version of the Prussian aristocrat and German chancellor; that he, too, would be sated once he had achieved his apparently nationalistic aims. If Nazi Germany had, in fact, been merely a nationalist state, the differences between it and France and Britain could probably have been resolved without precipitating a war. But Hitler harbored aims beyond restoring Germany's 1914 frontiers.

Churchill, from his understanding of British history, knew that Britain's foreign policy had long been one of opposition to any power seeking to dominate Europe, whether Philip II of Spain, Louis XIV or Napoleon of France, or the German kaiser. He perceived each of Hitler's limited demands and moves as part of a larger pattern that would lead to Germany's destruction of the European equilibrium. For this reason, he counseled opposition, condemned the Munich agreement, and ridiculed Chamberlain's claim that he had brought back "peace in our time." Rather, Churchill said bluntly, "We have sustained a total and unmitigated defeat." [28] As Churchill himself intimated, had he been prime minister in the late 1930s, World War II might have been avoided. Churchill's perception of Hitler and Nazi objectives was correct, Chamberlain's perception mistaken. Possibly Churchill could have convinced the British public of the true nature of the Nazi regime, placed the German dictator's repeated demands in their proper perspective, and led Britain to oppose his moves and speed up rearmament.

Vietnam illustrates the issue of perception even more poignantly. American participation in the Vietnam War, which ranks as one of the most unpopular wars in American history, has often been cited as an instance of misperception by the administrations of President John Kennedy and President Lyndon Johnson. Kennedy's inaugural address, it is said, was permeated with a sense of the bipolar conflict and confrontation of the 1940s and 1950s. [29] He pledged that the United States was "unwilling to witness or permit the slow undoing of those human rights to which this nation has always been committed, and to which we are committed today at home and around the world. . . . We shall pay any price, bear any burden, meet any hardship, support any friend, oppose any foe, in order to assure the survival and success of liberty." His conviction that the nation confronted a united and aggressive Communist bloc was reinforced by the Soviet Union's announcement that it would support wars of national liberation; these were "just wars" and would have the Soviet Union's full support. Not surprisingly, therefore, when such a war broke out in South Vietnam, the administration thought that the Soviets or Chinese had instigated it and, starting in 1961, sent in more than 16,000 military "advisers." [30] A few weeks before his death, Kennedy declared that, if South Vietnam fell, it would "give the impression that the wave of the future in Southeast Asia was China and the Communists." [31] Johnson, who relied for his policy advice principally upon his predecessor's counselors, certainly saw the issue that way and, in 1965, began massive U.S. intervention.

Critics of the war claim that the commitment of military advisers by Kennedy and of half a million troops by Johnson was based upon the "old myths" of the cold war instead of the "new realities" that had begun to emerge in the mid-1960s. [32] One of these new realities was that the Communist bloc was badly fragmented along nationalistic lines. An extension of Hanoi's control to South Vietnam, therefore, did not mean parallel extension of Soviet or Chinese power; indeed, it was argued, a nationalistic Communist Vietnam would be a barrier to an extension of Chinese power. Nor would the loss of Saigon mean the collapse of neighboring nations; whether successful guerrilla wars occurred in those countries would depend on their indigenous conditions. Even a successful counterguerrilla war in South Vietnam would therefore not necessarily "teach the Communists a lesson" and rule out other such conflicts, if internal factors in some of those states were conducive to wars of national liberation. In short, had the perceptions of the policy makers during the Kennedy-Johnson period more accurately reflected the changing nature of the international system, the United States could have avoided becoming involved in South Vietnam.

Different Policies, Different Policy Processes

Policy makers are, of course, involved in different types of decisions, the second aspect of decision making, and they arrive at them by different means, the third aspect of decision making. We shall describe three basic kinds of decisions and policies: crisis, security, and domestic. (The distinctions, although discussed here specifically in the context of American foreign policy, are broadly applicable to other democracies.) The first, crisis policy, is related primarily to great-power confrontations, especially direct U.S.- Soviet confrontations. They are considered crises because of the possibility of escalation to nuclear war. The frequent cold war crises over Berlin always posed this danger, although the most serious remains the Cuban missile confrontation in 1962.

The second, security policy, refers to the more normal noncrisis foreign and defense policies. Such policies range from foreign-aid bills and defense budgets to arms control policies, arms transfers to allies and other friendly nations, the organization and operation of the government's intelligence apparatus, and, not least, the conduct of limited wars. These policies are made by a process quite different from domestic policy, the third policy area.

Domestic policy revolves largely, though not exclusively, around the objective of welfare or prosperity. In most nations of the world, especially democratic ones, people increasingly expect their government to provide economic growth, jobs, rising incomes, and many social programs. For most citizens, these pocketbook issues are more important than most foreign policies. In recent years, however, many domestic issues have become increasingly entangled with foreign policy as the economic health of nations has grown more and more dependent on importing or exporting raw materials, manufactured goods, or food items. The escalating oil prices set by the Organization of Petroleum Exporting Countries (OPEC) during the 1970s, with their profound effects on employment, inflation, general prosperity, and way of life in the West, remain dramatic examples of the impact of foreign policy on domestic policies.

In the United States, crisis policy is usually managed by the president and a few advisers, while security and domestic policies are decided by the executive and legislative branches. In security policy, the executive takes the lead, although Congress is actively involved in the debate, approval (or disapproval), and funding of policy. In domestic policy, Congress plays a far larger role than it does in normal foreign and defense issues. Public opinion and interest groups are also more involved in the latter two policy areas than during crises, which, by their very nature, are generally short-term and over before critical public opinion is aroused.

Crisis Policy.   Crisis decision making, whether in the cold war period or before World War I, has received a fair amount of attention, and many hypotheses about how decisions are reached have been offered—some rather obvious, others more thought provoking. Although it is clear that crisis decisions require considerably more study, one hypothesis is that decisions in moments of crisis are made by a few people: the president, selected official advisers, and trusted friends and counselors from outside the government.[33] Another is that as decision making "goes to the top," the foreign policy bureaucracies are "short-circuited." Among the consequences of this is that crises are quickly brought to the attention of the government's leading officials, dealt with by them, and not subjected to prolonged bureaucratic infighting or managed according to routine operating procedures. A third hypothesis is that the decision makers feel under enormous pressure because crises tend to be short-lived phenomena, which further raises the already high level of tension. A fourth is that policy makers believe that inaction permits the situation to worsen, so that the disposition is to act. A fifth is that they depreciate the consequences of nonviolent responses and overestimate the effects of violent action. A sixth is that policy makers tend to have relatively little information at their disposal and the less information they have, the greater their reliance on broad stereotypes or emotional images of the enemy. And finally, there is the hypothesis that policy makers see themselves as having few alternative courses of action and the opponent as holding a number of options. What these hypotheses demonstrate is that, although crises are usually handled by the government's top officials, the decisions are most often made under adverse circumstances. In short, if these hypotheses are true, crises would frequently escalate to war.

For example, if U.S. and Soviet policy makers in a confrontation do not have sufficient time to obtain information and evaluate the meanings of their opponents' intentions, as well as to plan tactics to meet threats to their security while simultaneously avoiding the ultimate catastrophe of nuclear war, a dangerous miscalculation becomes a definite possibility. During the 1962 Cuban missile crisis, the Kennedy administration had one week for deliberation. Had it not received intelligence photos of the Soviet missile construction before the installation was completed, had it instead been confronted by an announcement of Soviet missile strength in Cuba, accompanied by a renewed demand for the West to leave West Berlin, nuclear war might have erupted. Washington might have decided to bomb the missile sites, as some of Kennedy's advisers counseled in the early stages of the deliberations, but that would have killed Soviet personnel, and the Kremlin might then have felt compelled to avenge the Soviet dead.

Security Policy. By contrast, security policy takes longer to formulate and involves a far larger number of participants. First is the executive branch, which takes the lead in making this type of decision. The many foreign policy bureaucracies, each with its own point of view and stake in a particular issue, each competing for money and influence, especially for influence in the White House, are all active participants. This situation has changed enormously since 1781, when the Continental Congress established a Department of Foreign Affairs to carry out "all correspondence and business" with other states and authorized it to hire "one or more clerks." Second, and of growing importance as presidents have increasingly assumed the direction of foreign policy, are those members of the White House staff concerned with national security affairs, led by the president's personally chosen assistant. Third is Congress, especially the Senate; power here, however, is widely dispersed among committees in both chambers, committees that are frequently jealous of one another. To mobilize the various factions in Congress in support of administration policies is therefore a time-consuming and often frustrating affair for the president, who may be tempted to make the decisions and sweep Congress along in the name of national unity. Fourth are the many interest groups—economic, veteran, religious, and others—that attempt to influence policies of concern to them. Finally, on the outer fringes, is the public, whose opinions or moods the different policy makers take into account in varying degrees, depending on the particular issue and the scope of public interest. When there is little interest, the decision makers are relatively free to pursue the courses they believe best; when there is a great deal of interest, when mass opinion is aroused and does not fully support government policy, the freedom of the responsible officials is more restricted.

Domestic Policy. Because domestic policy issues are essentially bread-and-butter matters that touch every citizen's pocketbook, they involve all of these categories of actors, only more so. The numbers in each category are multiplied many times by the bureaucracies, congressional committees, interest

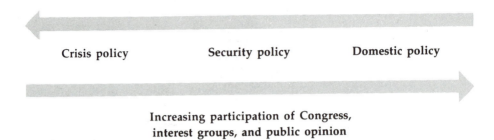

Increasing degree of presidential leadership

Crisis policy   Security policy   Domestic policy

**Increasing participation of Congress,
interest groups, and public opinion**

Figure 2-3 Different Policies, Different Actor Participation

groups, and the "publics" that are not usually concerned with foreign policies. Thus, presidential leadership in domestic policy is far more difficult, if it
is possible at all (see Figure 2-3).

Different Political Systems

There is one final distinction among different kinds of governmental structures that should be stressed: governmental organization leaves its imprint
upon policy "output" in a number of different ways. Kissinger has argued, for
example, that the personal experience of the Soviet leaders in a totalitarian
system affects their conduct of foreign policy. The absence of a constitutionally defined procedure for political succession to positions of real power
means continuous conflict over policy and power at the apex of the Soviet
political structure. Here the game is played in a quite nasty way, for climbing
upward usually means elimination of one's opponents. Stalin murdered most
of his former rivals and associates. Khrushchev purged many of those who
had supported his rise through the bureaucracy, and Leonid Brezhnev deposed and then denounced his former mentor, Khrushchev. The requisites for
upward mobility in the Soviet system of government are an enormous appetite for power, a single-minded dedication to attaining it, and a willingness to
denounce colleagues and confront the unpleasant, even dangerous, consequences of losing. Kissinger wrote, "Nothing in the personal experience of
Soviet leaders would lead them to accept protestations of good will at face
value. Suspicion is inherent in their domestic position. It is unlikely that their
attitude toward the outside world is more benign than toward their own
colleagues or that they would expect more consideration from it." [34]

This nonideological analysis, based upon observations of interaction among
the Soviet political elite suggests that long, tough, and patient bargaining is
necessary in negotiating with the Soviet leadership. Making concessions to

earn good will and elicit reciprocal concessions is a poor bargaining strategy, for the Soviets are unlikely to respond. Only a strategy of *quid pro quo* on each item will have a chance of success, and only after the Soviet rulers are convinced that their self-interest is incorporated in any resulting agreement and that no more concessions can be extracted from their opponent. Material interests are not sacrificed on the altar of good will and fellowship..

Yet it was precisely upon avowals of good will that Roosevelt relied to dissipate Soviet suspicions of the West. Roosevelt, a man of great personal charm and persuasiveness, was addicted to personal diplomacy. He could say "my friend" in eleven languages, and soon after meeting Stalin he was calling him "Uncle Joe." The president never doubted his ability to win Stalin's cooperation in the postwar world. He was too shrewd a politician and too good at manipulating men to fail; mutual good feeling and some hard bargaining had won over many an obstreperous member of Congress. The difficulty was that Roosevelt's technique, so well suited for success domestically, could not be equally successful applied in the quite different international arena.[35]

In domestic matters, Roosevelt and his fellow politicians shared certain common goals after the Great Depression—goals such as restoring the health of the economy, reducing unemployment, and providing for the greater security for all Americans by means of extensive social legislation. But in international politics, especially during wartime, the Allies disagreed not only on how the war was to be won, but also on the basic objectives for a postwar world. Each had a different vision of how that world ought to look. These differences, especially between the Soviet Union and the Western democracies, were too great to be overcome by cordiality.

COMBINING THE THREE LEVELS

The question that remains is: Which level of analysis should be used in understanding international politics? In this book we shall be using all three. Although the state-system level is fundamental, it cannot by itself explain the world politics of the postwar era. To understand why, let us look one final time at three different and previously mentioned historical experiences that have molded our present-day world.

British Policy After World War I

As we stressed earlier in discussing British policy toward Germany in the late 1930s, first-level or state-system analysis will tell us that Britain did not adopt the policies it ought to have adopted, largely because of the pacifist mood of the British public and Chamberlain's misperception of Hitler's intentions. Second- (nation-state) and third- (decision-making) level analyses explain why Chamberlain pursued the policies he did. And we also have suggested that, if Churchill had been prime minister, war might have been avoided, for he perceived Hitler's aims correctly. Had a British leader been able to explain to the public the dire threat to the nation's security with Churchill's eloquence and persuasiveness, Britain might have stood up to Hitler.

But is this analysis of what would have happened an accurate one? It is doubtful. Memories of World War I were too vivid, the desire to avoid its repetition too strong. Chamberlain's policy of appeasement was quite representative of British opinion. How horrible, he had said in a radio address when war with Germany over Czechoslovakia loomed, that the British should be digging trenches and trying on gas masks because of a quarrel in a faraway country between people of whom they knew nothing.[36] When Hitler's message that he would see Chamberlain at Munich arrived, the prime minister was addressing the House of Commons. Interrupting his speech with the news, he was cheered by the Commons. "At once pandemonium broke forth. Everyone was on his feet, cheering, tossing his order papers in the air, some members in tears. It was an unprecedented and most unparliamentary outburst of mass hysteria and relief, in which only a few did not join."[37] Upon his return from Germany, he was met by a jubilant crowd. Roosevelt sent a message: "Good man."

Perhaps the most significant and symbolic aspect of Churchill's career during the late 1930s was precisely that he was not a member of the government. Like Cassandra, he stood with a small group warning of "the gathering storm" over Europe. But Britain did not want to hear him. Churchill was widely condemned as a warmonger in the 1930s. Even when war erupted, Churchill did not take over the prime ministry from the man whose policies had failed so dismally. Chamberlain did not fall until after Germany's unexpected takeover of Denmark and the defeat of British forces in Norway in the spring of 1940. It took both the outbreak of war and a disaster to make Churchill prime minister.

Although the state-system level of analysis can suggest what Britain should have done, the nation-state and decision-making levels can best explain what did happen. The state-system level correctly predicted that failure to play by the rules of the game would mean loss of security and the necessity to fight a war to recover it. But the climate of British democracy ruled out doing what should have been done. As this example shows, we must be careful not to exaggerate the importance of a nation's leader. Foreign policy is not simply a reflection of his or her preferences and perceptions. The leader makes policy within the confines of a state system, a national political system, and a specific policy process.

U.S. Policy After World War II

Immediate postwar policy in the United States provides a striking example of the mutually reinforcing nature of all three levels of analysis. "Rarely has freedom been more clearly the recognition of necessity," Stanley Hoffmann said, "and statesmanship the imaginative exploitation of necessity. America rushed to those gates at which Soviet power was knocking." [38] At the nation-state and decision-making levels policy makers ended up doing what they had to do, but that was by no means a certainty at the end of World War II. After the surrender of Japan, eighteen months passed before the official declaration of the containment policy. Democratic opinion does not normally shift overnight. The American desire for peace, symbolized by a massive postwar demobilization, was too intense. Hostile Soviet acts were necessary before admiration for the Soviet Union, the result of the latter's heroic wartime resistance, could be transformed. Not until Britain's support for Greece and Turkey was withdrawn in early 1947 did President Harry Truman confront the fact that only the United States possessed the power to establish a new balance that would secure both Europe and America while preserving the peace. Whenever in this century British power had weakened and Germany had stood on the verge of attaining European hegemony, the United States had become involved to reestablish the equilibrium; with Britain's complete collapse after World War II, the United States had no choice but to take over Britain's former responsibility.[39]

Truman also showed that he had a keen awareness of the strategic significance of the eastern Mediterranean. When General Dwight Eisenhower, at a meeting with the president, showed his concern that Truman might not fully understand the gravity of the course he was embarking on in an area so far removed from the United States, the president responded by pulling an obviously well worn map of the Middle East out of a desk drawer and giving a group of top government officials, including Eisenhower, a "masterful" lecture on the historical and strategic importance of the area. Finishing, he turned to Eisenhower and good-humoredly asked whether the general was satisfied; Eisenhower joined in the laughter and said that he was.[40] By later going before a joint session of Congress and explaining to the whole country the new situation facing the United States, Truman was able to mobilize both congressional and popular support. In this example, therefore, the state-system level is of primary importance in explaining U.S. policy. The nation-state and decision-making levels tell us how accurately the policy makers perceived "reality" and how they were able in a democratic society to mobilize popular support for the new containment policy.

The United States and China in the 1970s

In the 1930s the public mood of appeasement meant that Churchill's warnings about Hitler were ignored, and Britain failed to do what it needed to do to preserve the balance. In the 1940s after World War II, Truman was able to arouse support to contain Soviet power after an initial military demobilization, an attempt to withdraw once more to the concerns of the Western Hemisphere, and a brief period of thinking that it was America's task to mediate between Britain and the Soviet Union. (The British, as usual, had begun to organize European' opposition to Moscow.) Years later, President Richard Nixon, together with Kissinger, his national security assistant, were also the right men at the right place at the right time. Even before he became president, Nixon favored exploiting the split between the two largest Communist states and attracting China into a Sino-American coalition against the Soviet Union. Kissinger was assigned the task of "opening the door" to the new China. They were able to pursue this policy because they were Republicans and because of the war in Vietnam. From 1950 until that time, the Republicans had made it impossible for any Democratic administration to recognize China by accusing the Democrats of being "appeasers" and "soft on communism." But a Republican president, who had been one of the chief accusers and had always had a tough anti-Communist stance, could hardly be accused of being an appeaser. Furthermore, Vietnam had largely disillusioned the nation with anticommunism, which appeared to be a chief reason why the United States had become involved in the war. Thus, Nixon and Kissinger could do in 1972 what they could not have done earlier. Even as Republicans, opposition within their own party would have been too strong, and anti-Chinese feelings still would have been widespread.

In the remainder of this book the three levels of analysis are discussed in three sections. In Parts II and III we focus on the state system; in Part IV we concentrate on the second and third levels. Part V then deals with the possible transformation of the state system. In fact, the division is not quite that neat. While analyzing the state system, we cannot separate it, for example, from the policy makers' perceptions of the system or from crisis decision making. And, in analyzing the second and third levels, it is not always possible to keep the specific political system separate from decision-making institutions and processes. Nevertheless, our broad distinction between the external environment in which states exist and the internal characteristics of the specific actors remains paramount.

Notes

1. Nicholas J. Spykman, *America's Strategy in World Politics: The United States and the Balance of Power* (New York: Harcourt, 1942), 21. Also see Raymond Aron, *Peace and War* (New York: Doubleday, 1966); and Stanley Hoffmann, *The State of War* (New York: Holt, Rinehart & Winston, 1965). For a more extensive discussion of the various ways in which analysts use the term *balance of power*, see Ernst B. Haas, "The Balance of Power: Prescription, Concept, or Propaganda," *World Politics*, July 1953, 442-477; and Inis L. Claude, Jr., *Power and International Relations* (New York: Random House, 1962), 11-39.
2. Claude, *Power and International Relations*, 43, emphasis added.
3. Edward H. Buehrig, *Woodrow Wilson and the Balance of Power* (Bloomington: Indiana

University Press, 1955); and Arthur S. Link, *Wilson the Diplomatist* (Baltimore: Johns Hopkins University Press, 1957), passim, esp. 61-90.

4. For the period from 1937 to 1941, the most detailed analysis will be found in *The Challenge to Isolation* by William L. Langer and S. Everett Gleason (New York: Harper & Row, 1952); idem, *The Undeclared War* (New York: Harper & Row, 1953). A briefer study is *The Reluctant Belligerent* by Robert A. Divine (New York: John Wiley & Son, 1965).

5. William H. McNeill, *America, Britain and Russia—Their Cooperation and Conflict, 1941-1946* (London: Oxford University Press, 1953), written for the Royal Institute of International Affairs; and Herbert Feis, *Churchill-Roosevelt-Stalin: The War They Waged and the Peace They Sought* (Princeton, N.J.: Princeton University Press, 1957). A shorter study is *American Diplomacy During the Second World War, 1941-1945* by Gaddis Smith (New York: John Wiley & Sons, 1965).

6. Robert E. Sherwood, *Roosevelt and Hopkins: An Intimate History* (New York: Harper & Row, 1948), 748.

7. Ibid., 70.

8. Cordell Hull, *The Memoirs of Cordell Hull* (New York: Macmillan, 1948), 2: 1314-1315.

9. Louis J. Halle, *The Cold War as History* (New York: Harper & Row, 1967), 10-19.

10. Thomas W. Wolfe, *Soviet Power and Europe, 1945-1970* (Baltimore: Johns Hopkins University Press, 1970), 10.

11. Ibid., 11; and Samuel P. Huntington, *The Common Defense* (New York: Columbia University Press, 1961), 33-39.

12. W. Averell Harriman, *America and Russia in a Changing World: A Half Century of Personal Observation* (Garden City, N.Y.: Doubleday, 1971), 44.

13. See, for example, Harold Nicolson, *The Congress of Vienna* (New York: Harcourt, 1946); and Edward V. Gulick, *Europe's Classical Balance of Power* (New York: W. W. Norton, 1967).

14. Paul E. Seabury, *The Rise and Decline of the Cold War* (New York: Basic Books, 1967), 59.

15. Halle, *Cold War*, xiii.

16. William J. Newman, *The Balance of Power in the Interwar Years, 1919-1939* (New York: Random House, 1968); Arnold Wolfers, *Britain and France Between Two Wars* (New York: W. W. Norton, 1966); and Winston S. Churchill, *The Gathering Storm*, vol. 1 of *The Second World War* (Boston: Houghton Mifflin, 1948), 90.

17. Frederick H. Hartmann, *The Relations of Nations*, 6th ed. (New York: Macmillan, 1983), 18.

18. Erich Maria Remarque, *All Quiet on the Western Front*, trans. A. W. Wheen (Boston: Little, Brown & Co., 1929), 289-290.

19. Among other sources on this period, see Churchill, *Gathering Storm*; Charles L. Mowat, *Britain Between the Wars 1918-1940* (Chicago: University of Chicago Press, 1955); and A. J. P. Taylor, *English History, 1914-1945* (New York: Oxford University Press, 1965).

20. Walter Lippmann has defined the role of democratic public opinion negatively. Precisely because of its emphasis on wealth and welfare, Lippmann argues, democratic opinion makes it difficult to take the necessary preparations to avoid war: "The rule to which there are few exceptions ... is that at the critical junctures, when the stakes are high, the prevailing mass opinion will impose what amounts to a veto upon changing the course on which the government is at the time

proceeding. Prepare for war in time of peace? No. It is bad to raise taxes, to unbalance the budget, to take men away from their schools or their jobs, to provoke the enemy." Walter Lippmann, *The Public Philosophy* (Boston: Little, Brown & Co., 1955), 19-20.

21. George F. Kennan, *American Diplomacy 1900-1950* (Chicago: University of Chicago Press, 1951), 65-66.

22. George F. Kennan, *Russia and the West Under Lenin and Stalin* (Boston: Little, Brown & Co., 1961), 33-36.

23. Kennan, *American Diplomacy*, 55-57, 68-69.

24. Henry A. Kissinger, *Nuclear Weapons and Foreign Policy* (New York: Harper & Row, 1957), 326; and Kissinger, *A World Restored* (New York: Grosset & Dunlap, 1964).

25. Quoted from Carlton J. H. Hayes, *The Historical Evolution of Modern Nationalism* (New York: Macmillan, 1950), 40.

26. Kennan, *Russia and the West*, 181.

27. Harold Sprout and Margaret Sprout, *The Ecological Perspective on Human Affairs* (Princeton, N.J.: Princeton University Press, 1965), 28-30.

28. The drama of Munich is captured by John Wheeler-Bennett, *Munich: Prologue to Tragedy* (London: Macmillan, 1948).

29. Townsend Hoopes, *The Limits of Intervention* (New York: McKay, 1969), 7-13.

30. Ibid., 13-16.

31. Tom Wicker, *JFK and LBJ: The Influence of Personality upon Politics* (Baltimore: Penguin, 1969), 192.

32. See J. William Fulbright, *The Arrogance of Power* (New York: Vintage, 1967), pt. 2; Arthur M. Schlesinger, Jr., *The Bitter Heritage* (New York: Fawcett, 1967); and Theodore Draper, *Abuse of Power* (New York: Viking, 1966).

33. Ole Holsti, "The 1914 Case," *American Political Science Review* (June 1965): 365-378; and Glen D. Paige, *The Korean Decision* (New York: Free Press, 1968), 273ff.

34. Henry A. Kissinger, *American Foreign Policy* (New York: W. W. Norton, 1969), 36-37.

35. Gaddis Smith, *American Diplomacy During the Second World War* (New York: John Wiley & Sons, 1966), 9.

36. *Times* (London), Sept. 28, 1938; and Wheeler-Bennett, *Munich*, 157-158.

37. Mowat, *Britain Between the Wars*, 617.

38. Hoffmann, *State of War*, 163.

39. Joseph M. Jones, *The Fifteen Weeks* (New York: Viking, 1955).

40. Ibid., 63-64.

Part Two

THE STATE
SYSTEM

CHAPTER 3

The Players:
States and
Other Actors

THE CHARACTERISTICS OF STATES

Since the Peace of Westphalia in 1648 the primary political actor in the state system has been the sovereign *state*. The number of states has more than doubled since 1945, when there were fifty-one members in the United Nations—nineteen from Europe and related areas, twenty from Latin America, only twelve from Asia and Africa. Twenty-five years later, the less-developed countries (LDCs) of Asia and Africa alone constituted more than half of the total United Nations membership. If the LDCs of Latin America are included, these states constitute a sizable majority. Altogether there are almost 170 states today, including a few that are not members of the United Nations. Some forecasters predict 200 states by the year 2000. Humanity, it is clear, is divided by nation-states. As different as these states are in terms of size, human and natural resources, and political and economic systems, they share certain characteristics: sovereignty, territory, population and nationalism, armed forces, and recognition by other states.

Sovereignty

Each state is considered sovereign and possesses both internal and external sovereignty. Internal sovereignty refers to a state's government—not that of any other state—deciding how it will manage its domestic problems. This may mean, as in the words of the U.S. Constitution, that it will "insure domestic tranquility, provide for the common defense, promote the general welfare...." All governments are concerned with maintaining domestic peace and national defense; how concerned they are with the general welfare

55

varies. In democracies, elections have provided not only an extension of freedom but also have created broadly based welfare states. But sovereignty in the case of undemocratic states can also mean the brutal treatment of their own population. In Cambodia, the Pol Pot regime killed an estimated 2 million to 3 million of its 8 million people, and 600,000 fled into exile. After it had unified Vietnam, the victorious North treated the southern population, especially the ethnic Chinese, so harshly that 900,000 fled in rickety boats, and many drowned in the process. At least 10,000 Vietnamese were imprisoned because they worked for the Americans. Hitler slaughtered the German Jews. Stalin killed an estimated 12 million to 15 million people in the forced collectivization of the peasantry and the elimination of the class of small landholders during the 1920s, allowed 5 million to die during the 1933 famine while he increased grain exports, and killed several million during the Great Purges in the later 1930s.

All governments, regardless of how they treat their citizens, reject foreign interference in their domestic affairs. The Soviets, for example, have repeatedly dismissed Western human rights campaigns on behalf of Soviet dissidents. But this does not stop governments from interfering frequently in one another's affairs. For example, the United States condemned the South African government for its treatment of its black population, and Congress imposed punitive economic sanctions in support of its condemnation of South Africa's racism.

In addition, the sovereignty of smaller states is severely constrained by their dependence on the good will and tolerance of the great powers, both neighboring and far off, upon whom they depend for their security and/or markets in which to sell their goods. The states of Eastern Europe used to be referred to as *satellites* because their governments, although nominally sovereign, were in fact under Moscow's control. Over the years, these states have become more independent, mainly in domestic affairs, but the Soviets intervened directly in 1953, 1956, and 1968 and indirectly (via the Polish army in Poland) in 1981, to ensure these nations' loyalty to Russia, the Soviet bloc, and the military alliance known as the Warsaw Treaty Organization. Sovereignty is even more questionable in Afghanistan than in the states of Eastern Europe. Since the 1979 invasion, the Soviet Union has run Afghanistan's government. Thus, although sovereignty acknowledges each government's exclusive jurisdiction over its nation's territory and people, in practice that concept does not always work. This is even true for more powerful countries such as the United States, which appears increasingly to be losing control over its borders and the flow of illegal immigrants. Sovereignty is never absolute. The 1970s demonstrated painfully that the Western industrial countries did not fully control their own economies as world oil prices escalated and Western inflation and unemployment followed. In the age of economic interdependence, sovereignty is relative.

External sovereignty refers to a nation's right to define its interests. It decides what its objectives are to be, the priority among these objectives, and how to pursue them, whether by alliances with other states or the use of force if it deems that necessary. Indeed, under international law, the state is the sole organization that has the legal right to use force. Usually only a defeat in war, the breakdown of the national frontier's protective shell, may permit a foreign state to take over sovereign control, to make and enforce rules for the vanquished state's people, as the United States did in Japan for a number of years after World War II. Sometimes neighbors intervene in a sovereign state and govern it, as when a nonstate actor, the Palestine Liberation Organization (PLO) and then Syria and Israel intervened in Lebanon during the 1970s. The Lebanese government was powerless during this period as the PLO in fact constituted a "state within a state," and Beirut was virtually *its* capital city rather than Lebanon's.[1] After Israel's full-scale invasion of Lebanon in 1982 and the expulsion of the PLO from that country, the Lebanese government disintegrated completely. The principal Lebanese factions—Maronite Christians (supported by the Israelis and, briefly, by U.S. Marines), Shi'ite and Sunni Muslims and Druse (backed by Syria)—found it impossible to establish a united government. After Israel's withdrawal, it was Syria that exercised authority in Lebanon, but there were limits even to Syrian control over events in a country where the civil war among these quarreling factions intensified in ferocity and violence. Lebanon after 1982 was a state in utter chaos; gunmen roamed the streets and the various militias attacked one another for control of what was left of that "nation."

Both the internal and external sovereignty of a state are exercised through its government. Official interstate relationships are conducted through representatives who are empowered to act on behalf of their states. The decisions made are binding upon the participating states if agreed upon according to each state's constitutional processes. In the United States, for example, a treaty negotiated and signed by the president is not binding until it has received the consent of two-thirds of the Senate. In the Soviet Union, if the Politburo agrees to sign a treaty, it is for all practical purposes in force. Furthermore, once a state assumes specific commitments, they are binding not only upon the present government that has agreed to them, but also upon future governments. Only occasionally do governments renounce such commitments; usually this occurs after revolutions have brought into power new regimes that denounce their predecessor's commitments.

In almost all forms of government, foreign policy decisions are made by a relatively small group of people, usually in the executive branch of the government. This is as true for democracies as for authoritarian states. The difference is that in the former, free elections regularly lead to changes in policy makers and that officials can be held accountable. Although presidents or prime ministers may possess a certain degree of discretionary power so that they can lead their nations, they and their colleagues are also subject to popular opinions and pressures; indeed, from time to time and on certain issues they may pursue policies they would prefer not to because they feel they have little choice. Had Neville Chamberlain been as prescient as Winston Churchill in the late 1930s, would he have pursued any policy other than the appeasement of Germany? After the withdrawal of U.S. forces from Vietnam in 1973, could any U.S. government have intervened two years later to save South Vietnam from collapse? Generally, however, democratic governments have a good deal of freedom to pursue policies they see fit within rather broad limitations.

Territory

Another characteristic of a state is its territory. Frontiers separate one state from another. When crossing a border or flying from one country to another, travelers normally have to show immigration officials some sort of identification and proof of their citizenship and have their luggage searched, if customs officials deem it necessary. Sometimes crossing a border can be a grim business, as when one is going through the Berlin Wall. The frontier dividing East Germany from West Germany is marked by barbed wire, watchtowers, and armed guards. One may, of course, be forbidden entry into some countries, and sometimes citizens can leave their countries only by escape. Most frontiers, admittedly, are not like that. Nor does the existence of borders mean that they are not, on occasion, contested.

In any event, all states possess territory; without territory there would be no state. When a state relinquishes control of a piece of territory, as the colonial countries of Europe did after World War II, another state is established and exercises authority over the territory. In this way the British gave up their colony in India and transferred its control to a sovereign native government. India defined her frontiers as those established by the British and defended them against Chinese territorial claims. When Austria-Hungary completely disintegrated after World War I, the separate states of Austria, Hungary, Yugoslavia, and Czechoslovakia governed the areas each inherited. It is this association of a state with land that is central to a state's conception of itself, and it is for the preservation of this territorial integrity that states go to war.

Population and Nationalism

States possess not just land; they have populations, ranging from the more than 1 billion people in the People's Republic of China to fewer than 100,000 people in the island of Dominica. The fact that we often use the terms *state* and *nation-state* interchangeably also suggests one additional characteristic of modern states: the national loyalty populations feel for their countries. Before 1789 and the French Revolution, most states were ruled by kings, and most people living within the territorial confines of such dynastic states did not really identify with them. At times, kings traded people and lands. But the nationalism born in France and then stirred up in the rest of Europe in reaction to French conquest led people increasingly to identify with their nations.

It is difficult to define a nation exactly, but we can say that it is a collective identity shared by people living within certain frontiers as a result of their common history (plus a good deal of mythology dramatizing the past), expectations of remaining together in the future, and usually a common language that allows them to communicate more easily with one another than with the inhabitants of neighboring nations who speak different languages. Ernest Renan, a Frenchman, characterized a nation as "a daily plebiscite," a continuous emotional commitment to a group of people distinct from every other segment of humanity, celebrating their "nationhood" with anthems, poetry, statues of heroes who have defended it, and other symbols.

But nationality and geographical boundaries do not always coincide in real life. The Soviet Union is a multinational state in which the Great Russians, who historically have controlled Russia, finally ceased constituting the majority of the Soviet people, and this shrinking of their minority status will grow. Often hated by the many other nationalities that comprise the contemporary Soviet Union, the Great Russians must be concerned about their future control and dominance of a nation that sprawls over one-sixth of the world's land surface. In the early 1980s Canada faced the possible secession of French-speaking Quebec, and, although that likelihood has lessened, many in Quebec still have a strong desire for self-government. Such a potentially divisive nationalism, leading ultimately to disintegration and civil war, occurs more frequently among LDCs than among the older, more cohesive nation-states of Europe. Maintaining national unity remains a primary problem for many of these new states because they are composed of various ethnic or tribal groups, often with different religious beliefs, different languages, and little in common except the shared experience of colonial rule. Thus, states such as Nigeria, Zaire, and India experienced civil wars upon becoming independent; others, like Pakistan, which emerged out of India, broke into even smaller sovereign states.

Even Communist states, which disavow nationalism in favor of the international proletariat, are fiercely nationalistic. In Eastern Europe, where the various Communist regimes have little legitimacy, they have increasingly appealed to nationalistic sentiment in order to boost their popularity. Elsewhere, nationalism in the Communist world has led to war: Vietnam against Cambodia, China versus Vietnam, and, very nearly, Russia against China, after the latter invaded Vietnam, Russia's ally, in 1979. And in non-Communist Iran, the fierce flame of Islamic fundamentalism has added great passion to Iranian nationalism. In its continuing war with Iraq, which began in 1981, thousands of Iranians, young and old, without much military training, have advanced into the withering fire of the Iraqi army, and, even if they were not yearning for martyrdom, have willingly sacrificed their lives. Other states, such as Pakistan and Saudi Arabia, have reacted by invoking Islam to rally their people and strengthen their own nationalism.

For the LDCs, as for developed nations, Communist or non-Communist, Islamic or not, the nation is the largest political organization with which most people can identify; they may give their loyalty to the family, tribe, religion, or region, but it is generally the nation that commands the ultimate loyalty and for which most have in the past been willing to sacrifice their lives if necessary. This is less a matter of blind patriotism than a recognition that the nation is the largest secular community in which a meaningful life can be lived. It may be that the nation as the fundamental actor in international politics may cause much danger and, in the atomic age, constitute a threat to survival itself; nevertheless, there is as yet no viable substitute for it.

Armed Forces

Given the claims that states are sovereign, that they have frontiers and populations, it would be remiss not to mention their ability to defend themselves and their potential to make war as another characteristic of statehood. Armed forces and the state are inseparably linked; they serve the state's interests. As organizations trained to inflict violence, armed forces historically have been used to do precisely that. War, indeed, "has been the instrument by which most of the great facts of political national history have been established and maintained.... The map of the world today has been largely determined upon the battlefield. The maintenance of civilization itself has been, and still continues to be, underwritten by the insurance of an army and navy ready to strike at any time where danger threatens." [2]

American history abounds in examples: wars among the European colonial powers largely determined the territory each acquired on the North American continent. The United States established its independence by war. The Louisiana Purchase was possible because France was deeply involved in a European war and expected to lose the territory anyway. It was the fear of war with the new republic that induced Spain to open up the Mississippi and surrender the Floridas. The threat of war was also used to resolve the Oregon boundary dispute. A war with Mexico ensued after the annexation of Texas, leading to the acquisition of the entire Southwest territory. Force was employed to dislodge the Indians when they blocked the westward expansion or were living on land the pioneers sought. Puerto Rico and the Philippines were taken during the Spanish-American War. Hawaii was annexed after the American settlers had overthrown the Hawaiian government. The War of 1812 was fought to preserve American independence and security. And the Civil War was fought to preserve the Union. American history would therefore suggest that war has traditionally played a crucial role in giving birth to new states, defining their frontiers, and preserving political independence and territorial integrity.

In this connection, David Ben-Gurion, the creator of the Israeli state and its first leader, placed this relationship between population and the armed forces in a crystal-clear light. He established the policy that Israel must always retaliate if the state or its citizens were attacked. The aim of such action would be not only to deter the Arab states, but to preserve moral and educational values as well. Israel was composed of Jews from all over the world, many from countries where to kill or harm Jews was not regarded a crime. Israel and its army would change that attitude by demonstrating that the consequences for shedding Jewish blood were serious. Jewish life and property had value.[3]

In short, states—city-states, feudal-states, or nation-states—have gone to war because they have felt it was in their interests, that on balance it was less costly to fight in defense or pursuit of their interests than *not* to fight. War was preferable to being eliminated, defeated, or failing to achieve a goal such as creating a new state or a larger and more powerful one. Armed forces and war, in short, receive their legitimacy from the existence of states and their determination to survive.

Recognition by Other States

Generally, a state is officially recognized by other states when it is perceived as having established control over the people within its boundaries. At that point it is customary to exchange ambassadors and undertake agreements. In reality, matters are not always so straightforward. For example, the state of Israel has existed since 1948, but, of the Arab states, only Egypt has recognized it, taking thirty years to do so; the others still refuse, even though they have fought four wars with Israel. Recognition means acceptance of a state as a legitimate political entity. Even without recognition, however, diplomatic relations can exist. The United States did not recognize mainland China until 1979, but, just as the Arab states have negotiated cease-fires and prisoner exchanges with Israel, the United States negotiated with China to end the Korean War, attended the great-power conference ending the first Indochina war in 1954, and occasionally met with Chinese officials to explore certain issues. The disadvantage of such relations is that they are intermittent and do not easily permit mutual and accurate assessment of intentions and capabilities.

The basic practice is to extend *de facto* recognition when a new state is born; the fact of its existence is the key. But some states will extend recognition only *de jure*, that is, when they approve of the new government. The United States was slow to recognize both the Soviet and the Communist Chinese governments, taking sixteen years and thirty years before officially extending recognition. Sometimes the situation becomes an awkward one. The United States recognizes the Sandinista government in Nicaragua, but President Ronald Reagan's administration made a clear commitment to its overthrow. Or different states recognize rival governments of another state. During World War II the Germans established puppet governments in conquered lands, but the Western Allies continued to recognize the former governments, which were usually quartered in exile in London. Poland at one time actually had three governments: one recognized by the West, one recognized by the Germans, and one (composed of pro-Moscow Communists) recognized by the Soviets.

Since World War II, Moscow and Washington have at times recognized rival governments: in East and West Germany, North and South Korea, North and South Vietnam, and Communist and Nationalist China. Both now recognize each of the Germanies. South Vietnam no longer exists, but the United States has not recognized the new unified Communist People's Republic of Vietnam. Washington has withdrawn recognition from the Nationalists on Taiwan and opened official diplomatic relations with Communist China. It continues, however, to supply arms to Taiwan. Because both the Communists and Nationalists agree that there is only one China, the United States is supplying weapons to a province that is in rebellion against the government that Washington recognizes as the legitimate ruler of China!

Even more bizarre is the situation of Hong Kong, a British colony leased from China for ninety-nine years until 1997. Adjoining the Chinese mainland, Hong Kong is a thriving capitalist society whose inhabitants enjoy Western-style freedoms. China and Britain have agreed to resolve Hong Kong's future status by a solution known as "one country, two systems." The Chinese Communist flag will wave over Hong Kong as it again becomes part of (Communist) China, but, for fifty more years, Hong Kong will be an autonomous administrative region of China with its own capitalist social and economic system and a Western way of life. Why does Beijing not just demand the Crown Colony's return or take it, as it could easily do? The reasons are twofold: one, Hong Kong's position as a trading and international financial center is economically beneficial to mainland China; and two, and even more important, Beijing would like to tempt the Nationalist Chinese on Taiwan to make the same kind of agreement. China could thus be reunited as a single country while Taiwan, like Hong Kong, enjoyed self-government, its higher standard of living, different economic and political systems, and its own army (supplied with weapons by the United States). Whether, of course, Beijing will tolerate both free trade and free speech in Hong Kong when the British lease expires remains to be seen, and whether an arrangement similar to Hong Kong's will be acceptable to Taiwan also only the future will reveal.

CLASSIFICATION OF STATES

Great Powers and Small Powers

The most widespread and traditional means of distinguishing among states is in terms of the power they possess. The components of power include geographic location, size, population, industry, and wealth (see Chapter 7). Most observers have long distinguished between "great powers" and "small powers." We can say, almost by definition, that the great powers generally have been considered the primary actors in the state system.

Table 3-1 The Great Powers

	Napoleonic Wars	World War I	World War II	Cold War and Détente
Austria-Hungary	x	x	—	—
Britain	x	x	x	x
France	x	x	x	x
Italy	—	x	x	x
Japan	—	x	x	x
Prussia-Germany	x	x	x	x
Russia/Soviet Union	x	x	x	x
United States	—	x	x	x

The Primacy of Great Powers. Particularly striking is the remarkable stability in the ranking of great powers, despite vast geographic, industrial, and social changes in Europe during the nineteenth century. We need only list the great powers since the French Revolution and the Napoleonic wars (see Table 3-1).

Stability in these rankings does not mean that changes in individual positions have not occurred. Prussia, which made its mark against Napoleon, became part of an enlarged and united Germany in 1870 after the defeat of France. Germany then replaced France as the Continent's preeminent power and became a rival to Britain, at that time the leading power in the world. Germany built a large navy in addition to the sizable and highly efficient army it already possessed. Austria-Hungary, by contrast, declined after the Napoleonic Wars and lost its place as the primary power in central Europe to Prussia, which, to the astonishment of the rest of Europe, defeated Austria in 1866 in only six weeks. By the turn of the twentieth century, Japan and the United States had joined the other great powers and had transformed the Europe-centered system into a global system. Germany made its bid for European, if not Eurasian, dominance in 1914, but American intervention in 1917, after Russia's defeat, ensured the failure of this venture. American withdrawal into isolationism again meant that the postwar European balance remained fragile. Germany was too strong for Britain and France to contain by themselves. Again, American intervention was the key factor in the failure of Germany's second drive for domination. But two world wars in this century had exhausted Britain, France, and Germany. Only two powers emerged still strong: the Soviet Union, despite its enormous losses in World War II, and the United States. Both were continental powers with populations and resources to match, dwarfing the great powers of the past. Hence the term *superpowers*.

The international system has always granted a special place to the great powers. During the nineteenth century the Concert of Europe was composed exclusively of the great powers; they were the self-appointed board of directors of the European "corporation," meeting from time to time to deal with significant political problems that affected the peace of Europe. This special great-power status and responsibility was reflected in the League of Nations Covenant, which gave such powers permanent membership on the Council; the Assembly, composed of the smaller nations, was expected to meet only every four or five years. In those days, "the world seemed to be the oyster of the great powers." [4] After Germany's second defeat, their privileged status and obligations were again recognized in the United Nations Charter provision that conferred upon the United States, the Soviet Union, Britain, France, and China (which at the time was still controlled by the Nationalists) permanent membership on the Security Council. The General Assembly was not expected to play a major role in preserving the peace. Interestingly enough, these same five states were, by 1971, when Communist China was admitted to the United Nations, also the only countries to have nuclear weapons.

Small Powers as Victims.   In contrast, small powers have often acted less than they have been acted upon. Their security frequently depends on the great powers. Even a state like Israel, which has fought its own wars, is very conscious of its dependence on the United States for modern weapons and money. Israel is also constantly concerned about U.S. diplomatic pressure to make concessions that it believes inimical to its interests but that Washington perceives as necessary to achieve an overall settlement in the Middle East. Even greater limits are felt by the states of Eastern Europe. Although they are no longer completely subservient to the Soviet Union and cannot be called satellites, Moscow has claimed in the Brezhnev Doctrine the right to determine when socialism is in danger of being subverted and to intervene militarily to prevent that, as it did in 1953 in East Germany, in 1956 in Hungary, in 1968 in Czechoslovakia, and in 1981 in Poland.

The United States under the Monroe Doctrine frequently has intervened in Latin America. Despite the failure of a 1961 U.S.-sponsored invasion of Cuba, the United States intervened either overtly or covertly on several occasions to prevent "another Cuba" and to contain Cuban and Soviet influence in the Western Hemisphere. In addition, the United States intervened in the Dominican Republic during the Johnson presidency, in Chile during the Nixon presidency, and in Grenada and Nicaragua during the Reagan presidency.

In general, a small country, if it lies close to a great power, must be very careful. It had better not give offense, and it must be especially aware and sensitive to the great power's interests. We have already noted the fate of Russia's neighbors, the countries of Eastern Europe. Latin-American, especially Caribbean, countries remember other U.S. interventions going back to the late nineteenth century. Since Fidel Castro assumed power in Cuba and allied himself to the Soviet Union, the fear of a second Cuba on the South and Central American continents has made the possibility of U.S. interventions a reality. The United States briefly invaded the small nation of Grenada in 1983 to rid the island of its pro-Cuban and pro-Soviet regime. After that invasion, Cuba told Nicaragua that, given U.S. power, Cuba would be unable to help its friends if the United States were to use force against them. That possibility certainly hangs over the United States' quarrel with Nicaragua, which is also pro-Cuban and pro-Soviet. But force is less likely to be used in a situation that Congress views as more comparable to Vietnam than to Grenada. For in Grenada the United States faced only light resistance; this would not be true in Nicaragua. Still, Nicaragua has to be careful to avoid actions the United States would interpret as provocative if, like many small countries throughout history, it does not want to become a victim.

The Hierarchy of States. Actually, the division of countries into great and small powers, although useful, is rather unsophisticated. It is useful because it simplifies the analysis and conduct of international politics. It allows the scholar and diplomat to focus on demands of the great powers and the interaction among them. Focusing on a relatively few states makes it easier to understand and analyze international politics. And it does tell the essential story. The needs of the weak have in the past been either ignored or received negligible attention. While oversimplified, the old axiom that the strong do as they please and the weak suffer as they must expresses a simple truth about the relations among nations. But the international hierarchy of states is in reality far more complex than the simple hierarchy of great and small powers.

At the top of the hierarchy since World War II are the two superpowers, the United States and the Soviet Union. Clearly, the very term *superpower* suggests their preeminence in the state system and their superiority even to the traditional great powers. The United States and the Soviet Union are in a category all by themselves. Usually their status is equated with their vast nuclear forces; the small forces of other nuclear nations are not yet comparable. But, even if nuclear arms had never been invented, these two countries would be superpowers. As countries with populations of more than 200 million people and sizable industries, they have also been able to afford large conventional forces and to use their wealth and technology to advance their aims. Their interactions at the top of the international pecking order have influenced, if not determined, the policies of more states than the interactions among lower-ranking members.[5] One of the paradoxes of the post-World War II state system has been that it has witnessed simultaneously a massive expansion of states—approximately one hundred new nations—and a significant contraction of primary actors, like the superpowers, in the system.

After these two powers are the second-rank powers—Britain, France, West Germany, China, and Japan—whose capacities to act in one or more of the regions beyond their own are relatively limited. The first three—pre-World War II members of the great-power club—have recovered from their collapse after 1945, but they can play a world role again only if collectively they succeed someday in extending the economic unity of the Common Market, whose leading members they are, to political and military unity in Europe. Individually, these nations will remain in their present status and feel vulnerable in a superpower world. In every postwar crisis outside of Europe, where the North Atlantic Treaty Organization (NATO) alliance has stood together against the Soviet Union, the Europeans have felt endangered. Whether it was U.S. involvement in the Korean or Vietnamese wars, the 1973 Arab-Israeli wars (which led to the first huge oil price increase), or the 1979 Soviet invasion of Afghanistan (which led to renewed American opposition to the Soviet Union), the Europeans have repeatedly sought to remain uninvolved. The United States, aware of its strength, acted in the belief it could influence events. The European nations, aware of their declining strength in this century, felt just the opposite, namely, that they could not influence these events. Therefore, they sought to distance themselves from the United States in case there were reprisals. Only by uniting can the second-rank European states regain the confidence to play a role proportionate to their population, wealth, and military experience.

One fact, however, is already clear. The frequent assertion in the late 1960s and early 1970s that Europe and Japan, economically recovered from World War II and very prosperous, would be able to use their economic power to attain great political influence died with the rise of the Organization of Petroleum Exporting Countries (OPEC). At that time the nine European Common Market states, which together have a population slightly larger and a productive capacity quite a bit larger than those of the Soviet Union, quickly folded before their former colonies and endorsed Arab aims in the 1973 war. So did Japan, even though it is regarded as an economic superpower. In subsequent years, dependent upon Arab oil, all these states remained sensitive to Arab political aims.

Although there is no one-to-one relationship between military power and political influence, such a relationship does exist. Those countries that have possessed the most military strength, have been willing to use it, and have gained a reputation for its successful use generally have exercised the most influence. Japan is attempting to disprove the rule. One observer has aptly commented: "Japan is allegedly intent upon the alchemist's 'grand experiment,' the transmutation of great economic into great political power without the use of any military catalyst." [8] OPEC, too, after a heady attempt at such a transmutation, found within a decade that it could not wield much political power. Great-power status without sufficient military power and some definition of the political role that the nation ought to play is not possible; economic capacity alone is not enough. Neither Europe nor Japan can defend itself without U.S. power or exercise influence commensurate with its economic productivity and wealth. Similarly, China, weak economically and even militarily, is only a potential superpower. The fact remains that the capacity to produce automobiles, steel, and video recorders does not translate into the type of influence the United States and the Soviet Union both exercise to shape events in areas both near and far from themselves.

From there on down we can divide nations into middle-rank powers such as Italy and Spain in Europe, India in Asia, and Brazil in Latin America (the latter two potential superpowers); minor powers such as Norway, Hungary,

South Korea, and Colombia; and microstates such as Grenada, Djibouti (population 394,000), Cape Verde (366,000), Brunei (240,000), the Seychelles (68,000), or Kitts-Nevis (65,000).[7]

Projection of Global, Regional, and Local Power

A closely related criterion for classifying states according to their power is the extent of their interest and capacity to intervene in affairs beyond their own frontiers. Power "makes ambitious projects feasible and increases ... their chances of success; weakness constrains, restrains and limits choice and independence."[8] The superpowers have the capacity to project their power throughout the entire state system. The United States, with its sealift and airlift ability, has long had a global reach. It could intervene overnight in Lebanon and fight a long war in Vietnam at the end of ten thousand miles of supply lines. (The generals in Moscow must have been envious.) The Soviet Union, the Avis of the superpowers, was initially a Eurasian power, although control of foreign Communist parties did extend its reach. But an enormous military buildup, including a blue-sea fleet and airlift capacity, has given Moscow a systemwide capability as well. Under both czars and commissars, Russian expansion has been concentrated around the nation's periphery. In the 1970s, for the first time it expanded its influence beyond Eurasia to Angola, Ethiopia, and South Yemen.

The second-rank states are essentially regional powers. The former colonial powers have largely limited their roles to Europe. Britain's last foreign intervention came during the war over the Suez Canal in 1956; it was a dismal failure, ending in the collapse of the British government. It was 1982 before Britain again acted far outside Europe. When Argentina seized the Falkland Islands off its coast, Britain sent a large naval unit to restore British sovereignty and wipe out the humiliation of the seizure. France, which had joined with Britain in 1956 to intervene in Egypt, reacted to that defeat by developing a nuclear bomb in order to recoup its prestige and to play an active role in Europe. In the 1970s, France increasingly used troops to support its interests, largely in former French Africa. In 1978 it intervened with small forces in Zaire, although it needed American planes to carry them. Middle-rank and minor powers have even less capacity to act beyond their regions or even their frontiers. Many of the smaller states have virtually no individual influence.

Nevertheless, if it were this easy to calculate power and predict who will influence whom and, in war, who will beat whom, it would have been difficult—if not impossible—to predict North Vietnam's victory over the United States or the quaking of the West European industrial countries before their former colonies in OPEC, most of whose member countries have tiny populations, no industry, and no military muscle, yet dared to raise the price of oil. Equally difficult to foresee was Israel's ability to defy American pressures for more conciliatory behavior, despite its almost complete dependence politically, economically, and militarily upon the United States or the substantial sums of economic and military aid that have to be paid by the United States to small countries for establishing military bases (for example, the Philippines). Indeed, if power calculations alone could accurately forecast how events would turn out, why have a contest of power, especially a war?

A ranking of states by power may give us an initial quick impression of which states are likely to achieve their aims and which are not, but though such a ranking is useful, even necessary, it is clearly not sufficient. States may be classified according to amounts of power, but power relations among states may be quite complex. The components of power, as we shall repeatedly emphasize in the next few chapters, are not automatically translated into equivalent influence or ability to achieve desired goals. It is even difficult to establish rankings below the level of the secondary powers. Is Cuba, which in 1978 and 1979 had more than twice the number of troops in Africa than France had, a minor power or a secondary power? In the early 1980s, Cuba had a population of almost 10 million but a military of 200,000 (for the American population, the equivalent would be 4 to 5 million, twice the size of current U.S. forces); 40,000 Cubans were reportedly serving overseas, 35,000 of them in Angola and Ethiopia.[9] Together with its two hundred jet fighters and fifty naval ships, Cuba had by the mid-1970s passed Brazil as Latin America's leading military power. And what about Saudi Arabia, a country even the United States feared to offend in the 1970s? Was it a superpower, a secondary power, or on a level lower even than the minor powers like Yugoslavia, Pakistan, and Israel? Rankings are not necessarily very accurate guides in a world in which arms may not confer more political leverage, economically advanced countries appear politically vulnerable and weak, and states with neither military nor economic strength often appear to dictate events.

Different Behavior Patterns

States may be differentiated not only by their power and the scope of their interests but also by differences of behavior.[10] States approximately equal in power—regardless of regime, according to Steven Spiegel—behave similarly; states very unequal in power act differently. Robert Rothstein has specifically warned that a small power is not a great power writ small, that its behavior is different in kind as well as in degree from that of its bigger brethren. A first-rank power can occasionally make a mistake without disastrous results, for it can, once it has recognized its error, exercise its great capability to correct the earlier blunders. At times it may even sustain setbacks, and this will not prove fatal. But a small power does not usually have that luxury. A great power can, more often than its small colleague, wait a little longer to see whether or not its adversary will really attack. Its margin of safety—especially in the age before nuclear weapons—has been greater, and thus it has been less likely to be tempted to strike preemptively. But for small powers, "it means, in sum, that the margin of error is small or nonexistent: To choose incorrectly may end the possibility of free choice. A lapse in vigilance can be fatal. Procrastination or 'muddling through' appears to be ruled out." [11]

We need only look at Israel's two successful preemptive strikes at Egypt and its allies in 1956 and 1967, as the Arab countries appeared to be ready to launch a war. For political reasons, this strategy was not employed in 1973. As a result of that decision, the fighting cost Israel heavy casualties and loss of prestige, which, in turn, affected its negotiating strength in the subsequent diplomatic efforts to achieve a more lasting regional peace. In those negotiations Israel was constantly afraid of being betrayed by the United States, of being forced to make concessions that it did not want to make to ensure oil for the United States. Israeli suspicions, occasionally bordering on paranoia, were striking, considering the long history of U.S. support for Israel and commitment to its existence. The difference reflected in good part the differences of power: the United States, as a relatively secure superpower, could suggest concessions it felt sure would lead to a comprehensive peace; Israel, as a small power, was very insecure despite repeated military victories over hostile neighbors and apprehensive that every concession would weaken it, especially in relation to the Palestinians. An Israeli prime minister might well have uttered words similar to those spoken by Nguyen Van Thieu, the last president of South Vietnam, to Henry Kissinger, when Thieu rejected the terms worked out by North Vietnam and the United States for ending the Vietnam War in late 1972:

> You are a giant, Dr. Kissinger. So you can probably afford the luxury of being easy in this agreement. I cannot. A bad agreement means nothing to you. What is the loss of South Vietnam if you look at the world's map? Just a speck. The loss of South Vietnam may even be good for you. It may be good to contain China, good for your world strategy. But a little Vietnamese doesn't play with a strategic map of the world. For us, it isn't a question of choosing between Moscow and Peking. It is a question of choosing between life and death. [12]

Status Quo States Versus Revisionist States

We can also classify states according to their aims in the state system: Are they generally willing to accept things as they are, or do they seek to change them? If they are largely willing to accept the existing situations, they are "status quo powers." The status quo can, therefore, be identified with words such as *satisfied, defense, preserve*. Revisionist powers are not content with things as they are, and revisionism is associated with words such as *expansion, offense*, and *change*. These terms have been particularly useful in the past, when they have been associated with peace treaties concluded at the ends of wars. As territorial settlements have usually been involved, the victors have sought to preserve the status quo, which has generally benefited them; the vanquished states have wished to arrange changes to alleviate some of the grievances outstanding from the war. At the end of World War I, for example, the

Versailles peace treaty included a number of provisions about Germany's frontiers with the new Poland and Czechoslovakia that most Germans disliked. France arranged for alliances with the countries to the east of Germany in order to contain German power. France was thus committed to these countries and their frontiers with Germany. There were also other provisions, such as limitations on the size of the German army and the kinds of weapons it could have. Germany wanted some changes, even before the rise of Adolf Hitler.

After World War II there was no formal peace treaty with the two Germanies, then divided between the superpowers. The frontier in Europe was the line between the Soviet and Allied armies when Germany surrendered. Over time this line between Western and Eastern Europe became accepted by both the United States and the Soviet Union. The nearest thing to a peace treaty was the Helsinki agreement in 1976, in which the *de facto* situation was mutually accepted and legally recognized. In general, the United States and the West have considered themselves the status quo powers during the cold war and détente; the Soviets have been viewed as revisionist, constantly probing for weak spots into which Soviet power can flow— initially around their own periphery, now in Africa, the Arabian peninsula, and Central America as well. The goal is less one of territorial change than of spreading Soviet influence to strategically located nations, and this effort is viewed as potentially damaging to American and Western interests. It ought to be added that the Soviet Union also views the United States as a status quo power—the defender of world capitalism—while it associates itself with the historical change from capitalism to socialism (Soviet-style), a change it seeks to speed up.

Designation of a state as favoring the status quo or as revisionist looks straightforward, but is often not. Germany in the interwar years wished to overthrow the status quo, but this did not appear so obvious to its adversaries at the time. Germany claimed that it wished to restore only the old pre-World War I Germany. Such aims were admittedly revisionist, but they would still have been limited and would have constituted little danger to Europe. Once satisfied, Germany would presumably have taken its place in the European subsystem as a status quo power. The British government believed Germany's claim and thus misjudged Hitler's intentions. He was unappeasable, but that was easier to see in retrospect. With Hitler's predecessors, whose ambitions had been limited to the restoration of pre-1914 Germany, this appeasement policy might have worked. Under Hitler, whose ultimate ambitions were unlimited, the policy was doomed to fail. But Hitler cleverly disguised the fact that he wanted a complete revision of the status quo; each time he made a demand, it was a limited one, and he claimed it was his last one. For a while his neighbors believed him.

During World War II, as we saw earlier, the United States thought the Soviet Union was basically a status quo power. After the war, the Soviet Union was redefined as revisionist. Is the Soviet Union today still a revisionist state? Or has it become basically a status quo power seeking primarily to protect its postwar domination over the eastern and central areas of Europe and its long frontier with China? Do Moscow's rulers still seek to fulfill their ideological objective of world revolution? Or have they become more and more conservative as their revolutionary fervor of an earlier day has evaporated, and as the Soviet Union—seventy years after the revolution—has become a highly bureaucratic and industrialized nation with much to lose in a nuclear war? In short, the questions of how revisionist a state is and on what issues or to what extent it has become *in practice* a status quo nation, even though it may still articulate revisionist purposes and slogans, are not easy to decide and become matters of controversy, if not confusion. What are the criteria of judgment—declaratory statements or acts and, if so, of what specific kind? How especially does the observer decide when a status quo power has become revisionist and the reverse? Nevertheless, for all of the ambiguities and difficulties involved in classifying states in this manner, it can be useful in analysis if used with care and awareness of the complexities involved.

West, East, and Nonaligned States (First, Second, and Third Worlds)

A tripartite classification of states, unlike those already given, is more contemporary. It is not based on power or goals but on states' relations with the superpowers—alignment with the United States (the West), with the Soviet Union (the East), or with neither, and those states are termed *nonaligned*. The three divisions are also known as the First, Second, and Third Worlds. This categorization was especially useful during the cold war years, when the Western alliance (NATO) and the Soviet Union and its allies in Eastern Europe, as well as China, confronted each other in two solid blocs, often called in the West the Free World and the Communist World. The third bloc incorporated the new nations. What united them was their former colonial history, their economically underdeveloped state or poverty, their sharing of the "revolution of rising expectations," and a foreign policy of nonalignment.

This threefold division is no longer quite so applicable. NATO, although it continues to exist and is likely to do so for a long time, can no longer be called a bloc, as if it were a cohesive unit with a single policy. Differences among the Western allies means that we must also speak of French or West German policies, for example. Divisions also exist among the Soviet Union's allies in Eastern Europe. Romanian policy does not mirror Soviet policy. And the Sino-Soviet alliance has completely split: China now aligns itself with the United States, Europe, and Japan. China even briefly invaded Vietnam after Vietnam had attacked Communist Cambodia to overthrow its pro-Chinese regime and replace it with a pro-Vietnamese and pro-Soviet government. Despite China's move away from the Soviet Union toward the United States, China publicly identifies itself as a Third World state. Yet it does not belong to the Third World "Group of 77," which has grown from the original 77 less-developed countries to more than 120 members. This group collectively defines and asserts issues of interest to the LDCs. China is instead aligning itself with the West politically and economically as it seeks safety from Soviet attacks and economic help to become a modern industrialized great power.

The nonaligned states, too, have become increasingly divided. Composed as they are of more than one hundred nations from different regions of varying sizes, history, ideology, and political and economic systems and divided between pro-American and pro-Soviet sentiments, they can no longer be considered a bloc. OPEC probably caused the sharpest division since it highlighted the enormous gap between the few resource-rich nations and the many poorer nations. Some of the smaller states have managed to develop thriving economies and become integrated into the international trading system. Thus, the Third World can be split into the oil-exporting countries; the newly industrialized countries (NICs), sometimes also referred to as "export platforms" (Hong Kong, Singapore, Taiwan, South Korea); and the Third World countries, LDCs with an average per capita income of $500 or less.

North-South States (Rich Nations and Poor Nations)

Another way of looking at the world is to divide it into North and South or rich and poor. These terms, like West and East, are handy tags, even though also oversimplified. *Northern* refers to all the industrialized, higher income states, both West and East. *Southern* includes the former colonial countries that had been governed from London, Paris, Brussels, and other Western capitals. During the cold war, these poorer or economically less developed nations used their status between the West and East to enhance their bargaining strength and attract economic assistance from both for their own development; in other words, they learned to play both ends against the middle. But during détente, as their leverage declined, the poor countries increasingly focused their attention on the richer Western states, which supposedly dominated the international economy and exploited them. The LDCs demanded a new international economic order.

The Soviets, insisting that they had never been a colonial power and therefore were not accountable for the lot of the underdeveloped countries, refused to do much to help improve the conditions of the latter, on grounds that they were the West's responsibility. Yet, by the standards of most southern nations (in Africa, Latin America, and Southeast Asia), the Soviet Union is also a rich nation, and therefore there is pressure on Moscow to upgrade its assistance. Since 1973 and OPEC's quadrupling of oil prices and the oil embargo against the United States, the conflict between rich and poor has shared center stage in the world arena with the older adversary relationship between East and West. The Southern nations' problems of overpopulation, hunger, and poverty are now very much part of the international agenda, and they are voiced especially in the United Nations Conference on

Trade and Development (UNCTAD), which has been called a "trade union of the poor." [13]

NONSTATE ACTORS

Individual nation-states are complemented by other actors. Some are groups of states: intergovernmental organizations (IGOs), or, as they were more commonly called in the past, international organizations. Others are nongovernmental organizations (NGOs).

Intergovernmental Actors

Intergovernmental organizations are voluntary associations of sovereign states, organized to pursue the many different purposes for which states feel they wish to cooperate through some sort of formal and often long-term structure. Decisions made by such IGOs are the product of negotiations among the governmental representatives assigned to them, including foreign and defense ministers, who attend specified meetings. The day-to-day business of each IGO is carried out by its bureaucracy, and their institutional machinery may be relatively small or large and complex, as in the European Economic Community (EEC).

IGOs may be classified by two factors: scope and function. First, the organization may be global or regional. The United Nations includes most existing states and strives for universal membership. The International Bank for Reconstruction and Development or World Bank, the International Monetary Fund, and General Agreement on Tariffs and Trade (GATT), are among the economic organizations whose membership is nearly universal, although they have been controlled by the Western powers led by the United States. The LDCs, believing that GATT's promotion of free trade was counter to their interests, started UNCTAD, in which they organized the Group of 77 to enhance their bargaining power. By contrast, the Commonwealth (no longer preceded by *British* because all of its members are regarded as equals) comprises states in almost every area of the world; far short of universal membership, it is nevertheless a global organization. Similarly, OPEC, the nucleus of which is Arab (Saudi Arabia, Algeria, Qatar, Kuwait, Libya, Iraq, and the United Arab Emirates), has other members in the Middle East (Iran), Africa (Nigeria and Gabon), southeast Asia (Indonesia), and Latin America (Venezuela and Ecuador). Mexico accepted "observer" status in OPEC in 1982. Other producer cartels also have multiregional or global membership.

Most IGOs, however, are regional. Many areas have organizations through which member states may promote regional cooperation or resolve common political problems or internal quarrels. The Organization of American States (OAS), the Organization for African Unity (OAU), and the Arab League are three examples. On the other hand, there are regional military alliances such as NATO and its Soviet counterpart, the Warsaw Treaty Organization (WTO), also known as the Warsaw Pact in Europe; or the defunct alliances, the Southeast Asia Treaty Organization (SEATO) and Middle East Treaty Organization (METO)—or, for a LDC regional IGO, the (Persian) Gulf Cooperation Council, composed of Saudi Arabia, Kuwait, Bahrain, Oman, Qatar, and the United Arab Emirates, to defend themselves against Iran.

A second method of classification is by function: political, military, economic, or social. The United Nations and the OAU are basically political organizations, even though they may carry out other tasks as well. NATO and WTO obviously have a primarily military purpose. The European Coal and Steel Community (ECSC) was established in 1950 to integrate these two sectors of the economies of West Germany, France, Italy, and the Benelux countries (Belgium, the Netherlands, and Luxembourg). The ECSC's success led to the formation of the European Economic Community (EEC), whose purpose was to integrate the economies of the six different countries into one single economy by eliminating trade barriers and other obstacles to the economic foundation of a United States of Europe (by 1986 the EEC had doubled its membership). The Soviet Union, Bulgaria, Hungary, Romania, Czechoslovakia, Poland, East Germany, Cuba, Mongolia, and Vietnam constitute the Council for Mutual Assistance or COMECON, whose stated purpose was to create a more rational division of labor among the Soviet bloc countries in Eastern Europe but whose real purpose always was to give Moscow greater control over these countries. Organizations dealing with health, education, communications, and food, such as the World Health Organization (WHO) and the UN Educational, Scientific, and Cultural Organization (UNESCO), focus on social purposes. It should be noted that few regional IGOs are concerned with issues of peace and security; most have economic or social functions (see Table 3-2).

From IGOs to Subregional Groupings

Membership in IGOs has been of particular value to some of the smaller, weaker states, which can gain extra leverage when they are involved in disputes with greater powers. Panama is tiny in comparison to the United States, the "colossus of the North." The canal running through Panama was long a symbol of American colonialism to Panamanians and other Latin Americans. The Panamanians wanted to run the canal and to regain control of the territory that the United States had leased when it built the canal. All the Latin American states supported Panama's determination to reassert its sovereignty over a piece of land that the United States treated as if it were American territory. Although it had dominated the OAS for years, the United States could not expect much support in a meeting, but Panama shrewdly informed the United States that, if a satisfactory agreement could not be achieved, the issue of the canal would be taken to the United Nations. In the

Table 3-2 A Select Group of Intergovernmental Organizations

Purpose	*Global*	*Regional*
Political	United Nations The Commonwealth	Organization of American States (OAS) Organization for African Unity (OAU) The League of Arab States Organization of the Islamic Conference
Military		North Atlantic Treaty Organization (NATO) Warsaw Treaty Organization (WTO)
Economic	Organization of Petroleum Exporting Countries (OPEC)	Arab Organization of Petroleum Exporting Countries European Economic Community (EEC) (includes European Coal and Steel Community, or ECSC) Association of Southeast Asian Nations
Social/ scientific	World Health Organization (WHO)	United Nations Educational, Scientific, and Cultural Organization (UNESCO)

world forum, where LDCs are in the vast majority, the United States would have been on the defensive. Panama thus benefited from membership in the regional and global IGO on this issue—from what might be called "group power."

Despite the obvious advantage to the smaller countries of pooling their strengths, regional organizations have in recent years become more and more divided and unable to act with a united front. In 1982, when Argentina forcibly seized the British-owned Falkland Islands, most of Spanish- and Portuguese-speaking Latin America, from democratic Venezuela to Communist Cuba, supported Argentina. Although the depth of this support for Argentina's aggression was questionable, there was a surface solidarity constituting a majority. The United States supported Britain and helped its military efforts to retake the islands. Yet the OAS was splintered because other English-speaking countries, mainly Caribbean countries, also refused to support Argentina. Indeed, the initial diplomatic efforts to resolve the conflict focused on the United Nations. Moreover, the OAS was not involved in efforts to resolve differences between the United States and Nicaragua resulting from the Sandinista revolution. Rather, this was attempted by the Contadora countries composed of Mexico, Venezuela, Columbia, and Panama. The Latin-American debt crisis was handled by the eleven-nation Cartegena group. In 1962 the OAS supported the United States during the Cuban missile crisis. But in 1983 the OAS did not approve the U.S. intervention on the island of Grenada; Washington, therefore, sought legitimation for its action in the previously little-known alliance of small Caribbean islands known as the Association of East Caribbean States. Similarly, in 1985, twenty-four Latin-American countries criticized the U.S. embargo imposed upon Nicaragua, called upon Washington to lift it, and promised to help Nicaragua. And Argentina's dispute with Chile over the Beagle Channel was mediated by the Vatican!

The OAS is not the only regional IGO whose unity is in peril. The intra-Arab conflicts make it difficult for the League of Arab States to stand together very often, despite the Arab-Israeli dispute. Egypt made its peace with Israel, but then found itself isolated in the Arab world. When Iran and Iraq went to war, Syria and Libya supported Iran, a non-Arab country, against Iraq. After its ejection from Lebanon by Israel, the PLO, with Jordan, sought the league's approval for what they claimed to be a joint diplomatic approach to Israel, but Syria, Lebanon, South Yemen, and Libya did not attend; of the sixteen Arab members attending, only ten were represented by heads of state.[14] The forty-year-old league was paralyzed by the more radical states and the reluctance of moderate states such as Saudi Arabia to confront them. The OAS, Arab league, and OAU, which was divided by intra-African quarrels, are all in need of revitalization if they are to survive.

Other IGOs have not done much better. The issue of economic sanctions against South Africa has deeply divided the Commonwealth. Several members have threatened to quit if Britain does not agree to sanctions. OPEC's members' failure to abide by the production levels set by the organization was a major cause for the downward topple of oil prices. Not surprisingly, in such circumstances where organizations of diverse membership have been unable to make collective decisions on regional security or economic matters, these functions have been shifting to subregional groups. Leading examples are the aforementioned Contadora and Cartegena groups in Latin America; the Gulf Cooperative Council; the Organization of Front-Line States (Angola, Botswana, Mozambique, Tanzania, and, since 1980, Zimbabwe), initially formed to help Zimbabwe become independent and more recently involved with South Africa's racial turmoil and independence for Namibia; and ASEAN, the Association of Southeast Asian Nations (Singapore, Malaysia, Thailand, Indonesia, the Philippines, and, since 1984, Brunei), which deals mainly with members' common economic issues, although the association has also been concerned with security as Vietnam has expanded into Cambodia and has been increasingly perceived as a regional threat.

Supranational Actor

There is one significant exception to the rule that in intergovernmental organizations the participating members maintain their autonomy. In Western Europe since 1950 there has been a revolutionary attempt to move beyond the nation-state toward a supranational actor. The six members of ECSC had joined in an IGO to transfer the authority of their governments in specified economic sectors to a new federal authority, which was to be established above them. Decisions were to be made by this higher authority; they would no longer be arrived at by negotiations among the member governments. By 1958 the ECSC had been succeeded by the EEC. This six-member organization was joined later by Britain, Denmark, Ireland, Greece, Spain, and Portugal, but it has been only partially successful. A monetary union has been established, but the EEC has not made much progress in shifting from an economic to a political union, although cooperation on some foreign policy and defense issues has increased. Still, the various European communities have moved beyond most of the more traditional IGOs in their decision-making processes.

Nongovernmental or Transnational Actors

Increasingly visible since World War II has been the transnational actor, the nongovernmental organization. It is characterized by headquarters in one country and centrally directed operations in two or more countries. The word *transnational* is appropriate because the NGO performs its functions not only across national frontiers but also often in disregard of them. The increase in the number, size, scope, and variety of NGOs since World War II has led observers to speak of a transnational organizational revolution in world politics.[15] NGOs differ from IGOs in a number of significant ways. The latter are composed of nation-states, and their actions depend upon their members' common interests; conflicting interests must first be reconciled through negotiations, which may not always be successful or rapid. The transnational organization represents its own interests and pursues them in many nations. "The international organization requires *accord* among nations; the transnational organization requires *access* to nations. . . . The restraints on an international organization are largely internal, stemming from the need to produce consensus among its members. The restraints on a transnational organization are largely external, stemming from its need to gain operating authority in different sovereign states. International organizations embody the principle of nationality; transnational organizations try to ignore it."[16]

Multinational Corporations.   The most prominent contemporary NGO is the multinational corporation (MNC), the usually huge firm that owns and controls plants and offices in many countries and sells its goods and services there. MNCs may be classified according to the kind of business activities they pursue:[17]

Extractive (resources)
  oil (Exxon)
  copper (Kennecott)
Agriculture (Standard Brands)
Industrial
  capital equipment (International Harvester)

automobiles (General Motors)
consumer goods (Colgate-Palmolive)
Service
tourism (Hilton Hotels, Holiday Inns)
retail (Sears, Roebuck)
transportation (Hertz, Avis)
public utilities (General Telephone and Electronics)
Banking (Chase Manhattan, Bank of America)
Conglomerates (International Telephone and Telegraph)

The sheer size of these MNCs is one of the reasons they are now often listed as actors of increasing importance internationally. Lester Brown, in ranking nations and MNCs according to gross national product (the total worth of goods and services produced) and gross annual sales, found that in the early 1970s the first twenty-two entries were the twenty-two largest nations, ranging from the United States to Argentina. The twenty-third was General Motors, followed by Switzerland and Pakistan; Standard Oil of New Jersey and Ford ranked twenty-seven and twenty-nine. Royal Dutch Shell was number thirty-six, ahead of Iran and Venezuela; General Electric and International Business Machines were forty-three and forty-five, respectively, ahead of Egypt, Nigeria, and Israel. Of the top fifty, forty-one were nations, and nine were MNCs; of the second fifty, eighteen were nations, and thirty-two were MNCs.[18] These rankings later changed somewhat because OPEC nations have greatly increased their wealth. Exxon, for example, replaced General Motors as the world's largest corporation—until oil prices collapsed in the middle 1980s, and the auto giant recaptured first place.

Regardless of the actual rankings, the implications are obvious. One is the strength of MNCs compared to that of the weaker countries, and the influence they can presumably exert within nations. The fear is that these "new sovereigns" will become more powerful than the governments of many countries, gain control of their economies, and thus dictate their futures. Another implication—and of even greater significance—is their possible effects on the state system itself. Because of the MNCs' multinational production, distribution, and service—and the trend is toward attaining global reach but with planning still centralized—some observers have argued that the nation-state may be rendered obsolete. The MNCs are viewed as ushering in a global economy, tying nations together with the cords of economic benefit. As the MNCs satisfy people's aspirations for higher standards of living, the territorial state may become outdated and irrelevant (see Chapter 19).

Until that happens, their role in helping the LDCs develop has become increasingly important. Since many government-run economies have been unable to induce sufficient economic growth and make their industries profitable, many LDCs reassessed the threat the large MNCs posed to their independence and welcomed American, European, and Asian MNCs to invest in their countries. Whether MNCs will continue to want to invest in the LDCs, even if the latter remain receptive to such investments, may depend on the outcome of a huge multibillion-dollar lawsuit against Union Carbide after a 1985 accident at a pesticide plant in Bhopal, India, killed two thousand people and injured many more. Pesticides have helped make India one of the few LDCs to become basically self-sufficient in food, despite its high birth rate. But these benefits mean little in the wake of a tragic industrial accident, even though the Indian government shared responsibility for this disaster by, for example, allowing thousands of people to live next to the plant. A huge settlement against Union Carbide, which might also bankrupt the company, might reduce future MNC investments in the Third World.

Religious, Humanitarian, and Professional Actors. One of the oldest and most visible NGOs is the Roman Catholic church, with a membership of half a billion people in the 1980s. To do its work, the church has learned to co-exist with all manner of governments, including Fascist ones. The political influence of the church can hardly be doubted. Even Communist governments treat the church with caution; Pope John Paul II's 1979 visit to his native Poland attracted huge crowds and was a matter of concern to the regime. The church played a leading role in trying to mediate the subsequent quarrels between the government and Solidarity, the independent labor union that was seeking not only to improve economic conditions but also to create a greater degree of freedom for Poles. The Pope reportedly warned the Soviets against military intervention and threatened to return to his native country if such an event took place. The Polish government finally cracked down on Solidarity by declaring martial law.

The church's influence is worldwide. In 1985 at a Synod of Bishops in Rome, the church had representatives from thirty-four African countries, seventeen from Asia, and twenty-two from Latin-America and the Caribbean. "Their voices were varied, but their message was clear: This is the new Catholic church, the church of the third world, and it is the church of the future." [19] Almost 50 percent of the world's 800 million Catholics live in the Third World. Despite its best efforts, the church is not always united. Disagreement exists over the use of artificial birth control, celibacy for the priesthood, and whether women should be admitted to the priesthood. Moreover, there are a growing number of priests in Latin America and in the Philippines who follow "liberation theology." Because of their involvement with the poor, they claim that Christ led them to Marx. They believe that American capitalism is the cause of poverty and that only through social revolution can economic injustice and political oppression end. These priests support Marxist guerrillas, as in El Salvador, or Marxist governments, as in Nicaragua, and, when opposed by the church, some have proclaimed themselves to be members of "the people's church." The pope has denounced liberation theology, but the church—conservative, liberal, as well as radical—is deeply involved with poverty, hunger, oppression, and human rights in the LDCs. It is also involved in social issues in the developed world. In the

United States, Catholic bishops have opposed as immoral the use of nuclear weapons, even for retaliation, and have called for a greater governmental role to help the poor.

Other well-known NGOs are the Communist International, through which the Soviet Union exerted its control over foreign Communist parties; the International Red Cross whose concern in wartime is with prisoners of war and in peacetime with natural and man-made disasters; and Amnesty International, an organization that has gained prominence because of its monitoring of the abuses of human rights in many countries. Less well known, but representative of the multifold professional and social NGOs, are organizations such as the International Political Science Organization, the International Studies Association (which includes many of the "famous" textbook writers students so enjoy reading!), the International Skeletal Society, whose members are radiologists, orthopedists, and pathologists, and the Rotary Club. Their main function is to link human beings in different countries. Most have little influence on the conduct of their nations' foreign policies, but they do foster many international friendships as well as advance professional knowledge.

'National Liberation' Groups.

An actor of increasing importance in the state system is the self-styled "national liberation" organization. Perhaps the best-known of these since the 1960s is the PLO; it claims to speak for the Palestinian people and seeks the establishment of a Palestinian state, which its leaders presumably would govern. It has been recognized as the legitimate representative of the Palestinians by the Arab states, has been granted observer status at the United Nations, and attends the meetings of the nonaligned countries as a full-fledged member, even though it is not a state. Its leader, Yasir Arafat, has been received by the Chancellor of Austria (a Jew), and by other political leaders in Europe and Japan, usually with the honors reserved for a visiting head of state. Even the pope received him in 1982. The Common Market countries have suggested that the PLO be associated with the Arab-Israeli peace talks and have called for Palestinian self-determination. Despite its military defeat in 1982 when Israel invaded Lebanon, and the subsequent further attempts to wrest control of the PLO from Arafat by President Hafez al-Assad of Syria, the PLO is diplomatically represented in more than one hundred nations, many more than recognize Israel!

Other national liberation organizations include the Patriotic Front, which fought a guerrilla war against the white-dominated government of Rhodesia, claiming that it represented the interests of the majority of black Rhodesians (it later won power in a free election and now controls the new state of Zimbabwe); the Southwest African People's Organization (SWAPO), which is seeking power in what it calls Namibia, a former German colony that has been administered by South Africa since the end of World War I; the Mau Mau in Kenya, which brought British colonialism to an end; the Polisario, which is fighting Morocco for control of the Western Sahara; the Farabundo

Marti Liberation Front, which is seeking to capture power in El Salvador; and the various tribes comprising the Afghan resistance to the Soviet occupation of Afghanistan.

Obviously, the PLO and some of these national liberation movements have exerted considerable leverage in international politics—more than many states—in their efforts to found states of their own. They may well be called "states-in-waiting." Their way of achieving this aim is composed of a mixture of public diplomacy and terror tactics. But a key means has been the waging of guerrilla warfare against the government in power. Communist national liberation groups have been particularly successful in this latter regard: in the liberation of Yugoslavia from German occupation in World War II; shortly after the war, the Greek Communist insurrection, which helped precipitate the American policy of containment; the long Chinese Communist civil war against the Nationalist Chinese government, which ended with China becoming a Communist nation; Castro's campaign against the Batista regime in Cuba, which turned Cuba into a Communist nation; the Viet Cong against the pro-American government in South Vietnam, which led to American military intervention; and the Sandinista campaign against the Somoza dictatorship in Nicaragua.

Note the names of some of their leaders: Tito, Mao Zedong, Castro, and Ho Chi Minh. All were charismatic leaders who became famous during their military struggles, which they won. These feats testify not only to their skill as military leaders but also to their ability to organize political discontent in their nations. They were, above all, astute and ruthless politicians and "nation-builders" who, after acquiring power, governed their nations. By contrast, no terrorist leader has successfully overthrown an established government and become a successful "father of his country."

Terrorists

Although national liberation movements do resort to terror, the features that distinguish them from terrorist groups are several. While the former organize the masses (for example, peasants who do not own their own land), the latter tend to be narrowly based. National liberation groups tend to originate in rural areas; terrorists in cities. The former are usually led by renowned individuals who have great appeal, but the latter are normally anonymous. One tends to carve out rural areas as "liberated territory"; the other hides among the multitudes in an urban environment. One wages a protracted conflict or guerrilla war, the other engages in sporadic violence. Both claim to be motivated by a good cause, and both start out from positions of weakness. The national liberation group, however, hopes to isolate the government by neutralizing public opinion while defeating government forces; the terrorist group expects to frighten its enemies into making concessions or surrendering.

A national liberation movement is a serious threat because it may defeat the government, but terrorism constitutes essentially a set of irritating pinpricks not likely to succeed. Nevertheless, given the multiplicity of causes, terrorism is increasingly resorted to by desperate or angry individuals and groups anxious to publicize their grievances and aspirations, whether the Party of God, the Iranian-sponsored Islamic fundamentalists whose favorite targets are Americans, or the Red Brigade in Italy. Hijackings, assassinations, kidnappings, attacks on embassies, and other acts of terror have drawn the world's attention to the demands of these groups and have compelled governments to take notice and in some instances even to negotiate with them.

The Principal Actor

Clearly, then, states are not the only actors on the world scene. Indeed, the proliferation of nonstate actors has led some to conclude that states are of declining importance and that nonstate actors are gaining in status and influence. Note, for example, what two writers have said about the multinational corporation: "The rise of the planetary multinational enterprise is producing an organizational revolution as profound in its implications for modern man as the Industrial Revolution and the rise of the nation-state itself." The MNC or planetary corporation is ushering in a world economy and the corporation itself is "the first institution in human history dedicated to centralized planning on a world scale." Where men like Napoleon and Hitler had failed in their conquest of much of the world, the managers of the corporate giants "proclaim their faith that where conquest has failed, business can succeed." [20] Even now, they make daily business decisions that have more impact upon our daily lives in terms of what we wear, eat, drink, what work we will do, and where we live than do governments.

More broadly, the rise of MNCs and the vast growth of so many other kinds of nonstate actors are said to challenge and weaken, if not actually undermine, the "state-centric" concept of international politics and replace it with a "transnational" world in which relationships are considerably more numerous and complex than just traditional state-to-state ones. There are three sets of relationships in fact. States deal with one another directly or as members of IGOs (for example, when the United States and the Soviet Union negotiate an arms control agreement, the Indian prime minister visits England, or a Brazilian official talks to the World Bank about a loan). States also deal increasingly with NGOs (for example, when the United States negotiates with Shi'ite Amal militia in Lebanon for the release of hostages seized on a TWA plane, Jordan's King Hussein negotiates with the PLO about a common diplomatic position for possible talks with Israel, or an LDC negotiates with an MNC to set up a factory in its country). Finally, NGOs deal with one another (for example, when Shi'ite, Druse, and Christian militia in Lebanon fight one another, when four anti-Soviet insurgent movements from Africa, Asia, and Central America meet and form an alliance, or, in a more pleasurable way, when the Montreal Expos play the Houston Astros).

Nevertheless, despite the proliferation of nongovernmental organizations, the state remains—as it has remained for three hundred years—the primary actor in the state system. The birth rate of new states has been high, and it continues. Nationalism seems especially rife in the LDCs. People can, of course, be loyal to more than one organization, but the nation-state remains for most people the object of their most intense loyalty. Before World War I, European socialist parties asserted that the loyalty of European workers was to each other; they would not fight one another on behalf of their nations, which were controlled by the capitalist class. Their cause was to eliminate capitalism so that workers would no longer be exploited and modern technology would be used to improve the lives of the workers and other underprivileged groups. But when Europe went to war, the workers in each country rallied to their respective national flags. After World War II, the various members of the Communist world were also divided by nationalism. Marxist rulers still claimed to be devoted to the international working class; nationalism was not supposed to motivate Communist states. First in Yugoslavia, shortly after World War II, and later in China, this nationalism exerted itself against the Soviet Union. In Eastern Europe it made Soviet control insecure, especially in Poland. It even led to a short war between China and Vietnam in Asia with the potential for Chinese-Soviet hostilities. Thus, a transnational loyalty, such as to communism, has become increasingly identified with specific nation-states. A similar phenomenon has been seen with other transnational loyalties: Zionism has become largely identified with Israel; feelings of European unity have been weakened by a revival of nationalism, reversing a postwar trend; and Islamic fundamentalism appears to be a tool mainly of Iran.

States also remain unique because of their control of territory. The MNCs need access to territory to make profits; the Roman Catholic church needs access to it to reach people and save souls; terrorists and national liberation groups need access to bases from which to pursue their campaigns. The PLO during the 1970s and early 1980s operated from its base in Lebanon; the former Patriotic Front conducted its war from the countries surrounding Zimbabwe. Such liberation groups cannot survive without at least the acquiescence of the states in which they are based and without the active support of other states like Libya, who supply them with weapons, training, and money. Finally, the state remains the principal user of *legitimate* force. It can enforce decisions at home and can decide whether to go to war and when.

Two authors have commented about the MNC, which some observers regard as the strongest competitor of the state, if not indeed a threat to the future viability of the state system:

> [T]he MNCs lack a fundamental characteristic which will quite probably not permit them to challenge the nation-state. And this characteristic is "territoriality." Whether a multi-national corporation executive works for IBM, Singer, Unilever, Volkswagen, or Hitachi, he lives in a nation-state which possesses some sovereignty, greater authority, and even greater control capacity over its environment. MNCs

have no jails, no courts and executioners, no passports, no armies, and very, very few weapons. In the last analysis, national governments control an overwhelming concentration of power and authority that would allow them to break up any MNC, provided there were adequate cause for such an operation.[21]

The state has survived since the Peace of Westphalia in 1648, but throughout this period it has never been the sole actor in the system. There have always been significant nongovernmental organizations, such as the Catholic church or the large European trading companies like the British East India Company, which had its own armed forces and controlled territory, something no modern MNC does.[22] But the state remains the principal actor and the system has long been defined by its major actors, not by all the types of actors within it.[23]

This does not mean that nonstate actors and transnational activities are unimportant. It only means that they have not yet rendered the state system obsolete. As long as states remain the major actors, the structure of international politics remains state-centric. States continue to dictate the terms of coexistence for themselves and other actors in the system. Kenneth Waltz has remarked that a theory of international politics that denies the central role of states will be needed only if nongovernmental actors rival or surpass the great powers, not just a few of the lesser ones. This is most unlikely. Moreover, states have a strong record of survival; few ever die. But business organizations do go out of existence. Who is more likely to be around in a hundred years, the United States or IBM? Given the longevity of the state as the principal actor, any analysis of international politics must start with the state, its motivations, objectives, and interaction with other states. Only then shall we also understand the role and impact of other actors.

Notes

1. Rashid Khalidi, *P.L.O. Decisionmaking During the 1982 War* (New York: Columbia University Press, 1985).
2. James T. Shotwell, *War as an Instrument of National Policy* (New York: Harcourt, Brace & Co., 1929), 15.
3. Amos Perlmutter, *The Partitioned State* (New York: Charles Scribner's Sons, 1985).
4. Inis L. Claude, Jr., *Swords into Plowshares* (New York: Random House, 1956), 53.
5. Steven L. Spiegel, *Dominance and Diversity* (Boston: Little, Brown & Co., 1972), 19.
6. Ian Smart, "Force in Modern Societies: Its Place in International Politics," *Adelphi Paper* 102 (London: International Institute for Strategic Studies, 1973), 22.
7. See Spiegel, *Dominance and Diversity*, for an attempt to construct such a hierarchy for the early 1970s.
8. David O. Wilkinson, *Comparative Foreign Relations* (Belmont, Calif.: Dickensen, 1969), 27.
9. James C. Goldsborough, "Dateline Paris: Africa's Policeman," *Foreign Policy*, Winter 1978-79, 174-190; F. Clifton Berry, "Cuba's Expanding Power Potential," *Air Force*,

April 1980, 43-47; and *New York Times,* Nov. 13, 1985.

10. Robert L. Rothstein, *Alliances and Small Powers* (New York: Columbia University Press, 1968).

11. Ibid., 5.

12. Quoted by John Stoessinger, *Henry Kissinger* (New York: W. W. Norton, 1976), 68. Reproduced by permission. This sense of Israeli vulnerability runs throughout the account of the post-1973 Yom Kippur War peace negotiations as recounted by Henry A. Kissinger, *Years of Upheaval* (Boston: Little, Brown & Co., 1982).

13. Robert L. Rothstein, *The Weak in the World of the Strong* (New York: Columbia University Press, 1977), 127.

14. *New York Times,* Aug. 8, 1985.

15. Samuel P. Huntington, "Transnational Organizations in World Politics," *World Politics,* April 1973, 333; and Richard W. Mansbach et al., *The Web of World Politics* (Englewood Cliffs, N.J.: Prentice-Hall, 1976).

16. Huntington, "Transnational Organizations," 338.

17. The following classification is based on the table in *The Politics of Global Economic Relations* by David H. Blacke and Robert S. Walters (Englewood Cliffs, N.J.: Prentice-Hall, 1976), 83.

18. Lester R. Brown, *World Without Frontiers* (New York: Vintage, 1973), 213-215; *1983 World Bank Development Report* (New York: Oxford University Press, 1983), 148-149; and *Fortune 500,* May 1983.

19. Quoted in the *New York Times,* Dec. 6, 1985.

20. Richard J. Barnet and Ronald E. Müller, *Global Reach* (New York: Simon & Schuster, 1975), 13-15.

21. Theodore A. Couloumbis and Elias P. Georgiades, "The Impact of the Multinational Corporations on the International System," in *The New Sovereigns,* ed. Abdul A. Said and Luiz R. Simmons (Englewood Cliffs, N.J.: Prentice-Hall, 1975), 164. Also see Hedley Bull, *The Anarchical Society* (New York: Columbia University Press, 1977), 272-273.

22. Bull, *Anarchical Society,* 271.

23. Kenneth N. Waltz, *Theory of International Politics* (Reading, Mass.: Addison-Wesley, 1979), 93-94.

CHAPTER 4

The Stakes:
The Objectives
of States

POWER POLITICS

The sovereign state is the heart of the state system, and the first and most fundamental prerequisite for any state to survive and remain independent is power. A state may have a large amount of power or relatively little, but, if it is to stay independent, it must have a sufficient amount to ward off potential threats. It may mobilize enough power by itself, or it can join together with other states in alliances. It is because of the pervasive nature of power in international politics that the term *power politics* often is used. Indeed, international politics cannot be anything but power politics.

Strictly speaking, as often as this term is used, it is misused. Power politics is a tautology; that is, it combines two words with the same meaning. Politics is inseparable from power. Whatever the objectives or goals, power provides a means to achieve them (for a definition and elaboration, see Chapter 7). Thus, to say power politics is repetitious and unnecessary. But one point about the term needs to be stressed. Power is a means to an end; it is not an end in itself, although some analysts claim that the accumulation of power is a continuous concern of states. Whatever the ultimate aim, the immediate goal is power. In this view, power is seen as desirable in itself and may be pursued for its own sake. "Whatever preserves and enhances power must be cherished. Whatever leads to the enfeeblement of power must be avoided." [1] Yet to treat power as an end in itself is analogous to discussing the accumulation of money without any reference to the purposes for which it is spent. An analysis of power must, therefore, start with a "theory of end." [2] States are not always preoccupied with enhancing power; sometimes they are satisfied with the power they have, and sometimes they will even reduce it. It depends on the objectives

86

they seek and how intensely these are pursued. Given the priority states attach to their security, for example, it would be better to substitute the term *security politics.*

What is at stake for any state in a particular conflict? The answer depends on how much importance policy makers give to the various "national interests" or objectives, which, in turn, depends on their perception of which state is the threat and their evaluation of the kind and degree of threat it represents. Stakes change. The stakes in a football game played before the season opens are lower than during the season; the stakes are higher during the play-offs. The Soviets initially made an arms deal with Egypt to weaken U.S. and British influence in the Middle East. Over the years the Soviets invested more and more in this relationship in terms of prestige, arms, and aid, so that in 1972, when the Egyptians demanded more weapons with which to drive the Israelis out of the Sinai desert, Moscow complied. The risk was that such a war, if it could not be prevented, would escalate into an American-Soviet confrontation; the alternative, the Egyptians made clear, was that Egypt would turn to other sources of political support and arms and the Soviets would lose their position of influence in Egypt after twenty-five years of investing in that relationship. This the Soviets were unwilling to do. The same was true for the United States in Vietnam where, from an initial position of aiding the French, the involvement grew. When South Vietnam looked as if it were about to go down the proverbial tube, the United States intervened militarily rather than lose prestige and influence. For both the Soviet Union and United States, there were gains to be made in their respective involvements; but even more, they wished to prevent losses or reversals in their objectives. Let us look at these objectives now in more detail.

SECURITY, WELFARE, AND OTHER AIMS

National Security

What are the most common objectives states seek? The first and most basic is *security.* But a state can expect to realize only some of what it wants. A state can expect a *degree* of security, not absolute security; it can feel only *relatively* safe, not completely safe. There is no such thing as absolute security in a state system composed of many national actors; a state could achieve such security only by universal conquest and the destruction of all other independent states—an unlikely possibility. All states, then, "live dangerously." The only question is how much or how little security does a state feel is enough? Although all states, even great powers, feel some degree of vulnerability, some have more control over their destiny than others. No state, however, is the absolute master of its fate.

The term *security* can be broken down into several categories. At the very least, security means simply *physical survival*. Israel, born in 1948, was surrounded by states that, at least until 1973, were sworn to its extinction. As Gamal Abdel Nasser, Egypt's leader during most of the 1950s and 1960s, reportedly once said, "Israel's existence is aggression." Israel had to fear for its survival if it lost even one of the wars it fought with its Arab neighbors. A loss would not just entail giving up territory; the Jews were to be "driven into the sea." The Arabs refused to recognize Israel's right to exist. Admittedly, this was an exceptional case, and later, under Anwar Sadat, Egypt made peace with Israel. However, no other Arab state has yet formally recognized Israel. Neither Jordan nor Syria, Israel's neighbors, nor the Palestine Liberation Organization (PLO) have explored through direct negotiations whether mutually satisfactory peace treaties could be arranged. Not too surprisingly in these circumstances, Israel is skittish and demonstrated that by bombing a partially built Iraqi nuclear reactor that Israel feared had the potential to produce bombs.

A second and more common meaning of security refers to the preservation of a state's *territorial integrity*. Because frontiers may change over time, states may redefine the meaning of this term. Poland, for example, has shifted its eastern and western frontiers westward since World War II. By the same token, the Soviet frontier has also moved westward. Communist China, on the other hand, frequently refers publicly to the Chinese territories seized by the Russian czars during the last century and wants the Soviets to acknowledge that these "unequal treaties" were imposed upon earlier Chinese rulers. The Soviet Union, however, has refused to do so. The issue of frontiers is particularly troublesome among the less-developed countries (LDCs), for their territorial integrity may not always correspond to ethnic and linguistic divisions. The new nations inherited their boundaries from colonial rulers, and it is this territorial integrity some LDCs seek to defend. Others states, however, claim pieces of their territory on the basis of reuniting ethnic groups. Somalia, for example, had claims against Ethiopia that led to fighting in 1978 and to Soviet-Cuban intervention to defend Ethiopia's territorial integrity. Frontiers are part of a nation's identity and dignity. Egypt demanded the return of the entire Sinai desert in exchange for peace with Israel. In 1967 Israel seized Syria's Golan Heights to improve its security, but Syria considers the area an integral part.

A third meaning of security is *political independence*, which means, negatively, a state's freedom from foreign control and, positively, the preservation of its domestic political and economic system. Security involves more than a state's physical survival and territorial security; it also includes the perpetuation of the values, patterns of social relations, life styles, and varied other elements that make up a nation's way of life.

This simple point is worth elaborating. Earlier we analyzed how the United States became involved in the two world wars and the cold war. The threat that precipitated U.S. involvement on all three occasions was the possibility that one power—Germany or the Soviet Union—would come to dominate Europe. We should note two points. First, this threat had little to do with ideology; it was certainly not anticommunism that motivated the United States against Germany, which was initially characterized by monarchical conservatism and later by fascism. Second, it was not related to physical danger, for neither Germany during either war nor the Soviet Union after 1945 had the air power to reach and destroy the United States, or even to invade it across three thousand miles of ocean.

The United States intervened on each occasion because its leaders saw the domination of Europe by a nondemocratic—indeed, *antidemocratic*—great power as a threat to the security of the United States and to the kind of world environment in which the United States could most comfortably exist. President Franklin D. Roosevelt explained his decision to aid Britain in 1940 and 1941 by stating that the United States should not become a lone democratic island surrounded by totalitarian seas to its east and west (Roosevelt included Japan's threat in the Pacific in this statement). He meant that, to defend itself in such circumstances, the United States would have to turn itself into a "garrison state"; democracy would have to be dumped overboard. He also meant that, as a *democratic* state, the nation wished to preserve an international order in which democracy could flourish. Committed to this milieu objective, the United States could not stand by and watch one democracy after another snuffed out by antidemocratic regimes. The result would be a hostile external environment, incompatible with American conceptions of what is just and unjust, whether that threat came from the extreme right or the left. That is why the United States today remains committed to the defense of Western Europe, even though the Soviet Union now has the capability to devastate the United States and the U.S. cost of protecting its allies has risen dramatically since the time the United States enjoyed its atomic monopoly and its vast strategic superiority.

National Prestige

A second objective important to many states is *prestige*. Precisely because prestige, as we shall see later, is closely related to power, especially military power, it may be defined as a nation's *reputation for power* among its fellow states. In a sense prestige is subjective and intangible because it depends on the perception of other states. Prestige, like love, is in the eye of the beholder. It is, to be sure, acquired as the result of past action. Victory on the battlefield or successful economic coercion gains prestige for a state. Other states note that a state is powerful, that it is willing to use its power to gain its aims, and that it has used this power effectively to achieve what it set out to do. In short, the state's power has credibility.

This reputation for power, given the nature of the state system, is not to be sneered at and shrugged off as "mere prestige." For a nation's reputation for power may mean it will not be challenged and will thus avoid war, or it may gain compliance with its demands, again without having to threaten or fight. Prestige is of special concern to would-be great powers; they expend major resources in quest of it and often even more to avoid its loss. When the Soviets first put Sputnik into orbit and particularly after they sent the first man into space in 1961, their achievements were widely interpreted as symptomatic of a changing distribution of power in favor of the Soviet Union. Within a short time of its first Sputnik, Moscow began to pressure the West to leave West Berlin. Moreover, Soviet achievements were seen throughout the world as a loss of prestige for the United States because U.S. power—especially in weaponry—was based to a very large extent on its technological ability and innovation, an area in which until then the United States was deemed far superior to the Soviet Union. President John Kennedy reacted to the Soviets' man in space by setting a goal for the United States of placing a man on the moon before the end of the 1960s. The effort cost more than $30 billion. But, by late 1962, after its success in compelling the Soviets to withdraw their missiles from Cuba, the United States had largely recovered its prestige. Once during his campaign for the presidency, Kennedy declared: "I believe that there can only be one possible defense of the United States. It can be expressed in one world. That word is 'first.' I do not mean first, *if* . . . I do not mean first, *when* . . . I mean first, *period*. I mean first across the board." [3]

By contrast, the American intervention in Vietnam was a less successful and far more costly (approximately $150 billion) effort to prevent the loss of prestige that Washington thought would attend the defeat of South Vietnam. The United States was unwilling to suffer this loss lest it erode the credibility of American power and commitments in other areas, perhaps more significant than Vietnam. A Pentagon memorandum written by an assistant secretary of defense assessed the reasons for American intervention as 70 percent to avoid a humiliating American defeat; 20 percent to keep South Vietnamese territory out of Chinese hands; and 10 percent to permit the people of South Vietnam to enjoy a better, freer way of life. [4]

The American defeat was an obvious setback and loss of prestige. Moreover, it emboldened the Soviet Union to extend its influence. In subsequent years, the Soviets and their Cuban proxies intervened in several places, among them Angola and Ethiopia. The Soviets also supported Vietnam's invasion of Cambodia to overthrow its pro-Chinese regime in favor of a pro-Soviet and pro-Vietnamese one. Even Iran, a much smaller power, which is as anti-American as it is anti-Communist, was bold enough to seize the U.S. Embassy and its personnel in Tehran in 1979. This was a completely unprecedented act, the seizure of what is considered "foreign territory," something not even Adolf Hitler or Joseph Stalin had tried against their opponents.

It was this series of setbacks that heavily influenced the administration of the newly elected Ronald Reagan to "get tough," perhaps more than it otherwise might have done, to denounce the Soviets vigorously and thereby alert Moscow that America's post-Vietnam psychosis was over; to remobilize American public opinion for the task of containing Soviet power; to launch a major arms program, including the modernization of U.S. strategic deterrent forces; and even to use conventional force to liberate the tiny Caribbean island of Grenada from "Soviet-Cuban domination." The latter was intended as a warning to Moscow, Havana, and the Sandinistas in Nicaragua that the United States would use force when it thought its vital interests were at stake. This demonstration was weakened considerably by the president's inept involvement of 1,200 U.S. Marines in Lebanon's civil war, in which 241 of them were killed in a terrorist suicide attack. Soon after, the United States withdrew, a Goliath brought to heel by its weaker opponents. But subsequent uses of force to capture several terrorists who had hijacked an Italian cruise ship and killed an elderly American, and to punish Libya for its alleged involvement in several anti-American terrorist incidents, restored the credibility of U.S. power and prestige.

Great powers historically have associated prestige with military power and, if necessary, the successful use of force. Indeed, the Soviet Union's status in the world since 1945 has stemmed largely from its military power, especially more recently its strategic nuclear capability. The Soviet Union's victory in World War II and expansion into eastern Europe transformed the Soviet Union into a superpower, even though it did not at the time have an atomic bomb. Over the past forty years, however, the Soviet Union has performed poorly in feeding and providing consumer goods for its people and has been unable to keep up with the new industrial revolution in electronics and petrochemicals. It has lost its appeal as a model of development for Third World states and has been unable to provide much foreign aid. In addition, Communist ideology has been regarded with increasing skepticism and boredom by the Soviet population. Consequently, the Soviet Union's prestige has increasingly depended upon its military strength. Unlike the United States, the Soviet Union is basically a one-dimensional power.

If nuclear weapons were abolished, the Soviet Union would have few claims to superpower status and would not be a threat to America's physical security. Indeed, it is precisely for this reason that the summit meetings with President Richard Nixon and President Jimmy Carter in the 1970s were so important to Moscow. For the Soviet leader, the meetings with the American presidents and the signing of arms control agreements constituted a recognition by the United States that the Soviet Union was an equal power in world affairs and entitled to equal participation with it in all important global and regional issues. The United States, by contrast, even without nuclear arms, would maintain its superpower status because of its economy, technology, its system of government, and cultural attraction.

It is not only the superpowers that are concerned with prestige. Countries such as Britain and France, former great powers reluctant to accept their secondary status, and countries such as China and India, striving to establish their status, have all become nuclear powers. Possession of the bomb is—and seems likely to remain—as much a symbol of prestige as empires were in an earlier age. Indeed, giving up the remnants of empire was sometimes painful just because it was equated with loss of prestige. France fought two wars, once in Indochina, another in Algeria, to prevent such a loss; even Britain, which did not generally try to buck the historic trend, reacted fiercely to Egypt's 1956 seizure of the Suez Canal. The United States, with its Central American sphere of influence, found it difficult to surrender its sole control over the Panama Canal, even though militarily and economically the canal had lost much of its former utility. When Argentina seized the British-owned Falkland Islands in early 1982, Britain sent a sizable fleet to recover them. The events surrounding the short undeclared war that followed also provide a dramatic example of the role of force in international politics. Argentina had long claimed these islands, which it called the Malvinas. Negotiations had gotten nowhere, not because Britain was unwilling to give up these far-away islands; after all, Britain had given India and other colonies their freedom. The stumbling block was the 1,800 English-speaking sheep farmers who were opposed to being ruled by a Spanish-speaking country whose government at the time was an arbitrary military dictatorship. Negotiations having been unfruitful, the Argentines sent in the military. The British, humiliated by this invasion of English territory and believing that the inhabitants should play a role in determining their future, sent the fleet eight thousand miles into the South Atlantic to recover the islands. Force settled the issue. Even though in the long run the islands might become Argentinian, Britain—like great powers historically—was willing to fight and suffer casualties to avoid humiliation.

Even smaller countries that do not have memories of past glory or entertain thoughts of future greatness are concerned about prestige. For them, it is not a sense of power but of simple dignity that is at stake; they wish to be treated with respect even though they are not strong countries. Even the smallest of them want to have the symbols of nationhood. Tiny island-states in the Pacific feel they need their own airlines, even when they run at a loss. Thus, Kiribati has Air Tungaru; Vanuatu, Air Vanuatu; Western Samoa, Polynesian Airlines; Papua New Guinea, Air Niugini; Fiji, Air Pacific; and the Solomon Islands, Solair.[5]

A last point is worth noting: a nation's prestige may outlast its power. The latter may be declining relative to that of other nations, but its reputation may save it from challenge for a while. When that challenge comes, however, from a state whose power is increasing, prestige vanishes if, as is likely, the waning state suffers a setback. The challenger now acquires prestige.

Economic Security

So far our discussion of security and prestige has focused on the military context within which security is traditionally defined. But, in fact, can security be defined only in terms of the most visible and most obvious threat? What about a healthy economy? Is a nation "secure" if its economic base is declining? Specifically, how "strong" was the United States in the first half of the 1980s as the Reagan administration's domestic policies transformed it into the world's largest debtor nation? Coming into office committed to a substantial increase in defense spending as well as a tax reduction to stimulate the economy, the fiscally conservative Reagan administration ran up a deficit of about $200 billion, the largest in the nation's history. Income taxes were cut by 25 percent, while defense received $1 trillion, about the amount that Reagan had increased the national debt by 1985.

The competition for money between the private sector looking for investment capital and the government looking for money to finance the deficit kept the nation's interest rates high. These interest rates attracted foreign capital, about half from Europe, sending the value of the dollar soaring upwards by about 30 percent against foreign currencies from 1981 to 1985. Billions in pounds, francs, yen, and other currencies were invested in the United States, doubling foreign investments in five years to $833 billion. The result was that American exports rose in price by 30 percent, making them too expensive in a competitive market; and conversely, the price of imports dropped by 30 percent, undercutting U.S. firms. While all this was a bonanza for American consumers and tourists, American farmers were deeply hurt as overseas sales dropped sharply; thousands of farms were foreclosed or were on the brink of foreclosure. Imports hurt industries such as autos and steel, which could not meet the competition; the resulting loss of earnings also meant a loss of capital to invest in their modernization. The nation's unemployed stood at 8 million, more than 2 million were jobs lost in industries that export and compete with imports. In April 1985, the United States became a debtor nation for the first time since World War I, as the United States borrowed $100 billion or more each year from the rest of the world to finance its growing trade deficits—that is, the imbalance between what the United States pays for imports and earns from exports. In 1986, the United States passed Brazil and Mexico, the world's two largest debtor nations. This external debt may approach $1 trillion by 1990, more than the total owed in early 1985 by all of the LDCs collectively!

The consequences were several. First, the decline of exports and growth of the imports led to a loss of jobs in the United States and to demands for protection for many of the injured industries. These protectionist demands, aimed mainly at America's allies, caused tensions with Japan and within the North Atlantic Treaty Organization (NATO) and threatened to set off "trade wars." Second, to stem the outflow of capital to the United States, the Europeans also raised their interest rates, hurting their own economic recovery from the ravages of the 1970s. This, in turn, threatened to reduce their defense spending at a time when the United States was urging its NATO partners to increase their allotment to defense. In fact, the U.S. Senate urged U.S. troop withdrawal if the Europeans did not shoulder a greater part of the defense burden of the alliance. Third, the LDCs—especially in Latin America—were badly hurt. Their huge debts owed largely to leading American banks, run up in the 1970s as they borrowed to help pay their oil bills, had to be repaid in dollars; simultaneously, protectionist measures limiting their access to Western markets made it almost impossible for them to earn the money to pay off their loans.[6] The resulting "debt bomb" threatened to cause serious economic and political problems, both among their debtors and Western leading countries (see Chapter 11).

Thus, although the defense buildup was strongly supported by U.S. public opinion because of the cuts in defense spending during the 1970s, the manner in which it was undertaken created an intolerable economic situation. As far as the U.S. economy was concerned, the experience was not only painful but also contributed to its declining influence in the world economy. The fact that, even as the dollar declined, the U.S. economy still remained sluggish was a symptom of its increasingly uncompetitive nature in world markets. This was aptly symbolized by the renaming in 1986 of US Steel, the former symbol of a once thriving and dominant economy, as USX (now mainly an oil company). Steel companies, the former backbone of industrial strength, continued to close plants and lay off workers.

Related to this decline was the deterioration of the American labor force, in turn a symptom of lower educational standards (reportedly among the lowest in the industrial world). The United States was graduating fewer engineers and scientists than Japan, which has less than half its population. American children attend school an average of 180 school days, Japanese children 240 days, and the average in Europe is 220. Moreover, American children go to school for six and a half hours per day, while the rest of the industrial world requires eight hours. It is hardly surprising in an increasingly technological world in which mathematics represents the cutting edge of development and research—a subject in which American children place lower than children of other industrial countries—that the United States also has difficulties competing in the new high-technology industries. Japanese and West German children simply learn more mathematics and science than American children because they are at school longer.

National Welfare

Economic wealth or prosperity has also long ranked high as a goal for states. First, wealth has been directly related to the military strength a state can afford; in an age before nationalism, the wealthy prince could buy a large army. Since the French Revolution, which mobilized the masses, and the Industrial Revolution, states with sizable populations and industrial capacities have ranked at the top of the power hierarchy. But industry and technology involve more than power; they also involve welfare, the desire of people in all societies for a better material life. Therefore governments—even dictatorial ones—must respond to their citizens' demands. The "revolution of rising expectations" is universal; if it is usually thought of in connection with underdeveloped countries, that is only because they are copying the large Western states, which, as the first to industrialize, have provided their people with the world's highest standard of living.

Until the recent concern with environmental problems, mostly the byproducts of industrialization, economic growth was the chief, if not the sole, criterion for social policy in the West. Raising everyone's living standards, including redistributing among those who had previously been denied more of an ever-rising gross national product (GNP)—the value of a nation's total production and services—was at the heart of all modern Western welfare states' social policies, including those of the United States. Attempts to redistribute existing or only slowly growing wealth among different classes or segments of society would have precipitated intense social conflict because one class would have gained at the expense of another. Rapidly expanding the "economic pie" so that everyone could have a larger share of it made it possible to avoid such conflict and any possible political instability while satisfying the vast majority of groups and people. The 1973-74 oil embargo by the Organization of Petroleum Exporting Countries' (OPEC) and its quadrupling of prices demonstrated Western industrial societies' vulnerability to interruptions in supply and price increases, for these nations depend on economic growth and affluence for social peace. During the 1970s, fear of future "energy crises," of other threats to a comfortable standard of living that might expose countries to political pressures, was very much a concern shared by all Western states. What became clear was the degree to which the prosperity of Western economies—income, economic growth, employment, ability to afford social services—was entwined with the fortunes of the international economy and international politics.

The desire for the "good life" is not limited to Western states. The drive for even higher economic growth rates and increased gross national product is shared by the Soviet Union as well. Every few years the Soviet leaders promise their long-suffering compatriots that, at the end of this or that five-year plan or decade, their standard of living will be comparable to that of the United States, the nation whose economic and social system they never fail to denounce as exploitative and inhumane. Precisely because in the Second Industrial Revolution of electronics, especially in computers, the Soviet Union was falling behind, and because this lag affected all areas of its economy and not just the sector devoted to consumer-goods production, it needed access to Western trade and technology as a "fix" for its own overcentralized, overbureaucratized, and often ideologically hamstrung economy. Otherwise, it might suffer some social unrest; worse, its military capability might be affected. Therefore, détente was partly the political price the Soviet Union was willing to pay to improve both its industrial and agricultural economies.

But, among all nations, it is the LDCs that have been most bent on modernizing—industrializing and urbanizing—themselves. To attract assistance from the competing superpowers, most of the formerly colonial states pursued a policy of nonalignment. When the cold war turned into détente, they began to press their demands more assertively. OPEC's aggressiveness, the attempts to organize other producer cartels to control supplies and prices of resources, and demands in the United Nations for a "new international economic order" (NIEO) all were aimed at changing the distribution of wealth and power between the First and Third Worlds. Whatever the ultimate outcome of these demands, they resulted in confrontation between the "haves" and "have-nots." With a rapidly growing world population, and the Third World's drive toward industrialization in an age of finite natural resources (especially oil), the desire of nations for economic growth and greater prosperity may well result in higher levels of conflict as economic issues rival political-military issues or, more accurately, as economic issues become so heavily politicized that to refer to them as *economic* issues is a misnomer.

Ideology

A final goal, which some states pursue more than do others, is the protection or promotion of ideology. An *ideology* is a set of beliefs that purports to explain reality and prescribes a desirable future existence for society and the world in general; it also defines the role for the believing nation in bringing about this future condition. Revolutionary ideologies in particular, which condemn the present state of existence as evil and intolerable, are expressed in terms of long-range goals that amount to a universal transformation of the state system (see Chapter 2); each tends to impart to the revolutionary state a strong sense of mission and commitment to the achievement of humanity's secular salvation. Each, in the name of justice, wishes to create the new Jerusalem here on earth. In the nineteenth century, protected by the balance of power in Europe, the United States regarded itself as the New World with a political system morally superior to the regimes of the Old World. The United States chose to isolate itself from possible contamination by the European nations. In the twentieth century, however, it has been increasingly drawn into the Old World's quarrels as Britain's power weakened. The United States has engaged Germany twice in hot wars and the Soviet Union in a cold war to defend democratic values. On the other hand, revolutionary regimes, like that of France after 1789, the Soviet Union after 1917, and China after 1949, have energetically sought to expand their influence and power in the international system to advance their respective faiths. The initial expectation after revolution is that it will spread from one country to another by means of "spontaneous combustion." Leon Trotsky, the first Soviet people's commissar for foreign affairs, did not expect his job to last long. "I will issue a few revolutionary proclamations to the peoples of the world and then shut up shop," he declared.[7] But the proclamations did not spark a global revolutionary fire. Later Soviet leaders preferred to rely on more traditional means to ensure that history would march their way by helping it along wherever and whenever possible.

One critical problem that arises for states that harbor universal or regional goals is that these goals are usually long range and frequently conflict with shorter-term and immediate national aims, like security; as a result, the long-term goals tend to become subordinated to more limited national objectives and demands. Communist China, for example, although born as a revolutionary state, proclaimed itself during the 1960s as the true heir of the revolutionary tradition of Marx and Lenin. China would spearhead the revolutionary struggle against American imperialism; the Soviet Union, it charged, had already sold out the revolution by its increasing cooperation with the United States. But, when China was faced with possible Soviet military action in the late 1960s and early 1970s, it turned to the world's most powerful "imperialist" state. Niccolò Machiavelli became a more important guide to policy than Marx.

Since the French Revolution, states have primarily promoted secular ideologies. But Iran, under the Ayatollah Ruhollah Khomeini, has advocated an Islamic fundamentalist revolution. Basically a reaction to the Westernization of Iran which, among other things, displaced the clergy from its prominent role in society, Islamic fundamentalism aims to restore traditional religious values throughout the Islamic world and to eliminate secular Western, especially American, values and power throughout the Middle East and West Asian areas. Much of this drive has become associated with Iranian-sponsored terrorism in Lebanon and other Middle Eastern countries against Western targets, as well as with the Iran-Iraq war, which Iran has fought with great zealousness and willingness to sacrifice life (see Chapter 12).

The impact of ideologies upon international politics generally has been to enlarge the scope and intensity of conflict between nations with opposing belief systems. It is difficult enough to resolve differences of interest; it becomes infinitely more difficult to reconcile nations with differences of philosophy. Each ideological nation sees itself as the representative of truth and morality and sees opposing states as wrong and immoral. Each becomes a crusader and seeks to transform other countries; that is, each becomes a "revolutionary state." Compromise among states in these circumstances is difficult because it is viewed as treason; how can a state claiming to possess a monopoly of wisdom and morality compromise with the "devil"? A nation believing itself to have a moral mission cannot violate its own principles.

GOALS OF 'HIGH' POLITICS AND 'LOW' POLITICS

It has become commonplace in recent years to distinguish between the objectives of "high" politics and "low" politics. High politics refers to political-security or strategic issues, and low politics to welfare or social-economic issues. Proponents of this distinction argue that the process of modernization is transforming the character of foreign policy and the means by which it is carried out.

The basic claim is that modernization has elevated low politics issues to a higher priority than high politics issues. The increasing mass participation in modern societies means that people's concerns are mainly with their standard of living. Since few, if any, societies are economically self-sufficient, fulfilling people's expectations of more jobs, higher pay, and a constantly improving way of life requires nations to cooperate with one another rather than fight. Anarchy and force, therefore, will be replaced by interdependence and co-operation. Inherent in this high politics/low politics distinction is the usually unstated maxim, "Politics bad, economics good." Politics is concerned with conflict and war and destruction, economics with humans and their welfare, a more positive and obviously more moral area of concern.

The high/low politics distinction, however, is hard to maintain in the real world. As suggested earlier, economic and political issues intersect. The economic productivity of the United States was obviously a key factor in transforming it into a political and military superpower in this century, just as Britain's industrialization in the nineteenth century made it the world's greatest power until the rise of Germany. Both nations' primacy also made possible an international free-trade system. On the other hand, states frequently use economic means to gain political objectives. The Arab members of OPEC wished not only to increase their income by raising oil prices but also to gain Western, especially American, recognition of the PLO as the representative of the Palestinian people, which the Arabs thought would speed up the creation of a Palestinian state and shift previously pro-Israeli American policies. The redistribution of wealth between the First and Third Worlds, like the struggle for scarce resources, became, in an anarchic system, a matter of power. The Hobbesian character of international politics is not limited to security and prestige issues; day-to-day events, such as an energy crisis, reinforce this struggle (see Chapter 11).

The issue is not whether economic interdependence exists in the contemporary world. One need only note the LDCs' debt problem and imagine the impact on Western societies if the LDCs defaulted. The issue is that the wrong conclusion is drawn, namely, that modernization is gradually reducing the former priority of security objectives and the role of force in international politics. There is little evidence to support this proposition. What is interesting is why proponents of this view think that interdependence should change historic patterns of state behavior (see Chapter 20).

POSSESSION AND MILIEU OBJECTIVES

We have been discussing objectives that states seek to defend or increase because they attach great value to them. And states pursue them in a competitive situation. Milieu objectives are concerned with nations' attempts to influence the nature of that competition—to shape the conditions of the state system beyond their own national boundaries.[8] States tend to perceive possession goals, such as security, in terms of a finite amount, which means that more for an adversary means an equivalent reduction for oneself. Milieu objectives, by contrast, are viewed as a gain for all because their aim is to improve the state system all states share. Arms control negotiations between the United States and the Soviet Union involve the security of both superpowers, but to the extent that they make the international environment safer, all states benefit. Thus, a possession goal may be a way station to milieu goals. The former is identified with the "national interest." The likelihood that milieu goals are also in the national interest of other countries only underlines the fact that nations share common interests.

In 1950 the United States went to war in Korea. It did so to protect its security interests (see Chapter 10). But another goal was to create a world environment free from aggression, one in which aggression would not be rewarded, and in which smaller nations would feel safe—in short, a world unlike that of the 1930s when aggressions unmet only whetted the aggressors' appetites. President Harry Truman wished to prevent World War III.

Another frequently cited example of a milieu objective is the redistribution of wealth between the First and Third Worlds. It might well be asked why the industrial nations, in this context often referred to as the rich nations, should engage in such an effort for the benefit of the poor. Samuel Huntington offers this explanation:

> [T]he United States is a tenant occupying the largest, most elegant, most luxuriously furnished penthouse suite in a global cooperative apartment house. . . . The United States does [therefore] have a basic interest in the structural soundness of the building as a whole. It is precisely that soundness which is in question. The condition of the building is beginning to deteriorate . . . [and is] liable to collapse or to go up in smoke. As the wealthiest tenant in the building, the United States has a clear interest in insuring that the structure as a whole is sound and that minimum conditions for decent human existence prevail in the building.[9]

THE COMPETITION OF OBJECTIVES

Some, although by no means all, of the principal objectives states seek have been identified. The resulting conflict among objectives suggests that *the acquisition of more of one objective often comes at the cost of another. Objectives are frequently incompatible.*

Guns Versus Butter

One such conflict is between security and welfare or, in more colloquial language, guns and butter. Realistically, the more a state spends on maintaining military forces, the less it can spend on foreign aid, on construction of schools, hospitals, and roads, on education, vocational training, and a "war on poverty." The more taxes it needs to buy bombs, the less the taxpayer has left to buy a new house or car, purchase family insurance, take a vacation, or send the children to college. Nations have limited resources, even if these are great, and they must make choices. The choice is not usually *either* guns *or* butter but how much of each. The question then becomes: How many more guns will yield how much of an increase in relative security—taking into account the fact that the opponent is also likely to increase the number of its guns to match our increase? Or conversely, how much *less* butter is an additional increase in security worth, assuming it is an increase? If such a reduction in butter, for instance, depresses the quality of life in the society and perhaps its cohesion as a functioning entity, will the extra arms have enhanced its security, even if the opponent does not or cannot match it in arms? These have been the kinds of questions widely and frequently asked in the United States since Vietnam and OPEC price hikes.

A rapidly growing economy would afford a lot of guns and butter. But the slow down of all Western economies has resulted in more of a conflict between military spending and social welfare. Already committed to cutting back the government's role in social policies, President Reagan proposed huge new outlays for weapons and simultaneous deep cuts in welfare spending. From the late 1940s to the early 1970s, the U.S. economy grew rapidly enough to afford high wages and standards of living, an extensive welfare state, and large outlays for defense and economic aid. Indeed, President Lyndon Johnson during the 1960s waged the War on Poverty and the war in Vietnam simultaneously. Since the late 1960s, however, the increasing "deindustrialization" of America—high U.S. wages had led industry to invest overseas where labor was cheaper—plus the high oil prices after 1973, added up to lower rates of economic growth in the United States. Therefore, the choice between guns and butter became sharper.

Between 1950 and 1969, congressional cuts in the defense budget averaged only $1.7 billion compared with $9.2 billion for nondefense expenditures. For the next six years the balance was reversed with defense being cut $5 billion while nondefense expenditures were raised an average of $4.7 billion. Defense spending hit 5 percent of GNP, the lowest since before the Korean War. The Nixon-Ford years saw the most sizable reduction of American military strength relative to the Soviet Union of the whole postwar period.[10] President Carter began to increase the size of the defense budgets by the late 1970s, as Congress's antimilitary sentiment began to weaken in the light of the continuous Soviet military buildup. Reagan continued the U.S. rearmament effort and increased that effort while cutting social programs. But in a democracy, voters do not like to have their benefits cut too much, and so there are limits to how much the butter can be cut without electoral risk.

In the Soviet Union, given the rulers' lack of accountability to public opinion, this choice is easier to make. After the Cuban missile crisis, Moscow began a program of sustained military growth in both nuclear and conventional areas, a program that came at the cost of a better life for Soviet citizens. Indeed, for the 1990s, it is questionable whether the stagnant Soviet economy can continue to channel such large resources into the military; more investment is desperately needed to revive the civilian economy. If the Soviet economy, which requires fundamental reforms as well as greater investment, continues to flounder, Soviet leader Mikhail Gorbachev may well face the need to reduce the Soviet Union's international ambitions. He may aspire to being America's equal and to playing the global role the United States does. As noted earlier, however, the Soviet Union is a superpower only because of its military strength. If he is unwilling to cut back Soviet international goals, Gorbachev of course can continue to exploit Third World opportunities with the use of force (Soviet or Cuban). But in that case he cannot reduce tensions with the United States, which he needs to do in order to focus on the economy and attract Western technology. Thus, Gorbachev confronts a major dilemma.

It is because guns are often believed to be bought at the expense of butter that military spending is frequently criticized as wasteful. Weapons are not only destructive; they also use up money that could be better spent on improving people's lives, some argue. In short, weapons are regarded negatively, while advancing the standard of living is thought of positively. Although this contrast is understandable, it also illustrates two characteristics of the guns versus butter debate. One is the emotional and moral context in which international politics issues are often framed. How can any rational and moral person possibly favor more guns and violence instead of greater economic prosperity and human happiness? Yet is it not false to pose this issue as if it were a simple matter of military spending versus social spending? Is a government's buying guns *not* a social service, comparable to maintaining police forces to preserve domestic tranquility? Military forces may be far larger and costlier, but this reflects the fact that law and order do not exist internationally. Because they do exist domestically, police forces can be relatively small compared to the size of the population. In any event, defense may not be cheap, but it is cheaper than fighting a war. Governments consider their first responsibility to be to keep their citizens alive, secure, and well. Only when a state feels reasonably secure can it enjoy its particular way of life. This does not sanction military spending at such high levels that it hurts the economy, as noted earlier; it is only to suggest the ordering of priorities.

A second characteristic of this debate is its historical and cultural context. The debate occurs in all societies, but not all consider spending money on guns at the expense of butter either a "waste of money" or a diversion of money that could be better spent elsewhere. Russia has had a long history of invasions and defeats, and Russian rulers have always given a prominent place to the military and have highly valued military power. Given their sense of insecurity, the Russian government and people did not view military expenditures as a waste of money but as necessary expenses. On the other hand, countries like the United States or Britain, which historically have felt much more secure because they were less easy to invade than Russia, were understandably more reluctant to fund larger forces than those absolutely needed. Generally domestic affairs received priority.

Security Versus Democracy: Domestic Dilemma

Security may be necessary to protect a nation's way of life, but this does not mean that states impose no limits on what they will do to accumulate power and thereby raise their sense of security. This is especially so for democratic states for whom the conduct of foreign policy raises both domestic and foreign policy questions, of which the most important is: Will security come at the cost of democratic values? During the cold war, the balance between security and democratic values generally was kept. Nevertheless, U.S. involvement in world affairs since World War II led in the 1960s and 1970s to the charge that, in trying to ensure the external safety of American democracy, the government had endangered democratic values domestically. The constitutional balance had been upset as the presidency had become "imperial," going to war either without congressional support or with support purportedly elicited by deceiving and lying to the legislature. The authority of Congress had been emasculated. The Central Intelligence Agency, among its other questionable activities, had helped to overthrow a legitimately elected government in Chile and planned a number of assassinations of leaders in other countries. The CIA and the Federal Bureau of Investigation, in carrying out domestic surveillance, had repeatedly broken various laws forbidding such activities. Indeed, it was charged that a "military-industrial complex" had come to dominate the American political process and had distorted the purposes of American society, benefiting Big Business, the Big Military, and Big Politicians while neglecting the poor and ignoring the nation's urban, environmental, and educational problems.

External Dangers. The external implications of the clash of security and democracy are starkly apparent when a democracy allies itself with undemocratic states. Can a democracy associate itself with dictatorial states without undermining its own cause? Or should it confine itself only to allies sharing the same political values, even to the point of jeopardizing its security by failing to take advantage of the strategic position, economic benefits, and added military strength that can be gained from alliance with certain undemocratic states? During World War II, Winston Churchill welcomed the Soviet Union as an ally after Hitler became the common enemy. The Soviet Union might not be a democracy, the prime minister said, but to beat Hitler he would eat supper with the devil—though he did admit that he would use a long spoon. But this alliance had been brought about by Germany's attack on the Soviet Union.

After 1945 and the outbreak of the cold war, the United States made alliances with many undemocratic regimes—Turkey, Greece, Spain, Nationalist China, Brazil, and Portugal, to name some of the more prominent—in the pursuit of the containment of Soviet- and Chinese-Communist power. Indeed, containment began with the Truman Doctrine, which somewhat ironically pictured the threat to Turkey and Greece from the Soviet Union as a conflict between democracy and totalitarianism. The Turkish and Greek regimes were hardly models of democratic purity. Were Truman's declaration and American policy hypocritical because they were inconsistent with the values of American democracy, or was the United States acting as the distribution of power after World War II obliged it to act? Truman's action demonstrated clearly that he believed that a democracy can align itself with undemocratic governments in strategically located areas at moments of perceived danger to American security.

Only in Western Europe did U.S. leaders view national self-determination and national security as compatible. In Eastern Europe, they also found it safe to advocate the principle of self-determination, for success would mean the retraction of Soviet power. In the meantime, the United States could point out that the Soviet-controlled people's democracies were a farce. But outside Europe the choice appeared to be in favor of safety and equilibrium. In Korea, for instance, the United States defended a governing regime that was undemocratic. The issue, however, as American policy makers saw it at the time of intervention, was American security vis-à-vis the Soviet Union or Communist China, not the democratic purity of the South Korean regime.

Nor was this view just a matter of simple cynicism or hypocrisy, although it may often have appeared that way. It was a matter of priorities. Japan is potentially very powerful; it has also been a democracy since the end of World War II. Historically Japan has considered the southern half of the Korean peninsula vital to its security. That was one major reason for the U.S. defense of South Korea when it was invaded by North Korea, a Soviet dependency at that time. That is also why U.S. troops are still on the peninsula more than thirty years after the Korean War was ended and why they can be withdrawn only if the timetable of such a pullout does not leave the Japanese insecure or in doubt about U.S. resolve and willingness to defend Japan from external threats (see map, page 259). South Korea, then, has contributed to the sense of security of a major democratic ally of the United States. Yet the South Korean government remains a repressive one.

Security, Democracy, and Welfare.
The security versus democracy issue can also be applied to the related issue of welfare. In the 1970s, as the United States was becoming an oil importer and Europe and Japan's dependence on oil from the Persian Gulf area was also growing, the United States—in an increasingly isolationist mood after the Vietnam War—selected Iran to look out for its interests in the region. If the United States was unable or unwilling to police the Persian Gulf, including the oil-rich sheikdoms on the Arabian peninsula, someone else must be found to do it, and the shah was willing. President Nixon and President Gerald Ford were, therefore, reluctant to

pressure him for liberal domestic reforms, including greater respect for political and civil rights. The shah, who did not participate in the 1973-74 oil boycott against the United States, who supplied oil to Israel, and who backed the Egyptian president's peace negotiations with Israel, ruled his country autocratically while supporting American policy objectives. In 1978, as his authority was eroding and it looked as if his days were numbered, the United States wavered. Should it give the shah all-out support and encourage him to use force, if necessary, to quell domestic disorder? Or should it discourage him from violent reaction and seek what Washington believed (falsely) would be, after the shah's departure, a more constitutional regime? President Carter, who had announced human rights to be the cornerstone of his foreign policy, could not decide whether to support the shah, the despot who was a friend of the United States, or to seek reforms that might risk weakening or displacing him, and thus make U.S. foreign policy more consistent with its democratic justifications.[11] American policy was ambiguous and fluctuated between the objectives of security and democracy.

Yet, after the collapse of the shah's government and the subsequent Soviet invasion of Afghanistan, the president declared what became known as the Carter Doctrine. It committed the United States to the defense of the oil sheikdoms on the Arabian peninsula, especially Saudi Arabia. Hardly shining examples of democracies, these kingdoms' importance to U.S., European, and Japanese welfare and security could still not be doubted because the industrial democracies had grown increasingly dependent on imported oil. President Reagan tried to make Saudi Arabia the keystone of his policy in the Middle East-Persian Gulf area, at one point warning that he would not allow Saudi Arabia to become "another Iran." He thus upped the U.S. commitment from a defense of the country to the survival of the Saudi regime itself. Compared to the vital issue of a continuing access to oil, democracy and human rights were secondary.

The Issue of Human Rights.   Clearly, in a world containing a minority of democratic states, the objectives of security (or welfare) and democracy (or human rights) are bound to compete on occasion. Deciding which objective is to be granted priority is often agonizing. If, for instance, in the name of security, a democracy somewhat indiscriminately supports a fairly large number of authoritarian allies to enhance its power, gain strategic position, ensure prosperity, or play off one country against another, it may cast doubt on its purposes. On the other hand, if in the name of democracy it refuses or minimizes alignment with authoritarian regimes, it may remain pure but ultimately weak against the principal enemies of democracy.

In the wake of the Vietnam War, critics frequently said that the United States should not again fight for the defense of dictatorships, that it should commit its blood and treasure only for the cause of democracy, as in World War II. Yet World War II broke out when Britain, a democracy, went to the rescue of Poland, an undemocratic country. Britain apparently did so (as the

United States did in Greece and Turkey) because it saw its own security linked to that of Poland, regardless of that country's government. Similarly, in 1980, the United States confronted a situation in which it had to decide whether or not to send military aid to Pakistan after the Soviet invasion of Afghanistan had made Pakistan vulnerable to possible Soviet incursions. The Pakistani military regime was no less repressive than South Vietnam's had been. Yet, given its strategic position and its ties to the United States, could Washington write Pakistan off? A comparable situation arose shortly thereafter in El Salvador, where the Reagan administration decided to support the government—despite human rights abuses—against left-wing guerrillas supplied with arms, it claimed, from Cuba and Nicaragua.

The dilemma is obvious. Note the Reagan administration's position on human rights, as spelled out in a State Department memorandum: "Human rights is at the core of our foreign policy because it is central to what America stands for. 'Human rights' is not something we pack into our foreign policy but is its very purpose; the defense and promotion of freedom in the world." Ultimately, this is the fundamental distinction between the United States and the Soviet bloc—otherwise, why arm, and why fight, if the two superpowers are morally equal? Yet the memorandum states that human rights considerations in U.S. relationships with allies and friends "must be balanced against U.S. economic security and other interests. We must take into account the pressure a regime faces and the nature of its enemies. . . . Human rights is not advanced by replacing a bad regime with a worse one, or a corrupt dictator with a zealous Communist politburo." [12]

The references were obvious. One was to the Carter administration's dislike of the shah for his human rights violations and its hope that if he fell a more democratic and liberal regime would come to power. The resulting failure of the United States to support the shah as his government crumbled is understandable. But the result was not a pro-Western, constitutional government but an Islamic theocracy that was militantly anti-American and murdered far more people than the shah's secret police ever did. The other reference was to Nicaragua where the revulsion of President Carter for the repressive regime of Anastasio Somoza led the administration to withdraw its support. Although the Sandinistas promised the Organization of American States that if they gained power, Nicaragua would pursue a policy of free elections, a mixed economy at home, and nonalignment abroad, the result, even before the Reagan administration came into office in 1981, was a regime increasingly dictatorial at home and aligned with the Soviet Union and Cuba in foreign policy.

Ironically, it was President Carter who took the initial steps against Nicaragua. But his successor vigorously pursued an anti-Sandinista policy by supporting Nicaraguan opponents or "contras" in their war against the government; Reagan in fact called the contras "freedom fighters." The president's policy was aimed at preventing the establishment of a "second Cuba" on the mainland and the expansion of Marxist influence throughout Central America, especially Mexico and Panama. Reagan also supported the government of El Salvador, Nicaragua's neighbor, in its civil war against left-wing guerrillas who, he claimed, were supported by Nicaragua and its friends.

Many critics in Congress opposed the president's policy, arguing that the human rights violations committed by the contras in Nicaragua and the Salvadoran military made them unworthy of U.S. support, that both nations had long records of political oppression and social injustice that had produced the Sandinistas and the Salvadoran insurrection. Nevertheless, the Reagan administration persisted. In Nicaragua, however, the administration was restrained by Congress, which was fearful that support for the contras would eventually result in U.S. military intervention if the contras failed either to overthrow the Sandinistas or compel them to agree to genuinely free elections. In El Salvador, Washington sponsored two free elections, one for a legislature and one for the presidency, and the Salvadorans turned out to vote in surprising numbers. Among the results were the election of a democratic reformist president and a decline of human rights abuses. The elections also demonstrated decreasing support within El Salvador for the rebels, who increasingly turned from their guerrilla warfare in the countryside to terror tactics within cities.

Despite the fact that in El Salvador the Reagan administration appeared to have found a democratic center—admittedly, a very fragile one—to support, it continued to be perceived as supporting right-wing regimes; indeed, the president strongly argued that support for such pro-American regimes was preferable to left-wing pro-Soviet ones. In early 1986, however, the administration changed its policy statements. After popular revolts against the dictatorial governments of Haiti and the Philippines, two long-time U.S. friends, the United States, which had helped smooth the transition to the opposition, asserted that in the future it would oppose repressive regimes of the anti-Communist right as well as the pro-Soviet left. "The American people believe in human rights and oppose tyranny in whatever form, whether of the left or the right." [13] Thus, the administration, which had bitterly criticized Carter's "destabilization" of friendly regimes, embraced the Carter human rights policy after having helped destabilize two regimes itself. In the Philippines the alternative was a democratic one; the opposition had won legitimacy in an election which, despite the widespread attempts by the government of Ferdinand Marcos to manipulate the vote, demonstrated extensive popular desire for an end of his regime.

What American policy would be where such a democratic alternative did not exist remains to be seen. Nevertheless, the Reagan administration's shift in rhetoric testifies to the continuing dilemma of a democracy seeking to enhance its security in a world in which democracies are a small minority. Support for human rights may enhance American security in countries where a democratic center may be found; in other countries, where no such center either exists or is very weak and ineffective against shrewd religious or Marxist-Leninist zealots and political operators, destabilizing pro-American regimes may result in future Irans and Nicaraguas. Because this outcome is undesirable, the United States is unlikely to abandon its support of all right-wing regimes.

Peace Versus Security

Earlier we emphasized that states pursue objectives such as security, prestige, welfare, and ideologies. One objective was not mentioned: peace. Its omission seems rather obvious, and there can be no doubt of its significance. Leaders constantly proclaim that their nations' goal is peace, and there is no reason to doubt their sincerity in most instances. No national leader would be so bold as to declare that he or she hated peace and wanted war, even if the leader agreed with Frederick Schuman that

> war is a habit men enjoy, as they enjoy drunkenness, gluttony, fornication, gambling and crime. Its vast superiority over all other forms of sin is that it embraces all the vices and casts over them the thrilling shadow of danger and the glittering cloak of honor, thereby making them "heroic" or at least permissible. This is so because all one's fellows, sharing vicariously in the experience of war, glorify and indulge those who bear the brunt of battle.[14]

Peace is obviously a desirable aim for states. Rarely have states gone to war lightly. Too many things can go wrong, so that few can feel certain of victory at the outset. Defeat may mean losing territory, having to pay reparations, loss of national honor—all in addition to human and material losses during the fighting. As long as other objectives can be satisfied in peacetime, the peace will be kept, as the basic objective of states is to ensure their own security. Most states feel secure when they are at peace, though clearly peace is the product of their sense of security. That is why their preferences for peace have historically not been unqualified and why, when they have believed their security endangered, they have sacrificed peace. No major nation has wanted "peace at any price," at least not before discovery of the atom bomb. Inasmuch as war was not tantamount to committing suicide before 1945, it was indeed a principal instrument for preserving the balance. Preventing the hegemony of any single power or coalition of powers took precedence over peace.

War in the twentieth century, however, has become increasingly costly, and the nuclear bomb now hangs over all civilization. Indeed, these weapons, the destructive potential of which exceeds that of all other weapons in history, both in the immensity and in the speed with which they can wipe out tens of millions of people, raise the central issue whether the nation-state system can survive a nuclear holocaust. It has become painfully obvious that in the nuclear age peace and security have become inextricably intertwined. In a sense the dilemma has sharpened. To the extent that the balance of power still depends largely, if not primarily, upon the superpowers' military strength, it is maintained by the *threat* of force, rather than by its actual use. The danger of war, therefore, cannot be eliminated. But such a total war can hardly be fought for the enhancement of a nation's security; it would doom the contestants to extinction. Britain and France during the interwar period had already sensed this danger and were therefore willing to go far—too far, it turned out—to avoid all-out war. Since World War II, both the United States and the Soviet Union have, as their behavior has shown, ruled out nuclear warfare as an instrument of policy. Both know that peace and security have become inseparable. The crucial question is how national power can be used so that it can simultaneously preserve security *and* peace.

WHAT PRICE SECURITY?

The central question raised by all these examples of conflicting goals is: *What price security?* Even the means of securing a nation's territorial integrity may be incompatible with the values by which it lives. Should a nation root out all possible "security" risks and dissidents at home, even though innocent people may well be hurt, even though the fear of expressing any criticism of governmental actions may stifle free speech, perhaps even lead to the censorship of books and the banning of debates on "controversial" topics (as occurred in the United States during the 1950s)? Is a democratic nation, in allying itself with patently undemocratic countries, augmenting its own security? Or is it weakening itself by staining its own reputation and impairing the credibility of its claim to be a champion of democracy? Should a democracy committed to holding free elections and abiding by the results help to overthrow a freely elected government elsewhere, as the United States helped to do in Chile in the early 1970s? Should a democracy intervene in the affairs of a major NATO member, financing anti-Communist political parties to prevent the Communist party from being included in a coalition government, thus weakening the alliance? Can a democracy launch a preventive war, firing the first shot? Obviously, security and other objectives may clash; so may the objectives and the methods by which states pursue their ends. For policy makers, deciding on the exact mix of goals the nation ought to pursue, the means by which to achieve them, and the level of commitment to them is controversial and difficult.

Notes

1. Frederick L. Schuman, *The Commonwealth of Man* (New York: Alfred A. Knopf, 1952), 38.
2. Arnold Wolfers, *Discord and Collaboration* (Baltimore: Johns Hopkins University Press, 1965), 89-90.
3. John F. Kennedy, *Final Report of the Committee on Commerce, United States Senate, prepared by its Subcommittee of the Subcommittee in Communications*, pt. 1 (Washington,

D.C.: Government Printing Office, 1961), 52.

4. *The Pentagon Papers* (Chicago: Quadrangle, 1971), 432.

5. *New York Times,* Oct. 24, 1981.

6. For a devastating critique of American economic policy, see Helmud Schmidt, *A Grand Strategy for the West* (New Haven, Conn.: Yale University Press, 1985).

7. Quoted in E. H. Carr, *The Bolshevik Revolution 1917-1923* (London: Macmillan, 1953), 16.

8. Wolfers, *Discord and Collaboration,* 73-76.

9. Samuel P. Huntington, "Does Foreign Aid Have a Future," *Foreign Policy,* Spring 1971, 130-131.

10. John L. Gaddis, *Strategies of Containment* (New York: Oxford University Press, 1982), 320-322. Also see the articles by Melvin R. Laird, by coauthors Colin S. Gray and Jeffrey G. Barlow, and by Robert W. Komer all appearing in "The 'Decade of Neglect' Controversy," *International Security,* Fall 1985, 3-83.

11. Michael A. Ledeen and William H. Lewis, "Carter and the Fall of the Shah: The Inside Story," *Washington Quarterly,* Spring 1980, 3-40.

12. U.S., Department of State, "Memorandum on Human Rights," *New York Times,* Nov. 5, 1981. Also see Lars Schoultz, *Human Rights and United States Policy Toward Latin America* (Princeton, N.J.: Princeton University Press, 1981); and Fred Baumann, ed., *Human Rights and American Foreign Policy* (Gambier, Ohio: Kenyon College, Public Affairs Conference Center, 1982).

13. "Text of Reagan's Message to Congress on Foreign Policy," *New York Times,* March 13, 1986.

14. Schuman, *Commonwealth of Man,* 49.

CHAPTER 5

The Security Game

FORCE IN DOMESTIC AND INTERNATIONAL POLITICS

The adversary game that nations play is the product of an anarchical international or state system. This does not mean anarchy in the sense of disorder and chaos; rather, it means the absence of legitimate governmental institutions with superior authority. Each state is responsible for providing for the realization of its own security and other objectives; no world government exists to provide for each member state's security, prestige, prosperity, or fulfillment of ideological goals. The state system, therefore, is fundamentally based on the principle of self-help; that is, each state decides for itself how to pursue these objectives, including when and over what issues to resort to force. Thus, the system is always in a state of potential war because war may erupt at any moment. The seventeenth-century English philosopher Thomas Hobbes caught the essence of interstate politics and the basic adversary game when he wrote:

> [T]hough there had never been any time, wherein particular men were in a condition of war one against another; yet in all times, kings, and persons of sovereign authority, because of their independency, are in continual jealousies, and in the state and posture of gladiators; having their weapons pointing, and their eyes fixed on one another; that is, their forts, garrisons and guns, upon the frontiers of their kingdoms; and continual spies upon their neighbours; which is a posture of war.[1]

It is often said that international conflicts are settled with bullets, while domestic differences are settled with ballots. The reason is that in international conflicts there is no legitimate central government whose policy decisions are accepted as binding, backed by a common political culture (rules or norms that govern the way a society resolves conflicts peacefully). Admittedly, this distinction between international and domestic conflicts is oversimplified. Not all quarrels between states result in war; most are settled without even invoking the threat of violence. Nor are all domestic clashes of interest settled without force or violent disturbance, even within contemporary Western democracies. Of the 278 wars fought between 1480 and 1941, 28 percent were civil wars.[2] And the incidence of civil war has risen since World War II. The large number of new states that have arisen out of the ashes of colonial empires is one major reason for this increasing frequency of internal violence within nations. Many of the less-developed countries (LDCs) are deeply divided by religious, ethnic, class, and racial differences, and the result has often been civil wars and the disintegration of the new states. The frequency with which governments have been overthrown and the recurrence of civil wars and revolutions suggest that, where legitimate governmental institutions and commonly shared political cultures have not yet been achieved, domestic politics tend to resemble international politics. The distinction between domestic and international politics is, then, not in the use or nonuse of force, but in the fact that national governments normally provide protection for their citizens. Unlike the international system, domestic systems are not usually based on self-help. Central governments that are legitimate have the authority or right to ensure that the law is obeyed by its citizens and to use force against any private use of violence.

The Role of Governmental Institutions

Nevertheless, in some nations, especially the older, more settled Western nations, the role of violence in resolving disputes is considerably less important than that of international war in the state system. Why? What conditions and processes of conflict resolution exist within these nations to account for their greater capacity to solve inevitable domestic problems?

The Executive Branch. One factor is the presence of executive branches of government to enforce the law and keep order. In Western systems the executive normally holds a preponderance, if not a monopoly, of organized force with which it can legitimately enforce the law, protect society, and discourage potential rebels. The executive controls the armed forces and the national police, and it disarms the citizens of the nation by regulating the ownership of arms and forbidding the existence of private or party paramilitary forces. Domestic peace is, therefore, always armed. If the executive ever loses this superiority of power, either because all or part of the army refuses to support it, as in Weimar Germany or Spain before the rule of General Francisco Franco, or because of the rise of political parties that possess their own armed forces, as did the Nazis in Germany, the Communist Chinese, the Viet Cong in South Vietnam, and the Sandinistas in Nicaragua, the government may be challenged and the nation plunged into civil war.

The Legislative Process.   A second factor is that Western political systems also have institutionalized legislative processes through which conflicts of interests within society, articulated by political parties and interest groups, are channeled and peacefully resolved. The term *legislative process* is used, rather than *legislative branch*, because the latter does not legislate by itself. In any Western political system, it is the leader of the majority party who, as president or prime minister, draws up the legislative program to be submitted for approval to the congress or parliament. In legislation, too, the executive plays the leading role. The significance of the process of legislation, however, is that law making is essentially synonymous with the issue of domestic war and peace. The most controversial, significant, and bitter conflicts in society revolve around questions of what the law should be. The legislative process is focused on the basic issue of politics, which—as Harold Lasswell once summed it up—is "who gets what, when, and how."

Politics, therefore, is a series of conflicts over the distribution of "goods" such as wealth, status, and power in society. Other political scientists have used more formal terms, like *allocation of values*. The more usual term is *justice*. Although various groups and classes in society define that term differently, they all are concerned with attaining justice—realizing group aspirations and redressing grievances. Should there be a redistribution of wealth? Should minorities be granted full equality in American society, and should discrimination in interstate travel, housing, and employment be banned? Should the poor, the unemployed, the aged, the sick, and the hungry receive assistance? What kind and how much? Should labor be permitted to bargain collectively? Should farmers be subsidized or rely on the free market? Should the country have a national health-insurance plan, and, if so, what type and at what cost?

These questions pose major social issues and arouse strong passions. Yet they are unavoidable; in a pluralistic society new demands are continually being advanced, and people differ on how to resolve the many problems confronting society. A political system that is not very responsive to demands for change and does not provide for sufficient peaceful change will sooner or later erupt in revolution, the domestic equivalent of international war. A political system must either meet important aspirations of rising and discontented new social groups with sensitivity and sufficient speed or confront violent upheaval. If discontent is widespread enough, the executive's superior power cannot prevent the government's fall because the army and police are recruited from the population. In the ultimate breakdown of society, many soldiers will refuse to fire on their own people; units of the armed forces will instead join the rebellion, as in Russia in 1917, in Iran in 1978-79, and in Afghanistan, where soldiers defected from the Soviet-imposed government and joined the rebels. The ordinary soldier-citizen will have no more vested interest in maintaining the system than will most other citizens.

The Judiciary.   The final factor is that a judiciary, together with the executive and legislative institutions, helps to maintain expectations of individual and social justice. Violence, domestic or international, is normally an instrument of last resort. While hope remains that peaceful change is possible through existing political processes, rebellion can usually be avoided. But, just as there is no international executive with a monopoly of organized force and no international legislative process to provide for peaceful change, the state system lacks an international judiciary with the authority to ensure this sense of justice and bring about peaceful change.

The Role of Political Culture

The state system lacks not only effective central political institutions for preserving peace and regulating the behavior of its members but also an international political culture or consensus of political values comparable to those existing within most Western states. A state's political culture includes the shared political values and attitudes of its people related to the general purposes for which society exists and, even more important, the rules or norms by which the domestic "game" is played. The consensus thus comprises both substantive values (agreement on what the country stands for) and procedural values (agreement on how government should be conducted—for example, majority rule and the supremacy of law.) Nondemocratic states can proclaim the same substantive goals as democracies (as, in fact, the Soviet Union does in its constitution). Therefore, it is the way of governing or making political decisions that is critical. If policies were not made according to rules, they would be disregarded and disobeyed; they would lack moral sanction or legitimacy. People obey the law because they agree that the government has the right to govern, not because the government has at its command superior power and the individual is fearful of punishment. "For, if force creates right," the French philosopher Jean Jacques Rousseau wrote in the eighteenth century, "the effect changes with the cause: Every force that is greater than the first succeeds to its right. As soon as it is possible to disobey with impunity, disobedience is legitimate and the strongest being always in the right, the only thing that matters is to act so as to become the strongest." But, Rousseau continued, "The strongest is never strong enough to be always the master, unless he transforms strength into right and obedience to duty." [3] If a government is considered legitimate, even people who disagree with the content of a law normally obey it because they acknowledge that the government has the authority to decide policies for the entire society.

Politics, to sum up, deals with conflicts among groups whose objectives clash. The peaceful resolution of such differences depends on several conditions. First, there must be an executive with superior power, which discourages potentially violent challenges and allows the government to enforce legitimate decisions (in Vernon Van Dyke's apt phrase, "A peaceful country is a policeful country"). Second, there must be a set of governing institutions, executive, legislative, and judicial, that provide for peaceful resolution of conflict and allow most people and organizations to attain justice or what they themselves regard as fair shares of what society has to offer. Third, and, perhaps most important, there must be widespread agreement on common purposes and rules of the game so that, even in major disputes, the differing views and needs can be expressed through acceptable political channels and not lead to confrontation and violence. Fourth, this consensus, which serves to legitimate the government, must be reinforced by a deep emotional commitment embodied in nationalism and its various symbols: the flag, the national monuments, the national anthem, national institutions, and national celebrations of key events in a nation's history. Such symbols are reminders of national history and the common beliefs and loyalty of a people, as well as of the supremacy of society and the common good.

Instead of such broad agreement, which can buffer and limit areas of conflict so that they do not shred the whole social fabric, the only common agreement on what may be called a minimal "international political culture" is the commitment to the existence of nation-states, their independence, and their security. But this commitment *maximizes* divisions and conflict among nations. The primary loyalty of the nation-state is to itself. The absence of the conditions for peaceful change and accommodation internationally means that the basic condition of the state system is one of potential warfare among its members; at least, there is a higher expectation of violence than in national political systems.[4]

Anarchy, Order, and Justice

Several points should be emphasized in this comparative analysis of the role of governmental institutions domestically and their absence internationally: first, the executive with its monopoly or preponderance of legitimate organized force helps keep public order; and second, the legislative and judicial processes concern themselves with peaceful change and the attainment of some sort of approximation of what various groups and classes in society deem to be *justice*. In the domestic sphere, indeed, justice is the central issue; in Western societies, both the political process and political writings are concerned with this issue, as the development of the modern welfare state suggests. The reason justice can be the focus of these national societies is that they have assumed the existence of order, even if they continue—as today— to show a heightened concern about public safety and personal security.

In international politics and theories of international politics, however, order is the central issue. This does not mean, of course, that the need to preserve international order is necessarily incompatible with just changes.[5] The decolonization of European empires in the name of national self-determination, a basic Western principle, is proof that order and justice can be reconciled to some degree. Decolonization took place, by and large, because the Western powers, weakened by World War II and recognizing the justice of the colonies' claims to independence, were willing to grant most of them statehood. A few colonies had to fight for independence, but, even in those cases, segments of domestic opinion in the Western colonial country favored the "war of liberation" because self-government is a democratic principle.

The cry of revolutionary groups is "Let justice be done," and sometimes they add "though the earth perish," since in their judgment the world is so unjust it deserves to be destroyed if it refuses to change. In fact, revolutionaries do not really expect that the earth will perish, but that they will be successful, capture power, and then consolidate the gains of the revolution in a "new order." This is as true for the Palestine Liberation Organization (PLO), seeking the establishment of a Palestinian state, as it was for the Bolsheviks who captured power in Russia in 1917.

But it is not only revolutionary groups that seek justice. States do as well. As suggested earlier, Russia in 1917 and France in 1789 considered themselves to be "revolutionary" powers, states that were going to transform the old regimes (capitalism in one case, monarchy and aristocracy in the other) to new orders in the name of justice. Because the old regimes were alleged to be the cause for poverty domestically and war internationally, their replacement would usher in an era in which people would no longer exploit each other as commodities; rather, they would live together in liberty, equality, and fraternity at home and in peace abroad.

Nevertheless, justice takes a subsidiary place to order internationally for two reasons. First is the anarchical nature of the state system. Order, meaning the survival and safety of its member states, must be ranked as a basic need. It is, as domestic politics amply demonstrates, the precondition for the realization of justice. Second, and closely related, is that there is no agreed-upon moral code among the peoples and governments of the world. Within a nation, the moral code may well be imposed upon those who disagree; for example, when laws sanctioning child labor or racial discrimination or the absence of a livable minimum wage are changed by a political process that is recognized as legitimate, and the government enforces the new laws that reflect the nation's conception of justice. Internationally, there is neither an acceptable common moral code nor a set of higher institutions that possesses the authority to impose this code upon recalcitrant states.

Indeed, states whose foreign policies reflect a strong sense of justice, as they define the term—France and Russia, for example, or, in the 1980s, Islamic Iran—tend to launch international crusades to impose their ideas of justice on other states by force. Neighboring states, as well as others who are not neighbors, see this as a threat to *their* security, including their political organization and values. In short, the realization of justice, whether in the name of Mohammed, God, or some secular cause, may well be the cause for war. *Preserving peace, ironically, may mean accepting many of the injustices and wrongs in the world.* Should the Western democracies have declared war on Hitler and invaded Germany in the 1930s to overthrow him? Should one applaud Tanzania's invasion of Uganda to overthrow its dictator, Idi Amin, or Vietnam's invasion of Cambodia to eliminate a regime that had killed approximately one-quarter of its own population in a slaughter reminiscent of the Holocaust? The fact that states do not usually invade other states to bring about domestic justice is the reason for the cry "Let justice be done, even if the world perish."

It is even more ironic that when, in the name of justice, states launch crusades "to set all men free" and "bring them the truth," there is only one way that other nations can maintain their security and right to live according to their own moral code, and that is to use countervailing power. Yet, to pile one irony on top of another, the use of power, especially violence, often offends people's concepts of justice. Reason and consent ought to settle differences, not force. But war hangs over the conduct of international politics; historically it has served as one of the principal instruments for preserving the balance of power, which is the basis for any kind of order in an essentially anarchical state system.

INTERNATIONAL POLITICS AS A 'STATE OF POTENTIAL WAR'

Self-Help and the Drive for Power

The primary distinguishing characteristic of the state system follows from this decentralized or anarchical nature. *Each state in this external environment can rely upon itself, and only upon itself, for the protection of its political independence, territorial integrity, and national prosperity.* In a condition of what might also be called "politics without government"—perhaps the shortest way of summing up the distinction between international and domestic politics—the issue of who receives what, when, and how is decided, not by a national government recognized as legitimate, but by the interactions of states in a system whose basic rule is "every state for itself." Since a human being's highest secular loyalty is to the nation, policy makers of all states are intensely committed to the maintenance of national security, the prerequisite for enjoyment of the nation's other values—its way or life. If it is further correct that the external milieu is anarchical, posing a constant danger to this way of life, policy makers responsible for protecting the nation react fearfully to perceived threats to their country.

More specifically, we may say that states living in an environment in which none can acquire absolute security are bound to feel insecure and are therefore driven to reduce their sense of insecurity by enhancing their power. As with human beings in the Hobbesian state of nature, so with states in the state system: they are haunted by continuous fear and danger of violent death.[6] It is the resulting mutual fear and suspicion among states that produce "power politics." When a nation sees its neighbor as a potential foe, it tries to deter potential attack by becoming a little stronger than the neighbor. The latter, in turn, also fears an attack and therefore feels that it too must be strong enough to deter attack or, if deterrence should fail, to win the resulting conflict. *The insecurity of all states in the system compels each to acquire greater security by engaging in a constant scramble for increased power.* But as each state watches its neighbor's power grow, its own sense of insecurity recurs: it then tries all the harder to gain even greater strength. The result is that each state is continually faced with a "security dilemma."[7]

The nature of the state system thus conditions the behavior of its members, committing each state to a continuing concern with power because of its security dilemma. Nations seek power not because simple maximization of power is their goal; they seek it because they wish to guard the security of their "core values," their territorial integrity, and political independence, as well as their prosperity. And they act aggressively because the system gives rise to mutual fear and suspicion: each state regards its neighbor state as a potential Cain.[8] The dilemma inherent in the state system is essentially "kill or be killed," to strike first or risk destruction. In this context, it does not take much for one state to arouse and confirm another state's apprehensions and thus to stimulate the development of reciprocal images of hostility, each of which will be validated by the adversary's behavior. Conversely, these images will be hard to dispel even by friendly acts; indeed, such acts may be construed as indications of weakness and may therefore be exploited.

The Role of Military Power

Perhaps a more apt way of defining this almost compulsive concern with power that is shared by all states is in terms of the high potential for violence in the anarchical state system. Threats of violence or actual incidents of violence are in the end the principal means by which one state can impose its demands on other states or, conversely, resist demands imposed on it by others. In domestic politics government performs a distributive function; in international politics force or coercion takes the place of government. It is for this reason that the international system frequently has been characterized as being in a state of potential war; it is war, or the constant possibility of war, that all too often determines who receives what and when. In an environment of conflicting demands in which there are no universally accepted supranational institutions to provide for the nonviolent resolution of differences, it is the power of the respective adversaries—the power to win a war should it erupt—that will settle who gains what and who loses what. The actual strength of each party will be clear from the outcome: defeat, stalemate, compromise, peace, or victory. This is not to say that wars are common or even the principal expression of power. War is the instrument of last resort, the ultimate test.

More frequently than war, states use the *threat* of force or coercion. The military power not used may be more potent than the power used. Lord Nelson, England's famous admiral, is reported to have said to a diplomat: "I hate your pen-and-ink men; a fleet of British ships of war are the best negotiators in Europe." [9] And Frederick the Great, Prussia's remarkable ruler and soldier, likened diplomacy without armaments to music without instruments.[10] With force a nation takes what it wants from another state; with diplomacy, supported by the threat of using that force, a nation may persuade another state to make concessions to its demands.

The characterization of international politics as a state of potential war does not therefore seem incorrect historically. Even had there been far fewer wars, it remains true, as Hobbes suggested, that war consists

> not in battle only, or the act of fighting, but in a tract of time . . . as it is in the nature of weather. For as the nature of foul weather lies not in a shower or two of rain, but in an inclination thereto of many days together, so the nature of war consists not in actual fighting, but in the known disposition thereto.[11]

Coercion, or the threat of force, generally stands in the background, affecting negotiations among conflicting states, just as the threat of a strike always affects the bargaining between labor and management. A given strike does not *have* to occur to demonstrate the power of labor; management knows what the effects of a prolonged strike will be on corporate production and profits. On the other hand, management knows that the workers do not like to be laid off and jeopardize their earnings and that the union eventually will run out of strike funds. The desire to avoid a strike—a long one, anyway—is thus an incentive for both sides to compromise.

Similarly, the possibility of violence does not mean that it will occur; war, as already noted, is usually considered the instrument of last resort. States do not go to war lightly, for the costs are high, and in the "fog of war" the outcome among evenly matched opponents can rarely be certain, no matter how carefully each has calculated its power and that of its adversary. The knowledge that war is a possibility is more likely to moderate demands and provide a stimulus for other means of conflict resolution like persuasion, rewards, and coercion. Renunciation of force, on the other hand, eliminates the penalty for an uncompromising attitude and gives the advantage to the party willing to invoke violence.

The Role of Nonmilitary Power

Although the structure of the state system makes it necessary for states to be constantly concerned about the ratio of power between themselves and other states, coercion does not always mean the threat of violence; it may mean the use of nonmilitary, especially economic, sanctions that can sometimes be more effective than the threat of force. Members of the Organization of Petroleum Exporting Countries (OPEC) in the 1970s dramatically demonstrated this point to the world. In a system in which, according to all conventional calculations, great powers should be influencing small powers, the reverse seemed to be happening. *One principal characteristic of power is the capacity to hurt.* A state that makes demands on another says, in fact, "Give me what I want, or I will hurt you worse than compliance will hurt." If the other state agrees that compliance will hurt less than resistance, it is likely to submit; if it calculates that the cost of resistance will be less than yielding what is demanded, it is likely to defy the demands made upon it. The threat of force is an obvious example of coercion matched by the "reward" of withholding it and not hurting the adversary; the threat of withholding resources vital to a nation's industry or of greatly raising the prices of these resources is also an effective form of coercion. Infliction of violent pain or deprivation of needed resources are just two of the many strategies that can hurt an adversary. In the OPEC instance, a small, unindustrialized country was shown to have great influence in its relations with far bigger and militarily stronger countries. As Sheik Ahmed Zaki al-Yamani, the Saudi Arabian oil minister, told an American television audience in 1979: "If you think in the West that there will be no interruption in oil without a settlement of the Palestinian question, you are mistaken." [12] The late Mao Zedong was often quoted as saying that power grows out of the barrel of a gun; Yamani added that power grows out of a barrel of oil. The military weapon can be replaced by the economic weapon—what Karl Marx called the replacement of the cannon by capital.

Economic means are not used only to achieve national security or high politics objectives. They may be invoked for economic or low politics purposes. Obviously, trade is a principal way of obtaining the goods, services, and other resources that a country needs for economic growth, high employment, and a satisfactory standard of living. Oil, for example, can be bought on the international market. Still, if oil-producing countries wish to earn more money, they can organize themselves into a cartel and withhold oil or cut back production. This creates shortages and raises prices, which may then create higher unemployment and inflation in oil-consuming industrial countries, threatening them with economic disaster. States pursue their own economic interests as they do their political interests. The state system's lack of a legitimate government to allocate economic goods peacefully and manage economic relations among the member states means that states pursue low-politics goals as they do high-politics goals.

The very language of international politics is indicative of the contentious nature of the state system and its susceptibility to coercion. We speak of war, economic warfare and aggression, diplomatic fronts, waging peace, cold wars, crusades for peace, war as the continuation of politics by other means, and peace as the continuation of the last war by other means. And, in the wake of OPEC actions, many Americans, recognizing that the United States had become the food basket of a hungry world, began in the 1970s to talk of "food as a weapon." In politics among nations, almost anything—oil, food, investments, technology, trade—can become a weapon, a means by which one state can seek leverage over other states. Indeed, in 1979 a country-western song entitled "Cheaper Crude or No More Food" was popular; the target clearly was OPEC. Hobbes would have understood the use of food exports as a weapon in the self-help system that is the state system; he also would not have been surprised by such terms as "investment wars" and "trade wars."

THE BALANCE OF POWER AS A SYSTEM

Power as a Neutralizer of Power

If states wish to deter potential attackers and ensure their own independence and their ways of life, they will pursue balance-of-power policies. The balance of power is sought because of fear that if one nation gains predominant power, it may impose its will upon other states, either by the threat or actual use of violence. In Arnold Wolfers's words:

> Under these conditions of anarchy the expectation of violence and even of annihilation is ever-present. To forget this and thus fail in the concern for enhanced power spells the doom of a state. This does not mean constant open warfare; expansion of power at the expense of others will not take place if there is enough counterpower to deter or to stop states from undertaking it. Although no state is interested in a mere balance of power, the efforts of all states to maximize power may lead to equilibrium. If and when that happens, there is "peace" or, more exactly, a condition of stalemate or truce. Under the conditions described here, this balancing of power process is the only available "peace" strategy.[13]

The term *balance of power* is often used in loose and contradictory ways. It may, for example, refer to any existing distribution of power between two states, whether it is an equilibrium, an approximate balance, or an imbalance (meaning either superiority or inferiority of power, as in the sentences "the balance has shifted toward Syria" and "the balance has shifted away from Israel").[14] As we shall use the term, however, it refers to a *balance-of-power system* in which any shift away from equilibrium in the state system leads to countershifts through mobilization of countervailing power. This definition suggests a mechanism, like the "invisible hand" in the classical free market, that preserves the equilibrium. The systemic nature of the balance of power is further explained by Wolfers:

> While it makes little sense to use the term "automatic" literally, as if human choices and errors were irrelevant to the establishment, preservation, or destruction of a state of equilibrium, there nevertheless is a significant element of truth in the theory of "automatism" which is valid even today. If one may assume that any government in its senses will be deeply concerned with the relative power position of hostile countries, then one may conclude that efforts to keep in step in the competition for power with such opponents, or even to outdo them, will almost certainly be forthcoming. If most nations react in this way, a tendency towards equilibrium will follow it; will come into play whether both sides aim at equilibrium or whether the more aggressive side strives for superiority. In the latter case,

the opposite side is likely to be provoked into matching these aggressive moves. Forces appear therefore to be working "behind the backs" of the human actors, pushing them in the direction of balanced power irrespective of their preferences.[15]

In short, states cannot be trusted with power, for they will be tempted to abuse it. *Unrestrained power in the system constitutes a menace to all other member states. Power is therefore the best antidote to power.* The fundamental assumption, of course, is that power will not be abolished, that it is inherent in a system characterized by competition and rivalry, and therefore that the principal task of the international system is the management of power.[16] This is not to say that in "real life" all states—especially the great powers—have always and everywhere sought to expand their power. They have not, as demonstrated by the United States' return to isolationism after World War I and Japan's unwillingness to play a major and active political role even in Asia since World War II. Nevertheless, states have sought to enhance their power often enough so that we can say that not doing so is the exception and often a cause of wonderment to other states, which may be tempted to exploit the situation. For this reason, even a state wishing to act with restraint usually acts preemptively, knowing that potential adversaries may seek such advantage and that it will then be compelled to react.

The Purposes of the Balance

Power thus begets countervailing power. But consider the twofold aim of countervailing power. The first aim is the *protection of the security of each state,* not the preservation of peace. As noted earlier, most states normally feel secure when they are at peace, but peace is the product of a balance that is acceptable to the leading powers because it ensures their individual security. Peace may be desirable in itself, but it is also only one of several objectives that states pursue. States historically have sacrificed peace to achieve any of these objectives, especially their security. "Peace at any price" has rarely been the aim. To put it simply, peace is the cart, security the horse. To place the cart before the horse is to court disaster. This is easier to conceptualize than to practice, for peace is obviously a desirable value. Most states are reluctant to sacrifice peace, and the difficulty arises in deciding exactly at what point preserving a nation's security is worth the costs of war. If the balance of power is kept, however, the motivation for any state to risk launching an attack may be reduced, if not eliminated.

The second aim is the *protection of the state system as a whole.* The rationale underlying the balance of power is that each state has the right to exist. The way to ensure each state's security and independence is to prevent the emergence of any preponderant state. States are rarely eliminated by other states. To destroy the right of another state to exist is to undermine one's own claim to that right. Thus, at the end of the Napoleonic Wars, despite twenty-five years of fighting, France was neither eliminated nor punished. A lenient peace treaty was signed so that France could once more take its place in the family of European states and contribute to the preservation of the system. A vengeful France might have started another war, instead of contributing to the European system's peace and stability.

By contrast, the Treaty of Versailles ending World War I was harsh. Germany considered it punitive, and many regard it as a central reason why Germany remained a threat to the stability and peace of post-1918 Europe. Had Britain and France signed a treaty of reconciliation or modified the Versailles pact in the 1920s when Germany was still weak, the German Republic might have weathered the Great Depression and become a pillar of support for the European settlement. Instead, Adolf Hitler was able to exploit German nationalism to help him achieve power, mobilize support for his regime, and proceed to destroy the Europe of Versailles. Ironically, it was only when Germany threatened to use force that the Western powers sought to appease Hitler—that is, ratify Germany's stated grievances in the hope that this would gain Germany's support for a stable European system. But by then German ambitions and power had outgrown any possibility of being satisfied and war became unavoidable.

The United States learned from this interwar experience. It signed a generous peace treaty with Japan after World War II and treated West Germany in a spirit of reconciliation. In the subsequent postwar containment policy, in which its former enemies figure prominently, the United States accepted the premise that the Soviet Union is a permanent player on the international chessboard. The aim of containment was not to eliminate the Soviet Union. There was no reason to believe that eliminating it would end the United States' international involvements, any more than had the earlier elimination of Hitler's Germany. The aim of containment was merely to prevent further Soviet expansion. The expectation was that the Soviet Union would "mellow," that the Soviet leaders would accept the international system and coexist peacefully with other states, regardless of their domestic complexion. In short, the Soviet Union's revolutionary ambitions would be subordinated to preserving the state system.

The Rules of the 'Games Nations Play'

In a decentralized system, the rules of the balance of power remain the basic norms for states. These rules of the game may be ignored or forgotten only at a nation's peril. They are usually so internalized that those who conduct foreign policy think almost "automatically," as Wolfers has put it, in balance-of-power terms. Policy makers become "socialized" by the system; even revolutionary leaders learn quickly and follow the logic of the balance of power, rather than the dictates of ideology. As we shall see in Chapter 6 and throughout Part III, the norms of behavior vary with the structure of the system, that is, with the number of principal actors or great powers and the distribution of power among them. These rules can be stated in general terms:

1. Watch a potential adversary's power and match it. (The emphasis on power, rather than on intentions, suggests that a peaceful state today may become warlike tomorrow if it gains superior power.)
2. Ally oneself with a weaker state to restore the balance of power.
3. Abandon such alliances when the balance has been restored and the common danger has passed.
4. Regard national security interests as permanent; alliances must therefore change as new threats arise.
5. Do not treat defeated states harshly through punitive peace treaties. (Today's adversary may be tomorrow's ally.)

BALANCE-OF-POWER TECHNIQUES

Because the balance of power plays such a central role in international politics, we need to look briefly at the principal techniques used in balancing power.

National Mobilization

The most obvious method of balancing power involves rearmament. Given the key role that force has played historically, the reliance on arms is not surprising. But mobilization comprises two other important components of power. One is the economy; obviously, a thriving economy can afford to support large military forces. But, equally important, it can also afford economic aid and can use its technological and scientific capabilities in industry and agriculture to advance national purposes. Computers and tractors may help technologically lagging nations, especially LDCs, to modernize. The other component is the psychological mobilization of a people, the arousal of popular support for government policy by means of appeals to patriotism and pride in their country.

Alliances

The formation of alliances is one of the time-honored balance-of-power techniques, whether the main purpose is to supplement the state's own power or to draw lines around its sphere of interest. The only relatively new features of some contemporary key alliances are longevity—the North Atlantic Treaty Organization (NATO) was founded in 1949—and the existence of permanent headquarters. The latter keeps the alliances functioning on a day-to-day basis and serves to organize the military forces of the various allies into unified forces. Alliances in the past have been shorter, and planning for war has consisted mainly of coordinating separate military plans of the member states for such an eventuality.

Compensation

Dividing a strategically located country to preserve a balance between major states is an example of compensation; if one state were to take all the territory, the balance would be upset and war might result. Poland, for instance, has been divided three times among its great power neighbors in efforts to deny any one of them an advantage over the others. The last partition came just before World War II when Germany wanted to destroy Poland but settled, for the time being, for the avoidance of war with the Soviet Union, Poland's other neighbor. The Soviet Union would not have tolerated German occupation of all of Poland. So the two powers split this country, maintaining the balance that had existed before partition. Each then invaded Poland, occupying the agreed-upon parts. At the end of World War II, the Soviet Union became allied with North Korea, the United States with South Korea. Again, neither big-power bloc would have tolerated a united Korea under the other's control. The possibility of this in 1950 precipitated U.S. intervention to preserve South Korea and later Chinese Communist intervention to preserve North Korea. As one side gains in power, the other seeks compensation in order to keep the preexisting balance.

Neutralization

A technique opposite to compensation is neutralization. Instead of dividing a country to preserve the balance, no one is granted anything. Switzerland is surrounded by Germany, Italy, and France. None of its neighbors could accept its addition to one or both of the other states; Switzerland is too strategically important. Therefore, the agreement has been to accept Swiss neutrality and to keep "hands off," maintaining the country as a buffer zone between the other three. Similarly, Belgium, surrounded by Britain, France, and Germany, was neutralized in the nineteenth century. When Germany violated that neutrality at the beginning of World War I, the British government—until then divided over whether to come to France's aid—declared war on Germany. German conquest of the channel ports facing England had to be prevented. After the Soviet invasion of Afghanistan, the Common Market foreign ministers suggested neutralization as a means of resolving the problem. Soviet troops would be withdrawn and the West would pledge noninterference. Moscow rejected the idea because it knew that the collapse of its puppet regime was inevitable without Soviet troops. Western intervention was not the problem; the unpopularity of the pro-Soviet regime was.

Intervention

States have long intervened in the affairs of other states when events in the latter were perceived as threatening. Such interventions have been carried out primarily by the military or by intelligence organizations—that is, they have been either overt or covert. The American record of postwar intervention speaks for itself:

Military intervention (including limited wars): Korea, 1950-52; Lebanon, 1958; Vietnam (including Laos and Cambodia), 1965-73; Dominican Republic, 1965-66; Grenada, 1983

CIA interventions (to overthrow or attempt to overthrow unfriendly governments): Iran, 1953; Guatemala, 1954; Cuba, 1961; Chile, 1970-73; Nicaragua, 1981-

Another category could be included: intervention with military advisers, as when the United States sent advisers to Greece in the late 1940s and to Vietnam in the early 1960s before the full-fledged military intervention. The Soviets have come up with a very visible and effective means of intervention in proxy forces—Cuban, for example—in Angola, Ethiopia, and South Yemen. Proxies are useful because they reduce the risk to the country that controls them. If the Soviet Union intervened directly, the risk of U.S. countervention would arise; proxies may help to avoid this response and make the conflicts look more like struggles for "national liberation."

Divide and Rule

The principle of divide and rule is time honored, and there are two versions. In the first, which may be called preemptive divide and rule, the aim is to prevent two powers from forming an alliance. For example, in the months before World War II, Winston Churchill exhorted the British government to form an alliance with the Soviet Union to contain Hitler and deter a war. But London moved too slowly and Hitler formed his pact with Stalin. Similarly, many critics of American cold war policy have argued that had the United States been more sympathetic to Mao Zedong earlier, rather than supporting his opponent in the Chinese civil war, it could have prevented the consolidation of the Soviet-Chinese relationship in the early 1950s. Post-1945 U.S. policy toward the Third World nations was launched because of the U.S. fear that if it did not help them modernize, they might be attracted to the Soviet bloc.

A much more common version of divide and rule is the attempt to create or exploit differences among the adversary's existing allies. Since 1972 the United States has exploited the Sino-Soviet schism; these moves, however, came after the division already existed. Whether U.S. policy could have precipitated this split earlier remains a matter of speculation. The United States has also improved its relations with some of the Soviets' East European allies, but it is cautious in this respect, lest the Soviets become so jittery about their client states' loyalties that they invade them again. In its turn, the Soviet Union tried frequently during the cold war to play on Western Europe's memories of German aggression, conquests, and brutality to drive a wedge between West Germany and the other members of NATO, the European Coal and Steel Community, and the European Economic Community (EEC).

During World War II Britain and the United States agreed with the Soviet Union not to lay down their arms until Germany had surrendered unconditionally. This approach was intended to prevent the Germans from trying to divide and rule. The Western allies were concerned that the Soviets, who had suffered enormously, might be offered a German withdrawal from Soviet soil and might be tempted to accept it, leaving the two Western states to fight Germany by themselves. They would then have to land in France and confront the might of the entire German army, greatly increasing the risk of failure. The Soviets, on the other hand, were fearful that their allies might be tempted to accept a separate peace, leading them to face the German war machine by themselves. Moscow wanted the allies to draw off part of the German army.

War

The final technique of balancing power is war. When the balance is about to be upset or has been upset, the threat of war or the outbreak of war may provide the only way in which a new equilibrium can be created. We have noted that as Britain's ability to keep the balance in Europe was weakened, the United States was drawn into two world wars to preserve that balance against Germany. According to Inis Claude, the threat or actual use of violence has been "serious enough to stimulate preventive measures, but mild enough to enable statesmen to invoke the threat, and on occasion the actuality, of force in support of policy. War should be imaginable, controllable, usable." [17] Whether these three requirements can be attached to warfare among the superpowers and their respective principal allies in the contemporary world is questionable. The emphasis, therefore, has been shifted to deterrence and the threat of force; the *use* of force has largely been in "limited wars." For nonnuclear countries not allied to any superpower, war remains an option.

WAR AND PEACE

Bargaining Among States

We usually think of war and peace as two quite distinct conditions separated by a formal declaration of war. War and peace are mutually exclusive. To cite one observation among many, "War means that diplomacy failed, that persuasion did not work, and that bargaining was unsuccessful." [18] This is quite wrong. It is more accurate to think of war and peace as existing on a continuum along which states have conflicting interests of increasing scope and intensity. Some of these conflicts will be resolvable by peaceful negotiations, but at some point one side will feel that the demands made upon it are excessive, that it can no longer offer concessions without endangering its own security. It may calculate that the distribution of power is sufficiently equitable so that it can reject the adversary's demands without war resulting. But the opponent may not be willing to accept this rejection, estimating that the ratio of power favors it. The opponent therefore attempts to intimidate the adversary and, when intimidation proves ineffective, resorts to force; or, if the opponent does not initiate the use of force, the side faced with the demands may declare war rather than accept them.

In either case, the outbreak of war does not mean that diplomacy has failed or that negotiations are discontinued until one of the sides has won the war and imposes its terms on the other. War is bargaining. As Carl von Clausewitz argues in *On War*, still the definitive book on the subject after a century and a half, war is the continuation of diplomacy or bargaining by other means— that is, force. War does not suspend the political relationship among sovereign states. "How could it be otherwise? Do political relations between peoples and between their governments stop when diplomatic notes are no longer exchanged? Is war not just another expression of their thoughts, another form of speech and writing?" Its grammar—the fighting—may be its own, Clausewitz said, but "not its own logic." [19] The logic is that of politics: war erupts because states have conflicts of political objectives that they cannot resolve by persuasion or pressures short of war; they therefore seek to achieve these objectives by combat. The fighting will decide who is the stronger and whether the side demanding a revision of the status quo or the other trying to defend it will achieve its goal.

Peace, in short, is not absolute but conditional. If a state can preserve its security in peacetime, it will do so, but, if it cannot, it will invoke force as the instrument of last resort, as Britain finally did when Hitler attacked Poland in 1939. Once fighting erupts it will always continue until one side surrenders conditionally or unconditionally or, more frequently since 1945, until both sides reach a new set of mutually acceptable terms and end the war, an event often symbolized by an official peace conference during which the new postwar balance of power is reached. After the cessation of World War II hostilities, the conflict over this new balance began so quickly that no formal conference was ever held. But the key point is that peace is conditional. Negotiations between North Vietnam and the United States from 1965 to 1973, for example, could have led to peace at any time, but neither side was willing to accept the other side's terms of peace. The fighting, and the bargaining, thus continued, for they held out the promise to each side of better or more acceptable terms later. *The price of peace was of greater concern than peace itself.*

The axiom "when diplomacy stops, war starts" is simply untrue. Bargaining, which in peacetime is called *diplomacy*, continues after the shooting starts. War is not usually considered an alternative to negotiations; it is a violent continuation of them. Power, especially military power, is always present. Although we talk of peaceful negotiations, power stands in the background—"on guard"—and, when needed, is brought to the fore. It is invoked as a threat, and, if that is insufficient, it will be used openly. Power is omnipresent. Peace and war therefore have much in common. As Hobbes said, "Covenants without the sword are but words."

What Is Peace?

Peace becomes difficult, perhaps impossible, to define in this context because it has so many different meanings. It may simply denote an absence of war (at least, of large-scale war, as distinct from more limited kinds). Another meaning is the absence of major political conflict and rivalry, like the intense form of competition called in our age *cold war*. It may even include a high degree of cooperation or rapprochement between states. A third meaning is more positive, emphasizing not what is missing but what is present, including global organizations such as the United Nations that provide an institutional setting in which most nations of the world meet. There they *should* resolve their differences in a spirit of concern for mankind as a whole, rather than with selfish regard only for their own populations. Even this expectation of peaceful and orderly change is not quite satisfactory for some observers. Peace, they insist, cannot coexist with continued poverty throughout much of the world, even within the rich countries. The oppression of millions of people in many societies is also inimical to peace. In this interpretation, peace must be not only the absence of warfare but also the presence of decent standards of living and social justice for all people. Such a "true peace" can occur only at a level higher than the United Nations, at the level of world government, which would institutionalize the processes of change more fully than the United Nations ever could. A global community in which national differences and jealousies had disappeared would allow the institutions to work so that all humanity would share the blessings of peace, prosperity, freedom, and justice. Reasons for differences among men and women would have evaporated, and a lasting peace would exist for the first time in history. World politics in such a global order would be domestic politics.

Why Wars?

Until that time comes, however, war—and certainly the threat of war—will continue to play a role. Are contemporary leaders, like those of the past, hypocrites when they profess their devotion to peace? Undoubtedly, some have used words of peace to disguise their militaristic and aggressive aims. The fundamental tragedy of the state system is that it traps all states in a security dilemma: they are compelled to prepare for the possibility of war, however much they may prefer to avoid it. But the fundamental reason most political leaders resort to war is their inability to bridge the gap between their desires for peace and preparations for war. Wars have occurred frequently enough that recurrence has been expected. The possibility of war is a fundamental assumption that national leaders cannot afford to ignore; to do so might well be fatal. Leaders may quite sincerely desire peace, but the very nature of their positions as guardians of their countries' security encourages suspicions about traditional enemies or rising powers. This may be true even when the latter publicly disavow hostile intentions and declare their desire for friendship. "Beware of Greeks bearing gifts" sums up the attitudes of states toward one another; "maybe that state is acting in a friendly matter to relax my guard just before it attacks me." It may be, of course, that the other state does have friendly intentions; a suspicious attitude may then result in conflict, even war. But if it does harbor unfriendly intentions, then "being on guard" may well help to avoid conflict. This dilemma clearly haunts policy makers.

Second, desirable as peace may be, it has not usually been the most important objective for a given state. When its security is endangered, any state may sacrifice peace and fight. Similarly, when other objectives, such as the defense of a nation's freedom or promotion of certain national or ideological views, are pursued, peace may be secondary. A state may be quite willing to forgo peace if it feels that it must help to achieve the national liberation of oppressed peoples. If peace were a state's primary objective, it could have that easily enough—it could simply give in to the demands of the opposing states, as Britain did to Germany's demands in the 1930s.

Third, wars have also been fought repeatedly because they have been effective instruments for achieving the objectives of states. War may be regarded as evil, a curse on mankind, and condemned as destructive and immoral, but the fact is that war has all too often been useful. Germany owed its unity after 1870 to war; Czechoslovakia and Poland owed their existence as states to World War I; Britain and the Soviet Union owed their survival to victory in World War II. Moreover, the threat of violence has protected the Western democracies since 1945. The actual use of violence has brought the Chinese Communists to power on the mainland and kept South Korea independent. It has provided European Jews who survived the Nazi Holocaust with a home in Israel and has allowed Communist leaders to unify Vietnam. It has provided Cuban forces serving as Soviet proxies in Africa with victories in Angola, Ethiopia, and Eritrea (with more perhaps still to come). It remains the principal hope of self-styled national liberation movements—such as the PLO and the Southwest African People's Organization (SWAPO) in Namibia—for achieving statehood or seizing the governments of already existing states, as occurred in Zimbabwe in 1980, when the Patriotic Front won an election that the white minority agreed to after a long civil war.

The idea that war is irrational or immoral or that it profits nobody except munitions makers is not particularly convincing to those who have benefited or hope to benefit from war. Even in this age of nuclear weapons, nonnuclear warfare is still widely regarded as a rational instrument of policy. Coercion and force, principal characteristics of much of international politics, spring from the basically anarchical nature of the state system and its fundamental rule of self-help. Nuclear weapons, for all their horror, have not changed either one of these features; they have affected the ways in which military power is used, but they have not yet led to a transformation of the current system to a new world order characterized by greater harmony and cooperation among states and the elimination of the uses of threats and force.

INTERNATIONAL POLITICS AS A 'MIXED' GAME

Conflict

International politics is synonymous with conflict. In the conduct of this conflict, adversary powers tend to become alike. For example, in unifying Germany in three quick wars in 1862, 1866, and 1870, Prussia demonstrated the superiority of its General Staff system; subsequently, all the other Continental powers adopted the system.[20] In World War I, all of the participants, once they discovered that the war would not be over in a few months as they had expected, learned to mobilize their economies for the long term. During World War II, the Germans quickly demonstrated that a combination of armor and fighter aircraft was the way to win victories; the British and American armies soon copied the pattern. Once the United States possessed the atom bomb, the Soviets too got the bomb. Later, when the question was raised whether the United States should try to build a hydrogen bomb, the secretary of state said the country really had no choice. The Soviets obviously thought the same. The United States tested its first hydrogen bomb in 1954, the Soviets in 1955.

A more profound impact of conflict upon states is their socialization—that is, the learning and internalization of the rules of the game.[21] The U.S. approach to international politics, as we shall see in Chapter 13, has been one that has considered conflict as abnormal, peace as normal, and has rejected power politics as something "un-American." But since 1945 the United States has been a constant player; it left its long history of isolationism behind and learned to play the game. The Soviets, just after 1917, expected their revolution to extend to central and western Europe. When the revolution failed to spread, the Soviet regime quickly learned to adapt to the state system and play the balance-of-power game.

Indeed, socialization not only means that states internalize the rules of the game; it also means that any people who share an identity seek two things: their own state and their own armed forces. Throughout history, Jews have been persecuted in many states, but not until Hitler did any ruler seek to exterminate them. After the Germans had killed 6 million of Europe's Jews, many of the survivors and the Jews in Palestine not surprisingly wanted a Jewish state. Since its founding, Israel has defended itself in three wars (1956, 1967, and 1972) against its Arab neighbors who wished to eliminate the Jewish state. The displaced Palestinians learned their lesson from the Israeli example. They too want their own nation, flag, and army.

Competition

States engage not only in conflict but also in competition. Great powers are particularly prone to compete with one another, even if they are not at the time in conflict with one another. They are very conscious of their prestige. When having an empire was a sign of great-power status, states aspiring to that rank sought colonies. At the turn of the century, Alfred Thayer Mahan, an American naval captain, published a book claiming that a nation's greatness was linked to its possession of a large fleet of battleships—a claim he based on the experience of Britain, an island-power and the world's first nation to industrialize. The other powers of Europe, as well as Japan *and* the United States, decided to build navies. But Germany's acquisition of a large battle fleet was seen as a security threat by Britain. Germany was already the Continent's strongest land power, and the kaiser had announced that Germany was about to embark upon a world policy beyond Europe. The German navy was, therefore, a major contributory factor to the increasing tensions between Germany and Britain preceding World War I.[22] Ironically, the battleship was already passé. It played virtually no role in deciding the outcome of World War I. Had the Germans focused on building more submarines, they might have won the war; in any case, German submarines almost succeeded in starving England into submission. But the battleship remained a symbol of great power until World War II.

The atom bomb has become a contemporary symbol. Whatever its deterrent value, its acquisition is required for great powers seeking to maintain their rank—for example, Britain and France—or for nations like India and China that are seeking to acquire such rank. Britain began to develop its bomb after World War II, but before the Soviet threat became clear. The effort was directed at maintaining British prestige; later, the British H-bomb and delivery capability were justified as a way of influencing U.S. policy. It is not accidental that all the great powers represented on the United Nations Security Council—the United States, the Soviet Union, Britain, France, and China—are nuclear powers and that some of the likely nuclear powers of the future—Pakistan, Brazil, and Argentina—aspire to great-power status.

When states are in conflict, competition between them increases. For instance, the United States began to aid the development of the LDCs during the Truman presidency. After Joseph Stalin died in 1953, the new Soviet leaders visited a number of Asian countries and began their own economic aid program to the LDCs. Influence in the Third World was not to be left by default to the United States. Each power continues to compete for friends among the LDCs and, occasionally, even to intervene on their behalf. But perhaps the most notable contemporary example is the competition in space. It is, in a sense, a natural extension of competition on land, sea, and air, for space is the next area of strategic significance. The real importance of President Ronald Reagan's Strategic Defense Initiative is probably not whether it will defend the population of the United States or partially defend the increasingly vulnerable land-based missiles against a Soviet first strike, or even whether it will serve as a bargaining chip to trade against drastic Soviet cuts of their missiles. Rather, it is that it may give the United States the capability to deny the Soviet Union, which has been interested in space for some time, a technological lead that might translate into military and political advantages. Space is becoming the new arena for superpower competition, just like oceans were at the turn of the century.

Cooperation

In the state system the struggle for security is basic. States perceive one another as adversaries, and, as Wolfers points out, "the insecurity of an anarchical system of multiple sovereignty places the actors under compulsion to seek maximum power even though this may run counter to their real desires." [23] The inherent fears and suspicions of states would be reflected even in a situation of general disarmament. States might well be better off if none was armed. But then one state might calculate that, if it armed, it would be able to gain an advantage; it could coerce unarmed opponents or go to war to impose its demands. Precisely because most states fear such a possibility, they not only refuse to disarm but also make sure that they are as strong as potential adversaries. States are enemies, then, not because they are necessarily aggressive or have ideological differences but because they see that they can harm one another and, being cautious, view one another as possible enemies.

On one hand, then, the structure of the system traps states in adversary relationships. On the other, states cooperate with one another as well. In their competitive pursuits, states form alliances. Even enemies cooperate; arms control negotiations between the United States and the Soviet Union during the 1960s and 1970s were almost routine. Trade negotiations have been another symptom of collaboration. Even while a war is going on states may cooperate. If nuclear warfare is to be avoided when "limited wars" erupt, both superpowers must work together to prevent the latter from escalating too far.

International politics is thus a mixture of conflict, competition, and cooperation, although cooperation occurs within the context of adversary relations. A state wants to attract the strength of allies to enhance its power position in order to compete better; an arms control agreement with an opponent may reduce the level of armaments, reduce international tensions, and make the world a slightly safer place, but such agreements are signed, after all, by states whose weapons are aimed at each other because they are political rivals. Cooperation, if brief, is a subsidiary part of a conflictual and competitive game.

There are, as always, exceptions in the real world. Britain and the United States can hardly be called potential adversaries anymore. The Common Market states are unlikely to go to war with one another; not long ago some of them were bitter enemies. Early in this century Britain recognized that Germany's growing power posed a possible threat and made it a deliberate policy to improve relations with France, czarist Russia, and the United States, as well as with Japan. Britain remained particularly anxious to maintain its American connection, for the United States was the most powerful country in the world, even though it did not exercise that power during the 1920s and 1930s. During World War II and most of the cold war, the two nations had what was widely acknowledged as a "special relationship." Similarly, when the Continental states that were the original members of the EEC decided to move toward what they hoped would one day be a powerful United States of Europe, they did so within the broader context of the rivalry between the United States and the Soviet Union.

The Limits of Cooperation

Indeed, the structure of the state system limits cooperation among states in two significant ways.[24] First, states concerned about their security or wealth cannot let themselves become too dependent on other states, for then they might become vulnerable to threats to reduce or eliminate whatever exchange of goods and services had been occurring. The 1973 Arab oil embargo—and the threats of future embargoes and price increases—led the Western oil consumers to seek non-OPEC oil, develop alternative energy sources, and practice greater conservation. The Soviet Union presents another example of the danger of dependence. Since the 1970s the Soviet Union has become increasingly dependent on the United States for large amounts of grain and desirous of all sorts of U.S. technology—and the United States has encouraged this dependency—but the Soviet Union has been careful to seek alternative sources of supply.

Obviously, if a state becomes too dependent for any of its critical needs on another, it can avoid a reduction or cutoff of supplies only if it submits to the demands made upon it. A preferable strategy, therefore, is to import critical resources or goods from several countries or to find several markets rather than a single one for any products it must export to earn foreign currencies to pay for imports. Smaller or more poorly endowed states long ago learned that the price of dependence is a restriction of national freedom, of being vulnerable to foreign demands.

Second, even when states cooperate on critical issues such as arms control because both expect to gain from such cooperation, each worries about the distribution of benefits. Who will come out ahead? Allowing another nation to gain an advantage might be potentially damaging. Even if the president had not withdrawn SALT II after the Soviet invasion of Afghanistan in 1979, the U.S. Senate might have defeated the treaty. Many senators thought it an unequal treaty advantageous to the Soviet Union and that it jeopardized, rather than enhanced, American security. Even among Common Market countries, which have grown close during two decades of economic cooperation, there are setbacks, delays, and bitter disputes over the distribution of benefits. Is French agriculture benefiting more than West German agriculture? Are the Continental states gaining more from Britain's annual contribution to the EEC than Britain receives from the community?

Similarly, the weakening of OPEC in the 1980s was due to the members' inability to decide how much wealth each was to earn. Most of them sought to enhance their national earnings by selling more oil than allowed under OPEC's allotment; the result was to increase the surplus of oil over international demand and lower the price of oil. In 1986, to retain its share of the market, Saudi Arabia flooded the market, leading to precipitous drops in the price of oil to the $10 to $15 range per barrel (42 gallons). This in turn has led to renewed efforts to agree on production limits in order to raise the price of oil again.

In sum, each state continues to be concerned about its national security and welfare. The state system remains an example of a primitive political system, the primary feature of which is anarchy moderated by a modicum of order imposed by the balance of power.[26] The fundamental assumptions are that nation-states place high value on national security to protect their "core values"; that states are responsible only to themselves; that self-help is the fundamental rule of the game; that relations among states are determined by the interactions of their respective power; and that in such a system, states' behavior is bound to be conditioned by concerns about their survival, degree of security, and share of economic benefits.

THE NATIONAL INTEREST VERSUS HUMANITY'S INTEREST

Although leaders, governments, regimes, and interest groups tend to interpret the *national interest* quite differently, the principal virtue of the term is its emphasis on the fact that *each* nation places what it defines as its interest—or, more accurately, its interests—ahead of those of other nations. That this is so is a frequent criticism. The national interest, it is said, should be subordinated to the greater interest of all people, regardless of which nation they are citizens. The good of mankind should take precedence. Should all nations be exposed to destruction because of the U.S.-Soviet quarrel? Would it not be better if these two states and their allies spent less on weapons and more on helping the poor nations of the world raise their standard of living? Do the main problems facing the world—population, poverty, pollution, and nuclear proliferation—not require all nations to cooperate in finding collective solutions before these transnational problems overwhelm them? Indeed, in what is asserted to be an increasingly interdependent world, can nations afford to continue to think in narrow or parochial nationalistic terms? Is it not in their own interest to think in more enlightened global terms? In the final analysis, has not religion taught people that their duty is to all of humanity?

However reasonable the plea to place mankind before "nationkind," it tends to fall on deaf ears. Just as differences in religious belief have given rise to many sects, even within the major religions of the world, so nationalism has split humanity. National decision makers are neither perverse nor immoral nor simply stupid, unable to understand the logic of those who argue that the days of giving priority to the nation's interests are past. The basic reason for their attitude is the nature of the state system. In an anarchical system each state's "incentive is to put itself in a position to be able to take care of itself since no one else can be counted on to do so. The international imperative is 'take care of yourself'!" [26] National leaders have no choice but to place a high value on national survival, national security, and national independence. How, in these circumstances, can they "resolve the tension between pursuing their own interests and acting for the sake of the system? No one has shown how that can be done. . . . The very problem . . . is that rational behavior, given structural constraints, does not lead to the wanted results. With each country constrained to take care of itself, no one can take care of the system." [27]

This does not mean that states, acting on the basis of self-interest, necessarily define their interests in narrow and short-sighted terms. This may, of course, happen. But, as we noted earlier, states pursue not only possession goals but milieu objectives. States since World War II, especially the superpowers, have been increasingly concerned with arms control issues that affect not only U.S.-Soviet relations but also the survival of the entire state system. The Western industrial democracies have also been concerned with the division of the world between rich and poor nations, for the resulting instability of such a division was unacceptable. National interests may also be pursued unilaterally, but, depending on how other states define their interests, they frequently cooperate with one another, too. They may do so as adversaries or as allies. Clearly, in preventing nuclear proliferation or in avoiding an international "class war," many states become collectively involved. But the basis for their behavior in the state system remains each state's definition of its national interest (see Table 5-1).

THE FOUR CHARACTERISTICS OF FIRST-LEVEL ANALYSIS

The Balance of Power

Analyzing the security games that nations play on the level of the state system will give us certain very specific notions of the behavior of states. *First,*

Table 5-1 The State System

Primary actors	Nation-states
	Intergovernmental organizations
	    Universal: United Nations
	    Regional: Organization of African Unity
	    Special interest: OPEC (producer-cartel); "Group of 77"
	      (representing the Third World countries)
	    Supranational organization
	    Regional: Common Market
	Nongovernmental or transnational organizations
	    Multinational corporations; religious, humanitarian groups;
	      national liberation groups; terrorists

Characteristics	Decentralized—composed of mainly sovereign and independent states Anarchical—absence of commonly accepted political institutions and legitimate rules of the game for allocation of values and enforcement of decisions High expectation of violence—coercion and force as the principal allocative mechanism, or substitute for government Balance of power—principal mechanism that provides systemic stability and individual national restraint
General rules	1. Protect and guard oneself. 2. Be concerned with systemic power distribution. 3. Calculate self-interest rationally on the basis of power, not ideology.

the interactions of states revolve around the axle of the balance of power. Systemic change affects the behavior of all member states. Whenever the system becomes unbalanced, trouble follows. When Britain weakens and can no longer contain a Continental power seeking European hegemony, a previously isolationist power, the United States, must step into play Britain's role. When Germany, in the center of Europe, is defeated, a conflict erupts between two previous allies, both superpowers on the periphery of Europe. Eliminating a troublesome member does not guarantee, therefore, the end of trouble and conflict. Nor can it. To alter the structure of the system is to change everyone's behavior; the new distribution of power merely leads to new alignments. But competition among states continues.

Uniformity of Behavior

Second, the system imposes a high degree of uniformity of behavior upon states, regardless of their domestic complexion. The same basic interests and motivations are ascribed to all members. The "necessity of state" overrides different national attributes such as political culture, economic organization, or class structure—or, at least, it is supposed to. The systems analyst will examine internal variables only if they seem to have interfered with how a state ought to have behaved.

In this connection, the systemic model also tends to minimize the importance of ideologies, which are generally used to justify whatever states do. States are motivated largely by their security interests and are therefore concerned with preserving or enhancing their power. Ideology is viewed as a function of this interest.[28] For example, despite its anticapitalist and antifascist ideology, communism did not prevent the Soviet Union from aligning itself with France in 1935, then with Nazi Germany in 1939, and in 1941 with the United States and Britain against its previous ally. And after World War II the Soviet Union acted very much as czarist Russia had done: it expanded into eastern Europe and attempted to extend its power into the eastern Mediterranean area. Ideology did not prevent Moscow from behaving in typical balance-of-power terms. Indeed, the wide range of policies seemingly compatible with a specific ideology is generally cited as evidence that ideology is essentially a rationalization of policy, rather than a motivation for it.

This deemphasis on ideology, then, suggests that the analyst of world politics need pay little attention to what policy makers *say* about their policies. Clearly, they will say whatever will make their actions look good. They will talk about freedom, national self-determination, liberating peoples from Communist or capitalist slavery, and bringing about a world of peace, law, order, and justice. But such concepts should not be confused with the concrete interests that are the real, underlying reasons for the state's behavior. Indeed, the analyst who assumes that state behavior is the product of an ever-changing distribution of power can, according to Hans Morgenthau,

> retrace and anticipate, as it were, the steps a statesman—past, present, or future—has taken or will take on the political scene. We can look over his shoulder when he writes his dispatches; we listen in on his conversation with other statesmen; we read and anticipate his very thoughts.... We think as he does, and as disinterested observers we understand his thoughts and actions *perhaps better than he*, the actor in the political scene, does himself.[29]

Whether Morgenthau is correct, less emphasis on ideologies and statements of intentions does tend to reduce the probability that international politics will be viewed as a morality tale, a conflict between good and evil, and it refocuses attention on the security dilemma shared by all states living in an anarchical environment in which they see other states as potential enemies and are therefore bound to be concerned with their power vis-à-vis one another.

Limitations of Choice

Third, the system places limits on the policy choices of states. Some observers refer to *system-determined behavior*. Although this term may understate the degree of a state's "free will" or the actual range of its choices, it is a healthy reminder that for states as for individuals the available options depend on external realities—in this instance, the distribution of power. As Hedley Bull notes, "The choice with which governments are in fact confronted is not that between opting for the present structure of the world, and opting for some other structure, but between attempting to maintain a balance of power and failing to do so." [30] The United States again presents a perfect example. Each time the European balance in this century has been upset, the United States has had but two options: to intervene and prevent the Continental powers from achieving hegemony or to remain isolationist. The latter course might have been preferable to the American public, but it might also have jeopardized future U.S. security. Three times, therefore, different administrations have rejected isolationism. The United States really had no choice.

Continuity

Finally, and closely related, continuity of policy is a characteristic of many nations. The political complexion of a great power—like Russia—may change, as may its perception of its role in the world and its definition of objectives. But it still lives in a system in which neighbors to the east and west remain the same; so therefore does the Soviet Union's need to secure Eastern Europe. Russia, czarist or Communist, has no natural protective barrier, like the English Channel for Britain or mountain ranges for Italy and Spain. Russia, regardless of regime, has historically sought greater security by expanding westward beyond its frontiers. Similarly, two U.S. interventions against Germany and one against Soviet Russia after World War II have demonstrated the remarkable continuity of U.S. policy.

A REMINDER: ANALYSIS AND APPROVAL

What we are examining is an analytical framework, and our observations about state behavior are deductive. A framework is just that: a representation from which in practice—in "real life"—there will be varying degrees of deviation. Nevertheless, constructing such a framework and deducing behavior patterns from it is a useful exercise; the conclusions can, after all, be checked empirically. If this method of analysis improves the observer's capacity to understand state behavior, it justifies itself.

Whether the observer personally approves of the "logic of behavior" that a particular framework seems to suggest is not the point. It is one thing to say, as we have done, that the state system condemns each state to be continuously concerned with its power relative to that of other states, which, in an anarchical system, it regards as potential aggressors. It is quite another to morally approve of power politics, or *security politics*, as we have renamed it.

The utility of the state-system framework is simply that it points to the "essence" of state behavior. It does not pretend to account for all factors, such as moral norms, that motivate states. But as a necessarily simplified version of reality, it does clarify what most basically concerns and drives states and what kinds of behavior we can expect. We may deplore that behavior and the anarchical system that produces it and we may wish that international politics were not as conflictual and violent as the twentieth century has already amply demonstrated. We may prefer a system other than one in which states are so committed to advancing their own national interests and protecting their sovereignty. Nevertheless, however much we may deplore the current system and prefer a more peaceful and harmonious world, we must first understand the contemporary one if we are to learn how to "manage" it and avoid the catastrophe of a nuclear war.

Notes

1. Thomas Hobbes, *Leviathan* (Collier Books, 1962), 101.
2. Hans J. Morgenthau, *Politics among Nations: The Struggle for Power and Peace*, 4th ed. (New York: Alfred A. Knopf, 1967), 490.
3. Jean Jacques Rousseau, *The Social Contract* (New York: Dutton, 1947), 6.
4. The domestic system in the United States assumes people will generally obey the law voluntarily. This is clearly shown by the limited number of police (national, state, and local)—certainly not enough to deal with massive resistance to the law and far, far fewer than the number of men in the armed forces to be employed outside the United States. For an interesting analysis in which the willingness of governments to use force against other governments is contrasted with their reluctance, if not unwillingness, to use it against their own populations, see E. E. Schattschneider, *Two Hundred Million Americans in Search of a Government* (New York: Holt, Rinehart & Winston, 1969), 17-22.
5. Hedley Bull, *The Anarchical Society* (New York: Columbia University Press, 1977), 77-98.
6. Hobbes, *Leviathan*, 104.
7. John H. Herz, *International Politics in the Atomic Age* (New York: Columbia University Press), 231-232.
8. John Herz characterizes the effects of such suspicion as follows: "[The] very realization that his own brother may play the role of a Cain makes his fellow men appear to him as potential foes. Realization of this fact by others, in turn, makes him appear to them as their potential mortal enemy. Thus there arises a fundamental social constellation, a mutual suspicion and a mutual dilemma: the dilemma of 'kill or perish,' of attacking first or running the risk of being destroyed. There is apparently no escape from this vicious circle. Whether a man is 'by nature' peaceful and cooperative, or aggressive and domineering, is not the question." John H. Herz, *Political Realism and Political Idealism* (Chicago: University of Chicago Press, 1951), 2-3.
9. Quoted in Geoffrey Till, *Maritime Strategy in the Nuclear Age* (New York: St. Martin's Press, 1982), 210.

10. Quoted by Geoffrey Blainey, *The Causes of War* (New York: Free Press, 1973), 108.
11. Hobbes, *Leviathan*, 100. Also see the important book by Robert Gilpin, *War and Change in World Politics* (New York: Cambridge University Press, 1981).
12. "NBC White Paper," *New York Times*, Sept, 4, 1979.
13. Arnold Wolfers, *Discord and Collaboration* (Baltimore: Johns Hopkins University Press), 83. For contrary interpretations correlating peace with a superiority of power and war with a balance, see A. F. K. Organski, *World Politics* (New York: Alfred A. Knopf, 1956), 325-333; and Blainey, *Causes of War*, 112-114.
14. Discussions of the different meanings of "balance of power" can be found in Morgenthau, *Politics among Nations*, 161-163; Ernst B. Haas, "The Balance of Power: Prescription, Concept, or Propaganda?" *World Politics*, July 1953, 442-447; and Inis L. Claude, Jr., *Power in International Relations* (New York: Random House, 1962), pt. I.
15. Wolfers, *Discord and Collaboration*, 123.
16. Claude, *Power in International Relations*, 6.
17. Ibid., 91.
18. Charles W. Kegley and Eugene R. Wittkopf, *World Politics* (New York: St. Martin's Press, 1985), 417.
19. Carl von Clausewitz, *On War*, trans. Michael Howard and Peter Peaet (Princeton, N.J.: Princeton University Press, 1976), 605.
20. Theodore Ropp, *War in the Modern World* (New York: Collier Books, 1962), 195ff.
21. Kenneth Waltz, *Theory of International Politics* (Reading, Mass.: Addison-Wesley, 1979), 127-128.
22. Paul Kennedy, *Strategy and Diplomacy 1870-1945* (London: Fontana Paperbacks, 1984), 109ff.
23. Wolfers, *Discord and Collaboration*, 84.
24. Waltz, *Theory of International Politics*, 105-106.
25. Roger D. Masters, "World Politics as a Primitive Political System," *World Politics*, July 1964, 595-619.
26. Waltz, *Theory of International Politics*, 107.
27. Ibid., 109.
28. Morgenthau, *Politics among Nations*, 83-86.
29. Ibid., 5, emphasis added.
30. Hedley Bull, *The Control of the Arms Race* (New York: Holt, Rinehart & Winston, 1961), 49.

CHAPTER 6

Same Game, Different Players

The distribution of power is the key to understanding the behavior of states, and first-level (state-system) analysis is based on the assumption that the *structure* of the system conditions this behavior. The structure of the state system is defined by the number of major actors, or *poles,* and the distribution of power among them. A pole is what is popularly known as a "great power," and the measure of that greatness has usually been military strength. State systems vary in the number of poles they contain. Further, there is a relationship between the structure of the international system and its *stability.* Stability is defined as the absence of any nation's predominance, the survival of most member states, and the absence of a major war. The concept of balance of power is based on the assumption that war may have to be invoked as a last resort to preserve systemic equilibrium or to restore it once it has been upset. War, then, is not per se destabilizing, especially if it is infrequent and/or limited. Major violence, such as a war among superpowers, however, will be destabilizing. Therefore, a stable system may be said to be characterized by minimal violence, the generally peaceful settlement of differences, and a desire to retain the principal features of the system. An unstable system is prone to major violence that may result in the hegemony of one pole; such hegemony will be a threat to the survival of the other major actors.[1]

UNIPOLARITY (STABLE)

Unipolarity would require one state to be dominant and capable of imposing its will on other states. World conquest by one state or a close alliance of states would produce a unipolar system. Obviously, such a system would be stable even if its members were unhappy to be governed by a foreign power and to have little say in how they were ruled. The Roman Empire was probably the nearest thing to a unipolar system. Rome—a city-state—ruled more than 100 million people and much of the known world. To the Romans, *empire* meant the inequality of states; those who rebelled against Roman rule were brutally crushed. Relations existed between the empire and the barbarian tribes whom Rome eventually intended to bring within its sphere of control.

Some analysts have asserted that the immediate post-World War II period was also a unipolar one. That suggestion is dubious. To be sure, France and Britain collapsed after Germany and Japan were defeated, but the Soviet Union was hardly impotent, although it had been badly hurt and did not yet possess the atomic bomb. Indeed, it was the Soviet Union's transformation of the states of Eastern Europe into satellites that ended its wartime alliance with the United States and Britain, and the Soviet attempts to expand beyond the lines where the Red Army stood at the end of the war that led to the cold war. If the postwar system had been unipolar, with the United States playing the role of Rome, it is hard to understand why Moscow was not more accommodating on the issue of free elections in Eastern Europe and did not refrain from its expansionist efforts. The fact is that the system after 1945 was bipolar, not unipolar.

BIPOLARITY (UNSTABLE)

In a *bipolar* structure, two opposing states or coalitions are involved in preserving the balance of power.[2] More specifically, a bipolar system is distinguished by the presence of two actors whose power is so far superior to that of other states that they are called *superpowers*; secondary powers and a host of lesser states may align themselves with these superpowers, but it is their interactions that are central. Immediately after World War II such a pattern emerged, with the United States and the Soviet Union as superpowers and most of the prewar great powers reduced to secondary status.[3] In such a bipolar system, conflict is unavoidable for each superpower regards the other as an adversary; it is the only state that can threaten its security. In short, in a two-pole structure, *conflict is structurally determined*, and friend and foe are clearly distinguished. Last, and very critical, *bipolarity intensifies international conflict because each of the antagonists tends to see any gain of power and security for the other as a loss of power and security for itself and is determined to prevent this consequence.* Each feels such a high degree of insecurity that it may be said to be "driven" or "compelled" to react against the perceived potential threat from the other pole. The balance of power is continuously seen to be at stake; each side fears that it will be upset, that the adversary will achieve hegemony, and that such hegemony will be irreversible—in short, that "the game" will be over. Consequently, both poles are hypersensitive to the slightest shifts of power.

Neither, in the perception of the other, can make an innocent move; each will see any move by the other—even if defensively motivated—as a deliberate and hostile attempt to enhance its own position. Counteraction is thus inevitable. Even moves in areas not normally considered of vital interest to the other superpower will be opposed for symbolic and psychological reasons. Each fears a *domino effect*: if one of its allies, friends, protégés, or satellites falls, others will follow and upset the equilibrium.

It is then not so much the single loss that is feared, for in itself it may not create a large deficit in the balance. What is feared, rather, is a series of small losses over a longer period, for together they could cause a sizable deficit. *When one power pushes, the other therefore feels compelled to push back.* Each constantly watches the other, and both are "trapped," in a real sense prisoners of the system. Neither can advance or retreat; positions must be held. Thus, *bipolar politics is the politics of confrontation.* When one side challenges the other at some spot, it is testing its adversary's will to maintain its own position. If the adversary reacts, crisis results. This involves serious threats of violence, possibly even the use of limited violence, with all its inherent potential for escalation into total war. Such crises recur frequently. Furthermore, the possibility of a surprise attack by one side to eliminate the other can never be excluded. Indeed, a bipolar division of power places a premium on such an attack. If done successfully, it leaves one side the clear winner, for the only threat to its security will have been eliminated. The ancient Greek historian Thucydides, in describing why war had erupted between Athens and Sparta, explained bipolar war in general. The Spartans, he said, attacked Athens because of Athens's growing power and the fear this caused in Sparta. The latter, therefore, launched a preventive war.[4]

Is a bipolar system that is both *simple* (because there are only two adversaries) and *rigid* (because most of the allies and friends of the two poles are tied to them and do not shift from one side to the other) stable or unstable? The answer seems clear from the basic rule for behavior in a bipolar structure: oppose any unilateral attempt by the adversary to upset the balance of power. If the opponent pushes, push back. The almost frantic search for allies; the cohesiveness of the principal alliances; attempts to undermine the opposing "camp" while preventing defections from one's own through interventions; the attendant arms race, spurred by the constant fear that the opponent may achieve an irreversible power advantage—and end the game—all mean frequent crises, occasional limited wars, and the persistent threat of general war. For these reasons, bipolarity has usually been judged an unstable system. By definition, the two powers are far stronger than any of their allies or friends and therefore cannot be restrained by them.

MULTIPOLARITY (STABLE)

A *multipolar* system, according to most theorists, is composed of at least five approximately equal great powers.[5] Such a system, it is usually claimed, is characterized by more restrained national behavior and is generally more conducive to preserving the peace. The reason is that, compared with the *simple* and *rigid* bipolar division, multipolarity is *complex* and *flexible*. When the division is simple and the major actors are aligned on one side or the other, friend and foe are easy to discover; this division is rigid because no realignment is possible. But a multipolar structure does not by itself distinguish between friend and foe; each pole views all other major actors as potential adversaries—and potential allies. *Among a larger number of great powers, each state has the mobility to align and realign itself.* Alliances are created as specific conflicts arise, and they usually last for only short periods, as the equilibrium shifts and alignments change. In contrast to bipolarity's confrontations and crises, in which antagonisms are constantly reinforced, *the greater opportunity for shifting combinations under multipolarity reduces the risk of mutually reinforcing hostilities between various "players."* Allies of today may be tomorrow's adversaries—and allies again the day after. Since a state may need its present opponent as an ally in the future, hostilities cannot be allowed to become too intense. Individual states have changing relations with so many other states that inevitably their loyalties will cut across one another.[6] A member of one alliance will have interests in common, as well as in conflict, with those of its partners, but some interests are also likely to overlap with interests of members in the opposing coalition. When the enemy of today may become the ally of tomorrow, it is a bit more difficult to become aroused about any specific state or cause.

In a particular dispute, for instance, the possibility that an ally may defect is claimed to be a restraining factor on the other members of the alliance. In a multipolar system, an *alliance* has the meaning that most of us give that term: a collection of states, most of approximately equal power, who by joining together strengthen themselves versus a potential enemy. The possible loss of one partner is, therefore, a serious matter because it weakens the alliance. If one member of an alliance should decide to sway the membership to change the status quo, another member's threat of "dealignment" is likely to block those efforts. The alliance cannot afford such a loss. Because the state threatening to defect might move into a nonaligned position or even join the opposition, members of the alliance bring collective pressure to bear on the dissenter to moderate its aims. Furthermore, if one state should enhance its power—for example, by increasing its armed forces or by seizing territory—another previously unaligned state may throw its weight onto the scales of the weaker side. In a multipolar structure, with its inherent flexibility, not only are friends and foes more difficult to distinguish than in a bipolar structure, but also the balance is not nearly as sensitive to changes in the power distribution. Changes do not seem irreversible because imbalances can be remedied. A multipolar system is thus inherently more stable than a bipolar one. If one of the two superpowers in a bipolar system wishes to act in a manner not supported by its allies, they cannot inhibit it. Because of the enormous difference in power between the superpower and its allies, the threat of defection cannot work; defection cannot appreciably reduce the superpower's power. In fact, the situation is quite the reverse: the far weaker ally needs the superpower's protection more than the latter needs its support.

One additional argument has been advanced to explain the restraining and peace-preserving characteristics of multipolarity. The more numerous the actors, it has been claimed, the less attention any single actor can give to any other. This is beneficial because "the average share of available attention for any one conflict drops sharply as soon as there are more than three power centers in the system, and more gently after there are more than five such centers." More specifically, if a conflict requires at least 10 percent of a government's critical attention before armed conflict can result, then the "minimal attention ratio for an escalating conflict would have to be 1:9 since it does not seem likely that any country could be provoked very far into an escalating conflict with less than 10 percent of the foreign policy attention of its government devoted to the matter." [7] Whereas in a bipolar system the contestants watch each other unceasingly and are able to devote themselves fully to their quarrels, in a multipolar system, with as many as eleven approximately equal great powers, it is possible to avoid major conflicts. To sum up, we can say that bipolar systems are prone to crises and the eruption of war, but multipolar systems, because of their flexibility, are more likely to maintain peace (see Table 6-1).

Table 6-1 Two Types of State System

	Bipolar System	*Multipolar System*
Number of powers	Two superior states	Many (usually cited as five to ten) approximately equal states
Nature of system	Simple and rigid	Complex and flexible
Principal characteristics	Confrontation, crisis, arms competition, preoccupation with adversary's preemptive or first-strike capability, search for allies	Self-restraint and emphasis on negotiating major political differences
Alliance relationship	Cohesive	Rapidly changing

OR IS BIPOLARITY STABLE AND MULTIPOLARITY UNSTABLE?

The preceding evaluations of bipolarity and multipolarity have not gone unchallenged. Kenneth Waltz has persuasively argued that bipolarity is stable and multipolarity unstable. His major reason for this conclusion is that in a bipolar system each state needs to watch only the other one and counter its moves. Both poles may have allies, but, because their allies have far less power, the two major actors need pay little attention to their wishes and complaints. The allies are so dependent on their poles' protection that, however disgruntled they may be, they are unlikely to defect.

To be sure, a two-pole system means confrontation that can lead to hostilities. But the occurrence of hostilities also suggests that the balance is being kept. War would be much more likely if one power did not respond to the other's challenge, for that would mean that the opponent had succeeded in enhancing its power. When power confronts power there may be danger, but when power confronts weakness the danger is far greater. Avoiding trouble when challenged does not mean that war has been prevented, only that it may well come later—indeed, that the possibility of war is very likely. In addition, among equals, a quick surprise attack is not likely to be successful. Sparta did not succeed in destroying Athenian power quickly; the war continued for decades. The same was true for the war between Rome and Carthage.

Consistent with this logic, Waltz argues that multipolarity is unstable. Multipolarity's flexibility does not make it stable because fluidity in relationships, with states shifting back and forth among alliances and counteralliances and nonalignment, renders every state's calculations uncertain. Will one's current allies defect, and when and under what circumstances? If one member of an alliance is determined to change the status quo, will other members of the alliance threaten to defect and, if necessary, do so to moderate this demand? Or will that power drag everyone with it into a dangerous situation that risks war because, in an alliance of equals, no state can afford to lose the assistance of the other members? Instead of moderating the arms race, will the uncertainty of future relationships not intensify all states' sense of insecurity, thereby fueling the arms race? Was it not the multipolarity in 1914 that helped precipitate World War I because Austria-Hungary was determined to squash Serbia in the Balkans, and Germany, unwilling to lose Austria-Hungary as an ally, was pulled into the war (admittedly, not at all reluctantly)? When czarist Russia opposed Austria-Hungary, did France, unable to face Germany alone, have any choice but to support its Russian ally? And did not Germany claim after the war that it would not have moved had it known that Britain—which did not have alliances with France and Russia, only ententes—would come into the war (that is, had the system possessed the clarity of a bipolar system)?

Waltz takes traditional arguments and reverses them. Whether one agrees or disagrees with him, one thing appears to be increasingly clear: it is not the number of poles that makes a system stable or unstable but the number of major *nuclear* actors. If we define a major nuclear actor as any power likely to survive an enemy's first strike that also has the capability of devastating its opponent's major cities in retaliation, we can accept Waltz's conclusion, but with a major difference: *nuclear bipolarity will be a stable system; nuclear multipolarity will be an unstable system.*

There are two reasons why nuclear bipolarity is more stable. First, unlike war during the prenuclear age, war among nuclear powers now involves the very real possibility that those who fight it will be committing suicide. When it did not involve such a fatal consequence, war could be used as "an instrument of state policy" because the gains were likely to exceed costs. That is no longer true. The certainty of widespread devastation and the knowledge that a nuclear war will mean the end of civilized society act as a restraint. Second, precisely because the confrontation is between only two powers, they need watch only each other and learn about each other's behavior patterns in a crisis situation. Long acquaintanceship results in their becoming more familiar with each other's ways of "crisis management"; there is definitely an upward learning curve. Not that major mistakes and misassessments cannot occur; but fewer miscalculations may happen between two warriors who have faced each other before and have become familiar with each other's behavior patterns. Thus, even if one rejects Waltz's logic and agrees that prenuclear bipolarity was unstable, nuclear weapons have produced a stable nuclear bipolarity system.

Many believe that nuclear multipolarity will be unstable and that nuclear proliferation, therefore, must be prevented or slowed and that the number of nuclear powers must be kept at a minimum (generally agreed to be the six current nuclear powers plus, if need be, only three or four more). The reasons for this conclusion are also twofold. First, in a multipolar system, the larger number of states means that frictions among them are likely to be far more numerous than if there were only two powers. Second, even if a degree of flexibility were restored in such a multipolar system, the chances of at least one conflict erupting into war remain high. The fewer fingers on the nuclear trigger, the better, sums up this position.

Currently there are only two major nuclear powers. By contrast, the other countries that have nuclear weapons or are suspected of having them— Britain, France, China, India, and Israel—have quite a small capability, although they are hardly impotent. Before the birth of a genuinely nuclear multipolar system composed of states of approximately equal power, we are likely to witness a tripolar system.

TRIPOLARITY

Because of the increasing importance of China in contemporary superpower relations, tripolarity is well worth analyzing. The relations among the United

States, the Soviet Union, and China do not constitute a genuine tripolar system because China does not possess the economic and military power equal to that of the other two. But the exercise is worthwhile to show how analysts derive their models. Furthermore, tripolarity raises a basic question: Is behavior in a tripolar system closer to that under a bipolar system or that under a multipolar system? Some analysts suggest the latter because each pole will have at least two incentives for self-restraint and moderation in its behavior. The first is that nuclear warfare between any two poles would weaken the participants so catastrophically that the third pole would attain a dominant systemic position. The "victorious power," if there were one, would confront a third power still untouched by nuclear havoc; and, even if that third power were to possess only an inferior strategic nuclear capability, it could still dictate the terms of peace. The second is that not only would each pole be opposed to such an outcome, but each would also wish to prevent the emergence of a dominant coalition composed of the other two poles. Such a coalition could result only if any of the three exhibited unduly aggressive behavior. Self-restraint would thus be a wise policy for each pole.[8] *Whereas in a bipolar system each power most fears becoming militarily inferior, lest the opponent achieve a dominance that may not be reversible, in a tripolar system each pole may fear diplomatic isolation the most.*

In a tripolar structure, maintenance of the system demands abstention from the kinds of confrontation and lower-level military engagements that may escalate into a nuclear conflagration; this implies nonintervention in one another's spheres of influence and relative moderation in each pole's demands and behavior. Each pole is also likely to concentrate its attention and energies on its relations with its two rivals, for to become too involved outside the triangular structure and to neglect relations with the other two poles may be disadvantageous to any of the actors.

The basic rules of behavior are as follows:

1. The existence of "adversary number one" leads to "objective collusion" with "number two."
2. Each of the three players aims to reduce collusion between the others to a minimum.
3. At the same time, it is in the interest of each to bluff or blackmail the chief adversary by threatening collusion with the other.
4. The surest way for any of the three to provoke the other two into collusion is to display undue aggressiveness.[9]

Notice the use of the word *collusion*. Although the term connotes an underhanded intention, such an implication is not necessarily present. Two powers may well seek a *rapprochement* on some particular issue for reasons having little or nothing to do with power number three. Nevertheless, the latter is likely to be suspicious of the motives of the other powers and therefore to perceive collusion, whether it exists or not.

A tripolar system, then, promises to be stable, perhaps more stable than a bipolar system for it need not be quite so sensitive to slight increments of power by any pole, as the emphasis shifts from continual crises toward maneuver and from rigid confrontation toward flexibility. In a bipolar system each state thinks that it must match the other, but in a tripolar system some gain in power can be permitted because, if the increase should become too threatening to the other two poles, they are likely to combine their power. If one of the poles has been aligned with the expansionist pole it will shift toward the third pole. Or the third pole, because it can throw its power on the scales on the side of the weaker state, may be in a position to act as moderator in the dispute. *Rational calculations of power and self-interest, not ideology, will be the basis of each pole's foreign policy.*

There is an opposing view: some analysts argue that tripolarity is closer to bipolarity than it is to multipolarity and is unstable. Again, there are two main reasons. First, precisely because tripolarity is bipolarity plus one, it may revert to bipolarity if two powers align themselves against the third pole on more than just a temporary basis. Each pole greatly fears a long-term alliance or collusion of the other two, and this fear is bound to raise tensions. The Soviet Union fears a Sino-American alliance against it, even if that alliance relationship is not formalized, just as during the cold war years the United States used to fear the growth of Chinese power within the context of the Sino-Soviet alliance. The Soviet fear focuses on China's future military strength as the Chinese seek to modernize their country with U.S. assistance. Second, even if tripolarity should not revert to bipolarity, the addition of one pole triples the number of possible interactions from the single pattern possible under bipolarity (see Figure 6-1). These patterns may be cooperative,

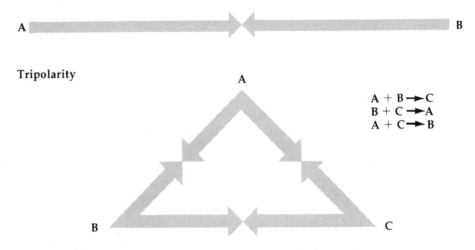

Bipolarity

Tripolarity

$$A + B \rightarrow C$$
$$B + C \rightarrow A$$
$$A + C \rightarrow B$$

Figure 6-1 Different Interactions in Bipolar and Tripolar Systems

but the likelihood of conflict is even greater as each strives for superiority in a three-way competitive system. Although the number of interactions increases, the flexibility of tripolarity is far more limited than that of a multipolar system in which several great powers may maneuver to maintain the equilibrium. Tripolarity therefore may be somewhat unstable.

SYSTEMIC STRUCTURES AND FOREIGN POLICY ORIENTATION

All states must deal one way or another with the "security dilemma" represented by the state system and the particular distribution of power within that system. Different distributions of power favor different responses. This is not to say that structure is the only condition affecting a state's response to the situation in which it finds itself. But it is a prime, if not *the* prime, factor in a system in which options are circumscribed by the environment in which states live. Among the principal responses have been isolationism-unilateralism, nonalignment, and alliances. None of these patterns is absolute; states do, however, tend to pursue one particular pattern more than another.

Isolationism-Unilateralism

For much of its history, the United States sought its security and the protection of its democratic way of life through a policy of isolationism. American practice can, therefore, reveal many of the conditions necessary for a state to adopt such a policy. But let us first clarify the meaning of the term *isolationism.* One thing it did not mean is what it seems to say, namely, a complete cutoff from all relations with other states in the system. Admittedly, something bordering on such a complete political, military, economic, and cultural isolation has been attempted in the past by China with its Great Wall and by Japan before Commodore Matthew Perry. These are clear cases of isolationism. The American case is more one of *unilateralism*, a "do-it-yourself" foreign policy in which a state relies on itself and not allies. The state has no commitments to other states and cannot be drawn into their conflicts; at the same time, no state is obligated to come to its assistance if it gets into trouble. American isolationism meant only noninvolvement and *political* isolation from the European state system's rivalries and conflicts.

Isolationism did not mean an abstinence from profitable commercial relationships, even with European states. Indeed, quite the opposite. George Washington expressed the essence of this isolationism best in his Farewell Address:

> The great rule of conduct for us, in regard to foreign nations, is, in extending our commercial relations, to have with them as little political connection as possible....

Europe has a set of primary interests which to us have none or a very remote relation. Hence she must be engaged in frequent controversies, the causes of which are essentially foreign to our concerns. Hence, therefore, it must be unwise in us to implicate ourselves by artificial ties in the ordinary vicissitudes of her politics or the ordinary combinations and collisions of her friendships or enmities....

Why forgo the advantages of so peculiar a situation? Why quit our own to stand upon foreign ground? Why, by interweaving our destiny with that of any part of Europe, entangle our peace and prosperity in the toils of European Ambition, Rivalship, Interest, Humor, or Caprice? [10]

Nor as it evolved did isolationism mean political abstinence in Latin America and Asia, both areas in which the United States was intermittently active politically, economically, militarily, and culturally, sending messages about democracy along with fundamental Christianity—especially in China. It was only from entangling alliances in Europe, the home of the world's great powers, that the United States kept its political distance until World War I. Even then, the United States referred to its allies as "associated powers," and, just to ensure that it would not again become involved in Europe's balance-of-power politics after the war, it legislated a series of neutrality laws. Congress attempted to banish "power politics" by legislating it away.

What were some of the conditions that enabled the United States for so long to pursue its unilateral course? One, which would appear to apply to China and Japan as well, is geographic remoteness from the centers of power as measured by the technological developments in transportation and communication at the time the policy was being practiced. By the standards of an era not acquainted with subsonic commercial jets that span the Atlantic Ocean in seven to eight hours, or supersonically in half that time, or large passenger liners that make the journey in four to six days, America was truly a world away from Europe.

A second condition, which would also apply to states less geographically remote, would appear to be a lack of power. The United States in 1795 was so militarily weak that it actually agreed to pay the Barbary states (Algeria, Morocco, Tunisia, and Tripolitania) $642,500 plus an annual tribute of more than $26,000 in naval stores for the release of American captives.[11] This arrangement continued until a sufficient navy could be built to extend U.S. power that far. For a state in this condition, it was prudent to follow President Washington's advice and avoid entanglements—the best way not to become a pawn on the interstate chessboard. As John Quincy Adams replied to Britain's proposed Anglo-American alliance to counter the threat of the Holy Alliance (Russia, Prussia, and Austria-Hungary) to reconquer Spain's former Latin American colonies, which had declared their independence, the United States would not become "a cockboat in the British man-of-war."

A third condition favoring isolationist-unilateral states is that they are not coveted by the great powers. They are, to put it another way, not major stakes, either because they are geographically remote or because they are weak, or both. More important concerns preoccupied the states of Europe: meeting the demands (either by accommodation or repression) of populations stirred by the promises of the French Revolution for self-government; coping with the equally profound impact of industrialization and urbanization, including the rise of the industrial middle class and working class; struggling with the changing map of Europe as new nations arose—especially Germany—and old empires, such as Austria-Hungary, began to crumble; rushing to divide up Africa; and, of course, attending to its small wars after a quarter century of exhausting total war following the French Revolution and the rise of Napoleon.

A fourth systemic condition favoring isolationism would seem to be a multipolar distribution of power. The European state system, composed of no less than half a dozen major actors, was kept balanced for much of the nineteenth century by Britain, which, when necessary, threw its support to the weaker side to deter any single state or coalition from gaining Continental hegemony. The Royal Navy stood guard over the Atlantic approaches to the Western Hemisphere. Any state attempting to project its power across the Atlantic Ocean could not hope to do so successfully unless it was also master of the Continent and able to organize its potential power for such a thrust. Keeping the European balance was thus tantamount to protecting the young Republic and permitting it further indulgence in its isolationism. That is why Adams could safely refuse the British offer of coalition against the Holy Alliance; he knew Britain would preserve the balance by itself. Therefore, the Monroe Doctrine could be publicly announced even though the United States was in no position to enforce it against a great-power intruder. London would do it!

America's emergence on the world scene after World War II as an active and continuous player of international politics coincided with the collapse of the European system and the emergence of a bipolar state system. Structural change compelled the United States to forsake isolationism once and for all. But for a nation that had become a great power and, therefore, acquired a major stake in the state system, the collapse of multipolarity—especially of Britain's role as "balancer"—meant the end of an era of aloofness from international politics and the transformation of an isolationist state into a prime player of power politics. The security of the United States could no longer be ensured by a unilateral orientation. If our analysis is correct, however—that is, if isolationism requires geographical distance from the centers of power, a low level of technology in transportation and communication, then isolationism-unilateralism is no longer a feasible foreign policy option for any major state.

Nonalignment

Nonalignment, the second policy response, has been widely adopted by the less-developed countries (LDCs) and mainly new, ex-colonial states in the contemporary world. It shares isolationism's unwillingness to become politically and militarily aligned and identified with any one of the major actors in the system, but differs from isolationism in that nonalignment is not incompatible with active political participation in the affairs of the international system. Let us look more closely at the similarities to, and differences from, isolationism. First, the nonaligned states are all economically underdeveloped and, in most cases, newcomers in the system; the Latin American states are the principal exception in the last respect. Second, the practitioners of nonalignment are mainly non-Communist states, although many call themselves "socialist" despite subscribing to a whole range of economic policies spanning state ownership to private enterprise. A few Communist states, China, Vietnam, North Korea, and Cuba, however, have been invited to meetings of the nonaligned states since the 1970s. But Soviet Russia, a developed state controlled by Caucasians, has always been excluded. Yugoslavia, another such state, has generally found its home among the nonaligned after Joseph Stalin ousted it from the Communist world. Nevertheless, the vast majority of nonaligned states are not Communist, but non-Western. Third, they are generally weak states either because they are small or because, if they possess large populations and rich resources, they have not yet developed their potential power and wealth. In any event, most of these states were former colonies, and they do not want to become puppets of the superpowers; nonentanglement is, therefore, the wise course.

But it is the systemic distribution of power that makes nonalignment not only feasible but also attractive for states wishing to maintain their freedom of choice in foreign policy. Given the desire of the LDCs to modernize themselves, whether they choose to do so by dictatorial or by democratic means is considered critical. An influential American study on the future of the underdeveloped countries, published as the bipolar rivalry entered the 1960s, said:

> Whether most of these countries take a democratic or a Communist or other totalitarian path in their development is likely to determine the course of civilization on our planet.
>
> Should that large majority of the human race which lives in underdeveloped countries turn to totalitarian ways for meeting its problems, the blow to the prestige of free institutions could not fail to affect the outlook for freedom in the United States itself. Americans have long believed, and with more reason today than ever, that our own institutions are in danger in a world where freedom does not flourish.
>
> ...The Communists offer a competing system which borrows the industrial technology of the West but repudiates Western political freedom and the dignity of the individual. Communism now directs its main drive toward the underdeveloped countries. The choice of these countries between taking the Communist path or modernizing with Western aid and friendship will probably determine whether the totalitarian or the democratic way of life eventually acquires throughout the world a preponderance of economic, psychological, and military power. In other words, it will probably determine our own security and the course of world civilization.[12]

The Soviets, in their turn, talked of a vast "peace zone" containing the majority of the world's population and comprising the socialist states (the

Soviets use the term *socialism* rather than *communism*) plus the nonsocialist but "peace-loving" LDCs. These states had achieved political independence but, while they were not members of the socialist world, they did not belong to the aggressive imperialist bloc either; indeed, they were highly nationalistic and anti-imperialist or anti-Western. Economic aid to the new states, which still needed to break their economic links with the West, would strengthen their independence, attract them to the socialist bloc, and fatally weaken the Western capitalist economies. By the middle 1950s, the Soviets had recognized the importance of the Third World, which had risen out of the crumbling Western empires and separated itself from the capitalist bloc, but had not yet joined the socialist camp. In short, the stakes were high. Both poles, having drawn clear lines between their respective spheres in Europe and protected them with their deterrent capability, extended their competition to the Third World. Each sought as its maximum objective adding the territory, population, and resources of the newly emerged nations—or, at least, the potentially stronger and politically more important new states. Their minimal aim was to prevent these states from joining the adversary's bloc.

For the new states, all of which were militarily weak and economically and politically underdeveloped, nonalignment made tactical sense in the context of this postwar distribution. An "in-between" posture presumably allowed them to maximize their bargaining influence. This was significant in at least two respects. First, the new nations desperately needed economic aid and technical assistance. Second, nations that had long been Western-controlled could reduce their political and economic dependence on the West with such aid. When a nation moved away from the West, the Soviet Union would offer it aid. Conversely, when it became too dependent on the Soviets or when it resisted them, a U.S. loan tended to be forthcoming. The middle position in the cold war was therefore politically and economically very useful, maximizing economic assistance and minimizing dependence on the principal donors. As Robert C. Good notes:

> The possibility of "blackmail" is built into the very structure of Cold War competition. But from the point of view of the excessively dependent, relatively impotent new state, this is not blackmail. It is the equally ancient but more honorable art of maintaining political equilibrium through the diversification of dependence, the balancing of weakness—in short, the creation of an "alternative" lest the influence of one side or the other become too imposing. The attraction of Communist aid is enhanced for radical governments whose wariness of the intentions of the former metropole extends to the "capitalist-imperialist West" in general. Yet [even] conservative governments are receptive to Communist aid. They want it partly to placate their radical oppositions and to hasten development, but also, one suspects, to pursue the first requirement of operational independence—the creation of a rough equilibrium among foreign influences in the life of the country. Conversely, radical governments that have developed extensive relations with the Communist bloc may seek the re-establishment of compensatory links with the West.[13]

A bipolar structure was thus conducive to a policy of nonalignment and to enhancing the leverage of the new states.

Alliances

If isolationism is largely a product of multipolarity and nonalignment an offspring of bipolarity, alliances are compatible with both types of balances.[14] If the first policy pattern is indicative of a very low level of involvement in the state system, and the second pattern of a medium level of participation, alliances are indicative of a very high level of activity. Comprised of states brought together by a commonly perceived external threat and concerned with their protection—peacefully if possible, by war if necessary—each alliance has been called "a latent war community." Nevertheless, depending upon the specific distribution of power, coalitions differ in composition and function.

Bipolar Alliances. In a bipolar system, alliances organized by the superpowers are inherently unequal because of the vast gap in power between the superpower and its allies. The nature of bipolar alliances follows from this enormous disparity in power. The superpower is the *producer of security;* its partners are the *consumers.* The partners cannot enhance their protector's security by significantly adding to its power; the superpower supplies the bulk of the alliance's strength. In the North Atlantic Treaty Organization (NATO) and the Warsaw Treaty Organization (WTO), the superpowers provide the strategic nuclear capability to keep the deterrent balance; they also furnish the conventional military backbones of both organizations. But the critical ingredient is the strategic nuclear protection that each extends to its allies. *A bipolar alliance, given the unequal internal power distribution, is in effect a unilateral guarantee extended by the superpower to its allies, which are really its protectorates.* The pledge of the allies to come to the superpower's assistance in the event of attack, a normal obligation for all coalition members when signing a treaty of alliance, is consequently a ritual. By contrast, the purpose of alliances in multipolar systems composed of at least five or six major actors is to add the power of other states to one's own. In these alliances, the mutual obligations of defense do matter. Indeed, because such an alliance cannot afford the defection of any great-power member without being seriously weakened in relation to the adversary alliance, constant attention must be paid to holding the coalition together. In a bipolar alliance, by contrast, one nation's defection normally would not seriously reduce the coalition's collective power.

The principal function of a bipolar alliance in these circumstances is deterrence, to "draw lines," and to leave no doubt in the other superpower's mind about which areas are considered vital and are to be left alone if war is to be avoided. The alliance clarifies the superpower's interests as dictated by the systemic structure. Just as bipolarity determines who the rivals will be, it also influences which states will align with one or the other. In a highly sensitive bipolar structure in which the principal competitors are continuously fearful that the balance will be upset, they will at the very least seek to enhance their protection, by extending their control over neighboring states in what one historian, noting Russia's establishment of the East European satellites after the war, has called "defensive expansionism." After all, if Russia did not do so, would not a potential adversary be tempted to extend its power to Russia's frontiers?

But, given the nature of the state system, once one of the superpowers expands into contiguous areas, its rival views this as an offensive move that increases the power of its opponent and decreases its own security. The countermove is inevitable. The result is that each pole stakes out its territorial claims and warns the other pole not to intrude into the areas it considers important enough to its security to risk war in their defense; it transmits that warning by extending its protection to these areas by means of an alliance. *A bipolar coalition, therefore, does not create new interests; it registers the interest of each superpower in the areas beyond those it already controls and seeks to dissuade the adversary from attempting to expand into them.*

The United States and the Soviet Union both stood in the center of Europe at the end of World War II. The American army and the Soviet army, by driving the German armies backward, had already drawn the lines between the American and Russian spheres as the postwar bipolar conflict erupted. Shortly after the European war had ended, a perceptive observer noted that "most of the lesser nations are being drawn by a sort of Law of Political Gravity into the orbit of one or the other Super-Power. So far neither Russia nor the United States has yet completed its protective belt of satellites. Some areas are being tugged both ways, like small planets caught between two stars." [15]

The purpose of NATO in 1949, the first American peacetime alliance in history, was to formalize the commitment and leave no doubt of it—if the Soviet Union harbored any doubt. (WTO, the Soviet-imposed response to NATO, only formalized an already existing relationship among its members, whose primary ties were party-to-party and had been organized in the Communist Information Bureau or Cominform in 1947.) If a bipolar alliance, then, is in reality a unilateral guarantee in the form of the superpower's extension of deterrence to those areas it wishes to protect against hostile attack, it follows that each such alliance is also *cohesive*. When the threat to the security of the alliance is seen as basic by all of its members, then they subordinate their diverse interests to the common fear of the enemy. It is this common perception of a high degree of external danger that binds the strands of alliance. Differences within the coalition tend to be essentially over the means of how to meet specific common dangers or opportunities.

But even when the threat diminishes and the individual members pay more attention to their national interests, the alliance holds. In an unequal alliance, the superpower need not do much to accommodate its partners; the latter have few options, no matter how much they disagree with the superpower's policies. They need its protection. The superpower decides what it thinks best, even if it means opposing its allies on occasion. The United States in 1956 could oppose the British-French invasion of Egypt and stop it without their defecting. NATO, originally signed for a twenty-year term, has lasted twice that long. Moreover, given the geographical fact that Europe, Eastern and Western, occupies the space between the two superpowers, and given the political fact that the superpowers' rivalry and conflict will also continue, moderated mainly by a common concern to avoid nuclear warfare and mutual suicide, there is reason to expect the continued existence of NATO, as well as WTO, in a bipolar Europe.

Multipolar Alliances. In a bipolar system friend and foe are structurally determined, but in a multipolar system amity and enmity can shift. *All major states regard one another as potential adversaries as well as allies.* When one or two of them begin to be very powerful and are perceived as a threat to the others, alignments begin to form, and each alliance is created to counter a specific enemy. Loyalty is critical to the survival of a multipolar alliance. Because the power of each member is so important to the security of the entire alliance, mutual defense obligations do matter. A dealignment or defection by any member reduces the alliance's collective strength and weakens it vis-à-vis the opposing alliance. Therefore, constant attention must be paid to holding the coalition together. In a bipolar alliance, one nation's defection would not seriously reduce the actual collective power. But in a multipolar alliance, such a loss would be serious and is always a possibility.

In addition, multipolar alliances, in contrast to bipolar alliances, add new interests. The alliance reflects the diversity of members' interests and may accept new interests as the price that must be paid to attract a state into coalition. Conversely, if it turns out that member states did not explicitly or implicitly understand this at the time of signing or if a member state changes its mind about supporting such additional interests, the alliance may become ineffective, if not paralyzed; possibly it may lead to defections. Contrast the ability of NATO, a multilateral and long-term bipolar alliance, to deter Russia with the inability of the interwar alliances—mainly bilateral with frequently shifting partners from one alliance to another—to contain German power and avoid World War II. France, after the First World War, established a set of coalitions to help it balance Germany as the latter recovered its might after the defeat. Germany's population, industrial strength, and military skills made it the strongest potential power in Europe. France signed alliances, therefore, with Germany's eastern neighbors—Poland, Czechoslovakia, Yugoslavia, and Romania—to contain Germany with the threat of an undesirable two-front war. France also had separate alliances with Britain and the Soviet Union. Why did this set of alliances fail to contain Germany? [16]

The European state system between the wars was composed of five major powers (Britain, France, Germany, Italy, and the Soviet Union) and several lesser ones (mainly Poland, Czechoslovakia, Romania, and Yugoslavia). But several of these powers—Poland, Italy, and the Soviet Union—shifted one or more times. This shifting made it impossible to form a stable alliance against Germany and difficult to calculate accurately what the power distribution was at various times during the 1930s between Germany and its opponents. This situation was aggravated by the fact that the alliances were mainly bilateral; that is, between one of the major powers and another: France and Britain, France and Poland, France and the Soviet Union (and, briefly, a close relationship, although not an alliance, between France and Italy). There was no large, multilateral, stable alliance like NATO with its supreme commander, integrated military staff and plans, and common strategy, which makes it clear to Moscow who its opponents are.

Worse was that France and Britain, the two status quo powers, could not even agree on what the status quo was! Britain would commit itself only to the defense of France at the French-German border; it refused until it was too late to commit itself to France's allies in eastern Europe on Germany's other side. The alliance with France created new interests for Britain, which Britain refused to accept. This difference allowed Germany to expand into eastern Europe, undermine France's allies, and erode the European balance. Only in 1939 did Britain commit itself to the defense of Poland and Romania and announce that Britain would declare war if Germany attacked Poland. But by then, after years of being appeased, Hitler did not believe that London would fight, and he sent his armies into Poland.

Worst of all, Britain did not seek a Soviet alliance. Britain could not make up its mind whether the real threat was Germany—in which case an alliance with Russia made sense—or Russia and communism—in which case the appeasement of Germany made sense, for Germany blocked the expansion of Soviet power. France was allied to Russia, but refused to help Russia's smaller ally, Czechoslovakia, in 1938. France would not risk war unless Britain would join in, which, of course, Britain would not do. Seeing this, Moscow decided to shift, signing a pact with Nazi Germany in 1939 that divided Poland and allowed Hitler to concentrate on the West, which, because Germany's rear was for the moment protected, signaled the beginning of World War II. Yet only by aligning themselves with one of Europe's two totalitarian powers could the two Western democracies have isolated Germany and avoided war. The constant shifting or defections from the various alliances, their basically bilateral rather than multilateral character, and Britain's ignorance of the principle of the conservation of enemies—never face two major enemies simultaneously, but align with the weaker one against the stronger one— were among the chief reasons that made it impossible to keep the peace in Europe's multipolar system.

Once the war had erupted, however, Britain (after France's defeat) was saved first by Hitler's turning on Russia, thereby driving Britain and Russia into an alliance (had it been formed earlier, this alliance might have avoided the war) and then by the United States, which, with its enormous power, ensured the Allied victory. In this way Britain was rescued from its own folly.

Notes

1. Joseph L. Nogee, "Polarity: An Ambiguous Concept," *Orbis*, Winter 1975, 1211-1212.
2. There is considerable disagreement about the dangers and virtues of bipolarity. On the dangers, see Hans Morgenthau, *Politics among Nations*, 5th ed. (New York: Alfred A. Knopf, 1972), 346-347; and on the virtues, see Kenneth H. Waltz, "The Stability of a Bipolar World," *Daedalus*, Summer 1964, 881-909; Waltz, "International Structure, National Force and the Balance of World Power," *Journal of International Affairs* (June 1967): 215-231; and Waltz, *Theory of International Politics* (Reading, Mass.: Addison-Wesley, 1979), 163-176. For a comparative study of the bipolar struggle between Athens and Sparta, see Peter J. Fliess, *Thucydides and the Politics of Bipolarity* (Baton Rouge: Louisiana State University Press, 1966). My own analysis throughout this chapter is heavily indebted to Glen H. Snyder and Paul Diesing, *Conflict Among Nations* (Princeton, N.J.: Princeton University Press, 1977), 419-450.
3. For broad analyses of the beginning of the cold war and American foreign policy during the cold war period, see Louis J. Halle, *The Cold War as History* (New York: Harper & Row, 1967); John Spanier, *American Foreign Policy since World War II*, 10th ed. (New York: Holt, Rinehart & Winston, 1985); and Seyom Brown, *The Faces of Power* (New York: Columbia University Press, 1968).
4. Thucydides, *History of the Peloponnesian War* (New York: Oxford University Press, 1960), 46.
5. Morton Kaplan, *System and Process in International Politics* (New York: John Wiley & Sons, 1957).
6. Karl W. Deutsch and J. David Singer, "Multipolar Power Systems and International Stability," *World Politics*, April 1964, 392-396.
7. Ibid., 396-400.
8. Ronald Yalem, "Tripolarity and the International System," *Orbis*, Winter 1972, 1051ff.; and "Tripolarity and World Politics," *The Yearbook of World Affairs 1974* (London: Institute of World Affairs, 1974), 23ff.
9. Michel Tatu, *International Negotiation: The Great Power Triangle, Selected Comments*, U.S. Congress, Senate, Committee on Government Operations, Subcommittee on National Security and International Operations, 92d Cong., 1st sess., 1971, 11.
10. See Felix Gilbert, *To the Farewell Address: Ideas of Early American Foreign Policy* (Princeton, N.J.: Princeton University Press, 1961), Appendix, 145.
11. Julius W. Pratt, *A History of United States Foreign Policy* (Englewood Cliffs, N.J.: Prentice-Hall, 1955), 110.
12. Eugene Staley, *The Future of Underdeveloped Countries*, rev. ed. (New York: Praeger Publishers, 1961), 3, 15, 37.
13. Robert C. Good, "State-building as a Determinant of Foreign Policy in the New States," in *Neutralism and Nonalignment*, ed. Laurence W. Martin (New York: Holt, Rinehart & Winston, 1962), 11.
14. Snyder and Diesing, *Conflict Among Nations*.

15. John Fischer in *Harper's,* August 1945, quoted by Norman A. Graebner, *Cold War Diplomacy,* 2d ed. (New York: D. Van Nostrand Co., 1977), 23.
16. Arnold Wolfers, *Britain and France between Two Wars* (New York: W. W. Norton, 1966); and Evan Luard, "Conciliation and Deterrence: A Comparison of Political Strategies in the Interwar and Postwar Periods," *World Politics,* January 1967, 167-189.

CHAPTER 7

The Ability to Play: Power and Intentions

THE PERCEPTION OF POWER

Power, great power, superpower, balance of power—we have used these terms repeatedly, but at no point have we stopped to inquire into the nature of power. In one sense, there hardly seems reason to do so, for *power* is a term with which we are all familiar; it seems so obvious what power is. The United States lands soldiers on the island of Grenada to overthrow a pro-Castro regime. The Soviet army invades Afghanistan to ensure the survival of a pro-Soviet Marxist regime. The United States demands the withdrawal of Soviet missiles from Cuba. The Soviet Union demands that West Berlin be turned into a "free city" (free of the Western allies, that is). Saudi Arabia threatens an oil embargo unless there is progress on Palestinian self-determination. In these instances we all know that power is being exercised.

It is a fact of life that some nations are more powerful than others and that international politics generally has been the story of the games played by the stronger members of the state system.[1] When we use adjectives like *more powerful* and *stronger,* we are usually referring to military capacity. No one thinks of Belgium or Burma as powers; their military strength, by either conventional or nuclear standards, is puny. The label *power* historically has been awarded to states that have won significant military victories. Until such a victory who could have known of the state's power? Without a demonstration, a state's power is undetermined, but military victory confers a reputation for power or prestige. In the nineteenth century Prussia's two rapid victories, the first over the ancient and redoubtable Austro-Hungarian Empire in 1866, and the second over Europe's strongest power, France, in 1870, left no doubt that the newly unified Prussia had become not only *a* power to be reckoned

161

with in Europe, but *the* power. The United States' defeat of Spain in Cuba in 1898 and Japan's defeat of Russia in 1904-05 similarly conferred great-power status on newcomers to the international stage. World War I confirmed these rankings.

Conversely, a military defeat such as the one suffered in 1940 by France, which had already been bled white during the 1914-18 war, jeopardizes a nation's reputation for power. There may not even have to be a defeat; the mere fact that a great power is unable to win a conflict with a lesser power hurts its prestige. Perhaps the great power should not have indulged in such a conflict in the first place, but, once it has done so, its ability to exercise power effectively is one of the issues at stake. Britain's inept use of force against Egypt during the Suez War in 1956, for example, made it plain to Conservative party leaders that Britain was no longer a first-rank power and that, as a nation-state, its status and influence could become great once more only if it joined Europe in its efforts to become a United States of Europe. A few years after Suez, therefore, Britain, a country that had long regarded a divided Europe as a prerequisite for its own security, applied to join the European Common Market. Just as Britain might have been better off had it not intervened in Egypt, so might the United States have better avoided entanglement in Vietnam. Once the United States was involved, Presidents Lyndon Johnson and Richard Nixon found it difficult to withdraw from the war, largely because of the high priority they gave to the "credibility" of American power.

There are, of course, variations on this theme of victory and defeat. During the 1960s, when all-out war was no longer viewed as a true test of a nation's power, the "space-race" replaced the test of battle. In 1960 President John Kennedy pounded home the message that the United States' poor performance in space during Dwight Eisenhower's years as president meant that Americans were not yet aware of the global political and psychological impact of bipolar competition in space. The first manned Soviet satellite to orbit the earth in April of Kennedy's first year in office convinced him that a second-rate effort was not consistent with his country's role as a world leader and a great power, whose reputation was based to a very large extent on its industrial-technological capabilities. The technology in this new sphere had come to symbolize the power, as well as the way of life, of the United States and the Soviet Union. Kennedy immediately ordered a review of various space projects in which the United States could surpass the Soviet Union.[2] The most promising was the landing of a man on the moon, and in May the president announced that this objective would be achieved before the end of the decade. Indeed, in July 1969 the first men stood on, the moon, and, although they talked of having come on behalf of all mankind, their shoulder patches read *U.S.A.*

An image of international power may also change as a result of policy decisions taken primarily for internal reasons. Joseph Stalin's massive purge of the Soviet general staff in the late 1930s was thought by Western observers to have left the Soviet military weak to the point of ineffectiveness, with the result that Soviet influence on the world scene plummeted. France then estimated Poland to be stronger than the Soviet Union, and later, when France and Britain were already at war with Germany, they almost took on the Soviet Union when they decided to help Finland in its courageous defense against a Red Army attack.

Three points are very important. The first, generally shared by many citizens and policy makers, is that *power is identified with military capacity* regardless of whether the estimate is based on power overtly applied, peacefully demonstrated (as in parades, maneuvers, and space shots), or held in check during bargaining. When books are written on power, they bear titles such as *The War Potential of Nations.*[3] Because war has been the *ultima ratio* of power in interstate politics, the emphasis on military strength is hardly surprising. The Prussian general Carl von Clausewitz's classic definition of war is the continuation of political relations by other means; turning this phrase around, peace may be called the continuation of the last war by other means. Earlier we suggested that the state system, unlike most modern domestic political systems in the West, is characterized by a condition of potential warfare. Each state's continuing concern with its military power has thus been very understandable. And it is military power that today, because of its enormous destructive ability, we most need to control and manage. To be sure, there are other ways of exercising power, especially by economic means. But coercion and the use of violence to achieve state ends in a system of politics without government has long substituted for governmental allocation of values.

The second point is that *power is what people think it is.* A distinction must thus be drawn between subjective (perceived) power and objective (actual) power. For example, the United States retired into isolationism after World War I. It did not participate actively in the state system, and its power was by and large discounted by other states. It pursued no political objectives outside the Western Hemisphere; it wished only to be left alone. It ranked behind France, Britain, Germany, the Soviet Union, and Japan in the great-power hierarchy, and yet was, objectively, the world's premier power, far stronger than Germany or its Western adversaries.

The third point is that *a reputation for power will confer power,* whether others' estimates of a nation's power are correct or not. If a nation or its leadership has prestige, it is less likely to be challenged; if its prestige is declining, challenges are likely, not only from powers of equal strength but also from less powerful states. These challengers will think that they can defy that nation's policies with impunity. After Britain's appeasement of Adolf Hitler at Munich in 1938 over the issue of the Sudetenland, Benito Mussolini said: "These men [the British leaders] are not made of the same stuff as Francis Drake and the other magnificent adventurers who created the Empire. They are after all the tired sons of a long line of rich men."[4] Shortly afterward, Hitler seized the rest of Czechoslovakia and began to look hungrily at Poland.

Having challenged Britain repeatedly without response, except for verbal protest, Hitler thought that it was safe to try again, that the British would back down as usual. Finally, the British government stood firm, and the result was World War II.

Twenty-three years later, in 1962, Soviet missile installations in Cuba precipitated the most dangerous crisis of the cold war. President Kennedy demanded their removal, believing that what was at stake was the United States' reputation for power. The Soviets apparently thought little of it; otherwise, how could they have believed that they could place strategic weapons in the United States' historic sphere of influence and so close to its shores? They had to be disabused of this notion before they mounted an even more dangerous challenge to American interests, which would have precipitated a nuclear war. For a great power to be viewed as weak by its adversaries, its allies, or even nonaligned countries is to court disaster. The United States learned this lesson dramatically after its prestige severely declined in Vietnam; not only the Soviet Union but also smaller countries felt that they could challenge the United States with impunity.

Whether leaders know that their nation's reputation is at stake is not always clear. They cannot know precisely the thinking of their adversaries, who may publicly deny holding low estimates of their prestige, even when such estimates actually motivate them. This key issue is thus a matter of judgment and often of controversy among policy makers. It poses a major problem because leaders must always be aware of the impact of their policies on other states. How other states perceive these policies is critical to making the policies. The leaders may come up with the best possible policy, but if it is not correctly perceived in the affected states, it may fail.

POWER: GETTING ONE'S WAY

Power may often be identified with military power and may exist only within the mind. But what is power? Probably the most common definition is the capacity to influence the behavior of other states in accordance with one's own objectives. Implicit in this definition is the understanding that, without the exercise of power, the other states will not accede to demands made upon them. Power, then, is several things. It is something that a state has; the exact quantity depends on measurement of each of the various components of power (as we shall see later in this chapter). It is also a means to achieve the state's various ends, or goals. Finally, and most important, it is a reciprocal relationship among two or more states. A influences B, and B influences A, but the amount of influence that each exerts is not necessarily the same: A's ability to influence B may be much greater than the reverse. Power relationships, though reciprocal, are not necessarily symmetrical.

It has been argued that power relations exist when four factors are present.[5]

First, *there must be a conflict of values or interests.* If A and B agree on objectives, B consents freely to A's demands or proposed course of action. Power is not used. One state may be stronger than the other, but, as there is agreement on what to do, power remains latent. Even when there are relatively small differences among states, as perceived by the parties to a dispute, persuasion is very likely all that is necessary to resolve the differences. There is an appeal to common interests, principles, and values; there may be attempts to introduce facts new to one party or interpretations of the situation that have not yet been considered; and the consequences of different courses of action may be pointed out.

Second, for a power relationship to exist, *B must comply, however unwillingly, with A's demands.* Compliance is necessary because, though the two may be involved in a conflict of interest, B may simply stand its ground and not give in. Then A must either give up its demands or resort to force.

Third, in a power relationship *one of the parties invokes sanctions that the other regards as likely to inflict "severe deprivations" or pain upon itself.* The cost of noncompliance for B must be greater than the cost of compliance. The threatened state B must believe that the adversary A's threat of sanctions is credible and not a bluff.

This emphasis on sanctions is not meant to imply neglect of *rewards* that A may offer B to promote resolution of their differences. When these differences are too large to be settled by persuasion but not of such magnitude that sanctions must be invoked, granting rewards may be the most effective way to exercise power. A reward might take the form of economic aid, lowered tariff barriers, or the sale of high-technology products. But a conflict involving deep disagreement may lead one party to invoke sanctions against the other. There are a wide variety of ways to punish or coerce an adversary: reduce imports, impose embargoes, raise prices, withhold arms (in peace or war), break off diplomatic relations, threaten the use of force, mobilize military forces. U.S.-Soviet relations during much of the cold war involved little economic intercourse, but they did involve the very visible presence of the military and frequent threats of its deployment.

Fourth, when differences between states are extreme, *force is most likely to be used.* If B complies when A exercises coercion, the use of force is, of course, unnecessary; A resorts to force only if B does not comply with A's demands. When A does resort to force, it admits failure to attain its objectives by threats of punishment. Using force does not, however, guarantee the attainment of these objectives. American intervention in Vietnam did not prevent the loss of South Vietnam. *Thus, the use of force may at times result in loss of one's reputation for power* (see Chapter 10). If the sanctions, once applied, do not inflict as severe a deprivation as A's threat had implied, B's future compliance with A's demands is even less likely. Other states also may not comply with A's demands until, at some point, A insists on compliance and is willing to enforce its demands to restore its prestige.

The different degrees of disagreement that lead states to use persuasion, rewards, coercion, and force depend on the parties involved, their demands, their disinclination to comply, and their perceptions of the stakes involved. Furthermore, these methods of exercising influence may in practice be mixed. If persuasion cannot quite resolve differences, rewards may be held out. Rewards may be enticing, but hints of threats for noncompliance may be useful. A threat may well be more effective if the belief is strong that force will be used unless agreement can be reached. Combinations of carrots *and* sticks may be more useful in resolving differences than either carrots *or* sticks. Carrying a "big stick" but "speaking softly" may be more fruitful than swinging the stick. Finally, coercion and force are more likely to be used against adversaries than against friendly states, but rewards may also accompany such threats if the adversary complies with the demands.

THE MEANS-END PROBLEM

Whatever a nation's objectives, or mix of objectives, and however it chooses to pursue them, it must have the power to achieve what it has set out to accomplish. The ideal foreign policy—one that balances the ends and means—is rare. The more likely situation facing a state is one in which its commitments exceed its power. Thus, it must decide on one of two courses: to cut its commitments or to mobilize more power. The U.S. involvement in global politics after World War II came precisely in such circumstances. When its power collapsed after the war, Britain cut its commitments, giving India independence and basically withdrawing from "East of Suez." West of Suez, Britain declared that it could no longer support Greece and Turkey, both at the time being pressured by the Soviet Union. The United States, which had demobilized after the war, then committed itself to defend Greece and Turkey with economic aid, which was followed by the Marshall Plan, a large-scale economic program for the recovery of Western Europe. The United States also began to rebuild its military strength and committed itself to the defense of Western Europe. Once Britain could no longer contain Russian power, the United States remobilized its power for that task.

The ends-means gap did not really present a problem for the United States until the late 1960s, early 1970s. With the world's strongest economy, the question was not whether the United States could mobilize sufficient power to meet its expanding commitments, first in Europe, then Asia, and finally in the Middle East. The question was whether it had so much power that it was making commitments indiscriminately rather than carefully distinguishing between vital and secondary interests. The war in Vietnam is generally considered an example of what happens if that distinction is not made. A frequently made recommendation after American forces were withdrawn from Vietnam in 1973 was for the United States to reduce its obligations. It could not be the "world's policeman." In fact, after the Soviet invasion of

Afghanistan in 1979, U.S. commitments, instead of shrinking, were extended to the Persian Gulf and then to Central America. Simultaneously, the American economy was weakened by its "deindustrialization" and enormous budget deficits. The nation had to make painful choices, as noted before, between guns and butter. In George Kennan's words:

> A country that has a budgetary deficit and an adverse trade balance both so fantastically high that it is rapidly changing from a major creditor to a major debtor on the world's exchanges, a country whose internal indebtedness has been permitted to double in less than six years, a country that has permitted its military expenditures to grow so badly out of relationship to the other needs of the economy . . . is simply not in a position to make the most effective use of its own resources on the international scene, because they are so largely out of control.[6]

The Soviet economy, although in far worse shape, could focus on arms production because the political system did not have to pay too much attention to the Russian people's desire for improved living conditions. Nevertheless, during the 1950s and 1960s the Soviet Union did not have the means to sustain overseas commitments and suffered setbacks when it made them. Its worst defeat came in 1962 in Cuba, where it tried to install missiles that could hit targets in the United States. When Washington demanded that the missiles be withdrawn, Moscow complied. The American navy was too powerful and the Soviet navy too small to challenge it in the Caribbean. Moreover, the Soviets, with just a few missiles, could not afford risking a confrontation that might result in a military clash with America's far larger nuclear forces.

The Soviet Union was humiliated on this occasion and resolved never to be humiliated again; it therefore embarked on a sustained program of military growth and modernization, building a large blue-sea navy, an airlift capability, and a missile force larger than that of the United States. Within a decade and a half the Soviets had acquired the means to support self-proclaimed Marxist forces or governments in sub-Sahara Africa and help them win or consolidate power. The means had been brought into balance with the ends. The big question was whether the Soviets, like the Americans, would increase their commitments as their military means grew. Traditionally a Eurasian power that expanded around its frontiers, the Soviet Union has become, for the first time in its long history, a global power like the United States. Indeed, the Soviet Union is actively improving that global military reach with the building of three large aircraft carriers. Soviet military writers no longer depict their country as capable only of defending the homeland and neighboring peoples' democracies in Eastern Europe, but also of developing forces able to engage the United States anywhere in the world.

There is, of course, a third course states can pursue when they face a commitments/power gap and that is to live with it. This could be dangerous if a state is challenged and the gap considerable. But it need not be so. After all, short of an all-out war, a state may not be able to fulfill all of its obligations, but it may possess quite enough power to respond to one or two challenges at a time. President Ronald Reagan's secretary of defense, Caspar Weinberger, admitted, "We can never afford to buy the capabilities sufficient to meet all of our commitments with 100 percent confidence." But, he also said, "The critical questions are: What risk are we prepared to accept in our plans for meeting particular contingencies? How much are we prepared to pay to reduce this risk?" These questions confront most states because means and ends are rarely in perfect balance. In turn, this raises the key question of how to calculate power.

CALCULATING POWER

Most readers have an idea of the principal components of power. They probably would include the following: geography, population, natural resources, economic capacity, military strength, political system and leadership, and national morale. Let us make several preliminary points before taking a brief look at each of these elements separately. First, any calculation of a nation's power and the power balance must include a mix of *tangible components* such as population, uniformed personnel, and numbers of tanks and missiles; and *intangible components* such as morale, efficiency and effectiveness of political systems, and quality of political leadership. The intangible components do not lend themselves to accurate calculations; they are matters of judgment.

Second, when doing such calculations, we must always remain aware of the distinction between *potential power* and *actual capability*—that is, power that has been mobilized. Except for periods of total war, states do not completely transform their economies into war economies or maximize their military strength. There is always a gap between potential and actual power.

Third, when we look at each component of power individually, we see that accurate assessment of even the tangible elements is not at all easy. Population figures for different states, for example, can be readily compared, and the rule of thumb "the bigger, the better" tends to be true for the more powerful states such as the United States and the Soviet Union. The trouble is that sometimes a large population may be a liability, rather than an asset. For China and India, the high birth rates that have led to anticipated populations of 1.5 billion and 1 billion respectively by the turn of the twenty-first century make modernization and economic development difficult. Progress is eaten up by the need to feed, clothe, and educate millions of new people. The problem of growing population in the less-developed countries (LDCs), many of which are already overpopulated, is likely to place major stress on the international system in the future.

For all countries, other factors also must be taken into account: age distribution, educational and skill patterns, and ethnic composition, for example. Any one of these factors can complicate the calculation of a single component. For countries deeply divided by various nationalities, religions, and races, we would surely have to "subtract" from the calculation, for in crisis or war such states may demonstrate low morale or even disintegrate. The LDCs are particularly subject to political fragmentation because of such problems.

Fourth, calculations of any single component of power make sense only when linked with those of other components. Large populations can ensure great-power status only when there is also an industrialized economy; it is the marriage of these two elements that constitutes power. The power rating is certain to be low in a nation characterized by poverty, a largely agrarian and unskilled population, a high birth rate, and great difficulties in urbanizing and industrializing.

Finally, the balance is dynamic, not static. Various components are always changing, and therefore the balance needs frequent recalculation. This makes it particularly difficult to project into the future. Policy makers are obviously concerned about the current balance, but they must also look at the balance five, ten years in the future to be prepared for new relationships with other states, especially adversaries.

Geography

The location and size of a nation are clearly very important. The United States and Britain have long been protected from invasions by bodies of water too wide for their enemies to cross easily. The United States was even able to isolate itself from the international political system for more than a century. Similarly, states such as Italy and Spain have been well protected by high mountain ranges—the Alps and the Pyrenees. Indeed, little of Western Europe's modern culture seems to have crossed the Pyrenees until late in the twentieth century! But little Belgium, not well protected and lying between great powers, was not so fortunate during the two world wars. Switzerland, by contrast, also lying between great powers but very well protected, has remained untouched. The countries on the axis from France to the Soviet Union all lie on a plain. The Rhine, separating Germany and France, was of little help in halting repeated German invasions of France. Russia has no natural protection at all and has been repeatedly invaded from the West. Russia also borders on Western Europe, the Middle East, and northern Asia; and the same lack of barriers that permits invasions also permits Russian expansion.

Note the correlation between the world's leading democracies and geographic protection: the United States, Britain, and the northern Scandinavian countries lie off the axis of repeated invasions. The states lying on the axis— France, Prussia/Germany, and Russia/Soviet Union—know war well, and not surprisingly they have developed large bureaucracies and standing armies to guard themselves. For these countries, notions of individual freedom, the rights of opposition, and criticism, in such circumstances, were luxuries that were subordinated to security and physical survival. Highly centralized governments and authoritarian politics have become the pattern. Even in France, the westernmost of these states, bounded by both the Atlantic Ocean and the Mediterranean Sea, the home of nationalism and democracy since the revolution of 1789, democracy continued to face challenges from the authoritarian tradition until World War II. But democracy was foreign to Prussia and Germany (Prussia unified Germany in 1870) until after World War II, when it was imposed upon West Germany by its conquerors; it was also foreign to czarist and Soviet Russia. And, although there is no suggestion that geography is the primary reason these countries have long been authoritarian, geography surely has been a major contributing factor. The farther east one goes in Europe, the more authoritarian it becomes; the farther west, the more democratic.

The United States, the most western power of all, had plenty of time to nurture its democratic roots and no need for large military forces. When drawn into Europe's wars in the twentieth century, each time the United States was unprepared. But, because it was far from the battlefields, it paid no penalty for this lack of readiness; it could mobilize its power after war had been declared. Not until the development of the long-range bomber and missile did the United States even become vulnerable to a direct attack. The disadvantage of this geographic location and the century-long protection it afforded was that, to come to grips with its enemies, the United States has had to project its power over vast distances. Not surprisingly, America's current allies and friends often get the jitters because, knowing they are far from the United States, they fear the possibility of being either insufficiently protected or abandoned in the future. President Reagan's plans for a strategic defense of the United States, which aims to guard against a missile attack, has aroused such concern in Western Europe. Why would the United States still need allies when it can once more protect itself without allies?

Had the United States been placed next to other great powers, isolationism would have been impossible. Instead, like Russia (against France and Germany) and China (against Japan), the United States would have been forced to make shrewd use of its vast interior space to neutralize an attack. The enemy would be drawn in, exhausting itself in the attempt to conquer such a vast territory, maintain long supply lines, and control a large and hostile population. (In Russia, of course, there was a long and icy winter as well.)

Today, location and size are no longer of such benefit in an all-out war because modern weapons can fly far and fast and are amazingly accurate over long ranges. More broadly, technology has reduced the significance of geography. For example, until recently only a few supply lines ran from European Russia to Central Asia and the Far East, and this hampered the application of Soviet power in Asia. Since the Sino-Soviet schism, transportation and communications have been greatly improved. Still, the 4,150-mile-long frontier with China obviously gives even the powerful Soviet Union a sense of insecurity, a feeling intensified by the improved relations between China and the United States. Should a war erupt between the Soviet Union and China, geography would certainly make it extremely difficult, if not impossible, for the Red Army to occupy, pacify, and govern a country as vast as China, with a population of more than 1 billion. These considerations are probably among the factors preventing a large-scale Soviet invasion.

Geography certainly continues to affect the sense of insecurity of small states, perhaps more so because they possess little room to maneuver in wartime. Negotiations in the Middle East since 1973 have foundered continually on the issue of the right of the Palestinians to a state of their own on the West Bank. Apart from any alleged biblical claims to that land and refusal to negotiate with the Palestine Liberation Organization (PLO), Israel wanted to keep control of the West Bank because otherwise Arab guns could fire into Israel. A long, narrow state, Israel's great insecurity is closely tied to geography, although even if Israel annexed the West Bank, it still could easily be hit by modern, medium-range missiles from Jordan, Syria, or even farther away. Objectively, Israel would be no more secure, but subjectively—in its feelings of security—it apparently would be. To ensure this, Israel in 1982 invaded Lebanon. It was determined to drive the PLO out of southern Lebanon—indeed, to destroy the PLO—believing that this would end the demands for a Palestinian state on the West Bank. Although Israel succeeded in driving the PLO out of Lebanon, at least temporarily, the result was a firmer Syrian hold on that country, the end of the Christian pro-Western and pro-Israeli influence, and the transformation of much of the southern Lebanese Shi'ite Muslims' pro-Israeli feelings into anti-Israeli ones. The war was hardly a success in terms of enhancing Israel's sense of security.

Population

Population figures are good initial indicators of a nation's power ranking and of possible changes in its ranking. In Table 7-1 we can immediately see how Prussia's unification of Germany in 1870 changed the map of Europe and finally brought the United States out of its isolation. Except for Russia in the east, the Continent's traditional great powers, Austria-Hungary and France, were displaced by Germany. France, which had the largest population (36 million) in 1850 was by 1910 just ahead of Italy, the least populous country in Europe. Germany's top ranking was underscored by its large-scale industrialization. Britain had become the world's greatest power in the nineteenth century. Steel production was usually the major indicator of industrial strength because of its association with the production of modern arms. In the first decade of the twentieth century Germany overtook Britain in steel production (and, by using much of that steel to build a sizable navy, obviously challenged the British navy and drove England into closer relations with France and Russia).

Only the United States was a match for Germany. With a population of 76 million in 1900 and 92 million in 1910 and with steel production more than twice that of Germany, the United States clearly would be compelled eventu-

Table 7-1 Population of Major European Powers, 1870-1910
(in millions)

Year	Austria-Hungary	France	Germany	Britain	Italy	Russia
1870	36	36	40	31	27	82
1890	41	38	49	38	30	110
1900	45	39	56	41	32	133
1910	50	39	64	45	35	163
1914	52	39	65	45	37	171

SOURCE: Adapted from *A Study of War*, I, 670-671, by Quincy Wright, by permission of The University of Chicago Press, copyright 1942 by The University of Chicago Press; and A. J. P. Taylor, *The Struggle for Mastery in Europe* (London: Oxford University Press, 1954), xxv.

ally to abandon its isolationism. In the words of A. J. P. Taylor: "By 1914 she was not merely an economic Power on the European level; she was a rival continent. Her coal production equalled that of Great Britain and Germany put together; her iron and steel production surpassed that of all Europe. This was the writing on the wall: economically Europe no longer had a monopoly—she was not even the centre of the world."[7] In Europe, however, Germany was becoming too powerful for its neighbors. It was acquiring the capability to become the dominant power and a threat to the independence of the other European great powers. World War I and the United States' participation in it were predictable from population and industrial figures alone. Also clear was the fact that no lasting peace in Europe was feasible even after Germany's defeat without continued American political involvement. After all, Germany was not broken up into separate states as the French had wanted. Unified Germany remained potentially Europe's most powerful state, despite some restriction on its armed forces. The United States' return to isolationism was certainly one factor responsible for World War II, which again required American intervention.

The example of Russia, France's ally in 1914, reveals the deceptiveness of population figures by themselves. It had a population two and a half times that of Germany, but that counted for little as czarist society was beginning to crumble. The giant Russia, as it was thought of, had been defeated by that "small upstart" Japan just a few years earlier, in 1904-05. This defeat was followed by widespread peasant revolts, which revealed inner social rot. The largest population in Europe therefore did not compensate for Russia's basic weakness: not only was its industry small—about the size of that of Austria-Hungary—but also much of the population was disenchanted with the regime. The peasantry (the bulk of Russia's population), the small working class, and the industrial middle class wished to be rid of the czar. Morale—popular support for a government—was low; Russia in 1914 already stood on the brink of revolution.

Even more revealing was the situation of Germany's ally Austria-Hungary, with a population larger than that of either France or Britain. Composed of a multitude of feuding nationalities who were beginning to demand self-determination, Austria-Hungary was determined to crush Serbia, a Slav state that was fanning the flames of nationalism. And so, on the brink of dissolution, Vienna decided that it could avoid death only by risking suicide in a war to eliminate Serbia. Because Russia supported Serbia, Germany supported Austria, and France backed Russia, the result of Austria-Hungary's ethnic composition was World War I.

The coming of World War I illustrates the value of changing population figures, as well as the limitations of looking only at such figures. Nonetheless, it remains true that a large population in a developed nation clearly confers an advantage. There are several reasons for this. First, it translates into a big army, especially if the age distribution is such that the country has a sizable percentage of youth.

Second, it means that the industries that develop to serve so many consumers tend to be large-scale and the country is likely to be very productive. This translates into large numbers of guns, as well as butter. In Sherman Kent's words, such a nation has a lot of fat in the economy, a lot of slack and flexibility. *Fat* refers to the economy's great productivity and wealth, so that a significant amount of money can be used for weapons without depriving the civilian population of consumer goods. *Slack* refers to unused productivity because of factors such as unemployment, the small proportion of women in the labor force, and the forty-hour week. *Flexibility* refers to the ability to turn the economy quickly from the production of peacetime goods to weapons.

In the past the U.S. economy has possessed all of these. In the future the amount of fat may be more sparse. A greater percentage of Americans will be over the age of 65; the increasing amounts of Social Security payments required may well cut into future military budgets. Indeed, the entitlement programs in an era of inflation and high deficit spending have already sharply raised the issue of guns (whose costs are also going up) versus butter as a major political issue. By contrast, a state such as Israel with its small population has never been able to afford both and needs foreign military and economic assistance. Israel cannot fight long wars because its armed forces are recruited from the civilian population; long absence from work therefore puts a strain on the economy. Israel has to fight short wars, and this necessity may be a powerful incentive to preempt when it believes the Arabs are preparing an attack.

Third, a large economy with many consumers means that many nations will want access to that nation's economy to sell their products. This circumstance gives that nation leverage.

Fourth, it also means that the nation can use its wealth as an instrument of foreign policy—foreign aid, for example. Because a large population with many scientists and engineers is also likely to produce high technology, this too can be employed to advance the nation's purposes internationally.

Table 7-2 Countries with Populations over
50 Million, 1985 (in millions)

Country	Population
China	1,055
India	759
Soviet Union	276
United States	240
Indonesia	161
Brazil	136
Japan	122
Bangladesh	102
Pakistan	95
Nigeria	94
Mexico	79
Germany (West)	61
Vietnam	60
Italy	57
Britain	56
France	55

SOURCE: Figures taken from the International Institute for
Strategic Studies, *The Military Balance 1985-1986* (Letchworth,
England: The Garden City Press, 1985).

Few nations have populations over 50 million, and many of these—eight,
including China—are already classified among the major actors or potential
great powers of the future. Indeed, China's population already exceeds 1
billion; by the year 2000 its population may reach 1.5 billion, with India
following at 1 billion (see Table 7-2).

National population forecasts reveal that Europe and the United States will
contain a minority of the world's population (see Figure 7-1). When these
figures are combined with productivity data, the trend toward a *division of the
world* between a minority of states that are rich and a growing majority that
are poor becomes clear. This trend is potentially very dangerous and is one
reason for growing concern about the North-South confrontation. By the year
2000 the population of the West (including the Soviet Union) will constitute
less than 20 percent of the world's population. The LDCs will have more than
80 percent.

Natural Resources

Industrialization married to population gives birth to power, but industrialization cannot continue to produce a nation's goods without natural resources. Britain, Germany, and the United States were able to industrialize

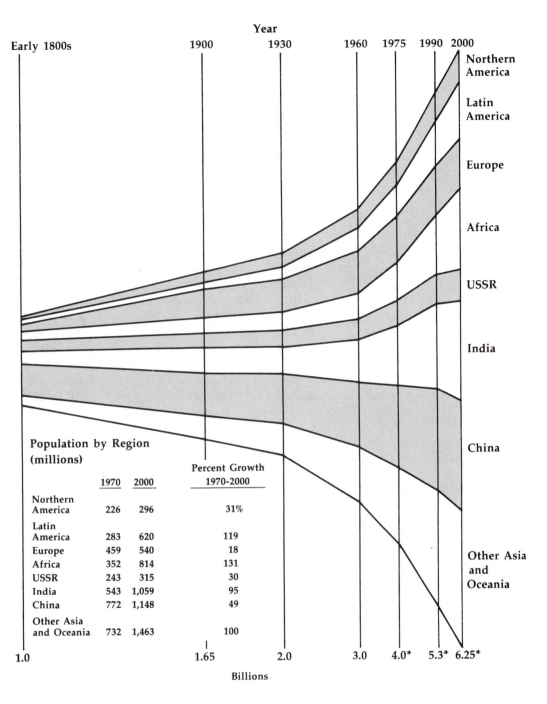

Year

| | Early 1800s | 1900 | 1930 | 1960 | 1975 | 1990 | 2000 |

Northern America
Latin America
Europe
Africa
USSR
India
China
Other Asia and Oceania

Population by Region (millions)

	1970	2000	Percent Growth 1970–2000
Northern America	226	296	31%
Latin America	283	620	119
Europe	459	540	18
Africa	352	814	131
USSR	243	315	30
India	543	1,059	95
China	772	1,148	49
Other Asia and Oceania	732	1,463	100

1.0   1.65   2.0   3.0   4.0* 5.3* 6.25*

Billions

*U.N. medium projection

Figure 7-1 The Population Explosion: Where the People Are Likely to Be in the Year 2000

because of plentiful supplies of coal, the major alternative source of energy for oil in the production of electricity. Coal is safer than nuclear energy, although coal does have environmental effects that make its social costs high. The United States has enormous reserves of coal, far more than Saudi Arabia has of oil. The index of economic development in the earlier stage of industrialization was steel, which was used for everything from railroad tracks to cannons to machinery. Iron and coal were key resources. The Soviet Union overtook the United States in steel production in 1974, about the same time that the number of Soviet missiles exceeded the American total. Was this change symptomatic, like the shift between Britain and Germany seventy years earlier?

After World War II, oil replaced coal, because oil was cheap. One has to wonder whether the oil companies, during the 1970s often accused of jacking up oil prices and earning "obscene" profits, did the West a favor by keeping oil so inexpensive for so long. Had oil remained more costly, especially in the United States, the industrial nations might have kept a better balance between oil and coal and become less vulnerable to the Organization of Petroleum Exporting Countries (OPEC) and its continual price increases from 1973 to the early 1980s. Not only bombers and tanks, but also the whole Western industrial structure and high standard of living have been based on oil. (Would southern cities such as Houston and Atlanta have become great cities and commercial and cultural centers without oil and air conditioning?) The United States, once an oil exporter, now imports about 40 percent of its oil. U.S. allies in the North Atlantic Treaty Organization (NATO) import about 85 percent of their oil (although Britain is becoming self-sufficient thanks to its North Sea reserves), and Japan imports 90 percent of its oil. The Central Intelligence Agency (CIA) several times has estimated that in the future the Soviet Union will begin to import oil. It is fair to say that energy production and consumption for all sources—coal, oil, natural gas, nuclear power, and the sun—are signs of modern and technologically advanced economies. What will replace oil tomorrow as the principal energy source remains unclear.

Table 7-3 shows other imported resources on which the United States is becoming increasingly dependent. Note the higher than 90 percent import level of chrome, cobalt, manganese, and other metals, many of which are used in manufacturing jet engines, computers, machine tools, tanks, and missiles. The availability of oil and these and other resources obviously depends on many factors, including the friendliness or unfriendliness of specific regimes. That is why President Jimmy Carter committed the United States to the defense of the oil sheikdoms on the Persian Gulf after the Soviet invasion of Afghanistan and why President Reagan strengthened this commitment to Saudi Arabia. The Reagan administration was also concerned about the racial situation in South Africa, a country in which fewer than 5 million whites rule about 1 million Asians and more than 17 million blacks in a system of rigid separation called *apartheid*. In this potentially explosive situation the United

Table 7-3 Key Minerals for Which the United States Is More Than 90 Percent Import Dependent (1978)

	Bauxite 93%	Chromium 92%	Cobalt 97%	Columbium 100%	Manganese 98%	Platinum-gr. 91%	Tantalum 97%
Indispensable Minerals or Ores Critical to High Quality in the Production of:							
Basic steel					X		
Stainless, tool, alloy steels		X	X	X	X		X
Basic aluminum	X						
Aluminum alloys	X			X	X		
Nickel-based and cobalt-based superalloys	X	X	X	X	X		X
Items Made Using Above-Mentioned Basic Products:							
Ordnance (tanks, fighters, bombers, missiles)	X	X	X	X	X	X	X
Power generating (turbines, controls, transmission)	X	X	X		X		
Electric motors, equipment (locomotives to mixers)	X		X		X		
All electronics (appliances, computers, phones, TV, navigation, controls, telecommunications	X	X	X	X	X	X	X
Nuclear application	X	X	X	X			X
Jet engines, gas turbines (hot parts)		X	X	X		X	X
Batteries, fuel cells					X	X	
Aerospace (airframes, hulls, rocket engines)	X	X	X	X		X	X
Projectiles, gun barrels, machine parts, crankshafts, axles, gears, machine tools		X	X	X	X		X
Mining, drilling (valve stems and systems, drill bits)		X	X		X		
High-tech medical (cryogenics, heart-lung, scanners)	X	X	X			X	X
Petroleum processing, drilling		X	X	X	X	X	X
Chemical processing		X	X	X	X	X	X
Glass products			X			X	
Pharmaceutical production						X	
Food processing, enrichment		X	X		X	X	
Synfuel production		X	X	X	X	X	X

NOTE: Since effective military technology requires highest possible performance, substitutes are not desirable. However, substitutes for purely commercial and civilian items are possible on a mixed basis—recognizing lower quality and performance would occur.

SOURCE: Uri Ra'anan and Charles M. Perry, *Strategic Minerals and International Security* (McLean, Va.: Pergamon-Brassey's, International Defense Publishers, 1955), 4. Reprinted by permission.

States has tried unsuccessfully to promote gradual, peaceful change and thereby keep a friendly government in power. The reason is obvious. From 1980 to 1983, South Africa supplied the United States with 61 percent of its cobalt, 55 percent of its chromium, 49 percent of its platinum, 44 percent of its vanadium (used as an alloy in making steel and a key component in aircraft bodies and engines), and 39 percent of its manganese. The United States is thus quite dependent on South Africa for some key industrial metals. South Africa, according to the Commerce Department, has more than 80 percent of the world's chromium and platinum, 70 percent of its manganese, and 47 percent of its vanadium.[8] For these reasons, President Reagan opposed economic sanctions against South Africa in 1986.

Western Europe and Japan, America's principal allies, are even more dependent on imported raw materials. Japan, for instance, imports virtually 100 percent of its petroleum, bauxite, wool, and cotton; 95 percent of its wheat; 90 percent of its coal and copper ore; and 70 percent of its timber and grain.

Economic Capacity

A common standard for comparison of national power, probably more reliable than population in this industrial age, is wealth or degree of economic development. Wealth is obviously related to military power, for the richest states presumably can afford to buy the most military power. Indeed, wealth can buy power of all kinds, which remains important for distinguishing the superpowers from the secondary powers. Britain, for example, cannot afford to build a sizable nuclear force or to keep up with the ever-changing state of the art in delivery systems and warheads. It must make a choice between trying to keep up with the leading members of the nuclear club, the United States and the Soviet Union, and developing sufficient conventional capacity to defend its many other interests. Its failure to make this choice, its decision instead to have some of each, meant that in the 1956 Suez War, for instance, it did not have a nuclear force to deter Soviet threats of rocket attacks against London (Washington had to tell Moscow not to try that one) or the conventional capabilities to occupy the Suez Canal and defeat Egyptian forces. The United States and the Soviet Union can mobilize both kinds of forces in sizable quantities, plus other kinds of power, like economic and technical assistance, if they wish to use those means as diplomatic tools. A nation's gross national product (GNP)—the total value of its production and services measured in currency—has thus frequently been used as a relatively accurate and measurable standard for comparing the power of different states.

A glance at Table 7-4 shows three things: the clear-cut distinction between the superpowers and the secondary powers over two decades; the ranking of the principal and secondary actors listed, which are pretty much as most observers would guess without knowing the GNP figures; and the wide gap between the Soviet Union and the United States. Japan is third to the United States. The figures for the LDCs with the largest populations are far lower:

Table 7-4 Ranking of Economic Capacity Among Great Powers (in billions of dollars)

Country	Estimated 1984 GNP
United States	3,619
Soviet Union	1,672-1,920[a] (estimated range)
Japan	1,163 (1983)
Germany (West)	613
France	492
Britain	400
Italy	348
China	309-362[b]

[a] At official exchange rates.

[b] China does not issue official statistics on GNP.

SOURCE: Figures taken from International Institute for Strategic Studies, *The Military Balance, 1985-1986* (Letchworth, England: The Garden City Press, 1985).

India ($189 billion in 1983), Indonesia ($72 billion in 1984), Brazil ($209 billion in 1983), Bangladesh ($12 billion), Pakistan ($31 billion), and Nigeria ($67 billion). For many smaller LDCs, the figures are even lower.

Still the GNP figure is not completely reliable. In the United States at least, it reflects the production not only of steel but also of about nineteen different brands of cat food and billions of hamburgers sold through fast-food chains. The Soviet Union, with a GNP of less than half that of the United States in the mid-1960s, launched a massive arms program; it can compete with the United States in arms and aerospace manufacturing because it devotes less of its wealth to consumer goods. Soviet cats, no doubt, do not eat as well as American cats. Whereas American military spending in the 1970s was about 5 percent of GNP, the lowest percentage since before the Korean War in 1950, Moscow was spending a steady 12 percent to 14 percent of its GNP on arms.[9]

GNP also does not reflect total production and services. The U.S. figure would be even higher if it reflected Mafia activities and the billions of dollars earned in the drug business. The cocaine trade among middle- and upper-income groups alone was estimated to exceed $15 billion a year in 1979,[10] and it has undoubtedly grown. The GNP also does not reflect volunteer work or women's household duties, for which wages are not paid.

Moreover, GNP, however calculated, does not always lend itself to ready comparison. Take, for example, Japan's GNP, which at the end of the 1970s was about two and a half times that of China, forty times that of Indonesia, and almost 70 percent of that of the entire region, comprising fourteen other nations, including China. (China's GNP, however, was approximately twice that of all the thirteen other countries put together, excluding Japan.) This comparison demonstrates how misleading GNP figures can be as measures of power. China possesses nuclear weapons, and, as a highly centralized state, controls the allocation of resources in order to concentrate on whatever objectives it chooses—for example, a nuclear capability at the cost of larger domestic investments. Japan is economically far superior and is likely to enhance its economic lead over China. Japan, however, has no nuclear forces and only a small conventional self-defense force; whatever influence it has is based solely on its economic strength. Indeed, Japan is probably the first major power in history—by all the indexes of population, industry, education, technical skills, and so forth—to attempt to project influence as an industrial power only, rather than as a military power with a self-defined political role.[11] Japan is not so much a nation as a large trading company—or, as some wag has called it, Sony Incorporated. Japan has been called an *economic superpower*, but the oil crisis of 1973 demonstrated that Japan's vaunted economic power was not enough to allow it to face up to Saudi Arabia. Politically and militarily it was only a potentially great power, still searching—and not too hard at that—for a role after years of American tutelage.

GNP reveals little about a nation's unity, the stability of its government, popular morale, military doctrine, and quality of diplomacy, which are relevant to analysis of a nation's power and foreign policy. At best, then, economic productivity—like population and military power—remains a crude indicator of power and a convenient shorthand means of comparison.

Sometimes per capita incomes are used as a standard of wealth. Again, the assumption is that individual income is highest in the most economically advanced nations. The figures for the United States, Western Europe, and Japan are indeed the highest, although the United States—which long enjoyed the highest standard of living in the world—has slipped since the oil crisis below Sweden, Switzerland, and West Germany. Britain has dropped to a level just ahead of Italy, which has the lowest per capita income of the larger European states. In a way, per capita income figures are more accurate indicators than GNP figures. The Soviet GNP may be second to that of the United States, but Soviet per capita income is below that of any major Western country, indicating a much lower standard of living. The United States could, at least until the inflation of the 1970s, afford substantial amounts of guns *and* butter, whereas the Soviet Union could choose only guns. The per capita incomes of the LDCs are the lowest. Actually, these figures can also be misleading on occasion. In the early 1980s Kuwait's per capita income was more than $20,000, about 60 percent higher than that of the United States. This high figure reflects Kuwait's enormous income from oil in the 1970s, but the income is not equally distributed; in fact, this figure hides the real distribution of income more than it reveals it.

Two final points must be emphasized. First, a nation's economic capability is enhanced if it possesses strength in the scientific and technological arenas. American technology is widely sought throughout the world—as are European and Japanese technologies—not only by LDCs but also by the Soviet

Union and China. China is looking to the United States and Japan for economic assistance and to Europe for military hardware. American computer technology is so advanced that it is sought even in Europe. As Robert Gilpin notes: "Whereas, beginning in the latter part of the nineteenth century, control over petroleum resources became essential once naval ships shifted from sail to diesel, so today an independent aerospace and electronics industry, along with the supporting sciences, has become crucial for a nation to enjoy diplomatic and military freedom of action." [12]

Second, the importance of agriculture is often underrated. A country such as Britain, which neglected agriculture while it industrialized, confronted the possibility of starvation during wars in this century. Germany almost succeeded twice in blockading the British Isles during the world wars. Today the LDCs in their eagerness to modernize—by which they mean industrialize—have tended to neglect agriculture, with the devastating results of widespread malnutrition and even starvation for their rapidly growing populations. Although most of the people in LDCs live on the land, agricultural production is inefficient and unscientific. By contrast, the United States, with only 5 percent of its population employed in agriculture, has become the breadbasket for the world. A balance between the agricultural and industrial sectors of the economy is clearly desirable and indeed necessary for economic growth and modernization.

Military Strength

Because international politics resembles a state of potential war, military power has become a recognized standard of measurement. Every new great power in the past proclaimed its appearance by a feat of arms, and the decline of a great power is equally signaled by defeat at arms, or what other states interpret as a defeat.

A nation's military power is usually measured by the number of people in uniform and by the number of different weapons it has. As might be expected, the countries with the largest populations have the largest armed forces, though not necessarily in proportion to their populations. Table 7-5 shows the military strength of the fourteen largest countries and the sizes of their armed forces in 1985. These figures do not include reserves, nor do they tell us much about the combat training, morale, and discipline of these forces. The American army in Europe during the 1970s, for example, was often reported to be suffering from a lack of discipline, widespread drug use, and racial strife. In the mid-1980s, however, with higher educational levels, a volunteer force, and better pay plus improved training, morale is up. Israel, with its population of slightly fewer than 4 million, is obviously not in the same league with the countries listed in Table 7-5. Yet in twenty-four hours it can mobilize 400,000 soldiers to supplement its permanent army of 164,000, and these forces are highly trained and well led, as four victories in four wars have shown. (Reportedly, there have also been several successful air encoun-

Table 7-5 Comparative Military Strength in 1985-1986

Country (in order of population)	Size of armed forces (the nearest ten thousand)
China	3.9 million
India	1.2 million
Soviet Union	5.3 million
United States	2.1 million
Indonesia	278,000
Brazil	276
Japan	243
Bangladesh	91
Pakistan	482
Nigeria	94
Germany (West)	478
Italy	385
Britain	327
France	476

SOURCE: Figures taken from International Institute for Strategic Studies, *The Military Balance, 1985-1986* (Letchworth, England: The Garden City Press, 1985).

ters against Soviet-piloted planes over Egypt; several MiGs were shot down by the well-trained Israeli pilots in the early 1970s.) Switzerland, with slightly more than 8 million people, can mobilize 625,000 troops in forty-eight hours; Swiss reservists train three weeks each summer. Sweden, with roughly the same population, can mobilize 750,000 troops within seventy-two hours. These countries can thus almost overnight raise forces as large as the standing armies of Britain, France, or West Germany!

The heavily populated industrial powers also have the largest nuclear arsenals. The United States and the Soviet Union are, of course, in a class by themselves, for they can wipe each other, as well as any other country, off the face of the earth. It is significant that the first five nuclear states were the five great powers whose status was reflected in permanent UN Security Council membership (the United States, the Soviet Union, Britain, France, and China). India has since joined this nuclear club. Possible future members include Brazil, Pakistan, and Japan; West Germany has forsworn acquisition of nuclear weapons. India too has great-power aspirations, and Brazil is said to share them. Pakistan is fearful of India. Japan could be a great power if it ever decided to play that role again.

The two superpowers are also producers of huge quantities of conventional arms, as are the Western allies. These nations are the world's largest arms suppliers. Furthermore, arms, including nuclear weapons, are becoming constantly more destructive and technologically sophisticated. The adjective *conventional* hardly does them justice. For one thing, they are becoming more accurate and increasing their chance of hitting and destroying the target to more than 50 percent; one result has been that opposing forces use war materiel at an ever-faster clip. A war can last only a few days under these conditions; a steady stream of new supplies is needed to continue hostilities. In such circumstances, a superpower's client state cannot be defeated. If defeat appears likely, the allied superpower must send more arms to avert it. As the Soviet Union poured in arms for the Arabs in the 1973 Yom Kippur War, the United States poured in even more arms for the Israelis, who were badly mauled in the opening phase of the war. Later, when Egypt stood on the verge of defeat, Moscow threatened intervention. Indeed, in Korea and Vietnam the United States did intervene to prevent defeat of its friends and protégés, but U.S. intervention was matched by help from the Soviets and the Chinese. Only countries with no superpower friends can still win wars! "[W]ars between small countries with big friends are likely to be inconclusive and interminable; hence, decisive war in our time has become the privilege of the impotent." [13]

Weapons balances are not easy to calculate. How do we compare an intercontinental ballistic missile (ICBM) with a single warhead to one with multiple independently targeted reentry vehicles (MIRVs) or several warheads; or a missile with a megaton (million-ton) warhead to one with a 200,000-ton warhead but with extreme accuracy? How do we compare bombers having quite different characteristics or compare tanks with antitank guns? It is also difficult to compare divisions of different sizes and compositions. In every war Israel's enemies have had more men, guns, tanks, and fighter planes, but the smaller Israeli forces have consistently outfought their enemies. Better leadership, training, discipline, motivation, and tactics have helped to beat numerically superior forces. In 1940 the stunning German defeat of France was accomplished, not by a much larger German army, as has usually been thought, but by forces of about the same size as those of the Allies. The Germans, with 134 divisions, beat 135 French, British, Belgian, and Dutch divisions; the numbers of tanks on each side were about the same. The German army won because of its better leadership, its mobility, and its unique tactical combination of tanks and fighter planes (the German air force was superior).

Moreover, what is really important is that the soldiers and their political superiors know what kind of war they are getting involved in. "No one starts a war—or rather, no one in his senses ought to do so—without first being clear in his mind what he intends to achieve by that war and how he intends to conduct it." [14] This common sense advice from Clausewitz is too often ignored. In the 1960s a proud American army of half a million, provided with all the latest equipment that American technology could invent, was unable to defeat the Viet Cong and the North Vietnamese army. American military leaders thought that they were fighting a miniature World War II and used essentially orthodox military tactics. But the North Vietnamese military leaders were fighting an unorthodox war.

The Political System and Leadership

It is one thing for nations to "have" power. But how is that power used and for what purposes? These issues must be decided by the political system. What role does the nation decide to play in the world? What are its objectives and the priorities among them? Can its leaders make decisions with reasonable speed, gain popular approval for their policies, and then carry them out with reasonable effectiveness? Are their policies appropriate to the circumstances? What methods are used to achieve the nation's various aims, and are they compatible with its values? Is overall foreign policy steady, or does it change from one administration to the next? Are governments stable, or do they frequently fall, to be replaced by new ones (as in Italy and in France before Charles de Gaulle established the Fifth Republic)?

These questions can be asked about any political system, and we shall not even attempt to deal with all of them here. Often the issue of the effectiveness of different types of governments in dealing with the outside world is presented as an issue between dictatorship, authoritarianism, or totalitarianism, on one hand, and democracy, on the other. Frequently the superior effectiveness of dictatorship is assumed. The reasons are obvious: first, decisions can be taken relatively quickly; second, there are no leaks or attempts to head off or dilute that policy while it is being formulated; and third, once the decision has been taken by the top officials, it can be executed immediately. There are no independent parliaments, parties, or interest groups and no free press or organized public opinion to question, criticize, or oppose it. On the other hand, making foreign policy in a democracy is like running an obstacle course without any certainty of reaching the end. The policy process is usually slow, and the result usually embodies a compromise among many conflicting points of view, which may weaken its effectiveness in alleviating the problem at which it is aimed. And, given ultimate dependence on public opinion and support, a democratic foreign policy may—as George Kennan has pointed out—be either too little or too much for the issues the nation confronts.

But are totalitarian governments in fact more effective in making policy on issues of war and peace? Not necessarily. Neither Hitler nor Mussolini nor the Japanese militarists who were responsible for World War II succeeded; their regimes were all defeated. This point raises a fundamental doubt about the wisdom of their policies. They started a war they could not win. Miscalculation, admittedly, is not a vice peculiar to undemocratic regimes; democratic governments miscalculate as well, but perhaps in systems in which policy is debated and criticism must be answered, the substance of policy may more often be wiser and more balanced. Dictatorships may have the advantage of being able to make more rapid decisions and to seize the initiative, but this freedom is no guarantee that they will give sufficient consideration to their moves. Democracies appear to be a bit slow because often so many decision makers are involved, and all interested parties have the right to be heard; it takes time to win legislative and public approval. Undemocratic states can act more quickly because relatively few policy makers are involved, and they need no one's approval except their own.

Actually, the dichotomy between democracy and totalitarianism on such issues is probably exaggerated. Obviously, both types of governments at times have acted successfully, at other times with folly. Even undemocratic regimes, unrestrained by consensus politics, can act slowly and hesitantly, and democratic governments on occasion can act speedily with the full support of public opinion. Undemocratic regimes can usually move more decisively and exploit unexpected opportunities more freely than can democracies. A sudden switch of policy—as when in 1939 the Soviets shifted overnight from alliance with France against Nazi Germany to alliance with Germany against France—is probably impossible for a democracy. Yet the Truman Doctrine in support of Greece and Turkey, as well as the Marshall Plan for the economic recovery of Europe, took only fifteen weeks to decide in 1946-47. The decision to demand the withdrawal of Soviet missiles from Cuba in 1962 took less than a week; the entire crisis lasted only thirteen days.

Whatever the differences in effectiveness between democracies and totalitarian regimes, there are also differences among democratic governments. After 1945, as the United States became a world power, American political scientists worried that the constitutional separation of powers would make it very difficult to conduct a coherent, responsible, and steady foreign policy. Quarrels between the president and Congress, lack of party loyalty, and the influence of pressure groups exploiting this political fragmentation were expected to result in a paralysis of policy or at best slow decision making, a change of policies with every administration, and constant pressure reflecting electioneering and the disproportionate influence of all types of interests seeking to impose their narrow demands. The British parliamentary system, with its unity of executive and legislative branch and its strong party discipline, appeared more likely to meet the requirements of the cold war. But the structure of the U.S. government could not be transformed. Friction between president and Congress has frequently occurred, especially in the years since the Vietnam War. Often the United States has spoken to the world with (at least) two voices. Executive policies have been weakened, undermined, or rejected by Congress, especially the Senate, and interest group pressures, especially from ethnic groups (Jewish, Greek, black, and so on), have been effective in constraining the president's freedom in negotiations and the conduct of foreign policy. Conflicts over priorities (for example, human rights versus arms control, détente with the Soviet Union versus opposition to the Soviets in Africa) have often remained unresolved because administrations could not make up their minds exactly what to do. Whether the conduct of U.S. foreign policy, however, would have been more effective under a parliamentary system is unclear. Britain's record in postwar foreign policy has hardly been outstanding; it has been characterized by indecision, procrastination, and mistaken choices (such as its slowness to join the European community and its maintenance of an "independent" nuclear force at the expense of conventional forces).[15]

By contrast, the Soviet Union built unprecedented military power and attained global status. But by the 1980s, its policies had driven virtually all the world's great powers together—the United States, Europe, China, Japan—in an anti-Soviet alliance. Soviet industry has lagged technologically, and its agriculture remains troublesome. After seven decades of communism, the Soviets' principal achievement has been the relatively efficient and massive production of arms. The proletariat and peasantry in whose name the revolution had been made remain without political or civil rights or the higher standard of living they have been promised for so long.

It may appear that the differences in decision making, continuity of policy, and flexibility between totalitarian and democratic regimes, as well as among the latter, are not very great. Furthermore, the wisdom of policy or lack of it can surely be attributed as much to the intelligence, ability, and drive of specific national leaders as to governmental structures and processes. We need only mention the names of some twentieth-century leaders whose special qualities have shaped history: V. I. Lenin, Joseph Stalin, Adolf Hitler, Woodrow Wilson, Franklin D. Roosevelt, Winston Churchill, and Charles de Gaulle. Others, perhaps not quite of the same stature, are Harry Truman and John F. Kennedy, who did not have sufficient time to demonstrate great leadership. These men had impact because they could articulate their nations' purposes, make significant domestic and foreign policy decisions—sometimes drastically changing their nations' directions—pursue their goals with vigor and flair, mobilize support for their courses of action at home, and even inspire their peoples to sacrifice and discipline. Some of these men reshaped history. Can we compare the current leaders of the Soviet Union with Lenin or even Stalin? How can we compare contemporary leaders in the West to the giants of yesteryear such as Roosevelt, Churchill, and de Gaulle? Only one thing is clear: all nations, democratic and otherwise, require leadership.

Still, the nature of the political system must be kept in perspective, regardless of who its leaders are at the moment. We noted earlier that, at the end of the Napoleonic Wars, France was not heavily punished, despite twenty-five years of destruction all over Europe. Instead, France was welcomed back as a great European power and expected to play a role in preserving this system. This surprising lack of vengeance meant that France accepted the system and its responsibility to help maintain it. At the end of World War I, the attitude toward Germany was quite different. After four years of enormous bloodletting and destruction, the Allies were in a vengeful mood. They tried to put Kaiser Wilhelm and some military leaders on trial for war crimes and imposed on Germany punitive measures such as astronomical reparations and limits to the size and character of German armed forces. It is easy to understand this mood and the hatred of the Germans, with their love of militarism and aggressive attitude. The desire to make them pay for the devastation they had caused seemed natural, and it was supposed to "teach them a lesson."

Unlike the earlier Napoleonic Wars, World War I was fought among states in which the people played active roles; instead of being passive subjects, they were citizens of nations. The length of the war and the endless killing aroused intense passions of patriotism and desires to punish the enemy. The war became a crusade against evil. These moods were reflected in the Versailles peace treaty. Germany was not to be accepted back into the European state system; it was not to be allowed to become a menace to its neighbors again as it had in 1862, 1866, 1870, and 1914.

The result, even before the rise of Hitler, was that Germany wanted to overthrow the Versailles settlement. Hitler was able to mobilize German nationalism to help him gain power by arousing German pride and patriotism against the treaty and for his regime. Had France and Britain not been democracies, their leaders might have been able—as after the Napoleonic Wars—to draw up a peace treaty less spiteful, less insulting, and less harmful to the Germans; they might have been able to arrange a settlement acceptable to all parties, but which allowed Germany to take its place in the European system again. Perhaps another war could then have been avoided because Germany would have been a member of the system with a vested interest in its preservation, instead of an outcast seeking its destruction. But the days of monarchical rule were over. The age of democracy—and punitive crusades—had dawned.

A more contemporary example can be cited in the Middle East, and here perhaps all we can do is ask questions. Would President Anwar Sadat, surely a leader in his own right, have been able to hold out the hand of peace and accept the legitimacy of Israel's existence had Egypt been a democracy? Despite popular yearnings for peace, would there not have been opposition party leaders, possibly in Sadat's own party, newspapers, and segments of Egyptian society that would have opposed his moves, perhaps successfully? If Israel, on the other hand, were an authoritarian state, would it not be easier for an Israeli leader to make greater concessions on the West Bank and Gaza Strip in order to resolve the Palestinian problem, which is an important element in a comprehensive peace for that area? Quite apart from Israel's genuine fears of a Palestinian state governed by the PLO, how can a government, which is composed of a coalition of two equally strong parties, give up the West Bank, when one party deeply believes that the West Bank rightfully belongs to Israel by biblical inheritance and that Jews should be settled there? How can they work out security arrangements that would enable Israel and a Palestinian state to live without constant fear of each other? These questions are not meant to suggest that democracies are obstacles to peace—probably because of their nature, they find it harder to go to war than do undemocratic states—but only to suggest that differences in political regimes do matter. Clearly, some institutional arrangements are more effective than others in permitting policy making and execution.

National Morale

National morale—also often called *national will*—can perhaps best be defined as popular dedication to the nation and support for its policies, even when that support involves sacrifice. Examples abound, and most of them have occurred in wartime, when identification with one's country is intense. The government, even in undemocratic states, cannot do without mass support, and a people's acceptance of military service, separation of families, and deaths measures its commitment to the nation. Indeed, whether morale in democracies is higher, more intense, or longer lasting is debatable. The German armies fought very well in two wars, despite the Allied blockade of World War I and the heavy bombing of World War II; widespread support for Germany's government lasted until near the end in each instance. Japanese soldiers demonstrated a tenacious fanaticism during World War II, which led them to fight hard for every inch of territory, to sacrifice their own lives freely in the process, and to impose heavy casualties on American marines.

Examples since 1945 are numerous; we shall mention only two. The Chinese Nationalist armies after World War II were all too often led by incompetent officers, who treated the troops like animals, stole their pay, sold their American equipment to the Chinese Communists (whom they were supposedly fighting), avoided battles, and retreated whenever possible. Discipline and morale were obviously low, and the armies' looting and raping hardly endeared the regime to its people. Similarly, the South Vietnamese army, with the exception of some elite units, fought poorly when it fought at all. The reasons included poor pay, no recreational leaves (one reason for the high desertion rate), knowledge that the rich could buy their sons' way out of military service, limited officers' commissions for well-to-do and educated officers, and a government that seemed to care little for the poor or for ending social abuses.

Bombing, which is frequently favored as a way of beating an enemy into submission, appears to be a positive factor in preserving and even raising morale. Before World War II it was widely believed that bombing cities would not only destroy the war industries supporting the front-line soldiers but also would break civilian morale. Civilians were not expected to be as tough as soldiers. The Battle of Britain after the German defeat of France proved otherwise. The German bombing of Britain, whose prime minister by then was the eloquent Churchill, probably did more to raise British morale than any other single factor. The American bombing of North Vietnam probably helped to maintain support for the Hanoi government. North Vietnamese general Vo Nguyen Giap, the mastermind behind his nation's strategy, predicted victory against the United States because he believed that democracies lose patience in long, drawn-out wars and will finally quit. As Giap had forecast, the war caused immense domestic turmoil in the United States, which in the end had no choice but to disengage from the conflict.

It is difficult to make definitive statements about American morale. The two world wars were fought far away, there was no physical damage to the homeland through invasion or sustained bombing, and civilians were not endangered. The loss of American life was very small compared with that of the other combatants. Standards of living were maintained at a fairly high level at home. Sacrifices were minimal and lasted for just over a year in the first war and a bit over three and a half years in the second—compared with four years for Britain and France in World War I and six years for Britain in World War II. The Vietnam War, because it was considered a "limited war," in response to a limited threat, was never popularly perceived to pose much danger to American security, and life went on pretty much as usual in the United States. There was little willingness to sacrifice butter for guns, as during the world wars. The draft of college students was resented, and there was widespread resistance to it; many youths emigrated to Canada and elsewhere. Perhaps it was the nature of that particular war only. There is still no record on how the national morale will hold up when sacrifice is demanded in a real crisis. The peacetime domestic gas crisis of the 1970s has shown that Americans do not like to do with less. The overall twentieth-century evidence remains fragmentary and ambiguous. American society has not really been tested yet.

What seem to be critical components in upholding national morale are patriotic feelings that can be rallied when the nation is attacked or insulted, even when the government may not be particularly popular (as in the Soviet Union during World War II), and a belief that the government places the nation's welfare first and pursues policies compatible with the nation's historic role. Many patriotic Americans felt that Presidents Johnson and Nixon were betraying the American heritage by fighting on the side of an authoritarian South Vietnamese regime against a regime that, although Communist, was nationalistic and committed to unifying Vietnam. Americans were simply tired of a long drawn-out war with no end in sight. They, who had rallied around the flag when the intervention in Vietnam first occurred, lost the will to continue. The costs in lives, inflation, domestic turmoil, and division were not worth continuing the war as it had been fought. By contrast, President Reagan has been able to mobilize Americans' patriotism, their pride in their country, their feeling good about the United States again. The country supported his use of force in Grenada (1983), Libya (1981 and 1986), and even in Lebanon (1982-83), although the president was forced to withdraw U.S. forces shortly after 241 marines were killed in a suicide terrorist attack. He wisely refrained from direct military intervention in Nicaragua because of widespread fears of "another Vietnam."

In this context, three problems deserve a quick reference. One is the Soviet-dominated states of Eastern Europe. In any war with NATO, could Moscow really count on the Polish and Czech armies? Another is that the Europe of the Common Market has 325 million people and a combined GNP larger than that of the Soviet Union and its allies. Why can this Europe, with its people, wealth, and military experience, not defend itself forty years after the end of World War II without 300,000 American forces in Europe against a nation of 276 million with more than 1 billion Chinese to its rear? Is the reason for this a lack of material strength or lack of will? A third, more general problem is the deep internal divisions of many nations, rent by quarrels among ethnic, tribal, racial, or religious groups who do not see each other as "countrymen," but only as enemies and rivals, even as potential persecutors should power change hands. In the early phase of the German invasion of the Soviet Union in World War II, many Soviets, especially Ukrainians, rallied to the German side until Hitler's secret police, the Gestapo, began large-scale massacres of the population. This killing drove all Soviet citizens to unite behind Stalin, who became during the war a symbol of traditional Soviet nationalism. The Soviet Union remains a country composed of many nationality groups, many of whom, like the Ukrainians, detest their subordination to the Great Russians. This will become a major domestic problem because the Great Russians lost their majority status among the Soviet people during the 1970s. In the postwar world, especially among the LDCs, this phenomenon of strong ethnic loyalties in competition with national loyalties has been remarkably widespread. It is present even in Western nations such as Canada, Belgium, Britain, and Spain.

WAR AND POWER CALCULATIONS

Overestimating One's Power

A war begins when the contestants disagree on their relative power; it will end only when they agree on their relative strength.[16] That is, war erupts because one of the nations in an adversary relationship has miscalculated the power distribution. The fighting will clarify the actual ratio of power; war is thus a bitter teacher of "reality." One state finally decides, correctly or incorrectly, that peaceful bargaining will not resolve the dispute and decides to continue bargaining over the terms of coexistence—who receives what—by war, "the continuation of politics by other means."

Power calculations have influenced decisions to go to war in two ways. The power of the adversary has either been underestimated or overestimated. The state that has underestimated its opponent's power may be emboldened to make reckless decisions leading to war; the state that has overestimated its opponent's power may become so fearful or cautious that it makes unnecessary concessions or, to avoid later disaster, strikes preventively before the enemy has grown too strong.

Examples are unfortunately plentiful. The German kaiser risked World War I in the summer of 1914 because he believed that the war would be over by the time the leaves fell. Hitler believed that the Soviet Union would collapse quickly and, confident of German power, invaded it before he had eliminated Britain, thus creating a two-front situation for Germany. Then, after Japan had attacked Pearl Harbor, the Nazi dictator declared war on the United States as well. He had contempt for the United States, a racially mixed society.

In 1950 North Korea invaded South Korea, certain of a quick victory. After the United States intervened to prevent the South's defeat, Washington made a similar error: U.S. troops advanced northward to China's frontier, despite Chinese warning that they would not tolerate this. General Douglas MacArthur disregarded these warnings because he had a rather low opinion of the Chinese forces. In Vietnam a few years later, the Joint Chiefs of Staff failed President Johnson badly when they predicted that 200,000 men could win that conflict in a reasonable amount of time—about two years. Few Americans rated North Vietnam's military strength highly. Presidential candidate Nixon expressed a widely shared view when he called the Communist state a fourth-rate power. Before 1965 and the large-scale American military intervention in South Vietnam, who would have doubted that it was but a matter of weeks, at most months, before the world's greatest military power would clobber North Vietnam, one of the world's smallest powers, a "half-country" with a population less than 10 percent of that of the United States and virtually no industry—"a bunch of peasants"?

In all of these examples, the power initiating the war not only overestimated its own power and therefore expected to win the war but also expected a *quick* victory. With the exception of the North Vietnamese, none of the states won the war they had started. The lesson: miscalculation of the power distribution is easy; especially, as one suspects, the confidence in one's own strength and high hopes of a quick victory lead to an underestimation of the opponent's power.

Underestimating One's Power

Quite the contrary phenomenon occurred just before World War II. The French and the British, remembering German military prowess in World War I and impressed by Hitler's aggressive speeches and bold international moves, consistently exaggerated German power on land and in the air and were therefore never sure that they could resist him without risking defeat in a war. Then, after Hitler had made several advances—in the Rhineland, Austria, the Sudetenland, and the rest of Czechoslovakia—the British finally declared they would defend Poland, against which Hitler also had claims. The German leader dismissed London's pledge of defense for Poland as mere words; he believed the British would retreat as before. But this time the British leaders meant what they said. World War II began as a result of Hitler's miscalculation.

Israeli policy makers, too, have consistently overestimated Arab power. Given the history of persecution of Jews, in particular Hitler's policy of extermination, the leaders of the new Jewish state in 1948 felt highly insecure among hostile neighbors who had tried to strangle Israel at birth. In 1956 and 1967, when these neighbors were forming joint commands, talking of war and of "driving the Jews into the sea," boasting of their imminent victories, and parading their Soviet weapons, Israel struck preemptively. Power seemed to be shifting to its enemies. Why leave them the initiative to strike? Why not hit them before they were completely ready? Overestimating an opponent's power can also result in war.

Vulnerability Analysis

In the final analysis, even if power were easier to calculate accurately, the calculation would still be gross. In this respect, a country's size, population, economic capacity, and military strength are handy for obtaining a quick initial picture of the power ratios and rankings among states. They can tell us that a nation like Canada, with a population of 24 million, cannot attain more than middle ranking, despite its large territory, modern economy, natural resources (including oil), and productive agriculture. They can tell us that Communist China will not achieve superpower status, despite its enormous population, territory, and potential oil reserves, until it has extensively industrialized.

Such calculations could also have told U.S. policy makers, before the fall of the shah of Iran in 1979, that their hopes of devolving some of the United States' guardianship role around the world on so-called regional superpowers were unrealistic. The idea of transferring some "policing" duties to Third World states in strategic positions and with populations, wealth, and military potential may have seemed sound as the United States sought to reduce its "global policemanship." Iran was to police the vital Persian Gulf, through which passes most of the West's oil. India, as the guardian of the Indian Ocean, as well as Brazil in Latin America, Nigeria in Africa, and Indonesia in southeast Asia, were all potential candidates for similar roles.

The problem was that the calculations of these nations' power potential did not include their general internal weaknesses. Their governments were often unpopular, repressive, corrupt, and authoritarian; they also suffered from lack of national cohesion and massive poverty. These characteristics would seem to disqualify them as leading regional actors, at least for the present. The shah's overthrow by means of work stoppages and mass demonstrations organized largely by Muslim religious leaders should be a lesson; not even his large, modern armed forces rallied to his cause. The political instability and social conflicts of many new nations are too great to impose this extra burden on them. They may look like regional superpowers, with all their modern weapons, but these warriors stand on the proverbial feet of clay.

In these gross power calculations, one fault deserves special mention: the tendency to heavily emphasize the military factor, the number of men in uniform, the quantity of arms, and so forth, in what is often called a *threat analysis.* In this analysis Soviet military power looks awesome: the total number of missiles and warheads, the size of its army and its equipment, its new surface navy and airlift capability.[17] But concentrating on military power overlooks Soviet weaknesses such as its economy, particularly its agriculture economy, and problems such as the enmity of China and the questionable loyalty of the states of Eastern Europe. For a careful calculation of the power of another state, it becomes critical that a threat analysis be balanced with what for want of a better term might be called *vulnerability analysis.* It is all too easy to add up the number of soldiers and tanks and not "look underneath" such figures.

A brief example: one reason the Germans felt 1914 was the right time for a war was that the German General Staff, looking strictly at Russia's population figures and men under arms, was becoming alarmed by the growth of "Russian might." Indeed, some German generals had been advocating a preventive war for several years; if such a war were not undertaken, they felt, Germany would be crushed.[18] What is incredible is that this threat analysis totally overlooked the fact that Russia, while always possessing forces larger than those of other European states, had just lost a war to Japan and had not done well in preceding conflicts. After its defeat by Japan, Russia had suffered widespread peasant unrest, a harbinger of the revolution to come. A vulnerability analysis would have shown that Russia's outer strength was matched by internal weakness and that this alleged "military colossus" was an "economic Pygmy."

The gross assessment of nations' power is also misleading in another way. Implicit in the "adding up" of the various components of power is the conclusion that the total represents all the power that is available and usable across the board. For example, if state A is a superpower because of its size, population, economic capacity, and military strength, then logically it should have its way on most issues, except when confronting the other superpowers. But the fact is that A may be able to deter superpower B from an attack on its homeland, but be unable to compel small nation C to halt an attempt to take over a country friendly to A. A may be able to mobilize some states to pass a resolution in the United Nations, but be unable to win the votes for another resolution. It may successfully negotiate a tariff reduction with some second-rank allies, but fail to prevent one of those allies from defecting.

An evaluation of why A is successful in some endeavors and unsuccessful in others may suggest one of two answers.[19] First, it may be that A did not try hard enough or was not sufficiently skillful. For example, it has been claimed that the United States did not win the war in Vietnam because political restraints were placed on the military. Had the United States bombed North Vietnam very hard from the beginning and made the war unbearably painful for the North Vietnamese, they would have had reason to sue for peace. No doubt there are occasions when such explanations of failure are correct, and it may be that Vietnam is one such case, but more often they are misleading and prevent our drawing the correct lessons from the experience.

A second explanation of why a state may achieve success in one situation and encounter failure in another is that a state may have the right kind of power for one but not the other. The variables are the kind of power being used or not used, the *purposes* for which it is used, and the *situations* in which it is used. These three factors account for the American failure to win in Vietnam and for its helplessness to prevent OPEC from raising oil prices, which damaged the United States far more seriously than the loss of South Vietnam ever did. A gross assessment of American power cannot explain such instances. Only an analysis of the specific context in which the relationship of the United States and Vietnam or the United States and OPEC occurred can do so.

The difference between power as a *possession*—involving the quantitative measurement of the components of national power—and power as a set of *relations* among states has been explained by James Rosenau in this way:

> For reasons having to do with the structure of language, the concept of "power" does *not* lend itself to comprehension in relational terms. Without undue violation of language, the word "power" cannot be used as a verb. It is rather a noun, highlighting "things" possessed instead of processes of interaction. Nations influence each other; they exercise control over each other; they alter, maintain, subvert, enhance, deter, or otherwise affect each other, but they do not "powerize" each other. Hence, no matter how sensitive analysts may be to the question of how the resources used by one actor serve to modify or preserve the behavior of another, once they cast their assessment in terms of the "power" employed they are led—if not inevitably, then almost invariably—to focus on the resources themselves rather than on the relationship they may or may not underlie.[20]

THE MISSING LINK: INTENTIONS

Judging Intentions

Another major problem with the traditional type of power analysis is its glaring omission of other states' intentions. In a way this omission is understandable. Intentions are unstable; friendly intentions today may change tomorrow, as leaders' views change or as the leaders themselves change. Capabilities may also vary, but they are not as likely to fluctuate dramatically from one day to the next. The underlying tangible components do not alter overnight; mobilizing them usually takes a few months, if not a year or more. "Playing it safe"—and what else should a state in the international environment do?— suggests that keeping up with a potential adversary's capabilities, even to anticipating a buildup in order not to be caught napping, is the safest course. Conversely, it seems wise to play down intentions as unreliable. The balance of power is capabilities, and they can be measured to a degree, whereas intentions cannot. The rule is "Never estimate intentions, only capabilities."

In addition, many calculations of capabilities are worst-case analyses. Since power calculations are not that accurate and leaders cannot be sure of the extent of an adversary's buildup, rule number two slips in almost unnoticed: "When in doubt, assume the worst." [21] The potential or actual buildup will then be assumed to be extensive, and the presumed threat to security will seem all the more grave. It makes eminent good sense in an anarchical environment, then, to assume the worst: "Better safe than sorry."

In real political life, however, policy makers do make judgments about intentions. Indeed, so do those whose advice is to ignore intentions. Implicit in their concern with capabilities—especially in "worst cases"—is an unspoken estimate of the adversary's intentions that they are unfriendly, indeed very unfriendly, and that the buildup had better be matched, if not exceeded, to serve as a deterrent. Capability analysis cannot be divorced from some sort of view of intentions.

Ironically, despite the quantifiable nature of weapons, calculations may not tell us much more than that they exist. What does their existence mean? That is a question of intentions. Judgments of an opponent's intentions may, of course, vary. Its leaders know the reasons for the buildup, but they may prefer to keep others guessing. If they reveal their reasons publicly, the first state may fear that they are telling only part of the truth or lying outright. Its own leaders are still left with the task of divining "the truth."

Was the purpose of the enormous Soviet strategic and conventional military buildup that started in 1964 to catch up with the United States, behind which it had lagged so long? Was it to achieve parity militarily, as well as psychologically, and attain recognition that it is equal to the United States? Or was it undertaken because the Soviet Union needed larger forces than the United States' to confront NATO to the west and China to the east? Was defense the primary motive for a country that had repeatedly been invaded throughout history? Or was the correct impression, widespread in the West, that the Soviet Union's new arsenal—including its airlift and sealift capabilities that had been developed over a decade and at huge cost—is offensive and far larger than anything required for defense? This power may not be used to attack anybody, but its very existence must be taken into account in Washington and other capitals. Its primary effect is political because it is available underpinning for the Soviet Union's efforts to expand its influence in areas possibly vital to Western interests. Counting weapons, therefore, is not enough; obviously more important is what people believe the weapons mean.

When a state seeks to preserve the balance of power with another state, it should take into account both the perceived power of that other state and its intentions, which are presumed to be potentially or actually hostile. After all, the United States does not increase the numbers of its weapons when Britain, France, or West Germany build up their military strength; these countries are allies, and their intentions are friendly. A threat to a nation's vital interests is perceived when another nation's intentions are *seen* as threatening; the other nation's capabilities simply confirm that it can carry out such intentions. The capabilities per se are not menacing. If they were, the United States would have been considered a major menace in the interwar years. It was potentially the most powerful country in the world, but it was isolationist and clearly had no intention of playing a political role in the world. Neither Germany nor Japan took much notice of the United States before World War II, and France and Britain knew that they could not count on help from the United States. Similarly, today Japan and Western Europe have great potential power, but neither has yet defined its political role and its aims beyond the minimum objective of defense—which is being mainly left to the United States.

Judging intentions is not easy, as the ongoing controversy over the meaning and consequences of the Soviet arms buildup shows. It is easy to make definitive judgments after events have supported a particular interpretation. Often there is evidence for each of the alternative interpretations of an adversary's intentions, and there may well be as much evidence for the wrong version as for the correct one. The proponents of each interpretation either will see the same evidence or "facts" and interpret them differently, or they will select different facts from the all too many that are available. Implicit in each interpretation of the Soviet military buildup is a specific view of the Soviet Union, of its roles and goals, and especially of whether it is a status-quo or revisionist state. If the latter, is it willing to run only minor risks to expand Soviet influence or bigger risks for high stakes?

Misjudging Intentions: The Question of Hitler

Let us take another look at the rise of Hitler, the example that seems so clear to everyone in retrospect. Even after more than four decades, people still wonder how it was possible to misunderstand his intentions. In fact, a strong case can be made for Britain's appeasement policy. (*Appeasement* was until that time a respectable word, not a word of accusation synonymous with cowardice. It meant satisfying those who had grievances partially in order to avoid otherwise inevitable conflict. Appeasement is in many ways the heart of democratic politics.)

Keep in mind the horror of World War I and imagine how strong the antiwar feelings were in Britain and France. But there was also sizable guilt about the Versailles peace settlement; the victors who had drawn up the settlement began to feel they had wronged Germany and that Hitler was a spokesman for legitimate German grievances. For instance, at Versailles the Allies had said that the limitation on Germany's military was only the first step toward a more general reduction of armaments. But after two wars with Germany—that of 1870 and the 1914-18 conflict—France was actually more concerned about maintaining its military strength than about disarmament. Hitler could therefore pose as the spokesman of an aggrieved Germany that had, in good faith, accepted a large measure of disarmament, whereas its former enemies, despite their avowals, had not. A great power, the equal of France and Britain, Germany was being treated as a second-class state; all it supposedly asked was to be treated fairly. Hitler's other claims were advanced in the context of the democratic principle of national self-determination, the very basis of the Treaty of Versailles. This principle had not been implemented fully because, as sometimes happens, when applied, it clashed with competing principles. National self-determination had been violated in the Rhineland, the Sudetenland, and the Polish Corridor, primarily for security reasons. Hitler could invoke a fundamental Western principle against the West in order to undermine the post-World War I settlement.

On which basis could France and Britain deny him any of these claims? Were equality and national self-determination all right for themselves but not for anyone else? Hitler's claims were recognized as just. Who could really say that he was insincere and that he was using the Versailles principles cynically? Had not the West—as Hitler repeatedly pointed out—violated its own principles? Was not the German leader therefore justified in demanding that the two Western powers correct the inequalities they had written into the peace treaty? No wonder the Western powers felt guilty about Versailles! They had preached one thing and practiced another; they had placed the moral validity of the Versailles settlement in jeopardy. France and especially Britain felt that, if war were to erupt, it would be their fault for clinging too stubbornly to the territorial settlement defined by Versailles. Hitler's bold speeches could be explained by the vigorous German resentment at the unjust treatment dealt it by France and Britain.

In other words, Hitler shrewdly disguised his ultimate intention of making Germany the world's most dominant power and paralyzed the will of his opponents to act against him. Each challenge confronted them with the question of whether they wanted to fight to preserve a morally dubious status quo. After the horror of World War I, the answer was obvious. Why should a war be fought to defend unjust positions, especially if it could be avoided? If Hitler was a nationalist who only wanted the return of German territory, would not the satisfaction of his demands for national self-determination end his claims and gain his support for the preservation of the European balance of power? The Nazi leader might be a repulsive person, but his personality was not the issue: peace was. He did, of course, also arrest those who opposed him, and he was a militant anti-Semite, sworn to the destruction of world Jewry. What he did within Germany, however, was a German affair: Germany was a sovereign state. Besides, who could really believe that any man would really kill millions of innocent people just because they had been born Jewish? Such monstrosity was simply unbelievable, beyond the imagination of decent people. It was all talk—"politics."

A post-World War II generation that thinks of Hitler as a warmonger has forgotten that, to people in the 1930s, his character was not so apparent. He could announce German rearmament while pledging Germany's willingness to renounce all offensive weapons or disband its entire military establishment—if only other nations would pledge to do the same. He could denounce a treaty with a neighbor while simultaneously issuing assurances that it was his own fondest hope to sign a nonaggression pact with that same neighbor. He solemnly guaranteed other countries' frontiers, promising not to interfere in their internal affairs, and he never tired of declaring that his present claim was the last one he would ever make. Ironically, Hitler became a most effective spokesman for peace. To his contemporaries, Hitler often appeared to be sincerely and honestly dedicated to resolving all problems that might stand in the way of peace in Europe. His constant refrain was that Germany would never break the peace. The real question is thus not why appeasement was attempted but why it should *not* have been attempted. Only in 1939 did it become clear that Hitler's ambitions were not limited by the principle of national self-determination. Britain then committed itself to Poland's defense, but it was too late.

The dilemma for a great power like Britain in the 1930s is clear, and such dilemmas still occur: if it is assumed too early that a potential adversary's intentions are expansionist when in reality they may not be, policy may create an enemy where otherwise there would have been none. On the other hand, since the revelation of a nation's "real" intentions can come about only during a long period of time and from careful observation of emerging patterns over a series of issues, it may be too late to act once it becomes clear that this pattern is expansionist; in any event, acting earlier would have been more advantageous and, in all probability, less risky and costly. Remember that if a state is genuinely revisionist, it is most likely to test its adversary on small issues, none of them too important in themselves to the defender of the status quo, certainly not important enough to risk going to war. Quick recognition of another state's intentions is thus difficult. What to do remains a problem for the policy maker, who frequently has to make decisions in an environment of uncertainty; the temptation is to wait and see, as did Neville Chamberlain. The consequence of a mistaken assessment, however, may be the outbreak of war.

Should we remember history? Not surprisingly, the events leading up to World War II have influenced policy makers ever since. The memories of Hitler and Munich, the symbol of appeasement, have had enormous influence, especially on American leaders. The lesson appeared crystal clear: dictators are expansionist; attempts to appease them only whet their appetites for more, instead of satisfying them; and their demands have thus to be opposed from the beginning—if necessary by force. It was only too easy after 1945 to think of Stalin as a left-wing resurrection of Hitler; of the Communist Soviet Union as comparable to Nazi Germany, a totalitarian state; of Soviet expansion in Eastern Europe and Soviet pressure on Iran and Turkey as emulating Berlin's expansionist course. Such analogies can be very useful; they may immediately highlight what the stakes really are in a conflict. But analogies must be drawn circumspectly.

Was the example of Munich really relevant after World War II? Before the

Vietnam War, U.S. policy makers certainly thought so, and they often invoked it as a reason for stopping Russian/Chinese/Korean/Vietnamese expansion or for not giving in to any of their demands. After Vietnam, however, the Munich analogy fell into disfavor. In retrospect, it appears to be the major reason for frequent U.S. intervention and expansion of the nation's commitments. The effect of the war was to turn U.S. opinion against further interventions and to be wary of new commitments. "No More Munichs" became "No More Vietnams." The question, however, was whether the latter slogan was relevant in the quite different circumstances after 1975. Drawing analogies helps to avoid repeating past mistakes, but can it also lead to new ones? The central issue in resolving the correctness or incorrectness of the analogy remains the issue of intentions. What, for example, are the intentions of Mikhail Gorbachev, Fidel Castro, or the Sandinistas in Nicaragua? On this issue, as with Hitler, the experts and public are often divided, and American policies toward them are therefore often controversial. [22]

Notes

1. Only recently have some analysts questioned this assumption that the great states are the primary actors. See Stanley Hoffmann, *Gulliver's Troubles or the Setting of American Foreign Policy* (New York: McGraw-Hill, 1968), 26-43. For a response to Hoffmann, see Kenneth N. Waltz, "International Structure, National Force, and the Balance of World Power," *Journal of International Affairs* 21 (1967): 220-228; and Waltz, *Theory of International Politics* (Reading, Mass.: Addison-Wesley, 1979), 161-193.
2. Theodore C. Sorensen, *Kennedy* (New York: Bantam Books, 1966), 589-592.
3. Klaus Knorr, *The War Potential of Nations* (Princeton, N.J.: Princeton University Press, 1955); and Knorr, *Military Power and Potential* (Lexington, Mass.: D. C. Heath, 1970).
4. Quoted by Winston Churchill, *The Gathering Storm* (Boston: Houghton Mifflin, 1948), 341.
5. Peter Bachrach and Morton S. Baratz, *Power and Poverty* (New York: Oxford University Press, 1970), 17-38. Also see Charles A. McClelland, *Theory and the International System* (New York: Macmillan, 1966), 68-88; and K. J. Holsti, *International Politics: A Framework for Analysis* (Englewood Cliffs, N.J.: Prentice-Hall, 1967), 191-209.
6. George F. Kennan, "Morality and Foreign Policy," *Foreign Affairs* (Winter 1985/1986): 215-216.
7. A. J. P. Taylor, *The Struggle for Mastery in Europe* (London: Oxford University Press, 1954), xxxi; and Paul M. Kennedy, "The First World War and the International Power System," *International Security*, Summer 1984, 23.
8. *New York Times*, Aug. 25, 1985. Also see President Reagan's speech on sanctions against South Africa, *New York Times*, July 23, 1986; and L. Harold Bullis and James E. Mielke, *Strategic and Critical Materials* (Boulder, Colo.: Westview Press, 1984).
9. William G. Hyland, "Brezhnev and Beyond," *Foreign Affairs* (Fall 1979): 61.
10. *New York Times*, Sept. 9, 1979.

11. See Robert E. Osgood, *The Weary and the Wary* (Baltimore: Johns Hopkins University Press, 1972); and Kunio Muraoka, *Japanese Security and the United States,* Adelphi Paper 95 (London: International Institute for Strategic Studies, 1973).

12. Robert Gilpin, *France in the Age of the Scientific State* (Princeton, N.J.: Princeton University Press, 1968), 76.

13. John G. Stoessinger, *Why Nations Go to War* (New York: St. Martin's Press, 1974), 220.

14. Carl von Clausewitz, *On War* (Princeton, N.J.: Princeton University Press, 1976), 579.

15. Kenneth N. Waltz, *Foreign Policy and Democratic Politics* (Boston: Little, Brown & Co., 1967).

16. Geoffrey Blainey, *The Causes of War* (New York: Free Press, 1973), 115-119, 122.

17. Andrew Cockburn, *The Threat* (New York: Random House, 1983).

18. Stephen Van Evern, "The Cult of the Offensive and the Origins of World War I," 58-107; and Kennedy, "The First World War and the International Political System," 7-40.

19. David A. Baldwin, "Power Analysis and World Politics: New Trends Versus Old Tendencies," *World Politics,* January 1979, 163-164.

20. James N. Rosenau, "Capabilities and Control in an Interdependent World," *International Security,* Fall 1976, 34.

21. Raymond L. Garthoff, "On Estimating and Imputing Intentions," *International Security,* Winter 1978, 22-32.

22. Ernest R. May, *"Lessons" of the Past* (New York: Oxford University Press, 1973). Also see May, ed., *Knowing One's Enemies* (Princeton, N.J.: Princeton University Press, 1984); and Richard E. Newstadt and Ernest R. May, *Thinking in Time* (New York: Free Press, 1986).

Part Three

HOW TO PLAY—POLITICALLY, MILITARILY, ECONOMICALLY

CHAPTER 8

The Balance
of Terror

BARGAINING AND CONFLICT RESOLUTION

The importance of the balance of power in the state system and the effects of different distributions of power on state behavior should be clear by now. The difficulties in calculating power and the dangerous consequences of miscalculating an adversary's capability and neglecting its intentions should also be clear. But, assuming that states act upon correct calculations, how do they use their power to protect or advance the objectives they deem important? We shall deal with these issues in the next five chapters, which focus on some of the principal ways states exercise their power: deterrence and crisis diplomacy, limited war, and various economic means. We shall note that, on different types of issues—or, as they are sometimes called, *issue-areas*—different actors are involved, and different kinds of power are exercised in different ways for different purposes. Finally, the differences of behavior among these actors in bipolar and multipolar systems will be discussed.

The essence of the relationships among the actors involved lies in bargaining. Bargaining is the centerpiece of relations among nations, for it is through bargaining that the distribution of the values or goods over which nations differ is decided. The leverage that each nation has in negotiations reflects its power, the ways in which that power is used, and the nation's willingness to use it. When force is used between states, the outcome on the battlefield usually decides the ratio of power, and the peace treaty reflects which state won or lost what and how much. But whether states use force, the threat of force, or economic means, *diplomacy* describes their actions. Our use of this term differs somewhat from common usage, which implies officials (diplomats) seated around a table, formally negotiating some compromise between conflicting positions to avoid more serious conflict. We shall use the term *diplomacy* regardless of who conducts negotiations—indeed, regardless of whether formal negotiations occur or not. Bargaining is going on between states not only when diplomats gather and talk but also when no formal meetings take place. Much of diplomacy, admittedly, is explicit, but in the next few chapters we shall focus on *tacit negotiations*.[1]

When the United States intervened militarily in Vietnam in 1965, it did so to prevent the loss of South Vietnam to the North. By destroying enemy forces, or at least by inflicting heavy and sustained casualties on the enemy, the United States hoped to weaken the Communist side and to strengthen South Vietnam. Either the North Vietnamese would then finally call off the war, or, if negotiations took place, the United States and South Vietnam would have more leverage. Thus, the fighting itself was the bargaining. There was no visible or explicit negotiating: U.S. diplomats did not meet with North Vietnamese diplomats at some neutral spot in Switzerland. Nevertheless, negotiations were going on constantly. North Vietnam had already stated its expectation of unifying Vietnam. Any solution short of taking over the South was unacceptable. The United States rejected that solution; it intervened massively to prevent unification from occurring as the South Vietnamese army failed. It expected an improved position on the battlefield to be reflected in the terms of any final settlement. Actual formal talking is only a minor part of such tacit negotiations, if it occurs at all.

A domestic comparison can be found in a strike. A break in formal talks between labor and industry does not mean that negotiations are not going on. They go on in a different form. Labor stays off the job and waits to see how long industry can hold out against its demands; management, in turn, waits to see how long the union's strike fund will last. The two parties test each other's power and determination to "win." From time to time, a formal bargaining session may be called, and the old terms may be altered to test whether the other party is ready to compromise. If so, the strike is over. But if one side hopes that by waiting longer it can further weaken the opponent, the strike continues. The strike itself is the means of bargaining.

Whether diplomacy is explicit or tacit, resolution of conflict does not necessarily always take the form of compromise. There are at least four different kinds of conflict resolution: (1) those in which both states lose, (2) those in which neither state wins, (3) those in which one state wins everything, and (4) those in which both states are partial winners and partial losers in a compromise agreement.[2]

Loss by Both States

The best example of the first type of conflict resolution is the concept of strategic deterrence. The deterring side prevents its adversary from defeating or eliminating it by announcing, in effect, "You may kill me if you strike me, but I will kill you before I die." The deterrent is based on the first nation's ability to retaliate even after the enemy's first strike. Mutual deterrence is frequently said to be equivalent to mutual suicide. The United States even calls its capacity to destroy the Soviet Union an "assured destruction" capability. The reciprocal capacity is called "mutual assured destruction," or MAD— probably not a bad name for a strategy in which everyone loses.

Victory for Neither State

When neither party can win, the conflict resolution is called a *stalemate*. It can occur under a variety of conditions: when both parties have exhausted themselves in struggle, when both are unwilling to invest greater resources in a struggle that is not critical, when both are unwilling to escalate because the risks are too great, when a third party (perhaps one or both of the superpowers or the United Nations) intervenes and calls a halt to the conflict, or when new problems and priorities arise.

In the Korean War the United States, unwilling to escalate the war by attacking China, sought instead to exhaust the Chinese through a war of attrition. In Vietnam the American strategy of physical attrition was designed to exact so heavy a price in bomb damage of North Vietnam and in soldiers killed in battle that at some point the North Vietnamese would stop trying to take over the South. In Korea a stalemate did result when the battle lines were drawn along the thirty-eighth parallel, approximately where the war had started. In Vietnam, however, U.S. strategy failed.

Victory for One State

Probably the most obvious form of conflict resolution is a clear-cut victory for one side. It occurs when one side is much stronger than the other or the issue no longer seems important enough to cause the other side to take great risks and pay a high price. The Allied victory over Germany, Italy, and Japan in World War II is one illustration; the American victory over the Soviet Union in the Cuban missile crisis in 1962 is another. The Soviet interventions to crush the Hungarian rebellion in 1956 and the Czechoslovakian uprisings in 1968 are others, as are the Vietnamese Communists' defeat of France in 1954 and of the United States two decades later.

Compromise

Conflict resolution through compromise is probably the most common. Both states win part of what they want and give up part of what they want. The two sides may "split the difference," or one side may gain more than the other. The settlement is likely to reflect the perceived power relationship of the two states, their respective willingness to run risks and make sacrifices, or the importance each attaches to the issue in dispute. A compromise may be easier to achieve among states friendly to one another than among adversaries; a higher degree of mutual trust may be the critical ingredient.

The search for compromise, especially among adversaries, may be promoted by the use of force (as in the Egyptian-Syrian attack on Israel in 1973), the threat of force (as in the conflict between the United States and the Soviet Union over Berlin in 1948-49), the offer of rewards (as when the United States offered North Vietnam the withdrawal of American forces, continued Communist control of captured South Vietnamese areas, and U.S. economic aid in 1973), or a mixture of the proverbial sticks and carrots (most agreements).

Economic Resolution

Some economic issues may be resolved by reliance on the free market and the "laws" of supply and demand. If supplies of a resource are greater than demand, the price will be low; if the supply is tight, the price will be high. The Third World, however, complains that such laws have benefited the West and kept its own members poor. These nations insist that the market is neither free nor neutral but biased in favor of the strong Western industrial powers. These laws have become a major source of dispute between the First and Third Worlds, with the latter seeking to change them through political intervention. The goal is a more equitable distribution of wealth. In the 1970s the Organization of Petroleum Exporting Countries (OPEC) became an effective cartel, managing to raise oil prices far above the original market price of $3 a barrel to more than $34 a barrel between 1973 and 1981. That was one way of receiving a higher price for their resources and changing the bargaining relationship with the oil-consuming First World.

But economic means are used not only on economic issues. The Arab members of OPEC wished to use the organization to pressure the United States and Western Europe to modify their pro-Israel diplomatic stance and support the demand of the Palestine Liberation Organization (PLO) for a homeland. And just as economic means may be employed to advance political/military purposes, so political/military means may be used to achieve economic ends. Had OPEC withheld oil in order to gain its objectives, can it be doubted that the United States would have used force to avoid being "strangled," as Henry Kissinger worded it at the time?

THE NUCLEAR REVOLUTION AND THE BALANCE OF POWER

The Democratic and Industrial Revolutions

A nation's military strength is an important component of its power, for, as E. H. Carr wrote, "War lurks in the background of international politics just as a revolution lurks in the background of domestic policies."[3] Ironically, democracy, which was expected to abolish war, multiplied the importance of this component many times over. One democratic assumption used to be that only irresponsible rulers are belligerent, that wars are for them merely an enjoyable and profitable "blood sport." In this view, it is the people who pay the price of wars with their lives and taxes. If peace-loving people could hold their rulers accountable, wars should be eliminated and peace secured. Democracy would then bring an era of good will—of individual freedom and social justice at home, of peace and harmony abroad. The world would be safe for democracy because it would be democratic. Government by the people, of the people, and for the people would ensure perpetual peace.[4]

Instead, democracy became tied to nationalism, and the two gave birth to the "nation in arms." Once people were freed from feudal bondage and granted the right to some form of self-government, they came to equate their own well-being with that of their nations, and it seemed only reasonable that the nations should be able to call on them—the citizens—for defense. Not surprisingly, it was the French Revolution that brought people into contact with the nation-state. One result was the first system of universal military service. When citizens' supreme loyalty was to the nation, the nation in arms followed logically. Democracy and nationalism thus enabled France to mobilize fully for total war and fight a war to destroy its opponents completely.

This change was one reason why the Congress of Vienna reacted with such horror to the revolution, which had unleashed mass passions and all-out war. Previous wars had been restrained because men had identified not with nations but with smaller units, like towns or manors, or with universal ties as embodied in the Roman Catholic church. The armies of the *ancien régime* were composed largely of mercenaries and lowly elements of society such as debtors, vagrants, and criminals—men who were animated neither by love of country nor by hatred of the enemy, but who fought because they were paid or compelled to do so. States lacked sufficient economic resources to maintain sizable armies. Indeed, their tactics were determined by the need to limit expenses, and, to keep casualties low, the emphasis was on maneuver rather than on pitched battle. But the revolution enlisted popular support, and mass armies aroused by nationalism began to fight in defense of their countries. Bertrand de Jouvenel describes this "new era in military history" as "the era of cannon fodder."[5]

It remained only for the Industrial Revolution to produce the instruments enabling men to kill one another in greater numbers. Modern military technology brought total war to its fullest realization.[6] Mass armies could be equipped with mass-produced weapons that were ever more destructive, making it possible for nations to inflict progressively greater damage on one another in shorter and shorter periods. In the seventeenth century it took thirty years for the states of Europe to slaughter half the population of central Europe. In the second decade of the twentieth century it took only four years for them to bleed one another into a state of exhaustion and, for some, collapse.

The Destructive Nature of Nuclear Weapons

With the ascendancy of strategic air power and the development of atomic and hydrogen weapons, human beings found the means with which to accomplish their own extermination. Cities—indeed, whole nations—could be laid waste in a matter of hours, if not minutes. The effectiveness of that kind of strategic air power against a highly urbanized and industrialized society is no longer a matter of dispute. Nuclear bombs are so destructive that they make World War II bombing attacks appear trivial by comparison. Atomic bombs, such as those dropped on Hiroshima and Nagasaki, were surpassed in destructive power within a few years by the new hydrogen bombs. Kilotons were replaced by megatons (1 megaton equals 1 million tons of TNT). A single U.S. Strategic Air Command B-52 bomber could carry 25 megatons of explosive power—12.5 times the entire explosive power of all bombs dropped during World War II, including the two atomic bombs! [7]

Physical Effects and 'Nuclear Winter.' A nuclear explosion has four physical effects: blast, fire, immediate radiation, and long-term radiation.

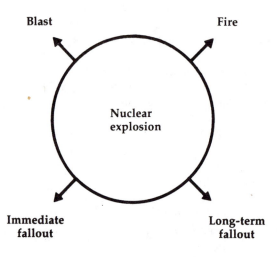

The blast, or shock wave, is the almost solid wall of air pressure produced by an explosion, creating a hurricane-type wind. The blast from a low-altitude bomb exploding in a city will collapse all wooden buildings within six miles of ground zero for a 1-megaton bomb, within fourteen miles for a 10-megaton bomb, and within thirty miles for a 100-megaton bomb. For brick buildings, the figures for the same bombs are four, nine, and eighteen miles; and, for sturdier buildings, the distance ranges from three to twelve miles.

The thermal impact of a bomb can be heightened by a higher altitude explosion or airburst. The heat generated by a 1-megaton bomb is tremendous, producing second-degree burns of the skin up to nine miles from ground zero; a 10-megaton bomb has the same effect up to twenty-four miles; a 100-megaton bomb up to seventy miles.[8] Furthermore, the heat in most instances would ignite wooden houses and other combustible objects (from plastics and furniture in homes to gas lines and furnaces) over the same range. World War II demonstrated that the real danger from fire, even when started with ordinary incendiary bombs, is the fire storm.[9] In a fire storm the intense heat from the fire rises, heating the air in turn. As the difference in pressure between the hot and colder air sucks in fresh oxygen to feed the hungry flames, the process builds in intensity. Air rushes in at ever greater speeds until wind velocity surpasses gale force. The flames, whipped by the wind and fed further by the gas, oil, and other incendiary materials of the homes and streets of the burning city, leap upward, stabbing high into the air, enveloping the stricken area. Everything burns in this tomb of heat and flame. There is no escape. Those who have not yet been crushed in their shelters are asphyxiated by lack of oxygen or by carbon monoxide poisoning; if they seek to escape into the burning streets, their lungs are seared, and their bodies, exposed to the intense heat, burst into flame. During the attack on Hamburg, the fire storm caused a ground temperature of 1,400 degrees Fahrenheit. Indeed, near the center of the fire storm the temperature exceeded 2,200 degrees Fahrenheit. A 100-megaton bomb could cause fire storms up to seventy-five miles from the point of explosion; woods, trash, and dry leaves all provide kindling.

The third and fourth effects of a nuclear explosion, the radiation impact, can be maximized by a surface burst or a low-altitude explosion. The resulting fireball—a large, rapidly expanding sphere of hot gases that produces intense heat—scoops up the debris and converts it into radioactive material. The fireball of a 10-megaton bomb has a diameter of six miles. The heavier particles of debris fall back to earth within the first few hours. Besides the immediate radiation in the area of explosion, longer-term, lighter particles "fall out" during the following days and weeks over an area the size of which depends on the magnitude of the explosion, the surface over which the explosion occurs, and meteorological conditions. The American 15-megaton thermonuclear explosion of 1954 in the Pacific Ocean caused substantial contamination over an area of 7,000 square miles (equivalent to the size of New Jersey). Under more "favorable" conditions, the fallout could have covered an area of 100,000 square miles (equivalent to the areas of New Jersey, New York, and Pennsylvania).

Fallout can emit radiation for days, months, even years. The power of this radiation depends on the amount absorbed.[10] A dose of 100 to 200 roentgens causes radiation sickness, a combination of weakness, nausea, and vomiting that is not fatal, although it can result in disability. At 200 roentgens, radiation becomes very dangerous: disability is certain, and death can come within a month. The possibility of death increases until, at 500 roentgens, it is certain for 50 percent of those exposed to the radiation. Above 600 roentgens, the number of deaths continues to mount, and deaths occur more rapidly.[11] Radiation also has two other effects: cancer and genetic transmutations that may affect subsequent generations.

Considering the overwhelmingly destructive character of a single nuclear weapon and the large number of them that the United States and the Soviet Union possess, a coordinated nuclear attack on either power's major urban and industrial centers would be catastrophic, reducing everything to rubble and leaving the population dead or injured, with little hope of help. Most hospitals, doctors, nurses, drugs, and blood plasma would be destroyed; so would the machinery for the processing and refrigeration of food and the purification of water. Medical "disaster planning" for a nuclear war is meaningless. Not surprisingly, nuclear war has been called "the last epidemic." In addition, there would be no transportation left to take survivors out of the smoldering ruins and into the countryside; most, if not all, of the fuel would have burned up. Estimates of casualties in such a coordinated urban strike range from 30 percent to 90 percent of the population, depending upon the yield of the bombs, the heights at which they were exploded, the weather, civilian protection, and preparations for coping with the aftermath of such an attack.[12]

If cities are the main targets in a nuclear war, Soviet premier Nikita Khrushchev's remark that the survivors will envy the dead appears all too true. A 1977 Department of Defense study estimated that 155 to 165 million Americans would be killed if all explosions were detonated at ground level and no civil defense measures existed. If half the explosions were airbursts, the casualties would be reduced to 122 million.[13] Other studies show equally high figures, although some differ by 20 million fatalities or so. Even "low" figures such as 55 million dead are staggering and unprecedented in the history of human existence, particularly when it is recalled that these are only the casualties that will occur immediately and within thirty days of the attack (see Figure 8-1). Deaths occurring afterwards from injury, radiation, starvation, and general economic chaos are not included. Total fatality figures would be much higher.

Today, we are more aware of some of the side effects of nuclear explosions. A 1974 study warned that nuclear war may destroy the ozone layer in the stratosphere. This layer protects all living things from ultraviolet solar radiation, which destroys protein molecules. In addition to death, destruction, and radiation, therefore, extensive ozone depletion could destroy the food chain of plants and animals upon which mankind depends for survival. As if this were not sufficient, scientists in 1983 concluded that fires from large-scale attacks on Soviet and American cities in a nuclear war would create so much smoke that it would filter out sunlight, thereby creating a "nuclear winter."[14] The Northern Hemisphere would be plunged into darkness by plumes of dust and soot suspended in the stratosphere; this would cause extensive freezing of the earth's surface, including lakes and rivers, even during the summer, leading to the extinction of a major portion of plant and animal life. Such a

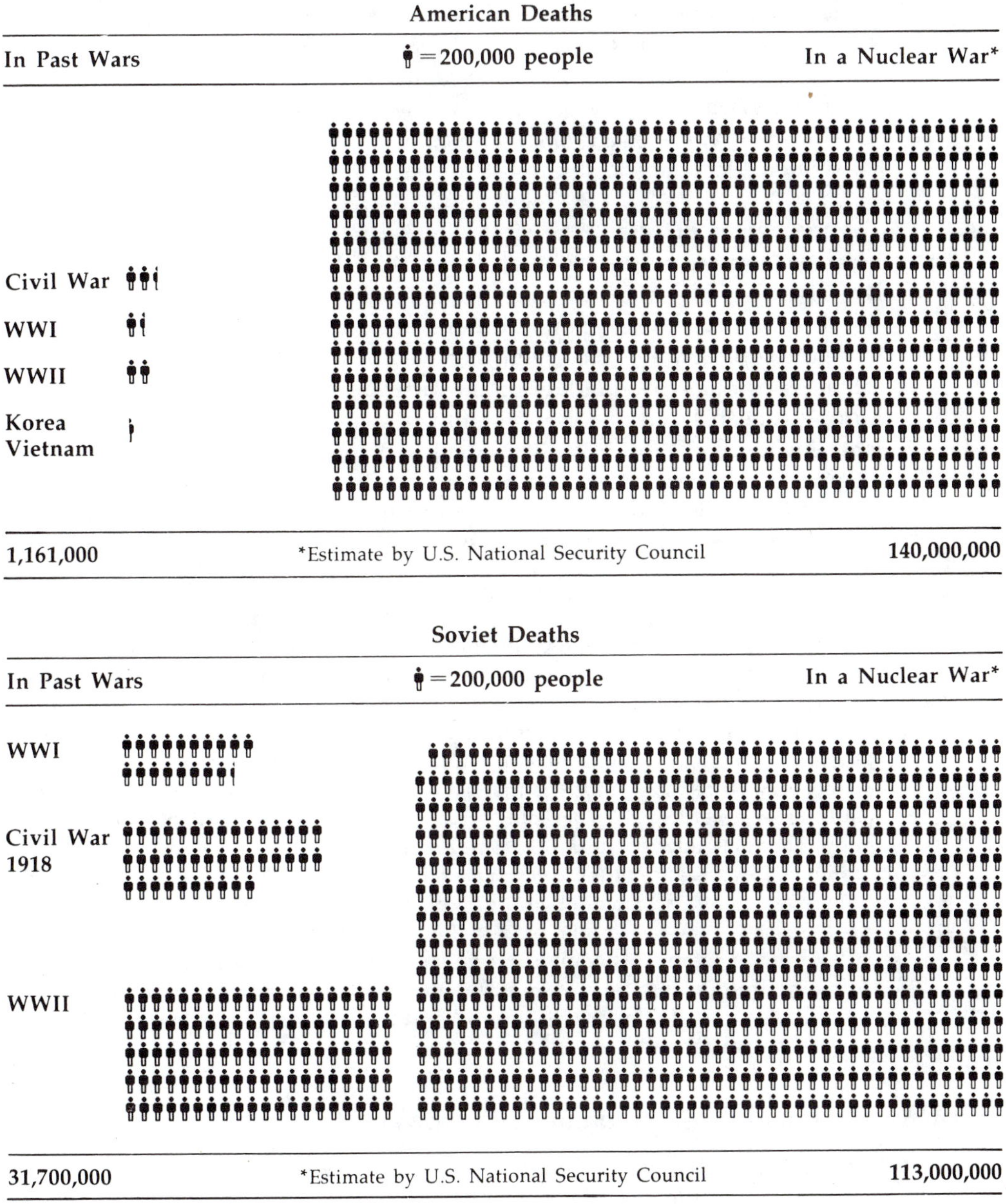

American Deaths

| In Past Wars | ⬩ = 200,000 people | In a Nuclear War* |

Civil War		
WWI		
WWII		
Korea Vietnam		

| 1,161,000 | *Estimate by U.S. National Security Council | 140,000,000 |

Soviet Deaths

| In Past Wars | ⬩ = 200,000 people | In a Nuclear War* |

WWI		
Civil War 1918		
WWII		

| 31,700,000 | *Estimate by U.S. National Security Council | 113,000,000 |

Figure 8-1 American and Soviet Deaths in Past Wars and in Projected Nuclear War

freeze might last weeks, months, possibly even years. The implications of a nuclear winter are twofold: (1) even if the initiator of a nuclear war could launch a surprise attack and destroy most of the opponent's retaliatory capability, the first-strike state would be a victor only briefly because the nuclear winter would soon cripple it as well; and (2) because the nuclear winter would spread from the Northern to the Southern Hemisphere, the human race could become extinct. Scientists continue to debate whether in fact nuclear war would unleash such a deep freeze and how long it would last. But clearly, the environmental effects of a nuclear war can no longer be considered secondary to the results of blast, fire, and radiation.

Psychological Effects. The psychological impact upon the survivors will be as devastating as the physical destruction. The elimination of a nation's largest cities, the deaths of more than 100 million of its citizens, and the wrecking of industries, communications, and transportation all would undermine the confidence of those who survived. A nation in ruins is not likely to retain its *élan vital* or entertain optimistic expectations for the future. It took Europe, especially France, more than forty years to recover from the psychological wounds of World War I and the loss of a generation on the battlefields. A quicker recovery after World War II was brought about primarily by extensive infusions of American economic aid. European losses then are minor compared with those incurred in a nuclear attack. Not only cities, but the very fabric of social life would be destroyed. Henry Kissinger noted in the late 1950s:

> Any society operates through confidence in an orderly succession of events, either natural or social. A catastrophe is an interruption in what has come to be considered natural. The panic it often produces is the reflection of an inability to react to an unexpected situation and attempt to flee as rapidly as possible into a familiar and, therefore, predictable environment. If a familiar environment remains, some confidence can be restored. Most natural catastrophes can be dealt with, because they affect only a very small geographic area or a very small proportion of the population. The remainder of the society can utilize its machinery or cooperative effort to come to the assistance of the stricken area. Indeed, such action tends to reinforce the cohesiveness of a society, because it becomes a symbol of its value and efficiency. The essence of the catastrophe produced by an all-out thermonuclear war, however, is the depth of the dislocation it produces and the consequent impossibility of escaping into familiar relationships. When all relationships, or even most relationships, have to be reconstituted, society as we know it today will have been fundamentally transformed.[15]

The Nuclear Impact on the Balance of Power

The impact of this awesome power on the conduct of international politics has been revolutionary.[16] Before 1945 war was still considered a rational instrument of policy, despite the rapidly increasing costs of modern warfare. States usually preferred to accept these costs rather than submit. Nuclear weapons, however, endanger the very substance of national life. Rather than helping to preserve civilization, the new instruments of violence promise to destroy it through the "assured destruction" of society. What possible goal could be "worth" the cost of self-immolation? How could a nation defend its political independence and territorial integrity if, in the very act of defense, it could be sacrificing itself? Nuclear war can know no victors; all the contestants will be losers. *Total wars may have been compatible with weapons of limited destructive capacity, but they are incompatible with "absolute weapons."*

The conclusion to be drawn from this general principle is that the main function of strategic military strength in the nuclear age is *deterrence* of an all-out attack. The purpose is to protect a nation's security by preventing an attack, rather than by defending the nation after an attack. The opponent is threatened with such massive retaliation that it dare not attack. The assumption is that, faced with the risk of virtual suicide, the enemy will desist. Mutual deterrence between two states, each seeking to protect its own security interests, thus becomes a matter of conflict resolution. "I won't destroy you, if you don't destroy me" is the offer of each side to the other. "We shall both lose if you attack me because I shall retaliate" is the answer.

In this extraordinary situation the role of nuclear power is that it is *not* to be used. Its primary value is in peacetime; if war erupts, it will have failed. The decisive test of arms is no longer vanquishing the enemy in battle; it is not having to fight at all. Furthermore, deterrence must be perpetual. There can be no margin for error. In previous periods of history, when deterrence failed, war resulted. Because no weapon was so destructive that failure spelled extinction, such mistakes were not irreparable. The critical issue for the military was not whether it could prevent the outbreak of hostilities but whether it could win on the battlefield. This is no longer true. The superpowers today possess overwhelming power yet are completely vulnerable to attack and destruction. We must conclude that modern nuclear warfare would be irrational. Nuclear technology has so vastly augmented the scope of violence and destruction that total war can destroy the very nation that wages it and can do so in a matter of hours, not years.

In sum, the balancing of power historically has had two purposes: protection of individual states and protection of the state system as a whole. Peace has not been the chief aim. When states have been secure, peace has followed; when states have not been secure, they have gone to war. The philosophy of "peace at any price" has been rejected by states. But nuclear weapons have changed all that; security can no longer be given priority over peace. Security and peace have become virtually identical. The deterrent function of the balance has therefore become supreme. To fight a war—a total war—to restore a balance that has been lost is no longer feasible.

DETERRENCE: SOME BASIC ASSUMPTIONS

The Stability of the Status Quo

Deterrence is based upon two assumptions; one is the acceptance of the territorial status quo, which, it is assumed, the opponent seeks to change. This acceptance, in turn, is founded upon either a belief in the justice of that status quo or in the virtue of stability. Deterrence thus could not have worked in the 1930s—and, as we know, it did not work.[17] The Versailles peace treaty was widely regarded as unjust, even by the victors of World War I. The result was that they did not enforce it. After World War II, however, memories of Adolf Hitler and of the appeasement policy that had led to that war reinforced the determination to defend the status quo. The failure of appeasement was attributed to the insatiable appetites of dictators; feeding them a few choice morsels would merely whet their appetite for more. Soviet behavior after 1945 was all too reminiscent of Germany.

The first requirement of American policy under these circumstances was to hold fast. Permitting changes in the status quo was considered appeasement that could only undermine the peace. In the 1930s appeasement had been expected to build a more solid foundation for peace; conversely, preserving the territorial status quo had been considered the sure way to war because Germany had legitimate grievances against this status quo. But after 1945 the division of Germany, for instance, may have not been "just," but both super-powers could live with it. At least it provided for a degree of stability in central Europe, and this protected Western Europe for the United States and Eastern Europe for the Soviet Union. When a challenge to the status quo occurred, the response was to demonstrate firmness rather than to make concessions. To give in would only make the situation worse.

Thus, "all the most important issues in dispute—Berlin, Germany, Formosa, the offshore islands—have remained in dispute even twenty years after the end of the war. There have been no 'betrayals.' But there have been no settlements either."[18] The challenge of the postwar world has often been just learning how to live with problems and defusing them to avoid nuclear catastrophe.

Rationality

The second assumption on which deterrence is based is that the policy makers on both sides are *rational*—that is, that they can calculate the costs and gains of any moves they contemplate and can keep a situation from getting out of control.[19] In the nuclear era especially, this assumption implies that they can recognize that the gains from destroying the adversary are completely dispro-portionate to the costs.

In the 1930s the British could not decide whether Hitler was rational. Some thought he was, believing that he would settle down once he had been appeased; others believed he was not, that he was reckless enough to engulf Europe in flames. If the Nazi leader was really such a raving maniac, it seemed the better part of valor to satisfy his demand for national self-determination and to give him his "last territorial demand in Europe."

No American policy maker in the postwar period thought of Stalin or his successors as irrational. Quite the contrary. George Kennan, in analyzing the sources of Soviet conduct during the early period of containment, noted the impact of both Communist ideology and Russian history:

> The Kremlin is under no ideological compulsion to accomplish its purpose in a hurry. Like the Church, it is dealing in ideological concepts which are of long-term validity, and it can afford to be patient. It has no right to risk the existing achievements of the revolution for the sake of vain baubles of the future. The very teachings of Lenin himself require great caution and flexibility in the pursuit of Communist purposes. Again, these precepts are fortified by the lessons of Russian history: of centuries of obscure battles between nomadic forces over the stretches of a vast unfortified plain. Here caution, circumspection, flexibility and deception are the valuable qualities; and their value finds natural appreciation in the Russian or the oriental mind. Thus the Kremlin has no compunction about retreating in the face of superior force. And being under the compulsion of no timetable, it does not get panicky under the necessity for such retreat. Its main concern is to make sure that it has filled every nook and cranny available to it in the basin of world power. But if it finds unassailable barriers in its path, it accepts these philosophically and accommodates itself to them. The main thing is that there should always be pressure, increasing constant pressure, toward the desired goal. There is no trace of any feeling in Soviet psychology that that goal must be reached at any given time.[20]

Studies of the "operational code of the Politburo" have confirmed this appraisal.[21] The Kremlin leaders did not believe in "adventurism" or "romanticism." They counseled against being provoked by the enemy into an untimely or unwise advance, and with every plan for advance they recommended a provision for retreat. Communist China's foreign policy during the years China and the United States were enemies was equally cautious, unlike the Beijing leaders' verbal militancy.

Conversely, the Soviets, first by their actions and later by their words, demonstrated that they believed U.S. policy makers to be rational as well. During the early years of the cold war, the United States held an atomic monopoly. Nevertheless, these were also the years of pressure in Iran and Turkey, of the Greek civil war, the *coup d'état* in Czechoslovakia, the use of Communist parties and Communist-controlled unions to try to undermine the Marshall Plan, and, of course, North Korean aggression. The latter in particular showed that the Soviets did not fear a retaliatory attack on Moscow. Even during 1958-62, the years of repetitive Berlin crises and the Cuban missile crisis, when Soviet leaders knew that U.S. strategic power was vastly more destructive than their own, they were confident that they could raise tensions *without* provoking the United States to war. To ensure that tensions would not go out of control, they either left themselves diplomatic escape hatches or were willing to make timely withdrawals whenever they underestimated American reactions. The Cuban missile crisis of 1962 attests to the Soviets' confidence that, short of major provocation—from which they carefully abstained—they could challenge the United States without fear of nuclear response.

Khrushchev later distinguished between American "madmen" and "realists" in Washington. The madmen allegedly believed that communism must be eliminated by military force, while the realists were committed to coexistence and arms control. The realists were in power in Washington; moreover, even madmen had a way of becoming realists.

Richard Nixon, the anti-Communist crusader of the 1950s, became the architect of détente in the 1970s. Ronald Reagan, who denounced the Soviet Union as an "evil empire," revoked Jimmy Carter's post-Afghanistan grain embargo on the Soviet Union and, despite his criticism of the 1979 SALT II agreement as "fatally flawed," observed its limits until 1986, when he stated that the United States would no longer observe it if the Soviet Union continued to violate its terms. Reagan also acted very cautiously, in striking contrast to his rhetorical fire.

THE DIPLOMACY OF COERCION

Deterrence equals diplomacy. It is not a military concept. The soldier's primary test has always been on the battlefield, and his primary professional concern has been with weapons and the exercise of violence. Deterrence, if it is to be successful, obviously must be based on weapons, but *the test is not in the use of force but in coercion, or the threat of force, to dissuade an adversary from attacking.*[22] The purpose is to influence the adversary's intentions. Such manipulation of the threat of violence is one aspect of diplomacy.[23] As already noted, a state's capacity to use nuclear arms to damage an adversary or destroy it if deemed necessary—or to reward it by refraining from such destruction—ensures the capacity to bargain.[24] The promise of not being made to suffer immense pain is an offer that nation B can extend to nation A even in peacetime, for nuclear weapons no longer make it necessary to defeat A in war first. A knows that it can be immensely hurt and does not have to engage in war to make this discovery. Indeed, A shares a *common interest* with B in avoiding war. The ability to inflict great damage can thus be exploited diplomatically before the eruption of war.[25] Modern technology has enhanced the importance of "threats of war as techniques of influence, not of destruction; of coercion and deterrence, not of conquest and defense; of bargaining and intimidation."[26]

The Credible Commitment

But how does B persuade A not to attack when A can threaten B in the same manner? Surely B's attempt at intimidation is less believable or credible when A knows that if B resorts to war it risks suicide. It is one thing to try to influence an opponent not to turn to violence, but quite another to make the opponent believe that the threats are genuine and that war will result, considering the price of such a war. More bluntly, how can the opponent be made to believe that a threat is *credible?* The principal answer: by means of a *credible commitment*.[27] But how is that achieved?

National Interests and Priorities

Credibility is basically a product of a nation's interests. Clearly, a nuclear power is most likely to go to war and to risk enormous losses if its home territory is attacked; it is also more likely to take this risk if its more important allies are attacked than when lesser allies or friends in areas of secondary importance are attacked. The potential attacker will understand this set of priorities. Moscow can have little doubt that an attack upon the United States will lead to a retaliatory strike. From time to time there may be some question in the Kremlin whether the United States will come to the defense of its North Atlantic Treaty Organization (NATO) allies in Europe. The precedent of participation in two world wars suggests that the United States takes its commitments in Western Europe seriously and that a Soviet attack would be extremely risky. In non-Western areas, however, U.S. commitments may be perceived as less credible, leading to exploratory probes to test them. Credibility is therefore largely the reflection of a nation's interests and the priorities among those interests. Not all areas or countries are of equal value. Nations may have great power, but none is omnipotent. Each has only so much power with which to achieve many different aims. This limitation is reminiscent of the old saw about having "champagne taste on a beer income." Choices must be made and priorities arranged.

Relinquishing the Initiative.   A key tactic in strengthening the credibility of a commitment is to commit the deterrer unequivocally to a course of action should the opponent move in spite of warnings. *The deterrer relinquishes the initiative.* By announcing that it will stand firm, regardless of the costs, the deterrer places on the other side the responsibility for the next move and therefore the responsibility for precipitating a conflict. The deterrer's "initiative that forces the opponent to initiate" thus becomes critical. In real political life, however, such irrevocable commitments are rare, for states seldom take stands from which they cannot retreat if their adversaries stand firm and hostilities appear to be both imminent and undesirable. Threats are usually more ambiguous and commitments somewhat more porous. While irrevocable commitments may give the adversary the choice of war or peace, they also surrender the defender's control over events. A mixture of firmness and flexibility is therefore a more normal pattern of interaction.[28]

The Necessity for Resolve.   Keeping commitments also depends on resolve. To understand why, we can subdivide the concept of balance of power into the *balance of resolve* and the *balance of capability*.[29] For bargaining purposes, the deterrer's requirements are threefold: possession of military capability, determination to use it, and evaluation of both by the potential attacker. Power, however massive, is ineffective without the willingness to use it, and, even when these two factors are present, deterrence will still fail unless the adversary perceives their presence.

$$\text{deterrence} = \text{capability} \times \text{perceived resolve}$$

Why, we asked earlier, did World War II erupt? The answer revolves around Britain's policy of appeasement. The German-Allied military balance was not as lopsided throughout the late 1930s as the swift German victories in the spring of 1940 suggest.[30] What was more significant was the balance of resolve. Even after Britain had publicly pledged assistance to Poland in the event of a German attack, Hitler continued to perceive a lack of British determination. After years of appeasement, this perception was not surprising. Perhaps it is more surprising that British leaders thought the Nazi leader would see their commitment as credible. In the deterrent equation, if either capability or political will is low (or perceived as low), the ability to deter declines.

This intangible element of resolve is particularly difficult to evaluate. Each power's perception of the other's resolve is likely to fluctuate with time and specific occurrences. Khrushchev's image of U.S. determination was apparently greatly influenced by John Kennedy's early policies: the failure to support with U.S. forces the abortive Bay of Pigs landing by anti-Castro Cuban refugees in 1961 and the inaction at the time of the building of the Berlin Wall a few months later. The result was that in 1962 Khrushchev was tempted to establish a missile base close to American shores, despite the Monroe Doctrine and Kennedy's warning against establishment by another power of a base in the Western Hemisphere.[31] After 1962 U.S. resolve was once again clearly established.

The danger is that if A acts—or does not act—consistently with B's image of the way A should act, B may push, expecting A to retreat. A may do so, and its resolve may then decline further. If at some point A vows to stand firm instead of retreating, but fails to make that vow credible to B, war will erupt because of miscalculation. Thus, the balance of resolve may be unstable in two respects: when one side is inclined to retreat and when one side fails to communicate its genuine resolve to its opponent.

Interdependence of Commitments

It is not surprising that both nuclear giants have been continuously concerned about the credibility of their commitments and have tended to see their commitments as interdependent.[32] If a specific commitment to preserve a particular line, or frontier, is no longer credible, regardless of how distant or unimportant that line may seem, B may come to believe that other commitments made by A are also no longer credible. That perception may then tempt B to seek further expansion of its own power.

As critics of the disastrous U.S. commitment in Vietnam have repeatedly stressed, a nation's interests and commitments are not all equally important; they are scaled hierarchically according to criteria of security. A country's defaulting on some commitments that are of low priority does not automatically signal to the adversary that there is a lack of resolve to honor more important commitments. According to this line of argument, not defending South Vietnam would not have meant that West Berlin would not have been defended. In the abstract, this qualification of the "interdependence of commitments" is correct.

But two key questions remain: First, how can B always be sure of A's ranking of priorities; and, second, even if B can make some pretty good guesses, will A's yielding of a lower-priority commitment not tempt B to test A's resolve in an area of greater importance? After all, without testing, B cannot really know whether A's determination is indeed stronger. The failure of A to honor a commitment in one area may thus be viewed by the potential attacker as an indication that other commitments will also not be honored. *States generally think that their overall reputation is more important than, and relatively independent of, the specific interest and commitment being challenged.*[33]

U.S. ARMS CONTROL DOCTRINE

The Rationale

For a state to deter its opponent, it must have the forces to launch a massive retaliation. Before World War II, states normally had military forces with which they hoped to prevent enemy attack, but these forces were never nearly as strong as the forces that could be mobilized if war actually broke out. Since war was not fatal, there was no reason to keep large and expensive forces continuously at the ready. Plowshares were to be converted into swords after the attack. This attitude was particularly prevalent in the United States. Protected by two oceans and thus not subject to invasion or even air attack, it had time to mobilize its vast power after it became involved in war. But nuclear deterrence requires peacetime readiness of all the forces that would be required for retaliation if an enemy attack occurred. If deterrence is to be permanent, the enemy must never doubt that it would be committing suicide should it strike first.

The need for a wartime offensive capability is thus constant and requires unfailing concern with effective delivery systems. This is a difficult problem because of the rapid technological changes that have occurred every few years since 1945. Like the factor of resolve, they have become critical in determining the stability of the nuclear balance of power. Even the early nuclear delivery systems tended to destabilize the postwar equilibrium because of the ability of fast bombers to execute surprise attacks. It is true, of course, that even before the development of high-speed bombers surprise attack had been possible. The Germans had achieved it against the Soviets in 1941, despite the large-scale movement of troops to Poland that it had necessitated, and the Japanese had been highly successful at Pearl Harbor a few months later. The speed of postwar bombers, however, made surprise attack even more feasible, particularly since it would no longer have to be preceded by massive troop or ship movements.

Although the United States during the first two decades of the cold war sought to deter a Soviet attack by threatening to drop enough bombs virtually to wipe the Soviet Union off the map, this threat would have been meaningless if most American bombers could have been destroyed in a surprise attack. The surviving bombers would then not have been able to retaliate with sufficient destructiveness. Not all of them would have had enough fuel to reach their targets. Soviet fighters and ground-to-air missiles, alerted for the arrival of those bombers that did reach Soviet territory, would have been able to shoot down many, if not most. The few that did manage to penetrate Soviet defenses might no longer have been able to wreak catastrophic damage. Indeed, the level of damage might have been acceptable to Soviet leaders if it meant the elimination of their deadliest enemy.

The vulnerability of bombers to a nuclear Pearl Harbor thus rendered the balance of power very unstable because of the enormous advantages gained by the side that struck the initial blow. Possessing only bombs was insufficient to ensure that war would not result. The possibility of eliminating the opponent's retaliatory bombers—bombers above ground being considered "soft" targets—constituted a powerful incentive to attack. The consequent balance was therefore a delicate one. What conditions might instigate an opponent's first strike against one's own retaliatory force? And what could be done to prevent such an attack and "stabilize" mutual deterrence?[34] These questions preoccupied students of arms control in the late 1950s and 1960s. Proponents of arms control rejected the feasibility of general disarmament and assumed that neither conflicts among states nor nuclear weapons would be abolished (see Chapter 17). Instead, the best hope for earthly salvation seemed to them to lie in the "control" of armaments. In a competitive state system, deterrence was recognized as the only feasible policy. It had to be improved, however, to be made "safe."

Preemptive and Preventive Strikes.   Arms control thus supplemented the more traditional defense policies, as its aim was identical: to protect the national security by deterring war. Whereas disarmament stressed the reduction of a nation's military capability, either completely or partially, arms control emphasized the elimination of American and Soviet incentives to strike first. Two presuppositions underlay arms control: despite the continuation of their political conflict, both nuclear powers shared a *common interest in avoiding nuclear war*; and both possessed delivery systems that raised tensions by providing a strong and *independent incentive for a first strike*.[35] Of paramount importance is hitting first because, in the nuclear age, to come in second is to lose. Policy makers thus might be tempted to launch a first strike.

Remember the first law of preservation in the state system: Be suspicious. One side's gain—and any proposal by a potential adversary is assumed to have advantages for itself—is usually considered the other side's loss. The fear of loss is particularly acute in the military sphere, where each party is hypersensitive to the possibility of being inferior. Few arms agreements have existed in history precisely because states, driven by their sense of insecurity, prefer to add arms to their already existing arsenals to ensure that they will not find themselves lacking. *Arms control thinking, however, is based on the assumption that one side's gain is not necessarily the other's loss; both sides can gain simultaneously.*

If the only defense is indeed an offense, then a *preemptive strike* is a particular danger during crisis periods. It differs from a *preventive strike*, in which the aggressor coolly plans the strike beforehand with confidence that it can obliterate the opponent; the attacker picks a specific date and then sends its forces on their way, regardless of possible provocation. In a preemptive strike, however, the attack is launched in order to forestall a strike by the enemy. In this instance the aggressor believes that the opponent is about to strike; it therefore strikes first to destroy the enemy's forces before they take off. The attack results from moves on the other side that are interpreted as menacing.[36]

The role of a possible miscalculation in precipitating a preemptive strike is clear. The signs that an opponent is about to launch an attack are likely to be ambiguous. The opponent may simply be taking measures to make its own strategic force less vulnerable and thereby to enhance its deterrent stance. For instance, during the years the United States and Soviet Union possessed mainly bombers, the opponent might have sent many of them into the air to avoid having them caught on the ground; by making them less vulnerable to sudden destruction, the opponent might try to prevent the other side from launching an attack. But the action itself could easily have been misinterpreted as the prelude to an attack. In a situation of mutual vulnerability, in which the "nice guy" finishes last, delay can prove fatal.

Offensive action may therefore be the only wise course. Thomas Schelling thus describes the odd logic of preemption: " 'Self-defense' becomes peculiarly compounded if we have to worry about his striking us to keep us from striking him to keep him from striking us." [37] What is important, in short, is not what A intends to do but B's perception of A's intentions. In this type of hair-trigger situation, the interpretation cannot be conservative. Because the survival of the nation is at stake, it is necessary to assume the worst. To return to our example, the strategic bombers of both sides were, of course, ready at all times to take off on their missions. When one side places a large number of them in the air, the possibility of a sudden attack increases. Even defensive actions, intended merely to enhance one's deterrent power, may intensify international tensions or touch off nuclear conflagration. Paradoxically, then, the very weapons intended to deter nuclear war may well precipitate it.

Stabilizing Mutual Deterrence.　How then can a preventive war and especially a preemptive strike be forestalled? The answer is to make each side's retaliatory or second-strike forces invulnerable. *A second-strike force is one that can absorb an initial blow and still effectively perform its retaliatory mission.* The deterrent force that matters is that part likely to be left after an initial enemy attack; the size of the force before the attack is less relevant. In the bomber era, an invulnerable deterrent force was impossible. The solution was twofold. First, instead of relying on one weapons system for deterrence, several systems were to be developed so that if one became vulnerable as technology changed, the others would still be safe and deterrence remain assured. It was best to err on the side of safety. Thus, the United States and the Soviet Union developed a triad consisting of bombers, intercontinental ballistic missiles (ICBMs), and submarine-launched ballistic missiles (SLBMs) (see Table 8-1 and Figure 8-2). Second, the backbone of the deterrent forces was solid-fuel missiles that can be fired instantly. They can be dispersed more easily than bombers, which are generally concentrated at a relatively small number of bases, the location of which is easily discoverable. Missiles, unlike bombers on the ground, can also be hardened, or placed in underground concrete silos that can withstand the enormous pressure from the blast of a nuclear explosion. Most important, sea-launched missiles—in contrast to stationary ICBMs—can be concealed and made mobile by placing them in nuclear submarines whose exact location is not known to the enemy.

The importance of the dispersal, hardening, mobility, and concealment of missiles lies in the fact that they deprive a surprise attack of its rationale. The entire justification for a first strike had been to surprise the opponent with its bombers on the ground and to destroy them. But when the opponent's retaliatory power is basically invulnerable, obliterating the enemy's cities will benefit the aggressor very little. Surprise no longer confers any significant advantage to the side that hits first. The enemy's first strike cannot destroy the ability to strike back. The fact that a second-strike force will remain is the

Table 8-1 U.S. and Soviet Strategic Launchers, Summer 1985

Type of Launcher	United States	Soviet Union
ICBMs	1,000[a]	1,398
SLBMs	640	930
Intercontinental bombers	324	170

[a] Actually, by mid-1985 the United States had ten Titan missiles left of the original fifty-four. All will be dismantled by 1987.

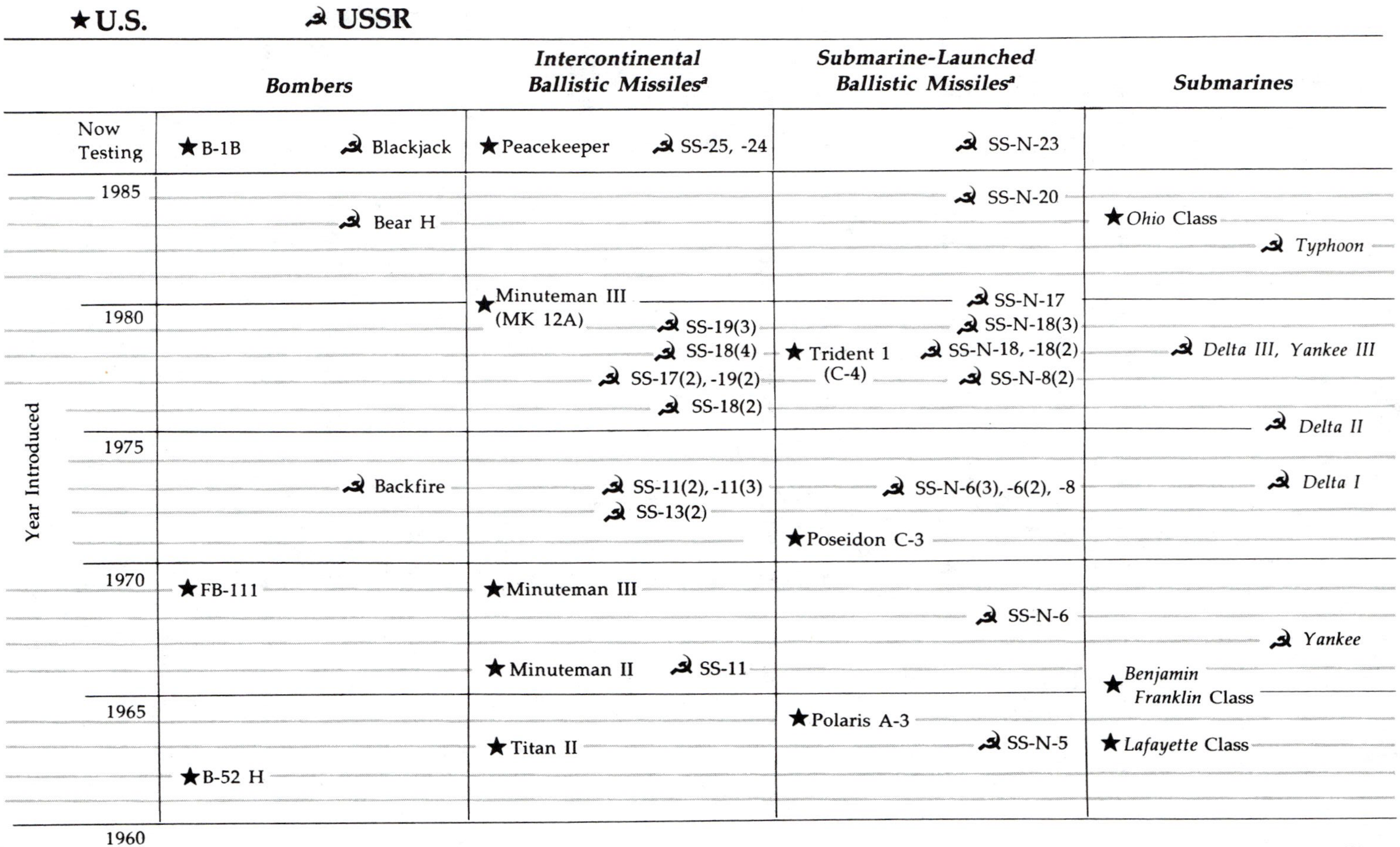

★ U.S.   ⋆ USSR

Bombers | Intercontinental Ballistic Missiles[a] | Submarine-Launched Ballistic Missiles[a] | Submarines

Year Introduced

Now Testing
- ★ B-1B ⋆ Blackjack (Bombers)
- ★ Peacekeeper ⋆ SS-25, -24 (Intercontinental Ballistic Missiles)
- ⋆ SS-N-23 (Submarine-Launched Ballistic Missiles)

1985
- ⋆ Bear H (Bombers)
- ⋆ SS-N-20 (Submarine-Launched Ballistic Missiles)
- ★ Ohio Class ⋆ Typhoon (Submarines)

1980
- ★ Minuteman III (MK 12A) ⋆ SS-19(3) ⋆ SS-18(4) ⋆ SS-17(2), -19(2) ⋆ SS-18(2) (Intercontinental Ballistic Missiles)
- ⋆ SS-N-17 ⋆ SS-N-18(3) ★ Trident 1 (C-4) ⋆ SS-N-18, -18(2) ⋆ SS-N-8(2) (Submarine-Launched Ballistic Missiles)
- ⋆ Delta III, Yankee III (Submarines)
- ⋆ Delta II (Submarines)

1975
- ⋆ Backfire (Bombers)
- ⋆ SS-11(2), -11(3) ⋆ SS-13(2) (Intercontinental Ballistic Missiles)
- ⋆ SS-N-6(3), -6(2), -8 (Submarine-Launched Ballistic Missiles)
- ★ Poseidon C-3 (Submarine-Launched Ballistic Missiles)
- ⋆ Delta I (Submarines)

1970
- ★ FB-111 (Bombers)
- ★ Minuteman III (Intercontinental Ballistic Missiles)
- ⋆ SS-N-6 (Submarine-Launched Ballistic Missiles)
- ⋆ Yankee (Submarines)

1965
- ★ Minuteman II ⋆ SS-11 (Intercontinental Ballistic Missiles)
- ★ Polaris A-3 (Submarine-Launched Ballistic Missiles)
- ⋆ SS-N-5 (Submarine-Launched Ballistic Missiles)
- ★ Benjamin Franklin Class (Submarines)
- ★ Lafayette Class (Submarines)
- ★ Titan II (Intercontinental Ballistic Missiles)

1960
- ★ B-52 H (Bombers)

[a] The modification series for Soviet intercontinental and submarine-launched ballistic missiles is shown in parentheses—for example: SS-19(3), SS-N-18(2).

Figure 8-2 U.S.-Soviet Strategic Arms: Modernity Compared

best guarantee against war. *Invulnerable deterrents stabilize mutual deterrence.*[38] Once the advantage of an initial attack has been greatly reduced, if not eliminated, the incentive to strike at all, and the possibility of war, also disappears.

Characteristics of Arms Control

There are three critical elements of U.S. arms control thinking: first, the numbers of nuclear weapons needed to achieve the "assured destruction" of the other society is the criterion of how many each side needs, not the number of weapons the opponent has; second, deterrence requires urban areas to be left vulnerable to attack as "hostages"; third, second-strike forces must be invulnerable, so that the enemy can never believe that he can destroy enough forces to survive a retaliatory strike. Each of these points will be considered in turn.

Parity in Numbers of Weapons.   *The balance of capability does not necessarily require equality in numbers of bombers and missiles.* A balance is achieved when each side has a second-strike force able to destroy the opponent's homeland after absorbing an initial blow. The best size for such a second-strike force may vary quite a bit in the views of U.S. and Soviet leaders. For example, SALT I, the 1972 agreement on offensive arms, froze the strategic missiles of the United States at 1,054 ICBMs, plus 656 more SLBMs. The Soviet Union was permitted to have 1,618 ICBMs, plus 740 SLBMs. The treaty seems to have given the Soviets a hefty advantage of 2,358 missiles to 1,710, but it seems less unequal when we note that approximately 450 U.S. bombers (as opposed to 150 Soviet bombers) were allowed.

According to U.S. leaders' arms control thinking, even if most U.S. land-based missiles were destroyed in their silos by Soviet ICBMs, a sizable bomber fleet plus (at that time) 41 nuclear submarines, each one armed with 16 missiles, would remain. Thirty-one of these submarines carry missiles that possess 10 warheads each, for a total of 4,960. Could Moscow, therefore, really risk launching a strike on the assumption that it might be able to destroy enough of the U.S. second-strike force to prevent the latter from inflicting overwhelming retaliatory damage on the Soviet Union? Would such a move not represent a reckless gamble—a "cosmic roll of the dice," as Harold Brown, Carter's secretary of defense, called it—even if the total Soviet strike force was larger than that of the United States by several hundred missiles? [39]

The superpowers can inflict unacceptable damage on each other. Long ago they reached a plateau—variously called *parity, sufficiency, mutual deterrence, nuclear stalemate,* and *balance of terror*—in their capability to destroy each other. The nuclear balance, or mutual deterrence, is not sensitive to numerical variations if each side retains an invulnerable deterrent force capable of the assured destruction of the enemy's society.

Vulnerable Populations and Economies.   *Urban industrial areas are deliberately left unprotected as hostages.* In 1964 the Soviets began to deploy an antiballistic missile (ABM) system around Moscow. By itself, the Soviet ABM constituted no problem. The problem lay in the possibility of an extensive ABM deployment to protect the Soviet urban population. If such ABMs were capable of shooting down a large percentage of missiles in a retaliatory strike—or if the Soviets believed they could—it might weaken the U.S. capability to deter. For deterrence depends upon the ability to hold the adversary's population hostage: a Soviet ability to greatly reduce America's capacity to inflict unacceptable losses upon Soviet cities might, by eliminating the possibility of suicide, tempt the Soviets to risk launching a preventive or preemptive first strike. Anything that detracts from the superiority of the offense to inflict assured destruction on the opponent tends to destabilize mutual deterrence, which is based on a *vulnerable population and invulnerable offensive forces.* An ABM protecting cities is a "bad" weapon in the sense that it can endanger nuclear deterrence.[40] In SALT I the ABM, for all practical purposes, was abandoned and cities left correspondingly vulnerable.

Invulnerable Retaliatory Forces.   Because invulnerable second-strike forces are the key to the stability of mutual deterrence, *the weapons produced and deployed must be the "right" kind.* Whether a weapon is right or wrong, good or bad, depends on whether it will help to stabilize the balance or to destabilize it; these terms have no moral connotations in this context. Bombers, when they constituted the backbone of deterrence, were bad because they were vulnerable to attack. Missiles, because they can be dispersed, protected in silos, or moved around and concealed underwater, are good; it is not so easy then for a surprise attack to destroy one's retaliatory capacity. Indeed, in the early 1960s it was believed that once both powers possessed invulnerable missiles, peace was guaranteed because there was no point in attacking; moreover, it was expected that once each power had reached the level it needed to retaliate, the arms race would end.

It was this kind of arms control thinking that during the 1970s led the superpowers to first freeze their offensive forces in SALT I and then set equal ceilings for both powers in SALT II, ceilings that were to be lowered in future agreements (see Table 8-2). Such an agreement has not yet been negotiated, in part because of changing technological and doctrinal developments.

THE THREATS TO STABLE MUTUAL DETERRENCE

Technological Innovations

Just as technology had stabilized mutual deterrence with single-warhead missiles that were not especially accurate—they were accurate enough to hit

Table 8-2 The Provisions of SALT

	SALT I (1972)		SALT II (1979)[a] United States and Soviet Union
	United States	*Soviet Union*	
Total of all strategic delivery systems	1,710	2,358	2,250 (including bombers)
Intercontinental ballistic missiles (ICBMs)	1,054 (550 with MIRVs)	1,618 (minus 210 older ICBMs that could be scrapped and replaced by SLBMs)	820 (all with MIRVs: Soviets could keep 308 heavy missiles such as the SS-18 allowed by SALT I)
Submarine-launched ballistic missiles (SLBMs)	656 (496 with MIRVs)	740 (plus 210 SLBMs)	1,200 (SLBMs *and* ICBMs with MIRVs)
Bombers	(450, excluded under SALT I)	(150, excluded under SALT I)	1,320 (SLBMs, ICBMs with MIRVs, plus bombers with ALCMs)
			930 (single warhead ICBMs, SLBMs, and bombers without ALCMs)

MIRVs = Multiple independent warheads or reentry vehicles
ALCMs = Air launched cruise missiles
[a] Unratified by the United States. The Reagan administration, however, observed its limits until 1986.

cities, but not accurate enough to hit missiles in their silos—so technology in the 1970s appeared to be undermining this stability, first with multiple warheads (or MIRVs, multiple independent reentry vehicles), and then with increasingly accurate guidance systems. The United States began "MIRVing" its missiles to overwhelm Soviet ABMs with more warheads than they could shoot down; this would help preserve the offense's superiority over defense and preserve the credibility of deterrence. In this context, MIRVs were intended to stabilize mutual deterrence.

But MIRVs' major long-run impact has been to destabilize mutual assured destruction (MAD); they once more made it possible for both superpowers to strike first. If both the United States and the Soviet Union had, for example, 1,000 ICBMs with single warheads, a surprise attack on the other would not be feasible. On the assumption that it takes two warheads to destroy one missile, it would take 2,000 ICBMs to eliminate the opponent's 1,000 ICBMs. If, however, one side had three warheads per missile and the other eight, then the latter gains the capability to destroy the former's missile sites with a fraction of its ICBM force. It will have ICBMs to spare.

More specifically, the United States has 2,100 ICBM warheads, 1,650 of them on 550 Minuteman III missiles. The Soviet Union has 1,400 ICBMs; 308 of these are the gigantic SS-18s, most with 10 warheads on each missile, and 350 SS-19s with 6 warheads apiece, for a total of more than 5,000 warheads. Theoretically, either the SS-18s or the SS-19s could destroy most of the 1,000 U.S. ICBMs.[41] Operationally, a Soviet attempt to do so would run into many problems—for example, missiles could malfunction, go off course, or not arrive at their targets fast enough to prevent a U.S. launch-under-attack. These problems would make the first strike less successful and leave the United States with a sufficient retaliatory capability. Moreover, the United States would still have its SLBMs, which have more warheads than ICBMs. Deterrence should therefore continue. Whatever temptation there may be to strike first and destroy the opponent's retaliatory capability, the likelihood of being able to do so is small. Certainly, given the awesome consequences of miscalculation—committing suicide if one fails—the United States and the Soviet Union have every reason to continue to be extremely cautious rather than rash.

Nevertheless, one worrisome feature is that in the late 1980s the United States, like the Soviet Union, added to its arsenal 50 to 100 MXs (missile experimental), large missiles with 10 accurate warheads. Trident II missiles, to be placed on U.S. submarines in the 1990s, will also have a counterforce capability. In short, both superpowers will continue to increase the already large numbers of accurate missiles capable of destroying the opponent's ICBMs. The danger will be that, as in the bomber era, each side's ICBMs will be vulnerable to a first strike, and that in a crisis, *each will feel that it must preempt.* Neither will think it can afford to wait and see whether in fact the other side will strike first. Fearing such an attack, each will be concerned to protect its retaliatory forces, and each will feel compelled to beat the other to the punch. Such "crisis instability" is obviously potentially dangerous.

The addition of MIRVs, however, was not the only problem. Accords reached during the SALT era were based upon a clear-cut distinction between strategic nuclear weapons and, for instance, theater nuclear weapons (arms whose range was limited to a "theater" of operations like Western Europe). This distinction made it possible to verify agreements. But increasingly this distinction eroded. During the SALT II negotiations the United States was greatly concerned that the Soviet Backfire bomber might be used in intercontinental bombing operations, despite Soviet disavowals of such a purpose. The Soviets for years considered as strategic any weapons that could reach Soviet territory, and thus they have long been concerned about U.S. planes on aircraft carriers in the Mediterranean and fighter-bombers in Western Europe.

In more recent years, the Soviets defined U.S. missiles such as the Pershing II and cruise missiles (very accurate, unpiloted planes), both stationed in Western Europe, as strategic. Indeed, under SALT II, each bomber, mainly carrying cruise missiles, is counted as equivalent to a MIRVed strategic missile. In short, what is or is not a strategic weapon is harder and harder to tell, and that difficulty is one reason for the lack of progress in arms control since SALT II.

But what technology puts awry, it can also put right. One proposed means for restabilizing mutual deterrence is the small, mobile, single-warheaded Midgetman ICBM. Since it was the addition of multiple warheads to missiles that constituted the main threat to the stability of the strategic balance, the idea was to revert to an earlier era of missiles with only one warhead. Admittedly, the accuracy of guidance systems could not be wished away, but the assumption was that if both superpowers possessed about the same number of missiles, neither would dare risk a first strike, especially if each side's ICBMs were mobile. The future of Midgetman remains unknown: the Soviets have not been asked whether such an idea was acceptable to them, and members of the Reagan administration, apparently not worried by arms control considerations, opposed the missile because with one warhead it had "too little bang for the buck."

Soviet Strategic Doctrine

Two years after the Cuban missile crisis in 1962, the Soviets launched a massive and sustained military buildup of both nuclear and conventional forces, the purpose of which was strategic parity with—if not superiority to—the United States. Also of concern to U.S. policy makers was the Soviet emphasis on extensive civil defense measures to protect the Soviet population. Most worrying, however, was the Soviet deployment, in the wake of the 1972 SALT I agreement, of the SS-18 and SS-19 with their first-strike capability at a time when the U.S. retaliatory capability was fundamentally a countercity, not counterforce, capability.

This growing number of missiles and accurate warheads, together with the civil defense measures and first-strike counterforce weapons, suggested an ominous development: a Soviet nuclear war-fighting capability quite contrary to a deterrent strategy through a retaliatory second strike.[42] In reality, the Soviet version of deterrence was quite different from that of the United States. The Soviet military believed that if war were about to erupt, Soviet strategy should be to seize the initiative and preempt in order to destroy as much of the American retaliatory force as possible. The purpose of such a strike would be to reduce the destruction the United States could inflict on the Soviet Union, destruction the Soviets expected would be reduced even more by civil defense efforts. By contrast, U.S. strategy concedes the first strike to the opponent, assuming that it could be deterred by the threat of ultimate punishment.

This difference in strategy did not mean the Soviets were not interested in deterrence. They were. Soviet political leaders repeatedly stressed that they sought only strategic parity, not superiority, and that only crazy people bent on suicide would start a nuclear war.[43] They rejected Washington's charge that the Soviet Union believed it could fight and win a nuclear war. Soviet military leaders believed, however, that if deterrence failed, they must fight a nuclear war. Therefore, they concentrated on the appropriate means of pre-empting in such circumstances, thereby limiting the damage to the Soviet Union. It was their conviction, in fact, that this Soviet capability to fight a nuclear war was the best means of deterring the United States. Unlike the United States, the Soviets see deterrence and war fighting not as mutually exclusive but as one and the same thing. The capability to fight a nuclear war was the best guarantee against a failure of deterrence. Nevertheless, the ambiguity between Soviet political leaders' stress on deterrence and the Soviet military's offensive orientation greatly worried the United States, leading it to adopt a counterforce posture as well.

U.S. Counterforce Planning

The increase in the numbers and accuracy of MIRVs, plus Soviet military doctrine, led the United States to imitate the Soviets rather than the other way around. (The Americans had hoped the Soviets would adopt the U.S. arms control doctrine revolving around mutual assured destruction.) The reason for this change in U.S. policy was the fear that, at a time of strategic parity, a Soviet first strike on U.S. strategic forces (ICBMs, bombers, and nuclear submarines) might no longer be deterred by the threat of retaliating on Soviet cities.[44] More specifically, a U.S. second strike might no longer deter a Soviet first strike because the Soviets, by launching a counterforce attack, would by and large avoid hitting America's cities. If the United States, therefore, retaliated against Soviet urban areas, the Soviets could use their remaining missiles to hit America's population centers. The critical question is whether the United States would risk committing suicide in these circumstances. Would the likelihood of a Soviet third strike against America's population deter America's second strike against Soviet cities? "If the Soviet leadership believed that in response to a nuclear attack by them we would be forced to choose between suicide and surrender, might they not conclude that we would not respond to an attack at all? Would deterrence not be gravely weakened?" asks Secretary of Defense Caspar Weinberger.[45]

To cope with this question, the United States also began deploying counterforce weapons. With the ability to respond tit-for-tat to a Soviet attack limited to specific military targets, such as ICBMs—and holding in reserve forces that could attack Soviet cities if the Soviets hit U.S. cities—the United States was trying to strengthen the credibility of its deterrence posture and avoid ever having to face a suicide-or-surrender alternative. This war-fighting capability—previously viewed as the very opposite of deterrence—was then viewed in terms similar to the Soviets': "not something separate from our strategy of deterrence," said Weinberger. "In fact, it forms the foundation of effective deterrence." [46]

The critics were less sure that a U.S. capability of fighting a limited nuclear war would fortify deterrence; rather, they feared its opposite. If both powers believed that they could avoid mutual annihilation, they might risk a nuclear attack. Others were skeptical that a limited nuclear war could be fought; the momentum of such a conflict was bound to escalate. Finally, the Soviets said that they did not believe in limited nuclear war; a nuclear war would be total. [47]

STAR WARS: ESCAPING THE NUCLEAR DILEMMA?

It was in this context that in 1983 President Reagan proposed his Strategic Defense Initiative (SDI). Its purpose, he said, would be to render missiles "impotent and obsolete." [48] A three-phase system, SDI would try to shoot down the missiles in their initial boost phase, which lasts approximately five minutes; next it would try to shoot down the warheads after they had separated from the missile in midphase flight; and last, a terminal defense would try to destroy those warheads that had escaped. The president stressed that rather than continuing to rely on a retaliatory strategy, which might kill tens of millions of people if deterrence failed, SDI would protect people, make retaliation unnecessary, and destroy weapons (rather than MAD, which protected weapons and killed people). And when the research and testing were finished, Reagan said, the United States would share its technology with the Soviets so that both powers could escape the nuclear nightmare.

Needless to say, SDI had its critics. Calling it "star wars," they said it was technically not feasible; that the first time it was needed, it would have to work perfectly, an unlikely prospect for an extremely complex system that could never be completely tested; that anything less than total effectiveness would still result in mass destruction; that it would spur the Soviets to an offensive buildup to overwhelm U.S. defenses; and that the Soviets would also match the United States in building up its defenses. [49] In short, the result would be two new prohibitively expensive offensive and defensive arms races that would violate the 1972 ABM treaty, and, at the end of these races, the United States would be less secure than before. According to the critics, the less costly and more realistic alternative was to negotiate a major reduction of offensive arms; there was no technical solution to the arms competition, only a political one.

As these arguments raged, the Reagan administration offered an interim defense of SDI: terminal defense, technologically already pretty much available, for the increasingly vulnerable ICBMs. This would help to restabilize the deterrent balance. This made sense to the degree that the Soviets, believing that such a defense might be reasonably effective, and calculating that they could not destroy most U.S. ICBMs in a preemptive strike, would be less likely to launch such a strike. Missile protection would thus strengthen U.S. deterrence.

However correct this forecast might be, the proposal was at odds with Reagan's SDI aim to eliminate missiles. Instead of doing away with offensive forces, this "interim" deployment assumed their continued existence. They were only to be made less vulnerable to attack so that they could retaliate. Ironically, if SDI technology were to be successful and deployed, the likelihood that it might shoot down many, if not all, incoming missiles might influence the Soviet Union (and the United States, once a Soviet SDI was in place) to retarget cities. If only a limited number of missiles would get through, the only way to assure the opponent's destruction would be to wipe out as many cities as possible. Thus, a system intended to protect the population might make its elimination all the more certain! Incapable of placing a dome-like shield over an entire country, SDI was more likely to spur on the arms race as the defense sought to catch up with the offense and the offense sought to reestablish its superiority over the defense. As the critics pointed out, it was dubious that SDI would render deterrence obsolete and eliminate the worry that the human race would become extinct. But technological development is not going to stop with SDI, any more than it stopped after World War I had established—briefly, as it turned out—the superiority of the defense over the offense.

Indeed, just as the United States had once worried that Soviet ABM deployment might tempt a Soviet first strike, the Soviets expressed their concern that SDI would lead to an American first strike on the Soviet Union. Neither the Soviet ABM nor the U.S. SDI could protect against an all-out strike by the opponent, but they might well be able to deal effectively with a retaliatory strike that had been seriously crippled by a first strike. Like the ABM earlier, SDI was perceived as not stabilizing, but destabilizing, the deterrent equation. Moreover, it blocked a new SALT, or what the Reagan administration preferred to call START (Strategic Arms Reduction Talks), agreement. Just as President Nixon had refused to limit U.S. offensive forces in SALT I without a simultaneous agreement on the levels of defense forces—if the Soviets wished to have a large number of ABMs, the United States would need to raise the numbers of its missiles to overcome an ABM defense—so the Soviets in the 1980s refused to radically reduce their offensive capability in the absence of an agreement limiting SDI to research while preventing any deployment. Thus, a potential bargain was visible, if the political leaders on both sides wanted an agreement: a 50 percent cut in strategic forces, which would significantly reduce the Soviet threat of a first strike against U.S. ICBMs, for a postponement of SDI deployment, and its possible elimination in future arms control agreements. But at the Iceland summit in 1986, President Reagan rejected such a deal; whether the president was simply bargaining hard or whether SDI is not a "bargaining chip" remains to be determined.

DETERRENCE AND THE NUCLEAR ARMS RACE

Would it be correct to say that the continuing nuclear arms race in offensive and defensive weapons is very dangerous and is likely to end up in a nuclear war? The very term *arms race* is consistent with the widely held view that arms races are the cause of war, that basically armaments and peace are incompatible—more specifically, that the more armaments there are, the greater is the danger of war. The logical conclusion is to reduce arms to ensure peace. Sir Edward Grey, Britain's foreign minister on the eve of World War I, made this classic statement on arms races:

> The moral is obvious: it is that great armaments lead inevitably to war. If there are armaments on one side there must be armaments on other sides. While one nation arms, other nations cannot tempt it to aggression by remaining defenceless. . . . The enormous growth of armaments in Europe, the sense of insecurity and fear caused by them—it was these that made war inevitable.[50]

This broad, sweeping generalization may sum up the conventional wisdom on the relationship of arms to war, but it is too simple. For one thing, arms races may result in war, but not all wars are the result of arms races. There is no evidence that arms races preceded the Spanish-American War (1898), the wars in Korea (1950-53) or Vietnam (1965-73), the Russo-Japanese War (1904-05), or the British-Argentinian war over the Falkland Islands (1983), to cite but a few of the many wars in this century. Among the causes of World War II, in fact, was Britain's refusal to match Germany's growing military strength, thus upsetting the European balance. Arms races have also sometimes been called off when they reached a certain point, as in the Anglo-German naval race, which ended in 1911 and was not the reason for Britain's declaration of war in 1914. After World War I, the Washington Naval Conference restricted the battleship fleets of the United States, Britain, Japan, Italy, and France according to a fixed ratio and declared a ten-year "naval holiday" for new capital ship construction (it was extended five more years in 1930).

Arms races, like wars, cannot be isolated from the political circumstances that produced them, and these races will take different forms. The race may be part of a process of competitive modernization among states seeking to preserve the status quo. Each fears falling behind the others in keeping weapons technologically up to date. Or it may be part of a political struggle between a status quo state and a revisionist state. In this context, the former's decision to match the latter's increase in capability sends a *political* message: that it refuses to acquiesce in a major shift of the power balance. The resulting arms race is a measure of their political rivalry. The arms race did not produce this rivalry, nor will the race end until there is some political settlement of these powers' differences. The arms race, in brief, is a test of national will, especially on the part of the status quo power (a test that Britain failed in the 1930s).[51]

To the extent that the balance will dissuade an adversary from attacking, arms racing by the latter can be considered a "necessary surrogate for war."[52]

And another observer, agreeing that the arms race is a substitute for war, said that while it may be an expensive substitute, it is cheaper than fighting a war. Athough frequently regarded as making war inevitable, the arms race would be better viewed as a deliberate postponement of war as well as an attempt to use a more powerful threat in preference to war.[53] In short, an arms race is a bloodless way to demonstrate to the adversary that he would lose if war should occur. Whether the race ends in war will depend, as noted earlier, on the accuracy of the involved states' power calculations and intentions.

The term *arms race* implies an action-reaction process; one side builds up, the other responds in an ever-upward spiral.[54] The implication is that at some point war will erupt in a "spontaneous combustion." It is inevitable as each side piles up more arms. (Those who assert this thesis apparently assume that the time when the war erupts, or the specific events and crises that are the immediate cause of the war, are of no importance!)[55] This action-reaction thesis, however, pays little attention to the fact that in the superpower arms race neither the Soviet Union nor the United States, by far the wealthier and more productive society, has ever built all the weapons it could. The United States built many bombers; the Soviet Union built relatively few. Moscow deployed an ABM system around the capital city; Washington did not deploy any ABMs. Further, the United States has greatly reduced—not increased— both the numbers of delivery systems (bombers and missiles) and the megatonnage they carried. In terms of megatonnage, the U.S. stockpile was four times greater in 1960 than in 1980. The number of delivery systems was one-third higher in 1967.

The action-reaction process inherent in the term *arms race* not only suggests that each state matches its opponent but also that if one state stops racing and begins to reduce its arms, the other side will reciprocate. Actually, quite the reverse may happen. The adversary may see a slowdown as an opportunity to strengthen itself and gain an advantage, not necessarily to attack, but to enhance its political leverage. During the Nixon-Ford years, when U.S. defense expenditures dropped to the lowest percentage of the gross national product (GNP) since before the Korean War in 1950, Soviet military spending is estimated to have increased to between 12 percent and 17 percent of the Soviet GNP.

Since 1945 there has been *not one single quantitative arms race but a series of qualitative arms races.* In a situation in which one failure of deterrence is one too many, in which the stakes are nothing less than the survival of society itself, neither superpower can afford *not* to be concerned with modernizing deterrent forces as technology changes. Thus, U.S. offensive strategic forces have undergone several transformations: from the propeller/jet B-36 bomber to the intermediate-range pure jet B-47 to the intercontinental B-52; from bombers to liquid-fuel missiles to solid-fuel missiles; from a single warhead to multiple warheads; from warheads inaccurate by miles, to warheads accurate within hundreds of feet. Similar technological advances occurred in strategic defenses.

It may well be, however, that both the United States and the Soviet Union in this process have acquired too many arms. But the key question is how many missiles does it take to deter the other side? No one really knows. For the United States, is it the 1,000 ICBMs already built? After all, no war has started. Or could deterrence be implemented by 500 or even 200 missiles? The level of arms needed for deterrence cannot be known for certain unless war breaks out. Then it can be said that the numbers one side possessed were not enough to deter the aggression. But, in the absence of a war, how can one prove that an event that did not occur did not do so because of a certain level of armaments? Thus, the numbers of weapons will always be a debatable and controversial topic.

This topic is complicated even more by the way one answers the following questions: How much of the deterrent forces will be operational at the time of the attack? How many of these forces are likely to be destroyed in an enemy attack (assuming the United States will retaliate only after it has absorbed a first strike)? How many surviving missiles will malfunction on takeoff or during flight? How many missiles will miss their targets? Because the number of forces operational at a time of a first strike and the numbers destroyed before they can retaliate are unknown, the caution against relying on forces that are too small is obvious. Ironically, there is another reason for caution: small forces would presumably be easier to destroy in a first strike and therefore would have less credibility as a deterrent because the surviving forces might not be able to retaliate. A small force, in other words, might tempt a strike. In the nuclear balance, there is safety in numbers. With sizable forces on both sides, the attacker cannot be certain of a successful first strike. Michael May describes it thus: "Numbers of nuclear weapons systems must remain high if the futility of a first strike is to remain obvious; if undetectable cheating is to remain unimportant; and if the U.S. and the U.S.S.R. are to remain secure in their deterrence regardless of what other nuclear powers may do." [56]

Closely related to the issue of high numbers of nuclear weapons is the issue of the composition of this deterrent force. Since deterrence is the chief aim, should one rely only on one system—for example, bombers—even if one possesses plenty of them? Is there not greater safety in diversity? Can one not legitimately argue that the three systems each superpower possesses—bombers, ICBMs, and SLBMs—make deterrence that much surer? One, having multiple systems guards against a technological breakthrough that could render one system vulnerable; two, several systems greatly complicate an attacker's ability to destroy all of the opponent's retaliatory forces; and three, several systems make it far more difficult to defend against a second strike. Thus, as already noted, MAD has become destabilized because U.S. bombers and ICBMs have become vulnerable as Soviet counterforce capability has grown, and MAD might be even more destabilized as U.S. counterforce capability grows. However, the fact that the submarine force, the third leg of the triad, is largely survivable (a few may be caught in port) and that it can deliver an overwhelming reprisal attack by itself surely eliminates any Soviet (or American) temptation to strike first.

In the final analysis, *the key threat to peace is less the numbers of strategic arms than the type of arms being deployed.*[57] Counterforce weapons are potentially destabilizing. But the saving grace is again threefold.[58] First, there is the enormous destructive power of each nuclear weapon, which, when multiplied by both superpowers' large stockpiles, means that nuclear war risks national survival. Second, if either side were ever tempted to preempt, the chances are that operationally many things will go wrong and therefore such a first strike will not succeed in destroying most of the opponent's ICBM/bomber retaliatory capability. Even the likelihood that a small percentage will survive and be used in a retaliatory blow means that a first strike becomes too great a risk to take. Third, this risk becomes even greater because of the multiplication of strategic forces. Submarines, especially American submarines, remain invulnerable; as the range of their missiles increases, they can roam over larger portions of the ocean, making themselves even harder to find. In fact, they could, if necessary, fire from their home ports and reach their targets. So can the latest Soviet submarines. Altogether, the likelihood of committing suicide remains very high if either side were to launch a first strike. A devastating second strike is unavoidable, and SDI is unlikely to change that for the foreseeable future. This should, as in the past, continue to eliminate any temptation to launch at all and thereby ensure future deterrence.

Ironically, the fear of a nuclear Armageddon, a fear shared by both the United States and the Soviet Union, remains the best guarantee of peace. For better or worse, regardless of specific weapons systems or military doctrines, we live in a MAD world; the likelihood that future attempts to control the use of nuclear weapons may fail, and that a "limited nuclear war" will escalate with results neither side wants, is a powerful disincentive to launching a first strike. The avoidance of nuclear war is the only course that makes sense in these circumstances.

Notes

1. The emphasis on tacit bargaining, as distinct from traditional diplomatic negotiations, was introduced by Thomas C. Schelling, *The Strategy of Conflict* (New York: Oxford University Press, 1963). See also Schelling, *Arms and Influence* (New Haven, Conn.: Yale University Press, 1966).
2. A similar typology may be found in *Politics and the International System* by Keith Legg and James Morrison (New York: Harper & Row, 1971), 69-70, 280-284.
3. Edward Hallet Carr, *The Twenty Years Crisis* (London: Macmillan, 1951), 109.
4. See, for example, Immanuel Kant, *Perpetual Peace*, trans. Carl J. Friedrich in *Inevitable Peace* (Cambridge, Mass.: Harvard University Press, 1948), 251-252.

5. Bertrand de Jouvenel, *On Power*, trans. J. F. Huntington (Boston: Beacon Press, 1962), 148.

6. The interrelations between war and industrial power are well treated in *War and Human Progress* by John U. Nef (Cambridge, Mass.: Harvard University Press, 1950); and Richard A. Preston and Sidney F. Wise, *Men in Arms: A History of Warfare and Its Interrelationships with Western Society*, rev. ed. (New York: Praeger Publishers, 1970), 176ff. For the impact of democratization and industrialization on U.S. military performance, see Walter Millis, *Arms and Men* (New York: New American Library, 1956).

7. Arthur T. Hadley, *The Nation's Safety and Arms Control* (New York: Viking, 1961), 4.

8. Ralph E. Lapp, *Kill and Overkill* (New York: Basic Books, 1962), 37; and Scientists' Committee for Radiation Information, "Effects of Nuclear Explosives," in *No Place to Hide*, ed. Seymour Melman (New York: Grove Press, 1962), 98-107.

9. A vivid account of a fire storm is given in *The Night Hamburg Died* by Martin Caidin (New York: Ballantine, 1960), 80-105, 129-141. The German estimate of those killed in Hamburg was 60,000. The U.S. B-29 attack on Tokyo, March 9-10, 1945, burned up sixteen square miles and killed 84,000 people, most of whom were burned to death or died from wounds caused by fire. In contrast, the Hiroshima atom bomb killed 72,000 people. The most destructive attack ever, however, was the two-day Anglo-American bombing of Dresden in February 1945: 135,000 people were killed. On this attack, see David Irving, *The Destruction of Dresden* (New York: Holt, Rinehart & Winston, 1964).

10. Lapp, *Kill and Overkill*, 53-54.

11. Ibid., 77.

12. Office of Technology Assessment, *The Effects of Nuclear War* (Washington, D.C.: Government Printing Office, 1980), 159.

13. Ibid., 159.

14. Paul R. Ehrlich, Carl Sagan et al., *The Cold and the Dark* (New York: W. W. Norton, 1984). In the same genre, though hardly "scientific," see Jonathan Schell, *The Fate of the Earth* (New York: Avon Books, 1982). For a critical appraisal of the "nuclear winter" and its impact on nuclear strategy, see Albert Wohlstetter, "Between Unfree World and None," *Foreign Affairs* (Summer 1985): 962-994; and for an appraisal of its scientific basis, see Stanley L. Thompson and Stephen H. Schneider, "Nuclear Winter Reappraised," *Foreign Affairs* (Summer 1986): 981-1005.

15. Henry A. Kissinger, *Nuclear Weapons and Foreign Policy* (New York: Harper & Row, 1957), 79. See also Office of Technology Assessment, *The Effects of Nuclear War* (Montclair, N.J.: Allenheld, Osmun & Co., 1979); and Arthur M. Katz, *Life after Nuclear War* (Cambridge, Mass.: Ballinger, 1981).

16. Glenn H. Snyder, "Balance of Power in the Missile Age," *Journal of International Affairs* 14 (1960): 21-34.

17. Evan Luard, "Conciliation and Deterrence," *World Politics*, January 1967, 167-189. Also see Arnold Wolfers, *Britain and France Between Two Wars* (New York: W. W. Norton, 1966); and John Wheeler-Bennett, *Munich: Prologue to Tragedy* (London: Macmillan, 1948).

18. Luard, "Conciliation and Deterrence," 174-175.

19. For a critical analysis of the themes of "rationality" and deterrence, see Patrick M. Morgan, *Deterrence* (Beverly Hills, Calif.: Sage Publications, 1977); and John

Steinbruner, "Beyond Rational Deterrence: The Struggle for New Concepts," *World Politics,* January 1976, 223-245.

20. George F. Kennan, *American Diplomacy 1900-1950* (Chicago: University of Chicago Press, 1951), 118.

21. Nathan Leites, *The Operational Code of the Politburo* (New York: McGraw-Hill, 1951); and Leites, *A Study of Bolshevism* (New York: Free Press, 1953), 27-63.

22. Schelling, *Strategy of Conflict,* 3-10.

23. Virtually all the seminal thinking on military force has been by civilian intellectuals, which is symptomatic of the fundamental change from the conduct of war to the implementation of deterrence through exploitation of coercion. The student interested in what is usually called national-security affairs does not go to works by generals and admirals; he or she turns to the civilian experts, mostly academicians. Those political scientists, historians, mathematicians, and physicists have concerned themselves with issues of strategy. Since the word *strategy,* historically meaning the use of battles to achieve the objectives of war, is now applied more to what Schelling has called "the manipulation of risk," it is to their writings that we turn. By taking the mystery out of a subject that civilians have usually thought only professional soldiers understood, analysts such as Bernard Brodie and Henry Kissinger have transformed interested laymen into experts and permitted them to question the soldier's judgment on matters of strategy, force levels, and weapons.

24. Schelling, *Arms and Influence,* 1-34.

25. Ibid., 22.

26. Ibid., 33.

27. Ibid., 43-55; and Schelling, *Strategy of Conflict,* 21-28.

28. See particularly the two chapters entitled "Resolve and Prudence" and "Freedom of Choice" in *The Politics of Force: Bargaining during International Crises* by Oran R. Young (Princeton, N.J.: Princeton University Press, 1968), 177-265.

29. Glenn H. Snyder, "Crisis Bargaining," in *International Crises,* ed. Charles F. Hermann (New York: Free Press, 1972), 232.

30. This point is well documented by William J. Newman, *Balance of Power in the Interwar Years, 1919-1939* (New York: Random House, 1967), 112-122, 131-146.

31. Elie Abel, *The Missile Crisis* (New York: Bantam Books, 1966), 24-26, 28; and Young, *Politics of Force,* 79-80, 87. Khrushchev's explanation in his "memoirs" emphasizes only his desire to defend Cuba from an alleged American invasion. For an evaluation of this motivation, see Arnold Horelick, "The Cuban Missile Crisis: An Analysis of Soviet Calculations and Behavior," *World Politics,* April 1964, 365-369.

32. Schelling, *Arms and Influence,* 56.

33. Snyder, "Crisis Bargaining," 232-233.

34. This continuing concern with different strategies and changing weapons systems is discussed by William W. Kaufmann, *The McNamara Strategy* (New York: Harper & Row, 1964). For overall views of U.S. strategy and arms control, respectively, see Lawrence Freedman, *The Evolution of Nuclear Strategy* (New York: St. Martin's Press, 1981); and Robin Ranger, *Arms and Politics 1958-1978* (Boulder, Colo.: Westview Press, 1982).

35. Fine introductions to the field of arms control can be found in *The Control of the Arms Race,* 2d ed., by Hedley Bull (New York: Holt, Rinehart & Winston, 1965); and Thomas C. Schelling and Morton H. Halperin, *Strategy and Arms Control* (New York: Twentieth Century Fund, 1961).

36. In Schelling's words: "The 'equalizer' of the Old West [the pistol] made it possible

for *either* man to kill the other; it did not assure that *both* would be killed. . . . The advantage of shooting first aggravates any incentive to shoot. As the survivor might put it, 'He was about to kill me in self-defense, so I had to kill him in self-defense.' Or, 'He, thinking I was about to kill him in self-defense, was about to kill me in self-defense, so I had to kill him in self-defense.' But if both were assured of living long enough to shoot back with unimpaired aim, there would be no advantage in jumping the gun and little reason to fear that the other would try it." Schelling, *Strategy of Conflict*, 232-233. (Emphasis in original.)

37. Ibid., 231.

38. Ibid., 232.

39. For an early discussion of the lack of any payoff from a position of strategic superiority that the Soviet Union might achieve, see Benjamin S. Lambeth, "Deterrence in the MIRV Era," *World Politics*, January 1972, 221ff.

40. Jerome B. Wiesner et al., *ABM: An Evaluation of the Decision to Employ an Antiballistic Missile System* (New York: Signet, 1969); and Johan J. Holst and William Schneider, Jr., eds., *Why ABM? Policy Issues in the Missile Defense Controversy* (New York: Pergamon, 1969).

41. Robbin F. Laird and Dale R. Herspring, *The Soviet Union and the Strategic Arms* (Boulder, Colo.: Westview Press, 1984), 53-54.

42. Ibid., 65-85. Also see David Holloway, *The Soviet Union and the Arms Race*, 2d ed. (New Haven, Conn.: Yale University Press, 1984), 29-64; and Fritz W. Ermath, "Contrasts in American and Soviet Strategic Thought," *International Security*, Fall 1978, 138-155.

43. Raymond L. Garthoff, *Détente and Confrontation* (Washington, D.C.: The Brookings Institution, 1985), 753-800.

44. For an early view, see Lynn Etheridge Davis, "Limited Nuclear Options: Deterrence and the New American Doctrine" (London: International Institute for Strategic Studies, 1975-76); and Caspar W. Weinberger, "U.S. Defense Strategy," *Foreign Affairs* (Spring 1986): 685-697.

45. Ibid., 680.

46. Ibid., 678-679.

47. Desmond Ball, "Can Nuclear War Be Controlled?" (London: International Institute for Strategic Studies, 1981).

48. See the series on weapons in space, *New York Times*, March 3-8, 1985.

49. McGeorge Bundy, George F. Kennan, Robert S. McNamara, and Gerard Smith, "The President's Choice: Star Wars or Arms Control," *Foreign Affairs* (Winter 1984-85): 264-278. For the pro and cons of SDI, see Dorinda G. Dallmeyer, *The Strategic Defense Initiative* (Boulder, Colo.: Westview Press, 1986).

50. Quoted by Paul Kennedy, *Strategy and Diplomacy 1870-1945* (London: Fontana Paperbacks, 1984), 165. Also see the annual studies by the Stockholm International Peace Research Institute, *SIPRI Yearbook*, for a similar contemporary viewpoint.

51. Michael Howard, *The Causes of Wars*, 2d ed. (Cambridge, Mass.: Harvard University Press, 1984), 18-20.

52. Ibid., 21.

53. Geoffrey Blainey, *The Causes of War* (New York: Free Press, 1973), 141.

54. See especially Albert Wohlstetter, "Is There a Strategic Arms Race?" and "Rivals, But No 'Race,' " *Foreign Policy* (Summer, Fall 1974): 3-20, 48-81.

55. Blainey, *Causes of Wars*, 137; also see Richard N. Lebow, *Between Peace and War* (Baltimore: Johns Hopkins University Press, 1981).

56. Michael M. May, "The U.S.-Soviet Approach to Nuclear Weapons," *International Security*, Spring 1985, 487; and Joseph S. Nye, Jr., "Farewell to Arms Control?" *Foreign Affairs* (Fall 1986): 1-20, for a balanced analysis of the effects of reductions on contemporary arms control negotiations.

57. On SALT I, see John Newhouse, *Cold Dawn* (New York: Holt, Rinehart & Winston, 1973); on SALT II, see Thomas W. Wolfe, *The SALT Experience* (Cambridge, Mass.: Ballinger, 1979); and Strobe Talbott, *Endgame* (New York: Harper & Row, 1979). More broadly, on the do's and don't's of arms control to avoid nuclear war, see Graham T. Allison, Albert Carnesdale, and Joseph S. Nye, Jr., *Hawks, Doves, and Owls* (New York: W. W. Norton, 1985).

58. Robert Jervis, *The Illogic of American Nuclear Strategy* (Ithaca, N.Y.: Cornell University Press, 1984); and Spurgeon M. Keeny and Wolfgang K. H. Panofsky, "MAD vs. NUTS: The Mutual Hostage Relationship of the Superpowers," *Foreign Affairs* (Winter 1981/82): 287-304.

CHAPTER 9

Crisis Management

CRISES AS SUBSTITUTES FOR WAR

Not only the practice of deterrence but also frequent crises characterized the postwar bipolar world. Crises are probably unavoidable in any international system characterized by anarchy. In a bipolar system, however, the insecurity, fear, and suspicion of both superpowers make avoidance of crises—situations of intense confrontation, usually of short duration, in which the perceived possibility of war rises significantly—particularly difficult. It may be correct to conclude, as Kenneth Waltz has suggested, that in a bipolar distribution of power "a large crisis now [is better] than a small war later."[1] A crisis is evidence that the balance is being kept.

Crises, then, serve a purpose when war is no longer the instrument of last resort. Earlier we characterized the state system as a state of potential war; war is the means for either demanding or resisting change. In a system in which no legitimate means for achieving change exist, conflicting demands, if they cannot be resolved peacefully, must be settled by force. War often decides who gets what; the power ratio when the shooting ends settles whatever issue is at stake. *But war is no longer the* ultima ratio *in the nuclear age. Crisis is now the substitute for war as the "continuation of politics by other means."*[2] The threat of coercion takes the place of all-out force as the means of deciding who gets what in a crisis, which may be defined as a situation in which one state demands a change in the status quo and the other resists because it perceives vital interests at stake. It is this confrontation that gives rise to the key characteristic of a crisis, the heightened expectation of the possibility of war. In such a confrontation, each party tests the measure of its adversary (including its firmness in defending its interests and its willingness to accept risks on

240

behalf of these interests) by means of what Thomas Schelling calls the "manipulation of risk." Successes or setbacks in individual tests are equivalent to victories and defeats in war. *In direct bipolar confrontation, in which it is too dangerous to fight and maneuvering becomes a surrogate for actual hostilities, each country's perception of the other's resolve is central. At stake is its reputation for power as judged by its adversary.* This perception, rather than the specific tangible issue at hand, is the axis around which the crisis revolves. On a nation's reputation for power rests the credibility of its commitments. If this reputation is intact, the nation is not likely to be challenged. If it is in doubt, challenge is likely to follow, and, unless the reputation is restored, the crisis cannot be ended.[3]

Change in Capability

The very eruption of a crisis suggests that the existing pattern of power has been "significantly disturbed" and that the relationship between the adversaries has become "politically fluid."[4] Two kinds of change are particularly significant. One is a change in capability. For example, in 1957 Sputnik was launched into space by an intercontinental ballistic missile (ICBM)—both Soviet "firsts." Soviet leaders, believing that the balance was changing, attempted to exploit diplomatically what they considered to be a military advantage. Nikita Khrushchev and his defense minister repeatedly boasted that the Soviet Union was producing ICBMs "on the assembly line" and threatened the United States with annihilating defeat. "We now have stockpiled so many rockets [ICBMs], so many atomic and hydrogen warheads, that, if we were attacked," Khrushchev said, "we could wipe from the face of the earth all of our probable opponents."[5] The Soviets shrewdly exploited resulting U.S. uncertainty about actual Soviet strategic strength.[6] By 1960, thirty Soviet ICBM tests had been reported in the American press, the Soviets had launched six successful space shots, and Americans who were informed about their country's defense efforts forecast a sizable "missile gap" lasting until the year 1964. Suddenly, Americans were startled by their new vulnerability to nuclear attack. The Strategic Air Command (SAC) was said to be particularly vulnerable to a surprise missile strike, and its credibility as a deterrent was in some doubt both in the United States and among the North Atlantic Treaty Organization (NATO) allies.

As if to demonstrate their claimed new strength and the weakened position of the West, the Soviets in 1958 demanded the withdrawal of Western troops from West Berlin so that it could be "demilitarized" and turned into a "free city." What was significant was that the Soviets made the demand at all. It was the most serious challenge to Washington's leaders since 1948-49. The Truman Doctrine, the Marshall Plan, the Berlin airlift, and NATO had made it very plain to the Soviets that the United States considered Western Europe vital to its interests and that Soviet domination over this rimland of the Eurasian continent was no more tolerable than German control had been twice before. Presumably this knowledge had deterred the Soviets in the late 1940s, and it was fear of war that had led them to redirect their challenges to areas outside Europe. But ten years after the first Berlin crisis the Soviets once more challenged the West in Europe. Indeed, the fact that, for the first time in the postwar era, they were publicly demanding that the Western powers abandon territory and were threatening them with an ultimatum suggested a new confidence in their own power to achieve their stated political aim of converting the western half of Germany's former capital into a "free city."

Change in Resolve

The other kind of change is in the balance of resolve. By 1962 Khrushchev had apparently become convinced that the United States would not use force to defend its vital interests. He talked openly of the American failure of nerve, and the West's passive acceptance of the Berlin Wall in 1961 was seen by him as one indication. Another was the debacle of the 1961 invasion of the Bay of Pigs by Cuban refugees, who were sponsored by the Central Intelligence Agency (CIA).[7] If eliminating Fidel Castro was a vital American interest, then, once the Cuban exile force had been defeated, U.S. forces should have been committed to accomplish that goal. On the other hand, if eliminating Castro was not important, then the Bay of Pigs operation should never have been launched. Khrushchev, who had used the Red Army to crush the Hungarian revolution in 1956, read President John Kennedy's unwillingness to follow through on his action in Cuba as a sign of inexperience and weakness; it therefore did not seem that the installation of Soviet missiles in Cuba would involve great risk. The Soviet Union merely had to confront the United States with a *fait accompli,* and the latter would retreat, rather than face a test of will. Past American inactions or ineffective reactions seem to have encouraged the Soviets to continue their probes—and, in the case of the missile installations, the probe reached within ninety miles of the American shore (see Figure 9-1).

Note that the Cuban missile challenge occurred even while the balance of capability favored the United States. Spurred by Khrushchev's statements about large-scale production of missiles and by his threats, the Kennedy administration, upon coming into office in 1961, launched the massive build-up of Minuteman ICBMs and Polaris submarine-launched ballistic missiles (SLBMs), which by 1966 were to total 1,000 and 656, respectively. The administration also soon discovered that Soviet claims about rocket production were greatly exaggerated. Furthermore, Khrushchev was aware that the Americans knew of this exaggeration. The Soviet medium- and intermediate-range missile installation in Cuba therefore could be interpreted partly as a technological shortcut to enhance Soviet strength. Obviously, the imbalance of strategic capabilities did not deter the Soviets from placing missiles so near to U.S. territory; equally obviously, the Soviet leadership thought that the imbalance

Figure 9-1 The Caribbean Region

of resolve favored the Soviet Union and that this imbalance was more important than the strictly military one.

CRISIS MANAGEMENT

In the nuclear era, crisis is a substitute for war. Two contradictory sets of motives are at work.[8] One is winning, compelling the opponent to retreat and to make concessions. The emphasis is on competition and conflict. In this sense, a crisis reflects the general nature of international politics painted in very bold colors. The contrary motive is to avoid war. *Perception of a grave threat to the security of at least the challenged party, the suddenness and unexpected nature of this threat, the "players'" sense that they must act quickly, and their heightened expectation of violence are the characteristics of a crisis.*[9] These conflicting objectives and the chances for miscalculations make crises very dangerous. The alternative to some sort of peaceful resolution, however, is so catastrophic in the nuclear age that caution and restraint—rather than impulsiveness and recklessness—become imperative. Given the unpredictability inherent in a crisis, the possibility that this "substitute for war" can get out of hand and blow up under certain circumstances places a premium on "crisis management."

The Cuban missile, or October crisis, provides a textbook example, partly because the unexpected discovery of the Soviet installations allowed the United States a week for debating the meaning of the buildup, what Soviet purposes might be, how these purposes would affect U.S. interests, the future of American-Soviet relations, and the alternative ways of getting the missiles removed. (There was virtually no debate on whether removal was necessary.) In a sense the October crisis was unique; usually the surprised party is not afforded the luxury of time for debate and careful consideration of options, and the resulting compression of time to make crucial decisions is obviously potentially critical to a nonviolent outcome. But in 1962 several factors favored the Americans' ability to manage the crisis and to achieve their objectives: to persuade Moscow's leaders to undo what they had already done—not simply to stop further activities—and simultaneously to avoid a nuclear war.

In seeking to coerce a challenger to desist, there is a difference between a demand that he stop his activities (as in Berlin) and a demand that he stop and surrender whatever gains have already been made (as in Cuba). An adversary may be more inclined to accept the former than the latter.[10] If the challenger is unwilling to "stop and undo," the only way to gain compliance is to escalate the pressures. But threats of escalation also enhance the risks and possibility of war.

Asymmetry of Motivation

The first, perhaps fundamental, reason why the United States was successful in achieving its purpose in the Cuban missile crisis was that U.S. motivation to succeed was far stronger than that of the Soviet Union; the "asymmetry of motivation" favored the United States because it had the greater stake in the issue. Whatever gains the Soviet Union might make if it won, the United States had far more to lose.[11] Passivity in the face of such a clear menace— underlined by both the stealth and the speed of the Soviet missile buildup— was perceived by Washington's leaders as humiliating to the United States, lending credence to repeated Soviet claims that communism was the wave of the future and that the Soviet Union was becoming the world's foremost power. To have acceded to a Soviet presence in Cuba would have demonstrated American impotence to a watching world; a United States unable or unwilling to prevent the installation of Soviet missiles in its traditional sphere of influence—as Ronald Steel has observed, the Monroe Doctrine was really a Caribbean Doctrine[12]—would also be thought too weak or fearful to defend vital interests farther away. Soviet medium-range ballistic missiles (MRBMs) in Cuba to some degree would have enhanced the Soviet capacity for a first strike, for the U.S. early-warning lines were all positioned in the north to detect a strike across the North Pole. When confronted by U.S. inaction, the Soviets might have shipped many more such missiles to Cuba.

Nonetheless, as President Kennedy recognized, it was less the balance of capability that was affected than the balance of resolve. Not the strategic balance but the *appearance* of the balance, as he worded it, would be substantially altered.[13] In these circumstances the Soviets would undoubtedly have renewed their pressure on Berlin; they had already announced that they wished to resume "negotiations" on this subject after the American midterm election in November. They would also have furnished "proof" that U.S. allies in Europe, the Middle East, and Asia could not rely upon the United States in any major crisis. The future existence of these alliances would have been seriously jeopardized. And, in the Western Hemisphere, this evidence of American impotence would have encouraged Castro and other leaders of anti-American movements by sharply reducing the authority of the "colossus of the North" in Latin America.

All in all, Kennedy thought that the Soviets had broken a fundamental rule of the game in Cuba. The United States had not established bases in Eastern Europe; it had not aided anti-Soviet revolts. In return, the Soviets were not to encroach militarily in the United States' own sphere of influence. Castro's takeover of power, which resulted from internal Cuban conditions and despite the opposition of the Cuban Communist party, had not represented such an encroachment. Soviet missiles did. If the Soviet action were to pass with impunity, the terms of bipolar coexistence and competition would have been redefined. There were, of course, major risks in demanding the withdrawal of the Soviet missiles, but the consequences of *inaction*, despite the United States' greater strategic striking capability, were perceived to be disastrous. The Soviets had much to gain. Because potential American losses were vastly greater, Kennedy saw no choice but to react in Cuba and to demand the withdrawal of Soviet missiles. The asymmetry of interests, and therefore of motivation, favored the United States.

Asymmetry of Capability

A second reason for American success was that the balance of capabilities also favored the United States, and the president could be reasonably confident and resolute. Kennedy made his demand for the withdrawal of the Soviet missiles in a public speech, thus committing the country to this course of action. There could be no compromise or retraction of this demand without humiliation and a loss of national prestige. The president had staked his own and the nation's reputations publicly. Establishment of a blockade was evidence of this determination to succeed. American warships on the high seas were to stop Soviet missile-carrying vessels, and SAC was placed on a state of alert. Both measures were part of a show of force, which lent Kennedy's demand credibility. If Khrushchev thought of the president as an inexperienced and bumbling young man, he had to be disabused of this notion if war was to be avoided. Kennedy himself wanted to reduce American-Soviet tensions. But détente was impossible if Khrushchev continued to push and push to enhance Soviet influence because he thought Kennedy had—as Theodore Roosevelt once said of William McKinley—a chocolate éclair for a backbone. The minimal condition for negotiations was Soviet respect for American power.

Given U.S. strategic strength, Kennedy could slowly pressure the Soviets while avoiding any dangerously quick use of an ultimatum. He remained cautious until just before Soviet missiles were to become operational. Once Kennedy delivered the ultimatum, Khrushchev assumed a conciliatory tone and promised to dismantle the missiles and ship them back to the Soviet Union. The Soviet leader did not, as some expected, take any retaliatory action in Berlin, where conventional Soviet power was dominant. Quite the reverse: Khrushchev followed his Cuban surrender by speaking more reasonably about Berlin too. The balance of resolve and capability, which the Berlin crises had placed in some doubt from 1958 to 1962, had once more become settled. American-Soviet relations were no longer "politically fluid."

The outcome reflected the strategic balance at the time (see Table 9-1). It has occasionally been said that it was America's conventional superiority in the Caribbean that was the decisive military element in the resolution of the crisis. But had the strategic balance been reversed, would Kennedy have made his demand at all, even though, from his perspective, the pullout of Soviet missiles was a must? Did the favorable balance of nuclear capability strengthen his resolve? Would a strategic balance favoring the Soviet Union have made him more hesitant in responding to the challenge confronting him, even though the United States had local conventional superiority?

Shortly after becoming president, Kennedy, having watched Khrushchev's behavior in Berlin in the late 1950s, accelerated the U.S. missile buildup and raised the levels of land-based and sea-launched missiles substantially over those maintained by his predecessor. If the Soviets could demand that the West leave West Berlin and precipitate a series of crises over this issue at a time when the balance of capability did not favor them, what demands would they make—and how far would they then push—when they did acquire strategic parity? After the Cuban crisis Khrushchev's successors began an enormous strategic buildup that was detrimental to the rest of the economy (especially the consumer-oriented sector). This was due in part to the Soviet "defeat." By the 1980s the combined total yield or payload of the Soviets'

Table 9-1 U.S. and Soviet Srategic Strength in 1962

Type of Launcher	United States	Soviet Union
ICBM	229	44[a]
SLBM	144	97
Bombers	1,300	155

[a] Plus six training launchers.

land- and sea-based missiles greatly exceeded that of the American deterrent. The Soviets certainly thought that it was the strategic balance that had been decisive in 1962. Otherwise, why did they not use their local conventional superiority around Berlin to strangle the Western part of the city to recoup their prestige?

The Escalation Ladder

A third reason for Kennedy's success was the way in which the pressure on the Soviets was exerted. To the extent that crises are substitutes for a war the contestants wish to avoid, the nuclear threshold has to be raised, allowing for a wide range of physical maneuvers to test each other's will or nerve. Unlike in the prenuclear era, when the transition from peace to war tended to be rather fast, in the nuclear era the quick resort to force must be avoided. Coercive moves must precede any use of force and must start on a low rung of what has been called an "escalation ladder." The pressure should be raised only after careful observation of the adversary's response and full consideration of how the adversary is likely to react to one's own moves. Ultimatums should be delivered only when absolutely required by the situation. Between the low and high rungs of the escalation ladder there must be an extensive series of possible steps to increase the pressure short of war. This requirement is critical for the contestants, who must preserve some freedom of maneuver. On the one hand, they make commitments and appear to surrender their initiative in order to impress their opponents with the credibility of their demands; on the other, they cannot afford to be caught out on a limb. Each side can state its basic aim, sound menacing, and keep up the pressure, but to maintain tactical flexibility it can take only small upward steps at first. If these steps elicit no resistance and if demands remain unmet, it can then move up a few more rungs.

Commitments to physical moves are taken only gradually and at low levels of pressure. That is how the Soviets sought to erode the Western position in Berlin between 1955 and 1958. For three years they had watched the Allies' response to their declarations and moves in Berlin, assessing their own possible responses if publicly challenged. In 1961 construction of the Berlin Wall was preceded by placement of barbed wire and establishment of numerous crossing points between East and West Berlin to see whether the Allies would do more than protest feebly. When no demands or moves were made for its removal, the barbed wire was replaced by a massive brick wall. Although all these moves were clearly Soviet-designed, the Soviets shrewdly let their East German proxies carry them out to avoid a direct confrontation with the United States and its allies.

Similarly, Kennedy began his solution to the Cuban crisis with a blockade. He did have other options: a private warning to Khrushchev, a protest at the United Nations, an air strike on the missile sites, or a full-fledged invasion. But the blockade was selected. Kennedy realized that, although it might prevent more Soviet missiles from entering Cuba, it would not rid the island of those already there. The blockade was intended as a signal of American determination (which a private warning or protest might not have accomplished so successfully); if Khrushchev then failed to remove his rockets, the pressure could be stepped up. In the meantime Khrushchev would have to decide his response, while Kennedy could delay the even more agonizing decision on what he would do if missile construction continued. No great power presents an ultimatum to another lightly.

Khrushchev was not so afraid of war that, when the president announced the blockade, he immediately desisted. The Soviet leader was not a man to panic easily. He accepted the blockade, and Soviet missile-carrying ships did not try to run it, but he accelerated efforts to make the missiles in place operational. In the midst of the crisis, Khrushchev thus confronted Kennedy with a new and much more difficult challenge. American warships could keep more missiles from coming into Cuba, but, short of an ultimatum, how could the president have the missiles already on the island removed?

It was the ultimate test. Kennedy responded with the same steel nerves he had shown throughout: at the end of the week of crisis, he escalated the challenge by intensifying the pressure. He informed the Soviet leadership that if the missiles, which were about to become operational, were not removed immediately, the United States would remove them.[14] This ultimatum he presented not publicly but privately, through his brother Robert Kennedy, to the Soviet ambassador in Washington. Simultaneously, he gave his personal assurance that the few American missiles in Turkey would be dismantled. This was supposed to have been done even before the Cuban crisis erupted, and the Soviets publicly demanded their removal quite late in the course of the crisis, as a quid pro quo for the removal of their own missiles from Cuba.

Careful Tactics

A fourth reason why the U.S. threat of coercion was successful was the careful handling of the details of the crisis. Leaders in Washington seized and held the tactical advantage, fully exploiting the "initiative that forces the opponent to initiate."[15] The blockade of offensive missiles left it to Khrushchev to decide whether to break this quarantine and, if so, how. Kennedy, however, managed the details of the blockade shrewdly. Khrushchev had to make the key decisions, but he was not to be confronted in such a way that he would have no alternative but to respond militarily. He was also to be given time to think over what he should do; he was not to be forced into hasty and ill-considered actions.

Although the U.S. Navy wished to intercept Soviet ships eight hundred miles from Cuba, so as to be out of range for the MiG fighters based there, the president reduced the distance to five hundred miles.[16] Furthermore, the first ship to be boarded and searched was not to be one owned and manned by the

Soviets. A Soviet tanker, which had identified itself and its cargo to U.S. Navy ships, was allowed to pass because it was unlikely to be carrying missiles. An East German passenger ship was also cleared. The first ship that was finally halted and searched was an American-built Liberty ship, Panamanian-owned, registered in Lebanon, captained by a Greek, and bound for Cuba under a Soviet charter.[17] It is vital in a crisis—one of the chief characteristics of which is the perceived need for quick decisions—to slow the momentum of interaction and to introduce "pauses" for careful reflection and calculation. Kennedy's management of the blockade showed his careful attention to every detail of the crisis, no matter how small, and his control over all phases of the operation, especially those involving military forces.

All the moves and countermoves during the crisis were part of the opponents' testing of each other's resolve and willingness to run risks and of the strength of their respective interests in Cuba. No words were exchanged between official representatives of the two governments at a diplomatic table, yet the moves were all part of the bargaining process. In a crisis words are not enough. Diplomacy also involves action. The antagonists communicate their intentions, expectations, attitudes, and determination by means of the moves that they make. The bargaining is tacit, not verbal. Yet, though words alone are not sufficient, they are nevertheless indispensable. Terms must be outlined, possible compromises must be explored, time limits may be set, and the order of the steps in de-escalating the crisis should be agreed upon. Explicit negotiations are thus necessary as well. But how are they to be conducted? The telephone "hot line" between Moscow and Washington was not established until a year after the Cuban missile crisis. There was no quick, informal way to make contact, only the slower official channels. The two leaders improvised. Messages were passed between Kennedy and Khrushchev, as well as between Robert Kennedy and the Soviet ambassador. Perhaps most important were the meetings of a Soviet embassy official and an ABC television reporter, in which the Soviet unofficially proposed the bargain that ended the crisis—removal of the missiles in exchange for an American pledge not to invade.

When the crisis was over and the Soviets had acknowledged defeat by withdrawing their missiles, Kennedy refused to humiliate Khrushchev. With the United States' reputation for power restored, he did not have to gloat over his victory; instead he praised Khrushchev's "statesmanlike decision to stop building bases in Cuba [and to dismantle] offensive weapons. . . . This is an important and constructive contribution to peace."[18] This is the reason why he gave the Soviet leader a pledge not to invade Cuba, which he had no intention of doing anyway. As a result, Khrushchev had his own loophole: the claim that he had sent the missiles to Cuba to defend Castro from a U.S. invasion and that, having received a pledge of noninvasion, he could bring them home.

Note that Kennedy's demand at the end was the same as at the beginning: withdrawal of Soviet missiles. Castro and communism in Cuba were not made additional issues. The Soviets were not asked to pull their missiles out and also to stab Castro in the back as they left (as later the North Vietnamese insisted that the United States do to the Saigon government). The greater the demand, the greater the disinclination to comply and the riskier the confrontation. Had the United States added the downfall of Castro to its demands, the Soviets would surely have thought that they had to respond either in Cuba or, more dangerously, in Berlin. But Kennedy kept the agenda of demands limited to the Soviet missiles, and he "won." The crisis started because Khrushchev had misread American resolve; the crisis ended when the balance of resolve was restored.[19]

MILITARY COERCION: HAVE NUCLEAR WEAPONS MADE MILITARY POWER USELESS?

Former secretary of defense Robert McNamara expressed a widely held view when he wrote that *"nuclear weapons serve no military purpose whatsoever. They are totally useless—except only to deter one's opponent from using them."* [20] Absolute power, to put it another way, equals absolute impotence. Strategic power is useful only as a means of denial, but not of positive gain. The strategic superiority the United States enjoyed until the late 1960s did not confer any political advantages. The United States—like the Soviet Union—was paralyzed by its inability to use a form of power that risked destroying itself.

What this view overlooks is that military power is often most valuable when it does not have to be used. The gun that has to shoot often must do so because a state has failed to achieve its aim otherwise; the gun that does not have to shoot is useful because it supports its nation's diplomacy and manages to achieve its purposes by means of persuasion. Powerful states throughout history have had to resort to force less often than weaker states because strong states have had at their disposal more means—economic, for example—to work their will. The "nonrecourse to force" is a doctrine of the mightier states.[21]

Moreover, it is a serious error to confuse the nonuse of force—in this case of nuclear force—with a lack of usefulness. As Waltz has suggested, such confusion is like saying that the police force that seldom employs violence is weak and that a police force is useful only when the officers are swinging their clubs. Or, to use another analogy, it is like suggesting that a man with huge assets is not rich if he spends little money and that he is wealthy only when he spends a lot of it.[22]

Nuclear weapons have meant that military power is used in a more sophisticated way than it often was in the prenuclear age. In this age of deterrence and crisis management for the two most powerful nuclear states, military power is exerted without force having to be employed. To say that nuclear weapons are useless except to deter the adversary's use of them is to forget that preserving the status quo and peace at the same time is no mean achievement. Historically, great powers have gone to war to protect the status quo, just as revisionist powers have gone to war to change it. The period of more than forty years of peace following World War II is significant. For Western Europe, which despite the horrors of World War I stumbled into another war only twenty years later, the period since 1945 has been its longest time at peace in the twentieth century.

Indeed, the principal impact of nuclear weapons for the last four decades has been to restrain the exercise of power by the United States and the Soviet Union. Despite the problem of preserving the stability of mutual deterrence, the unlikelihood that a first strike would successfully disarm the enemy means that the two superpowers continue to face the very real possibility of mutual suicide.

This, in turn, has meant that a bipolar system, which might have been unstable in the prenuclear era, has become stable in the nuclear era. There has been no total war between the superpowers and their allies for more than forty years: crises have not escalated to the use of force. *Rather than nuclear weapons eliminating man, they appear to be eliminating large-scale war among the most powerful states—both nuclear and nonnuclear war.* In this respect, the remarks of Marshal Nikolai Ogarkov, former chief of the Soviet General Staff, are very instructive:

> The strategic nuclear forces of the United States can fire at a single launching 12,000 warheads with a total yield of 3,400 megatons. This is 170,000 times more than the yield of the first atomic bomb that the United States dropped in Hiroshima. 170,000 times! Just think of it.
>
> Moreover, this is only part of the story. If we add to this total the retaliatory capacity of the Soviet Union, which can hardly have fewer nuclear systems at its disposal, I think the matter speaks for itself. . . .
>
> As a result, a paradox arises: on the one hand, it would seem, there is a process of steadily increasing potential for the nuclear powers to destroy the enemy, and, on the other hand, there is an equally steady and, I would say, even steeper reduction in the potential for an aggressor to inflict a so-called disabling strike on his principal enemy. The point is that, with the quantity and diversity of nuclear missiles already achieved, it has become impossible to destroy the enemy's systems with a single strike.
>
> A crushing retaliatory strike against the aggressor, even with the limited quantity of nuclear warheads remaining to the defender, a strike inflicting unacceptable damage, becomes inevitable in present conditions.[23]

In other words, "We shall both lose if you attack me because I will still be able to retaliate." And if the nuclear winter thesis is correct, retaliation may not even be necessary. Even if the aggressor succeeded in disarming its adversary with a first strike, success would be short-lived; the nuclear winter it had unleashed would soon devastate the entire world.

The overall consequence of the realization that there are no victors, only losers, has been to discipline the exercise of power. Not only has it prevented a total war between the United States and the Soviet Union despite the scope and intensity of their rivalry, but it has also led them to manage their crises very carefully when they have erupted: in Berlin (1948-49 and again repeatedly from 1958 to 1961), in Quemoy and Matsu in the Taiwan Straits (1954-55 and 1958), and in Cuba (1962). If the possibility of the use of violence lies behind much of international politics, this possibility rises close to the surface during crises. In this sense crises stand at the crossover point from peace to war, even if their occurrence suggests that the balance is being kept. As dangerous as they are, none has escalated into war, as would probably have occurred in the prenuclear period when the penalty for going to war did not include the ultimate price of extinction. In both deterrence and crises the powers resort only to the threat of force, not to the use of force. That significant shift is the result of nuclear weapons and the reason why the period since 1945 has been called the age of deterrence and crisis management.

Deterrence has a historical record that is usually ignored by those who focus on "the day after" and on the catastrophe to come.[24] Little attention is given to "the day before." This is not to say that one should be complacent about the prospect of a nuclear war, but the fact that forty years of nuclear weapons have been forty years without nuclear war suggests that such a war is not inevitable and that the policy makers on both sides take this matter seriously. Those years "are not only evidence that war can be avoided but are themselves part of the reason why it can be; namely, increasing experience in living with the weapons without precipitating a war, increasing confidence on both sides that neither wishes to risk nuclear war, diminishing necessity to react to every untoward event as though it were a mortal challenge."[25]

Ironically, if nuclear weapons were eliminated, relieving fears of a nuclear holocaust, wars between the major powers might become more likely because such hostilities would be considerably less damaging. There is clearly a trade-off between the destructiveness of war and the likelihood of war. Total wars are incompatible with "absolute weapons," but they are not incompatible with weapons of more limited destruction. Thus, the abolition of nuclear arms, if it were possible, would present a cruel dilemma: it would remove the fear of national, if not global, suicide, but it also would make it feasible once more to use war as an instrument of state policy whose gains might exceed its losses.

The overall impact of nuclear arms on the superpowers' conduct of policy might be summed up as in Figure 9-2. More specifically, the nuclear revolution dramatically illustrates that one of the aims of the balance of power is to preserve the state system. The U.S.-Soviet conflict, the scope of which exceeds all previous historical conflicts, might well have burst into flames before invention of "the bomb." But regardless of each power's goals, both have been compelled to place coexistence over nonexistence and to claim a stake in maintaining the present state system. It is in this context that the most likely use of force is one that is compatible with maintaining that system—limited war.

Increasing likelihood of conflict

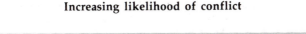

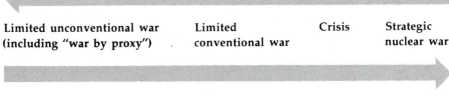

| Limited unconventional war (including "war by proxy") | Limited conventional war | Crisis | Strategic nuclear war |

Increasing risk and cost

Figure 9-2 Likelihood of Conflict Versus Risk and Cost

Notes

1. Kenneth N. Waltz, "The Stability of a Bipolar World," *Daedalus*, Summer 1964, 884.
2. Glenn H. Snyder, "Crisis Bargaining" in *International Crises*, ed. Charles F. Herman (New York: Free Press, 1972), 220. See also Glenn H. Snyder and Paul Diesing, *Conflict Among Nations* (Princeton, N.J. : Princeton University Press, 1977).
3. For an excellent and detailed analysis of crises that result from deterrence failures, see *Deterrence in American Foreign Policy* by Alexander L. George and Richard Smoke (New York: Columbia University Press, 1974).
4. Oran Young, *The Politics of Force* (Princeton, N.J.: Princeton University Press, 1968), 63-95.
5. Arnold L. Horelick and Myron Rush, *Strategic Power and Soviet Policy* (Chicago: University of Chicago Press, 1966), 50-58.
6. The forecast of Soviet and U.S. strength in ICBMs in 1960 was 100 to 30; in 1961, 500 to 70; in 1962, 1,000 to 130; in 1963, 1,500 to 130; in 1964, 2,000 to 130. This forecast was based on interviews with persons presumably knowledgeable about the defense effort. The gap would be closed after 1964. Quoted from *New York Times* in ibid., 51.
7. Theodore C. Sorensen, *Kennedy* (New York: Harper & Row, 1965), 326-346; Arthur M. Schlesinger, Jr., *A Thousand Days* (Boston: Houghton Mifflin, 1965), 219-250; and Tad Szulc and Karl E. Meyer, *The Cuban Invasion: The Chronicle of a Disaster* (New York: Ballantine, 1962).
8. Phil Williams, *Crisis Management* (New York: John Wiley & Sons, 1976), 27-31. This book is an excellent summary of the crisis literature. For a view that emphasizes misperception as the cause for crises, see Richard N. Lebow, *Between Peace and War* (Baltimore: Johns Hopkins University Press, 1981).
9. Charles F. Herman, *Crises in Foreign Policy* (Indianapolis: Bobbs-Merrill, 1969).
10. The whole strategy of coercion to "asymmetry of motivation" and balance of power is explored in *The Limits of Coercive Diplomacy: Laos, Cuba, Vietnam* by Alexander L. George, David K. Hall, and William E. Simons (Boston: Little, Brown & Co., 1971), 23-24.
11. Ibid., 86-136.
12. Ronald Steel, *Pax Americana* (New York: Viking, 1967), 195.

13. The best accounts of the missile crisis can be found in Sorensen, *Kennedy*, 752-809; Schlesinger, *A Thousand Days*, 726-749; and Elie Abel, *The Missile Crisis* (Philadelphia: Lippincott, 1966). The most detailed analysis of American policy may be found in *Essence of Decision* by Graham T. Allison (Boston: Little, Brown & Co., 1971). For an analysis of Soviet motivations, see Arnold L. Horelick, "The Cuban Missile Crisis: An Analysis of Soviet Calculations," *World Politics*, April 1964, 363-370. For an account of the rescue of the merchant ship *Mayaguez* from the Cambodians in 1974, a more recent although considerably less important crisis, see Richard G. Head, Frisco W. Short, and Robert C. McFarland, *Crisis Resolution* (Boulder, Colo.: Westview Press, 1978).

14. Robert F. Kennedy, *Thirteen Days: A Memoir of the Cuban Missile Crisis* (New York: Signet, 1969), 107-109; and George, Hall, and Simons, *Limits of Coercive Diplomacy*, 115-134.

15. Young, *Politics of Force*, 348-361.

16. Kennedy, *Thirteen Days*, 67.

17. Ibid., 82.

18. Quoted in Abel, *Missile Crisis*, 183.

19. For a comparative analysis of Chinese-American crises, see J. H. Kalichi, *The Pattern of Chinese-American Crises* (Cambridge: Cambridge University Press, 1975).

20. Robert S. McNamara, "The Military Role of Nuclear Weapons," *Foreign Affairs* (Fall 1983): 79.

21. Kenneth N. Waltz, *Theory of International Politics* (Reading, Mass.: Addison-Wesley, 1979), 185.

22. Ibid.

23. *New York Times*, Sept. 13, 1984.

24. Quoted by Charles Krauthammer, "On Nuclear Morality," *Commentary*, October 1983, 49.

25. Thomas C. Schelling, "What Went Wrong with Arms Control," *Foreign Affairs* (Winter 1985/86): 233.

CHAPTER 10

The Use
of Force

LIMITED WAR IN THE NUCLEAR AGE

Nuclear weapons have made an all-out war suicidal for the superpowers. The only type of war they may use safely to advance their purposes is limited war.[1] Although the use of total force may be irrational, it does not follow that *any* use of violence is irrational. If one of the superpowers can directly or indirectly through allies and friends present a limited challenge to its opponent to which the latter can respond *only* with all-out war, the latter confronts an agonizing dilemma: if it does so, it will risk suicide; if it wants to avoid that disaster it can simply not respond and surrender. It is one thing for a nuclear giant to threaten its adversary with all-out war in response to an attack on its own homeland. Such a threat is credible. The same type of threat is credible when the protection of key allies is involved. But the same threat is not credible as a deterrent to attacks on less important allies or friends. The ability to drop the bomb on the opponent's capital is not very useful in deterring limited incursions into areas of less vital interest (see Table 10-1).

Following World War II the United States enjoyed virtual immunity from attack until the mid-1950s, for the Soviets did not explode their first atomic bomb until late 1949, and the Soviet long-range air force did not undergo major development until 1954. Conversely, the Soviet Union was vulnerable to Strategic Air Command (SAC) bombers, whose American bases were supplemented by a global string of bases around the periphery of what was then the Sino-Soviet bloc. Yet, even under such favorable conditions, it was not rational for the United States to fight a total war in response to limited provocation. The credibility of commitments is related to the importance of the interests at stake. A power may risk a major war in defense of itself and its

Table 10-1 Levels of Coercion

Using the Threat of Force			Using Force
Deterrence	*Crisis*		*Limited War*
Persuade adversary not to initiate action	Persuade adversary to stop short of objective	Persuade adversary to surrender gains	Compel opponent to desist and/or restore the status quo

SOURCE: Adapted from Alexander George et al., *The Limits of Coercive Diplomacy* (Boston: Little, Brown & Co., 1971), 24. Reprinted with permission.

principal allies, but not of lesser states in areas of secondary concern. The ineffectiveness of threats of all-out war in deterring limited Soviet probes was clearly demonstrated when North Korea attacked South Korea in June 1950. The Soviets were apparently quite willing to acquiesce in, if not initiate, this use of force by an ally, despite the United States' overwhelming strategic superiority. Obviously, they did not expect direct U.S. retaliation for their limited Communist challenge on the Korean peninsula. The subsequent war in Korea, however, did become a model for the only kind of warfare possible between nuclear powers.

A Definition of Limits

Limited war may be defined as war fought for limited political purposes.[2] In contrast to the aims of total war, which generally include the complete destruction of the enemy's military forces and its government, the aims of limited war fall far short of total victory and unconditional surrender. Perhaps the most obvious goal is the capture or recapture of strategically located or economically important territory. In the Korean War, the North sought to take over the South and to establish Communist control over the entire Korean peninsula; the North would then, in the metaphor used by the Japanese, have "pointed the Korean dagger straight at Japan's heart." It helps to recall that the precipitating cause of the Russo-Japanese War of 1904-05 was Russia's penetration of Korea from Manchuria. Japan at that time offered to divide Korea at the thirty-eighth parallel, but the czarist government refused. As a result, Japan attacked Siberia. Japanese security demanded that the southern half of Korea remain free of Russian control. In June 1950, when Japan served as a base for American forces, the United States' reaction was similar. One reason was that after Nationalist China's collapse, the United States needed Japan as an ally. It had to defend South Korea; otherwise Japan would have been neutralized.

Another reason for the U.S. intervention was to preserve the recently formed North Atlantic Treaty Organization (NATO). The Europeans remembered America's retreat into isolationism after World War I. The United States had just committed itself to Western Europe's defense, but was it a credible commitment? South Korea was not, admittedly, an ally of the United States, but it was a friend. Through the United Nations the United States had sponsored an election that had brought the South Korean government into power and then assisted the new government with military and economic aid. Would the United States now defend its protégé or abandon it? The United States had little choice but to defend South Korea to keep the confidence of the NATO allies.

Moreover, the United States was concerned with a milieu goal. President Harry Truman recalled that during the 1930s the democracies had not stopped the aggressions by Germany, Italy, or Japan. The failure to halt the initial aggressions eventually led to World War II. The United States wanted a postwar world free from aggression. A failure to act in South Korea might encourage further Communist inroads.[3]

All of these objectives could be ensured by defending South Korea; they did not require, as in past American wars, the complete defeat of the enemy. In short, U.S. goals were limited and compatible with restoring the status quo. They did not require the enemy's unconditional surrender or the removal of its government. To forget the goal was to risk escalating the war.

The Victor's Restraint and the Opponent's Survival. If limited war is an alternative to fighting all-out nuclear war while preserving the balance of power, the existence of the opponent's state cannot become the issue. Halting the opponent's violations of one's interests is the issue. Unconditional surrender or total victory cannot be the goal. The "winner" on the battlefield must, therefore, forgo winning a total victory; the "loser" will then not be compelled to escalate the conflict by, for example, calling on friends to intervene. The Korean War again provides a good example of this situation. The United States at first sought only the restoration of the status quo. But once the North Korean forces had been driven back to the thirty-eighth parallel, the United States, seeing an opportunity to unify all Korea and to destroy a Soviet satellite regime, changed its objective. By turning around the dagger once aimed at Japan and thus endangering the political survival of the North Korean regime, the United States provoked Chinese intervention.[4] China's entry into the conflict intensified the fighting and risked escalating the war even more. But leaders in Washington, afraid that striking back against China *in* China would trap the United States into a full-scale war on the Asian mainland or precipitate World War III, reverted to their original aim. They had learned the consequences of what could occur in the nuclear age if the United States followed its historic policy of seeking a total victory on the battlefield.

Noninvolvement of Major Powers. In addition to this basic political constraint, the forces of the superpowers must not engage each other directly if the war is to be limited. Not that total war would be inevitable if U.S. and Soviet forces (and during the early days of the Chinese-Soviet alliance in the 1950s, Chinese forces as well) were to clash. But their participation in combat would increase the difficulty of controlling the conflict. The great powers seem to be well aware of this second constraint. The United States and the Soviet Union have been extremely careful about where they have confronted each other, as in Western Europe—like porcupines making love! Incidents involving direct clashes between American and Soviet forces have been scrupulously avoided.

It is significant that a limited war, such as the Korean War, occurred outside of Europe and in an area from which U.S. forces had been withdrawn. After the U.S. intervention, the fighting was between the troops of North Korea, the Soviet Union's ally, and the troops fighting under the flag of the United Nations. The Communist Chinese troops that later intervened were not sent officially by the Chinese government. The government in Beijing never declared war and never accepted responsibility for the Chinese troops in Korea, which were declared to be "volunteers." Nor did the United States declare war on North Korea or on Communist China; U.S. troops were regarded as part of the UN force fighting a "police action." The absence of a declaration of war and the use of volunteers may seem rather obvious fictions, yet such fictions help to keep wars limited.

Geographical Constraints.   A third constraint is geographical: limited wars generally have been confined to the territory of a single nation. The Yalu River served as the frontier between North Korea and China during the Korean War, and even after the Chinese intervention the war was not extended beyond it. Bombers were not sent to hit factories, railroads, or military supply depots in Manchuria. If fact, even the bombing of bridges crossing the Yalu into China was restricted to the North Korean side. The Korean War was thus fought only in Korea (see Figure 10-1). Moreover, each side allowed the other some clearly demarcated "privileged sanctuaries"— inviolable areas for reserve troops, supplies, and air and naval bases. In a limited war, to attack these areas is to risk removing one of the constraints on the scope of the conflict. Manchuria was such a sanctuary for the Communists during the Korean War. Although its use as a sanctuary was known in the United States, especially by those who demanded that Manchuria be bombed, it was less well known that the United States also possessed privileged sanctuaries within the actual area of the fighting. No air attacks were launched on either Pusan or Inchon, the two largest ports through which most of the supplies for the UN forces were channeled. If either port had been frequently bombed, UN operations might have been seriously hampered. Similarly, Communist Chinese jet fighters did not attack UN troops in the field, American air bases in South Korea, or aircraft carriers off the coast; instead, they were limited to the Yalu River area, defending the bridges.

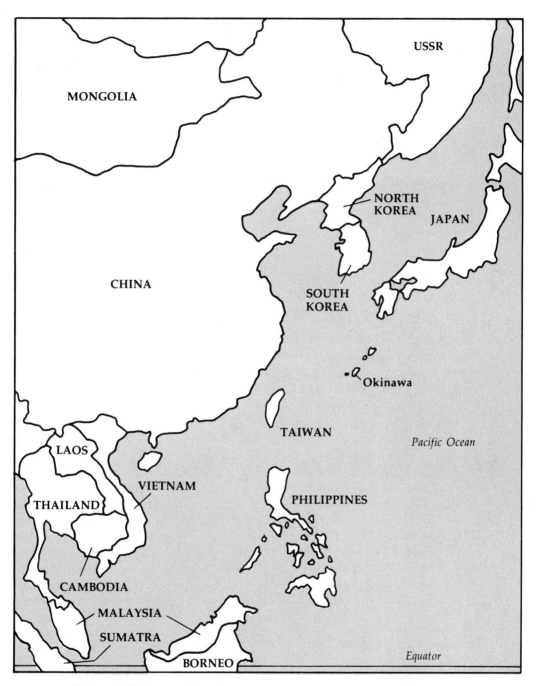

Figure 10-1 Eastern Asia

The Nonuse of Nuclear Weapons.   A final constraint on limited wars is the refusal to use tactical or battlefield nuclear weapons. These weapons, which did not become available until the mid-1950s, were once advocated in the West as means of equalizing the superiority of Soviet and Chinese military personnel. In fact, they do not necessarily favor the defending side. A more powerful reason for not using them is that once employed, escalation from tactical to strategic nuclear weapons is likely. In the heat of battle, the pressure will be to use ever more powerful nuclear arms. But most important, tactical nuclear weapons are a political liability. Few nations want to be "saved from communism," or from anything else, by means of nuclear weapons that could devastate them.

Limitations and Escalation.   If these principal constraints are present, wars can be limited. The belligerents agree to these limits by *tacit* bargaining on the battlefield. However ridiculous such restrictions may appear from the military point of view, the principal aim of observing them is to provide an incentive to the enemy to accept similar restraints. The limitations must be clearly drawn: precisely because they are *not* formally negotiated but tacitly agreed upon, the terms must be qualitatively distinguishable from possible alternatives. Frontiers and the distinction between conventional and nuclear weapons are so crystal clear that it is relatively easy to agree on them tacitly; once these limits have been violated, however, it is far more difficult to draw new lines. Nonuse of tactical nuclear arms is simple and unambiguous, easily understood and observed.[5]

In addition, the restraints tend to reinforce one another; conversely, the more they are violated, the more tenuous the limitation. No single step in escalation will lead immediately and automatically to total war. Because the removal of each constraint tends to weaken the capacity to limit the conflict, when one side does escalate, this step should be taken only after the most careful consideration. After each step upward on the ladder, cautious leaders should pause to see whether the opponent will desist as a result of this escalation and fear of the greater risks this poses of even further escalation and costs. If the opponent does, there may be no need for further escalation; if not, further escalation may be necessary. The important point is that at each rung of the escalation ladder there should be time for either tacit or explicit bargaining.[6] The side against which the escalation is directed must have time to evaluate its next move, and it can do so only after it has decided what the escalation signifies about the opponent's intentions. It is thus very important to slow down the momentum of military operations in order to maintain political control and keep the war limited.

But, if one side persists in its original goals and refuses any concessions to conclude the war, the conflict becomes more difficult to restrain. In such circumstances escalation appears necessary. Only by imposing more severe sanctions and by exacting a greater price for the continued fighting can the side that escalates hope that the opponent will back off, give up some of its objectives, and end the hostilities. The result is a paradox. On the one hand, limited goals are established in order to avoid escalation. On the other, if one belligerent refuses to accept limited goals, escalation is necessary to compel more self-restraint.

REVOLUTIONARY WARFARE

Revolutionary or guerrilla conflict, even more than conventional limited war, reflects the restraints imposed upon the use of force by nuclear weapons. The Soviets and the Chinese Communists, who used it to come into power, call this kind of conflict wars of "national liberation." In the less-developed countries (LDCs), guerrillas aim to capture state power in order to completely transform the social-political structures and economic organizations.

One advantage of such wars is that they do not raise the issue of aggression as clearly as do conventional limited attacks; the initiators remain free of the stigma *aggressor*. There is no single moment when a major attack across a well-defined frontier occurs. David Galula thus compares conventional war and revolutionary war:

> In the conventional war, the aggressor who has prepared for it within the confines of his national territory, channeling his resources into the preparation, has much to gain by attacking suddenly with all his forces. The transition from peace to war is as abrupt as the state of the art allows; the first shock may be decisive. This is hardly possible in the revolutionary war because the aggressor—the insurgent—lacks sufficient strength at the outset. Indeed, years may sometimes pass before he has built up significant political, let alone military, power. So there is usually little or no first shock, little or no surprise, no possibility of an early decisive battle. In fact, the insurgent has no interest in producing a shock until he feels fully able to withstand the enemy's expected reaction.[7]

Furthermore, because guerrilla forces generally are preponderantly native, a guerrilla war has the appearance of being a domestic conflict or civil war. Finally, guerrilla wars tend to be lengthy. If the guerrillas were as strong as, or stronger than, their opponent, they would seek quick victory in conventional battle. But their very weakness compels them to whittle away at the enemy's strength bit by bit. This process of attrition can go almost unnoticed in the outside world until the last stage of the war, when the guerrillas are poised to defeat their weakened and demoralized opponent. By then, it is usually too late for effective countermeasures. Waging guerrilla warfare is thus considerably safer than fighting a regular war in the nuclear age.

Guerrilla Strategy and Tactics

In the initial phase of a revolutionary war, the weaker guerrillas are strategically on the defensive; tactically, though, they are always on the offensive. To wear down the enemy they adopt *hit-and-run tactics.* Mobility, surprise, and rapid military decisions characterize their operations. They fight only when there is a good chance of victory; otherwise, they do not attack and, if engaged, quickly disengage. Their attacks are swift, sudden, and relentless. There is no front line in such a war. The front is everywhere, and the guerrillas can strike anywhere. Guerrilla tactical doctrine is perhaps most aptly summed up in Mao Zedong's well-known formula: "Enemy advances, we retreat; enemy halts, we harass; enemy tires, we attack; enemy retreats, we pursue." [8]

Rather than inflicting major defeats on the enemy, these tactics result in harassment, confusion, and frustration. The guerrillas do not engage in conventional battle until the last stage of the war because they are too weak throughout most of the hostilities. Physical violence is important, but it is the *psychological impact* of the war that is decisive. Although the enemy cannot be beaten physically, its *will to fight* can be eroded in two ways. Basically, the regular army can be demoralized. Suffering one minor defeat after another, rarely engaging the enemy directly in battle, forced increasingly on the defensive by the guerrillas' tactics, the army loses its offensive spirit as it finds its conventional tactics useless. Determination to stay and fight decline, and stamina is sapped.

Even more important in undermining the enemy's will to fight is to isolate the government either by capturing the support of most of the population or by neutralizing it. Control of the population is essential if the guerrillas are to achieve their objective of "internal conquest." The populace provides them with recruits, food, shelter, and, above all, intelligence. If the guerrillas are to surprise the enemy, they must know where to strike and when. They must know all the opponent's moves to be able to choose favorable moments to fight and to escape when government reinforcements suddenly arrive.

Victory is naturally one way of impressing the people, who at the beginning of a revolutionary war are likely to be divided into three groups: a fervent minority favoring the guerrillas, a militant minority favoring the government, and a majority of the population—perhaps 50 percent to 70 percent—who are neutral. This last group will remain passive until it becomes clear which side will win. Its neutrality favors the guerrillas because it hampers the government forces; the people will not provide the government with the information necessary to locate the guerrillas. As the government's troops become demoralized and defensive, as increasingly they appear unable to provide the population with elementary security in daily life, the government loses whatever allegiance it has had. It is the peasants, generally removed from any contact with their government, who are most concerned about their own future. If they think the guerrillas will win the war, they are unlikely to antagonize them but will instead cooperate.

Selective terrorism also helps to elicit cooperation. Its aim is to reaffirm the weakness of the government by attacking mainly local government officials. Obviously, wholesale and indiscriminate terrorism would only alienate the very people whose support the guerrillas seek to win, though on occasion massive execution or the burning of an entire village is used to influence other villages and towns. The guerrillas have made their point vividly when they can show the peasants that the government is not able to protect even its own officials.[9] Furthermore, by eliminating these officials, often with all the villagers forced to watch, the guerrillas break the link between the government and the majority of the people, restricting the government's authority mainly to the cities as well as intimidating anyone from helping the government and its army.

Even in the cities, this authority may not go uncontested. In the Tet offensive of 1968 the Viet Cong infiltrated major South Vietnamese cities and district capitals. The populations were shocked into recognition that they were not safe either. Just as the Viet Cong's executions of some villagers who cooperated or sided with the government conveyed to the peasants the message that they had better support the guerrillas—or at least remain "neutral"—so the attacks on cities were intended to warn their inhabitants that they had better be careful about which side they supported. These attacks further undermined confidence in the Saigon government as well as in the United States. If after three years of intensive warfare neither side could apparently guarantee the safety of the cities it was supposed to control, why should the population expect any better in the future?

Guerrillas, however, achieve popular support mainly because of an effective *social strategy* in which they are identified with a popular cause or grievance.[10] Communist guerrillas do not usually present themselves as Communists, nor do the people support them because they are Communists or desire the establishment of a Communist state. The guerrillas present themselves simply as spokesmen for existing social causes and aspirations. If the people are resentful of continued colonial rule or of a despotic native government, the guerrillas take up the cry. If certain classes seek social and economic justice, the guerrillas demand it on their behalf. The guerrillas identify themselves as liberators and reformers, promising that they can satisfy rising expectations. In South Vietnam the Viet Cong appealed to the peasants by pointing out that they were working in the landowners' rice fields for the landowners' benefit. When the landlords fled to the cities, the Viet Cong told the peasants that they no longer had to pay exorbitant and exploitative rents (or taxes); the peasants owned the land, and the Viet Cong would protect them if anyone sought to take it away. The result was a deep schism between the government in Saigon and the peasantry.

This social strategy is basic to the guerrillas' revolutionary warfare. Although the military component is important, it is neither the most significant nor the distinguishing characteristic of this particular kind of war, especially as it is waged by Communist parties whose entire social outlook is based on a class analysis and class struggle. Indeed, the struggle begins before the military phase of the war begins. In each village and hamlet the revolutionary party establishes its cells, seeks local control and support, and thus diminishes the base of popular support for the government. The fact that a large proportion of the population tends to be neutral in the war, waiting to see who is likely to win, is partly the result of this *preemptive* social strategy. Whereas the revolutionaries' maximum goal is to mobilize the population to fight with them against the government, their minimum aim is to prevent the population from fighting on the government's side.

When the war has gone on long enough for the revolutionaries to have won widespread popular support, the government will have become increasingly isolated socially and weakened militarily, so that only a final blow is needed to topple it. This last step involves conventional battle—unless, as in Cuba and South Vietnam before American intervention, the entire governmental structure and authority have already disintegrated. The guerrillas must, of course, be extremely careful in their timing. If they engage in conventional fighting too early, before the enemy army has lost most of its will to fight and before they themselves are properly trained and equipped, they may be badly defeated. But if they have the patience and are able to calculate correctly the moment of transition, the war will end in victory for them. The defeat of the French forces at Dien Bien Phu in Indochina in 1954 broke France's determination to hold onto its old colony, yet the French garrison at Dien Bien Phu consisted of only one-fifteenth of the total number of French troops in Indochina. The French suffered 12,000 casualties, including prisoners, but the estimated Vietminh casualties were greater, 15,000. Since its total force was not as large as that of the French, the Vietminh clearly had been badly hurt. Nonetheless, this single battle sapped France's will to resist.[11] The French decided to end the long and—for them—futile fighting.

Guerrilla warfare may at times seem militarily primitive, for guerrilla weapons do not begin to compare with the highly intricate weapons in Western arsenals. Guerrillas may receive sophisticated weapons, but their success does not depend upon them. Politically, however, guerrilla warfare is "more sophisticated than nuclear war or . . . war as it was waged by conventional armies, navies, and air forces." [12]

The Primacy of Political over Military Factors

No counterrevolutionary war can be won by conventional military means alone: *a purely military solution is impossible.* Interestingly, the successful guerrilla and counterguerrilla leaders of the past two decades have not been military men.[13] In China, Mao—a student, a librarian, and subsequently a professionally trained revolutionary—defeated Chiang Kai-shek, a professionally trained soldier. In Indochina, Ho Chi Minh, a socialist agitator, and General Vo Nguyen Giap, a French-educated history teacher, defeated four of France's senior generals. Fidel Castro was a lawyer and Ramon Magsaysay, who led the counterguerrilla war in the Philippines, was an automotive mechanic turned politician. In short, the orthodox military officer has generally been unable to cope with the unorthodox nature of guerrilla warfare.

In the final analysis the government can win its war against the revolution-aries only if it alleviates the conditions that have led the peasantry to support the revolutionary party in the first place. For example, in Malaya, the British promised independence during the war there from 1946 to 1960. Because they had already granted independence to India, Pakistan, and Burma, their word was credible, and the Malayans had a stake in the government's struggle. The Communists were thus stripped of their guise as liberators from colonialism. Many Malays fought alongside British troops. The contrast with the situation in Vietnam is striking. In the first Indochina War the people supported the Vietminh as national liberators because the French refused to grant them full independence. Ho Chi Minh became a symbol of Vietnamese nationalism. Anti-Communist Vietnamese who had fought with the French against the Vietminh (as anti-Communist Malays had fought with the British) were never able to compete with Ho for this nationalist identity. After 1954 they ap-peared to many—including many in the West—as puppets of France. This image was reinforced by their lack of social conscience and concern. Indeed, the government's suppression of political opponents, critics of the war, and advocates of settlement with the Viet Cong only fortified this image.

Popular confidence, then, is the indispensable condition for successful antirevolutionary warfare. Military countermeasures alone can never be ade-quate; troops trained in the tactics of unconventional warfare must be sup-ported by political, social, and economic reforms. It was this kind of combina-tion that defeated the Communist-led Huks in the Philippines during the 1950s. The government won the allegiance of the peasantry by instituting reforms to improve their lives; the Communist appeal was weakened, and the Huks lost their support.[14] A British colonel summed up the essence of counterguerrilla warfare in this way: "There has never been a successful guerrilla war conducted in an area where the populace is hostile to the guerrillas. . . . The art of defeating the guerrillas is therefore the art of turning the populace against them."[15]

The major task of antirevolutionary warfare is fundamentally *political*. Guer-rillas are a barometer of discontent. This discontent must be ameliorated, for it is the decisive element in bringing about victory or failure. Perhaps the French experience in Algeria offers the clearest evidence. The French actually won the military war against the Algerian guerrillas. By 1960 the Algerian National Liberation Army no longer possessed even a battalion-sized unit. By the end of the war in 1962, the Algerian guerrillas had, according to French army sources, fewer than 4,000 troops left (10,000, according to other, more sympathetic French sources) out of a total of almost 60,000 three years earlier.[16] French military tactics had been as effective in Algeria as they had been ineffective in Indochina. Nevertheless, the French lost the war because it could not be won *politically*. The Algerian population was hostile; so were France's NATO allies and the nonaligned states. The suppression of a nation-alist movement was politically unpalatable and infeasible in an age when the right of all former colonies to rule themselves was almost universally recognized and asserted. *In certain circumstances war is revolution. Consequently, conventional military force may be self-defeating.*

U.S. POWER AND THE 'RULES OF THE GAME' IN VIETNAM

The preceding analysis should largely explain why it was difficult for the United States to cope with guerrilla warfare in Vietnam.[17] American military leaders had been traditionally trained. They saw this war like other wars, as essentially a military, not political, undertaking.[18] All that was necessary, they believed, was to apply American technology and know-how to the problem. Could the world's mightiest nation, with its huge army led by well-trained officers and supported by the might and knowledge of American industry, not defeat a few thousand black-clad Asian guerrillas? It was easy to indulge in the "illusion of omnipotence." The United States had, after all, beaten far greater powers. France's earlier failure was blamed on the alienation of the Vietnamese nationalists and on an army that was not well equipped or led and had poor air support. None of these factors, presumably, would hamper the United States.

Hubris (the Greek word for overweening pride) proved a great impediment, however. In effect, the United States was so powerful and so sure of success that it believed it could fight a guerrilla war simply by changing the rules and fighting according to the American concept of war.[19] The concept emphasized the achievement of victory through attrition of the enemy's forces. The soldier's concern was strictly military; politics was not his business. This division of labor suggests that the crucial political reforms would be postponed until after the guerrillas had been defeated. The additional advantage, according to the military, was that the United States would be fighting the war, thus avoiding the difficulties and frustrations of cooperating with the ineffective South Vietnamese army, which was expected only to stay out of the way. This policy and ordering of priorities guaranteed failure. Surely the war could not be won primarily by foreign troops; rather an indigenous army with a will to fight and support from a sizable portion of its people was required. Indeed, how could the South Vietnamese government establish its own identity and claim the allegiance of its people if it was seen as essentially an American puppet, completely dependent on the United States politically, militarily, and economically?

U.S. Strategy and the Erosion of Public Support

To defeat the North Vietnamese forces sent into South Vietnam, the U.S. military adopted a conventional offensive strategy of "search and destroy." Translated into daily operations, this strategy allocated 80 percent of U.S. forces to the central highlands and frontier areas, where only 4 percent of the population resided. More than 90 percent of the people lived in the Mekong delta and coastal plain, and it was in those areas that the actual guerrilla war was being fought.[20] While the United States sent in more troops to decimate the North Vietnamese forces, the Communist government in Hanoi matched the buildup. *America's aim was physical attrition; North Vietnam's was psychological exhaustion.*[21] The American victories in battle and the heavy casualties inflicted on the opponent could not, as a result, be transformed into lasting political success.

The United States was irrevocably committed to a seemingly interminable war that eventually eroded the patience of the American public. Indeed, the search-and-destroy strategy that left the cities essentially undefended was an invitation to a Viet Cong attack. The dramatic Tet offensive of 1968 not only revealed the folly of U.S. strategy but also forced Americans to ask whether the war could be brought to a successful political and military conclusion at all.[22] Psychologically, the Tet offensive was the beginning of the end for the United States in Vietnam, as the American public, increasingly beset by doubts about the wisdom and costs of a war that seemed to have no end, became more and more disillusioned. It was the United States' Dien Bien Phu, sapping American will and determination. It was not an American military defeat. Quite the contrary: the Viet Cong suffered such an enormous defeat that the North Vietnamese bore the burden of the fighting thereafter.

But Americans like to win their wars quickly. President Lyndon Johnson could recall the challenge in Korea. Within one year Americans had been fed up with "Truman's war" and the continuing, apparently futile, loss of American lives. This mood contributed to the defeat of the Democrats in the 1952 presidential election. A long-drawn-out, indecisive engagement does not fit the traditional American all-or-nothing approach, and guerrillas can exploit this impatience simply by not losing.[23] In total war, when the public perceives a serious threat to the nation, it is willing to mobilize fully and make sacrifices; guns are automatically placed ahead of butter. In a limited war, where by definition the security threat is a limited one, the public does not automatically give priority to the prosecution of the war. When the national security is seen as directly and greatly threatened, people are willing to accept tax increases, a draft, rationing, and inflation; in a limited war situation, this is not so. Neither in Vietnam nor in Korea did the United States mobilize fully. Because the aim was not the total defeat of the enemy, most men were not drafted and industry was not generally converted to military production. For the vast majority of Americans, life went on pretty much as before, and guns, therefore, had to compete with the continuing demands for butter by the many interest groups in society. Before Tet, the United States suffered 15,000 casualties—one for every 15,000 Americans—and during the entire war less than one-quarter of 1 percent of all Americans served in Vietnam. Nevertheless, the consensus of support for the war disintegrated. The political right demanded that the political restraints on military operations, which presumably prevented the war from being won, be lifted; the political left, arguing either that vital American interests had never been at stake or were not worth the cost, recommended withdrawal.

The erosion of public support testifies to the fact that in a guerrilla war like Vietnam there were two battlefields: "one bloody and indecisive in the forests and mountains of Indochina, the other essentially nonviolent—but ultimately more decisive—within the polity and social institutions of the United States." [24] The Viet Cong could not invade the United States; nor could they militarily defeat American forces in Vietnam. Their entire strategy was one of protracted conflict to wear down the adversary's will. General Giap, the victor over the French at Dien Bien Phu and the strategist of the war in the South against the United States, had a shrewd political estimate of the Western democracies' determination to continue fighting an inconclusive war for very long: "The enemy will pass slowly from the offensive to the defensive. The blitzkrieg will transform itself into a war of long duration. Thus, the enemy will be caught in a dilemma: He has to drag out the war in order to win it and does not possess, on the other hand, the psychological and political means to fight a long-drawn-out war." [25]

Orthodox military doctrine thus led to the adoption of counterproductive strategy. American officers had not heard the axiom that a conventional army in a guerrilla war loses if it does not win, whereas guerrillas win if they do not lose. They could not grasp the fact that the United States could win all the battles, yet lose the war. Winning this kind of war demands a strategy that does not downgrade the political and psychological factors. The United States military, however, selected a strategy guaranteed to lose and then blamed its lack of success on the flow of men and weapons from North Vietnam. In this way military leaders could avoid acknowledging their faulty strategy in the South, the main place where the war could be won.

The Failure of the Air War

The military's argument was that the war was not being won because it did not have enough men, enough helicopters, enough gunships. More of everything would ensure local victory. But most of all, the military argued that the main arena of contest was not the war in the South but in North Vietnam. And there it was prevented from destroying and punishing the real enemy by various restrictions on targets. If unleashed, the U.S. military could win the war; the obstacles were the politically imposed restraints.

In fact, there was already an air war against the North. The North Vietnamese were to be punished for their role in the war and made to pay an ever-increasing price until they had suffered enough to quit. The air force was to be the instrument for administering this punishment, but the task was beyond the ability of the air force. For one thing, an air force's ability to affect the enemy's capacity to fight lies in its ability to attack the sources of enemy supplies and the supply lines; it requires that the army then engage the enemy on the battlefield. [26] The Vietnamese sources of supplies, however, were the Soviet Union and China; furthermore, it was the North Vietnamese who generally chose the times and lengths of engagements in this unconventional war. Only the trails running to South Vietnam and, of course, roads, rivers, and a few factories in North Vietnam were left to attack. The trails through the jungle were difficult to find and ran mostly through Laos and Cambodia. The supplies, therefore, kept on coming. Indeed, the flow of men and ammunition increased, and the trails were not even used to full capacity.

The real difficulty with the bombing campaign of 1965-68, however, was making it work against an underdeveloped country; an industrial state simply has more to lose. No doubt, there must be some level of punishment that would affect even an underdeveloped nation's will. But in Hanoi the motivation to succeed the French in all of Indochina was so strong, had been held so long, and had been so near to fulfillment—only to be repeatedly betrayed— that the will to fight on was intense. The North Vietnamese were willing to pay the price of bomb damage, civilian casualties, and heavy losses in military personnel for their fundamental belief that they were the rightful heirs of French power throughout all of Vietnam, if not all of Indochina.

It can be argued that more bombing and quicker escalation would have raised the price of noncompliance higher than that for compliance. Perhaps that was the reasoning behind President Richard Nixon's heavy bombing of much of North Vietnam, including its capital city and principal harbor, after the North Vietnamese conventional invasion of South Vietnam in the spring of 1972. The United States resumed heavy bombing at Christmas to end the war. The first bombing helped stop the enemy offensive; the second brought a peace agreement in January 1973. But the Christmas bombing took place in circumstances different from earlier attacks. The Nixon administration, through its détente policies with the Soviet Union and China, had isolated North Vietnam politically. Even after this heavy bombing, however, the final settlement could not compel the North Vietnamese to withdraw their forces from the South.

In the first three years of air war against North and South Vietnam, the United States expended three times the tonnage dropped in Europe and the Pacific area during World War II (at a cost of 50 cents per pound of bomb, a total cost of $3 billion).[27] For North Vietnam, as for any other country, there must have been a level of pain at which the government in Hanoi would "break" and give up its attempt to expand its control into South Vietnam. The enormous casualties accepted by the Hanoi government suggests that that level had not yet been reached. John Mueller has argued that the military costs suffered by the North Vietnamese were "virtually unprecedented historically," even though the North Vietnamese—unlike the combatants of World Wars I and II—were not fighting for their survival.[28] The American goal was to deny them victory in the South, not to eliminate Vietnam altogether. Hanoi leaders have admitted to Communist battle deaths at about 500,000 to 600,000; Mueller notes that these figures are equivalent to 2.5 to 3 percent of the prewar population of Vietnam, a percentage twice that suffered by the fanatical Japanese during World War II. In the last 160 years only a few of the participants in more than one hundred wars have lost as much as 2 percent of their prewar populations. In World War I Germany lost 2.7 percent; in World War II the Soviet Union and Germany each lost 4.4 percent. The North Koreans had stopped fighting in 1953, after far fewer casualties; the Vietminh had done the same in 1954.

Under "normal" conditions, therefore, the expectation that the government in Hanoi would desist if punished heavily was a rational one. But, clearly, its willingness to suffer immense physical losses while psychologically wearing out the United States gave it the upper hand: its determination to succeed was simply greater than the American will to continue. The bombing of North Vietnam, then, had little effect on North Vietnamese determination or ability to infiltrate. Quite the contrary. The government may have benefited through bombing by receiving greater domestic support for its efforts in the South. As the Battle of Britain epically demonstrated in World War II, people who are bombarded daily are strengthened in their resolve. Without the bombing, Ho might not have been able quite so easily to rally his people to support a long war with a high casualty rate.[29]

Worse, the bombing, more than any other issue, deeply divided the American population and antagonized even friendly Western nations. To have bombed Hanoi "back to the Stone Age," as one air force general summed up his recipe for victory, would have aroused even greater political hostility. As it was, the bombing made the United States appear a bully and North Vietnam the underdog. It aroused international sympathy and support for the Hanoi government, and it stirred many an American conscience. The fact that the bombing brought many people out for anti-American demonstrations all over the world was as significant as the actual battles—and seemingly more decisive; it made it even more difficult to handle the war "politically at home and diplomatically abroad." [30] It shifted the onus of the war from Hanoi to Washington.

Who Won, Who Lost?

In the final analysis the North Vietnamese won the war two years after the American withdrawal in 1973—despite a settlement that left the South Vietnamese government with a reasonable chance of survival. The North won for three reasons: (1) the American public "had had it," and, when North Vietnamese forces invaded South Vietnam openly in 1975, the United States refused to intervene again; (2) the South Vietnamese regime fell, not only because of its military errors and panic but, more fundamentally, because of its political weakness in mobilizing broad popular support throughout South Vietnam; and (3) the North Vietnamese were absolutely determined to win, unify, and govern all of Vietnam, regardless of cost.

The Vietnam War showed the limitations, if not the outright uselessness, of employing force in unfavorable political circumstances. The fact that President John Kennedy acquiesced in the South Vietnamese military's overthrow of Ngo Dinh Diem was evidence of the political bankruptcy and catastrophic failure of American policy. As Theodore Draper points out, "Kennedy's decision in 1963 to back Diem's overthrow was the most deadly criticism of Kennedy's decision in 1961 to back Diem to the hilt." [31] Long before Johnson's massive escalation in 1965, the situation in South Vietnam had clearly become unpromising. After the first Indochina War between the Vietminh and French, General Walter Bedell Smith, head of the American delegation to the 1954 Geneva conference, reportedly said that any second-rate general should be able to win in Indochina if there was a correct political atmosphere. Without such an atmosphere, not even a first-rate general could win. "Sound politics in Vietnam was the precondition of military victory, not that military victory was the precondition of sound politics." [32] *Resorting to force in unfavorable political circumstances can result only in political failure and the loss of a state's reputation for power or prestige.*

One unfavorable political condition was the lack of legitimacy of the governments the United States supported. The United States had too many men and too much firepower in Vietnam to lose, and, had the various governments in Saigon been able to arouse sufficient loyalty among South Vietnam's population, the U.S. forces, presumably with a better trained and a more motivated South Vietnamese army, could have won. As it was, the United States almost did anyway because the North Vietnamese made a critical miscalculation in timing. They launched the Tet offensive in the hope of stimulating a popular uprising in the South's cities and defections in South Vietnam's army. Neither happened. What occurred instead was that the Viet Cong got slaughtered. By exposing their guerrilla forces on the false belief that South Vietnam was ripe for the final thrust that would end the war, the North Vietnamese ensured the Viet Cong's destruction. After Tet, the North Vietnamese army did most of the fighting, and it increasingly fought a conventional war. When this army rolled into Saigon in 1975 as the victor, it did so as a regular army that had won with orthodox tactics. Hanoi's victory was not a victory for revolutionary or guerrilla warfare. That had died with Tet.

Ironically, if a conventional war had been fought from the beginning, the U.S. military would have won. But by 1972, when the North Vietnamese marched into South Vietnam in conventional military formation, the American army—troops that had not yet been withdrawn—could no longer participate in the fighting. President Nixon's "re-Americanization" of the war—the commitment of U.S. air power and the blockade of North Vietnam—had already aroused great opposition in the United States. The war on the second battlefield had already been lost politically; the American public wanted only to disengage from the war. It is surely correct to say that "in losing a people's war, the Communists went on to win the war itself. But in adopting a conventional war strategy, they won by a means they should have lost. The United States, on the other hand, won a war it thought it lost, and lost by default what it could have won." [33]

One final question must be addressed: Did North Vietnam really win and the United States lose? In one sense yes, even if we "did a far better job of defeating [ourselves] than the Communists ever did."[34] But in another sense North Vietnam lost and the United States won. Hanoi, after its victory and the unification of Vietnam, mismanaged the economy and alienated some of the country's most productive elements, especially its Chinese ethnic minority. The Communists might have claimed popular support as the rightful heirs to French rule because they were nationalists and sought Vietnam's national independence, but, once that had been achieved, they could hardly claim mass support by modernizing Vietnam's economy and raising the people's living standards. The final irony is that many of the "boat people," who fled Vietnam at great risk to their lives, came to the United States where, as have Castro's Cubans in Miami and elsewhere, they flourished and contributed enormously to the energy and entrepreneurship of the U.S. economy. The United States may have lost militarily, but can it not be said that ultimately it won the war economically and politically and the Communists lost?

SOVIET-STYLE GUERRILLA WAR IN AFGHANISTAN

In revolutionary warfare the guerrillas seek victory by separating the government from the people and winning their support for the guerrillas' cause. Mao used the analogy of fish (guerrillas) in water (the people) to underline the guerrillas' need for the people's support. The guerrillas base their conduct of the war on a "social strategy," and the government side must respond with the same strategy if it is to win. However, the Soviets with 120,000 troops in Afghanistan, supported by 30,000 troops stationed in the Soviet Central Asian republics to the north, have reassessed Mao's strategy since their 1979 invasion, which was intended to ensure the survival of the Marxist regime in power. Because resistance to the government is based on popular support, "the easiest way to separate the guerrillas from the population is to empty the fish bowl and capture its contents. In other words, an effective counterstrategy in the face of guerrilla action involves massive reprisals, sometimes including the extermination of a large part of the population."[35]

The assumption that underlies this approach is that "the war would be won by the side that succeeded in making terror reign."[36] When Soviet troops enter an Afghan village they frequently level it, shoot, bayonet, or kill with hand grenades the population that has not fled (often old men, women, and children), and then they plant grenades on the corpses, burn the crops, and kill all livestock. More frequently, because it is less costly in personnel, Soviet air power is used to attack resistance holdouts and retaliate against nearby villages with indiscriminate bombing, including the destruction of all food production in rebel-held areas. Even children are not exempt as targets. A French doctor with the rebels has mentioned the use of booby-trapped toys to blow off the hands and feet of children. This tactic is not meant to kill, but to demoralize the adults who must witness their children's suffering and to convince them that it is futile to support the rebels. Antipersonnel mines intended to wound adults serve the same purpose; in the case of resistance fighters, the intention is not only to intimidate those who oppose the Soviet army but also to eliminate, however briefly, the injured fighters and those who must assist them to get away. Other well-substantiated reports document widespread use of torture, rape (often in front of the family), and other means of terrorizing the population, including the deliberate attacks on hospitals set up by a team of French doctors to help the insurgents.

The principal impact of this deliberate use of mass terror is to empty the countryside and cut the resistance off from its base of popular support. Afghan refugees are not, as in most wars, an unfortunate consequence of war but a deliberate creation of Soviet strategy. The people living in the country and villages are forced to flee either to neighboring Pakistan and Iran or into Afghanistan's main towns, which are under Soviet control. More than 4 million refugees—about a quarter of Afghanistan's population before the invasion—have fled to Pakistan (approximately 2.6 million) and to Iran (about 1.8 million). Two million people are "internal refugees." The same strategy has been applied in Ethiopia, where the province of Ogaden revolted against the Marxist regime. With Soviet-Cuban advice and help, one town and village after another was leveled, creating 1 million refugees—almost the entire population—who fled to Somalia. Nevertheless, the size of the Afghan refugee flow is historically unprecedented. Amazingly, resistance continues, and this Soviet war has lasted longer than the four-year Soviet war against Nazi Germany.

But time may be on the side of the Soviets. The reason is twofold: in the towns they control, Russian has been made the compulsory language in school, and Marxism-Leninism has been introduced into the curricula. Thousands of young Afghans have been sent to Soviet and East European universities, and the Afghan economy is being steadily integrated into the Soviet economy. The second reason is that the Soviet Union, unlike Western nations, *can* fight a long counterguerrilla war. Soviet public opinion does not influence policy; the press does not report a lack of successes, let alone any major defeats or sizable personnel losses (estimated at 30,000 casualties, with 10,000 killed); no street demonstrations and chants of "How many kids did you kill today?" are heard by the Soviet Union's leaders. Western journalists and television have basically ignored the war, not even reporting the stories of the refugees to Pakistan. No Western government has held up agreements with Moscow in protest—quite the opposite: criticism has been deliberately muted in order not to jeopardize relations with Moscow. There is not only no world pressure on the Soviets but little moral support for the Afghan "freedom fighters." Moscow can, therefore, feel reasonably confident that time is on its side. Bordering on the Soviet Union and out of mind to the Western world, Afghanistan may be slowly annexed by its huge northern neighbor.

WAR BY PROXY

Nuclear weapons have made nuclear war too costly to fight. The use of force, as distinct from the threat of using force, is safe only in limited wars. It is not accidental that it is the age of suicidal weapons that has witnessed this revival of a more limited form of conflict; nor that the superpowers, anxious, to control the risk of escalation, have been inventive in coming up with a variety of ways of engaging each other without direct confrontation. One of these ways became especially prominent during the 1970s and became known as war by proxy. The Soviets used it in both Angola and Ethiopia by supplying military advisers, arms, and large numbers of Cuban troops to fight on the side of the government. In addition, to ensure governmental control for the self-proclaimed Marxist regimes, the Soviets sent East German policemen and other Soviet-bloc personnel.

The point of using proxies is to avoid direct superpower confrontation. Employing a "stand-in" makes the attempt to change the status quo less dangerous. It is not that in any of these instances the Soviet Union would have confronted the United States directly, but Moscow thought that its actions might be perceived in Washington as a challenge to U.S. interests, thus provoking some sort of American reaction. (Only once—in Korea—were U.S. interests sufficiently threatened. North Korea in 1950 was among the first Soviet proxies after World War II.) The main benefit of proxies is that Moscow can keep a lower profile than if it intervened itself. There is also another benefit; namely, that someone else does most of the dying. Proxies, then, allow the danger of a possible superpower confrontation to be avoided, another refinement of the techniques devised in the nuclear era. Under the so-called Reagan Doctrine, the United States has been increasingly active in supporting national liberation movements against Marxist regimes (for example, in Angola, Afghanistan, and Nicaragua). These proxy wars not only provided the same benefits but also, as we shall see, furnished an alternative to the open use of American forces. The fact that both superpowers resort to war by proxy shows that, in the age of absolute weapons, the superpowers have increasingly shifted their conflict to the "lower levels" of the spectrum of violence, when they have used force at all.

A DECLINE IN THE USE OF FORCE?

Growing Third World Capacity to Resist

The widely asserted view that force is of declining utility is based on: (1) the notion that weapons of mass destruction are useless and (2) the effects of the failure and high cost of the U.S. effort in Vietnam. The first idea, we have already noted, confuses the lack of use with a lack of political usefulness. The correlation between nuclear arms, the absence of any great-power war, and the careful managment of crises, testifies to the utility of military power in peacetime. The second has more substance, for the use of force by Western democratic states against Third World countries has declined. There are several reasons for this change.

One significant factor that has made it more difficult to apply force to the LDCs than in the nineteenth century—when resistance, when it existed, was quickly crushed—is the rise of nationalism. Ever since the French Revolution, the growth of nationalism has made it increasingly difficult to conquer *and* pacify foreign territories and populations. The conquered peoples of Europe resisted their Nazi oppressors. If Britain had toppled Gamal Abdel Nasser of Egypt in 1956 or if the United States had successfully overthrown Castro in 1961, each would have found itself confronting the lengthy and expensive task of pacification. A weak country with a strong sense of national identity— and foreign attack can be a powerful stimulant to nationalism—can make the use of force against itself extremely costly. American forces were involved in Vietnam for eight years; by the time they disengaged in 1973, the costs far exceeded any conceivable gains. The loss of 50,000 American lives, thousands of injuries, expenditures of approximately $150 billion, and the use of over-whelming firepower on behalf of an authoritarian government were too costly in terms of the nation's self-image. The army, which suffered from discipline, drug, and racial problems, paid the price in low morale and was saved from collapse only by the ending of the war. The political turmoil and social divisions within the United States were a heavy additional price. Pacification can thus be made so costly and difficult for a foreign power that it will give up its effort, if it is not deterred from intervening in the first place.

Increasing Northern Costs

It was Western technology in the nineteenth century that helped the European colonial countries conquer much of the non-European world. In the words of the English couplet, "Whatever happens, we have got/The Maxim gun, and they have not." A technological advantage in combat is unlikely in the future. Not only nationalism but the lethal character of modern conventional weapons may deter future great-power interventions because of the cost in lives and material that the LDC may exact. Arms are becoming lighter, more portable, and more accurate. Precision-guided munitions (PGMs) are also becoming sufficiently cheap so that even smaller countries, if they do not receive them from one of the superpowers, can buy them on the international arms market. When a relatively inexpensive missile presents a genuine threat to a multi-billion-dollar aircraft carrier off its coast or to a multi-million-dollar aircraft in its sky, a great power will think twice about intervening. Even in brief uses of force, such as the United States employed in Libya in 1986, the aircraft carriers have been kept well out to sea and the attacks carried out in the evening or at night to minimize losses. The fact is that states such as Syria, Iran, Cuba, and Nicaragua, although small, are well armed and that the United States would have to use substantial forces and expect sizable losses in actions against them.

Northern Moral Constraints

National self-determination is a fundamental democratic principle. It is in the name of national self-determination that the colonies demanded their freedom after World War II. For a Western nation with a predominantly white population and a colonial past to attempt to coerce one of the non-Western, largely nonwhite former colonies arouses guilt and moral repugnance in democratic societies. Note the opposition within Britain and the Commonwealth countries to the Suez War in 1956, America's domestic resistance to the Vietnam War (as well as criticism in allied countries), and President Kennedy's apprehension that the use of U.S. forces in Cuba in 1961 would alienate the very progressive elements in Latin America whose support was necessary to the success of the Alliance for Progress.

In addition, where the guerrillas appear to be fighting against political oppression and social injustice, U.S. intervention on the other side, the side of apparent repression, arouses opposition. Unlike the two world wars—straightforward fights between dictatorships and democracies that aroused moral support rather than repugnance—an intervention on the side of those less than 100 percent democratically pure mobilizes political opposition. If interventions occur, the public is likely to be divided and world opinion critical.

Nothing stimulated domestic protest more than the air war against North Vietnam, and the protest influenced the conduct of the war. The Johnson administration felt so vulnerable on this issue that it limited its attacks to certain kinds of targets, such as bridges and railroad lines, which would not cause extensive civilian damage and loss of life. President Nixon was unable to use ground forces because of the uproar about American casualties, and he gradually withdrew them. When he blockaded and heavily bombed North Vietnam in 1972, he precipitated intense protests from members of Congress, influential journalists, and the public. The Christmas bombing, which Nixon claimed would compel the Hanoi government to accept a cease-fire (which it did shortly afterward, whether because of the bombing or not), was especially harshly criticized.

The constraints on the use of force because of domestic opposition to a war tend to narrow the gap between the power of the Western Goliath and the LDC David. Goliath, beset by inner doubts about the merits of his cause and accused of ruthlessness, finally gives up since he calculates that the costs of continuing his attempts to coerce David are no longer acceptable. They are disproportionate to the end to be achieved. David, highly motivated by a strong sense of nationalism and determined to win (or, at least, not lose), is encouraged by his enemy's problems, which, he expects, will sooner or later force Goliath to quit. David therefore calculates that the cost of complying with Goliath's demands is far greater than that of not complying.

The balance of resolve, in short, is as critical in the conduct of revolutionary warfare as it is in deterrence and crisis management. If a country's will to keep on fighting can be eroded, its superior military capability can be neutralized; indeed, the capability may as well not exist. A British scholar has said that, for this reason,

> the [Chinese Communist] slogan "imperialism is a paper tiger" is by no means inaccurate. It is not that the material resources of the metropolitan power are in themselves underestimated by the revolutionaries; rather, there is an acute awareness that the political constraints on their maximum deployment are as real as if those resources did not exist, and that these constraints become more rather than less powerful as the war escalates.[37]

Adding up the components of power—even the conventional ones—therefore would not have resulted in an accurate prediction of the outcome of the Vietnam War. *Big Western democratic nations have tended to lose small wars since 1945.*

Public scrutiny of every aspect of war has made a tremendous difference. When the democracies use force, they cannot do so as they did a hundred years ago. The press and television report on every facet of the hostilities, no matter how embarrassing or politically damaging it may be to the government. After the Argentinians seized the Falkland Islands and the British launched a successful expedition to recover them, Meg Greenfield of *Newsweek* wrote about the sinking of the Argentinian cruiser *General Belgrano*, which resulted in a heavy loss of life. British sentiment appeared to be that, if provoked, "you may fight but you shouldn't kill, and, if you kill, you shouldn't kill too many, and you may not—repeat, not—use all the means at your disposal to do the job." Western governments and publics might fight if they had to but there no longer seemed much satisfaction in punishing those who had provoked the conflict. "There was horror, here and everywhere else, at the deaths of those Argentine boys. Far from being able to savor a military victory of this cost to the enemy, one is these days almost obliged to mourn it, or to mourn its awful human effects."[38]

Also note the following British observations about the sinking of the *General Belgrano*:

> It was an important military victory for Britain, yet it turned into a political defeat because of the premium that the international community put on the appearance of avoiding escalation. Any military action which is not self-evidently for defensive purposes ... becomes an outrage. *Measures such as economic sanctions or blockades are deemed more acceptable than any military action which tends to lead to direct casualties.* (Emphasis added.)[39]

In short, the Western democracies can no longer act in accordance with the phrase that "in love and war everything is fair."

The Prerequisites for Future Interventions: The Dominican Republic Model

It would appear that the principal prerequisites for future Western interventions are a worthy cause, the assurance of relatively few casualties, and good chances for a successful achievement of the objectives in a short period of time. The U.S. intervention in the Dominican Republic in 1965 to forestall "another Cuba" in the Caribbean was virtually without cost; the U.S. Marines ended the domestic fighting, withdrew, and a free election established a stable government. In Grenada in 1983, the operation again was quick, relatively painless, ending with a withdrawal of U.S. troops and an election (see map, page 243). These operations were the opposite of those in Korea and Vietnam, which were lengthy, did not achieve their objectives quickly, and were expensive in lives and materiel, as well as economic and political costs in the United States.

There were, of course, reasons for the U.S. successes in the Dominican Republic and Grenada. Both are islands and therefore could be isolated by air and naval power. In both, U.S. troops held overwhelming numerical and technological superiority; in Grenada, 8,000 troops faced only 700 Cubans, most of them not professional soldiers. It still took the United States three days to conclude its military task. British operations against the Falkland Islands were similarly successful because the site was isolated and the Argentinian troops, although larger in numbers, were not as well trained as the British.

The situation was quite different when 1,200 U.S. Marines were sent into Lebanon in 1983 as part of an international peace-keeping force. As the U.S. government took the side of the pro-Western, pro-Israeli, Christian-dominated government in what was a civil war in that country, the marines increasingly came under attack. The opposition Muslim factions, supported politically and militarily by Syria, proved too strong; after they staged a suicide attack on the marine compound, which killed 241 men, the United States withdrew. The United States had sent too few marines to have any real peace-keeping power. Moreover, military power alone cannot resolve the political issues that cause civil wars, and Lebanon could not be isolated militarily. Syria was determined that the Muslims should win and change the government's pro-Western orientation. It is doubtful that the suicide attack could have taken place without Syrian knowledge, if not assistance. The United States probably should not have taken sides in the civil war once it became clear that no peace-keeping force could overcome the deep and bitter divisions within Lebanon. There was no peace to keep because it proved impossible to overcome Lebanon's political and social factionalism. Even Syria, the dominant power in Lebanon after the withdrawal of the international peace-keeping forces and of the Israeli army, which had invaded Lebanon in 1982, was unable to establish a stable government of national unity and peace.

There is only one problem with the Dominican Republic model. There are only so many small islands! What about other areas where the United States' "vital interests" are involved? The secretary of defense in 1984 defined such interventions in terms that, if followed, virtually preclude any intervention.[40] Not only did he demand that if the United States intervene, it should do so with "the clear intention of winning"—presumably achieving the complete defeat of enemy forces—and with no political constraints on the conduct of the war; the action should have the support of the American people and Congress. Yet such support existed initially in both Korea and Vietnam; the problem was that it evaporated as the war continued. To require continued support as a precondition of intervention is in fact an excuse for nonintervention.

It is perhaps because the United States has run out of small islands and weak opponents and seeks to avoid future protracted land wars as in Korea or Vietnam, that covert operations and air strikes such as those against Libya in 1986 in response to terrorism have some appeal (see Chapter 12). But if such air strikes were to be carried out against more formidable opponents like Iran and Syria, which are also engaged in supporting terrorism, and American losses in planes and crews rose, would the approval ratings for U.S. actions remain high or decline? Similarly, covert operations, supposedly benefiting from existing in a zone between "diplomacy and war," suffer from exposure in America's open society. Long-term commitments, such as U.S. support of the contras' war against the Marxist government of Nicaragua, cannot go on without news leaks. What is the point of covert operations when they headline American newspapers and television news? Even covert wars are difficult to sustain if the public, Congress, and the administration are all at odds, as a comparison of Nicaragua with Afghanistan demonstrates. There is considerable support and no opposition to assisting the Afghan resistance to the Soviet occupation of that country.

Perhaps the only thing that will unite the United States in the use of force in the future is the sinking of an American ship, if one may be only partly facetious. The blowing up of the battleship *Maine* in Havana precipitated the Spanish-American War; German submarine attacks on American shipping led to U.S. intervention in World War I; the Japanese attack on Pearl Harbor propelled the United States into World War II; and two reported attacks on U.S. destroyers in the Gulf of Tonkin (only one of which occurred) preceded the U.S. military involvement in Vietnam. Only Korea proved to be an exception. There must be something holy, or at least symbolic, about a ship, especially a warship, in the American psyche. Anyway, administrations seeking to intervene somewhere must obviously place some kind of warship—a huge carrier?—near to the enemy and hope the enemy will not only attack it but sink it! Of course, how well U.S. forces will perform remains debatable, after efforts such as the abortive 1980 rescue attempt of the American hostages in Iran and the three-day effort by thousands of U.S. troops to subdue 679 Cubans in Grenada, 673 of whom were construction workers.[41]

Non-Western States and the Resort to Force

Since World War I the rising costs of war have led the industrial democracies—Western Europe, Japan, and, increasingly, the United States—to question the legitimacy of war or, at least, offensive war. The issues that are likely to compel them to use force are becoming more and more narrowly defined in terms of self-defense, however difficult it is in reality to distinguish between the offensive use of force and self-defense. Nevertheless, there is a growing perception by the public that war and even the threat of force for coercive purposes is illegitimate. Since the ill-fated Suez invasion of 1956, European military forces have had a declining capacity to project their power beyond Western Europe. Britain had to stretch itself and remove much of its navy from NATO duties to recapture the Falkland Islands. Even then the United States had to help with certain supplies. Europe's defense of itself seems a growing and unwelcome burden for the Europeans. The states of Europe, with their large combined pool of military personnel, great industrial and technological strength, and potential military power continue to rely on the United States for their defense to a far greater degree than their resources suggest they should. As a British observer has noted, "The countries of Western Europe are superior to the Soviet Union in population, wealth, technology and military potential, and the idea that Russia is the naturally dominant power in Europe, against which Europe can construct no counterbalance without importing outside help, is a very recent one." [42]

In the era since the Vietnam War, American vital interests also have been defined more and more selectively. The memory of the war has haunted U.S. policy makers; when they have considered intervention in the Third World, with the exception of Grenada and a half-hearted effort in Lebanon, force has not been used. In both El Salvador and Nicaragua, Congress and U.S. public opinion were strongly opposed to intervention—hence the increasing reliance on covert intervention and supporting proxies with military aid and advisers.

Communist and Third World states, unlike most Western states, are not similarly constrained by the principle of national self-determination and calculations of costs and gains. The United States tends to accept national self-determination almost as an absolute value, but the Soviet Union interprets it only in terms of its own struggle against the West. Self-determination is regarded as illegitimate by the Soviet Union, and therefore it has used force several times in Eastern Europe. Opposition to Soviet domination is defined as "counterrevolutionary" and "reactionary," rather than as legitimate attempts by Hungary, Czechoslovakia, and Poland to gain control of their own destiny. The Soviet government regards the existing regimes throughout Eastern Europe, as well as the Marxist government installed by a coup in Afghanistan in 1978, as legitimate. On the other hand, in the non-Western world, the Soviet Union regards activities to reduce or eliminate Western influence as legitimate. The governments or movements that the Soviet

Union supports are defined as movements of national liberation, and those who oppose them are condemned as "reactionary" and "imperialist."

The LDCs themselves strongly support national self-determination, the legitimizing principle on which rest their claims to independence from colonial masters. But they interpret it in two ways: against the West and against one another, for many of the former colonies lay claim to people and territory of neighboring states on the basis of ethnic identification. For the LDCs the principle of self-determination can thus also justify intervention. The absence of open societies is beneficial to the Soviet Union, other Communist states like Cuba, and most LDCs, for they can more easily sustain the costs of intervention. Public opinion does not play a strong role and cannot therefore exert a restraining or inhibiting influence on governmental leaders. The Soviet Union has not only repeatedly intervened in Eastern Europe, as well as Afghanistan, but, together with Cuba, it has also intervened in Angola, Ethiopia, and South Yemen. North Vietnam intervened in South Vietnam, and later a reunited Vietnam invaded Cambodia. China, in turn, temporarily invaded Vietnam. Egypt intervened in Yemen in the 1960s; and Yemen and South Yemen clashed in the late 1970s. Syria sent its forces into Lebanon during the latter's civil war in 1975-76, and their presence seems permanent. And since the early 1950s, India has seized the Portuguese colony of Goa on the Indian subcontinent, intervened in East Pakistan during the Pakistani civil war, and been instrumental in depriving Pakistan of its eastern territory and destroying it as a rival. In addition, Tanzania invaded Uganda to overthrow its dictator. Iraq attacked Iran, Somalia invaded Ethiopia, Argentina seized the Falkland Islands, and Libya invaded Chad. Rather than a decline in the use of conventional force, there has been a global shift in attitudes toward the utility of force.[43] Can it be doubted that it was the Argentinians' belief that Britain would do nothing that led them to seize the Falklands by force? Increasingly, in any event, many newer states are behaving just as states have behaved for centuries.

Notes

1. The two best introductory books on limited war are Henry A. Kissinger, *Nuclear Weapons and Foreign Policy* (New York: Harper & Row, 1957); and Robert E. Osgood, *Limited War: The Challenge to American Strategy* (Chicago: University of Chicago Press, 1957).
2. Kissinger, *Nuclear Weapons,* 140.
3. See Harry S. Truman, *Years of Trial and Hope,* vol. 1 of *Memoirs* (Garden City, N.Y.: Doubleday, 1958), 332-333.
4. See John W. Spanier, *The Truman-MacArthur Controversy and the Korean War* (Cambridge, Mass.: Harvard University Press, 1959), 84-134; and Allen S. Whiting, *China Crosses the Yalu: The Decision to Enter the Korean War* (New York: Macmillan, 1960).

5. Thomas C. Schelling, *Strategy and Conflict* (Cambridge, Mass.: Harvard University Press, 1960), 75; and Schelling, *Arms and Influence* (New Haven, Conn.: Yale University Press, 1966), 137-141.

6. Hermann Kahn, *On Escalation* (New York: Holt, Rinehart & Winston, 1965), 38-41. On controlling escalation, also see Richard Smoke, *War* (Cambridge, Mass.: Harvard University Press, 1978).

7. David Galula, *Counterinsurgency Warfare* (New York: Holt, Rinehart & Winston, 1964), 9-10.

8. *Mao Tse-tung on Guerrilla Warfare*, trans. Samuel B. Griffith (New York: Holt, Rinehart & Winston, 1961), 103-104. For the Vietminh's seven rules for the conduct of guerrilla warfare, see Otto Heilbrunn, *Partisan Warfare* (New York: Holt, Rinehart & Winston, 1962), 78-79.

9. In South Vietnam, for instance, more than 15,000 village officials were murdered between 1957 and 1965. See Bernard B. Fall, *Viet-Nam Witness: 1953-56* (New York: Holt, Rinehart & Winston, 1966), 293.

10. Jeffrey Race, *War Comes to Long An* (Berkeley: University of California Press, 1972), 141ff; Heilbrunn, *Partisan Warfare*, 145-146; and George K. Tanham, *Communist Revolutionary Warfare* (New York: Holt, Rinehart & Winston, 1961), 143. On the different components of strategy, see Michael Howard, "The Forgotten Dimensions of Strategy," *Foreign Affairs* (Summer 1979): 975-986.

11. Tanham, *Communist Revolutionary Warfare*, 32, 97.

12. Griffith, Introduction to *Mao Tse-tung on Guerrilla Warfare*, 7.

13. Charles W. Thayer, *Guerrilla* (New York: Harper & Row, 1963), 42-60.

14. See Frances L. Starner, *Magsaysay and the Philippine Peasantry: The Agrarian Impact on Philippine Politics, 1953-1956* (Berkeley: University of California Press, 1961). For views of the contrasting situation in South Vietnam, see Bernard B. Fall, *The Two Viet-Nams: A Political and Military Analysis*, 2d rev. ed. (New York: Holt, Rinehart & Winston, 1966); and Denis Warner, *The Last Confucian* (New York: Macmillan, 1963).

15. Quoted in Heilbrunn, *Partisan Warfare*, 34. On the decisiveness of civilian loyalties, see Chalmers A. Johnson, "Civilian Loyalties and Guerrilla Conflict," *World Politics*, July 1962, 646-661. Also see Johnson, *Autopsy on People's War* (Berkeley: University of California Press, 1973).

16. Fall, *The Two Viet-Nams*, 346-347. The Algerian example also clearly demonstrates that counterterror is not effective in ending guerrilla warfare.

17. We are not concerned in this section with judgments on whether the United States should have intervened in Vietnam. We focus only on the manner in which force was used. Judgment is, of course, implicit in such an analysis. Ultimately, it reflects on the issue of the original intervention, for, if the conclusion is that force was exercised ineffectively—indeed, counterproductively—it may also be deduced that the intervention should have been avoided in the first place. This judgment, to be sure, is pragmatic, not moral. For moral and legal judgments on the war, see, among others, Telford Taylor, *Nuremberg and Vietnam: An American Tragedy* (New York: Bantam Books, 1971); and *Crimes of War*, ed. Richard A. Falk, Gabriel Kolko, and Robert J. Lifton (New York: Vintage, 1971). For a contrary point of view, defending the war's legality, see Guenter Lewy, *America in Vietnam* (New York: Oxford University Press, 1978), 223-270, 343-373. My final pragmatic judgment on Vietnam is much the same as Donald Zagoria's in *Vietnam Triangle: Moscow, Peking, Hanoi* (New York: Pegasus, 1967), xiii, namely, that Amerian strategy and tactics

raise "serious doubts in my mind whether we as a nation have the wisdom, the skills and the manpower to cope with civil wars."

18. General Lewis W. Walt, assistant commandant of the U.S. Marine Corps, confessed in 1970 that when he visited Vietnam in 1965 he thought of it as a conventional war like the Korean War. *New York Times*, Nov. 18, 1970. General Earle Wheeler, chairman of the Joint Chiefs of Staff, held the same opinion, as reported by Roger Hilsman, *To Move a Nation* (Garden City, N.Y.: Doubleday, 1967), 426.

19. Robert Thompson, *No Exit from Vietnam* (New York: McKay, 1969), 13-17; and Lewy, *America in Vietnam*. Both authors stress that the United States, by waging a conventional conflict, was guilty of misconduct of the war.

20. Henry A. Kissinger, *American Foreign Policy* (New York: W. W. Norton, 1969), 102.

21. Ibid., 104.

22. Thompson, *No Exit*, 40-74.

23. Andrew J. R. Mack, "Why Big Nations Lose Small Wars: The Politics of Asymmetric Conflict," *World Politics*, January 1975, 175-288. Also see John E. Mueller, *War, Presidents and Public Opinion* (New York: John Wiley & Sons, 1973); and Larry Elowitz and John Spanier, "Korea and Vietnam: Limited War and the American Political System," *Orbis*, Summer 1974, 510-534.

24. Mack, "Why Big Nations Lose Small Wars," 177.

25. Quoted in Fall, *Two Viet-Nams*, 113.

26. Townsend Hoopes, *The Limits of Intervention* (New York: McKay, 1969), 75-79. For an assessment of "coercive violence" in Vietnam, see Wallace J. Thies, *When Governments Collide* (Berkeley: University of California Press, 1980), 349-374.

27. Raphael Littauer and Norman Uphoff, eds., *The Air War in Indochina* (Boston: Beacon, 1972); and Lewy, *America in Vietnam*.

28. John E. Mueller, "The Search for the 'Breaking Point' in Vietnam: The Statistics of a Deadly Quarrel," *International Studies Quarterly* (December 1980): 497-519; and Thies, *When Governments Collide*, 414-420.

29. Thompson, *Political Realism*, 139-140.

30. Hoopes, *Limits of Intervention*, 82.

31. Theodore Draper, *Abuse of Power* (New York: Viking, 1967), 59.

32. Ibid., 29, 30.

33. Timothy J. Lomperis, *The War Everyone Lost—and Won* (Baton Rouge: Louisiana State University Press, 1984), 176.

34. Ibid., 173.

35. Claude Malhuret, "Report from Afghanistan," *Foreign Affairs* (Winter 1983/84): 427.

36. Ibid., 428.

37. Mack, "Why Big Nations Lose Small Wars," 139-140.

38. Meg Greenfield, "Dismaying Victory," *Newsweek*, May 17, 1982, 49.

39. Lawrence Freedman, "The War of the Falkland Islands, 1982, *Foreign Affairs* (Fall 1982): 209.

40. For Weinberger's speech, see *New York Times*, Nov. 29, 1984. See also Harry Summers, *On Strategy* (New York: Dell Publishing, 1984); and General Palmer Bruce Jr., *The 25-Year War* (Lexington, Ky.: University of Kentucky, 1984). Eliot A. Cohen's "Constraints on America's Conduct of Small Wars," *International Security*, Fall 1984, 151-181, provides a good analysis of why the U.S. military resists fighting what he prefers to call small wars.

41. For two books very critical of the armed forces' preparations for fighting in the

future, see Edward N. Luttwak, *The Pentagon and the Art of War* (New York: Simon & Schuster, 1984); and Arthur T. Hadley, *The Straw Giant* (New York: Random House, 1986).

42. Hedley Bull, "European Self-Reliance," *Foreign Affairs* (Spring 1983): 878.

43. A similar thesis has been suggested in "Is International Coercion Waning or Rising?" by Klaus Knorr, *International Security,* Spring 1977, 92-110; and Knorr, "On the International Uses of Military Force in the Contemporary World," *Orbis,* Spring 1977, 5-27. Also see Chapter 18 for a further analysis of this theme.

CHAPTER 11

The International Political Economy, Statecraft, and Interdependence

THE SEPARATION OF POLITICS AND ECONOMICS

Until 1973, the year of the oil embargo against the United States and the quadrupling of oil prices by the Organization of Petroleum Exporting Countries (OPEC), analysts of international politics had largely ignored the economic dimensions of relations among states. Security considerations were primary, and, not unnaturally, the shadow of "the bomb" had led to an emphasis on deterrence, crisis management, and limited warfare. The behavior of states was explained primarily in terms of the state system. Economics was relegated to a subordinate, indeed peripheral, position.

In part, this separation of politics and economics sprang from the nineteenth-century *laissez-faire* or free-market economic theorists. The classical capitalist economists painted a natural economic order that was independent of politics and worked best when governments interfered as little as possible with the laws of supply and demand. The economic sphere, which was based on private property and the profit motive, would provide for the citizens' material wants. Private enterprise, through the laws of the market place, would maximize the manufacturers' profits by providing what the consumer wanted. The political sphere, that of government, was concerned with safeguarding the nation from foreign threat and preserving law and order domestically. But it was not to intervene and upset the market. Economics and politics were thus conceived of as two separate orders, divorced from one another. Because they enhanced the standard of living, economic activities were regarded as good. Politics, on the other hand, was tolerated only as a necessary evil because the government had to tax citizens to raise the revenues to support the army and police. Concerned with such things as fighting wars and keeping order at home, the government's activities were regarded as not having much to do with improving the lives of ordinary people. Politics, therefore, was thought to be "bad."

The effect of this separation of economics from politics is not of historical interest alone. Rather, this legacy from nineteenth-century economics continues to influence thinking about international politics. For example, after Adolf Hitler was already in power, a Peace Ballot in England in 1935 showed that a very large number of Britons favored economic sanctions against aggression but not many favored military ones. The preference for taking economic rather than military measures against regimes that have displeased a particular country continues to this day, even when great powers face weaker countries. This reluctance reflects more than second thoughts about risking war. More fundamentally, it reflects the belief that power is divisible. Yet economic sanctions are ineffective in most circumstances unless backed up by the belief on the part of the target country that force may be used later. If it is true that military coercion of weak states by the strong has become less likely because of the increasing moral and material cost of doing so, then the economic power of the powerful states cannot be expected to do what the military power might have done. Economic power is not a substitute for military power, even in situations where the targeted state's economy is vulnerable to economic sanctions. As Robert Tucker has perceptively noted:

> The limited effectiveness of economic coercion may in some measure be attributed to the same sources that limited the effectiveness of physical coercion. While the legitimacy of the former has not been subject to the same standards as has the latter, economic coercion has been called increasingly into the question. . . . This argument draws added force once it is recognized that economic coercion can only have its full effects to the extent it leaves open the option of physical coercion.[1]

Another part of the legacy is seen in the distinction between security and welfare. Every government must choose: How many guns and how much butter does the nation need, and how much can it afford? This distinction between the military services and the social services again reflects the difference between politics and economics. The former suggests a concern with power, the latter with people's well-being. The often heard criticisms that military spending is wasteful and that greater amounts should be allocated for welfare reveal this widespread belief in the distinction between politics and economics. *Yet only the welfare states can afford both guns and butter:* their economic growth has been sufficiently great that they can have both. States that have a lower growth rate or live nearer to subsistence spend their money first on arms. It is precisely the welfare states that have tended to be the strongest; *power states,* those that spend mainly on guns, squeeze their economies and deprive their citizens of a better standard of living to buy more weapons.[2] The obvious difference between the United States and the Soviet Union in this respect suggests again why the security/welfare, politics/ economics distinction is unpersuasive. A state's economic strength has always been associated with its political-military power, just as states have long used economic means to achieve their political purposes.

A final product of the legacy from the nineteenth-century economists is the distinction between "low" and "high" politics so central to contemporary interdependence theory (see Chapters 1 and 4). Essentially an update of the free-market theory projected globally, interdependence emphasizes that transnational economic and technological forces will bind nations together; the fact that they are not self-sufficient—not even the United States or the Soviet Union today—is said to compel them to work together for their own well-being. Thus, cooperation on welfare issues will supersede the conflict of power issues. Chapter 20 will analyze in detail this new, sophisticated, and quite persuasive modern version of an older theory. But note here that all of the preceding examples point to the wisdom of bringing back an old term, *political economy*, to emphasize the inseparability of politics and economics.[3]

NATIONAL INDEPENDENCE AND SELF-SUFFICIENCY

... In Wartime

Sovereign nation-states guard their independence jealously, even when they believe the world is becoming more interdependent. In pre-World War I Europe most professional soldiers thought that no war could last very long precisely because of the high degree of economic interdependence.[4] Countries would not be able to afford such a war and mobilize large armies without risking mutual bankruptcy and social revolution. War plans aimed at quick victories, but what happened was the opposite. Once it was realized that the war was not going to end quickly, the industrial economies demonstrated their enormous potential power when they were mobilized for the long haul. The war lasted four years before Germany's exhaustion led to the end of hostilities.

The fate of Britain during the war underlines the importance for great powers of being as self-sufficient as possible. The first nation to industrialize, the world's most powerful country for most of the nineteenth century, and the country that demonstrated that a prerequisite for the industrial revolution was an agricultural revolution, Britain neglected its production of food as industry demonstrated its capacity to raise the country's wealth and power. By World War I Britain had become a food importer. Moreover, as a resource-poor state, Britain had to import the raw materials needed for the manufactured products it exported to earn a living. A new weapon, the submarine, became a threat to Britain's lifelines. The Germans, who had built only a small fleet of submarines (like the British, they had spent most of the money allocated for the navy on battleships) almost managed to starve Britain into submission. But by declaring an unlimited submarine campaign against all shipping to England, including neutral American ships, the Germans provoked the United States to enter the war.

During World War II the German threat to British lifelines was even greater. After France's defeat in 1940, when Britain was left alone to carry on the fight against Germany, the Battle for the Atlantic became critical for Britain's survival as well as the prerequisite for an ultimate victory over Germany. Especially after the United States declared war in December 1941, this battle was waged fiercely until the Allies won it in May 1943. Once the sea lanes to Britain were secured, the U.S. troops, landing craft, and other supplies needed for the invasion of France, together with British troops, could be shipped to the British Isles. The risk Britain ran during both world wars underlines the importance for great powers to be as self-sufficient as possible in order to better withstand other states' pressures in peacetime and avoid defeat in wartime.

As the Germans used submarines, the British used the naval blockade. Although Germany was by 1914 Europe's most industrialized state, it had also maintained its agriculture. Nevertheless, the four-year blockade—on top of the strains imposed on Germany by the years of fighting virtually alone against Britain, France, Italy, Russia, and, after 1917, the United States—took its toll. For that reason, British strategy during World War II was to impose another blockade and to defeat Germany by slow strangulation.[5] But it was a strategy doomed to defeat. For German industry produced synthetic oil, rubber, and wool; the neutral states, such as Russia (until Germany attacked it), Sweden, and Spain, supplied materials Germany needed; and, of course, Germany conquered most of Europe and looted it for whatever it wanted. Without these supplies, Germany would have been vulnerable to a blockade. Germany instead built up its military forces quickly and then rapidly conquered the raw material and financial base needed for a long war.[6]

... In Peacetime

Because states are not generally self-sufficient and must obtain what they need through trade in the absence of conquest, one of the economic tools they frequently use in conflict is an embargo. *The purpose of an embargo is to prevent the shipment of certain products or even all products to the targeted country.* During the cold war, in what might be called economic warfare or a strategy of denial, the United States regulated exports to the Soviet Union. All products that might have had some sort of military application or could have contributed to the economic strength of the Communist state were placed on the embargo list. Although America's allies in the North Atlantic Treaty Organization (NATO) were somewhat less restrictive in the goods they embargoed, the overall consequence was that the economies of the West and the East remained separate and independent. There is no evidence, however, that these Western attempts at coercion resulted in Soviet political compliance, and the cold war years until 1962 were among the most tense and conflict-filled of the postwar era.

As the cold war gave way to détente, it was part of U.S. diplomatic strategy to bridge this gap and make the Soviet economy more dependent upon that of the United States. When Henry Kissinger became President Richard Nixon's national security adviser, he recognized two opposite factors at work internationally. The first was a tired and disillusioned United States, weary of the burden of its many cold war commitments—which had ended in the quagmire of Vietnam—and wary of new obligations. The mood of the country was isolationist. In a poll taken at the time, more than 50 percent of the people said that the United States should defend only one foreign country—Canada! The percentages favoring defense of Europe, Israel, and Japan were far lower.

This popular desire to limit American involvement in the world coincided with the emergence of the second factor at work internationally: the Soviet Union had achieved strategic parity with the United States. Moreover, the Soviet Union had considerably upgraded its conventional capabilities, developing a sizable surface fleet plus airlift capability. Czarist and Soviet Russia had always been essentially a Eurasian, or continental, power. Now, for the first time in its history, it had become a global power. As the Soviet Union's ability to neutralize U.S. nuclear power grew, its capacity to project its conventional power beyond Eurasia grew as well. Would the Soviet Union, in these new circumstances, continue to expand its influence only on land and in territory contiguous to its own? Or would it feel a new confidence and take greater risks, challenging the United States in new areas farther away from the Soviet Union? Would the United States, on the other hand, be more cautious and hesitant to react? At the very moment when the United States was experiencing its greatest doubt about its own international role and when its strategic superiority that had allowed it to "contain" the Soviet Union with the threat of force had eroded, the Soviet Union was more powerful and self-assured than ever before. The question was how could the United States contain the Soviet Union now? How could it be induced to follow a path of self-restraint? Was there a nonmilitary lever to supplement, or even to replace, the military one?[7]

One tactic was to use the productivity of American industry and agriculture and offer the Soviets "carrots." The Soviet economy was stagnating in both the industrial and the agricultural sectors. During the 1950s the Soviet economy had grown at a rate of 6 percent a year; during the 1960s this rate declined to 5 percent, and by the mid-1970s it had fallen to 3.5 percent. The Central Intelligence Agency (CIA) forecast for the 1980s was 2.5 percent.[8] Stagnation was especially serious in the electronic, computer, and petrochemical industries. The Soviet Union was falling behind in the new industrial revolution. The implications for its military power, for its ability to satisfy the cravings of its own people for more consumer goods, and for the attraction of Soviet communism as a model for the less-developed countries (LDCs) were serious. Moreover, the regime was unable to deliver on its promise of more

meat and a balanced diet for the Soviet people. Because they judged fundamental structural reforms of their centrally controlled and directed economy
as politically too risky, it was logical for Soviet leaders to turn to the West for
technology, food, and credits with which to buy what they needed. Kissinger
and, after him, President Jimmy Carter were quite willing to offer the Soviet
leaders economic "rewards" if they acted with greater restraint in foreign
policy.

If the American-Soviet relationship was fundamentally one of conflict, and
the Soviets needed to trade with the United States, the U.S. government could
use trade as a political lever. Seen from a historical perspective, however, the
proposition seemed a little shaky. During the 1920s and 1930s, as Premier
Joseph Stalin launched his drive to modernize the Soviet Union, U.S. corporations became actively involved; their involvement, however, did not create
any dependence on the United States or alter the Soviet regime's anticapitalist
views. But, had conditions not changed? Some experts on the Soviet economy
certainly thought so. Contemporary trade might indeed entangle the Soviet
Union so deeply in the world economy that the price of disruption would be
very high and therefore would deter political efforts to advance Soviet
influence.[9] Before World War II, when technology was simpler, the Soviets
could manufacture their own spare parts. Today, however, in electronics and
in petroleum and mineral extracting, for example, technology is highly sophisticated and requires continuous servicing and upgrading if productivity
is to be increased. In many instances the Soviets must turn to the West for
technological expertise and products. In agriculture, furthermore, the Soviets
may no longer be self-sufficient, especially as they want to upgrade their diet
to include more meat. This step requires more feed grain for cattle. Because of
the Soviet Union's climate and its inefficient collective and state agricultural
system, the nation grew more dependent on imports. The United States
produces large agricultural surpluses that can be exported. A degree of
dependence upon the United States and the rest of the capitalist world could
perhaps be generated.

It needs to be clearly understood that Kissinger's efforts were an attempt to
create a *tactical linkage* that sought to use trade to change Soviet international
behavior. The Soviets were asked to pay not only an economic price for what
they wanted, but also a political price. When the Soviets acted with self-
restraint in ways acceptable to the United States, they were to be rewarded;
when they did not, they were to be punished. The economic spigot was to be
turned on and off. The sanctioning state's assumption was that the adversary's
needs were sufficiently important that it would behave in the desired manner
to avoid a cutoff of trade. In other words, the Soviet Union would contain
itself! Another assumption was that "the sanctioning state must control a
significant portion of the target's trade—either absolutely or in a few key
commodities."[10] If it does not, it must build up that trade to achieve political
leverage in the future. The Kissinger strategy, in short, was a way of testing
whether the Soviet Union's economic needs could be used to create greater

economic interdependence with the United States, enhance their joint interest in economic cooperation, and moderate Soviet foreign policy behavior.

Limitations of Using Trade as a Political Lever

Practice, as distinct from theory, quickly revealed the limitations of using the Soviets' need for computers, oil drilling equipment, and wheat as a political lever to reward their restraint and punish their expansionism.

Domestic U.S. Objections. The United States, it soon became clear, could turn the economic spigot on but could not so easily turn it off.[11] American farmers let President Gerald Ford know in 1975 that, if he expected their votes, he had better not try another grain embargo against the Soviet Union. He did not. But in 1979, after the Soviet invasion of Afghanistan, President Carter embargoed 17 million tons of grain, most of it earmarked for livestock feed. Simultaneously, to cushion the fall of prices and quiet the farmers' protests, the government took a series of remedial measures. Patriotism also stilled farmer protest—but not for long. Presidential candidate Ronald Reagan promised the farmers that he would end the embargo if he were elected, and he did so despite his tough anti-Soviet rhetoric. He did so also despite the fact that U.S. grain exports had risen by 2 percent in 1979. The customers of Argentina, Canada, and other countries from whom the Soviet Union bought its grain after the Carter embargo now bought their grain from the American farmers. And Reagan ended the embargo despite the fact that the Soviet purchases of feed grain fell short of what was needed and that this resulted in shortages of meat. Had the embargo been continued, and given the repetitive bad Soviet harvests until 1984 and the ineffective farm system, Moscow might indeed have confronted a disaster.[12]

Clearly, the eagerness of U.S. banks, corporations, and farmers to trade with the Soviet Union and the pressures that they can exert on Washington means that this kind of leverage cannot be used frequently. We cannot dismiss the possibility that the Soviets may manipulate U.S. economic interests more skillfully than American leaders can because American interest groups will seek to avoid confrontation and "unpleasantness" in order to protect their profits. (So much for capitalist enmity toward communism!) Thus, if the cost of sanctions to domestic interests is too high, public support for sanctions will erode. The lesson is clear: shooting yourself in the foot is not painful for the targeted nation.

Availability of Alternative Supplies. A second limiting factor is that the Soviets can buy technology and wheat from Western Europe, Japan, and other countries. Trade and credits are satisfactory bargaining tools only when the items that an adversary needs cannot be obtained elsewhere. Even if the U.S. government were to stand firm, foreign businessmen and farmers overseas would be all too happy to receive the contracts. The Soviet Union could, in fact, play off one Western country against another and gain economic benefits despite its political behavior. Embargoes, in short, tend to be "leaky." This was one major reason why, after the Polish army imposed martial law in 1981 to crack down on the independent labor movement Solidarity, the United States imposed only symbolic, rather than punitive, sanctions. It knew that in the absence of a Soviet invasion of Poland, its NATO allies would not want to lose profitable markets. Thus, the symbolic sanctions against Poland would satisfy America's sense of outrage and provide some moral support for the Polish resistance. In fact, the irony was that it was the Western countries that appeared to become doubly dependent. They depended on the repayment of Soviet (and East European) debts amounting to a staggering $90 billion by early 1982, and they needed markets for specific Western industrial, technological, and agricultural products. Or, to state it another way, the Soviets could hold the West hostage and manipulate Western countries if they did not wish to see some of their banks go broke and their industries lose orders and jobs.

Lack of Soviet Dependence on Trade.   Last, there is the question of whether the Soviet Union is so dependent on trade that even if the United States could turn the economic spigot on and off and America's allies and friends were more cooperative, it could use this economic leverage for "high politics" purposes. Despite a report by the Commerce Department in 1982 that the Soviet Union was dependent upon foreign trade to a "far greater" degree than Western analysts had assumed in the past—and was presumably more vulnerable to economic sanctions—the record suggests that Soviet leaders are not easily pressured. They rejected a trade agreement in 1975 when the Senate decided to link it to Jewish emigration. The United States may have overestimated the intensity of Soviet economic needs and, therefore, its bargaining power on issues the Soviets consider of political importance.

The Soviet-European Gas Pipeline.   All of these factors became even clearer in the Soviet gas pipeline dispute in the early 1980s. Western Europe, trying to reduce its oil dependency on the Middle East, saw the Soviet Union as a promising source of natural gas. The Europeans agreed to finance and help construct an overland pipeline to Siberia. The United States feared that this pipeline would create a European dependency on the Soviet Union for a critical fuel and give Moscow a future means of achieving its political objectives in the contest for political influence between the superpowers. The Reagan administration also saw the Soviet sale of natural gas to Western Europe as a means of earning large sums of Western currency at a time when Soviet industrial growth had slowed to a crawl and the Soviet grain harvest had fallen short four years in a row. Soviet military spending remained at an all-time high, more than twice American spending. Washington's aim was to reduce Soviet earnings in Western markets, forcing Moscow either to cut back on its military investments to pay for Western technology and food or to invest more in consumer goods and food at home. Presumably, this would slow down the Soviet arms buildup.

The problems with this attempted coercion were several. First, the United States was trying to put the economic squeeze on the Soviet Union—against the wishes of its closest allies—at a time when Washington, in response to farm lobby pressures, was extending a grain agreement and thinking about a longer-term grain agreement with Moscow. Under this agreement the Soviets were required to purchase a minimum of 6 million tons of wheat per year, clearly a boon to the American farmers who were overproducing grain and whose prices were declining.

Second, the American effort to wage economic warfare against the Soviet Union by damming up the "leaks" from Western Europe became a source of divisiveness within the alliance. The French government ordered French firms making oil and gas equipment abroad under American license to honor the contract with Moscow despite the U.S. embargo (and the licensing contracts these firms had signed with American firms). Other European countries followed the French lead at a time of recession and unemployment. In short, the European countries were determined to follow their national interests, regardless of the legalities involved or American concerns about European dependency.

Third, however eager the United States may have been to let the Soviets live with the consequences of their inefficient economic system and high military budgets, it was doubtful that the U.S. opposition to the pipeline would do more than slow it down. It was unlikely to stop it or compel the Soviets to either cut military spending or become politically more restrained and accommodating. The United States, concerned about its own grain sales, not only appeared a hypocrite but also divided the Western alliance while proving unable to block the European deal with the Soviet Union or to advance American political aims in the competition with Moscow. Economic coercion was hardly likely to collapse the Soviet system. It might force some belt-tightening and further worsen American-Soviet relations, but Soviet political objectives would surely not change. Ironically, what weakened European enthusiasm for the pipeline was the decline of world oil prices relative to the Soviet "floor price" for the gas purchases. In any event, was there any reason to believe that Western Europe, seeking to reduce its energy dependence on the Arab oil producers, was going to do so by becoming dependent on the Soviet Union? Rather, did the Soviet natural gas supplies not give the European states greater national freedom by permitting them a greater degree of flexibility?

To repeat: democracies whose governments are pressured by various domestic interest groups with economic stakes in trade are not usually able to pursue a consistent and effective strategy of economic denial. Indeed, these constituencies may render Western nations vulnerable to Soviet pressures because they want to minimize the economic costs of Soviet political adventures. The Soviets thereby gain two opportunities to exploit: they can exploit domestic Western divisions between governments that may want to use economic sanctions and business interests that do not, and they can play one Western government off against another. Even if the Soviets' need for Western trade were greater, economic coercion is not likely to work very well in restraining their political behavior internationally. Moscow may want more Western technology to modernize its economy; it may wish to increase the amounts of protein in Soviet diets with Western grain. No nation, not even the Soviet Union with its rich endowment of natural resources, is an island unto itself. But very clearly, its leaders will not permit their economic needs to be used either to weaken their control of the Soviet economy or to restrain them from acting in foreign policy in what they believe to be the Soviet Union's interests.[13] Still, if economic sanctions cannot change Soviet behavior, they may be able to punish the Soviet Union by compelling it to pay a price for its actions. The question remains how much pain can be inflicted at what price to those who impose the sanctions.

THE SUPERPOWERS AND THEIR ALLIES: AID AND TRADE

In the difficult years that followed World War II, the United States, the Soviet Union, and their respective allies took economic measures to strengthen their positions. The United States created the Marshall Plan, several Western European states formed an economic union, and the Soviet Union created economic ties with Eastern Europe and other allies.

The Marshall Plan

The United States resorted to economic means to advance its foreign policy goals from the very beginning of the cold war. It was, in fact, Western Europe's economic collapse that finally made it impossible for the United States to return to isolationism, as it had done after World War I. Just as Britain's weakening position had brought the United States into World War I in 1917 and close to World War II in 1941 even before Pearl Harbor, so Britain's postwar collapse left the United States no alternative but to commit itself in Western Europe.

On the surface Britain's crisis was an economic one. As an island nation it depended for survival on international trade. It had to trade or die because, as noted earlier, in the nineteenth century it had become almost completely urbanized and had neglected its agriculture. Except for coal, it had to import most of the raw materials for its industries: cotton, rubber, wool, iron ore, timber, and oil, upon which it was becoming increasingly dependent for the fueling of its factories.

Before 1939 Britain had paid for these foods and raw materials by three means: in services such as shipping, in income from foreign investments, and in manufactured exports. But the war had crippled the British merchant marine, liquidated most of the nation's foreign investments, and destroyed many of its factories. Britain thus had to increase its exports to an enormous extent; to regain its 1939 standard of living, it had to raise exports by 75 percent. By December 1946, despite an American loan and a severe austerity program that included rationing bread, Britain had only reached its prewar level of production. In those circumstances nature delivered what was almost a knockout blow: in the winter of 1946-47 Europe suffered one of its severest cold spells in history, with temperatures below zero. In Britain the transportation system came to a virtual standstill; trucks and trains could not move, barges were frozen in rivers, and ships could not leave their moorings. Industry could not be supplied with fuel, and factories were closed. By February 1947 more than half of Britain's factories lay idle. Coal was not even being mined any longer, and gas and electricity were in short supply. Electricity to industrial consumers was cut off for several days, and domestic consumers had to do without electricity for three hours every day. When the thaw finally arrived, Britain was beset by floods. It took months to recover.

In the meantime, the export drive had completely collapsed. Britain had come to the end of its economic rope. The financial editor of Reuter's press service saw the true dimensions of the winter disaster: "The biggest crash since the fall of Constantinople—the collapse of the heart of an Empire—impends. This is not the story of a couple of snowstorms. It is the story of the awful debility in which a couple of snowstorms could have such effects." [14] The future looked bleak: millions of Britons were unemployed, cold, hungry—and worn out by the long years of war and determined efforts to recover. Despite all the sacrifices they had made, their efforts had come to nothing. Britain's fate could have been worse only if it had lost the war.

Germany, which had been defeated, and France, which had never recovered from its defeat in 1940 and the years of German occupation, were in no better shape. All Europe stood on the verge of collapse, and everything appeared to compel dependence upon the United States. Most of the items necessary for reconstruction—wheat, cotton, sulphur, sugar, machinery, trucks, and coal—could be obtained in sufficient quantities only from the United States. Yet Europe, with a stagnating economy, was in no position to earn the dollars to pay for these goods. Furthermore, the United States was so well supplied with everything that it did not have to buy much from Europe. These two conditions led to the ominous *dollar gap*—a term that frightened Europeans as much as *cold war*. [15]

In former times, the closing of this gap would have been left to the mechanism of the international market. The European states, unable to pay for the machinery or the raw materials they needed, would simply not have bought them. Although this alternative would have meant the closing of factories, large-scale unemployment, millions of hungry and cold citizens, and widespread social discontent, that would have been merely unfortunate. In the long run, though, it would have brought about the desired result: the unemployed would have no money with which to buy goods manufactured with imported resources or machinery, and demand would therefore be driven down to the point at which trade would be in balance once more.

This "remedy" could not be adopted in the mid-twentieth century. The Europeans had not fought the war and suffered so much to face that kind of future. The war had been fought for a better future, in which people could live decently. In addition, the old-fashioned way of closing the dollar gap simply seemed incompatible with the humanitarian basis of Western civilization. It was no longer politically possible. When people elect their representatives, governments can hardly allow them to remain unemployed, to live in cold houses, or to starve.

The European collapse thus posed a fundamental question to the United States: Is Europe vital to American security? The answer was never in doubt. Two world wars had demonstrated it, and the collapse simply reaffirmed it. The U.S. commitment was demonstrated by the grant of billions of dollars in Marshall Plan funds to stimulate economic recovery and in the establishment of the NATO military alliance. The American role in Europe was akin to that of a doctor in relation to a patient—the prescribed cure was a massive injection of dollars. This large-scale program of economic aid was to be administered in the form of grants, rather than loans, which would have intensified Europe's dollar problems. Only such a grant program could restore Europe's prewar agricultural and industrial production, close the dollar gap, and stimulate a revival of European *élan vital*, political stability, economic prosperity, and military strength.

The Common Market

The infusion of Marshall Plan dollars was imaginative, but the French use of economics was revolutionary. France, after the experiences of 1870, 1914, and 1939, suffered a natural fear of Germany. The French were alarmed at American plans for the revival of the German economy, even though these plans were intended to benefit the economies of all the countries of Western Europe. For the French, the question was how to contain Germany's great power. Since the unification of Germany in 1870, France had attempted to deal with the greater inherent strength of this aggressive and militaristic neighbor by forming alliances to balance German power. Before World War I, France had found an ally in czarist Russia; in the interwar years, Poland, Czechoslovakia, Romania, and Yugoslavia had all been allied with France. Yet none of these alliances had saved France from attack. British and especially American power had been more important. As World War II was coming to a close, the French responded as they traditionally had done. Because Germany was still regarded as its number-one enemy, France entered into the French-Soviet Treaty of Mutual Assistance of 1944, which was quickly rendered obsolete by the cold war.

The failure of the traditional balance-of-power technique, by which an inferior power seeks to balance a stronger one, led France to seek a new way of exerting some control over German power. The French found a revolutionary means: European integration. It was through the creation of a supranational community, to which Germany would transfer certain sovereign rights, that German power was to be controlled. Only in this manner would German strength be prevented from harming the rest of Europe. Instead it would be channeled into support for European welfare and security.

France made its first move in the direction of a united Europe in May 1950, when it proposed the formation of the European Coal and Steel Community (ECSC), to be composed of "Little Europe" (France, Germany, Italy, Belgium, the Netherlands, and Luxembourg). The aim was to so entwine German and French heavy industry that it would become impossible ever to separate them. Germany would never again be able to use its coal and steel for nationalistic and militaristic purposes. The German use of political and military power derived from the industrial Ruhr area was to be eliminated for all time. War between Germany and France would become not only unthinkable but even impossible.

The French idea was not based on emotional appeals for a united Europe or a call to discard narrow nationalistic loyalties in favor of a broad European allegiance. A united Europe could not be created out of sentiment alone. The French rejected "the rosy mists of idealism" and determined to erect the new Europe upon a solid foundation, building from the bottom upward. A united Europe, they knew, could be forged only by binding together the interests of politically powerful and economically important groups across national boundaries. For instance, the removal of all trade barriers in the coal and steel sector of the economy would encourage modernization of mines and plants, as well as elimination of those that continued to operate inefficiently. Once the efficient producers had adjusted to the wider market and its opportunities, leaders would want to remove national barriers in other areas. Furthermore, as production increased, Europe's standard of living would rise, French and Italian workers would receive what they believed to be their fair share of income, and labor in general would recognize that the goal of a welfare state could be achieved only at the European level. Free trade, in short, would be the engine of integration.

The French also showed great political astuteness in their selection of heavy industry as the first to be integrated. Coal and steel are the basis of the entire industrial structure, a sector that cannot possibly be separated from the overall economy. Success of the ECSC would exert pressure on the unintegrated sectors of the economy, and, as the benefits of pooling heavy industry became clear, other sectors would follow suit. The ECSC was regarded as the first stage of an attempt to create a wider market in one particular area of the economy, and it was expected that this approach would be gradually extended to other areas, such as agriculture, transportation, and electricity. Eventually it would lead to the creation of a single European market and efficient mass-producing industries. Clearly, the basis for this shrewd plan was material.

Industry, labor, and agriculture would all benefit. The ECSC was thus the forerunner of the European Common Market (the European Economic Community, or EEC). The EEC's express purpose was to integrate the entire economies of its members and eventually to transform the separate nations into a United States of Europe, in which countries such as France and West Germany would become states in a federal union.

The Common Market was formed in 1958. Apart from its integrative function (see Chapter 19), it adopted a new goal in the late 1970s. With a membership already expanded from the original Inner Six to nine (including Britain, Denmark, and Ireland), the EEC elected to enlarge its membership again to twelve to include Greece, Portugal, and Spain (see map, page 632). The inclusion of these three semideveloped countries in a community of industrialized states was significant and to some people disturbing. It was disturbing because earlier additions, especially of Britain, had already complicated the integration process. The addition of three more states, all on the periphery of Europe and among the Continent's less-developed states, would place even greater strains on the EEC's institutions, policies, and distribution of resources.

The reason the members of the EEC proceeded with this enlargement, however, was to encourage democracy. The three new members had been ruled for long periods by authoritarian right-wing regimes, and their new democratic governments remained fragile. Many of their citizens came to Western Europe seeking jobs. The EEC employed millions of foreign workers, including Yugoslavs and Turks. A new fascist regime in Spain or Portugal or another colonels' coup in Greece would seriously affect the security and the democratic basis of the EEC. For this reason the community decided to help these nations lay the social and economic foundations for stable democracies and thus ensure the security of all the democracies in Europe. This new role was predictable when, after the collapse of Portugal's right-wing government and subsequent turmoil between the democratic parties, on one side, and the Communist party and radical military officers, on the other, the EEC offered help in rebuilding Portugal's shattered economy—but only in a "democratic" Portugal. This offer provided an incentive for those Portuguese who sought democracy; they struggled harder and won the government.

COMECON

The Soviets had a different way of organizing the economies of Eastern Europe following World War II. After initially forming "mixed" companies (the Soviet Union held a 50 percent interest but wielded total control), the Soviets founded the Council for Mutual Economic Assistance, known in the West as COMECON. When Stalin died, his successors decided to treat all of Eastern Europe as a single economic region, in which each country would produce certain items for the whole region. Poland would mine bituminous coal, East Germany would produce lignite and chemicals, and Czechoslovakia would manufacture automobiles. If each country were specialized, all countries would have to cooperate. The aim was to link the political and economic interests of the Communist countries and to create a high degree of interdependence among them. Economic specialization was to be the means of making Eastern Europe dependent on the Soviet Union and of isolating the Soviet bloc's economy from the West. (After 1962 Mongolia, Cuba, and Vietnam joined COMECON and were integrated into the Soviet bloc.)'

Despite these underlying political purposes, neither COMECON nor the national planning of the individual East European countries could quite meet national aims, especially that of providing a higher standard of living. The regimes in Eastern Europe are kept in power by the Soviet army, but the nationalistic outlook of most of them conferred a degree of legitimacy upon them. Economic improvements, as in Hungary in the 1970s, helped strengthen this legitimacy, just as economic failure, as in Poland in the late 1970s and early 1980s, weakened the authority of the regime. It is in this connection that Western economies are important, for they provide a standard of comparison and a constant reminder to the regimes in Eastern Europe of their lower living standards. The success of the EEC puts pressure on these regimes to do better.

Ironically, given the poor performance of the Soviet economy, the states of Eastern Europe turned to the West. The consequence was that East European trade with the West, including the United States, rose rapidly during the 1970s. From 1974 to 1982 East European debt grew from $13 billion to more than $60 billion! The political implications of this debt, owed primarily to Western banks, had to concern Moscow. If East European economies like Poland's became more dependent on the capitalist countries, these Western nations might gain some influence over East European nations' domestic policies. To obtain a new loan, Poland in 1979 permitted Western banks to monitor its economic policies. It was made clear to the Poles that, if they were to meet their payments on the $15 billion they owed the West, they would have to adopt a policy of austerity. This meant slowing down Poland's rate of economic growth and freezing the military budget, despite Soviet pressure to increase military spending. The Poles provided their private creditors with comprehensive financial information on the country's total foreign debt and debt-repayment schedules. The resulting austerity led in 1980 to widespread workers' strikes and demands not only for higher pay but also for an independent trade union.

After it was formed, however, the trade union Solidarity did not limit itself to economic demands, but also made political demands (for example, for less press censorship). Initially successful, frequently threatening or holding brief strikes, Solidarity became a mass protest movement. The government continued to retreat, and the union increasingly eroded the Communist party's monopoly of power. The Soviets have never accepted such a weakening of Communist control, and they exerted great pressure on the Poles to crush Solidarity, especially after the union wanted a national referendum on the

Communist system. Either because they wished to avoid a Soviet invasion or in response to Moscow's demands, the Polish army in late 1981 declared martial law and eliminated the people's immediate hopes to change the political system. The Communist type of highly centralized economy and the Soviet trading system clearly could not match the appeal of the West.

Aid to Cuba

Outside of Eastern Europe, the Soviet Union had more economic problems with its allies and friends. Given its difficulties in providing its population with sufficient food, its lack of experience with tropical agriculture, and its industrial economy oriented toward heavy industry and arms rather than consumer goods, the Soviet Union was little able to assist its new-found friends in Angola, Ethiopia, and other countries. With an economy that could not produce prosperity for its own people, it could do even less for its allies and friends, whether Communist or not.

Cuba was the most visible example. In more than two decades it had been unable to diversify its economy and become less dependent on sugar exports for earning its living. Indeed, Fidel Castro, having broken what he condemned as the "imperialist" economic relationship with the capitalist United States—in which Cuba was largely dependent on the U.S. market for the sale of its principal commodity—found himself in the same type of imperialist relationship with the Soviet Union! He still supplied mainly sugar; only his client had changed. Because Cuba was the Soviet Union's foothold in the Western Hemisphere, Moscow subsidized Cuba's economy. During the 1970s Cuba's attraction grew as Castro represented Soviet interests as a leader of the Third World's supposedly nonaligned states. Cuban troops helped Moscow's friends achieve power in Angola and consolidate power in Ethiopia. By the early 1980s, the estimated yearly Soviet subsidy for Cuba was said to be $4 billion and rising to $5 billion. It is not surprising that the Soviet Union was unwilling to repeat this costly experience in Chile, Ethiopia, and Nicaragua.

In one thing the Soviet economy did excel—weapons production. The Soviets, often with Cuban assistance, could help friendly, self-professed Marxist-Leninist groups come to power, but could do little for them afterwards economically. The possibility of Western economic aid and technology was in these circumstances a tool of potentially great influence and a limit on how far some of these states could turn toward the Soviet Union.

THE SUPERPOWERS AND SECONDARY ADVERSARIES: QUOTAS, BOYCOTTS, AND EMBARGOES

Economic pressures are not only used by the superpowers in dealing with one another and their chief allies. They are also frequently used in other conflict situations. Three examples have involved the United States and countries in Latin America.

Cuba, Chile, and Nicaragua

After Castro assumed power in Havana, Cuba's relations with the United States grew more contentious. The signing of the Soviet-Cuban trade agreement in 1960 was symptomatic of Cuba's shift toward the Soviet bloc. When Castro demanded that several American- and British-owned oil refineries process Soviet imported crude oil and they refused, the refineries were expropriated. This evidence of Cuban alignment with the United States' principal enemy led the administration of Dwight D. Eisenhower to try both to punish and to warn Castro. The United States suspended imports of 700,000 tons of sugar that remained unshipped out of Cuba's total 1960 U.S. quota of approximately 3 million tons. *A quota is an import level for a particular product established by the importing government for a specific time period.* This amount can be sold at a special price, above the international market price. For Cuba, whose entire economy was based on sugar production, this suspension was a form of pressure. The United States' aim was to punish Castro, if not to eliminate him. (When two countries trade with each other normally, and no quotas exist, one nation may attempt another form of pressure by boycotting, or cutting off, a major import or all imports from the other country.) Despite the loss of a sure American market, Cuba was not deterred from turning politically and economically toward the Soviet bloc, even after the United States embargoed all exports to the island (except food and medicine) and stopped its own citizens' travel there. Havana had been a great tourist center.

A decade later in Chile, Allende came to power, despite U.S. attempts to prevent his doing so because of his radical left-wing views. The Nixon administration then cut off all American short-term bank credits for Chile. To make up for this loss, Allende obtained even more credits from the Soviet Union, China, a number of Eastern European countries, Argentina, Brazil, Mexico, Finland, France, West Germany, the Netherlands, Spain, Sweden, and Japan. Most of these credits, however, were tied to purchases in the creditor countries to boost their own exports. Chile, therefore, could find no substitutes or spare parts for its American-made machinery and no comparable industrial technology. The copper industry, the source of Chile's international earnings, and the transportation system (cars, buses, diesel trucks) were seriously affected. Only massive Soviet financial support could have saved Allende's regime. The Soviet Union did extend considerable aid, but, after spending so much to support the Cuban economy from 1967 to 1972, it was not prepared to underwrite the runaway inflation and socially divisive domestic policies, which resulted from Allende's own policies rather than from American pressure.[16]

The Sandinistas initially came into power in Nicaragua in 1979. The Carter administration, opposed to the dictatorship of Anastasio Somoza, had cut off all U.S. assistance to the regime. It hoped that the Marxist Sandinistas, along with the business groups, trade unions, students, and the Catholic church, who had cooperated with the Sandinistas in a genuinely popular revolution against Somoza, would give Nicaragua political democracy, a mixed economy, and a nonaligned policy in world affairs. These were the goals the Sandinistas listed to the Organization of American States (OAS). After they acquired power, however, the Sandinistas gradually squeezed their former allies out of the government, progressively restricted their freedom, introduced censorship, and increasingly consolidated their grip on the government; internationally, they aligned themselves with Cuba and the Soviet Union. Once this became evident, Carter turned against the regime. Reagan's displeasure with Nicaragua has taken the form of support, through the CIA, of the "contra" guerrillas who are attempting to overthrow the Sandinistas. Direct U.S. military intervention was out of the question: Congress and public opinion were strongly opposed to "another Vietnam." The covert intervention through the contras dragged on but without any major victories. In 1985 the administration imposed an embargo.

What conclusions can be drawn from these three examples? In Cuba, U.S. economic pressure was unsuccessful. In fact, the elimination of the sugar quota strengthened Castro's popularity at home, diverted Cuban attention from the regime's failures, and allowed Castro to use the United States as his scapegoat while simultaneously urging his people to work harder and rally to his cause. Attempted economic coercion also brought him admiration throughout Latin America precisely because of his successful defiance of the United States. It probably strengthened his determination to continue playing David against the North American Goliath because "he might have overestimated the enemy and . . . it might be worth while to see whether history had destined him to play the role of liberator of the entire continent." [17] Probably no amount of U.S. economic aid could have dissuaded Castro from enacting his role as a revolutionary leader. Economic sanctions by the United States served only to arouse Cuban nationalism and to rally public support for Castro's regime. They had the opposite effect from the one sought.[18]

A second lesson to be drawn from the Cuban experience is that sanctions will inflict only temporary pain if alternative sources of supplies and export markets are available. A nation is vulnerable only if it is largely dependent on one product and trades mainly with one country. Castro was able simply to switch markets. Cuban sugar was sold to the Soviet bloc, which also became the source of products that Cuba had previously imported from the United States. Given the diversity of available markets, any targeted regime can survive with very little discomfort.

The Chilean example confirms these lessons, although at first the collapse of Allende's regime suggested the opposite; that is, that American economic pressures abetted by CIA activities can subvert a regime. Allende's government could have survived if Allende, like Castro, had presented himself as the leader of all his people. Instead, he declared, "I am not president of all

Chileans"; that is, he saw himself as representing only some Chileans—the poorest segments of society and not the others. The latter included not only the rich but also the middle classes, even the *petit bourgeoisie*. Allende deliberately relinquished the possibility of arousing nationalist sentiment in support of his policies. Instead, he divided the Chileans and pursued a highly inflationary policy to satisfy "his" Chileans. Paul Sigmund thus described Allende's mistakes and the lesson that can be learned from them:

> Defiance of international corporations and foreign governments need not lead to economic or political collapse. The Allende policy, however, which combined inflation with deliberate class polarization, was a formula for disaster.
>
> The lesson, if there is one, in the relations between the United States and the Allende government is that a government which is determined to nationalize U.S. companies without compensation and to carry out an internal program which effectively destroys its ability to earn foreign exchange cannot expect to receive a subsidy to do so from either the U.S. government or from U.S. private banks. It may, however, receive some assistance from other countries either for political (aid to a fellow "socialist" country) or economic (encouragement of exports) reasons—at least for a time. What it cannot do is blame all its problems on foreign imperialists and their domestic allies, and ignore principles of economic rationality and effective political legitimacy in its internal policies. No amount of foreign assistance can be a substitute for these, and *no amount of foreign subversion or economic pressure can destroy them if they exist.* (Emphasis added.) [19]

A government that enjoys domestic support can successfully resist attempts at economic coercion and subversion.

The economic pressures against the Sandinistas are as unlikely to succeed as those brought against Cuba and Chile. The Sandinistas had already survived several years of economic hardship, mostly because of their own mismanagement. Like Castro, they had built up a powerful police apparatus and nationwide political organizations to control domestic turmoil. Trade with the United States had been sharply reduced as the Sandinistas had diversified markets for Nicaragua's products as well as imports. Because the Latin American countries opposed the embargo, as did most other states, the embargo was, at best, another sign of U.S. displeasure. Symbolic acts such as this may be of some value, but if they are carried out unilaterally and are widely opposed by other states their message may well be lost.

Economic Coercion and High Politics

Economic sanctions, like force, are political instruments. Like war, they seek to achieve specific political aims: to compel the targeted state to comply with the preferred policies of the sanctioning state (Kissinger's economic linkage policy toward the Soviet Union); to deter, or if not to deter, to punish an adversary (Carter's grain embargo against Moscow); to eliminate a perceived hostile regime (Castro and the Eisenhower sugar quota or the Reagan embargo on Nicaragua); or to communicate disapproval toward an adversary (all of the preceding examples).

But almost all of these examples of publicly imposed sanctions have failed to achieve their political objectives. The main reason for failure is not only that the targeted nations usually have been able to avoid economic pain, but also that their leaders and populations have recognized that their stake in maintaining their policies is high. Compliance is considered a surrender of a nation's dignity and independence to decide its own future. The Soviets learned this lesson in the late 1940s, when Stalin cut off all trade and aid to Yugoslavia after his quarrel with Marshal Tito. Stalin failed in the effort to eliminate Tito, who simply shifted to American and Western European markets, while the people rallied to his support. Indeed, as a leader of the Yugoslav guerrilla movement against the occupying Nazi armies during World War II, Tito had come to symbolize Yugoslav nationalism. The Chinese taught this same lesson to the Soviets in the late 1950s. Despite the damaging withdrawal of all Soviet advisers and technical experts, the Beijing government refused to follow Soviet policies. The Chinese "decided to go it alone, whatever the problems and costs, determined to end their economic dependency and vulnerability." [20] They repaid Soviet loans so that they would not be financially indebted to Moscow. As A. Doak Barnett points out: "[W]hereas in the mid-1950's China had seemed well on its way toward full incorporation into a Moscow-dominated 'Communist world system,' by the end of the 1960's it had nothing more than minimal diplomatic contact with Russia." [21]

Ironically perhaps, it is a lesson that the Soviets taught the United States, when they rejected a commercial agreement in 1975 because of American demands that they change their policy on emigration, especially for Jews. No power, and certainly not a great power, will admit publicly that it has mistreated its own citizens; none will promise to improve its behavior under pressure and in return for certain material goods. Domestic affairs are considered the business of the national government and of no one else. To insist on domestic changes is an affront. The Soviets, therefore, turned down the agreement. (In contrast, quiet, behind-the-scenes diplomacy had gained the release of 35,000 Soviet Jews in 1973.) Even after the Soviet invasion of Afghanistan, the grain embargo and other economic measures, while communicating strong disapproval, could not compel Soviet withdrawal. For one thing, the Soviets bought grain elsewhere, demonstrating once more that unless the major suppliers of a product all agree to go along with an embargo, the sanctions imposed by one country cannot work. "Leaky" sanctions are ineffective, even when the sanctioning country is a major supplier.

Even more fundamentally, in a clash between a nation's vital interests and economic benefits, the latter are sacrificed to the former. High politics takes priority over low politics. *Attempts at economic coercion are generally self-defeating when the target state believes high politics issues are at stake;* instead they strengthen the morale of the targeted nation and stiffen its resistance to negotiations. Indeed, what is usually overlooked when sanctions are applied is that even if the leaders of the targeted state wished to comply, they could not. They would be accused of capitulating to foreigners' demands and jeopardizing their nations' security and independence. In short, to avoid losing domestic support, they could not comply; sanctions restrict their ability to change their policies.

One has to ask why, given this failure rate, states indulge in applying sanctions at all. One reason is that sanctions represent a way of expressing displeasure with another nation's policy. The United States knew that its European allies would not join it in applying sanctions against Poland, but these sanctions not only articulated American anger but also gave the appearance of doing something in a situation where little could be done. They may have shielded the administration from the anger of Polish-Americans and gained their electoral support.

The sanctions against South Africa were initially intended to achieve the same objectives: to express U.S. anger at apartheid and to defuse domestic opinion. Banning South African gold coins from sale in the United States, or barring bank loans to South Africa (which the banks were already doing) were symbolic sanctions, and they were not intended to impose any real pain. But mass media attention and other factors led to growing popular anger and demands for more severe sanctions. The administration, resisting, was dragged behind public and congressional opinion. There was strong sentiment that as the leading democratic nation, the United States had to impose more than symbolic sanctions. Otherwise, the critics asserted, the United States would appear as if it approved of the South African regime and apartheid; the United States would be bitterly criticized by the black African nations; and it would alienate those blacks who would some day govern South Africa. One U.S. senator expressed the view that South African racism was viewed by many as an American civil rights issue and that was why it aroused the same strong emotions. Given these reasons, it was not surprising that Congress overrode President Reagan's veto of its sanctions measure; the president, it was stated, was out of step with public opinion on this issue.

Domestic pressures played no role in decisions on Nicaragua; the embargo was applied because there was little else that could be done. Reagan could not send in U.S. forces and Congress had limited help for the contras to humanitarian aid. With military action ruled out, sanctions were seen as better than nothing; at least they avoided—or were supposed to avoid—the appearance of the United States as a helpless giant. Carter had done the same thing in 1979 when Iran seized the U.S. Embassy; unable to gain the hostages' release, the president halted the purchase of Iranian oil. Since the United States purchased only a small amount of Iranian oil, this cutoff was basically symbolic. To a frustrated American public, the president's move gave the impression of some action short of the use of force, which, it was widely believed, would result in the hostages' death. The real hope of the president was that the action would limit the political damage. For a while it did, but Carter's failure to secure the hostages' freedom month after month finally hurt him in the next presidential election, contributing to his defeat by Reagan. Why, then, do governments—especially democratic ones—continue to use sanctions? In large part, they do so to minimize domestic damage and to avoid the image of impotency at home and abroad.

THE SUPERPOWERS AND THE THIRD WORLD: ECONOMIC AID

The unequal distribution of wealth between the First and Third Worlds was the original cause for Western economic aid to the less-developed countries (LDCs). The fear was that if the gap between the rich and poor nations widened, the resulting social instability and political turmoil would give rise to revolutionary conditions. In the postwar bipolar system, it was believed, that situation would benefit the Soviet Union and its allies.

For the LDCs, the distribution of power in the immediate postwar world enhanced their ability to attract the funds needed for their development. Because the superpowers were unwilling to risk total war, and each hoped to win friends and influence people in the developing areas, foreign aid became an instrument of policy. In the nuclear age, aid was a substitute for arms: "In our times, economic activities are not an alternative [to war]; they are a substitute. They are no longer a preferable alternative to clearly feasible war and to equally despicable but apparently dispensable power politics. They are instead a substitute for practically self-defeating major war, and they are more than ever an instrument of the again respectable politics of power."[22] Foreign aid thus became for a while an instrument of economic warfare.

Soviet Aid

The Soviet aid program, begun in the mid-1950s, was generally concentrated in just a few countries, even during its first decade.[23]

Criteria.   Aid was given to states that were either politically vital (such as India) or strategically located (such as Afghanistan). In particular, aid was given to those states that were perceived by the West as "troublemakers"— Egypt, Iraq, Algeria, and Cuba, for example. Furthermore, the Soviets did not necessarily demand economic justification of a project as a condition for aid. They furnished aid to build the Aswan High Dam in Egypt and a steel mill in India, in each instance responding to a request by the host country for such support. They were not especially concerned with how a particular project fitted into a country's overall plan for development. If it served Soviet purposes, it received support. One such purpose was public relations, or prestige; they therefore spent their money on highly visible projects like the dam at Aswan, the paving of Kabul's main street, buses for the Afghans, and sports stadiums in Rangoon, Burma, and Jakarta, Indonesia. They were quite willing to send modern weapons to the new states, providing the recipients with the symbols of modern nationhood and the illusion of national strength.

During the cold war they entered into close alliances with Arab states in a joint effort to eliminate Western influence from the Middle East.

Type of Aid.   The Soviets largely provided credits, while the United States relied on grants. It was often argued that the former offered a distinct psychological advantage over the latter. Unlike grants, which supposedly made the recipients feel they were accepting charity, credits, it was claimed, enabled borrowers to retain their dignity. Because they would pay for loans, they could perceive themselves as engaged in normal business transactions of mutual benefit. Furthermore, the Soviet loans were extended at lower interest rates than American loans. The Soviets could accuse the West of exploiting the developing countries in typical capitalist fashion and stress the advantage to a developing country of receiving Soviet aid. The Soviets also seemed more willing to accept repayment in local currencies or in exports, which often helped to relieve surpluses of cotton, rice, fish, or sugar and to preserve a country's slim dollar or sterling reserves.

Although the Soviet loan policy may have had many advantages for the developing nation, it was also geared to specific Soviet purposes, which actually had little to do with the recipient's well-being. The Soviets used loans not to preserve the recipient's self-respect but to keep down costs; a loan was always less expensive than an outright grant. Furthermore, because loans must be repaid, the number of applications was limited. Equally important, loans helped to establish bilateral trading relations with the recipients; the Soviet Union could thus obtain the commodities it needed and, more important, could try to tie the recipients to Soviet products.

Results.   The Soviet Union's aid program was not as successful as one might expect, and the results speak for themselves. Soviet aid to a particular country was often initiated at a point when relations between the recipient and the West were poor. Aid to Iraq began after its pro-Western government had been overthrown by a new nationalist government. Having denounced Western imperialism and withdrawn from the Middle East Treaty Organization (METO), the new government sought new sources of support. When Guinea left the newly formed French Commonwealth and France accordingly withdrew all its aid, Soviet rubles began to pour into the former colony. As Egypt grew increasingly anti-Western in the mid-1950s, and sought to overthrow pro-Western governments throughout the Arab world, the Soviet bloc offered it a huge supply of modern weapons. When the United States then retracted its offer to build the Aswan dam, partly because of Egypt's new ties with the Soviet Union, the Soviets took over the financing of that project.

Yet Iraq did not become Communist, and the new government eventually arrested the Iraqi Communist leaders. Sékou Touré of Guinea sent the Soviet ambassador home for allegedly plotting to overthrow his government and then began to reestablish relations with France. And Gamal Abdel Nasser arrested Egyptian Communists and denounced the Soviet Union on several occasions, while his successor shifted toward closer relations with the United States. Indonesia aligned itself with China against the Soviet Union. In no developing nation did Soviet aid result in Soviet client states—except in Cuba, where the Communists were already in power before the Soviet aid program began. Even Castro, who in the 1960s received about $1 million a day from the Soviet Union, criticized the Soviet regime for refusing to support revolutionary action in Latin America before the 1979 Sandinistas' assumption of power in Nicaragua. The Soviet leaders presumably did not want a dangerous confrontation with the United States in an area of traditional American dominance, and they probably still do not, but currently they can work in El Salvador through proxy states—Cuba and Nicaragua.

Reasons.   Why did the Soviet Union have such limited success with its aid program? One reason was Soviet performance. The Soviets at times failed to deliver the quantities of goods promised. They engaged in questionable practices (such as reselling Egyptian cotton at prices lower than the world market and thus underselling Egypt's own cotton).[24] They delivered poor-quality crude oil, wormy wheat, and unsatisfactory machinery, and they permitted shoddy construction. The Aswan dam, for instance, had all sorts of unanticipated ecological effects. Some of these failures, indeed, might have been expected. The Soviets generally perform best in the area of heavy industry, where they have considerable experience, rather than in light industry and production of consumer items. Soviet experience in agriculture, the Achilles' heel of the Soviet economy anyway, had little applicability to the tropical farming that characterizes most of the underdeveloped areas.

Yet the defects of the Soviet aid program should not be overstressed. The American program suffered similar failures and was inferior to the Soviet program in certain respects.[25] Not needing legislative approval of annual foreign-aid appropriations, the Soviets were able to commit themselves for years in advance, thus allowing the recipient nation to plan a long-range economic program. They also had the flexibility to exploit favorable new situations as they arose. The Soviet government could mobilize its best engineers and technicians if it so desired, for there were no private Soviet corporations with higher wages to attract top talent away from government-sponsored aid projects. Finally, no citizen, official, ethnic group, or farm lobby in the Soviet Union embarrassed the government by denouncing the recipient country or by attempting to block payment through the sale of products in competition with Soviet products.

The fundamental reason why Soviet aid during the cold war years did not achieve more was that Soviet long-range political aims did not coincide with the aspirations of the LDCs. Short-range Soviet goals often were compatible with national independence and nonalignment in foreign policy. Indeed, one of the attractions of Soviet aid was that it strengthened the newly independent nation by reducing its otherwise exclusive dependence on its former colonial country or on the United States. But ultimate Soviet aims diverged sharply from the objectives of the new states.

The people of most of these nations keenly remembered their long colonial subjugation; they were not about to substitute Soviet colonialism for the Western variety. Their nationalism was directed against *any* foreign control, and this posed a real dilemma for the Soviets. When the Soviets did not interfere in domestic politics, they enjoyed good relations with the recipient nations (as with India). But when they sought to pressure a government to support Soviet positions, attempted to overthrow governments, or refused to support governmental goals, they alienated friendly states (such as the Sudan, Egypt, and Somalia). In more recent years this trend has started to reverse as the Soviets helped a number of self-proclaimed Marxist regimes come to power and/or consolidate their power. Although regimes in Angola, Ethiopia, and Yemen, for example, are nationalistic, they have looked to Moscow for arms, military advisers, and Soviet-bloc personnel to help organize the government, including police forces, Cuban troops, and general political support.

American Aid

For the United States, the principal purpose of an aid program—after emphasis had shifted from Europe to the LDCs—was to help stop communism.

Military Aid.   Indeed, the term *economic aid* is actually something of a misnomer.[26] The giant portion of American aid since the Korean War has been *military aid* to support mainly the armies of allied nations around the Sino-Soviet periphery: Nationalist China, South Korea, South Vietnam, Pakistan, and Turkey. Such military assistance may be viewed as a form of economic aid, for the recipient nation spends less of its own resources on military forces and can instead invest more heavily in economic development, assuming it would invest in a military force without aid.

Bribery.   Another form of aid may be called—for want of a better term— *bribery aid.* Much of the aid extended to Latin American republics before the formation of President John Kennedy's Alliance for Progress could be included in this category. In addition to military equipment, the money sent to these countries, supposedly for economic development or collective hemispheric defense, was actually intended to prop up the ruling classes and the military, neither of which was particularly interested in modernization. The United States was preoccupied in Europe, Asia, and the Middle East—that is, outside Latin America, whose grave social, political, and economic problems it ignored until Castro suddenly and dramatically drew attention to the vulnerability of the United States in its own backyard. Up to that point, the United States had been interested primarily in preserving hemispheric stability and securing votes in the United Nations. Latin American armies, hardly threatened by the Soviet or Chinese military and useless as fighting machines anyway, could nevertheless be strengthened to deal with unrest at home. Outside Latin America as well, "bribery" money was from time to time given to key leaders to help them maintain stability in their countries.

Development Loans. The most significant form of aid, in view of the almost global scope of the "revolution of rising expectations," has been the *development loan.*[27] American policy makers were eager to promote economic growth. They feared that some of the more important new nations, should they fail to transform themselves into unified, urban, industrialized societies, might adopt communism as a more efficient way of modernizing. In nations with ineffective political institutions, the appeal of communism was that it made government possible. "They may not provide liberty, but they do provide authority; they do create governments that can govern." [28] Implicit in American promotion of economic growth was the assumption that poverty would benefit the Communist cause; aid was intended to prevent Communist expansion.

Conversely, it was frequently assumed that economic development would nurture more open societies and democratic institutions,[29] which would in turn ensure peaceful international behavior. Although these assumptions are questionable, it is true that democracy cannot develop amid conditions of poverty. Aristotle pointed out that "poverty is the parent of revolution and crime. . . . When there is no middle class, and the poor greatly exceed in number, troubles arise, and the state soon comes to an end." Aristotle believed that political stability depends upon the absence of extreme wealth and poverty:

> Thus it is manifest that the best political community is formed by citizens of the middle class, and that those states are likely to be well-administered, in which the middle class is large, and stronger if possible than both the other classes, or at any rate than either singly; for the addition of the middle class turns the scale, and prevents either of the extremes from being dominant.[30]

In other words, widespread, moderate affluence is a prerequisite for democratic government. When the majority of people live in dire need, democratic government cannot establish roots. A higher national income and a more equitable distribution of that income are more likely in a developed economy, and such an economy does tend to promote democracy. The society that can afford to "deal everyone in" can afford to be democratic.[31] Economic growth does not, of course, automatically produce a democratic society—Germany and Japan in the 1930s and the Soviet Union today are obvious examples. In each of these instances an economically developed nation has been controlled by an authoritarian or totalitarian regime bent on regional or global expansion. Freedom and democracy are not the necessary results of economic development. But, if economic development is not a *sufficient* condition to ensure the maturation of a democratic society, it nevertheless remains a *necessary* condition.[32] Therefore, the United States sought to promote peaceful evolution, economic development, and political democracy, if possible, thus building an international environment in which Western democratic values would continue to flourish.

Changes in U.S. Policy

Since the 1970s, however, there have been significant changes in U.S. as well as Soviet aid policies, for a number of reasons. Both of the superpowers were aware that "instant development" was an unrealistic expectation. Modernization (the urbanization and industrialization of a mainly agricultural society) is a very long and very complex process, not to be achieved in a "Decade of Development" or by a simple transfer of factories and machinery to a cultural environment unable to cope with modern industry and its accompanying social, political, and psychological demands. The enormous efforts already made and the disappointing results tired and disenchanted the two principal competitors. Both also recognized that aid did not necessarily buy allies or votes. The Soviet Union became increasingly disillusioned with the more radical leaders it had once sought as partners against the West. By 1965 several of them had been deposed; in addition, in each instance the successor regime had claimed that a principal reason for the *coup d'état* had been economic stagnation and domestic chaos. Furthermore, the recipients of Soviet aid often did not repay their loans. The United States, on the other hand, grew more sophisticated. While accepting nonalignment even before the fall of radicals such as Mohammed Ben Bella in Algeria, Kwane Nkrumah in Ghana, and Sukarno in Indonesia, it became disenchanted with those who had bitten the hand that was feeding them. Finally, competition for the Third World seemed less urgent as other external and domestic commitments became more pressing, especially in the early to mid-1970s when Western economies were hit by high oil prices, inflation, and unemployment all at the same time. Once the rivalry resumed after 1975, the principal instrument of competition was military aid.

As a result, American aid has declined in relation to the rising gross national product (GNP). In the late 1940s Marshall Plan aid totaled 2.75 percent of GNP. By the beginning of the 1970s nonmilitary aid had fallen to 0.29 percent of GNP, the lowest of all major donor countries. In 1986 American aid constituted 0.18 of 1 percent of GNP! The Reagan administration asked for $22.6 billion for economic assistance in 1987, but is not likely to get more than $17 billion. The United States remained last of the leading seventeen economic powers; the Netherlands, by providing 1 percent of its GNP, was in first place. As Robert Rothstein has noted, American aid has been extended to seventy countries, but eight of them received 75 percent of the total up to the late 1970s. Seven of those eight—South Korea, Taiwan, South Vietnam, Pakistan, Turkey, Jordan, and Brazil—are either formal allies or generally closely aligned with the United States. The eighth country is India, in the 1950s and early 1960s a leader of the nonaligned movement and one of the few democracies in the non-Western world. (Indeed, India has often been called "the world's biggest democracy.") In contrast, most LDCs receive "so little aid that it is difficult to see why aid became so controversial an issue."[33] Since 1980 more than one-third of U.S. economic assistance went to Israel, Egypt, and Turkey.

Greater emphasis recently has been placed on technical assistance programs that would emphasize teaching skills and knowledge in areas such as health, education, and food production and, especially during the Reagan years, on a larger role for American private enterprise. One main criterion for aid has been economic rather than political: Could the recipient mobilize its resources and adopt policies to make sound use of the proferred funds? Of course, there have been exceptions (for example, pressuring international institutions to withhold loans from Allende's Chile and extending more aid to Egypt as it became more accommodating toward a settlement with Israel after 1973). But generally the United States now offers what it believes to be sound advice to the LDCs: try "the magic of the market place," as President Reagan phrased it. Less government intervention in the economy, more private enterprise, and attractive conditions for foreign capital investment are the prescription.

Changes in Soviet Policy

The Soviet Union has followed suit. Indeed, ideologically, the shift in its attitudes toward foreign aid has been startling.[34] In the early 1960s Soviet advice to the new states was drawn straight from Marxist-Leninist theory. Expand the public sector of the economy to gain control over the economy. Expropriate and nationalize private foreign and domestic firms to keep profits for reinvestment, rather than letting them go into private hands at home or abroad. Orient economic relations toward the Soviet Union and its friends to break the Western imperialist economic chains that allegedly kept the LDCs underdeveloped. This approach has changed. Soviet aid policy since the mid-1960s has emphasized economic criteria more heavily than political criteria; aid is to be given for economically viable projects. Soviet leaders deemphasized—in very un-Marxist fashion—state control and nationalization of industry and have suggested that private capital, even *Western* capital, can play an important role in the modernization of new nations. They have also pointed out the need for more balance between industrial and agrarian development. And, of course, the amount of Soviet aid has declined.

Since the Brezhnev years, Soviet economic assistance has reached a low point.[35] The inability of the Soviet Union to provide economic development assistance on the scale expected by its Third World friends is a serious handicap. The Soviets simply have too many economic problems at home to afford the endless demands for economic aid. One Cuba to support at $8 million to $10 million per day and a Vietnam costing approximately $2 million a day are enough! Angola, Ethiopia, Nicaragua, and other pro-Soviet Marxist states, which, even among the LDCs, are the least economically successful, have been told to rely basically on their own efforts; the Soviets would only help "to the extent of our ability." This attempt to discourage the expectations of its client states reflected Moscow's rising costs, from an estimated range of $13.6 billion to $21.8 billion in 1971 to $35.9 billion to $46.5 billion in 1980.[36] The Soviet Union has lost its earlier appeal as a model for economic development, a model that the Soviets themselves constantly held up before the LDCs in earlier days.

With the decline of both American and Soviet aid, and facing the high cost of oil during the 1970s, the LDCs began to borrow billions of dollars and to go deeply in debt. The result was the "debt bomb."

THE TICKING OF THE INTERNATIONAL 'DEBT BOMB'

By 1985 about thirty LDCs had collectively run up an astronomical $970 billion debt, most of it loaned by some of the West's largest multinational banks and the rest by governments and the international lending agencies such as the International Monetary Fund (IMF). Approximately $380 billion was owed by Latin American countries, and three-quarters of this amount was owed by Argentina ($45 billion), Brazil ($104 billion), Mexico ($98 billion), and Venezuela ($35 billion).[37] Should a significant amount of this debt be repudiated, it would bankrupt many banks, creating a financial crisis in Western countries.

The root of the debt crisis is the rise in oil prices from $3 a barrel to $34 a barrel, which took place from 1973 to 1982. The oil-producing countries earned huge amounts of "petrodollars," much of it then invested in the West or deposited in Western banks. But the LDC oil consumers were hard hit by this steep increase of their oil bills. Simultaneously, Western economic aid also dropped off as the Western economies slumped. The LDCs therefore had to choose between greater belt tightening or going into debt to buy oil and continue their economic development. Eager banks, holding surplus petro-dollars, were only too eager to lend them money. This was, of course, very profitable for the banks, which competed with one another to extend loans and did not worry very much about being repaid. The LDCs' collateral was their commodities; a few of the borrowers, like Mexico and Venezuela, were oil producers and wanted the money to develop their oil resources further.

The LDCs, however, could not repay their loans because commodity prices fell sharply. A main reason for this was that the industrial countries' econo-mies were in a recession, and their demands for raw materials declined. If an oil producer like Mexico could not make enough money to pay off its debt in these circumstances, how could other countries, especially those like Kenya, Bangladesh, and Zaire that depend on the export of one item, such as coffee, jute, and copper? Chile, also dependent on copper exports, suffered a painful setback as a debtor when copper prices fell by more than 50 percent from

$1.50 a pound in 1980 to 62 cents a pound by 1985. It lost $29 million for each penny drop in the copper price. For the agricultural economies of Central America, this was a disaster. They suffered several years of no growth or negative growth and increased unemployment in a region already suffering considerable domestic upheaval and international strife.

There was another reason that the debts the LDCs had incurred became such an unbearable burden. When they had borrowed the money, the LDCs thought that the dollars could be repaid easily. The United States was suffering a major inflation in the late 1970s, and the LDCs expected to repay their loans with cheaper dollars. But in the early 1980s the dollar's value rose sharply relative to other currencies as a result of the huge Reagan budget deficits.

Even to pay off the annual interest on their loans, the LDCs had to borrow more money. To prevent the LDCs from defaulting on the loans they could not pay back, the banks, ironically, loaned them more! The debtors had their bankers over a barrel; the bankers feared that the debtors might organize a debtors' cartel and repudiate their loans. Increasingly, in fact, the debtors did rebel. To obtain more funds, the banks or the IMF asked the recipient governments to cut government spending, balance their budgets, bring down inflation with wage controls, and get their economies in order. The resulting austerity, as subsidies for social programs were cut and food prices rose, led to riots in the Dominican Republic, the invasion of supermarkets in Rio de Janeiro, and strikes throughout Latin America. Over the preceding forty years, Latin America's economy had grown, permitting limited benefits for the people in housing, health, and education. All that was wiped out as exports fell.[38] Paying the annual interest of more than $45 billion left little capital for investing in economic development, let alone in social programs. In fact, to the degree that they pay back their loans, the LDCs are exporting capital they need.

Their dilemma is obvious: if they default on their loans, the debtor nations will endanger their credit ratings. Or they can tighten their belts and receive new loans, but risk domestic political explosions as living standards fall even lower and the division between the rich and poor grows. The implications for American security interests are obvious. Most of the Latin debtors are democracies, but several of these democracies are new and fragile. Their political futures may be endangered and dictatorships of the left or right may return in an area where authoritarianism has a long tradition. It was debt or democracy for new democracies such as Argentina and Brazil.[39]

Peru in these circumstances decided to repay only 10 percent of its export earnings (and lost its credit worthiness when it defaulted on a $180 million repayment). Brazil declared it would not pay its debt with recession, unemployment, and hunger. Castro advised the Latin states not to pay their debt at all—a proposal that will have more appeal as living standards continue to decline, unemployment grows, and social disorders spread from the poor to the middle classes.[40] The Latin countries were not totally without a case. The

U.S. deficit, which had raised the value of the dollar, was a major reason for their difficulties in repaying their loans. Each percentage increase of American interest rates added tens of millions, if not hundreds of millions, of dollars to what they owed. A 1 percent increase in 1984 had added $600 million to Argentina's debt, and, in the words of its president, "jeopardized his country's social peace." [41] The short-term solution of rescheduling the debt—that is, simply stretching out the time for repayment—was thus insufficient. While avoiding crises in the short run, it only postponed the critical issue of eventual repayment.

In recognition of this fact, the United States in 1985 accepted the Latin position that growth-oriented policies were more likely than austerity programs to enable the Latin American countries to meet their financial obligations. The American plan would try to encourage economic growth by rewarding countries that adopted market-oriented policies with increasing support from the commercial banks as well as the World Bank. How successful this shift in policy would be in Latin America and other regions remains to be seen, especially if oil prices continue to fall, thus making it even more difficult for Mexico and Venezuela to repay their debts. Among other things, would the United States and other industrial countries not surrender to domestic protectionist demands to keep LDC products out? More important, will the industrial democracies see that the "debt bomb" is not just a financial problem, but part of the greater issue of the distribution of the world's resources between the rich nations and the poorer LDCs? It was, after all, the concern for what would happen to the stability of the world if this gap grew that had been the original motive for economically aiding the LDCs.

U.S. TRADE WITH THE LDCs

The American interest in preventing the debt bomb from exploding is not just a question of saving U.S. banks; it is a matter of national interest. American exports to the Third World have become larger than those to Canada and Western Europe. The Common Market used to be America's premier export market, but U.S. prosperity has now become increasingly intertwined with the LDCs. The United States, in brief, has a growing interest in the development of Third World countries. The following figures from the State Department underscore the importance of the LDCs to the U.S. economy:

U.S. benefits from LDC prosperity: Partly as a result of post-1973 income growth in the oil-producing countries, LDCs have become an increasingly important market for U.S. manufacturers.

Over the last decade, the proportion of our manufactured exports purchased by LDCs has increased by one-third. In 1983, LDCs purchased more than $75 billion worth (about 38%) of U.S. merchandise exports, exceeding U.S. exports to Western Europe and Japan combined. . . .

LDCs are an important market for U.S. agricultural goods. Of the $36 billion of agricultural products we exported in 1983, $15 billion worth (about 43%) went to LDCs; more than 70% of our wheat exports and more than two-thirds of our rice exports went to LDCs.

At the end of 1983, U.S. private direct investment in the LDCs totaled $51 billion, about 22% of our total private direct investment abroad. As the LDCs become more stable and prosperous, they become more attractive candidates for investment, which should stimulate further economic growth. . . .

LDCs produce materials critical to the functioning of the U.S. economy. They supply more than half of our imports of such important metals as tungsten, bauxite, tin, and cobalt and provide 100% of the natural rubber, cocoa, and hard fibers we consume.

It has been estimated that about 70% of bilateral U.S. assistance disbursements and 50% of our contributions to multilateral development banks are spent on U.S. goods and services. In 1983, our total economic assistance to LDCs was $8 billion, $4.9 billion of which was bilateral. Hence our bilateral economic assistance expenditures last year can be expected to generate about $3.5 billion worth of U.S. exports of goods and services.[42]

By the 1980s the LDCs were the sources of key minerals and other commodities besides oil, and they provided a growing market for American products. American stakes in this trading relationship with the LDCs had grown in ten years to the point where the LDCs' growth or nongrowth—indeed, collapse— would affect the United States' well-being and economic performance. The consequences of this growing, mutually beneficial relationship with the LDCs are therefore not only economic, but also political. The United States, for example, needs to help the debt-ridden Latin American states because debtors cannot buy American goods (the debt has deeply cut exports to these countries, raising the U.S. unemployment level). Many of the debtors are new democracies whose future political stability is in the interests of the United States.

OPEC: 'POWER GROWS OUT OF THE (OIL) BARREL'

The Energy Crisis

The year 1973 was marked by the Yom Kippur War in the Middle East. That same year OPEC's Arab members, which held the world's largest oil reserves, instituted an embargo against the United States and the Netherlands to protest those countries' political support of Israel. The Arab states also planned monthly production cutbacks for the other non-Communist industrial states. In addition, OPEC raised oil prices from $3 to $12 a barrel. It was this ability to control supplies and prices that made OPEC a powerful producer-cartel. The impact upon the Western industrial countries, as well as upon many LDCs, was devastating. OPEC's actions caused not only minor inconveniences to consumers, who had to pay more for gasoline and other oil-based products, but also a profound upheaval in entire economies, ways of life, and standards of living. They also upset the plans for economic growth of many states, developed and less developed alike. Governments and citizens the world over learned the true meaning of the word "interdependence" (see Chapter 20). Economic issues rose to the top of the international agenda and became intensely politicized. The "energy crisis"—high oil prices and a lack of secure supplies—was born.

In the Western industrial nations and Japan the quadrupling of oil prices—and later rises, especially in 1979—immediately affected living standards. Families could no longer buy as much because gasoline, heating oil, and plastics, and other oil-based materials like clothing, became much more expensive. Food prices also rose, for cultivation and distribution depended upon energy. The rising price stoked Western inflation, already high, and simultaneously precipitated the worst recession since the Great Depression of the 1930s, with very high unemployment rates. This "stagflation" in turn made recovery more difficult. The economic growth rates of all industrial countries were set back. Western Europe and Japan, the United States' principal allies, were hit much harder than the United States, for they were far more dependent upon OPEC oil. The large consuming nations no longer appeared to be in control of their own economies. Anti-inflationary policies could not be effective as oil prices continued to rise. By the spring of 1980 the Western countries had 18 million unemployed, and the figure was still going up. An estimated $240 billion to $250 billion worth of industrial capacity lay idle. The reported 1982 unemployment figure for the twenty-four major industrial democracies was more than 30 million people!

The energy crisis starkly demonstrated the fragility of all Western economies, including that of the United States. Relatively inexpensive oil had led to the neglect of vast coal deposits in Europe and the United States. From 1955 to 1972, Western Europe's use of coal had shrunk from three-quarters of total energy sources to about one-fifth, while the share of its energy from oil rose from one-fifth to three-fifths. The American experience was similar. In 1964 the United States was still the world's leading oil producer; in 1965 the Middle East overtook that position. In 1970 U.S. production peaked and then started declining. By 1976 the industrial West—Western Europe, the United States, and Japan—consumed 65 percent of the world's oil production. This meant that increasingly they used other nations' oil. The Middle East and Africa, who have two-thirds of the world's oil reserves, consumed only 4 percent.

As Alan Madian has pointed out,

> the artificially low prices from 1945 to 1973—in the late 1960s oil was priced at under $2 a barrel—turned the industrialized countries into petroleum junkies. Had oil been priced with due respect for the scarcity value of supplies, the present price might well be lower. Producers would have far less market power, since oil would

have a significantly lower market share. There would be both less demand and more supply under U.S. control, and probably a more developed synthetic crude oil industry and other substitutes.

The major oil companies are now accused of creating artificial shortages. Yet for 28 years they were responsible for producing capacity surpluses in what are now the OPEC countries. Low prices subsidized the development of the industrialized nations and contributed to unprecedented growth rates. Cheap petroleum kept other energy prices low and eroded their market share. This bargain led to distortions in the industrial economies, and petroleum use doubled each decade. Investments in plant and equipment were based on the assumption that petroleum and other energy alternatives would remain cheap.[43]

It was this oil-hungry world that OPEC faced when it broke the monopoly of Western oil companies. The extent of OPEC power, directly reflecting Western dependence on oil, is very clear from the American example. The United States became an importer in the 1970s. By 1976 it was importing 42 percent of its oil at a cost of $35 billion a year. Of its total 17.4 million barrels per day (mbd), it was importing 7.3 mbd (with 42 gallons per barrel). Almost 40 percent of this imported oil came from the Arab members of OPEC (AOPEC), four of which, Saudi Arabia, Kuwait, Iraq, and the United Arab Emirates, along with Iran, possess more than 50 percent of the world's known reserves and produce 40 percent of its supplies (see Figure 11-1).

In 1977 American oil imports cost more than $40 billion. The major suppliers were, from largest to smallest, Saudi Arabia, Venezuela, Nigeria, Libya, and Iran. In the summer of 1979, the United States was importing 45 percent or 9 million barrels *each day* out of a total of 21 million barrels used *each day.* From 1973 to 1979, American oil imports had increased more than 40 percent. Despite the clear warnings of 1973-74, it increased, rather than decreased, its dependence. In 1973, 70 percent of the oil the United States imported was from OPEC; by 1977 this figure had risen to 86 percent. The percentage of these imports from AOPEC rose from 22 to 43 percent. Then in late 1978 and early 1979, disaster struck. The Iranian cutback in oil production after the collapse of the shah stretched supplies so tightly that prices increased almost 100 percent in less than one year.[44] By December 1979 the price of oil stood at $24 a barrel, up from about $13 a barrel in January 1979. (Some countries, however, were already selling their oil for up to $40 a barrel in the tight market.) American oil costs for that one year alone rose $28 billion. By the spring of 1981, the average price had risen to $36 a barrel, an increase in just over a year of more than 100 percent. In 1982 the price stabilized at $34 a barrel, $21 higher than the price in 1973. Forecasts were unanimous that the future would be one of scarcity and persistent price increases.

Minipowers Versus Great Powers

There was an irony in this situation. None of the oil-producing states could be considered a major power, not even Iran with its substantial population. Most

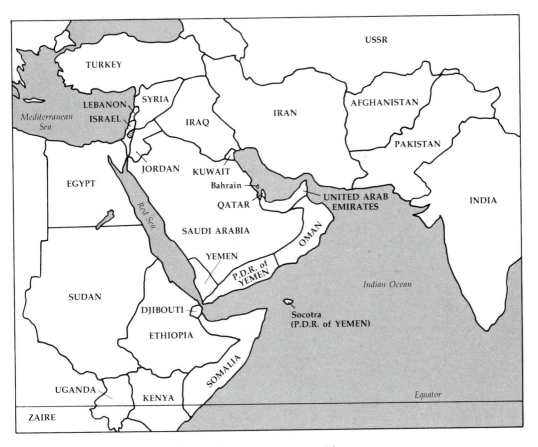

Figure 11-1 The Middle East and Northeastern Africa

of these states had small populations, little industry, and virtually no military muscle. All they had was oil! But with that oil they were able to influence not only the domestic affairs but also the Middle Eastern policies of the non-Communist industrial states. Japan first and then Western Europe acceded to Arab demands to show more sympathy for the Palestinian cause. Even the United States, long a major supporter of Israel, decided to play a more even-handed role, and, shortly after the 1973 war, Kissinger began trying to bring about a more lasting peace in the region. The weak had come to seem omnipotent, the strong impotent. It appeared that the world had turned upside down as one by one the Western states, former rulers of these small countries and still military giants relative to OPEC's members, complied with some Arab wishes. Clearly, power relations do not always follow the rule that the nation that can produce "more bang for a buck" can achieve its demands and successfully resist the demands of others.

Some OPEC members' highly public and dramatic use of their economic power seems to contradict our earlier conclusion that the exercise of economic sanctions is counterproductive. The most powerful military states in the world passively accepted high rates of inflation, recession, the declining value of the dollar, and continual oil price increases. Could there be much doubt that OPEC's price increases were far more damaging to the West than the loss of West Berlin, the placement of Soviet missiles in Cuba, or the loss of South Vietnam could ever have been? Can we disagree with Robert Tucker's conclusion that "it is the oil cartel, and not the rising military power of the Soviet Union, that has formed the greatest threat in the 1970s and early 1980s to the structure of American interests and commitments in the world."[45]

The key question, however, remains: How could modern countries, far larger in population and with sizable armed forces, repeatedly acquiesce in the raising of oil prices, which devastated their economies? One need but look at the obvious disparities in population and the size of the armed forces between some of the leading Arab oil producers and Western consuming nations at the time oil prices were at their peak (see Table 11-1). Were the oil barrels of the Arab and non-Arab OPEC members more powerful than the West's gun barrels? The very question suggests part of the answer: the West refused to use force in a situation that a half-century earlier would have resulted in a swift recourse to force.[46] OPEC claimed it had the right to determine prices for its oil and to deny that oil to Western nations through an embargo or reduced production. The West, by its acceptance of such measures, legitimated OPEC's claim. It has interpreted the principle of national self-

Table 11-1 Armed Forces of Leading Arab and Western Nations, 1981-1982

Country	Population	Armed Forces
Arab Oil-Producing Nations		
Saudi Arabia	10,395,000	51,700
Kuwait	1,460,000	12,400
Iraq	13,835,000	252,250
United Arab Emirates	950,000	42,500
Qatar	230,000	9,700
Western Consuming Nations		
United States	225,300,000	2,047,100
Britain	55,968,000	343,000
France	53,800,000	504,630
Germany (West)	61,665,000	495,000
Italy	57,200,000	366,000

SOURCE: Figures taken from International Institute for Strategic Studies, *The Military Balance 1981-1982* (Dorking: Bartholomew Press, 1981-1982).

determination to mean that, if another country owns resources it can do with them what it pleases, regardless of the difficulties inflicted on themselves and the rest of the world. In these circumstances, the use of force could only be considered illegitimate.

Indeed, this interpretation of the principle of national self-determination by the West led it to acquiesce in the virtual disregard by some OPEC members of their contracts. As Walter Levy, a noted oil expert, said in 1980 at the end of a decade of rising oil prices:

> The producing countries ... in fact do not recognize as binding supply or price arrangements even if freely concluded by them. Recently they have gone so far as to change agreed-upon prices retroactively. This, they argue, they are entitled to do under the doctrine of sovereign control by producing countries over their natural resources. ...
>
> Because of the fear of being arbitrarily cut off from supplies, Western nations and their [oil] companies now accept within a wide range practically any economic or political terms that a producing country may impose upon them.[47]

It was this subservience that encouraged OPEC continually to raise prices.

Leverage, Cartels, and Oil Gluts

OPEC's strong bargaining position from 1973 to 1979 reflected the following conditions:

> The West's substantial dependence on imported oil, so that even sharp increases in price did not quickly reduce demand by very much.
>
> Limited possibilities of substituting other energy sources for oil in the short run.
>
> A small number of producer nations that control most international trade in this commodity.
>
> Common political or economic goals among the exporting nations.
>
> The producers' invulnerability to embargo by consumer nations.

OPEC's attempt to exploit the market after the shah's fall from power proved to be the best antidote to its efforts to ride the oil-price escalator even higher. The conditions that had given OPEC its leverage during the 1970s began to change. First, the steepness of the price increases during this period resulted in genuine conservation measures, such as designing more fuel-efficient cars, commercial jets, housing, and appliances. Second, the number of non-OPEC oil sources increased; for example, Alaska, Mexico, and the North Sea (Norway and Britain). Third, this non-OPEC oil and the production of alternatives such as coal and natural gas were increasing at 4 percent a year. The high price of oil was also making coal and natural gas more profitable, resulting in expanded production. In addition, it stimulated research into areas such as oil shale, solar energy, and synthetic fuel, although the subsequent oil glut led to cutbacks in this research. Only nuclear energy was not expanding much because of popular opposition in many Western countries.

Fourth, OPEC members were often at odds with one another. As the 1980s began, Iran and Iraq were at war, and Libya sought the overthrow of the Saudi monarchy for allegedly allying itself with the United States and Israel and betraying the Arab cause. Fifth, the global recession led to a sharp reduction of demand for oil.

The consequence of the decreased demand for oil was an oil glut in the early 1980s and a downward pressure on prices. OPEC's eightfold increase in prices from 1973 to 1980 had by 1982 resulted in a drop of its share of the world oil market from almost 60 percent to less than 40 percent. Production was down 22 percent from 1981 and 45 percent from 1979. The official price of $34 per barrel of oil fell to $28. The decline of oil consumption continued, and non-OPEC oil production increased. OPEC's future as a producer cartel was in jeopardy. No longer able to firmly control the price of oil, its production by 1985 was down to 16 mbd from the 1979 high of 32 mbd. OPEC's members competed with one another for the largest share of the remaining oil market (while non-OPEC oil increased from 17 mbd to more than 27 mbd). The unofficial price at which members were willing to undersell one another fell further to below $20 by early 1986, dropping to the $10 to $12 range. Since 1973-74, the West has paid more than a trillion dollars to OPEC, the largest forced transfer of wealth since the Spanish conquistadors plundered gold from ancient Peru. This economic "bleeding" ended. The United States had by 1985 cut its dependence on oil imports to less than 30 percent from the 1977 peak of 46 percent; and, more important, it had shifted the source of most of its oil imports to Western Hemisphere countries (Canada, Mexico, and Venezuela).

OPEC, trying to survive, urged its members to eliminate the oil glut by sticking to the production cuts it set for each member. But that only gave rise to internal tensions. The oil-producing states with large populations needed all the money they could earn to stoke their development plans (Nigeria) or pay for their wars (Iran); cutbacks in production and revenues tended to be resisted. Preferred policy was to ignore national production levels established by OPEC, and produce more and sell at discounted prices. The burden of cutbacks therefore fell upon the large oil producers with smaller populations. They, too, had expensive economic plans for their modernization. The question was whether they, Saudi Arabia in particular, would reduce oil production enough and cut their earnings correspondingly to benefit states that were unwilling to cut back to the same degree, if at all. Some of these states, Libya and Iran, for example, were not even on friendly terms with the larger producers. Would a few states make such sacrifices for the organization when they could maximize their earnings by underselling other members?

The answer was no. Saudi oil income had declined from $100 billion in 1980 to $25 billion by 1985. The Saudis, therefore, announced that having reduced oil production from more than 10 mbd to a low of 2.5 mbd to shore up world oil prices and OPEC, they would no longer accept cuts of the Saudi quota of 4.3 million mbd; indeed, they would maintain their market share in the future by offering competitive prices and no longer selling at the officially set price. In short, the Saudis threatened to undersell other OPEC members if these members continued to sell more than the OPEC quotas set for them. But even had this move unified OPEC, it would not have been enough, for non-OPEC producers, like Britain, Norway, and Malaysia, also wanted to increase their earnings and therefore dropped their prices. The result was that in December 1985 OPEC decided to abandon its official policy of trying to defend its $28-a-barrel oil price through cuts in production.[48] OPEC thereby recognized as official policy what it was already practicing: most members were already producing over the levels set by OPEC or selling below the official price—or doing both.

The OPEC decision also meant that the organization was readying itself for a price war with non-OPEC oil producers, especially Britain, which had become a large producer (1 mbd). OPEC's goal was to retain its share of the world oil market, which had dropped from more than a half to only one-third in ten years. Nigeria, for example, desperate for income, could now match a British or Norwegian price reduction in order not to lose sales. In effect, OPEC was no longer even pretending to be a cartel. Oil prices were expected to fall unless the non-OPEC oil producers, also fearful of rapidly falling price, would agree to maintain prices. If not, the possibilities for cutting inflation, price reductions of all goods made with oil, and savings on transportation costs were promising; for countries like Mexico, seeking to repay their huge loans with oil money, the news was less happy, as it was for the banks that had made the loans.

Can OPEC be pronounced dead? Not yet. Consider these facts: oil remains an essential fuel; oil consumption still exceeds new discoveries by a ratio of 2:1; OPEC controls three-quarters of the world's known oil reserves; an upswing of the Western economies, stimulated by cheaper oil, will raise the demand for OPEC oil, strengthen its bargaining position; and render the Western industrial states vulnerable again to pricing pressures and possible supply disruptions; and political upheavals and political uses of oil remain a possibility.

Five main threats remain: (1) the producers' manipulation of oil supplies for economic or political purposes (the Yom Kippur War, 1973); (2) shortages of oil as a result of domestic unrest and revolution (Iran, 1979); (3) conflict among oil-producing states, reducing oil production (Iran-Iraq War, 1980—); (4) OPEC may once more pull together, cut production, and raise prices because of the large common losses (indeed, it attempted to overcome past differences in late 1986); and (5) either a possible Soviet invasion of the Persian Gulf area (a possibility that is not too likely, but one that U.S. policy since 1979 is committed to deter) or Soviet competition with the rest of the world for OPEC oil. The Soviet Union, not Saudi Arabia, is the world's largest oil producer, but in the mid-1980s its production declined somewhat. Whether that was the beginning of a major decline, as the CIA had first forecast in 1977, remains to be seen, but the CIA may have been correct that

Soviet oil production would peak, even if its forecast was several years too early. If the Soviet Union were to become an oil importer, would it seize the oil so near its southern border, or buy it, sending oil prices upwards in a more competitive environment?

ECONOMICS AND POWER

The Instrument of the Wealthy

Historically, the advanced economic powers have been able to exercise the most influence. Welfare states have been the powers because money buys arms. Wealthy states have been able to afford not only butter but all sorts of guns. Today the United States can afford to build strategic nuclear weapons and sizable conventional capabilities that are becoming increasingly more sophisticated and expensive and to exert economic influence. Britain, once the world's greatest military and economic power, can afford only relatively small conventional forces, which in 1956 could not even quickly defeat Egypt. Unable to afford to keep up with rapidly changing military technology, Britain has based its small "independent" nuclear force on American weapons. In 1979 U.S. military transport planes had to carry the British peacekeeping force to Rhodesia (now Zimbabwe); Britain did not have planes that could carry helicopters and jeeps. In 1982 Britain had only two small aircraft carriers, one of which had already been sold, to recover the Falkland Islands. The Royal Navy had been reduced to pay for Britain's nuclear deterrent.

Wealthy nations, however, have been able to afford not only all types of guns but also a whole range of nonmilitary instruments. As a result, they have not had to resort to force in the pursuit of their objectives as often as have weaker states. The more economically advanced states have been able to use their "economic weapons," such as their technology, food, economic aid, or access to their markets. Kenneth Waltz reminded us earlier that this " 'non-recourse to force' is the doctrine of the strong," or what Karl Marx called the replacement of the cannon by capital. E. H. Carr illustrated the point long ago: "Great Britain's unchallenged naval and economic supremacy throughout the nineteenth century enabled her to establish a commanding position in China with a minimum of military force and of economic discrimination. A relatively weak power like Russia could only hope to achieve a comparable result by naked aggression and annexation." [49] This does not mean that wealth per se confers power. During the 1960s it was popular to think that economic power could even substitute for military power. But the oil crisis of 1973 demonstrated convincingly that being an economic superpower like Japan or the EEC was not enough. Their very dependence upon imported oil made them vulnerable to Arab economic coercion.

It is, of course, this issue of the superior economic power of the West that is at the heart of Third World countries' current complaints about their continued poverty. The LDCs perceive the international political and economic order as grossly unfair, dominated by the First World, which makes the economic rules, receives the giant share of economic and political benefits, and keeps the Third World poor and subordinate. With some notable exceptions, the poor countries have had difficulties modernizing. The majority of the former colonies have been unable to earn enough to pay their way. They see the international laws of supply and demand as "stacking the deck" against them.

First, many of these countries have only one or two commodities to sell for foreign exchange with which to buy machinery and food. But this situation means that their income depends upon the health of the Western economies; their earnings fluctuate with the swings of the business cycle. Second, competition among raw-materials producers means that, as each nation works harder to produce more to raise its income, it merely succeeds in lowering the price through oversupply, thereby driving its income down. The increasing use of synthetic materials in Western states has made the situation even worse. Finally, the LDCs claim that what they buy in the West costs them more because of inflation. The "terms of trade," the difference between what they earn for the commodities they export and what they pay for Western imports in the so-called free market, favor the economically powerful over the economically weak.

To sum up the Third World's case—the rich have become rich by "plundering" the poor; Western industrialization, prosperity, and power have been built on the LDCs' cheap resources. Even with foreign aid and, in years of high employment in the West, increased export at world market prices, most Third World countries have not been able to earn sufficient revenues to modernize by organizing producer cartels and raising their own prices. Even OPEC's prices fell in the 1980s. In short, the LDCs, according to this view, are the victims of an international economy controlled by the rich industrial states. The poorer nations need access to their markets to earn a living, and they require Western economic aid, technical assistance, and technology to help them develop.

The Third World countries in the UN General Assembly have demanded a fairer international distribution of wealth in a new international economic order (NIEO). Underlying their demands is a sense of deep frustration and anger at their past subordinate status and exploitation, as well as a determination that their fate should be in their own hands. They are tired of their position in the international economy. The issue is one of power. The LDCs, while no longer colonies, are now what many of them call *pseudocolonies*. That is, they have not yet gained control over their own economic, and therefore political, destinies. Their economies remain tied to Western industry and are dependent for prosperity on exports and foreign markets, rather than on domestic consumption.

These complaints would not have surprised Friedrich List, a nineteenth-century German political economist, who, after studying the economy of Britain, the world's first industrial state to champion free trade, advised Germany against free trade.

> I saw clearly that free competition between two nations which are highly civilized can only be mutually beneficial in case both of them are in a nearly equal position of industrial development, and that any nation which owing to misfortune is behind others in industry, commerce, and navigation ... must first of all strengthen her own individual powers, in order to fit herself to enter into free competition with more advanced nations.[50]

The free market may well be a superior mechanism for allocating goods, when those competing and exchanging goods are of approximately equal power. When one nation is clearly more advanced economically, however, free trade benefits that nation more because it is able to penetrate the markets of weaker countries; if the latter do not protect themselves with tariffs to keep cheaper foreign imports out, home industries can never develop. During the initial stages of development, new industries are bound to be more expensive. Free trade is thus the weapon of the strong; tariffs to protect "infant industries" while they grow to efficiency are the weapon of the weak.

The laws of the free market are *not* neutral. Power is the "invisible hand" determining the distribution of wealth. Among nations that are equal in economic power, economic relations may well breed interdependence, as in the EEC and between the community and the United States. But between the economically strong and the economically weak, the inevitable result is the dependence of the latter. Economic weapons, then, remain "pre-eminently the weapons of strong Powers."[51]

Conditions for Economic Coercion

If wealth gives states a position of general influence, the actual exercise of economic coercion by any state depends upon three conditions: a high degree of control over the supply of goods and/or services the targeted state needs; an intense need of the targeted state for the economic goods and/or services; and a calculation by the targeted state that compliance with the demands made on it is less costly than doing without these goods and/or services.[52] These conditions gave OPEC leverage, even though its members possessed few of the normal components of power. The industrial countries' lives were so dependent upon imported oil that any major disruption would have played havoc with their economies. Paying higher prices was preferable to doing without. But these three conditions are frequently not present, as the examples of sanctions against Cuba and Yugoslavia, among others, show.

Sanctions are most effective if applied collectively; individual national sanctions are rarely effective. Even OPEC's collective influence has decreased as other sources of supply or alternative energies became available, and the need for energy declined as societies became more energy efficient. The critical condition is the cost calculation. Compliance is least likely if the cost to the targeted or coerced nation is perceived to be its national independence or what is sometimes called its national honor or prestige. States prefer to suffer economic or low politics deprivation before yielding to high politics demands.

Sanctions also involve costs for the nation imposing them. It is one thing to be angry at another nation's actions and to apply sanctions to demonstrate disapproval and compel the target nation to change its policies or simply desist from what it is doing. But sanctions are not cost-free, as farmers, businessmen, bankers, and even Olympic competitors in the United States and Western Europe have learned. Indeed, sanctions may involve substantial costs to the nation(s) seeking to punish or coerce another nation; and, as the quarrel among the Western allies over the Soviet pipeline showed, these costs may be political, not mainly economic. The key question, therefore, is always whether imposing sanctions is worth it, given the repeated demonstrations that economic sanctions provide little political leverage. Sanctions may, however, be applied for moral and political reasons (for example, to register disapproval of the Soviet invasion of Afghanistan or South Africa's treatment of its black population) and to cut domestic political losses.

Economics and Morality

Appearances of morality are not unimportant in the relations among nations and in the shaping of national reputations. The exercise of the economic weapon appears more moral than the military one, or perhaps we should say less immoral. In reality, it may be no more or less immoral. A wartime blockade may cause just as many—or more—people to starve to death as would be killed by high explosives in a series of air raids. Similarly, granting a nation political independence, even though economically it is dependent on foreign markets and not really in control of its own destiny, generally seems less immoral than direct political control by a foreign occupying power. Carr called the popular distinction between dollars and bullets an illusion. Power, he argued, is "one and indivisible."

> It uses military and economic weapons for the same ends. The strong will tend to prefer the minor and more "civilised" weapon because it will generally suffice to achieve his purposes; and as long as it will suffice, he is under no temptation to resort to the more hazardous military weapons. But economic power cannot be isolated from military power, nor military from economic. They are both integral parts of political power; and in the long run one is helpless without the other.... But generally speaking, there is a sense in which dollars are humaner than bullets even if the end pursued be the same.[53]

The Visible and 'Invisible' Uses of Coercion and Rewards

States have been more successful in attaining their aims by offering economic rewards than by depriving target nations of economic products and services.

Rewards promise economic improvement and higher standards of living. Such rewards led to Western Europe's economic recovery after World War II and to the strengthening of NATO. They provided the foundation upon which European nations have been integrating their economies and laying the basis for possible political union and status as a third superpower. They attracted the Soviet Union to détente. And, although economic aid in its various forms may not have given either superpower control over the LDC recipients or helped the latter to develop, it has helped stabilize regimes (at least in the short run) and enhanced the independence of some new nations, allowing them to resist seduction or pressure from the other superpower. Nor have all economic projects and technical-assistance programs been failures. Economic reward at least provides an incentive for improved political relations.

Whereas rewards can help to cement relations, economic punishment has generally proved ineffective in achieving high political purposes. That should not be surprising. Economic coercion cannot succeed if other markets or sources of supply are available to the target nation or if its leaders and people perceive the demands as affecting national integrity, pride, and independence. Richard Olsen has suggested, however, that the many instances of failure are all examples of publicly visible coercion. Economic coercion, he claims, can also be exerted "invisibly"—and more effectively:

> In most cases of economic coercion, the sanctions are more subtle; they are applied in areas in which the target is the solicitor: aid, investment, finance, and technology. Trade sanctions are usually highly visible. . . . Furthermore, trade, however unequal the terms, is a partnership in which groups in both the sender- and target-countries stand to lose when sanctions are applied. This is much less the case in the more subtle and complex areas of international technology transfers, finance, investment, and aid. Ours is a capital- and technique-scarce world, with keen competition among LDCs for what is available. . . .
>
> First World governments, their aid agencies, international financial institutions such as the World Bank or the regional development banks, private bank consortia, and multinational corporations are, for many LDCs, integral and influential parts of the domestic economy and policy-making apparatus. Dependency is indeed vulnerability; as George Ball has asked in apparent commiseration: "How can a national government make an economic plan with any confidence if a board of directors meeting 5,000 miles away can by altering its pattern of purchasing and production affect in a major way the country's economic life?" [54]

Publicly applied economic sanctions tend to fail to achieve high political goals, but "relatively covert, subtle economic sanctions will ultimately be *politically* effective with only moderate, purely *economic* effects." [55] Dependence thus allows for the exercise of economic coercion without publicity and patriotic rallying around the flag in the target state. Not publicly announced cuts in quotas or embargoes but delays in delivery of spare parts, drying up of credit, decline in value of investments, reduction of multilateral and bilateral loans, and refusal to refinance debts are more effective, though less visible, means of coercion. They can create economic pain while avoiding the mobilization of nationalism in the targeted state, which would allow it to resist efforts at coercion.

TRADE AND THE NEW MERCANTILISM

International economics, like international politics, occurs in a decentralized system.[56] In the absence of a legitimate world government to allocate goods peacefully and manage economic relations among states in accordance with their needs, states fall back on their own resources to achieve their economic aims. If international politics is "politics without government," it is the distribution of power that largely determines "who get what, when, and how." The efforts by states to maintain or enhance their wealth or welfare is as much a Hobbesian struggle as is their quest for security and prestige. Or, perhaps more accurately, economic goals are pursued by states by much the same mix of conflict, competition, and cooperation as are the noneconomic goals. The pursuit of prosperity in a world in which wealth is unequally distributed and resources are finite is bound to lead to conflict over access to markets and control over, or assured access to, certain natural resources. At the same time, states often share certain goals, such as expanding international trade, even if they disagree on how to do it, or, negatively, how to avoid disaster, such as preventing the debt bomb from exploding.

Indeed, what is striking about international economics is the degree to which politics shapes economic policies. Diplomatic and strategic goals frequently influence trade policies. Great powers may try to become as self-sufficient as possible to avoid depending on foreign sources of supply. The U.S. reaction to OPEC's price rises was to reduce dependence on Arab oil; Western Europe sought to diversify its energy dependence on the Middle East by seeking natural gas from the Soviet Union; Moscow would not allow itself to become too "interdependent" with the United States, despite its need for American technology, lest its freedom of political action be constrained. States also use embargoes and boycotts. The United States has been particularly prone to use them, as in the embargo on all strategic goods against the Soviet Union during the cold war and after Afghanistan and another on grain and modern technology, or the embargoes against Nicaragua and South Africa. Foreign aid has also been an obvious instrument of influence for the two superpowers, as well as a means for the former European colonial powers to maintain some degree of influence in LDCs. Perhaps the most devastating political usage of economic power was the Arab OPEC members' embargo and hike in oil prices in an effort to persuade the United States, Western Europe, and Japan to be more accommodating to Palestinian interests in the Middle East peace process. Western Europe and Japan, far more dependent on Arab oil than the United States, did succumb to this pressure, although it is only fair to add that they were generally more sympathetic to the possibility of a

Palestinian state than was the United States.

Even more striking than that governments should use economic tools to advance their interests is the degree to which the structure and operation of the international economy reflects that of the international political system. When Britain was the greatest power in the nineteenth century, the international economic system was one of free trade. Because Britain had the most advanced economy, free trade—that is, access to other nations' markets—was in its interest. After World War II, the United States, preeminent because of its enormous industrial capacity and technological skills, also established a free-trade system in the West; the result has been a high degree of interdependence among Western states (which may include Japan). The Soviet Union in its sphere organized a centralized economy. As adversaries, East and West remained independent of one another politically and economically until the detente of the 1970s. As the Third World countries emerged from colonialism, North-South economic relations remained basically as one of inequality or dependency. Thus, the threefold political divisions of the world had their economic counterparts. Politics and economics are simply inseparable, and the term *political economy* appropriately describes everything that happens in the international economy.

Ironically, it was in the Western system that the United States was having economic difficulties in the 1970s and 1980s. This economy became increasingly characterized by interdependence as the open, capitalist economies interacted with one another in a vastly expanded system of trade, investment, production, and marketing. The United States historically has not been dependent upon foreign trade. In 1939, 1949, 1959, and even 1969, it constituted no more than 5 percent of the nation's GNP. If imports had been cut as late as 1969, it would have affected few Americans; some might have missed their Mercedes-Benz automobiles and a few more the bananas with their breakfast cereal. But by 1979, had imports been cut, millions of Americans would have felt it immediately had they been deprived of their Japanese cars and video recorders.

The United States, long isolated from the world economy, had become part of an interdependent economy. This fact was one of the chief reasons for America's "de-industrialization." American workers are highly paid: to remain competitive, industry moved overseas where workers earned lower wages and where markets were closer and transportation costs less. Moreover, as the Europeans formed a Common Market by eliminating trade barriers between their countries and protecting Europe's industries with a common tariff against foreign competition, U.S. industry invested in Europe as well. The escalating oil prices of the 1970s, as noted earlier, speeded up the decline of U.S. industries like steel, automobiles, textiles, and electronic appliances.

Not only traditional industries but also new high-technology industries are affected. The American tool industry has declined. Not a single video recorder, a high-technology product, is manufactured in the United States; many computers with American names, like IBM, are manufactured in Japan and South Korea. The overvalued dollar of the early 1980s further hurt American industry, but its decline did not significantly reverse the growing trade deficits. These deficits with Canada, Europe, and Japan had grown to a record $148 billion by the end of 1985; with Japan it had grown to an enormous $50 billion. In January 1986 America's deficits with Canada, the Common Market, Japan, OPEC, and the LDCs ran $1.7, $2.5, $5.5, $1.8, and $6 billion, respectively. For selected products the largest deficits were in petroleum and petroleum products ($4.7 billion), automobiles ($3 billion), and clothing ($1.4 billion); only agriculture showed a small surplus.[57] For the first six months of 1986, the deficit was $84 billion, and the estimated total deficit for 1986 was $156 billion.

The decline of American industry and the huge trade deficit, however, were due only partly to the growing inefficiency and uncompetitiveness of some segments of the economy and to Reagan budget deficits as the administration launched its military buildup at the same time it cut taxes. They were also the result of a new mercantilism, a reaction to the new interdependence.[58] Mercantilism was the prevailing policy from the fifteenth to the eighteenth centuries as states sought to enhance their power by increasing national wealth then associated with the accumulation of gold. State-directed mercantilism was a policy under which political concerns directed economic activity. The relevance of this policy for today is that it has been increasingly adopted by America's partners in the Western economy in an effort to maintain employment and stoke economic growth. The Common Market countries and Japan adopted aggressive export policies, subsidizing the products of their less competitive industries so that they could undersell American products in the United States; simultaneously, they tried to keep imports down.

Japan has been especially aggressive in this respect. In its case, the efficiency of industry, the inventiveness of its engineers (thanks to its educational system), and the quality production and consumer appeal of many of its products are major reasons for the large trade imbalance with the United States. Japanese stereo equipment, televisions, video equipment, cameras, calculators, watches, and office machinery are everywhere; Japanese steel is cheaper in Ohio than Ohio-made steel, and Japanese cars have taken an increasing percentage of the U.S. market. The Japanese may well be ahead of the United States in robotics and in the next generation of computer chips (which they are accused of selling at substantially below production costs). The reason for this success has been the close working relationship of government and industry. In Japan the Ministry of International Trade and Industry (MITI) selects the industries that are to grow and targets the countries whose markets are to be penetrated; it coordinates these plans with research and investment capital. Since 1945 Japan has passed the Soviet Union in industrial production and is second only to the United States; at its current rate of expansion, it may emerge as a greater industrial power than the United States within the next two decades!

State-guided national trade policy, in brief, has made Japan an economic giant. President Reagan's secretary of commerce, in calling Japan's trading practices "unfair," asserted, "Japanese export policy has as its objective not participation in, but dominance of, world markets." [59] All of America's trading partners have to varying degrees adopted mercantilist policy, even if Japan is by far the most efficient and effective. And behind Japan, sometimes called the "Big Dragon," stand the "four little dragons," Hong Kong, Singapore, Taiwan, and South Korea, which we usually more politely call the Newly Industrialized Countries (NICs).

States, we need to remind ourselves in this age of growing economic interdependence, remain driven by their national concerns. As each country seeks to increase its employment and prosperity by exporting as much as possible while holding down imports, the United States, because it still believes in free trade and is a very large market, attracts these exports. Protectionist demands in the United States in order to promote "fair trade" are a loser's response to this intense economic competition. The fact is that world trade has become another form of international conflict among states as international commerce has been increasingly managed by governments in all countries except, until recently, the United States.[60] In these circumstances, the "voluntary" quotas by some countries on certain imports to the United States, the tariffs, and other means of protecting American goods will not work well over the long run.

Protectionist pressures, however, are likely to grow stronger in an increasingly competitive—and changing—world economy. The trend in industrial economies is for production to become "uncoupled" from employment. Peter Drucker has argued that it is less the American economy than American labor that is becoming "de-industrialized" and that this is true in all industrial states. "If a company, an industry or a country does not in the next quarter of a century sharply increase manufacturing production and at the same time sharply reduce the blue-collar work force, it cannot hope to remain competitive—or even to remain 'developed.' It would decline fairly fast." [61] The reasons: "robotization" or "automation," the shift in industries from labor-intensive to knowledge-intensive industries, as well as the trend from large manufacturers to middle-sized and smaller plants.[62]

American farmers will also seek protection or other kinds of government help. U.S. agricultural production has for years been very efficient, and the United States has been a food basket for the world. In 1981, a banner year, American farmers exported a record 162 million metric tons worth $44 billion.[63] Throughout the 1970s, when dollars were flowing out at a record level to pay for oil, large agricultural sales on the international market were the main reasons the trade imbalances did not become even larger. But since 1981 the volume of these exports has declined, due in part to the high value of the dollar and the practice of other countries of underselling the United States. Morover, the 1979 U.S. grain embargo against the Soviet Union (above the level set by an earlier Soviet-American agreement) led the Soviets to look for suppliers who would not cut off shipments for political reasons. (The anti-Soviet Reagan administration, admittedly, signed a new agreement with Moscow stating that the United States would not embargo future food shipments to the Soviet Union, presumably regardless of political circumstances!)

The trade patterns in world food exports are changing drastically (see Chapter 14). India is beginning to export grain; China's agricultural production has greatly increased in recent years; other LDCs, such as South Korea and Thailand, will soon become greater agricultural producers and exporters; and the European Economic Community is greatly overproducing food items (see Chapter 19). Many of these developing and developed countries were until recently food importers. Intense competition among old and new food producers for a share of the international market is thus a prospect for the future. Indeed, 1985 American grain exports were down by about 50 percent from the 1981 level of 48 million metric tons, and this surplus grain cost the United States approximately $20 billion per year to store. The United States therefore decided in 1985 to do what other countries have been doing: subsidize farm products for export and sell them at competitive world prices. But it is doubtful the United States will recover much of its share of the world market lost since 1981 because America's competitors are determined to preserve their market shares.

The problem is not limited only to grain. American farmers are faced with increasing amounts of food imports in everyday staples. The prospect is of an even greater trade deficit in farm products, once the source of huge export earnings. As in industrial goods, the high value of the dollar has hurt, but so has cheaper farm labor. Apples can be picked in Chile and flown to Boston, where they can be sold cheaper than apples grown in New York State. Lower costs like this have encouraged American food companies to sign contracts abroad for meat, fruits, and vegetables, and many have built food processing plants there.[64] Obviously, all this will add to protectionist pressures.

Allies and friendly nations trying to advance common security interests, as a result, are becoming economic competitors, waging "trade wars," and working at cross-purposes with one another. For example, in the future we may talk specifically of "orange juice wars," the United States, especially Florida, versus Brazil. More accurately, a trade war of this type may be called a *subsidy war*. Such conflicts are, however, bad economics. Protectionism and subsidies invite retaliation, permit the survival of inefficient producers who cannot compete, raise domestic prices for these goods for consumers whose taxes are keeping the producers in business, and decrease exports because if other states cannot earn dollars with imports, they cannot afford to buy as many American goods.

Given the ever widening trade imbalance among the West's leading traders (the United States and Japan, as well as West Germany), the piling up of agricultural surpluses as subsidies for farmers have skyrocketed, and the crushing debt bomb a new trading system, will have to be negotiated. Indeed, in an effort to stimulate economic growth and stop the increasing move to protectionism, global trade negotiation began in late 1986 when seventy-four nations met under the sponsorship of the General Agreement on Tariffs and Trade, an organization committed to drawing up the rules of free trade. The United States may also have to think of a national industrial strategy, a form of business-oriented national planning. In a world in which trade has become a source of conflict even among allies, the stakes in terms of employment levels, national prosperity, and alliance relationships are great.

Notes

1. Robert W. Tucker, "A New International Order?" *Commentary*, February 1975, 44.
2. E. H. Carr, *The Twenty Years' Crisis 1919-1939* (London: Macmillan, 1951), 120.
3. The books in which the impact of economics on international politics and the uses of economic means for political ends were first explored are David H. Blake and Robert S. Walters, *The Politics of Global Economic Relations*, 2d ed. (Englewood Cliffs, N.J.: Prentice-Hall, 1983); Joan Edelman Spero, *The Politics of International Economic Relations*, 2d ed. (New York: St. Martin's Press, 1981); and C. Fred Bergsten, *The Future of the International Economic Order* (Lexington, Mass.: D. C. Heath, 1973). See also various articles by Bergsten: "The Threat from the Third World," *Foreign Policy*, Summer 1973, 102-134; "The Responses to the Third World," *Foreign Policy*, Winter 1974-1975, 3-34; and "Coming Investment Wars?" *Foreign Affairs* (October 1974): 153-175. Finally, see C. Fred Bergsten and Lawrence B. Krause, eds., *World Politics and International Economics* (Washington, D.C.: The Brookings Institution, 1975).
4. Theodore Ropp, *War in the Modern World*, 2d ed. (New York: Collier, 1962), 203-204.
5. Paul M. Kennedy, *The Rise and Fall of British Naval Mastery* (Malabar, Fla.: Robert E. Krieger, 1982), 306-309.
6. Williamson Murray, *The Change in the European Balance of Power* (Princeton, N.J.: Princeton University Press, 1984), 4-27.
7. For analyses of the feasibility of economic leverage, see Samuel P. Huntington et al., "Trade, Technology and Leverage," *Foreign Policy*, Fall 1978, 63-106; and Herbert S. Levin, Francis W. Rushing, and Charles M. Movit, "The Potential for U.S. Economic Leverage on the USSR," *Comparative Strategy*, I (1979), 371-404.
8. *New York Times*, June 29, 1979.
9. Marshall I. Goldman, "Will the Soviet Union Be an Autarky in 1984?" *International Security*, Spring 1979, 18-37.
10. Michael Mastanduno, "Strategies of Economic Containment: U.S. Trade Relations with the Soviet Union," *World Politics*, July 1985, 515.
11. See Walter C. Clemens, Jr., *The U.S.S.R. and Global Interdependence* (Washington, D.C.: American Enterprise Institute, 1978) for a skeptical interpretation of the likely impact of interdependence on the Soviet Union. See also Elliot Hurwitz, "The Politics of Soviet Trade," *New York Times*, Aug. 25, 1980.
12. Mikhail Bernstein and Seymour Martin Lipset, "Punishing Russia," *New Republic*, Aug. 5, 1985.
13. Clemens, *U.S.S.R. and Global Interdependence*.
14. Quoted in *The Fifteen Weeks* by Joseph M. Jones (New York: Viking, 1955), 80.

15. An excellent book that conveys the feelings of this period in both Europe and the United States is Theodore H. White, *Fire in the Ashes* (New York: Sloane, 1953). See also White, *In Search of History* (New York: Warner Books, 1979), 263-306.

16. Joseph L. Nogee and John W. Sloan, "Allende's Chile and the Soviet Union," *Journal of Interamerican Studies and World Affairs* (August 1979): 339-365.

17. Andrés Suarez, *Cuba* (Cambridge, Mass.: M.I.T. Press, 1967), 86.

18. Richard S. Olson, "Economic Coercion in World Politics: With a Focus on North-South Relations," *World Politics*, July 1979, 472-479; and Anna P. Schreiber, "Economic Coercion as an Instrument of Foreign Policy: U.S. Economic Measures Against Cuba and the Dominican Republic," *World Politics*, April 1973, 387-413. Also see Otto Wolff von Ameringen, "Commentary: Economic Sanctions as a Foreign Policy Tool?" *International Security*, Fall 1980, 159-167; and James M. Lindsay, "Trade Sanctions as Political Instruments: A Re-Examination," *International Studies Quarterly* (June 1986): 153-173.

19. Paul E. Sigmund, "The 'Invisible Blockade' and the Overthrow of Allende," *Foreign Affairs* (January 1974): 339-340.

20. A. Doak Barnett, *China and the Major Powers in East Asia* (Washington, D.C.: The Brookings Institution, 1977), 41.

21. Ibid., 41-42.

22. George Liska, *The New Statecraft* (Chicago: University of Chicago Press, 1960), 3.

23. See Joseph S. Berliner, *Soviet Economic Aid* (New York: Holt, Rinehart & Winston, 1958), 179-180; and Hans Heymann, Jr., "Soviet Foreign Aid as a Problem for U.S. Policy," *World Politics*, July 1960, 525-540. Also see Wynfred Joshua and Stephen P. Gibert, *Arms for the Third World* (Baltimore: Johns Hopkins University Press, 1969).

24. Berliner, *Soviet Economic Aid*, 171-177.

25. Heymann, "Soviet Foreign Aid," 538-539.

26. For the classification of aid generally followed here, see the excellent article by Hans J. Morgenthau, "A Political Theory of Foreign Aid," *American Political Science Review* (June 1962): 301-309.

27. For a good study of cold war American aid programs, see Joan M. Nelson, *Aid, Influence and Foreign Policy* (New York: Macmillan, 1968).

28. Samuel P. Huntington, *Political Order in Changing Societies* (New Haven, Conn.: Yale University Press, 1968), 8.

29. This assumption was never made explicit in the doctrine of foreign aid, for reasons analyzed by Robert A. Pakenham, "Developmental Doctrines in Foreign Aid," *World Politics*, January 1966, 194-225; and Packenham, *Liberal America and the Third World* (Princeton, N.J.: Princeton University Press, 1973).

30. William Ebenstein, ed., *Great Political Thinkers*, 3d ed. (New York: Holt, Rinehart & Winston, 1960), 105.

31. David M. Potter, *People of Plenty* (Chicago: University of Chicago Press, 1954), 118-119.

32. See Eugene R. Black, *The Diplomacy of Economic Development* (New York: Harper & Row, 1966), 19, 23. For a general analysis of the conditions necessary for democracy to flourish, see Seymour M. Lipset, *Political Man* (Garden City, N.Y.: Doubleday, 1959), 45-67.

33. Robert L. Rothstein, *The Weak in the World of the Strong* (New York: Columbia University Press, 1977), 160.

34. Elizabeth Kridl Valkenier, "New Trends in Soviet Economic Relations with the Third World," *World Politics*, April 1970, 415-432; and Valkenier, *The Soviet Union*

and the Third World (New York: Praeger Publishers, 1985). Also see Jerry F. Hough, *The Struggle for the Third World* (Washington, D.C.: The Brookings Institution, 1986).

35. Carol R. Saivetz and Sylvia Woodby, *Soviet-Third World Relations* (Boulder, Colo.: Westview Press, 1985), 134-135, 142-147.

36. Francis Fukuyamu, "Gorbachev and the Third World," *Foreign Affairs* (Spring 1986): 715-731.

37. Diana Tussie, *Latin America in the World Economy* (New York: St. Martin's Press, 1983).

38. Carlos Fuentes, "The Real Latin Threat," *New York Times*, Sept. 15, 1985.

39. Abraham F. Lowenthal, "Threat and Opportunity," in "America and the World 1985," *Foreign Affairs* (1986): 558-561.

40. *New York Times*, Sept. 26, 1985; also see Harold Lever and Christopher Huhre, *Debt and Danger* (Boston: The Atlantic Monthly Press, 1986).

41. *New York Times*, May 11, 1984.

42. U.S. Department of State, Bureau of Public Affairs, *U.S. Prosperity and the Developing Countries* (Washington, D.C.: Government Printing Office, January 1985).

43. Alan L. Madian, "Oil Is Still Too Cheap," *Foreign Policy*, Summer 1979, 173-174.

44. On the collapse of the shah, see George Lenczowski, "The Arc of Crisis," *Foreign Affairs* (Spring 1979): 796-820; and Richard Cottam et al., "The United States and Iran's Revolution," *Foreign Policy*, Spring 1979, 3-34; and especially Gary Sick, *All Fall Down* (New York: Random House, 1985).

45. Robert W. Tucker, "Oil and American Power," *Commentary*, September 1979, 39.

46. See Louis J. Halle, "Does War Have a Future?" *Foreign Affairs* (October 1973): 20-34; and Klaus Knorr, *On the Uses of Military Power in the Nuclear Age* (Princeton, N.J.: Princeton University Press, 1966); and Knorr, "The Limits of Power," in *The Oil Crisis*, ed. Raymond Vernon (New York: W. W. Norton, 1976), 229-243.

47. Walter J. Levy, "Oil and the Decline of the West," *Foreign Affairs* (Summer 1980): 1003-1004.

48. *New York Times*, Dec. 9, 1985.

49. Carr, *Twenty Years' Crisis*, 130.

50. Quoted in Edward Mead Earle, "Adam Smith, Alexander Hamilton, Friedrich List: The Economic Foundations of Military Power," in *Makers of Modern Strategy* (Princeton, N.J.: Princeton University Press, 1943), 140.

51. Carr, *Twenty Years' Crisis*, 131.

52. Klaus Knorr, "International Economic Leverage and Its Uses," in *Economic Issues and National Security*, ed. Knorr and Frank Trager (Lawrence, Kan.: Allen Press, 1977), 99-125; and James A. Nathan and James K. Oliver, "The Growing Importance of Economics: Can the United States Manage this Phenomenon?" in *Evolving Strategic Issues*, ed. Franklin D. Margiotta (Washington, D.C.: National Defense University Press), 73-99.

53. Carr, *Twenty Years' Crisis*, 131, 132.

54. Olson, "Economic Coercion," 477, 481.

55. Ibid., 485.

56. See especially Spero, *Politics of International Economic Relations*, 1-18.

57. Department of Commerce figures, *New York Times*, March 9, 1986.

58. Kevin T. Phillips, *Staying on Top* (New York: Random House, 1985); also see Miles Kahler, "European Protectionism in Theory and Practice," *World Politics*, July 1985, 475-502.

59. Quoted by Theodore H. White, "The Danger from Japan," *New York Times Magazine*, July 28, 1985, 43.

60. Phillips, *Staying on Top*; and Daniel Patrick Moynihan, "Centralize Trade Policy," *New York Times*, Jan. 16, 1983.

61. Peter F. Drucker, "The Changed World Economy," *Foreign Affairs* (Spring 1986): 777.

62. Ibid., 777-778.

63. *New York Times*, April 20, 1986.

64. *New York Times*, Aug. 3, 1986.

CHAPTER 12

Multipolarity and the Proliferation of Conflict

STABLE NUCLEAR BIPOLARITY—AND BEYOND

Our analysis of bipolar international politics has revealed two main powers, watching and countering each other's every move. As a consequence, the bipolar system has been characterized by numerous confrontations and crises, and each nation has anticipated the possibility of a preventive or preemptive strike by its opponent. Not surprisingly, many observers consider such a bipolar structure unstable and prone to erupt into war. Yet in the forty years since World War II, total war has not occurred. How can that be explained?

Although Kenneth Waltz has argued that bipolar systems are stable, we have tried to demonstrate (especially in Chapters 8 through 10) that regardless of whether nonnuclear bipolarity was unstable or stable, the existence of nuclear arms provides the key to the two superpowers' success in preserving peace, despite the scope and intensity of their rivalry. They have repeatedly tested each other, but the fear of committing nuclear suicide has imposed the restraint they might not otherwise have exercised. Before nuclear weapons, nations overestimating their own power and underestimating that of their adversaries frequently caused wars; in the nuclear age, policy makers have had to be more careful. The result has been an emphasis on deterrence, crisis management, and limited war. Total war no longer seems a rational instrument of national policy; crises have become the ultimate instrument, the substitute for war, as one state has attempted to shift the status quo and the other has resisted. The post-1945 nuclear bipolar balance, unlike the prenuclear bipolar balance, therefore, has been a stable balance.

To ensure this, the two powers have negotiated a number of arms control agreements (see Table 12-1). Though adversaries, they have found it necessary

Table 12-1 Arms Control

Objective	Agreement	Year
Quantitative and qualitative limits	SALT I ABM agreement	1972
Strategic delivery systems	SALT I interim agreement on offensive arms	1972
	Vladivostok guidelines	1974
	SALT II[a]	1979
Direct communication between U.S. and Soviet leaders during crises	Hot-line agreement	1963
	Hot-line modernization agreement	1971
Barring nuclear weapons from specific regions	Antarctica treaty[b]	1959
	Outer-space treaty[b]	1967
	Seabed treaty[b]	1971
Discouragement of nuclear proliferation	International Atomic Energy Authority[b]	1954
	Nonproliferation treaty[b]	1968
	Nuclear Suppliers' Club	1975
Limiting of nuclear tests	Limited test-ban treaty[b]	1963
	Threshold test-ban treaty[a]	1974
	Peaceful nuclear-explosion treaty[a]	1976
Banning nonnuclear weapons of mass destruction	Biological-weapons convention	1972

[a] Signed but not in force because of Senate refusal to ratify.

[b] Multilateral agreements.

to cooperate on this issue. Arms control agreements constitute a mutual antisuicide suicide pact that transforms their relationship from a purely adversary one to an *adversary partnership* composed of elements of both conflict and cooperation.

The passing of bipolarity is not, however, likely to produce a genuine multipolarity in which half a dozen or more powers have approximately equal capability. That cannot develop until countries such as China, India, and possibly Brazil become full-fledged powers, with sizable populations, large-scale industries, and military strength to match the capabilities of the present superpowers, and until the countries of the European Economic Community (EEC) can unite politically to form a United States of Europe. None of these events is likely to occur in the next decade or two.

A system between bipolarity and multipolarity might be called *bipolycentric*. As awkward as that term is, it aptly represents the two elements of the contemporary international system. The *bi* refers to the continuing superpower status of the United States and the Soviet Union. Their relationship is still critical. Since the dangerous confrontation of the Cuban missile crisis, this relationship has become more complex, mixing elements of conflict, competition, and cooperation. Given the stark alternatives of coexistence or nonexistence and the recognition that their fate is inextricably bound together, the need to negotiate and reduce tensions, if possible, is obvious. Hence the two powers have become locked in what we have referred to as an adversary partnership, combining a changing mix of cold war and détente, competition and accommodation over time.

The *polycentric* in bipolycentric refers primarily to the many new state actors, or centers of foreign policy. In a multipolar system, there are a number of roughly equal great powers; in a polycentric system, there are numerous actors whose power varies considerably, although none of them is the equal of the superpowers, who remain at the top of the state hierarchy. But weak or relatively strong, compared to neighboring states, their actions affect events in the international system, and the consequences of their behavior may be dangerous, whether it is Egypt and Syria going to war with Israel, Bangladesh seceding from Pakistan, Iran seizing American hostages, or Iraq going to war with Iran. The world is no longer as dominated or controlled by the superpowers as in the bipolar days; even their allies who continue to rely upon them for their security have regained a considerable measure of diplomatic freedom. In a sense, it is precisely because the superpowers are stalemated while continuing to be the producers of their allies' security, that the latter have been able to take advantage of this stalemate to become once more independent centers of foreign policy decisions.

This system will not enjoy the stability that generally characterizes a multipolar system, partly because nuclear weapons have tended to reverse the characteristics of bipolarity and multipolarity. That is, nuclear bipolarity tends to be stable, and nuclear multipolarity will tend to be unstable. The reasons for the probable instability of a nuclear, bipolycentric system are complex and numerous.

THE MULTIPLICATION OF STATES

One reason for such instability is the multiplication of states. In 1939, on the eve of World War II, there were only 60 states in the world. Thirty-five years later, in 1974, Guinea, a Portuguese colony, became the Republic of Guinea-Bissau, the 150th state; by 1986 there were nearly 170 states, and this birthrate continues. Whether there are 175, 200, or even more states in another decade or two, the number will be unprecedented. Furthermore, this proliferation of states poses unprecedented problems. In the year 2000, if U.S. State Department estimates are reasonably accurate, many of the existing states will have tiny populations. About 60 percent of them will be smaller than metropolitan Chicago; about 50 of them will have populations too small to fill the Astrodome. The increasing number of microstates, such as the Cape Verde Islands, the Seychelles, and the Maldives (each of which has a population of fewer than 300,000), and submicrostates, such as Grenada, Nauru, Ifni, and Tonga (with fewer than 100,000 people), that in the United Nations General Assembly will have a vote equal to that of larger countries, raises basic questions about the legal fiction and international practice of equality among states.

In spite of the right of peoples to be politically independent and to manage their own affairs, are such states "irrespective of their size and ability to fulfill their responsibility .... also ... entitled to sovereign equality in the affairs of the community of nations? " [1] Does the right to self-determination justify the equal participation of such Lilliputian countries in the affairs of the state system? Should eighty member-states of the United Nations, each paying 0.02 percent of the organization's budget—for a total of 1.6 percent—be able to impose their views on a country such as the United States, which pays 25 percent of the budget but also has only one vote? With a few other small states, which together contribute 2.5 percent of the United Nations' budget, these ministates would actually be able to mobilize two-thirds of the vote in the General Assembly. More broadly, are the richer nations, including the Soviet Union, obligated politically and morally to support these wards of the system because it is the "democratic" thing to do? Does the system have to be fragmented, or decentralized, even further for the sake of national self-determination, a principle that is being invoked increasingly on behalf of secessionist movements in existing states (many of which are new states)? Who is supposed to take care of these states? Many of them do not meet any but legal criteria of statehood; they usually do not have viable economies or the capability to defend themselves. Because these states have equal votes in the General Assembly, a majority of them can demand that the wealthier states take care of them. Will the rule of "one state, one vote" survive this demand?

THE INCREASE IN CONFLICT

A second reason for the instability of a polycentric system follows from the multiplication of Third World states in the wake of the collapse of European colonialism: the more states there are, the greater are the opportunities for conflict.

No Safety in Numbers

The competing aims of many states are a likely source of conflict. The logic of earlier forms of multipolarity does not apply. For example, it has been claimed that a major cause of multipolar stability is that each state must divide its attention among many other states. It is unable to concentrate on any single state, thus reducing the possibility of the intense interaction, confrontation, and enmity associated with bipolarity (see Chapter 6). In a system of nearly 170 states, it may be that each will be compelled to divide its attention among several possible adversaries, but it is also true that the number of potential occasions for friction among states will vastly increase. Furthermore, the attention of involved states will not be divided equally. Some conflicts will clearly attract more attention than others because the perceived interests and stakes will be higher. It can be predicted that the amount of strife and the passions aroused will surely make the system increasingly dangerous. Stanley Hoffmann said rather pessimistically:

> An elementary rule of the game is this: every player, from the lowliest to the most eminent, will try to find, develop, and exploit some asset in order either to maximize his influence or to ensure his security. But when all do this simultaneously, the outcome on the chessboard, inevitably, may be frustration for many and a threat of chaos for all.[2]

Intranational Divisions

More specifically, conflict among the many new states will arise from a variety of causes, particularly the continuing ethnic, religious, racial, and linguistic divisions within the highly nationalistic, less-developed countries (LDCs). The basic problem, inherited from the colonial rulers who drew the frontiers of these "nations," is that many ethnic groups were at that time divided among two or more colonies, and at the same time other ethnic groups suddenly found themselves lumped together in the new colonial country. The postcolonial states have inherited these boundaries, and the results have been, on the one hand, irredentism and, on the other, separatism.

Irredentism.   *Irredentism* is the movement by one state to incorporate within its boundaries the portion of its predominant ethnic group that has been separated from it plus the territory on which that portion lives. Political borders, it is claimed, should coincide with ethnic and regional boundaries. In the drive to reunite divided "peoples," frontiers become objects of conflict among the less-developed countries. For example, Somalia has claimed the right to portions of Ethiopia and Kenya; the claim against Ethiopia led to an undeclared war, in which Soviet and Cuban intervention prevented Somalia from incorporating part of Ethiopia.

Separatism.   *Separatism* is a movement for self-determination. The new LDCs have invoked this principle to legitimate their claims to independence from colonial rulers. But now it is being invoked against them by ethnic groups in their own populations, which could lead to national disintegration. An attempt to secede may lead to civil war as the government resists (as in Zaire after it became independent from Belgium, or in Nigeria). It can even lead to international war if another state becomes involved. For example, when East Pakistan sought to secede from Pakistan in the 1970s, its people were dealt with brutally by the Pakistani army; millions fled to India. The cost of feeding and caring for all these refugees was so high that war seemed cheaper. India therefore fought and defeated Pakistan and established the state of Bangladesh in what formerly had been East Pakistan. This move also weakened Pakistan so that it could no longer seriously rival India on the subcontinent. Some secessionist movements are successful, as in the instance of Bangladesh; others, such as those in Nigeria and Ethiopia, have failed; and still others smolder and flare up once in a while.

Rivalry for Regional Leadership

More frequent conflict in a polycentric system may also stem from the fact that, among the many member states, some will seek to become more influential than others, generating further friction. Sometimes such nations are called regional powers; some examples are India, Brazil, Nigeria, Iran, Iraq, and Syria. The term *new influentials* may be more accurate, for some of these states may not only be leading regional powers but may also wield influence in other areas, as does an oil-rich state such as Saudi Arabia. Their influence may even be global. Whatever strengths and weaknesses such states bring to the exercise of regional or global influence, their mere presence is likely to create jealousies and conflicts and to rekindle historic rivalries in their regions.

A vivid example is notable in the Middle East where the Arab-Israeli problem has been complicated by competition among Arab states for leadership of the Arab world. Egypt, Syria, and Iraq especially have all competed at different times for this leadership role and have generally claimed to represent overall Arab interests against Israel. A premium has been placed on intense Arab nationalism and extremist rhetoric and policies. The state that most actively opposes Israel, that most militantly calls for war, that most adamantly refuses to recognize Israel, seems the most genuinely Arab. Peace with Israel thus has been extremely difficult to negotiate. Arab political leaders willing to live with Israel have been assassinated, isolated, or silent. Egyptian President Anwar Sadat, unlike his predecessor, Gamal Abdel Nasser, rejected the role of a new Saladin leading the Arabs in a holy war and instead made peace with Israel. Egypt has been isolated in the Arab world since the peace treaty with Israel was signed in 1978, and Sadat was assassinated in 1981. Another consequence has been to fill the vacuum left by Egypt's isolation; first Iraq, and then Syria, have sought Arab leadership by opposing Israel.

The point is that, even though Israel is only a Middle Eastern state, rival claims for regional primacy—which exist in other areas as well—enhance the possibilities of conflict. India and Pakistan have fought several wars, and the government of what is left of Pakistan since the secession of Bangladesh now is believed to be seeking an atomic bomb to match India's. In Southeast Asia, a new, strong, and self-confident Vietnam dominates Laos and Cambodia, and

Vietnam's other neighbors, especially Thailand, watch it apprehensively. Both the Soviet Union and China have been drawn into this friction-prone area. To sum up, the result of internal problems of the LDCs, regional rivalries in a world of many states, and an increasing trend toward "regionalization," is more—not less—conflict.

DECLINING CONTROL OF THE SUPERPOWERS

A third reason why a nuclear polycentric system is likely to be unstable is that the great powers no longer can exercise the degree of influence over the many weaker states that they once could exercise among fewer states. In past multipolar systems, the great powers, because of their superior capabilities, provided a degree of stability in an anarchical environment. States were not born equal. This inequality owing to differences in geographical position, size, population, and natural resources, was accentuated by the Industrial Revolution in the nineteenth century.

Decreasing Ratio of Great Powers to Small States

But the great powers' capacity to impose some degree of order has declined as the number of lesser

> states has thus been steadily increasing throughout the twentieth century. In 1910 there was one great power for about every five and a half states; one for about eight in 1930; one for about fourteen in 1950; and one for over every eighteen by 1970. Since there was a closer degree of parity among the great powers in 1910 and 1930, in 1950 and 1970 it would perhaps be more accurate to include only superpowers, which makes the ratio one for about every 37.5 states in 1960 and one for every 63.5 in 1970. The relevance of these figures is that each great power had to deal with a progressively larger number of independent governments, no matter how weak, as the twentieth century progressed.[3]

In 1950 the United States and the Soviet Union were still able to preserve a high degree of control. In the bipolar system their allies were subject to the respective superpowers. The American alliance admittedly permitted some give-and-take among the allies and some respect for national independence and sensitivity. In contrast, Soviet leader Joseph Stalin totally controlled his allies in Eastern Europe as he did his own people. Yet both alliances were called blocs because they behaved as if they were single actors. Differences in point of view, which at least were expressed in the North Atlantic Treaty Organization (NATO), centered on means of achieving collective goals. On the goals themselves there was a large measure of genuine agreement.

By 1970, when the 1950 ratio of 1:37.5 had changed to 1:63.5 (by 1979 it was 1:77.5), the fragmentation of the First and Second Worlds was well advanced. Of the Western alliances, the Southeast Asia Treaty Organization (SEATO) ended in 1975, and the Central Treaty Organization (CENTO) died when the shah of Iran was overthrown. The NATO alliance was also in disarray as the Western allies were increasingly divided by political and economic issues. Similarly, the Soviet-controlled world showed signs of discord. In Eastern Europe most states sought greater freedom from Soviet direction. In Asia, China and the Soviet Union not only denounced each other harshly but did not renew their alliance in 1980, and when Vietnam invaded Cambodia to overthrow a pro-Chinese regime and replace it with a pro-Soviet one, China "punished" Vietnam with a short and limited invasion, and the Soviet Union threatened to "punish" China in a similar manner. The effects of nationalism, however, were not limited to the weakening of the once-cohesive First and Second World alliances; the LDCs were affected as well. Despite a common anticolonial attitude, which was reinforced in the 1970s by bitter resentment of what was perceived as Western control of the world economy and Western responsibility for their continued poverty, the Third World also showed signs of fragmentation. Different stages of development, political systems, economies, ideologies, and sympathies for the West or the Soviet Union all constituted divisive factors. Even issues on which there appeared to be unity—such as demands for higher and stable guaranteed prices for natural resources— were divisive because such prices would benefit some considerably more than others.

Decreasing Western Willingness to Use Force and Sanctions

As noted earlier, Western states are reluctant to use force, the ultimate instrument of self-help, against the ex-colonial Third World states because of rising material and moral costs. Britain's use of force against Egypt in 1956 was widely condemned even in Western countries, as well as at home, where the government fell; the United States did not even attempt to intervene and overthrow Fidel Castro at the Bay of Pigs after the Cuban emigrée forces had failed; and American intervention in Vietnam was not only widely criticized outside of the United States, as well as inside, but the memories of Vietnam have prevented further unilateral interventions (with the single exception of Grenada). It is striking, as has already been mentioned, that confronted by steeply rising oil prices, the United States and its even more oil-dependent allies during the 1970s did not even talk of using force to halt the enormous damage the oil-producing countries were inflicting upon them. A few decades earlier, there would have been no such reluctance to resort to force against "the colonies" when such vital interests were at stake. During the 1980s, however much it might have wanted to use American troops to overthrow the Sandinista regime in Nicaragua, Ronald Reagan's administration was prevented from doing so by public opinion and Congress. In the absence of more clear-cut provocation by Nicaragua and its friends, the Soviet Union and Cuba, it became hard even to deliver military assistance to the "contras," the regime's opponents whom Reagan called "freedom fighters."

Congress at one point restricted aid to "humanitarian assistance"—food, medicines, and so forth—not weapons. And in 1986, an American air strike on Libya in response to a reportedly Libyan-directed terror bombing of a West Berlin discotheque frequented by American service personnel was widely condemned in Europe and elsewhere, even though there had been other terrorist acts against the United States involving Libyans.

Because physical coercion of the weak has lost some of its former utility, it has become more difficult to preserve the traditional hierarchy in the state system. The almost equal reluctance to substitute economic coercion—admittedly ineffective in most instances—means that the weak are in a better position to challenge the historic inequality of states.[4] Weak states can do things within their territories—such as quadruple oil prices—that in an earlier age would have led to great-power intervention, and they hesitate less to challenge stronger states in the international arena. Iran seizes American diplomats and holds them hostage for 444 days. Cuba sends its soldiers to fight and/or advise friendly forces from Latin America to Africa. Libya, a country of only 3.5 million, does not hesitate to act as a virtual "outlaw state," sending hit men or hiring gunmen to murder Colonel Muammar al-Qaddafi's opponents in other countries. (A British policewoman was killed in London when a Libyan "diplomat" opened fire from the embassy.) Qaddafi allegedly subverts neighboring regimes and provides bases in Libya, funds, and arms to various terrorist groups, including a radical Palestinian group that in 1985 murdered passengers at the Rome and Vienna airports.

THE GREATER BARGAINING LEVERAGE OF SMALLER STATES

A fourth reason for polycentric instability, then, is the fact that the weaker states are no longer as subservient or passive as they once were. The system increasingly appears to favor the weaker countries, most of which are not Western.

Resource Cartels

How do the weak gain such leverage? How do they exert pressure on the stronger Western states? Resource-rich LDCs that remain unaligned with either of the superpowers can form a coalition, pooling their collective bargaining power. One such coalition has been the Organization of Petroleum Exporting Countries (OPEC). OPEC's 1970s strategy involved withholding needed resources, raising or threatening to raise prices, and keeping production at a level close to that of demand, so that consumers remained fearful about the availability of supplies. This strategy was pretty successful for a decade. It has been less successful in the 1980s.

Whether such "resource diplomacy" can be effectively carried out with nonoil commodities depends partly on whether the West becomes more dependent on imported resources. Even though the United States is the least vulnerable of Western societies, it too appears to rely more and more on imports and therefore to be potentially vulnerable to external pressures. In 1950 the United States depended on imports for only 15 percent of its resource needs (as measured in dollars); by 1970 the figure had reached 25 percent, and the projection for the year 2000 is 60 to 70 percent. Simultaneously, the United States' population, which constituted only 6 percent of the world's total, consumed 30 to 35 percent of the world's petroleum, 55 to 60 percent of its natural gas, 15 percent of its coal, 20 percent of its steel, 35 percent of its aluminum, and 30 percent of its copper.[5]

LDC producer-cartels for nonfuel resources probably will not achieve the bargaining power OPEC did. The consumer countries became immensely dependent on oil imports because they neglected other sources of energy. A limited number of producers accounted for most of the world's oil trade and shared common political and economic goals. Oil cannot be recycled, and substitutes are not easily found. Even the initial price rises did not result in significant reductions of demand; it takes years and enormous capital to develop either new sources of oil or alternative sources of energy. The consumer countries also had little retaliatory economic capacity; many producer states are relatively small and, therefore, less dependent on imports.

Nonenergy producer-cartels face more severe problems. Stockpiles against short-term disruptions can be built up; substitutes can be found more easily and synthetics developed; recycling can reduce the need for imports; resources that become too costly may in the future be extracted at less expense from the seabeds. At the same time, producer countries with large populations will be more dependent on imports from the consumer nations. The Western states appear to have more leverage—including the ability to resist LDC demands—when commodities other than oil are in question. This leverage is, furthermore, enhanced by two other factors. One is that the industrial countries possess about 60 percent of the nonfuel, nonfood raw materials and the less-developed countries only 30 percent (the Communist countries account for 10 percent). The second is that many of the Third World countries want Western technology, machinery, and know-how (as well as arms) for their modernization. Still, the United States—and Western Europe and Japan even more so—will become more dependent on imports of some raw materials and this may enhance the leverage of those LDCs producing them, although there is an opposing trend toward using fewer raw materials in the production of many items.

The United Nations as a Platform

Third World coalition strategy is also reflected in the UN General Assembly where the LDCs have effectively exploited their equality with the stronger and richer states (see Chapter 15), and in the UN Conference on Trade and

Development (UNCTAD). Outside the United Nations such strategy is represented at annual meetings of the nonaligned nations and specially organized conferences on population, environment, food, women, and the law of the seas. All these conferences, attended by members from all regions, have essentially symbolic, public-relations functions as the participants seek to affect attitudes toward the distribution of wealth in the world.[6] The size of the Third World majority in the United Nations, the 120 or so members of UNCTAD (from which the "group of 77" emerged as an informal working coalition to coordinate and push issues of interest to the LDCs), and the various conferences, keep the international spotlight focused on the relationship of rich and poor nations, of "haves" and "have nots." The LDCs thus have several forums in which, in full view of the world (because of the ever-present Western press), they can dramatize their grievances, express their anger and resentment, blame the West for their continued underdevelopment, and push for "equality" and "justice." This propaganda campaign has been unrelenting.

The purposes of this campaign are several: to enhance Third World leaders' awareness of their common interests and to bring them closer to one another, to convince Western leaders and their peoples that they cannot ignore the "poor of the world" any longer, and, most of all, to persuade the West to formulate plans to remedy their grievances. Howard Wriggins has likened these activities to "consciousness raising," an unrelenting effort to change the "symbolic environment" of North-South negotiations by influencing the agenda of these negotiations—that is, which issues are discussed—and by trying to influence the outcomes of specific issues. The Third World has thus seized the initiative and has placed the Western powers on the defensive in negotiations over these problems. Many Westerners also believe that the West exploited the LDCs during the colonial period and that Western nations still take advantage of LDCs' generally cheap resources whenever they can. The related sense of shame and guilt probably strengthens the LDCs' hand. For the weak, invoking morality is very practical. It strengthens the "justice" of their case and weakens that of the powerful.

The general relations between Western initiative and non-Western defensiveness and dependence that prevailed before 1973 has been reversed. Not that the West has capitulated or even acknowledged officially that it is responsible for the poverty of the LDCs. Western leaders frequently claim the opposite. The fact that they demand progress at all is said to reflect Western influence. Indeed, during the Reagan years, the advice has been to try private enterprise in the free marketplace. Furthermore, in specific bargaining sessions on concrete issues, short-term national interests often erode the Third World participants' united front, which is based mainly on common resentment and aspiration. The material welfare of each state usually outweighs the symbolic common front. Yet clearly the LDCs have done quite a lot by focusing on symbolic issues such as equality and the gap between rich and poor states.

THE PROLIFERATION OF NUCLEAR ARMS

Hovering over the entire polycentric system is the threat of proliferation of nuclear weapons. Before considering the most likely consequences of such proliferation, we must understand why states seek nuclear arms.

Why Seek 'the Bomb'?

Do potential nuclear states not know that a few bombs or missiles constitute neither an effective deterrent nor a credible retaliatory force? Are they unaware that the extremely high cost of the special delivery system adds enormously to the estimated cost of obtaining a minimal nuclear strike force? The United States could afford to go through five stages—from subsonic bombers to supersonic bombers to stationary missiles (powered by liquid and solid fuels) to mobile missiles with single warheads to those with multiple warheads. But Britain could not. The cost perhaps could be reduced if national deterrents could be based on missiles from the start and if the rate of technological change in delivery systems could be slowed or stabilized by agreement among the major powers. Yet the costs would remain immense. Are the potential aspirants not aware that the costs far outweigh the potential benefits of weapons that may not be usable without staking one's very existence? If nuclear power basically confers upon its possessor the capacity to deny demands made upon it, why seek such dangerous power? [7]

National Security.   One answer is that, despite the costs and the sacrifice of other needs, national security considerations remain foremost. Allies of the United States have become increasingly concerned about the credibility of American defense commitments made in a period when the United States had an atomic monopoly and vast strategic superiority, but that now have to be carried out in an era of parity. The United States could easily honor its pledge of protection when it was essentially immune from destruction, but can it afford to do so when keeping its word may spell its own destruction? First Britain and then France have acquired small nuclear capabilities because they have been unsure, in view of the growing number of Soviet intercontinental ballistic missiles (ICBMs), that the United States would always and in all circumstances unhesitatingly come to their defense. Doubts arising from the changing strategic balance have been reinforced by concern that the United States, since the Vietnam War, has experienced a mood of withdrawal and is retracting its overseas commitments; at least, it is doubted that U.S. leaders will fulfill commitments undertaken before the Vietnam War.

We need ask only one question: What would West Germany, South Korea, and Israel do if they felt unprotected? The first two are U.S. allies, and West Germany was forbidden to produce and deploy nuclear arms in the treaty admitting it to NATO. Yet can it be doubted that, if West Germany or South Korea felt isolated or vulnerable to external pressures from a hostile state (the

Soviet Union or North Korea), either country would seek nuclear arms? And, although Israel is not formally a U.S. ally, it is so in all but name. Can it be questioned that, if it had not had American diplomatic support and extensive military assistance, Israel might already have declared itself a nuclear power? It is widely believed that Israel already has such arms and that it developed them because it is surrounded by neighbors openly vowing to destroy it and because it could not be sure that friendly and helpful countries would always remain so. Perhaps its friends would change their minds, as France did after Charles de Gaulle became president. When a country believes that the protection of a nuclear superpower is no longer credible or is suspect, it may feel compelled to seek nuclear weapons.

A state such as Israel, increasingly isolated politically and pressured by friends to settle conflicts with its neighbors, is particularly likely to try to enhance its security by acquiring nuclear arms. Another such state is Taiwan; the United States dropped its security treaty with the Nationalist Chinese government when it recognized the Beijing government in 1979. South Korea could be another if American troops were withdrawn from the peninsula. More broadly, if other countries should feel that the United States was reducing its role in the world, the possibility of nuclear diffusion would increase. The United States cannot have it both ways: it cannot reduce its global security role and at the same time expect its allies and friends to accept nonproliferation of nuclear arms. There is a political cost to be paid, whatever the choice, and the choice is basically political. Should the American-Japanese security treaty lose credibility in Tokyo, will Japan not cast off the "nuclear allergy" that has characterized it since the bombing of Hiroshima? Since India exploded its first nuclear device, Pakistan, its bitterest enemy on the subcontinent, has reportedly moved closer to acquiring the bomb. Indeed, quests for the bomb often appear to come in pairs. The United States and the Soviet Union both exploded their first bombs during the 1940s; as the Chinese-Soviet split grew, China exploded its bomb in 1964, and India's rivalry and past border conflicts with China undoubtedly were as influential in leading to India's 1974 detonation as its bitter quarrel with Pakistan.

Prestige.   Another answer to the question why states seek to become nuclear powers is prestige. "Nukes" have become status symbols. Just as a great power once demonstrated its primacy by acquiring colonies and a strong navy, so, after World War II, it had to acquire nuclear weapons. For nations that were once great powers and continue to harbor the "great-power syndrome" and for nations determined to become great powers, nuclear weapons are symbols of strength. In their view, not to possess such weapons is to retreat from greatness and to abandon power and international respect—and therefore self-respect. For, in the nuclear age, is a nation not impotent if it does not own such arms? Can a nation still claim authority to make its own decisions on vital issues if it is dependent on another power's nuclear protection? National pride has been a powerful incentive to the development of national nuclear deterrents.

For Great Britain, nukes became a desperate matter of keeping the *great* in its name, despite its rapid decline in power after 1945. These weapons also fitted its image of itself as the United States' junior partner. For France, defeated during World War II and then suffering the loss of Indochina, humiliation at Suez in 1956, the lost war in Algeria, and a status in Europe second to Britain and later to West Germany as well, the nuclear bomb became a means of seeking to regain international respect and self-respect. China, carved up during the nineteenth century by the European powers, including Russia, regards the bomb as a symbol of great-power status and national dignity as well as a weapon for protection. It is, indeed, difficult not to associate such status and influence with possession of nuclear weapons because the United States, the Soviet Union, Britain, France, and China are also all permanent members of the UN Security Council. The bomb seems to be the "admission fee" to a rather exclusive club that discriminates against nonnuclear states.

India is a rival of China, its competitor for leadership in Asia; it is also the leading power on the subcontinent. And it was the first nation to break the nuclear membership barrier in 1974. Another aspirant for at least regional influence before 1979 was Iran: the shah had spoken publicly of turning Iran into the Germany of the Persian Gulf area; presumably he dreamed of reestablishing the ancient Persian empire. Brazil, which is poor in coal but rich in uranium, has sought both abundant energy and political greatness as the number-one power in Latin America. Brazil and Argentina in the past were jealous rivals; after its defeat by Britain in the Falkland Islands, a humiliated Argentina had an even stronger reason to seek nuclear arms. But in 1986, Brazil and Argentina's new civilian leaders, both succeeding military governments, dampened this rivalry, at least momentarily. If states like these, however, should acquire nuclear arms, can countries such as West Germany and Italy forgo them? Can Japan continue without them if South Korea and Taiwan achieve them? The desire for nuclear arms as symbols of status and modernity, especially in Third World countries, is also reflected in the huge purchases of the most sophisticated conventional arms by countries such as Iran and Saudi Arabia. The have-not states not only want to become haves; they want all the symbols too—airlines, computers, and the latest conventional arms. Some will also want nuclear weapons.

Domestic Politics.   A third and final reason why states seek to acquire nuclear arms is related to domestic politics. Such considerations may reinforce the other two reasons. A nation beset by economic and social problems and low morale may—if it possesses the technological capability—seek the bomb to boost morale, restore national confidence, divert attention from domestic problems, and, of course, mobilize popular support for the government. Great powers have traditionally held military parades to stimulate patriotic feelings, and Indira Gandhi of India benefited politically from national pride in the first Indian nuclear explosion. The benefit may be only temporary, for it does not alter the domestic conditions that may underlie political unpopularity, but that possibility does not lessen the incentive to join the nuclear club.

The Role of Nuclear Reactors.   Security, status, and domestic politics are three major reasons for the proliferation of nuclear arms. The possible use of nuclear energy as an alternative to oil will provide those nations with the opportunity to acquire such arms. The United States is no longer the only nation exporting nuclear reactors to produce energy. Such plants are very expensive, which means sizable profits, jobs, and improved balances of payment for the exporting nation. The United States had 102 nuclear power plants in 1986; 272 plants were operating in the rest of the world. But since the late 1970s, the United States and countries such as Sweden have halted or slowed down plans for domestic nuclear expansion; the Soviet program may also slow down in the wake of the disaster at Chernobyl which spread radioactivity to Scandinavia, Poland, and Western Europe. Other countries, such as France, which receives 65 percent of its energy from nuclear reactors, have continued to invest in nuclear energy. The problem is that reactors that produce the energy to meet legitimate economic and industrial needs also yield the by-product from which bombs can be built. There are three ways of recovering this material: first, the spent fuel from a nuclear power plant can be reprocessed and the critical plutonium extracted; second, the uranium burned in these power plants can be enriched; and third, a plutonium-fueled breeder reactor, which produces more fuel than it consumes, can be used. Multiplying the number of reprocessing and enrichment facilities thus greatly enhances the prospects of raising the number of nuclear states.

> Civilian nuclear energy programs now under way assure that many new countries will have travelled a long distance down the path leading to a nuclear weapons capability. The distance remaining will be shorter, less arduous, and much more rapidly covered. It need take only a smaller impulse to carry them the rest of the way. There is a kind of Damoclean overhang of countries increasingly near the edge of making bombs.[8]

The Likely Results

The diffusion of nuclear power may thus endanger the peace achieved with such difficulty and diligence by the United States and the Soviet Union. Admittedly, the possibility that more nations may acquire reactors does not mean that they will necessarily seek nuclear weapons. Whether they do so involves *political* decisions and depends on each particular nation's political circumstances and objectives. There is no technological momentum that automatically requires nuclear reactors to be followed by nuclear bombs. Several European states, as well as Japan and Canada, have both the reactors and the requisite nuclear skills, but have not decided to build bombs.

Nor would diffusion have equal impact throughout the world. A Japanese decision to go nuclear would have profound effects, a Swedish decision little. A small Indian nuclear force may frighten Pakistan, but it is not likely to intimidate China. An Israeli nuclear force may overwhelm Israel's neighbors, but it would not be effective against the Soviet Union. Indeed, one nuclear explosion does not turn a country into a nuclear power. A token nuclear force does not constitute a militarily significant force, which requires a credible delivery system and for many countries a much larger investment of economic and technological resources than do conventional military forces.[9]

Nonetheless, in a system of nearly 170 nations, the diffusion of nuclear weapons to perhaps 20 or 30 nations will considerably raise the statistical odds of nuclear conflict. It may be unfair to think of non-Western nuclear states as "juvenile delinquents" of some sort, but such thoughts are generated by the instability of some governments and the fanaticism of some leaders, which raise the specter of irresponsible behavior. Imagine what might have happened had Fidel Castro been in charge of Soviet missiles in 1962 or what Qaddafi might do with a few nuclear bombs. But, even if all leaders were stable, wise, and careful in their calculations, would they be able to avoid accidents or miscalculations in every single confrontation that might occur? Will some nuclear states not be tempted to strike at their enemies before the latter also acquire nuclear arms? Will even the superpowers be safe then? The relatively tiny forces that most potential nuclear states might muster do not appear to threaten the superpowers. Yet could not some of them perhaps "rip off an arm," to use de Gaulle's vivid term for what he thought his small French force could do to the Soviet Union? Most disturbing is the vulnerability of many of these states to *coups d'état*. Among potential nuclear states that have experienced *coups* or civil wars since 1958 are Argentina, Brazil, Chile, Greece, Indonesia, Iraq, Libya, Nigeria, Pakistan, South Korea, Syria, and Turkey.[10] Let us take the example of a civil war in one of those countries

if that country had had an indigenous capacity to reprocess reactor fuel and to extract plutonium, even a small pilot plant. Who would have guarded the facilities? Who would have destroyed them, from nearby or from afar, at the risk of spreading deadly plutonium locally to keep bomb material from falling into mischievous hands? What outside country might have invaded if the spoils of war would have included a nuclear-weapon capability, even only to deny that capability to some other greedy neighbor? What neutral outsiders might have been invited in by the President or the Prime Minister, to guard or to abduct the dangerous stuff; and would all parties have willingly cooperated with the removal of such an awful prize, or would that have added merely one more armed group fighting its way to the cache? There may be some useful international understandings and procedures to be worked out for that kind of emergency. One thing is certain: in years to come there will be military violence in countries that have sizable nuclear power industries.[11]

Strategies to Slow Proliferation

Technological Strategy.   One possible way to halt or slow down nuclear proliferation is to use a technological strategy. The United States now refuses to export plutonium-reprocessing and uranium-enrichment facilities. To set an example for other nations, President Jimmy Carter announced in 1977 that the United States would not use plutonium as a commercial-reactor fuel within its own boundaries. Congress, in fact, has approved a law banning economic or military aid to any country that sells or receives such facilities not subjected to adequate safeguards.[12] West Germany and France have sold nuclear-fuel cycles in the past,[13] though both have declared that they will not export reprocessing plants in the future. The pressure to sell remains, however, because it is a profitable business. But there are other reasons besides profits. For example, France and especially Italy provided nuclear assistance to Iraq—a radical and militant anti-American and anti-Israeli state—until its war with Iran in 1979; Italy, importing one-third of its oil from Iraq during the 1970s, was seeking to ensure long-term access to Iraqi oil.[14]

The basic approach, however, has been multilateral. The United States, the Soviet Union, Britain, West Germany, France, Japan, and Canada have jointly devised a series of principles for regulating their nuclear exports. The seven original members of this "suppliers' club" (Belgium, the Netherlands, Sweden, Italy, Switzerland, East Germany, Poland, and Czechoslovakia have since joined) agreed upon the following guidelines: recipients of nuclear technology must apply internationally accepted safeguards drawn up by the International Atomic Energy Agency (IAEA) and they must give assurances that they will not use these imports for making nuclear explosives, even for peaceful purposes such as excavation.[15] President Carter was particularly insistent on tighter safeguards and controls. He proposed that the IAEA inspect "all nuclear materials and equipment" of countries receiving nuclear fuel from the United States for their reactors, so that closer supervision could be exercised over their nuclear energy programs.[16] (India has been a major exception.)

But the IAEA is grossly understaffed; it can only report violations, but cannot apply sanctions. Indeed, it is questionable whether the agency is capable of detecting all diversions to nuclear weapons. For plutonium-reprocessing and uranium-enrichment plants, inspectors in residence are probably needed. Whether IAEA inspectors visit nuclear plants from time to time (after giving advance notice of their visit) or are stationed there all the time, the implementation of safeguards to ensure against the diversion of nuclear materials requires the cooperation of the nations possessing the nuclear reactors. Iran, for example, has forbidden any IAEA inspection of its nuclear facilities since the 1979 revolution. In addition, the IAEA is powerless to act even if it detects diversion. International indifference and inaction was the response when the IAEA raised the likelihood that Pakistan might have diverted spent fuel to extract plutonium. Israel in 1981 took no chances when

Iraq was about to complete its nuclear reactor. Israel's antiproliferation policy was simple: it bombed the reactor. Israeli policy was to use a preemptive strike to prevent possible enemies from acquiring nuclear bombs.[17] The technological strategy may in fact be deficient even if all members of the suppliers' club cooperate. For the club may find itself outflanked by the club of "nuclear outcasts," composed of states that are very insecure—such as Israel, South Africa, and Taiwan. These states can help one another while evading international restrictions. In return for uranium from South Africa, Israel reportedly has shared its nuclear expertise. Other potential suppliers are Argentina, Brazil, India, and China.

It may be, therefore, too late to turn back the technological clock. In 1980 nuclear experts from sixty-six countries that had participated in the International Nuclear Fuel Cycle Evaluation concluded after two years of study that the U.S. strategy for curbing nuclear weapons' diffusion by banning the manufacture and use of plutonium was too late. A country could not be stopped from building a bomb by outlawing plutonium-based technology; too much scientific knowledge and explosive material were already available.

Legal Strategy.   In addition to the technological strategy, there is a legal one. Under the Treaty on the Nonproliferation of Nuclear Weapons (NPT), for example, the almost 130 current signatories agree that, if they are already nuclear powers, they will not provide nuclear weapons to other countries and that, if they are not nuclear powers, they will not try to manufacture nuclear devices. They will also accept IAEA-administered safeguards for their peaceful nuclear activities; this will ensure that nuclear materials are not diverted into weapons making. The legal strategy for halting proliferation involves gaining maximum adherence to the treaty. All Warsaw Pact countries are treaty signatories, reflecting Soviet concern about nuclear diffusion. The weakness of this approach is that any country can terminate its adherence to NPT with only ninety days' notice. Furthermore, Argentina, Brazil, the People's Republic of China, Cuba, France, India, Israel, Pakistan, Saudi Arabia, and South Africa have not signed the pact. The majority of NPT members would not be able to build nuclear weapons anyway; of those capable of eventually producing such weapons, only a small number have signed.

It is worth reemphasizing in this context that IAEA serves only as a monitoring agency for verifying national accounting systems for nuclear materials, and that it is also an agency very dependent upon the good will of the nations whose facilities it is inspecting. A nation bent on cheating can probably do so. Some experts have suggested either a multilateral agreement banning the export of enrichment and reprocessing plants or a market-sharing agreement guaranteeing each supplier country a minimum number of reactor sales a year as a solution.[18] This approach might at least reduce commercial competition and permit greater control by Western suppliers.

Political Strategy. Finally, there is a political strategy, based on ensuring the security of nonnuclear states. The question asked by such states is, "If we forgo becoming nuclear states, who will defend us against possible nuclear threat or attack by neighboring states?" The answer is, "We (the United States or the Soviet Union) will." But neither superpower is in fact willing to make such a definite commitment; vague pledges at the time the nonproliferation treaty was signed have not been convincing enough. American and Soviet reluctance to tie their futures to states they do not control and over which they may have little influence is understandable. But, as already stressed, so is the motivation of very insecure states to acquire nuclear arms. The Reagan administration even stated that the United States must continue nuclear testing to halt proliferation! In the past, the belief has always been that a comprehensive ban on testing would be a major step to preventing proliferation. The administration, however, is opposed to such a ban because it needs to test components of the Strategic Defense Initiative and has argued that friends and allies might become unsure of America's "stockpile reliability." If that occurred, they might build their own deterrent forces.[19]

In any event, regardless of this rationale, the choices remain fundamentally political, rather than technical, as in the refusal to sell nuclear power facilities, and they are agonizing political choices because conflicting values and consequences are at stake.[20] A number of policy options are available. One is to protect the security interests of potential nuclear states by supplying them with conventional arms and/or giving them a sense of security through an alliance relationship with the United States. For example, the United States can reduce South Korea's or Pakistan's insecurity in these ways (although, providing conventional weapons may risk starting a local conventional arms race). A second option is for potential rival states to try to settle some of their differences and perhaps even cooperate on specific nuclear programs. Political talks in recent years between Argentina and Brazil show promise; India and Pakistan too have talked but theirs is a long and bitter rivalry, and Pakistan not only faces a more powerful India to its rear but also Soviet power in Afghanistan in its front yard. In the Middle East, progress in the peace talks between Israel and the Arab states would help relieve regional insecurities; admittedly, prospects for a resolution of Israeli-Arab differences do not look good. Thus, we return to the state system, its anarchical nature, and the security problem that it poses for all member states: "There are no simple solutions that are feasible, no feasible solutions that are simple, and no solutions at all that are applicable across the board."[21] Or, as two physicists and one political scientist wrote:

> In the final analysis, it would be illusory to think that nuclear weapons proliferation could be severely limited by imposing controls on the sale of nuclear power facilities. The fundamental problem remains: minimizing the motivation nations have to acquire nuclear weapons altogether. This involves issues far beyond the realm of a nation's interests and involvement in the development of nuclear power to generate electricity.[22]

One hopeful sign in this respect is the nonproliferation treaty. It has become a politically powerful symbolic norm. Whether nations acquire nuclear weapons depends on their leaders' calculations of the gains and costs. The strong international support NPT has drawn means that they must take into account the increasing international disapproval for states with nuclear ambitions. Thus security, prestige, and domestic motivations for seeking nuclear weapons must be balanced not just against financial costs and military advantage, but against the widespread belief among nonnuclear states that states wanting such weapons are a threat to peace. The strong international support for NPT has raised the political price for acquiring nuclear arms and thereby perhaps lowered the incentive to do so, at least for some nations. It also maintains the pressure on the nonsignatories. Communist China, formerly critical of NPT, has in recent years pledged not to assist other countries to acquire nuclear weapons. Nevertheless, the issue remains less whether nuclear proliferation can be halted than whether a nuclear world is manageable. And if that is true, even under the best of circumstances—a slowing down of proliferation—the key issue is whether the nations acquiring them can all be stopped from using them.

THE DIFFUSION OF CONVENTIONAL ARMS

The possible spread of nuclear arms is still largely in the future. The actual spread of conventional arms is already a reality. It has been a rapidly growing trade, symptomatic of the diffusion of power in the state system from the Western industrial states to the LDCs. During the 1970s, it also reflected the need of the former to earn money to pay for oil, as well as the continuing competition of the superpowers for influence in the Third World. Arms have become not only big business (for the Soviets as well as the West) but also a key instrument of contemporary diplomacy. For both the United States and the Soviet Union arms sales represent ways of gaining influence and competing for the allegiance of certain LDCs. Sales have also, in a sense, become a *substitute* for traditional means such as alliances and the stationing of forces in other countries for their protection.

Arms sales ... have become a key instrument of diplomacy for the weapons suppliers, in some cases the best one available to them. There has been a decline in the traditional instruments of reassurance and diplomacy, such as formal alliances, the stationing of forces abroad, and the threat of direct intervention. At a time when the major powers are less likely to intervene with their own armed forces, they are more prone to shore up friendly states through the provision of arms or to play out their own competition through the arming of their proxies. *A contributing factor has been the reduction of other instruments of diplomacy, such as developmental aid. Both the United States and the Soviet Union now give less in economic than in military assistance.*[23] (Emphasis added.)

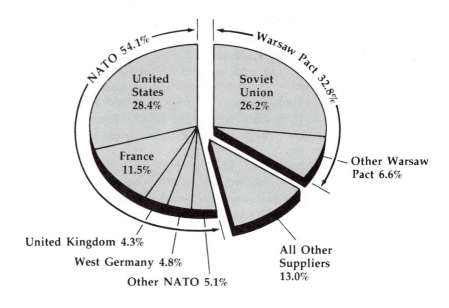

Figure 12-1 Shares of World Arms Exports, 1983

Size of Sales

Several features about these arms sales are worth noting. First is the sheer magnitude. Arms sales rose to more than $20 billion in 1980 (in constant 1977 dollars). The United States and the Soviet Union were the largest suppliers; in 1978 each sold about 40 percent of the total. French and British sales quadrupled; by the late 1970s arms sales accounted for more than half of their trade surpluses. For the Soviet Union, arms sales became a major means of earning dollars with which to buy Western technology and food. From 1979 to 1983, the United States and the Soviet Union were responsible for 57 percent of the world total of arms exports. American exports of $40 billion were 40 percent less than Soviet exports of $56 billion; the Soviets accounted for one-third of all arms exported during this period. During the closing years of the 1970s, it exported more tanks, self-propelled guns, surface-to-air missiles, and supersonic aircraft to the Third World than did the United States.[24] The 1983 shares of arms exports among the leading Western powers and Soviet-bloc states are shown in Figure 12-1.[25] In 1984, however, the value of the weapons provided by both the superpowers to the Third World was the lowest since 1977. The United States fell behind both the Soviet Union and France.

Expansion of the Market

A second important feature is the expansion of the arms market. As noted, earlier arms transfers went from the superpowers to their NATO and Warsaw

Pact allies. In the 1970s members of OPEC with large trade surpluses, such as Saudi Arabia and Iran under the shah, bought arms from the United States and other Western states. Iraq and Libya bought their arms from the Soviet Union and the Eastern bloc nations. Israel and Syria too received large arms shipments from the United States and the Soviet Union, respectively. By 1979 about 35 percent of all arms shipped to the Third World went to the Middle East. In 1983 the Middle East received 42 percent of the world's arms imports.

But other LDCs in Africa, Asia, and Latin America were also increasing arms purchases. India, for instance, signed a $1.6 billion arms deal with Moscow; Ethiopia, a very poor country, bought more than $1 billion worth of arms from the Soviet Union. All in all, more than three-quarters of the global arms trade now goes to the Third World. In addition, the LDCs are expanding their own arms production and sales. Brazil, Israel, and India, for example, have all become arms manufacturers.

These sales declined in the 1980s as the LDCs faced increasing foreign debt problems and, for OPEC members especially, sharply reduced oil sales. By 1984 the value of the arms delivered to the LDCs was the lowest in a decade. Still, the Middle East remained the largest arms purchaser due to the Arab-Israeli conflict and the Iran-Iraq war. The leading arms importers in order were Iraq, Saudi Arabia, Libya, Egypt, Syria, and Jordan (see Figure 12-2).[26]

'Conventional' Weapons

A third feature is the character of the weapons. In many instances these weapons can hardly be described as conventional. If the adjective *conventional* meant *nonnuclear*, it was accurate; if it meant *just ordinary* arms, that is, surplus arms or arms that were becoming obsolete, the adjective was not always accurate. The arms sales of the 1970s often included very sophisticated weapons, the same ones that were in the arsenals of the Western suppliers and the Soviet Union (for example, U.S. F-15 fighters and AWACS surveillance planes and Soviet MiG-23 fighters and T-72 tanks).

More and more frequently, conventional weapons have become anything but conventional. Many are precision-guided munitions or missiles (PGMs), which operate surface-to-air, surface-to-surface, and air-to-surface. Unlike the older generations of arms, which needed many rounds to hit the target, one or two shots with these new weapons will usually suffice. These new arms are guided to their targets by television, laser beams, or heat (infrared) rays. Also referred to as "smart bombs," they are becoming commonplace despite their technological sophistication. Many are, by modern standards, reasonably priced, light, and able to be fired by a small team. Because the weapons are highly accurate and not too expensive, they can make an attack very costly for the victim. When a $100,000 surface-to-air missile can shoot down a $35 million fighter, or a surface-to-surface missile costing a few hundred thousand dollars can hit a very expensive warship, the costs can be prohibitive, even for a major power, and will probably deter it from efforts to coerce

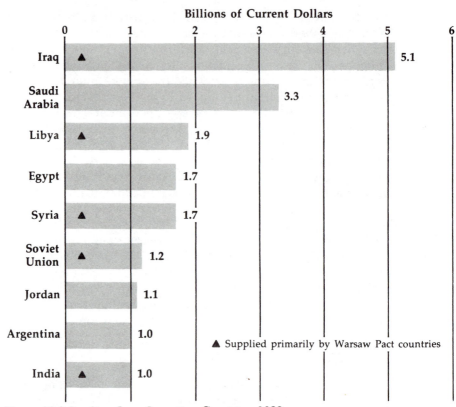

Figure 12-2 Leading Arms Importing Countries, 1983

smaller countries. For example, during the Falkland Islands fighting, $200,000 French Exocet missiles fired from French-built fighters, piloted by Argentinians, hit and destroyed a couple of British ships—one of which was a $50 million destroyer—from twenty miles away.

PGMs tend to favor the defense and make any military engagement very costly because they destroy so much war materiel very quickly. The diffusion of modern arms is thus not to be regarded lightly because they are conventional. In the 1973 Arab-Israeli war the highly trained Israeli army and air force suffered enormous initial losses and were driven back by Egyptian and Syrian forces, equipped by the Soviet Union with electronic warfare capability. Israel had none at the start of hostilities, but later received the means for electronic countermeasures from the United States and reversed the early defeats. Nevertheless, the 1973 war was a dramatic turning point in modern warfare.

Obviously, given the prevalence of regional rivalries, this diffusion of weapons may make it easier for states to decide to resolve their differences by force or attain their ambitions. Examples include Argentina's 1982 invasion of the Falkland Islands and the subsequent war with Britain; the Iran-Iraq War, which has continued since 1980 despite a stalemate; the Indian-Pakistani war in 1971; and Syria's "assistance" in Lebanon in the early 1980s against Israel and the United States.

POLYCENTRISM: SUPERPOWER INTERVENTION IN QUARRELS BETWEEN WEAK STATES

The real danger in the multiplication of states and interstate conflicts in the bipolycentric system is the presence of two superpowers. Militarily, they remain in a class by themselves. No state, including China and a potential united Europe, can match them. The United States and the Soviet Union would still be superpowers even without nuclear weapons, which only symbolize their superiority. The only military threat that each one has to fear to its physical survival is from the other. Their competition for influence, however, continues; it is no more likely to be abandoned than earlier historic great-power struggles.

A serious question is how the changing balance of power is likely to affect this competition. The Soviet Union's enormous strategic arsenal can now neutralize American strategic forces. During the cold war, strategic superiority allowed the United States to respond to Soviet challenges and to compel the Soviet Union either to desist or retreat. This superiority no longer exists. In these changed circumstances, the Soviet Union may be emboldened to use its conventional forces or proxy forces to expand Soviet influence in the world's trouble spots. It has built a sizable sealift and airlift capability and can now for the first time in its long history send its forces to other continents. Previously, it had been limited to expanding around its own frontiers. Essentially, the Soviet Union was a Eurasian power. Under Leonid Brezhnev, it became a global power, matching its aspirations as a Communist state and its perception of itself as a great power equal to the United States.

In these circumstances, U.S.-Soviet competition will in all likelihood not only continue but will probably also be intensified owing to the increased opportunities in the bipolycentric system. Extended into the Third World, this competition is potentially very dangerous because of the many local conflicts that may draw the superpowers in and produce explosive confrontations. The best model for understanding and explaining the future is, surprisingly, the situation before 1914, which led to World War I.

The 1914 Scenario

The war began as a quarrel between Austria-Hungary and Serbia. Austria-Hungary was one of Europe's oldest empires, composed of many different ethnic groups. In an age of European nationalism and the desire of various nationalities for self-determination, Austria-Hungary was on the verge of breaking apart. Serbia, a Slavic state, was encouraging this disintegration, which would have left it as a leading Balkan power. When, on a visit to Serbia, Archduke Francis Ferdinand of Austria was assassinated, Austria-Hungary was determined to punish Serbia. The government in Vienna thought that once Serbia had been crushed, Austria-Hungary might survive and that internal dissolution could somehow be avoided.

The problem was that all of Europe's great powers were allied with one or the other of these two countries. As a Slavic state Serbia was bound by culture and religion to czarist Russia. Furthermore, Russia could not afford to let Serbia be crushed, lest Austria-Hungary become predominant in the Balkans and thus pose a threat. At the same time, Russia was allied with France. After losing a war with Germany in 1870, France found it natural to form an alliance with the largest country lying to the east of Germany. The common French-Russian interest was to contain German power. If Russia went to war, then France would back it up. France had no choice; if Germany defeated Russia, France would have to face Germany alone. Clearly, it would then have to comply with German demands.

On the other hand, Germany was not about to let Austria-Hungary be humiliated or dissolved; Austria-Hungary was Germany's major ally. In addition, Germany was ambitious. As the strongest nation on the Continent, it was in an expansive mood. It was quite willing to take advantage of the Balkan crisis to fulfill its ambition to become the dominant European power. It had defeated France before and thought it could do so again quickly, in the opening stages of hostilities. Then it could shift its armies eastward and defeat Russia, already weakened by defeat at the hands of Japan in 1904-05 in the Russo-Japanese War and by domestic revolutionary conditions. A local conflict in the Balkans, on the periphery of Europe, thus broadened into a European war because of rivalry among the great powers. This rivalry had existed before the Balkan crisis erupted, but it had remained quiescent until events in an area of secondary importance triggered the war.

Present-Day Parallels

A similar danger that regional conflicts will embroil the two superpowers is inherent in the contemporary emerging bipolycentric system.

The Middle East.   The United States and the Soviet Union have actively competed for influence in the Middle East since 1955, when the Soviets and the Egyptians concluded an arms agreement. The rivalry of the superpowers was superimposed on Arab-Israeli hostility and intra-Arab competition. Diplomatic support, economic aid, and military assistance from the two superpowers fueled the Arab-Israeli conflict through several wars. Without this competition for influence, the fundamental struggle could not have continued. From whom would the Arab armies and the Israeli army have received their equipment?

In any event, with each war, the possibility of superpower involvement has become greater. In 1956, when the British, French, and Israelis captured the Suez Canal, the Soviets threatened to send volunteers and rain rockets on Paris, London, and Tel Aviv. The Soviets were putting on a show, but a good show. Hostilities had already ceased, thanks to American pressure on its allies, but the Arabs, apparently believing that Soviet threats had led to the cease-fire, were grateful to the Soviets. The Soviets were probably primarily responsible for precipitating the 1967 war, for they had deliberately floated false rumors of an Israeli force poised to invade Syria. The Syrians reacted immediately; what could Egypt, then the acknowledged leader of the Arab world, do but mobilize its forces and send them into the desert? Moreover, the Soviet fleet made its first appearance in the Mediterranean, presumably as a symbol of Soviet commitment to the Arabs and as a warning to the United States not to interfere while the Arabs defeated the Israelis with their enormous amounts of Soviet military equipment and training. Israel won again, even more quickly than in 1956. This time it kept the territories that it had captured; they were to be traded for genuine peace and recognition by the Arabs of Israel's right to exist. But no Arab leader would even sit down with Israeli representatives to talk.

In 1973 Egypt and Syria launched still another attack to recapture the 1967 territories. Despite initial successes, their armies were finally thrown back. As Egypt's armies stood on the verge of defeat, the Soviets mobilized paratroopers and threatened unilateral intervention if American forces would not join Soviet troops to enforce the cease-fire that the two superpowers had agreed upon. The United States placed its forces throughout the world on alert as a warning to the Soviet government against such an intervention. The crisis passed as the United States pressured Israel to obey the cease-fire. The administration of Richard Nixon was also seeking to avoid an Egyptian defeat and complete Israeli victory; a total humiliation for one side and total victory for the other were not judged conducive to persuading the two sides to sit down together and talk about troop disengagement and a possible peace settlement.

Another Arab-Israeli war, Washington leaders feared, might precipitate the dreaded superpower clash, a possibility perhaps even more frightening than the oil embargo by Arab members of OPEC. Each Arab-Israeli war had brought the two superpowers closer to conflict. How many wars can the Middle East sustain without engulfing the world in nuclear flames? For both superpowers the stakes in the area are enormous. Each has its "client" states, which depend upon it for political, military, and economic support. If a client state does not behave itself, the sanction supposedly will be withdrawal of part or all of this support. Yet the danger is that no client is fully controllable; each has its own interests and ambitions and in pursuit of them may draw its "patron" into the conflict. Who really manipulates whom? The patron may be able to cut off aid, but the client is not really helpless, for its leaders know that the patron is supporting them to advance its own interests. The client can threaten to find another patron, thus negating years of investment and support from the current patron and undermining all the political benefits the patron has enjoyed in that time.[27]

In 1967, after Egypt had felt compelled to respond to the Soviet-inspired rumor of a threatened Israeli invasion of Syria, the Egyptians made a series of military moves that the Soviets had not expected and evidently did not like because these actions increased the risk of war. The Soviets lost control of the crisis as tensions between Israel and Egypt rose. The initial Soviet error had been to assume that they could control Syria, a small and highly unstable country that was attempting to challenge Egypt's primacy in the Arab world. Syria ran with the rumor, taunting Egypt and suggesting that it was not fit to be the defender of Arab honor and the standard bearer of the Arab cause if it sat by passively. Similarly, in 1972, when the Soviets apparently refused to supply Egypt with offensive arms to launch a war to recapture the territories lost in 1967, Egypt sent its Soviet advisers home. For the men in the Kremlin the possible defection of Egypt from the Soviet camp would have been a serious blow, jeopardizing all the Soviet Union's political gains in the area. Therefore, in 1973 the Soviets supplied Egypt with the arms it wanted, and the Yom Kippur War was the result. Who manipulated whom? It appears that the tail wagged the dog. The so-called client state appeared to dictate its patron's policy. A great power is not necessarily in complete control and cannot necessarily fully restrain its client (even if it so desires). The crisis therefore may balloon beyond its control.

In a bipolar crisis, only two states are involved, and that is a major reason why crises can be "managed" and war avoided. In a multipolar alliance in which the allies are of approximately equal strength, or even in an alliance between a superpower and a client in which the former is eager not to lose the latter, attention is focused not on the opponent but on holding the alliance together. Quite apart from the fact that the less attention given to the adversary, the greater the opportunities for miscalculation, the desire of the superpower to preserve the coalition gives the advantage to the weakest and least responsible party, provided that the latter is willing to defect if its demands are not met. Egypt thus received the Soviet weapons that it wanted and went to war and, once that war had begun to go against Egypt, President Sadat appealed to the Soviets to rescue it. The global alert of American strategic forces deterred the Soviet Union in 1973, but will it, with its more powerful current strategic forces, be deterred in similar situations in the future?

Why should the United States and the Soviet Union become involved when two smaller states, whether they possess nuclear weapons or not, engage in conflict? Would not both superpowers have every reason to dissociate themselves from the belligerents? Past behavior suggests that neither the United States nor the Soviet Union will permit any other country to involve it in a conflict in which its survival is at risk. For example, the Soviet Union would not let China involve it in its quarrel with the United States over Taiwan in

1958, for that might have precipitated a nuclear confrontation. But can we be sure? Political interests may incite one superpower to intervene, leading the other to intervene as well, if shifts in regional balances are perceived to affect the central balance as in October 1973, when the United States and the Soviet Union appeared to stand on the brink of a duel. The stakes for the two superpowers are high in the Middle East, but they may be even higher in other areas.

Africa.   Since 1973 the Soviets have found opportunities to expand their influence in sub-Saharan Africa. Owing to their new sealift and airlift capabilities, they were able to intervene in Angola, Ethiopia, and South Yemen. In Angola in 1975-76 the Soviet Union supported one of the three ethnic factions struggling to control the country as Portuguese colonialism came to an end. The Soviet Union organized a large-scale airlift. More than 10,000 Cuban forces, as well as automatic weapons, armored vehicles, mortars, rockets, antiaircraft guns, jet fighters, and surface-to-surface missiles were transported into Angola to defeat the two opposing factions (ineffectively supported for a time by the United States, before Congress, afraid lest Angola become "another Vietnam," cut off the small amount of assistance).

In Ethiopia in 1977-78 the Soviets and Cubans intervened in another indigenous struggle. Somalia, ironically a pro-Soviet Marxist state that had received extensive Soviet military aid in return for allowing the Soviets to establish naval and air bases on its territory, turned on Ethiopia, in order to fulfill its irredentist ambitions and to incorporate the Ethiopians of Somali origin. Ethiopia, a much larger country that had recently fallen under control of pro-Soviet military officers, was facing disintegration as a result of numerous rebellions, secessionist movements, and civil war. This time the Soviets supplied several generals to work out the military strategy, 3,000 Soviet military technicians, 20,000 Cuban troops, and an estimated $2 billion worth of weapons, including 300 tanks.[28] A Somali attack on the Ogaden area was repulsed. In South Yemen the Soviets, Cubans (reportedly 6,000 to 7,000 troops), and East Germans were also involved.[29] In Afghanistan the Soviets intervened with their own troops in December 1979 to consolidate a pro-Soviet Marxist regime. One of the additional Soviet aims may have been to achieve a series of Marxist states along the strategic sea lanes of the Indian Ocean, Persian Gulf, and the mouth of the Red Sea.

In a sense, the Soviets have found a new and perhaps "safer" type of warfare, involving diplomatic and military moves in areas far beyond their periphery. (In neighboring states, such as those in Eastern Europe and Afghanistan, they have consistently used the Soviet army.) In an age in which force must be restrained or at least disciplined, in which the world has witnessed a resurgence of "limited warfare," the Soviet combination of military advisers (including East German security men), large-scale transfer of military equipment, and Cuban troops constitutes *proxy warfare*. The use of proxies is considered less provocative and dangerous by the Soviet leaders;

Soviet troops are far more likely to stimulate an American political or military response. In Afghanistan, for instance, the United States exacted a series of political and economic reprisals. Clearly, political circumstances in Africa during the 1970s encouraged Soviet exploitation of regional conflicts, and the Soviets gained widespread African approval because they helped to defend national frontiers (in Ethiopia) and supported the cause of black majority rule (in Zimbabwe-Rhodesia, Namibia, and South Africa). In such favorable conditions for interventions, a few thousand soldiers make all the difference, and Soviet leaders have skillfully established Soviet influence. This new form of proxy warfare is a formidable instrument of political and military policy.

The United States failed to react, except for verbal protests. Congress did not consider Angola an area of vital interest and cut off U.S. aid. In Ethiopia, the government had a right to invite Soviet help, and the United States could hardly support Somalia, which was seeking to incorporate an area of a neighboring state on the basis of an ethnic claim. Virtually every state in Africa is liable to similar claims and therefore supported Ethiopia's fight to maintain its territorial integrity. In the early 1960s, the United States itself had intervened, through the United Nations, in the Belgian Congo (now Zaire) to guard its territorial integrity against the secession of Katanga province. Had the United States intervened on behalf of Somalia, the Organization for African Unity (OAU) would have been alienated. If Ethiopian forces had crossed over the legally recognized frontier into Somalia, the United States could have intervened. Only when fighting did erupt between South Yemen and North Yemen in 1979 did the United States send some military equipment to North Yemen, because the Saudis felt insecure and had begun to question whether the United States understood its vital interests and would defend them.

Whether American restraint resulted from disillusionment after the Vietnam War and weariness with commitments in faraway places or from indigenous political conditions, Soviet leaders presumably calculated that they could expand their influence with impunity. The American government each time denounced the Soviet and Cuban intervention, pointing out that such unilateral exploitation of political opportunities was a violation of détente, which presumably obliged both superpowers to restrain themselves in order not to jeopardize their more important bilateral relationship. The Soviet leaders rejected these charges; détente did not commit them to the status quo and would not prevent them from supporting "national liberation" movements against Western imperialism.

But at some point a political situation may arise in which vital American interests are at stake, and the United States—after using force on several occasions during the Reagan years—may risk intervention. A rapid deployment force, composed of the three main services, has been organized to protect American interests around the Indian Ocean. Local conflicts arising from indigenous ethnic, racial, religious, and linguistic issues may well draw in both superpowers and escalate into war. This danger could be increased several times if the Central Intelligence Agency (CIA) is correct in its forecast that, in the 1990s, the Soviet Union, which has so far been self-sufficient in oil, will begin to import oil from the Middle East. Incentives to enhance Soviet influence in that region will then be even stronger. Control over the Persian Gulf with its vast oil reserves may then become a key struggle for both the Soviet Union and the West. The Soviet Union is in an excellent position for such a struggle. It borders on several Gulf states, and its invasion of Afghanistan has brought it even closer. The Soviets are also in a position to exploit regional ethnic conflicts. The Baluchis, who straddle the borders of Iran, Afghanistan, and Pakistan, have a rebellious history, and Soviet help for the Baluchis in Pakistan may unsettle that country even further. Should a People's Republic of Baluchistan ever be established, the Soviets could establish a naval base near the entrance to the Persian Gulf, through which most Western oil from this area passes.

Nor are other areas immune. In East Asia, for example, the adversary nature of relations among Communist states may draw the United States into conflicts among China, the Soviet Union, and Vietnam. In southern Africa, conflicts between whites and blacks and among blacks have already led to diplomatic involvement. And since 1979, Central America has become more of a strategic stake for both superpowers. The world has become more inflammable than ever, and the United States, while not forgetting Vietnam, has become, under President Reagan, more assertive once again.

TERRORISM AS WARFARE

Along with concern about the diffusion of nuclear arms and superpower involvement in regional quarrels, there is also increasing concern about the widespread use of terrorism. The basic reason for this terrorism is the number of causes and people determined to achieve their objective, even at the cost of their lives, in the contemporary world. As long as there are these "just" causes—and in a world of multiplying ethnic and religious divisions, such causes seem to be increasing—there will be groups who resort to terrorism because they believe that there are no legitimate ways to redress their grievances and realize their aspirations. Stemming from the Latin *terrere*, terrorism seeks to achieve its goals by frightening those it believes stand in its way.[30]

Categories of Nonstate Terrorists

There are three basic categories of nonstate terrorists. One is the national liberation group or what earlier we called "states-in-waiting." Most such groups resort primarily to guerrilla warfare. Examples are plentiful: the Communists in China, the Vietminh and Viet Cong in Vietnam; Castro's rebels in Cuba; the Sandinistas in Nicaragua; the former Patriotic Front, which sought majority rule in white-dominated Rhodesia and is now the government of Zimbabwe; the Southwest African People's Organization (SWAPO), which seeks independence for Namibia from South Africa; the Polisario, which wants to establish its own state in the western Sahara independent from Morocco; and, not to be forgotten, the Afghan resistance to the Soviet Union. But some national liberation movements resort mainly to terror; for example, the Palestine Liberation Organization (PLO), which seeks a Palestinian state; the Irish Republican Army (IRA), which wants a united Ireland; and several Puerto Rican groups that wish an independent Puerto Rico.

The second category is the revolutionary group, many of which exist within Western societies. Such groups proclaim their goals as the overthrow of capitalism because it is unjust domestically and aggressive internationally. They include the Italian Red Brigade, the German Baader-Meinhof gang, and the Red Army Faction and Direct Action in France. Some of these groups and others since late 1984 have cooperated in attacks on NATO targets ranging from U.S. airbases to European arms manufacturers.

Third are ethnic and/or religious groups seeking either redress for past injuries or greater autonomy within a state, if not independence. Examples are the Basques in Spain; the Armenians, who have carried on their campaign against Turkey in both the United States and Europe; and the Sikhs in India, who have assassinated both its prime minister, and later, one of its moderate leaders. Sikhs are also suspected of blowing up an Air India 747 over the ocean and of attempting to do the same with another plane. In the latter incident, the bomb went off in Tokyo after the passengers were off the plane (see Figure 12-3).

Terrorism as Television Theater

Terrorists resort to various means: assassination, seizure of embassies, hijacking of airplanes (even one ocean liner), kidnapping, and bombing. Although these acts are criminal in character, the groups' political aims make such terrorism a form of political violence. Fundamentally, terrorism is a weapon of the weak; the terrorists would lose a straight test of strength with the forces of "law and order." Terrorism—like guerrilla warfare—is consistent with Carl von Clausewitz's definition that war is the continuation of politics by other means.

As weak as they may be, terrorists wage their "war" by attracting publicity for their cause through their acts. Whether it is the seizure of an airliner or ship, the kidnapping of government officials or nongovernmental personnel, including tourists, or the murder of one or more individuals, these dramatic acts are viewed by millions on television and covered by all the media. Television coverage especially provides an incentive for the performance of such acts. It provides a world stage on which the terrorists play and draw global attention, and the jet airplane allows them to strike quickly anywhere

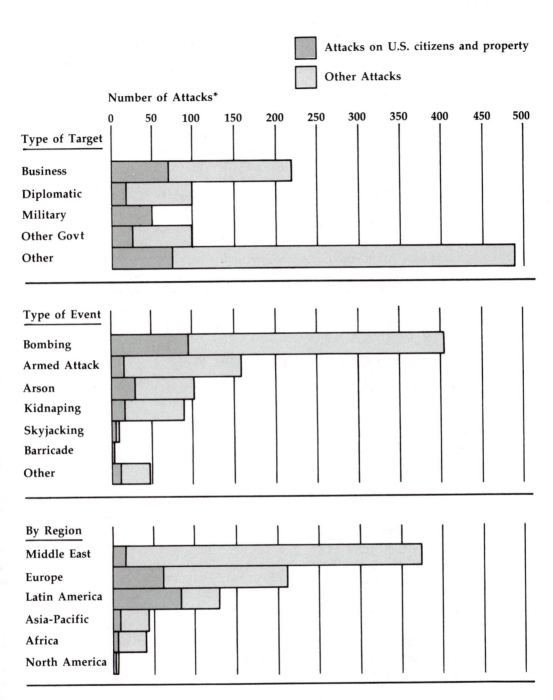

* Based on preliminary 1985 figures, which may be subject to review and revision. Number may be higher than total number of attacks because of capability of recording multiple victims and/or installations attacked.

Figure 12-3 International Terrorist Attacks, 1985

in the world and then fly to safety. Terrorism is public theater in which there are no innocent bystanders. For the terrorists, everyone is a player; there are no distinctions between soldiers with rifles and tourists carrying Michelin guides. The audience may condemn their acts as senseless and brutal and decry these acts all the more so when the victims are educators, clergy, and tourists. But these actions, while brutal, are not senseless or random; rather, they are the actions of fanatical advocates of a cause—not madmen—who know what they want and are willing to kill themselves and others for this cause. If the terrorists believe, rightly or wrongly, that a particular country— for example, the United States—is the cause of their grievances or blocks them from achieving their goal, they will consider *all* Americans guilty. Therefore, attacks on U.S. embassies or the seizure of diplomats or just "plain Americans" publicize their anti-Americanism. They are also intended to exact a cost, show the impotence of the United States because it cannot prevent such attacks, humiliate it, and undermine the legitimacy of the pro-American governments of those countries such as Lebanon and Kuwait where such acts occur. The terrorists want people to feel helpless and defenseless, and to lose faith in the government's ability to protect them. In the name of their cause, the ends justify all means.

Differences Between Terrorism and Guerrilla War

While both terrorism and guerrilla warfare are the weapons of the weak, they are also very different. One need but list the leaders of guerrilla movements: Tito, Mao Zedong, Ho Chi Minh, and Fidel Castro. All of them were charismatic leaders. All, except Tito, successfully organized the people in the countryside and by means of guerrilla warfare overthrew governments in power to become the heads of those governments themselves; Tito did it by waging war against German occupation forces in World War II. All became *national* leaders and symbols of their countries. They organized political discontent in their countries and pursued a long-term socio-political strategy, not just a military strategy, to capture power. Both in their own countries and widely outside, their cause was considered morally and socially just, the opposite of the government's position.

By contrast, terrorists are basically urban-based. Among the reasons for this are the anonymity of cities, the fact that the media are concentrated in cities, and that, in the wake of their acts, cities are easy to hide in. Terrorist leaders are seldom charismatic, and they do not pursue a broad-based strategy to arouse and organize the masses because in most cases their cause does not attract popular support. One need but note how often terrorists wear hoods to cover their faces at television press conferences or if filmed in some act. Intimidation is the terrorists' stock-in-trade. For the guerrilla leader, terror may be an instrument of use as well, but it is not the basic reason for success. Indiscriminate terror as distinct from selective terror against government officials may alienate the mass support the guerrilla needs.

States as Terrorists

A new phenomenon appeared in the 1980s—terrorism by states.[31] Given the greater military weakness of smaller states, or their relative dependence upon external supplies of arms, the constraints imposed upon such states to go to war makes terrorism an attractive alternative means. Brian Jenkins has called terrorism a form of "surrogate warfare."

> Finding modern conventional war an increasingly unattractive mode of conflict, some nations may try to exploit the demonstrated possibilities and greater potential of terrorist groups, and employ them as a means of *surrogate warfare against another nation.* A government could subsidize an existing terrorist group or create its own band of terrorists to disrupt, cause alarm, and create political and economic instability in another country. It requires only a small investment, certainly far less than what it costs to wage a conventional war, it is debilitating to the enemy, and it is deniable. . . .
>
> We are likely to see more examples of war being waged by groups that do not openly represent the government of a recognized state: revolutionaries, political extremists, lunatics, or criminals professing political aims, those we call terrorists, perhaps the surrogate soldiers of another state. Increasingly, there will be *war without declaration, war without authorization or even admission by any national government, war without invasions by armies as we now know them, war without front lines, war waged without regard to national borders or neutral countries, war without civilians, war without innocent bystanders.* (Emphasis added).[32]

Terror, then, shrinks the power differential between the United States and countries like Iran, Syria, or Libya. Terrorists can do things governments cannot; moreover, the beauty is that governments that use terrorists as proxies can disavow them. Thus Iran can, through its support of radical Shi'ite Muslim groups such as Islamic Jihad (Holy War) or Hezbullah (The Party of God), seek to weaken, indeed eliminate, U.S. power from the Middle East-West Asian areas. Syria, an ally of Iran against Iraq and seeking to bring Lebanon within its sphere of influence, can use such groups to undermine American support for Lebanon's pro-Western and pro-Israeli Christian-dominated government. (The United States had intervened militarily in Lebanon's civil war, and Syria, therefore, supported the Sunni and Shi'ite Muslims and Druze factions, all pro-Arab. The attack on the American marine barracks with 12,000 tons of gas-enhanced explosives was organized in Syrian-controlled territory in Lebanon. It was either agreed to by the Syrians or, more likely, assisted by them, for this attack took careful planning and was carried out with military precision. Only an organization skilled with explosives could have assembled the bomb.) And Libya can help radical Palestinians who fear that Yasir Arafat's PLO may recognize and negotiate with Israel to undermine Arafat and stop the peace process.

To the radical Shi'ite groups, the United States, the West's leading country, represents a civilization that is secular and has achieved great political, economic, and military power; it is also democratic, liberal, culturally preeminent, and dynamic, spreading to the Islamic world, which is weak, poor, and less developed. Iran and those who follow its leader, the Ayatollah Ruhollah Khomeini, are bent on eradicating this Western influence, including its music, sexual customs, and business and diplomatic presence, and are determined to revive the greatness of Islamic civilization (and, of course, Iranian influence). The seizure of the U.S. Embassy in Tehran, the bombing of the embassy in Kuwait (4 killed), the two bombings of the embassy in Lebanon (63 and 14 killed), the suicide bombing of the U.S. Marine compound in Beirut (241 dead), the attempt to blow up the U.S. Embassy in Rome (foiled by the Italian police), and the kidnappings in Beirut of American citizens (only one of whom worked for the U.S. government and he was murdered) all testify to the fact that these Muslim radicals see themselves as waging an undeclared war against the United States. Hence, this anti-American pattern is practiced by those who follow Khomeini. In the words of the graffiti on a Beirut wall, "We are all Khomeini."[33] To them, the United States is the "Great Satan," the devil to be exorcised. (None of this is intended to suggest that other Western states and friends were not targets; French and Israeli soldiers in Lebanon were also attacked.) Simultaneously the Iranians want not only to revive but spread Islamic—and especially, Shi'ite—civilization.

Many reasons usually accompany terrorist acts, such as U.S. support of Israel, revenge of a victim of retaliation (as Israel usually does), and, not unexpectedly in a world of terrorists, the release of comrades who were captured and jailed. In the TWA hijacking in 1985, for instance, the demand was for Israel to return the Lebanese taken by the Israelis as they withdrew from that country. The Israelis claimed that these Lebanese had been involved in acts of terror against their forces; whether taking such civilians was legal, the Israeli aim was to protect their soldiers as they withdrew. The Islamic Amal, whose leader was Lebanon's Minister of Justice and which took over the U.S. hostages when the TWA plane landed in Beirut, sought to equate the seized Americans with the Lebanese taken by Israel. The Americans were hostages, as the Lebanese were, and Amal demanded the release of the approximately seven hundred Lebanese for the Americans. This demand was obviously a rationalization for the seizure, not the reason for it. The Israelis had already begun releasing the Lebanese and had announced a quick release for the remaining prisoners.

There are literally thousands of causes; if it were not one, it would be another. The TWA hostage-taking was simply another blow to the United States, a humiliation all the more painful because it occurred at the same airport where U.S. Marines had been attacked, which finally caused the United States to pull out of Lebanon. And once seized, the Americans became central in a domestic struggle. The Shi'ite Muslims, represented by Amal, are the largest population group in Lebanon, long subservient to the Christians and Sunni Muslims, and the hostage crisis offered Amal the opportunity to enhance its influence. Neither Israel nor the United States was responsible for the Shi'ites' long oppression and backwardness; nevertheless, they came to play a role in Lebanon's domestic power struggle. Similarly, while Palestinian grievances are a major reason for Middle East terrorism against Israel, the settlement of the Palestinian problem would not end terrorism. Even if some factions within the PLO were willing to accept such a settlement, other factions sponsored by Syria and Libya would not. Their aim is the elimination of Israel and thus their terrorism is also directed against moderate Arab leaders who might negotiate a solution.

State terrorism is not limited to the Middle East-West Asia areas. The North Koreans blew up most of South Korea's cabinet officers on a 1983 visit to Burma; Qaddafi's gunmen have shot several exiled Libyan critics; President Ronald Reagan has in fact accused Cuba, Iran, Libya, North Korea, and Nicaragua of sponsoring terrorism. Because Syria had just helped (for reasons of its own) to secure the release of the TWA passengers, Reagan diplomatically omitted naming Syria, although it cannot in fact be excluded from such lists. South Yemen, a radical left-wing state aligned closely with Moscow, probably should also be on such a list, and Iraq, before its war with Iran, used to be on the list.

Reprisals Against Terrorists

Secretary of State George Shultz in 1984 expressed the anger and frustration of most Americans when he said that the United States must not allow itself to become "the Hamlet of nations, worrying endlessly over whether and how to respond" to terrorist attacks. After the assault on the marine barracks in 1983, the United States, despite talk of retaliation, did not act. However, the Israelis and French, who had also been attacked, did strike back.

The dilemma is obvious. On the one hand, if terrorists can carry out attacks and their victims remain passive, they are incited to further attacks to demonstrate their strength and the target's impotence. Only by exacting a heavy price can a nation discourage such attacks. On the other hand, punishment depends on knowing who the members of a terrorist group are, where they are, and then having the right means with which to retaliate. Even if one has that information, such as the whereabouts of the Iranian-controlled radical fundamentalist Muslims, how does one punish an enemy who deliberately surrounds himself with innocent civilians? Should this be allowed to discourage retaliation? A country such as the United States is restricted—and should be—by its standards of morality. The problem of retaliation is especially problematic when terrorists operate on another state's territory. Lebanon was too weak to expel the PLO; constant Israeli air attacks and a successful invasion to drive the PLO out left Lebanon in shambles. Its former pro-Western government collapsed; the civil war intensified among all religious and ethnic factions; Syria gained control; and millions of formerly friendly Lebanese, especially the Shi'ites living in southern Lebanon on Israel's border, grew to hate Israel. Some of the more extreme Palestinian radicals, who consider the PLO too moderate and too willing to compromise with Israel in a political settlement, reportedly hide in Libya and/or Syria.

In the case of state-sponsored terrorism, is the alternative to strike at the source? If the United States retaliated militarily against Iran, would this lead Iran to look to its big northern neighbor for help and would this not facilitate the achievement of Soviet control of the Persian Gulf? Does the United States want to align itself with the formerly anti-American and anti-Israel regime in Iraq, which is at war with Iran? Surely, the answer is no. What about other kinds of sanctions? The aftermath of the seizure of the Italian passenger liner *Achille Lauro* in 1985 suggests that this too is unlikely. After the Egyptians had secured the release of the ship and its passengers on the understanding that the hijackers be let go, it turned out that a crippled American in a wheelchair had been shot and thrown overboard. The United States asked the Egyptians to hold the perpetrators of this crime, presumably to deliver them to the United States. When the Egyptians attempted to fly them out, U.S. fighters intercepted the plane and forced it to land at a NATO base in Sicily. One of the men captured with the hijackers was the leader of their faction of the PLO and a close friend of PLO leader Arafat. The Italians, while holding the hijackers for trial since the murder was committed on an Italian ship, let the man who was suspected of planning the operation go. Just as the Egyptians had said that this man had been sent by Arafat to help negotiate an end to the ship seizure, so the Italians said that they had no evidence of his involvement and that he carried an Iraqi diplomatic passport. (Later, the Italians found the evidence and sentenced him to life imprisonment, a sentence he will never serve.)

The United States expressed its anger toward the Egyptians and Italians. In turn, Egyptian bitterness over the "piracy" of one of its airliners boiled over into angry anti-American crowds in the streets of Cairo and the possible weakening of its pro-American president who was maintaining the peace treaty with Israel and seeking to reenergize the peace negotiations between Jordan, the PLO, and Israel. In Italy, the government fell; it had been a government closely aligned with U.S. policy, even at the risk of popular displeasure on some issues.

Retaliation is not as easy as it might appear; each act reverberates, sometimes in ways that cannot be controlled. Repercussions may range from violating one's own moral standards, to endangering relations with friendly states, to driving an unfriendly state into Soviet arms with even more damaging consequences. The fact is that there are no easy solutions. Each case has to be decided on its own merit. And there is no agreement among states about what to do. After the TWA hijacking, the Arab world protested against and the Europeans refused to go along with a U.S. plan to close the Beirut airport. For one party a terrorist may be a freedom fighter, for another inaction is at least unprovocative. Why act and buy trouble? That appeared to be largely the reaction in Europe and elsewhere when the United States in 1986 struck Libya for its sponsorship of terrorism. Most U.S. allies refused American bombers from England the right even to fly over their territory, and the British government's permission to use bombers based in Britain was widely condemned there so that it may not grant such permission again. America's moderate Arab friends also protested.

Nevertheless, one of the ironies of this situation was its aftermath. Previous efforts by the United States to forge a common policy against Libya had been rejected. The Europeans had refused weak actions, such as reducing the personnel at Libyan "people's bureaus," or closing the embassies, which were also being used to support terrorism, as well as stronger actions such as economic sanctions. Only after the United States, frustrated by this lack of cooperation, acted unilaterally, did the allies denounce Libya and restrict the numbers and mobility of Libyan "diplomatic" personnel in their countries. They felt they had to do these things to prevent those "crazy Americans" from using force again!

The Future of Terrorism

Six factors favor continued international terrorism. The first is that contemporary conditions in the world encourage resort to terrorist tactics. These conditions include: the political fragmentation of states and/or unstable regimes in all areas and of groups holding grievances against the established order; commercial jets that provide both hostages and the means to transport them and their captors; states that are sympathetic to the terrorists and provide them training, money, and sanctuary; and mass media, especially television, that provide instant coverage and publicity for the terrorists' demands and cause.

The second is the trend toward smaller, lighter, more portable, more accurate, and cheaper weapons. A small number of people can today inflict the same kind of damage that earlier could have been inflicted only by large military units. These arms can now be acquired relatively easily by terrorists. What is especially frightening is that some fanatical group may in the future steal or divert nuclear materials, sabotage a nuclear reactor, or threaten to blow up a city. One expert wrote:

> Sometime in the 1980s an organization that is not a national government may acquire a few nuclear weapons. If not in the 1980s then in the 1990s.... By "organization" I mean a political movement, a government in exile, a separatist or secessionist party, a military rebellion, adventurers from the underground or the underworld, or even some group of people merely bent on showing that it can be done.[34]

Third, modern industrial society is very complex and integrated, its fragile technology susceptible to breakdown and failure. If "natural" failures (like the great Northeastern power blackout in the United States in 1965 or the breakdowns caused by severe winter weather in 1977), labor strikes, and even peaceful demonstrations can cause major disruptions, the potential for sabotage and terrorism—bombs in buildings, the destruction of industrial plants, hydroelectric stations, and nuclear reactors, and the poisoning of urban water supplies—is frightening.

Fourth, terrorism is relatively easy to carry out against free societies. It is not surprising that terrorism is not heard of in totalitarian states. Their control of society is too pervasive and, even if a terrorist action occurred, control of the news media would prevent a leak. By contrast, terrorism flourishes in the environment of free Western societies with their ease of coming and going (aided frequently by lax airport security) and accessibility to the mass media. Moreover, the high regard in Western culture for individual lives closes down the option of ignoring a terrorist's threat to murder hostages.

Fifth, state-sponsored terrorism may become more widely used by weaker states, allowing them to achieve objectives that before could be attained only by regular armed forces. This is particularly true against stronger adversaries. This kind of terrorism falls within the classical definition of war as a continuation of political activity by other means. The new battlefields—the embassy, aircraft, city street, powerplant, and other vulnerable targets in a complex modern society—are novel and give the advantage to the attackers; they pick the target and time. Not everything can be defended at all times.

Sixth, terrorists have a vested interest in continued terrorism. On the one hand, terrorists genuinely hate their enemies, seeing them as the embodiment of evil, making it extremely difficult to meet their stated grievances. On the other hand, within their own communities, being a terrorist confers status and prestige and, for the organization, money. Given these conditions, terrorism is not likely to end soon.[35]

FROM INTERNATIONAL POLITICS TO FOREIGN POLICY

The utility of analyzing international politics in terms of poles and the distribution of power among them is by now clear. We have seen how helpful it was in explaining the behavior of states in a bipolar system, particularly the virtually global nature of the two-pole confrontation, the hypersensitive nature of the balance, and the particular preoccupation with military power. We noted that the nature and function of alliances differ in bipolar and multipolar systems and that, as a result of these differences, for example, crises are more likely to be successfully "managed" in a bipolar balance than in a multipolar one.

But knowledge of the power hierarchy can be only a starting point for an analysis of the relations among states. Measuring power by adding up the various tangible and intangible components, even with great care and sophistication, all too often does not allow the analyst to predict the outcome of a specific set of interstate bargaining. An examination of actual power relations has shown us that the bargaining relations between big and small states are far more equitable than differences in population, natural resources, industrial capacity, and military strength might suggest. Indeed, one is sometimes tempted to say—admittedly, with some exaggeration—that the postbipolar era is the age of small and assertive countries that act as if they were great powers, and of great powers that frequently act as if they were powerless.

This observation certainly raises the question whether the concept of *poles* still makes sense. The world is no longer the great powers' oyster; to switch metaphors, *the giants must increasingly share the global stage with the pygmies. This fact certainly appears to limit the usefulness of any analysis based on the number of poles alone.* Over and over we have witnessed the limits of the great powers' ability to use their power to achieve their political, economic, and military objectives. Whether these limits are the result of the character of the state system or domestic conditions, they are real. The awesome nature of nuclear arms, the strong sense of nationalism among the LDCs, the diffusion of highly accurate modern conventional arms, the availability of alternative sources or markets for economic goods and raw materials, democratic public opinion, and changing views about the legitimacy of the use of force are some of the factors inhibiting or limiting the success of the great powers, especially in their policies toward smaller and less powerful countries. Indeed, as was noted earlier and is worth repeating, the natural order of things often seems turned upside down; the powerful appear weak, if not impotent, and the weak appear at least powerful enough to prevent the great powers from getting their way at a cost they are willing to pay, and sometimes the weak achieve their aims despite the great powers' opposition.

Polarity and Stability

The principal focus of our first-level analysis has been on the relation between the structure and the stability of the state system. Theorists in the past have generally concluded that bipolar systems are unstable and that multipolar systems are stable, but, in our lengthy analysis of these different structures, we have concluded that these propositions ought to be reversed. The principal reason is the impact of nuclear weapons. This conclusion, in turn, suggests a deficiency in the models. If multipolarity is stable because of its inherent flexibility and the diffusion of attention, the nature of weapons should not matter. If, however, despite the ability of states to shift from alliance to counteralliance and their alleged inability to become preoccupied with any single conflict, multipolarity's more numerous conflicts do arouse concern in the nuclear era, the traditional model is no longer valid. Similarly, if bipolarity is unstable because of the continual confrontation, the resulting frequent crises, and the adversary's temptation to launch preventive and preemptive strikes, war should erupt sooner or later, regardless of the nature of the weapons that each possesses. The fact that war has not occurred suggests that nuclear bipolarity provides stability.

As one analyst has perceptively remarked, stability may in fact be independent of polarity. Peace or war, stability or instability, seems less a matter of the number of poles *per se* than of poles plus a combination of other factors such as actors' objectives, the domestic sources of international behavior, policy makers' perceptions of the nature of the state system, and the threats and opportunities posed for their countries.[36]

The United States, for example, would undoubtedly have been the world's greatest power from 1919 to 1939—had it been willing to mobilize its power and use it. But it was not willing, preferring to return to an earlier isolationist position made temporarily possible again by Germany's defeat and the absence of external threats to France and Britain until the late 1930s. The United States, refusing to be a political and military player, thus ranked behind the various European powers, including the Soviet Union, and Japan during that period. The question was one of motivation. This is also what differentiates contemporary China from Japan and the European Common Market. China has the determination to play a key role in Asia, as well as in other geographical and ideological (Communist) subsystems. Japan and Europe have not yet been able to define for themselves the political roles they wish to play; both are still dependent upon the United States for their defense, though they possess the industrial strength, technological and scientific skills, and population to develop great power and to defend themselves. Thus Japan and Western Europe remain stakes over which the superpowers contest rather than influential actors themselves.[37]

The most significant factor in what Steven Spiegel has called "motivational power" is the nature of the regime, as has been apparent in the change of regimes from czarist Russia to Soviet Russia, from Weimar (democratic) Germany to Nazi Germany, and from Nationalist China to Communist China.[38] Such transformations are, in general, more significant in their impact upon national goals than are changes in leadership within a single regime. David Wilkinson has specifically distinguished between two broad classes of states, one characterized by the presence of a conscious, policy-controlling will, the other by its absence. He has suggested that

> the more one finds of this kind of hostile, dynamic leadership, the more its nature and peculiarities explain policy, while the less one finds of such "will," the more one will be able to explain policy by referring to traditions, history, and stable bureaucratic habit. Conversely, abrupt shifts of policy should more often than not coincide with the presence or appearance of a leadership of this kind.[39]

The will to play an active and major role in the international system is therefore a prerequisite to becoming deeply involved in both the competitive and the cooperative relations that characterize the power struggles in the state system.

Polarity and Other Variables

First-level analysis, as this example suggests, must be supplemented by second- and third-level analysis. In Joseph Nogee's words:

> In short, it is highly plausible to view the number of polar actors as an indeterminant variable. No single structure can guarantee stability, yet all have a

potentiality for it. Polarity relates to stability only when combined with other variables, but the nature of that relationship changes with circumstances and cannot be specified in advance. . . . The object of this critique is not to suggest the abandonment of bipolar and multipolar models. It is simply to stress their limitations for both policymaker and theorist. Polar concepts can provide useful descriptive labels for different historical periods. One step in the right direction might be to develop a more refined concept of an international "pole." We must, of course, have knowledge of the international hierarchy, including a description of its essential actors, in order to understand the international system. That must be determined empirically and can only be the starting point of analysis. To know which are the great powers of the moment is important but not enough. Power relationships are enormously complex and always changing. The great difficulty is that power, which is such a central variable, is an illusive one, difficult to measure. This is particularly true of those ingredients related to motivation and those which have a nonmaterial basis. That in part explains why the study of international relations has a greater tentativeness than most of the other social sciences. Theoretical models (especially polar ones) may have limited utility for predictive purposes, but we can, as Stanley Hoffmann reminded us, "project into the future a limited number of possible trends and rank them conditionally." If we cannot eliminate uncertainty, it is not a small thing to reduce it.[40]

Notes

1. Elmer Plischke, *Microstates in World Affairs* (Washington, D.C.: American Enterprise Institute, 1977), 9, 23.
2. Stanley Hoffmann, "Notes on the Elusiveness of Modern Power," *International Journal* (Spring 1975): 191.
3. Steven L. Spiegel, *Dominance and Diversity* (Boston: Little, Brown & Co., 1972), 120-121.
4. Robert W. Tucker, "A New International Order?" *Commentary*, February 1979, 43-45.
5. Zbigniew Brzezinski, "American in a Hostile World," *Foreign Policy*, Summer 1976, 78.
6. W. Howard Wriggins and Gunnar Adler-Karlsson, *Reducing Global Inequities* (New York: McGraw-Hill, 1978), 43-76.
7. See Leonard Beaton and John Maddox, *The Spread of Nuclear Weapons* (New York: Holt, Rinehart & Winston, 1962); Beaton, *Must the Bomb Spread?* (Baltimore: Penguin, 1966); Raymond Aron, "Spread of Nuclear Weapons," *Atlantic Monthly*, January 1965, 44-50; George H. Quester, *The Politics of Nuclear Proliferation* (Baltimore: Johns Hopkins University Press, 1973); Quester, "Can Proliferation Now Be Stopped?" *Foreign Affairs* (October 1974): 77-97; Lincoln Bloomfield, "Nuclear Spread and World Order," *Foreign Affairs* (July 1975): 743-755; Daniel Yergin, "Terrifying Prospect: Atomic Bombs Everywhere," *Atlantic Monthly*, April 1977, 47-65; Richard K. Betts, "Paranoids, Pygmies, Pariahs and Nonproliferation," *Foreign Policy*, Spring 1977, 157-183; Lewis A. Dunn, "Half Past India's Bang," *Foreign Policy*, Fall 1979, 71-88; Lewis A. Dunn and William H. Overholt, "The Next Phase in Nuclear Proliferation Research," *Orbis*, Summer 1976, 497-524; Ernest W.

Lefever, *Nuclear Arms in the Third World* (Washington, D.C.: The Brookings Institution, 1979); Dunn, *Controlling the Bomb* (New Haven, Conn.: Yale University Press, 1981); and Jed C. Snyder and Samuel F. Wells, Jr., *Limiting Nuclear Proliferation* (Cambridge, Mass.: Ballinger, 1985).

8. Albert Wolhstetter, "Spreading the Bomb Without Quite Breaking the Rules," *Foreign Policy*, Winter 1976-77, 148-149.

9. Lefever, *Nuclear Arms in the Third World*, 9-11.

10. Ibid., 500.

11. Thomas C. Schelling, "Who Will Have the Bomb?" *International Security*, Summer 1976, 89. Reprinted by permission of *International Security*.

12. In 1979 it appeared that the United States might be relaxing its opposition to the use of plutonium by its principal allies. *New York Times*, Oct. 25, 1979. Also see Michael Brenner, "Carter's Bungled Promise," *Foreign Policy*, Fall 1979, 89ff.

13. On West Germany's plan see Norman Gall, "Atoms for Brazil, Dangers for All," *Foreign Policy*, Summer 1976, 155-201; and Steven J. Baker, "Monopoly or Cartel?" *Foreign Policy*, Summer 1976, 202-220.

14. *New York Times*, March 18, 1980.

15. *New York Times*, Feb. 24, 1976.

16. *New York Times*, April 28, 1977.

17. Shari Feldman, "The Bombing of Osirag—Revised," *International Security*, Fall 1982, 114-142.

18. Abraham A. Ribicoff, "A Market-Sharing Approach to the Nuclear Sales Problems," *Foreign Affairs* (July 1976): 763-787.

19. *New York Times*, April 22, 1986.

20. Betts, "Paranoids, Pygmies"; and Lefever, *Nuclear Arms*.

21. Betts, "Paranoids, Pygmies," 178.

22. Ted Greenwood, George W. Rathjens, and Jack Ruina, *Nuclear Power and Weapons Proliferation* (London: International Institute for Strategic Studies, 1977), 32. Also see Lewis A. Dunn, "Building on Success: The NPT at Fifteen," *Survival*, May/June 1986, 221-233.

23. Andrew J. Pierre, "Arms Sales: The New Diplomacy," *Foreign Affairs* (Winter 1981/82): 269; also Pierre, *The Global Politics of Arms Sales* (Princeton, N.J.: Princeton University Press, 1982).

24. U.S. Arms Control and Disarmament Agency, *World Military Expenditures and Arms Transfers* (Washington, D.C.: Government Printing Office, 1985), 18.

25. Ibid., 10.

26. Ibid., 9.

27. On an analysis of patron-client relations, especially during multilateral crises, see Christopher C. Shoemaker and John Spanier, *Patron-Client State Relationships* (New York: Praeger Publishers, 1984).

28. Donald Zagoria, "New Soviet Alliances," *Foreign Affairs* (April 1979): 734.

29. Ibid., 735.

30. Walter Laqueur, *Terrorism* (Boston: Little, Brown & Co., 1977). Also see Claire Sterling, *The Terror Network* (New York: Holt, Rinehart & Winston, 1981); Yonah Alexander, *International Terrorism*, rev. ed. (New York: Praeger Publishers, 1981); and Benjamin Netanyahu, *Terrorism* (New York: Farrar, Straus, Giroux, 1986).

31. Ronald Reagan, "The New Network of Terrorist States"; and Robert B. Oakley, "Terrorism: Overview and Developments" (Washington, D.C.: United States Department of State, Current Policy No. 721 and 744 respectively, 1985).

32. Brian M. Jenkins, "High Technology Terrorism and Surrogate War: The Impact of New Technology on Low-Level Violence," in *The Other Arms Race*, ed. Geoffrey Kemp, Robert L. Pfaltzgraff, Jr., and Uri Ra'anan (Lexington, Mass.: Lexington Books, 1975), 102.

33. Daniel Pipes, "Undeclared War," *New Republic*, Jan. 7 and 14, 1985, 12-14; and "Fundamentalist Muslims," *Foreign Affairs* (Summer 1986): 939-959.

34. Thomas C. Schelling, "Thinking About Nuclear Terrorism," *International Security*, Spring 1982, 61.

35. Conor Cruise O'Brien, "Thinking About Terrorism" *Atlantic*, June 1986, 62-66.

36. Joseph L. Nogee, "Polarity: An Ambiguous Concept," *Orbis*, Winter 1975, 1219-1220; and Joseph L. Nogee and John W. Spanier, "The Politics of Tripolarity," *World Affairs*, Spring 1977, 319-333.

37. George F. Kennan, "Europe's Problems, Europe's Choices,' *Foreign Policy*, Spring 1974, 13-14.

38. Spiegel, *Dominance and Diversity*, 71-78.

39. David Wilkinson, *Comparative Foreign Relations* (Belmont, Calif.: Dickensen, 1969), 27.

40. Nogee, "Polarity," 1219, 1223-1224.

Part Four

THE SECOND AND
THIRD LEVELS

CHAPTER 13

National and Elite Styles in Foreign Policy: American and Soviet Perceptions and Behavior

THE CONCEPT OF STYLE: THE AMERICAN AND EUROPEAN CONTRAST

We now turn from the game of international politics analyzed in terms of the interactions among the states. We have assumed up to this point that states are similar in interests, motivations, and internal structure and that their behavior is the product of the state system. In using the first level of analysis, we have therefore had no reason to look inward—except in those instances in which states have not behaved as expected. Although assuming the identical nature of states is conceptually useful, it clearly does not suffice. If we wish to analyze and more fully understand the actual behavior of states, we must look not only at their interactions but also at individual states and their foreign policies; that is, their perceptions of themselves, their roles in the world, and their behavior.

It is our claim that nations develop distinct personalities or "styles" that affect the manner in which they conduct themselves in the international arena, whether they take the initiative or react to what other states are doing. This style reflects a country's historical experience, geographical position, political values and organization, and economic resources. Nations have unique histories; each reads its own past and draws certain lessons from it—or misreads it and learns the wrong lessons. Each state develops a certain picture of the system and possesses a repertoire of acts and responses derived from its domestic and foreign experiences. Each, to put it another way, perceives "reality" selectively from its particular perspective of *Weltanschauung* (world view) or "cognitive map"; in practice, each has a corresponding "operational code" or national style.

385

In no two states is this more obvious than the United States and the Soviet Union; their styles could not be more different. The United States is a product of its long isolationism. Surrounded by fish to the east and west and weak neighbors to the north and south, the United States had had no security problem for most of its history. It took security for granted. It possessed only a small army and, until the turn of the twentieth century, a small navy; the military and its values were generally despised and felt to be the antithesis of the nation's democratic values. Indeed, when needed, the army was drawn primarily from citizen-soldiers or militia. The nation's main task was internal; domestic concerns held an absolute priority. It is no wonder that in the United States (and to a lesser extent in Britain, protected so long by the English Channel) foreign and domestic policies were thought of as entirely distinct. Events overseas appeared to have little to do with the development of democracy at home. Continental European powers, bordering one another, could never afford to think of the domestic and foreign arenas as separate or independent. Unable to take security for granted, they gave priority to the conduct of foreign policy.[1]

For the United States, Britain, and to some extent all democracies, including continental European ones, the stark contrast between the intense conflicts, violence, and often perceived immorality (sometimes disapprovingly referred to as Machiavellianism) of international politics, and the law and order, consensus, and generally peaceful change of democracy, reinforced this tendency to separate international anarchy from domestic affairs. This contrast may not exist in the minds of people who have experienced internal tyranny from dictatorial regimes, revolution, or other forms of domestic violence; these peoples' experiences are closer to those of states living in an anarchical environment. Unfortunately, such domestic terror by governments against their own people, revolutionary violence, and the breakdown of law and order are spreading in the contemporary world.

This democratic, largely American and British, distinction between international and domestic systems, the result of both countries' foreign and domestic experiences, led them to draw a further distinction between policies of "choice" and "necessity." The American approach to international politics, more than that of the British who, after all, did not live in isolation, was based on two beliefs: (1) that the United States had a choice about whether it would participate in international politics; and (2) that if it did, it could apply the same moral principles that governed domestic affairs. Americans, once they had gained independence from Europe, told themselves that they were different from the Europeans (Continental Europeans, anyway), who were addicted to "power politics." Americans tended not only to associate the European states' behavior with the character of their class societies but also saw a causal relationship between them. Conflict and war were associated with Europe's aristocratic and/or undemocratic governments; the United States, an overwhelmingly middle-class society whose outlook was liberal and democratic, was peaceful in its behavior. Almost a century of experience seemed to support the belief that democracies were peaceful in their foreign policies.[2]

Rejecting the power politics approach, unsocialized by the state system's rules of the game, American political leaders were concerned primarily with realizing proven democratic principles in foreign policy as the United States became involved internationally. This contrasted to the continental tradition. Influenced mainly by geography, European leaders spoke of the "necessities of state," and learned to cope with the conflict between morality and "reasons of state." They were in no position to accept the American assumption that statesmen did not have to act out of necessity. Living far from Europe, Americans, as democrats, believed that they had freedom of choice and that, in fact, they could choose the moral path in their foreign policies as they did in their internal ones. The resulting American approach has often smacked of excessive moralizing, if not self-righteousness, in the conduct of external affairs; indeed, not to pursue policies believed to be consistent with democratic and moral principles arouses a sense of guilt and subjects these policies to moral condemnation.

The Soviet approach to international politics is quite different. Perhaps we ought to say *Russian* for Russia was an old country before the Soviet regime came to power. Unlike the United States, Russia has a long history of invasions. It was attacked by, among others, Mongols, Turks, Poles, Swedes, French (1812), Japanese (1904-05), and Germany (1914-17 and 1941-45), and was defeated by many of them. Russia's leaders, like most leaders of the Continental states, always felt vulnerable. Not protected by any natural barriers—oceans, channels, rivers, or mountain ranges—the many times Russia has been invaded and beaten, or almost so, has rendered its leaders virtually paranoid about security. They did not assume the good neighborliness of surrounding states, but their natural enmity. Not surprisingly, therefore, they thought that one way of increasing security was by pushing outwards and keeping foreign threats as far away as possible.

Not all of Russia's expansion over the centuries, however, can be considered defensive. The same lack of natural barriers that did not stop invasions also could not prevent Russia's outward thrust of power for offensive purposes. Russia is the world's largest territorial state, covering one-sixth of the earth's surface. It no more became that large merely by suffering invasions than a man becomes rich by constantly being robbed. Russian history is indeed one of sustained territorial expansion that has been regarded as a threat by neighbors such as Japan, which attacked Russia at the turn of the century. Russia's advantage is that it lies in what is usually referred to as Eurasia's heartland at the crossroads of Europe, Asia, and the Middle East; this strategic location allows it to probe all along their borders for weak spots and expand where these exist. Zbigniew Brzezinski, President Jimmy Carter's national security assistant, said that Russia historically has been a "persistent aggressor" against its neighbors rather than their victim. That expansion, of course, alarmed Russia's neighbors and, instead of increasing Russian security, *decreased* it because those neighbors reacted by strengthening themselves. Thus, even if Russian foreign policy is interpreted mainly as defensive, a cycle is set up: "Insecurity generated expansion; expansion bred insecurity; insecurity, in turn, would fuel further expansion." [3]

Russia's leaders understood the meaning of the phrase "reasons of state" and recognized that foreign policy frequently had to be given priority over domestic policy. This primacy, as noted before (Chapter 7), was associated with the centralization of power in the state and a central role for the military. Democracy with its decentralization of power, as practiced in the United States, did not take root in Russia; an American-style neglect of military power would have been an open invitation to foreign threats and would have negated opportunities for expansion when they presented themselves. Soviet leaders inherited this historical experience when they came to power. They merely carried on the traditional way, with its emphasis on conflict and struggle, the potential enmity of other states, the importance of military power, and self-reliance.

These examples suggest that the concept of style can be very useful in clarifying the ways in which a nation and its policy makers are likely to view a specific situation, alternative courses of action, and the course selected. It can be very helpful in analyzing a particular situation, although institutional and other pressures that also help to shape the final decision cannot be ignored.[4] In a way, the idea of style is familiar to the reader from stereotypes about certain categories of people—for example, capitalists, trade-union leaders, military men, Germans, Englishmen, and the Irish. Such stereotypes are often crude and impressionistic, and sometimes they are gross distortions used to justify prejudices (about blacks or Jews, for example). But the fact that stereotypes may sometimes be misleading or false does not mean that they have to be. They are of course likely to be simplifications of reality. All concepts, however sophisticated and however careful the researcher, are distorted to a degree, for they are means of organizing, and therefore of imposing some sort of order, on masses of existing data. They always involve selection—inclusion of some facts and exclusion of others. But selection is necessary if we are to gain some insight into the understanding of what is going on. With some care we can see, for example, that a certain nation has repeatedly behaved in a particular fashion in similar situations and can then suggest that it has demonstrated certain distinctive characteristics in its foreign policy.

THE AMERICAN NATIONAL STYLE

The U.S. national style is distinguished by seven characteristics in its external behavior that are uniquely "American." [5]

Swinging Between Isolationism and Interventionism

We start with the recognition that fundamental to American experience is the nation's lengthy isolation from the quarrels of the great European powers. For almost a century the United States was able to devote itself to domestic tasks: strengthening the bonds of national unity, expanding westward, absorbing the millions of immigrants attracted by the opportunities of the country, and industrializing and urbanizing an entire continent. This freedom to concentrate on internal affairs cannot be explained entirely by the presence of the Atlantic Ocean and weaker neighbors to the north and south. As a democratic nation, the United States and its internal orientation must also be explained by the preferences of the electorate. Citizens in a democracy are concerned primarily with their individual and family well-being. All Western democracies, responding to public demands, have become welfare states to some degree.[6] Government demands for service in the armed forces or for higher taxes to finance international obligations are bound to be viewed as burdens. And foreign policy will, on the whole, be considered a distraction from primary domestic tasks. The American citizen's intense concern with private and material welfare and almost compulsive striving for economic success—the measure of individual self-esteem—have long been noted. If, in an egalitarian society, a citizen is judged primarily by his or her material achievements, which indicate ability and bring varying degrees of respect, he or she will concentrate on "getting ahead." Money becomes the symbol of status and prestige; it is a sign of success, just as failure to earn enough money is considered a token of personal failure.

Given such a profound inward orientation, it is not surprising that the United States turned its attention to the outside world only when provoked. First there had to be a danger so clear that it could no longer be ignored. This point cannot be overemphasized: the United States rarely initiated policy; the stimuli responsible for its foreign policy usually came from beyond its frontiers. Historically the result was that U.S. foreign policy was essentially both reactive and discontinuous, a series of impatient responses to external pressures whenever there was "clear and present danger" and of returns to more important domestic affairs as soon as danger had passed. Long-range commitments and foreign policy planning tended to be rare.

The pattern, instead, was that of a pendulum: when it believed itself to be provoked, the United States swung from isolation to intervention; once the provocation was over the United States withdrew again. The unrestricted German submarine campaign in 1917 led the United States into World War I; after Germany's defeat, the United States returned to its traditional isolationist stance. Then the Japanese attack on Pearl Harbor in 1941 brought the United States out of this posture again; after the victory over Germany and Japan, the country attempted to withdraw once more. Britain took the first moves in containing the Soviet Union; the United States, considering itself a friend of both, attempted to mediate impartially between the two! Only gradually did Washington come to see its interests in the British-Soviet conflict, and it took Britain's collapse in the winter of 1946-47 for the United States to engage in the cold war.

Moralism and Crusadism

The American attitude was further characterized by a high degree of moralism and missionary zeal arising from the nation's perception of itself as a unique and morally superior society. The United States was the world's first democracy, committed to improvement of the lot of ordinary people. Americans regarded themselves as the "chosen people." The New World stood for opportunity, democracy, and peace; the Old World for poverty, exploitation, and war. Abraham Lincoln phrased the point aptly when he said that the United States was "the last best hope on earth." Woodrow Wilson during World War I and Franklin Roosevelt during World War II expressed much the same view. Just as in 1862 the United States had not been able to remain half free and half slave, so in 1917 and again in 1941, Americans thought that the world could not continue half free and half slave. Each war was considered an apocalyptic struggle between the forces of darkness and the forces of light.[7] Moralism in foreign policy reflected the awareness and pride of a society that believed it had carved out a better domestic order, free of oppression and injustice.

Isolation from European power politics was therefore basically a means of safeguarding American morality and purity. Quarantining itself was the best way to prevent the nation from being soiled and tainted by the undemocratic domestic institutions and foreign policy behavior of European states. The American experiment had to be safeguarded against the corruption of power politics, and withdrawing from the state system and providing the world with an example were the only correct course. On the other hand, once it became impossible to remain aloof, in the twentieth century, the country went to the other extreme and launched crusades to destroy the nation that had made it necessary to emerge from its isolationism. As a self-proclaimed superior country—morally and politically—the United States could remain uncontaminated only by eliminating those that might infect it. Once provoked, the nation acted as a missionary power and sought to make the world safe for American democracy by democratizing or Americanizing it. American crusading and American isolationism sprang from a single source.

America's wars fitted the pattern. Kaiser Wilhelm II's Germany in 1917 was a semiabsolutist monarchy; Adolf Hitler's Germany was a fascist totalitarian regime; and Joseph Stalin's Soviet Union was a Communist totalitarian state. They were all antidemocratic, evil systems led by evil men, they had to be destroyed (or, at least, contained). American power was "righteous power." Either it was not to be used at all, or it was to be used totally in a moral cause—in defense of democracy. The German submarine campaign in 1917 was regarded as more than a series of attacks on American ships. President

Wilson called it "warfare against mankind. This is a war against all nations.... The challenge is to mankind." And again, "...the right is more precious than the peace, and we shall fight for the things which we have always carried nearest our hearts—for democracy ... [and] for a universal dominion of right by such a concert of free people as shall bring peace and safety to all nations and make the world itself at last free."[8]

Similar words, although perhaps not quite so eloquent, were used during World War II and the cold war. Note these thoughts from President Harry S. Truman's 1947 speech, which became known as the Truman Doctrine: "At the present moment in world history nearly every nation must choose between alternative ways of life.... One way of life is based upon the will of the majority.... The second way of life is based upon the will of a minority forcibly imposed upon the majority ... it must be the policy of the United States to support free peoples who are resisting attempted subjugations by armed minorities or by outside pressure."[9] Almost every succeeding president spoke similar words at some point during his term.

Depreciation of Power Politics

A third characteristic follows from the liberal democratic values upon which the nation was founded and the resulting high moralism: a depreciation of power politics, with its connotations of conflict, destruction, and death. Strife was considered abnormal and only transitory; harmony was viewed as the normal condition among states. The use of power within the national political system is legitimate only in the service of democratic purposes; its employment in the state system can be justified only in the service of a moral cause. Specifically, in the state system power cannot be employed, at least without arousing guilt feelings, unless the nation confronts a morally unambiguous instance of foreign aggression. And, when that happens, the United States must completely eradicate the immoral enemy that threatens the nation and its democratic principles. The presumption is that democracies are peaceful states because the people, who elect their rulers, do not like to go to war and suffer the resulting hardships and losses in lives and property. Therefore, the eruption of hostilities is attributed to authoritarian and totalitarian states whose rulers, unrestrained by democratic public opinion, wield power for their own personal aggrandizement. Their removal becomes a precondition of peace and the end of power politics itself.

Distinction Between Peace and War

Arising from both this moralism and the depreciation of power is a fourth characteristic: the tendency to draw a clear-cut distinction between peace and war. Peace is characterized by harmony among nations, and war and power politics in general are considered atypical. In peacetime, little or no attention need be paid to foreign problems; indeed, such problems would divert people from their individual, materialistic concerns and upset the whole scale of social values.

Once Americans are angry and the United States has to resort to force, however, the use of force can be justified only in terms of the universal moral principles with which the nation, as a democratic country, identifies itself. Resort to the evil instrument of war can be justified only by noble purposes and by the goal of the complete destruction of the immoral enemy that threatens the integrity, if not the existence, of these principles. Since American power has to be "righteous" power, only its full exercise can ensure salvation or absolution from sin. The national aversion to violence thus becomes transformed into national glorification of violence, and wars become ideological crusades to make the world safe for democracy—by converting authoritarian adversaries into peaceful, democratic states and banishing power politics for all time.[10] Once that aim has been achieved, the United States can again withdraw into itself. Although foreign affairs are annoying diversions from more important domestic matters, such diversions are only temporary; maximum force is applied to aggressors or warmongers to punish them for provocation and to teach them that aggression is immoral and will not be rewarded. As a result, American wars are total wars, fought to achieve total victory and the enemy's unconditional surrender. "There is no substitute for victory," said General Douglas MacArthur in Korea. To stop short of victory is to fight "a half-war." There can be no compromise with the enemy. Only his total defeat is acceptable.[11]

Divorce of Diplomacy from Force

Not only does the United States consider peace and war two mutually exclusive conditions, but also it divorces diplomacy from force, so that in wartime political considerations are subordinated to military considerations. Once the diplomats have failed to keep the peace through appeals to morality and reason, military considerations become primary. During wartime, the soldier is in charge. Just as medical doctors have the responsibility for curing their patients, so the military "doctors" must order the treatment of international society when it is infected with the disease of power politics. The United States, then, traditionally has rejected the concept of war as a political instrument; war has not been viewed as the continuation of politics by other means. Instead, it has been regarded as a politically neutral operation that should be conducted according to its own professional rules and imperatives. The military officer is a nonpolitical technician who conducts the campaign in a strictly military, efficient manner. And war is a purely military instrument whose sole aim is the destruction of the enemy's forces and its despotic regime, so that after its defeat the people can be democratized.

The same moralistic attitude that is responsible for the American all-or-nothing approach to war also militates against the use of diplomacy, in its classic sense: to compromise interests, to conciliate differences, and to moderate and isolate conflicts. Although Americans regard diplomacy as a rational process for straightening out misunderstandings among nations, they also have been extremely suspicious of diplomacy. If the United States is by definition moral, it obviously cannot compromise, for a nation endowed with a moral mission can hardly violate its own principles. National principles would be violated, national interests undermined, and national honor stained. Moreover, to compromise with the immoral enemy is to be contaminated by evil. To reach a settlement with the enemy, rather than wiping it out, is to acknowledge American weakness. This attitude toward diplomacy, viewed as an instrument of compromise, reinforces the American predilection for violence as a means of settling international problems. War allows the nation to destroy its evil opponent, while permitting it to pursue its moral mission uncompromised.

Belief in U.S. Omnipotence

The fact that twice in the twentieth century the United States has successfully dealt its enemies total defeat has highlighted yet a sixth characteristic: the belief that the United States is omnipotent and, once engaged in a conflict, can "lick anyone in the system." [12] Indeed, even in the earlier history of the country, American actions had met with quick success whenever the United States had been drawn into the international arena. At one time or another, it has beaten the British, the Mexicans, the Spaniards, the Germans, and the Japanese. Furthermore, the United States had never been invaded, defeated, or occupied (as most other nations had been). It had made mistakes, to be sure, but with its great power, it usually had been able to rectify them. For a nation that had the confidence to promise "the difficult today, the impossible tomorrow"—a nation that, after all, could even turn Jesus into a superstar—failure would be a new experience.

American history had included only victories; the unbroken string of successes seemed evidence of national omnipotence. This belief in American invincibility tended to be reinforced by domestic successes. Historically, the United States was unique for, with the single exception of the Civil War, it had never experienced national tragedy. Few other states have managed to avoid defeat and conquest. American policy makers usually have not been deterred by thoughts of failure, but, had failure in fact occurred, they could have expected a major political reaction. For in a country that is believed to be all-powerful, the public will understand failure or defeat only as the result of national incompetence or treason. The nation cannot admit that its situation may not be resolvable through the proper application of force.

Pragmatism

A seventh and final characteristic is generally known as pragmatism. Again, it has been part of the nation's experience that when problems have arisen, they have been solved with whatever means were at hand. Americans have always been a "can-do" people and have prided themselves on their problem-solving abilities. Europeans invented radar and the jet engine, but it was Americans who refined and developed these inventions, produced them on a large scale, and marketed them more effectively than the countries of origin. All problems have seemed solvable; they are only matters of "know-how." The question is not *whether* but *how*—and how quickly at that. This approach to foreign policy may be called the engineering approach:

> A pragmatic or instrumental approach to world problems typifies the Western policymaker. Not theoretical conceptions enabling him to relate policy to the general trends of events, but know-how in the face of concrete problem-situations is what he typically emphasizes. He wants to "solve" the immediate, given concrete problem that is causing "trouble," and be done with it. Accordingly, diplomatic experience—always of great importance, of course—is exalted as the supreme qualification for leadership in foreign policy. For experience is the royal road to know-how. It teaches the statesman how to negotiate with the Russians, how to coordinate policy with the allies, how to respond to emergencies, and so on.
>
> In facing foreign-policy problems it is not the Western habit to attempt first of all to form a valid general picture of the world-setting events in which the problems have arisen. The tendency is rather to isolate the given problem-situation from the larger movement of history and ask: what can and should we do about it? [13]

More specifically, the United States tackles each problem as it arises. In the abstract, this approach may make sense. After all, until a situation has occurred and the "facts" are in, how can one react? The trouble is that, by the time sufficient facts are in, the situation may well be so far developed that it is too late to do much about it or, if one does try, the difficulties abound. The American quest for certainty is usually carried too far. Policy making should involve tackling problems early enough so that influence can still be usefully brought to bear; but often it can only be brought to bear when there is still insufficient information. By the time the situation is clear, a crisis may be near or at hand, and it may be too late for any effective action short of applying military power; it may even be too late for that. Pragmatism thus reinforces the reactive and discontinuous nature of the American conduct of foreign policy, along with the emphasis on the immediate and short run to the detriment of longer-term policy consideration. [14]

AMERICAN POLICY AFTER WORLD WAR II

The American approach to international politics reflects a series of simple dichotomies: domestic policy versus foreign policy, good nations versus bad nations, isolationism versus crusading, war versus peace, force versus diplomacy. But fundamental to all of them is the self-image of the United States as the epitome of democracy and the defender of the democratic faith. The

United States, the shining "beacon lighting for all the world the paths of human destiny" in peacetime (in the words of Ralph Waldo Emerson) has been like a democratic St. George battling against evil aggressors.

During World War II this moral attitude led the United States to divide nations between those that were "peace-loving" (the United States, the Soviet Union, and Great Britain) and those that were "aggressors" (Germany, Italy, and Japan). The former had to destroy the latter and thus sought unconditional surrender. The Western democracies crusaded for total victory. Once that objective had been achieved, the aggressors were to be entirely disarmed and peace preserved through the cooperation of peace-loving nations within the new United Nations. Power politics would be ended. Alliances, spheres of influence, and balances of power, President Roosevelt said shortly before his death, were to be replaced by international organization, which would furnish an alternative and better means for preserving peace. As the evil nations had been defeated, no new aggressors were expected. The Soviet Union, an ally, was certainly not expected to become an adversary.

Although Soviet behavior had already changed by the time hostilities ceased, a period of eighteen months was to elapse before U.S. policy toward the Soviets was reassessed. The American public attitude toward the Soviet Union was still generally friendly and hopeful for peaceful postwar cooperation. The United States wished to be left alone to occupy itself once more with domestic affairs and the fulfillment of American social values. The end of the war presumably signaled the end of power politics and the restoration of harmony among nations. The emphasis was therefore on rapid demobilization. Only when Britain pulled out of the eastern Mediterranean and there was no longer any countervailing power on the European continent—and only after continued Soviet denunciation and vilifications of the United States and Britain—did America's leaders again commit themselves. For this commitment to be made, a major external stimulus was needed.

The Cold War Crusade

American identification of the Soviet Union as an enemy and aggressor therefore resulted from Soviet actions in Eastern Europe, Iran, and Turkey. The Soviet Union now became the new enemy. Since international conflict was viewed as a contest between good and evil states, instead of a competition among states who all had legitimate interests, the American-Soviet struggle became transformed into another moral crusade. The Korean War and the Chinese Communist intervention in it especially turned a conflict that had been previously limited to Europe and aimed against the Soviet Union into a "global" conflict against communism. The antithesis between American democratic values and Soviet Communist values was striking; it was a clear instance of good against bad, and it fitted the traditional dichotomy of New World democracy versus Old World autocracy.

The impact on policy was readily visible. American policy makers, for instance, during the cold war years from 1946 to 1969 put off any attempt to achieve a major political settlement with the Soviet Union until after communism had "mellowed"—that is, changed its character. Until then, negotiations were thought to be useless not only because of the expansionist aims of the Soviet leadership but also because such diplomatic dealings with the devil in the Kremlin would be immoral. Recognition of Communist China became impossible, and China's intervention in Korea only confirmed the American appraisal of Communist regimes as evil, even though the United States itself had precipitated this intervention with its march up to the Chinese frontier with North Korea.

If communism per se were the enemy, then the United States had to oppose it everywhere or, at least, wherever it seemed that counterbalancing American power could be applied effectively. Thus the United States built up alliances in Europe, the Middle East, and Asia, and fought two limited wars on the Asian continent. It also supported numerous anti-Communist regimes, mostly outside of Europe, whether they were democratic or not. Most of them were right wing; Chiang Kai-shek (Nationalist China) and Ngo Dinh Diem and Nguyen Van Thieu (and several in between them in Vietnam) were typical of the dictators. Viewing communism as truly wicked, Americans counted all Communist states as uniformly evil. The recognition of differences among Communist states—and the exploitation of these divisions—was therefore difficult. Nationalism as a divisive factor within the Communist world was played down because of the belief that all such states were equally immoral. Above all, every issue of foreign policy tended to be framed as part of a universal struggle between democracy and totalitarianism, freedom and slavery.

The anti-Communist justification for American foreign policy came back to haunt the policy makers. In Europe, communism was contained, but when Nationalist China collapsed, the Truman administration was attacked as "soft on communism." Indeed, the unquestioned assumption that the United States was omnipotent suggested that the American failure in China had been caused by treason within the U.S. government. If the nation was supposed to be omnipotent, then it could not be lack of strength that accounted for its "defeat." It could not be that there was a limit to the nation's ability to influence events far away from its shores. Such setbacks seemed to have resulted from American policies.

It was argued that China had fallen because the "pro-Communist" administrations of Roosevelt and Truman had either deliberately or unwittingly "sold China down the river." This charge, which came primarily from the strong conservative wing of the Republican party (including Joseph McCarthy and Richard Nixon), was simplicity itself. American policy had ended in Communist control of the mainland. Administration leaders and the State Department were responsible for this policy. The government must, therefore, be harboring Communists and Communist sympathizers who were "tailoring" American policy to advance the global aims of the Soviet Union.[15] The "loss" of China was the fault of disloyal American leaders. Low morale among the Nationalist Chinese, their administrative and military ineptitude, and repressive policies that had alienated mass support were ignored, as were superior Communist organization, direction, morale, and the ability to identify with popular aspirations. When supposed omnipotence failed, conspiratorial interpretations were the result.[16]

The effects on American foreign policy makers were several. Above all, they wanted to avoid being accused of "having lost" country A or B, or of "appeasing communism." The Democrats, accused by the Republicans during the 1952 presidential election (in which the Democrats were defeated) of having lost China, were supersensitive to such charges. The principal result was to make American policy more inflexible and interventionist than it might otherwise have been. This was especially true of policy in Asia where one result was the inability of any administration to recognize Communist China and exploit Sino-Soviet differences before Nixon's visit to mainland China in 1972. (That visit took place after the Vietnam War had weakened America's anti-Communist consensus, and Nixon, a conservative Republican, who could hardly be accused of being "soft on communism," had been elected. The irony is that it was conservatives, who claimed to be strongly anti-Communist, who could be more accommodating in policy toward China and the Soviet Union than liberal Democrats.)

Intervention in Vietnam

The ultimate cost of this crusading policy was not the failure to recognize Communist China or exploit the Sino-Soviet split but the intervention in Vietnam. As the situation in Vietnam worsened in late 1961, it is not surprising that President John Kennedy introduced American military "advisers," particularly after the Bay of Pigs fiasco in Cuba and American inaction at the time of the erection of the Berlin Wall. Kennedy did not want the Democrats accused of being the party that had "lost Indochina," as it had "lost" China. The military advisers temporarily kept the situation in Vietnam from deteriorating. Kennedy's successor, however, had to deal with forestalling a defeat of the South Vietnamese. He intervened with American forces, the logical culmination of his predecessor's actions. From Truman on, each president had done just enough to prevent the loss of South Vietnam.

For each post-World War II president, increasing involvement in Indochina led to a major military intervention calculated as *less costly* than doing nothing and disengaging from Vietnam. In the context of American domestic politics, acquiescence in defeat was believed to be unacceptable. The costs of nonintervention in terms of the loss of congressional and public support was considered to outweigh the costs of intervention.[17] The basic rule was "Don't lose Indochina." Daniel Ellsberg summed up this imperative for each White House incumbent: "This is a bad year for me to lose Vietnam to communism." [18] Each time the American administration came face-to-face with the possibility of disaster, it escalated the involvement and commitment not to lose Vietnam. Note the negative nature of the goal: to prevent a disaster. It was hoped that, if the North Vietnamese found they could not win, they would finally just give up.

The United States was reasonably optimistic, seduced by its "illusion of omnipotence." After all, where had American power ever failed? Such optimism was expressed most strongly by the civilian policy makers. When a leading civilian government official was told that eliminating the guerrillas in Vietnam might take as long as it had in Malaya, he curtly responded, "We are *not* the British." [19] Indeed, the assumption was that Hanoi was so fearful that the United States would intervene that, should Washington indicate its willingness to do so, Hanoi would desist from helping the Viet Cong. Saigon and Washington would only have to mop up. A major war to prevent the loss of South Vietnam and, in the administration's opinion, the consequent loss of Southeast Asia, might therefore be averted if North Vietnam could be convinced of American determination; in the event of noncompliance, the Hanoi government would be subjected to ever-increasing pressure. A slow squeeze on the North Vietnamese thus began in 1964, and the administration started contingency planning for U.S. air strikes to begin in early 1965.[20]

Once the United States was involved, American pragmatism, the belief that proper techniques can solve all problems, was the guiding philosophy. The result was a resort to force. Policy makers characteristically regarded the subsequent war as essentially a "military" war, in which superior fire power and helicopter mobility would enable the United States to destroy enemy forces. The political aspects of the war, above all the basic land reforms necessary to capture the support of the peasantry, were by and large ignored, and therefore no South Vietnamese government could win popular support. Indeed, the unpopular successive regimes in Saigon seemed almost irrelevant. The fact that counterguerrilla warfare can be conducted successfully only if political conditions are ripe was ignored. The war in South Vietnam in fact could not be won. Policy makers, especially military ones, told themselves that the reason the war could not be won was primarily military: the infiltration of North Vietnamese troops and weapons. The bombing of the North was expected to remedy this problem by pounding the enemy into submission. The bombing did not, however, decrease the volume of men and supplies flowing southward, nor did it destroy North Vietnamese morale or pressure the government into ending the war. Quite the contrary: techniques employed in a political vacuum were bound to fail.

As hostilities in Vietnam dragged on and as American casualties and impatience grew,[21] American domestic politics became divided between those who advocated further escalation in the hope of attaining a clear-cut military victory and those who proposed withdrawal because victory seemed elusive. Indeed, these alternative responses sometimes were put forth by the same people, and President Lyndon Johnson found himself increasingly subject to opposing political pressures. To appease those calling for escalation, mainly conservative and hawkish elements in Congress, he did in fact escalate U.S. involvement. This decision was temporarily popular, but backfired when it failed to achieve victory. The other pressure was to withdraw, but to do this was to risk the charge of "appeasement." If he chose the middle course of neither expansion nor retreat, domestic opinion would split further, leaving the center weaker than ever. Whatever he did, the president was trapped, and he could count on little aid from his deeply divided party.

Post-Vietnam Withdrawal

Not only did this all-or-nothing attitude erode Johnson's support, leading him to forgo seeking a second term and producing a Republican victory in the 1968 presidential election; it also led to widespread American disillusionment with foreign policy and the use of power, especially the use of force. Power politics, it has been suggested, historically has been considered wicked, to be engaged in only by the states of the Old World. American power was supposed to be righteous power. The Vietnam War, which could be watched nightly on television in "living color," seemed to prove only that, in the exercise of power, the nation had been carried away and had forsaken its moral tradition. Driven by anticommunism, which exaggerated the cohesiveness and threat of the "Sino-Soviet bloc," tempted to intervene in many places and to make widespread commitments in the name of anticommunism, and aligning itself with many a disreputable reactionary regime in the name of freedom, the United States appeared to have violated its own democratic and liberal principles. This use of power in Vietnam created guilt feelings. Power was viewed as a corrupting factor. It seemed better to concentrate on domestic affairs and to return to a historic duty: to complete the unfinished tasks of American society, create a truly democratic nation in which the gap between profession and performance would be minimal and serve as an example for all mankind.

Whereas power is viewed as evil and its exercise as tantamount to abuse, providing an example of a just and democratic society to the world is considered the moral thing to do. In the words of former senator William Fulbright, chairman of the Senate Foreign Relations Committee until 1974, power had made the United States "arrogant." He counseled that the United States should focus its attention and resources "to serve as an example of democracy to the world" and to "overcome the dangers of the arrogance of power." More specifically, "the nation performs its essential function not in its capacity as a *power* but in its capacity as a *society*." [22] Ronald Steel, in criticizing the *pax americana*, has said the same thing more eloquently:

> It is now time for us to turn away from global fantasies and begin our perfection of the human race within our own frontiers. There is a great deal to do at home within a society which a century after the liberation of the slaves still has not been able to grant the Negro full equality, a society which has been plagued with violence in the streets and guilt in the heart, which has achieved unprecedented material riches and

yet is sick from a debilitating alienation, where the ideals of American democracy are mocked by the reality of racial prejudice, where individual decency is in constant conflict with social irresponsibility, where prosperity has assured neither justice nor tolerance, where private affluence dramatizes the shame of public squalor, where wealth has brought psychoanalysis, and where power has bred anxiety and fear. This is a society whose extraordinary achievements are now being overshadowed by the urgency of its unfulfilled promises and by dangerous strains in its social fabric.

America's worth to the world will be measured not by the solutions she seeks to impose on others, but by the degree to which she achieves her own ideals at home. That is a fitting measure, and an arduous test, of America's greatness.[23]

The optimistic faith that the United States, with its power and missionary zeal, can improve the world was thus replaced by a mood of disillusionment as, in the wake of the Vietnam War, it appeared that the wicked world outside could not be quickly or totally reformed and that the attempt would corrupt the nation. The characteristic swing pattern, which began with an attempt to reform the world, ended with the fear that the nation would forfeit its soul in the effort. It also renewed the determination to concentrate on the United States, to improve national life so that the presumed American superiority and greater morality could once more spread to the world and be worthy of imitation. Setting an example for the rest of the world, instead of adulterating its own purity with power politics, was said to be the American task.

In reality, such a policy is a cop-out. It implies that, before the United States can play a large role in the world and lead a coalition against an antidemocratic or immoral power, it first must purify itself and be fully democratic and moral. It no longer must be plagued by racial strife, crime, a wasteful way of life, or political hypocrisy. The United States must be perfect. Corrupted by power politics and deeply immersed in international politics, which drains its resources and diverts its attention from improving the quality of domestic life, the nation no longer must expend its energies on "foreign adventures." It must renew itself by withdrawing from power politics and devoting itself to social politics, building the shining society promised by the Founding Fathers which, if realized, would be the envy of and model for the world. Fulbright and Steel were thus arguing for the same policy that isolationists had formerly favored.

Most societies throughout history have not believed that they could achieve perfection. Mortals have hoped for this state of grace in the next world. It is possible, of course, to aspire to a better life and to create it here on earth. But it is quite another thing for critics of American foreign policy, as they have become disillusioned with the cold war, to compare *actual* conditions of society with some *imaginary* state of perfection and then to draw the conclusion from the rather obvious gap that the United States is not worthy to participate in international political life, especially to champion the cause of democracy against totalitarian regimes. In the critics' view, foreign policy is replaced by domestic policy, and virtue, not power, becomes the key. American influence should be derived solely from the United States' moral standing as a good and just society. Arms, alliances, and spheres of influence are not the answer. A redistribution of income, racial justice, environmental concerns—worthy ends in themselves—are favored as *substitutes* for a foreign policy that demands an extensive role in the world. The shift from military services to social services will presumably bring happiness to the United States and protect the peace of the world. The American approach to foreign policy thus still seems to be one of dichotomies: between peace and war, abstention and total commitment, no force and maximum force, and passionate crusading and disillusioned withdrawal.

The 1970s were a period of withdrawal. As noted earlier (Chapter 12), in a period of domestic pseudo-isolationism and strategic parity, détente for Secretary of State Henry Kissinger became a holding operation until the American people would "recover their nerve." In the meantime, Kissinger was going to exploit the Sino-Soviet split and the Soviet Union's need for Western economic help in order to keep it restrained. For if Moscow were to assert itself, the United States was unlikely to respond as in the cold war days—as later events demonstrated.

While the administrations of Richard Nixon and Gerald Ford sought to counter Soviet moves, although at times restrained by Congress and public opinion, the succeeding Carter administration embodied much of the national mood of withdrawal and guilt about the misuses of American power. Until the Soviet invasion of Afghanistan in December 1979, it rejected "power politics." Was it not this approach that had been responsible for America's involvement in Vietnam? The administration therefore deemphasized the East-West struggle while focusing its attention on the Third World and the problems of nationalism, self-determination, racial equality, human rights, and poverty. Balance-of-power politics was being transformed into "world order" politics. In the dawning new age of interdependence among states, security as the primary issue was being replaced by a concern with welfare, the hierarchy of nations by greater equality, and the use of force by more peaceful cooperation among states to advance the greater good of all nations, with special emphasis on human welfare and individual dignity (for a detailed analysis, see Chapter 21). Presumably, the wicked days of power politics were over. A more peaceful and just world was within grasp.

Humiliation and the Reassertion of U.S. Power

The Iranian seizure of American diplomatic personnel in Tehran as hostages in late 1979 sharply shifted the nation's mood again. The 444 days the hostages were held were considered a national humiliation. One month after the attack on the embassy, the Soviets invaded Afghanistan, and again the United States felt helpless. It was not just the other superpower that felt it could act without considering U.S. reactions; even a middle-range power such as Iran, in the midst of revolutionary turmoil, thought it could act against

American interests with impunity. All nations could see that in the wake of Vietnam the United States was determined to play a lesser role in the world. Congressional restraints on the president's ability to use the armed forces and Central Intelligence Agency (CIA) for overt and covert intervention raised questions about America's will to act.

As a further demonstration, defense budgets plummeted from 8.2 percent of the gross national product in fiscal 1970 to 5.2 percent in fiscal 1977, the lowest figures since before the Korean War. At a time when the Soviets were spending an estimated 12 percent, if not more, this meant that the 1970s witnessed the largest reduction in American military strength relative to the Soviet Union in the entire postwar period.[24] Large defense requests citing the continuous and enormous growth of Soviet military strength were dismissed by Congress as a "Pentagon scare tactic" in the annual budget fight. When the sharp increases in Soviet missiles were presented, the response was that the Soviets were just "catching up." When they caught up, the reaction was that now they would stop. When they did not stop, the excuse was that the Soviets, after all, confronted not only the United States and the North Atlantic Treaty Organization (NATO), but China as well. And as Soviet military power continued to grow steadily year after year, it was pointed out that the Soviets suffered from paranoia because of past invasions. Finally, as Soviet strength in strategic and conventional weapons grew beyond any conceivable defense needs—as Washington saw it—the ultimate excuse was that force no longer played a role in the post-Vietnam War world. The Soviets were wasting their money, and apparently they were too stupid to realize that the forces they were buying were no longer useful. In this political atmosphere, is it really surprising that the multiple indications of American impotence led to the humiliation at Tehran? Or that this slap in the face would once more arouse the nation to reassert itself?

President Carter's reaction to Afghanistan was twofold: the Carter Doctrine, committing the United States to the defense of the Persian Gulf oil kingdoms, and the imposition of economic sanctions on the Soviet Union. But despite Carter's belated recognition of the Soviet threat and that power politics was not quite dead, Ronald Reagan, the former governor of California, was the beneficiary of this change of public mood. Why reelect Carter, the belated convert to the "hardline," when Reagan had been the genuine hardliner all along? The pendulum had swung at least part of the way back to involvement and the reassertion of American interests and power in the world.

President Reagan refocused the nation's attention on the Soviet Union, the East-West struggle, and the central issue of American security. He did so in characteristic American style by depicting that struggle as a moral conflict. The Soviet Union was "the focus of evil in the modern world." He said to a Baptist convention, "There is sin and evil in the world and we are enjoined by the scripture and the Lord Jesus to oppose it with all our might." Reagan also stimulated and exploited a renewed pride in the nation and frequently praised the military and its service to the country. In operational terms, however, Reagan pursued essentially the post-1979 Carter politics: the strategic buildup from which he, however, cut the 200 MX missiles to 100 but resurrected the 100 B-1 bombers Carter had eliminated; the U.S. response to the Soviet intermediate-range missile deployment in Europe with equivalent U.S. arms; the growth of NATO conventional forces; increased military spending; the Carter commitment to the Persian Gulf; the strategic relationship with China, despite Reagan's personal anticommunism; the support of El Salvador's government against the insurgents; and the anti-Sandinista policy Carter had initiated in his last days as he realized the new regime in Nicaragua, which he had helped bring into power, was increasingly repressive at home and aligning itself with Cuba and the Soviet Union.

Reagan's support of Nicaraguan "contras," whom he called "freedom fighters," probably exceeded what his predecessor had done. Reagan might also have preferred to intervene with U.S. troops in Nicaragua, if not also in El Salvador. The administration appeared convinced that the Sandinistas were committed to a "revolution without frontiers," that is, undermining its pro-American neighbors in Central America. A second Cuba, or a first Cuba on the mainland, was unacceptable. Nevertheless, American opinion stood somewhere between "No More Vietnams," meaning, no more long limited wars, and "No More Irans," meaning, no more humiliations. Thus, in the absence of a direct provocation, such as the establishment of a Soviet base or shipment of major Soviet weapons systems, the administration's temptation to use force was foreclosed because a speedy Grenada-type operation was unlikely in Nicaragua. Nevertheless, there could be little doubt that much of the post-Vietnam mood had evaporated and been replaced by a "new patriotism" and a willingness to assert American power where the nation's vital interests were generally agreed to be at stake.

THE SOVIET ELITE STYLE

Because foreign policy decisions are made not by nations but by a few decision makers, some analysts have suggested that perhaps the styles or operational codes of the political elite, the small group that makes policy, may be analytically more useful. The United States has frequently been called a one-class society; the basic values of American society have been essentially those of the liberal middle class. For this country, it can be argued, the policy elite and the masses share a fundamental set of beliefs, values, and attitudes: democratic liberalism. But in other countries, where class differences are more obvious and the political elites are clearly separated from the mass of the population, the beliefs and values of the elites are usually easily identifiable. Even in countries such as the Soviet Union, which reject class distinctions and claim to be classless societies, the political elites are much more visible and far smaller in size than in Western societies, even those with clear class structures. For V. I. Lenin, who led the revolution in 1917, and his successors, the desire to overthrow czarism and capture power and the goals that they have sought internationally since that time have been shaped by their ideological outlook.

Ideology and Interest

Almost all debates over Soviet foreign policy revolve around this fundamental issue of the Soviet leaders' self-proclaimed adherence to the official ideology. Are they really motivated by Communist ideology, or do they merely use it to justify and expand their power? Are they seriously bent on fomenting world revolution, or are they trying to increase the strength of the Soviet Union as a nation? That is, are the Kremlin leaders fundamentally revolutionaries or nationalists? We saw earlier, in our first-level analysis, that ideologies are viewed as justifications for what leaders believe they must do to preserve and enhance their security interests in the state system. Ideologies are instruments for rationalizing what would have been done anyway. Ideology, therefore, is not a motivating force. All leaders, including Soviet leaders, think in terms of "national interest"; it is this interest that motivates the behavior of nation-states. Ideology, it is said, has not led the Soviets to adopt any policy that Soviet national interest has not demanded. It has been merely a means of promoting that interest. The manipulation of ideology to justify any and every change of foreign and domestic policy only "proves" that it is too flexible to be a guide to action.

The opposing arguments have been stated by Brzezinski:

> To dismiss ideology as an irrelevant criterion to an understanding of the political conduct of Soviet leaders . . . would be to assume that it is possible to build up a large organization ostensibly dedicated to certain explicit objectives, in which individuals are promoted on the basis both of their professional ability and their demonstrable ideological dedication, but in which an inner sanctum operates, makes decisions with a complete disregard of the ideological principles of the movement, indeed remains immune to the constant pressures for ideological justification, and cynically disregards the official creed.[25]

If this view is correct, then the Soviet Union's "national interest" is filtered through an ideology that, first of all, provides Soviet leaders with "a comprehensive, consistent, closed system of knowledge, to which its adherents turn to get answers to all questions, solutions to all their problems."[26] Marxism-Leninism is such a system of knowledge or *Weltanschauung*, an all-encompassing picture, a complete explanation of man, society, and history. As a *total conceptual framework*, it embraces not only economics and politics, but also philosophy, science, the arts, and even spiritual matters. No sphere of life is exempt. The ideology is also *official*, and its interpretation is the task of Communist party leaders, who regard their reading as embodying the only true view of society and history; as "true believers," such ideologues have been quite dogmatic. Finally, it follows that this kind of ideology and any other are *mutually exclusive.* By its very nature, Marxism-Leninism is intolerant of contrary beliefs—even when different interpretations of the truth have been offered by fellow believers. These dissidents, as we already know, are dismissed as heretics who have deserted "the faith."

Ideology and Perception

This stress on ideology as the key factor influencing foreign policies of the Soviet Union does not mean that, in a specific situation, Soviet leaders go to the library and find a statement of what to do clearly spelled out in Karl Marx's *Das Kapital*. It means only that the ideology provides them with a way of perceiving and interpreting "reality"—with *their* model of the world. Ideology in this context is what earlier we called an analytical framework that "organizes reality" for its devotees. It is through ideological lenses that the latter selectively perceive the world, define and understand it, and decide how to act in it. The basic characteristics of this Marxist-Leninist ideology will be elaborated in Chapter 14. We shall only summarize them briefly here:

- Economic forces are fundamental. The organization of the production and the distribution of wealth is the foundation, or substructure, upon which society is built.
- The capitalist superstructure consists of the owners of the means of production and wealth and of those who work for them and are exploited by them. Class relations are essentially based on opposing interests and conflict. According to Marx, all history is the history of class struggle between the rich and the poor—between the slave owners and the slaves, the feudal, land-owning nobility and the peasantry, the capitalist owners of industry (the bourgeoisie) and the working class (the proletariat).
- The capitalist political system, like the class structure, reflects the nature of the economic system. The owners of wealth control the state and use its instruments—the army, the police, and other levers of governmental power—to keep control. They can also manipulate other means of control, such as the legal and educational systems and religion, to maintain their power.
- This type of system cannot be reformed. Superficial, or cosmetic, changes may be attempted in order to "buy off" the underprivileged and the exploited, but they cannot save the system. Contemporary capitalism is based upon private property and the profit motive. Their abolition is the prerequisite for productive use of industry for the benefit of the many, rather than for the luxury of the few. But the nature of capitalism cannot be changed; attempts to create a socialist society will be resisted.
- The injustices of capitalism will, however, come to an end with the proletarian revolution. This revolution will occur when the proletariat has become the majority and politically conscious of its own exploitation. This day of reckoning is historically inevitable.

- Lenin explained the failure of this "inevitable" revolution to occur in the Western industrial countries by imperialism and the massive capitalist exploitation of non-Western, or colonial, peoples. This global exploitation was so profitable that some of the profits trickled down to the industrial proletariat, so that its standard of living was improved, its revolutionary consciousness eroded, and its vested interest in capitalism strengthened. Domestic revolution was thus avoided by means of a policy of imperialism.

- The Marxist class struggle within the capitalist states was projected onto the global plane. The rich are now defined as the Western industrial states, the poor and exploited as the LDCs. This worldwide class struggle has become the critical conflict in the world.

- Only when the industrial states lose the cheap raw materials previously provided by the LDCs and the economic growth rate slows, so that unemployment increases and the standard of living declines, will the domestic proletariat again recognize that its interests clash with those of the bourgeoisie. Then the class conflict will resume and will end in the proletarian revolution.

Inherent in this general analytical framework is a critique of contemporary society, which is condemned as utterly sinful and beyond redemption. Marxism-Leninism is deeply rooted in the belief that social relations in capitalist societies are evil, the products of the private ownership of property and the profit motive. It is the prevailing capitalist order that is responsible for the fact that the mass of human beings live in poverty, ill health, and ignorance. And it is capitalism that is the main reason why humanity is cursed with war. People can be freed from economic exploitation, political subjugation, and international violence only through the destruction of capitalism. According to the laws of economics developed by Marx, history has doomed capitalism; the proletarian revolution, which will usher in a better and more peaceful world, is inevitable.

Revolutionary Aims

Marxist-Leninist ideology, therefore, assigns to Soviet leaders the historically appointed task of helping to bring about the new, postcapitalist order. The ideology does not merely embody a critique of contemporary capitalist society. It also projects communism as the desired state of existence for humanity; if justice is to be realized in this world, poverty erased, discrimination eliminated, and people to be truly free in brotherhood, Communist values will have to be universal. The ideology thus dictates extensive economic and social changes. As Marx said, his purpose was not merely to philosophize about the world but also to change it. His followers feel compelled to give history a helping hand, to speed it up a bit to liberate people from their capitalist chains and ensure their secular salvation. Ideology is a motivating force and not merely a rationalization. It provides its "true believers" with both a conceptual framework *and* a long-range aim.

The Bolshevik Revolution of 1917 brought to power in a major country a group of men who were convinced that domestic justice and international peace could be realized only if the old capitalist order were swept away throughout the entire state system; all people were to be liberated from the social tyranny of capitalism and the scourge of war. This purpose transformed Russia, a traditional great power, into *Soviet* Russia, a revolutionary state, committed to the secular mission of eliminating world capitalism. The Soviet leaders denied the legitimacy of what they regarded as the prevailing international capitalistic order and the right of non-Communist states—which, by definition, were called capitalist—to exist. This ideology is contrary to the basic assumption of the balance of power: that each state has the right to exist, regardless of its domestic structure. The balance is supposed to protect all members of the state system. But the revolutionary state is revolutionary just because it *claims universal applicability for its values and ways of organizing domestic society and thus makes the domestic structures of all other states the central issue of international politics.* It seeks to extend the revolution to all other states and to convert their peoples to the faith "that makes men free"; this mission becomes its historic *duty.* Only the worldwide victory of the "new order" can lead to the establishment of a universal society in which human beings will be for the first time in history genuinely free from oppression, need, and war.

No state in a pluralistic system, obviously, can feel absolutely secure; yet each, though greatly concerned with its security, normally does not feel *so* insecure that it becomes completely preoccupied with its survival, seeking universal domination in order to eliminate threats from all other states. It seeks security within a balance-of-power system that provides for its survival, as well as for the survival of other states. Conflicts are therefore *limited* and *pragmatic;* no state seeks another's elimination. Each recognizes the right of the others to exist. Communist ideology, by repudiating the legitimacy of capitalist states, however, transforms the international struggle between the revolutionary power and its adversaries into a *total* and *ideological* conflict. If one state feels compelled to destroy the domestic structures of other states and to transform them according to its own ideological values, that state must seek dominance or hegemony so that it can impose its will on them. It seeks to overthrow the balance as a prerequisite to remaking the system in its own image.

In a brilliant and eloquent passage, George Kennan described how this revolutionary approach to foreign policy has made a "mockery of the entire Western theory of international relationships, as it evolved in the period from the seventeenth to the nineteenth centuries":

> The national state of modern Europe, bitterly as it might feud with its neighbors over the questions of *relative* advantage, was distinguished from the older forms of state power by its abandonment of universalistic and messianic pretensions, by its general readiness to recognize the equality of existence of other sovereign authori-

ties, to accept their legitimacy and independence, and to concede the principle of live and let live as a basic rule in the determination of international relationships. . . .

It was this theory that the Bolsheviki challenged on their assumption of power in Russia. They challenged it by the universality of their own ideological pretensions—by the claim, that is, to an unlimited universal validity of their own ideas as to how society ought to be socially and politically organized. They challenged it by their insistence that the laws governing the operation of human society demanded the violent overthrow everywhere of governments which did not accept the ideological tenets of Russian Communism, and the replacement of these governments by one that did. . . .

The significance of this situation has been somewhat obscured by those Western historians and commentators who have been unable to perceive any difference in principle between the attitude of the Soviet Union toward the Western countries and that of the Western countries toward the Soviet Union. After all, they have said, were not the Western governments equally hostile to Russia? Did they not attempt to overthrow the Soviet regime by their intervention in 1918-1919? Could the challenge to existing concepts of international relations properly be laid only at the Soviet door? Was not the Western rejection of socialism as a conceivable governmental system just as important in the breakdown of the established theory of international life as the Soviet rejection of capitalism?

It is my belief that the answer to the question is "No." Any unclarity on this point can lead to a grievous misunderstanding of some of the basic elements of Soviet-Western relations. There were, in those initial years of Soviet power, some very significant differences between anti-Sovietism in the West and the hostility which the Soviet leaders entertained for the Western powers. This hostility from the Communist side is preconceived, ideological, deductive. In the minds of the Soviet leaders, it long predated the Communist seizure of power in Russia. Anti-Sovietism in the West, on the other hand, was largely a confused, astonished, and indignant reaction to the first acts of the Soviet regime. Many people in the Western governments came to hate the Soviet leaders for what they *did*. The Communists, on the other hand, hated the Western governments for what they *were*, regardless of what they did. They entertained this feeling long before there was even any socialistic state for the capitalists to do anything to. Their hatred did not vary according to the complexion or policies or actions of the individual noncommunist governments. It never has. . . .

Surely, this approach cannot be equated with that of the pragmatic West, where for forty years the argument over the attitude to be taken toward Soviet power has revolved around the questions of interpretation of the behavior of the Soviet regime. There have undoubtedly been individuals here and there in the Western countries whose hatred of what they understood to be socialism has been so great that they have felt it should be rooted out with fire and sword, on straight ideological grounds, wherever it raised its head. But such people, surely, have been few; and I do not think that their views have ever been dominant in any of the major Western governments. . . . Had the Soviet leaders contented themselves from the outset with saying that they felt that they knew what was good for Russia, and refrained from taking positions on what was good for other countries, Western hostility to the Soviet Union would never have been what it has been. The issue has never been, and is not today, the right of the Russian people to have a socialistic ordering of society if they so wish; the issue is how a government which happens to be socialistic is going to behave in relation to its world environment.[27]

Marxism-Leninism, then, provided the new rules of *Soviet* Russia with a comprehensive analytical framework; it presented them with a way of perceiving the world; it defined the principal operational economic and social forces; it helped them to discriminate between friend and foe; it established Soviet long-range purposes; and it provided for continuing commitment to these purposes. Soviet policy makers perceive national security in the context of world revolution, a goal that the czars had never adopted.

Marxism-Leninism as a Method of Analysis

Marxism-Leninism provides the Soviet leaders with more than a broad *Weltanschauung* and a definition of ultimate purpose as a guide to policy; it also provides a method of analysis that makes it possible to identify, explain, and comprehend the particular historical era that the world is passing through on the way to postcapitalism. In contrast to the more pragmatic American approach, in which leaders tend to react to each problem as it arises and to deal with each on its "merits," the Soviet approach is based on a type of broad conceptual approach that is rare in the United States. This conceptual approach means that those in the Kremlin start with a broad picture of the world, the principal forces at work in it, and the direction of contemporary history.

For example, Lenin, asserting that capitalism had used imperialism to avoid domestic revolution, claimed that the basic struggle between capitalism and communism had become worldwide and that revolution would begin in what we now call the Third World. Instead of starting in the most highly industrialized nations, as Marx had predicted, the revolution would erupt in less economically developed nations, where the majority of the population are peasants, not proletarians. From the beginning, the Soviet leaders have seen their own revolution not as simply a single event in one country but as part of a larger, continuing historical process.[28] Until 1917 the international system had been controlled by the West; European colonial rule had spread to all parts of the globe, and by the beginning of the century the United States, already dominant over Latin America, had begun to play a role in the Pacific area. The Russian revolution signaled the first defection from this Western-dominated international capitalist system. Furthermore, the revolution was the beginning of the end of this basically European-centered world order; the defection of Russia was only the first one.

The projected decline of Europe was to be paralleled by the emergence of a new world order, the nucleus of which would be postcapitalist Soviet Russia. As the West's "raw-materials appendages" in the Third World became increasingly conscious of their subordinate status, their exploitation, and their poverty, they would become more and more resentful. In their "proletarian revolution" against the West, they would be drawn to the Soviet Union. In stage one—World War I—the defection of Russia had occurred; in stage two—beginning after World War II—the "peoples' democracies" of Eastern Europe and China defected from the weakening world capitalist order. Initially Soviet Russia had been alone, confronted by "capitalist encirclement"; after 1945 it was no longer alone, and the conflict became one between the capitalist and Communist worlds. As a greater number of Arab, Asian, and African nations became independent from colonial rule, Moscow leaders saw "the breakdown of the structure of Western dominion in the non-European parts of the world, the disappearance of most of what remained in the interwar periods (1919-39) of the great European colonial empires." [29] "Nonalignment" was defined as nonalignment with the West and was perceived as a radical shift in world affairs. "In an important sense ... the nineteenth century finally came to an end in the aftermath of World War II." [30]

It is hardly surprising, then, given this interpretation of contemporary history, that the Soviet Union is committed to what is now called *national liberation*. It sees its support for national liberation movements, on the one hand, as helping to administer the final blow to the old international order, propped up by the United States since 1945, and, on the other, as promoting the creation of a new postcapitalist system centered on the Soviet Union. Even during the period of détente, Moscow always openly declared that détente did not mean the end of the ideological struggle and the abandonment of support for national liberation. The Soviet-Cuban-East German interventions in Afghanistan, Angola, Ethiopia, and South Yemen during the 1970s were consistent with this perspective. That these interventions undermined American influence and enhanced Soviet influence in the strategically vital Indian Ocean-Persian Gulf area was an extra incentive to support "the struggle against imperialism." An ideology that provides its leaders with a general world view, an understanding of the principal social and political forces at work in the world, and sufficient insight into history to grasp the "essence" of contemporary international politics is obviously not meaningless, a mere rationalization of policies that would have been pursued even if the ideology had never existed.

Commitment to Struggle

Indeed, once Marxism-Leninism had committed the Soviet leadership to elimination of the old order, the conflict between the Soviet Union and the Western industrial states, all of which are regarded as capitalist, became total and irreconcilable. To the Soviets, the basic "fact" of history is the condition of continuing and unending conflict between classes or, more specifically, between states controlled by antagonistic classes, until the moment of victory. Politics is no longer a means of reconciliation. It is instead an unending series of campaigns to defeat the capitalist enemy. The only question is *kto, kovo?* (Who, whom?, meaning "Who will destroy whom?")[31] though history has already predicted the outcome. But this formula is symptomatic of a basic outlook. Between adversaries, one of which has been condemned to extinction by history and the other one selected to triumph, there can be no final agreement or settlement. A genuine lasting peace can come only after the elimination of capitalism and the victory of communism. Until then, agreements can be only temporary, each only a tactical move in the struggle, and real peace remains impossible while the conflict between the two social systems continues.

The struggle to achieve this goal must be prosecuted with vigor and persistence; to relax from the historical struggle would be tantamount to betrayal of the revolutionary mission. Victory over capitalism is the raison d'être of the movement—which does not mean that "peaceful coexistence" until the moment of victory is impossible. There is no special emphasis in Communist doctrine on the use of force, as there was in Nazi doctrine.

> The Kremlin is under no ideological compulsion to accomplish its purpose in a hurry. Like the Church, it is dealing in ideological concepts which are of long term validity, and it can afford to be patient. It has no right to risk the existing achievements of the revolution for the sake of vain baubles of the future.[32]

Soviet doctrine does not, therefore, reject temporary relaxation of tensions or détente when time is needed to recoup the nation's strength; nor does it reject accords with adversaries. Such tactical moves are required by the ebb and flow of circumstances, but the ultimate objectives remain constant. The scope for accommodation is clearly limited.

The question is not whether ultimate objectives are to be abandoned, but how they can best be realized. The struggle must go on, for the long-range aims are unchangeable; only the methods to be employed are flexible. Cooperation and negotiations do not mean the end of conflict; rather, they are ways of conducting it. Even high-risk methods are not foreclosed if circumstances favor them. The only qualification is that the risks not be so high that they might endanger the "bastion of the revolution." Marxism-Leninism has infused Soviet policy with a compulsion to expand Soviet influence whenever and wherever the opportunity presents itself and does not endanger the home base of the revolution. It is virtually treason not to take advantage of favorable circumstances when they arise; equally it is tantamount to treason to resort to "adventurism" or "romanticism" and take unnecessary risks that might threaten Soviet Russia itself.

Ideological Perceptions and World War II

Not surprisingly, the impact of the Soviet leaders' ideological perceptions greatly enhanced the degree of suspicion and fear among the states coexisting with the Soviet Union. Perhaps the most significant characteristic of the Soviet leaders' thinking is their distinction between objective and subjective factors. The former are those fundamentally economic, *objectively existing forces* that determine the social structures and political behavior of any state. Any group of Soviet leaders who are convinced that they have superior insight into history is bound to see the international environment as *extremely* hostile and to regard with deep distrust any Western state, however benevolent its expressed intentions. Indeed, as the Soviet Union has assumed that the Western states are out to destroy it—as it is bent on destroying the Western states—the Soviets' attitude toward what they regard as a capitalist-dominated system borders· on paranoia.

Consequently, it was immaterial during World War II whether Stalin personally liked Roosevelt. Roosevelt's expressions of hope for peace and cooperation after the defeat of Germany were dismissed as "sentimental gestures," not reflecting "reality." Current Soviet leader Mikhail Gorbachev was reported, on the eve of a 1985 summit conference with President Reagan, to believe that the United States was a land controlled by wealthy capitalists and conservative business interests." [33] This image of the United States as an "implacable foe" corresponded closely to the Marxist-Leninist view of a nation in which ordinary citizens are exploited by the ruling class and the purpose of government policy is to ensure the vested interests of the rich. Stalin *knew* that the deeper objective forces of the economic substructure, upon which the prevailing social and political superstructure rested, would determine Roosevelt's actions; in his view, the American president was merely a puppet—though perhaps a likable puppet—of Wall Street interests. Governmental decisions simply reflected the "law" of capitalism. How could anyone have persuaded Stalin otherwise, when he, like all other Soviet leaders, was absolutely convinced of his deeper insight into history, arising from his Marxist-Leninist training?

This suspicion of capitalist states has been constant since 1917. When any state defines another as an enemy long enough and acts upon that assumption, it will come to see confirmation for its suspicions in the reaction of the other state, whether that reaction is firm or conciliatory. Toughness will be viewed as confirmation of the other state's enmity; conciliation will be seen as an attempt to soften, in order to strike when vigilance has been relaxed. All actions by capitalist states are regarded as reflecting only their hostility toward Soviet Russia; their behavior is never attributed to friendly motives or mistaken but correctable policies. Enmity toward the Soviet Union is always present, though perhaps carefully camouflaged; the capitalist states *always* know exactly what they are doing. Errors and misperceptions are not the causes of conflict.

The intervention by Russia's former World War I allies after the Bolshevik capture of power in 1917 was seen as an attempt to restore the czar and the old order. The French attempt to contain Germany between the two world wars by means of an alliance with Poland and several other eastern European countries was viewed as an effort to keep the Soviets out of Europe. The appeasement of Hitler was perceived as designed to turn Nazi Germany away from attacking the Western states to an attack on the Soviet Union. Appeasement "opened the gates to the East" by letting Hitler swallow Austria, the

Sudetenland, then the rest of Czechoslovakia. To avoid further Western appeasement of Germany, Stalin made his own deal with Hitler, dividing Poland with him and turning Hitler's attention back toward France and Britain; he thus gained some time before Hitler once more moved to attack the Soviet Union.

During World War II, from 1941 to 1945, Moscow therefore saw the United States as a temporary ally only. Once Germany had been defeated, the United States, the strongest Western capitalist power, would become the Soviet Union's principal enemy in the continuing struggle against capitalism. Leaders in the United States, thinking in terms of the country's historic approach to international politics, saw World War II as a temporary interruption of the normal, peaceful condition among nations. After the conclusion of hostilities, U.S. policy makers expected to live in harmony and friendship with the Soviet Union. The chief American objective in Europe in 1941-45 was strictly military: the unconditional surrender of Germany in the quickest possible time, total victory, and the elimination of Hitler. A postwar balance of power against the Soviet Union played no role in the formulation of American wartime planning and strategy. Soviet policy makers, however, foresaw the postwar conflict and remained highly suspicious of the capitalist West.

To cite only one of many examples, the Soviets not unnaturally wanted the Western allies to invade western Europe to relieve the pressure on the eastern front. They did not believe any of the Western explanations of why that could not be done in 1942 or 1943, especially the claim that the West lacked sufficient landing craft for an operation of such magnitude or that the United States and Britain were unwilling to risk cross-channel invasion of France unless there were assurances that the invading forces would not be driven back into the water with enormous loss of life. The Soviets dismissed these as mere excuses. Why should the Western allies delay? Because, in the Soviet view, they were waiting to invade the Continent until Germany and the Soviet Union had bled each other white. Then they could administer the final blow to Germany and dictate postwar terms to the Soviet Union as well. In the wake of the retreating German armies, the Soviet Union consolidated its hold on eastern Europe as a buffer zone to give it greater protection in the postwar conflict.

Ironically, given Stalin's expectations, the war years had created a great reservoir of good will toward the Soviet Union both in the United States and in western Europe. The Soviet Union had borne the brunt of the German armies, and the heroism of the Red Army and the Soviet people was acclaimed everywhere. Stalin, the dictator who had collaborated with Hitler in 1939-41, became "Uncle Joe," as American leaders spoke of a new era of good relations with the Soviets. In the United States and Britain, hopes for the postwar period were high; in France, where Communists had played a leading role in the resistance movement, the Soviet Union was also much admired. By and large, the Soviet Union was described in glowing terms— virtually as a democracy—just as it was later depicted in almost satanic terms.

Concerned as the Soviet Union was about its security in eastern Europe, in this atmosphere it should have been easily reassured.

Had the Soviet Union left Poland, Hungary, Romania, and Bulgaria to govern themselves domestically while securing control of their foreign policies, as it did in postwar Czechoslovakia, it could have avoided arousing and alienating the United States and Britain. The Western states accepted the Soviet contention that Eastern Europe was the Soviet Union's security belt, but they argued that freely elected coalition governments that included Communists could be friendly to both the Soviets *and* the West. President Eduard Benes in Czechoslovakia seemed a symbol of this model for Eastern Europe, for the Czech Communists had, in a free election, won a plurality of the vote and were therefore the dominant partner in the coalition government. But even that kind of coexistence was unacceptable to the Soviet Union. Non-Communist parties were regarded by nature as anti-Communist because they allegedly represented class enemies; they were therefore to be eliminated from the Czech government, as they already had been in the rest of Eastern Europe. The Soviets overthrew the coalition government in Prague.

The Soviet Union had quickly emptied the reservoir of good will that would have guaranteed its minimum objective, Soviet security. Why? One reason lay in the fact that their exclusive and intolerant ideology was incompatible with, and hostile toward, an open society and multiple competing groups. Another was the presence of the Red Army throughout most of the area. Above all, it was the result of the anticipation that the United States would suffer another depression once war production had ceased and that, as a result, it would withdraw once more into its traditional isolationist posture. During the war Roosevelt had in fact told Stalin that American troops would be withdrawn from Europe within two years of Germany's surrender. The opportunity brought on by the fluidity of the immediate postwar situation thus had to be seized.[34]

It may be that much of Soviet expansionist policy in the wake of the retreating German allies can actually be explained in systemic terms. Russian leaders long ago had been socialized by the state system. But it can hardly be doubted that their traditional power politics outlook has been sharpened greatly by the Soviet leaders' ideological perceptions: that it has raised their sense of insecurity; strengthened their view of capitalist states as extremely hostile; committed them to accept the idea of a long-run struggle; intensified their suspicion of capitalist states' professions of peace and friendship as tricks to deceive them and lower their guard; and deepened their reliance on themselves, especially their nation's military power. During World War II, Stalin, knowing that Roosevelt was the political leader of a capitalist state—in effect, a tool of "Wall Street"—could not believe that the president's statements of good intentions and good will were genuine, and that they reflected the hopes of the American people who had come to respect and admire the Soviet Union because of its war effort, endurance, and courage. Stalin's perception of Soviet Russia's role in the world also made it impossible for him to abstain from exploiting weaknesses to the south and west of the Soviet Union in an effort to extend socialism to a larger area. The relative security that the Soviet leader could have gained for his country by acting more cautiously was squandered because of his ideological thinking and behavior. This aroused British and then American opposition; the conflict and high international tension resulted in good part from this ideological thinking, rather than from just the distribution of power.

The Soviet Union and the Western States

Communist ideology also influenced the Soviet ability to form alliances with non-Communist states, as for instance against Germany in the 1930s. France in the mid-1930s signed a treaty with the Soviet Union, which in turn signed one with Czechoslovakia. But the French were never to implement their alliance. The French were highly suspicious of Communist Russia, partly because of the existence of a sizable French Communist party and the French bourgeoisie's fear of social revolution. Another reason was the government's fear that, if it aided Czechoslovakia, the Soviets would stand by until France and Germany had weakened each other sufficiently to leave the Soviet Union in the predominant position on the Continent. Yet France and czarist Russia had been allies before World War I. It was only after that conflict and the ensuing Bolshevik Revolution that French-Soviet relations became so loaded with mutual suspicion that no meaningful alliance was possible.

In Great Britain as well, behavior between the wars was influenced by strong suspicions of Soviet motives. After the Munich conference, the British government responded to pressures from Winston Churchill and other anti-appeasement conservatives and sought an alliance with the Soviet Union, but it was so suspicious of Soviet revolutionary aims that it moved at a snail's pace. Probably to Britain's relief, Hitler signed up Stalin first. During World War II these suspicions were reduced because Roosevelt and Churchill came to view the Soviet Union as primarily a czarist state. Various factors influenced this assessment; namely, the apparent identity of Soviet aims with traditional Russian foreign policy objectives—for example, concern for the security of eastern Europe and the search for a warm-water port. The Soviet stress on the "Great Patriotic War," which highlighted Russian nationalism and tended to obscure Soviet communism, was another. Others were the dissolution of the Comintern; the replacement of the *Internationale* with a specifically Soviet national anthem; relaxation of restrictions upon religion; and the West's own hope that wartime cooperation would mitigate, if not remove, Soviet suspicions of the West—particularly if the West proved its sincerity by recognizing Russia's historic security interests.

Even the anti-Communist Churchill of the prewar period spoke of a postwar peace guarded by the "Four Policemen"—the United States, Britain, the Soviet Union, and China: "I wished to meet the Russian grievance, because the government of the world must be entrusted to satisfied nations, who wished nothing more for themselves than what they had. If the world government were in the hands of hungry nations, there would always be danger." [35] If they were jointly to preserve the peace, all four states would have to be satisfied. Churchill's assumption was that, although Stalin might be hungry, his appetite was limited and an appropriate meal could therefore be served to satisfy him. Uncle Joe was viewed merely as an heir to Nicholas II, which was the pose Stalin was striking. To be sure, this assumption was based more on hope than on reality, but it was based on genuine hope. Perhaps wartime cooperation would erode Soviet suspicions and fear of Western intentions; in any event, the attempt to win Soviet friendship had to be made if a major postwar conflict was to be avoided.

Not until the Allied invasion of France in June 1944 were Churchill's apprehensions about Communist policy reawakened by Soviet behavior in eastern Europe. But it was the postwar Labour government in Britain that took the initiative in mobilizing opposition to Soviet moves in Europe (though revisionist writers tend to forget this point). Even then, American policy makers were still hopeful. Indeed, throughout the war years and immediately thereafter, they thought of themselves as mediators between the Soviets and the British. Assuming that the Soviet Union and Britain would police the Continent, the demobilized United States preferred to act as the impartial referee between two friends whose ambitions clashed in eastern Europe and the eastern Mediterranean. Not until the Truman Doctrine in 1947 were wartime assumptions about the Soviet Union as a state with legitimate and moderate aims replaced by recognition that Soviet aims were of a greater scope and that the United States would have to take the initiative in organizing the West to contain Soviet power.

Effects of Ideology on Communist State Relationships

Communist ideology intensified the suspicions that already existed in the state system and hindered the establishment of alliances with Western states, but at the same time they impeded the formation of smoothly working alliances with other Communist states.[36] For the Soviet Union was also suspicious of other Communist states, as was revealed when, right after the war, Stalin expelled Yugoslavia's Marshal Tito—a loyal Stalinist until then— from the Soviet bloc. Soviet suspicion was revealed even more dramatically in the Soviet Union's relationship with Communist China; it simply proved impossible for these two giants of the Communist world to maintain a long-term mutually beneficial alliance. Conflicts among Communist nations were supposed to be nonexistent, for antagonism among states was ostensibly the result of the competing interests of their dominant classes. Communist states professed to be classless societies, and no strife between them should have occurred. The problem was that the Soviet Union was no longer the only powerful Communist state and that its monopoly of "truth"—that is, its total control of decision making—was being challenged.

In part the Kremlin leaders had only themselves to blame for this undermining of their authority. One of the functions of Communist ideology is to legitimate those who hold authority. Communist ideology was therefore designed to legitimate the Soviet leaders both as the rulers of the Soviet Union and—when the Soviet Union was the only socialist state—as directors of the international Communist movement. Just as there can be only one pope, there can be only one source of ideological pronouncements in a secular movement like communism. Moscow was this infallible source. But Beijing's leaders challenged this authority and the Soviet monopoly of political wisdom. In the resulting interparty conflict, each contender claimed the correct interpretation of history and the true interpretation of party theology. Within years of Stalin's death, each country was denouncing the other for heresy. Claiming to be fundamentalists, the Chinese saw themselves as remaining true to Marxism-Leninism, which they believed the Soviets had betrayed. Moscow, the Communist Rome, and Nikita Khrushchev, the new Communist pope (and later Leonid Brezhnev), were thus challenged by Mao Zedong's Eastern Orthodox Church.

Compromise on common policies between the *Communist* Soviet Union and *Communist* China was to pose an insuperable obstacle. In matters of doctrine, when the purity of ideology is at stake, does not a policy of give-and-take represent contamination? How can mutual adjustments be made between two members of a movement in which differences of emphasis become issues of loyalty to the faith? How could the primacy, infallibility, and doctrinal purity of the Kremlin leaders be reconciled with Chinese claims to an equal voice, Maoist infallibility, and ideological fundamentalism? The Western allies, themselves pluralistic societies, can cope with pluralism and diversity. Communist states cannot, for their parties impose uniform domestic patterns in accordance with their ideological interpretations. Each is a totalitarian society precisely because the Communist party claims to be the bearer of revealed "truth," which must be imposed upon society because "the truth will make men free." Heresy must be ruthlessly eliminated. How can two such states, each convinced that its interpretation of the truth is the only correct one, coexist?

Nonrevolutionary great powers at least share a degree of toleration. If they are allies, as are France and the United States, they can resolve differences as mere conflicts of interest without the additional burden of a superimposed conflict between good and evil. When differences of interest continue to exist, they do not necessarily lead to complete rupture. The self-righteous—for the righteous always tend to become self-righteous—exhibit no such tolerance, however. When ideology is so intimately linked with power, as it is in Communist policy and decision making, then there can be only one "correct" answer. Divergent policies cannot be compromised, and these differences affect the entire range of relations. The resulting bitterness between Soviet and Chinese leaders over who is orthodox and who is heretical can be appreciated best through their own exchanges:

> After Stalin's death [said the Chinese] Khrushchev, a capitalist-roader in power hiding in the Soviet Communist party ... usurped party and government power in the Soviet Union. This was a counterrevolutionary *coup d'état* which turned the dictatorship of the proletariat into the dictatorship of the bourgeoisie and which overthrew socialism and restored capitalism. [The Soviet Union is] a dictatorship of the German fascist type, a dictatorship of the Hitler type.[37]

> Matters have gone so far [replied the Soviets] that Hitler's raving about the need to "save" the people from the "Slav threat" has been taken out of the mothballs. The people in Peking [Beijing] emulate the ring-leaders of the Nazi Reich in attempting to portray the Soviet Union as a "colossus with feet of clay...."
>
> By their action the Peking leaders leave no doubt that they strive to use the heroic freedom struggle of the peoples in their global intrigues that stem from the Great Han dreams of becoming the new emperors of "The Great China" that would rule at least Asia, if not the whole world.[38]

In these circumstances, it is clear that the essence of any give-and-take is blocked by the insistence on doctrinal purity. One "correct" answer demands a single center of political authority and ideological orthodoxy. *Any relationship between Communist states must therefore be hierarchical in nature; it cannot be one of equality.* Either Moscow or Beijing must be the center of Communist theological interpretation *and* the source of policy in most, if not all, issue areas.

A COMPARISON OF AMERICAN AND SOVIET STYLES

The styles of the two superpowers have contrasted sharply since the cold war began and still do.

The American Search for an End of Conflict

In their perception of the nature of politics—especially in their image of conflict—the Americans emphasized an international harmony of interests, which stood in stark contrast to the emphasis in the state system on the inevitability of conflict and differences of interests among states. The American view was that conflict is an abnormal condition, whereas the Soviets viewed harmony as an illusion. The United States, long isolated from Europe and therefore not socialized in the state system, did not accept the reality and permanence of conflicts among members of that system. Differences between states were not considered natural and certainly not deep or long lasting; rather, they were attributed to wicked leaders (who could be eliminated), authoritarian political systems (which could be reformed), and misunderstandings (which could be straightened out if the adversaries approached each other with sincerity and empathy). Once these obstacles had been removed, peace, harmony, and good will would reign supreme.

Therefore every change of Soviet leadership aroused hopes in the United States for an end of the cold war. Perhaps, it was said, a more moderate leader would succeed, a more peaceful man. Adjectives such as *liberal* and *dove* were frequently used, in contrast to *conservative* and *hardliner*. These hopes and adjectives were heard after Brezhnev's death in 1982 and his eventual succession by Gorbachev, just as they had been heard after Khrushchev was ousted as the Soviet leader almost two decades earlier, as well as after Stalin's death in 1953. Or, it was believed, the Soviet system would be transformed from within. Over and over again, the Soviet Union was expected to behave with restraint because it needed Western economic assistance (right after World War II and again, during the détente of the 1970s); or because its own industrialization would make the totalitarian regime superfluous; or because the need of the Soviet leaders to satisfy their people's hunger for a higher standard of living would require them to shift resources from the military sector to investment in consumer goods.

Or, if evil men were not replaced or evil systems not fundamentally changed, there was always the hope that, if "misunderstandings" had given rise to the superpower struggle, they could be corrected, especially at summit conferences. Here American leaders could prove to their Soviet counterparts that they were sincere when they talked of peace and demonstrated their good will. The goal was to reduce the Soviet leaders' suspicions of American intentions and, if possible, win their friendship. If the leaders could just talk to each other face to face, realize that neither was a devil with horns but just an ordinary mortal, they could more easily see each other's point of view and, given good will, resolve their differences. The problem, then, appeared to be merely Soviet misperception of American leaders' desire for peace. Conflict could be resolved by correcting this misperception.

In this way the search for a cooperative, stable relationship with the Soviet Union goes on, regardless of past disappointments. An adversary relationship remains unacceptable to Americans; conflict and war are signs of failure. Even President Reagan, as strong an anti-Communist as any president since World War II, said on the eve of his 1985 summit conference with Gorbachev that he planned to tell the latter "that we mean him no harm. I am going to make every effort to try to reduce the mistrust and suspicion that seems to exist between the two powers." [39] Poor Gorbachev! He misunderstood us; the cold war would evaporate once this personal misunderstanding and mistrust—the cause for the cold war—was cleared up.

Thus it is hardly surprising that the United States becomes disenchanted so frequently, as with détente shortly after it was launched in the early 1970s. For if the cold war was over, peace and a moderation of conflict should be the consequence. "Negotiations rather than confrontations" were to be rule. But Soviet activities in Vietnam, Cambodia, Angola, Somalia, Ethiopia, South Yemen, and Afghanistan were seen as incompatible with the "spirit of détente." Americans expected the Soviet leaders to contain themselves—in short, to restrain themselves, or, to put it another way, to behave themselves quite unlike Soviet leaders. Soviet ideological perception makes the acceptance of the status quo impossible. Changes in Soviet leadership may bring changes of emphasis in policy or tactics, but it does not change the *fundamental* perception of the United States as the enemy and a commitment to a long-term and unavoidable struggle. The United States is the enemy because of what it is (a capitalist-imperialist state) and not because of what it does; that is, whether American policies at the moment are conciliatory.

The Soviet Focus on Conflict

The Soviet emphasis, then, totally unlike that of the United States, was on the inevitable and irreconcilable struggle with capitalist states. Conflict was viewed not as the result of wicked capitalist political leaders—they might be very decent and likable—but as the inevitable result of the system they represented. There was nothing accidental about conflict. Genuine peace and harmony could come only after capitalism, the real cause of rivalry between states, had been eliminated and replaced by world communism; until then, it was only natural, indeed imperative, to exploit existing opportunities in the Third World to advance Soviet influence. Attempts to explain or demonstrate to Soviet leaders the peacefulness or accommodating nature of American policies ran head-on into the fundamental conviction of Soviet leaders that history is inevitably going in their direction, that they have a superior—indeed, exclusive—insight into this historical process, and that they are obligated to help history along.

In contrast to the United States, which expected that détente would result in the modification of Soviet behavior, Soviet leaders never believed or said that détente was incompatible with continued struggle. While Americans became disillusioned with détente, and cynicism about Soviet intentions replaced the initial confidence, the Soviets claimed not to understand why Americans should be so disappointed in détente. They were not doing anything very different from what they had been doing all along. The United States seemed to be overreacting. There had been no understanding between the two powers on freezing the status quo, and there had therefore been no violations. The United States and the Soviet Union clearly perceived détente differently and had quite divergent expectations. The former assumed détente would result in mutual restraint. The latter perceived that détente was the result of the new strategic parity; the loss of U.S. strategic superiority as the result of the massive Soviet missile buildup "compelled" the United States to behave with greater restraint. The logic was clear: continued Soviet strategic growth would require the United States to behave very cautiously while allowing the Soviet Union to act more boldly and exploit opportunities to extend its influence, as during the 1970s.

Let us be very clear on this point: détente was seen as a symptom of America's growing weakness vis-à-vis the Soviet Union. It was the growth of Soviet strategic power that was "forcing" the United States to behave with "moderation." Military power—not the Soviet economy—had been the reason the Soviet Union regarded itself, and was regarded by the world, as a superpower. And because the Soviets also believed that it was their new-found strength that was the cause for a less confrontational posture by the United States, the logical step was to add more. Military power "paid off." In the 1970s, while U.S. defense budgets declined significantly, the Soviets continued to invest heavily in the military, despite their having overtaken the United States in numbers of missiles, and despite the fact that this investment came at the cost of improving the Soviet people's standard of living. The defense budget was not just a necessary burden to be borne because of external enemies. It was willingly paid by the regime because military might was a measure of Soviet standing and political achievement in the world.

Above all, the contrast in attitudes toward power could not be more striking. The United States has always considered itself a morally and politically superior society because of its democratic culture. Its attitude toward the use of international power has therefore been dominated by the belief that the struggle for power need not exist, can be avoided through isolation, or can be eliminated. Moralism in foreign policy had proscribed the use of power in peacetime; power was to be employed only in confrontation with unambiguous aggressors, at which point the United States would be obliged to fight on behalf of a righteous cause. Power, internationally, just as domestically, can be legitimated only by democratic purposes; otherwise, its exercise is evil and necessarily arouses guilt.

The Soviet belief in unceasing and irreconcilable conflict means acceptance of power as an instrument of policy, dedicated to the pursuit of Communist ends. But this power is used with care and restraint:

> [The Kremlin] has no compunction about retreating in the face of superior force. And being under the compulsion of no timetable, it does not get panicky under the necessity for such retreat. Its political action is a fluid stream which moves constantly, wherever it is permitted to move, toward a given goal.... But if it finds unassailable barriers in its path, it accepts these philosophically and accommodates itself to them. The main thing is that there should always be pressure, increasing constant pressure, toward the desired goal. There is no trace of any feeling in Soviet psychology that the goal must be reached at any given time.[40]

The Soviet use of power is not subject to cyclical swings from isolationism to crusading and back again, as the American pattern has been. Power is the raw material of international politics, to be applied discriminatingly and cautiously in the effort to achieve specific objectives. Its use arouses no guilt; the only requirement is that it successfully advance Soviet goals. It is used to probe for soft spots in the adversary's positions. In the past "adventurism" and "romanticism," which might have provoked the enemy and endangered the base of the world revolution, were avoided. The question is whether this attitude will prevail in the future as the regime, unable to provide its people with a higher standard of living and balanced diet, will seek to substitute foreign policy successes for domestic failures, and whether, in this quest for mass support and to demonstrate its own legitimacy, the Soviet leaders will be tempted to resort to military power, the one asset they have in abundance.

Americans, believing that peace is a natural condition and that differences between states usually can be resolved through demonstrations of sincerity and good will, cannot comprehend an attitude so dedicated to struggle. Soviet leaders, because of their commitment, never hesitate to sacrifice opportunities to win good will in exchange for strategic gains. The expansion and consolidation of Soviet power in Eastern Europe, which helped to undermine the wartime alliance, was not the only time that the Soviets torpedoed good relations with the West. In 1955 the summit conference and the "spirit of Geneva" quickly fell before the Soviet arms deal with Egypt, which helped to precipitate the Suez War a year later. The ink was hardly dry on the first strategic arms limitation treaty when the Soviets supplied Egypt with the offensive arms that led to the Yom Kippur War in 1973 and nearly led to a military confrontation with the United States. During all the years of negotiations on SALT II, the Soviets never hesitated to extend their influence in Africa. Even while the Senate was debating SALT II and the survival of the treaty was in doubt, the Soviets expanded their influence to the Indian Ocean and Persian Gulf areas, intervening with their own troops in Afghanistan. Believing in economic determinism and irreconcilable class struggle, they rejected the idea that opportunities for advancing their cause should be passed up; good will among enemies locked in a deadly struggle seemed to them an illusion anyway.

The Revisionist Explanation of U.S. Foreign Policy

In contrast, perhaps the most telling symptom of the American egalitarian style in conducting foreign policy is the appearance after every major war of works reinterpreting the country's participation. The *revisionist* histories have certain common themes: the conflicts in which the nation had been entangled had not in fact threatened its security interests. The politicians had seen a menace where none existed, and this illusion had been promoted by propagandists, who had aroused and manipulated public opinion. The illusion had also been promoted by soldiers with bureaucratic motives and, above all, by bankers and industrialists—the "merchants of death" of the 1930s, the "military-industrial complex" of the 1960s—who expected to benefit from the struggle. The United States' engagement in two world wars in this century (and in the cold war) was mistaken; these wars had really been unnecessary, immoral, or both. Yesterday's apparent aggressor and *provocateur* thus had not represented a threat to American security after all; on the contrary, the threat turns out really to have come from within. Except for certain *domestic forces*, the United States could have continued to isolate itself from international politics.

Such revisionism is perhaps the deepest symptom of the American aversion to power politics. The distinguished American diplomatic historian Dexter

Perkins wrote that revisionists always seek to convince the public that "every war in which this country has been engaged was really quite unnecessary or immoral or both; and that it behooves us in the future to pursue policies very different from those pursued in the past."[41] What is most striking about the revisionists' claim that the cold war was avoidable (based on second-level analysis) is that they really believe that, but for the United States' purported anticommunism and lack of sensitivity to Soviet interests, the conflict between the superpowers would not have erupted. It was *American* policy that aroused Stalin's fears and suspicions and led him to react aggressively and angrily. Stalin's ambitions were limited to Eastern Europe where the Soviet Union had legitimate security interests. Thus the cold war could have been avoided had the *United States*, animated by anticommunism, acted less provocatively. The revisionists were apparently unaware that in the state system, according to first-level analysis, conflict is inherent, *regardless* of the nature of the states and that, after World War II, a new distribution of power had to be arranged to provide a modicum of safety and stability in an anarchical international system.[42]

A change in *American* behavior is seen as the remedy. If Americans abandoned their anticommunism, revisionists argue, there would be no need for cold wars, interventions, or large military budgets. Instead, they could build a truly just society at home, a wiser and more moral goal. An observer in the late 1960s wrote:

> The reluctance, or the inability, to face the humiliating facts of international life is as noticeable in America as it was in the Britain of 30 years ago—at least among the young and the intellectuals. When they could no longer see their country as the noble, disinterested guardian on the ramparts of freedom, when the competitive pursuit of security could no longer be glamorized as a fight for the highest values, many sought refuge in the old illusion that one only has to recognize the beam in one's own eye to remove the splinter from that of one's opponent and thus live happily together forever after.[43]

Such an attitude, which seeks to deny the reality of international struggle and suggests that it can be avoided, is not to be found among the characteristics of Soviet style.

A CRITIQUE OF NATIONAL AND ELITE STYLES

Is There a National Style?

At this point, we might ask if there is really such a thing as national style. How can we be sure that when a decision is made, it is the result of a national style? Can we even distinguish between the style of a single nation and those of several nations whose governments and political system are similar? Robert Tucker spoke of pragmatism in policy making as Western, not just American; the British have long been proud of what they call their pragmatism in foreign affairs. George Kennan has always focused on the international behavior of democracies, not merely on the United States' crusading style. Fred Iklé, in comparing Western and Soviet negotiating techniques, notes certain distinctively Western features: letting the opponent determine the issues to be negotiated, being shy about making counterdemands, being fearful of offering unacceptable proposals, and forswearing the use of the threats. Why? Because the Western leaders, experienced in compromise and conciliation at home, believe in meeting opponents halfway, in splitting the difference; not to do so is considered improper, and to make counterdemands or invoke threats seems wrong. Good will and a sincere commitment to settle are believed to be desirable—though not exploiting a particular threat may leave one's own interests unsatisfied. Reluctance to put forth an unacceptable demand will encourage the opponent, fortify its commitments, and narrow the parameters of the Western diplomatic position. In Berlin after 1958, the refusal to state counterdemands left only Soviet demands on the books, which meant that any compromise would have undermined the West's own position. Luckily, it was part of the Soviet style to "ask for a whole loaf where they could get a half loaf—and end up with nothing." [44]

In Iklé's analysis of Western and Soviet diplomacy, Western states' national styles tend to be lumped together whereas the Soviet style is treated as distinctive. When dealing with regimes characterized by a Marxist-Leninist perspective, we no longer in fact speak of how the Communists do this or that; rather we speak of Soviet Communists, Chinese Communists, Yugoslav Communists, and Romanian Communists to stress the fact that the perceptions of any set of Communist leaders are infused with national attitudes. Yet can we really deny that certain American or British ways of perceiving and handling foreign policy problems are uniquely national or that certain forms of behavior are common to most, if not all, Communist elites?

Or Is It the Policy Maker's Style?

A second question is more obvious: Are we not really talking of the style of the policy makers, rather than of the nation? Policy is decided by a relatively few people on behalf of the nation; the people themselves do not make policy. At best, they have the opportunity to change their leaders every few years if they do not like the government's policies. Public opinion may also affect policy between elections, but by and large the public—in a democracy at least—reacts to decisions after they have been made and sets the outer limits within which the responsible officials make their decisions. Would it not, therefore, be analytically more useful to focus on the styles of these officials, as we did when we defined the Soviet style, rather than on broad national styles? Do the few who make policy share national preference, attitudes, and ways of behaving? The difficulty of distinguishing an elite style from a national style is particularly apparent in the Soviet example, where it ought to be easier to separate the Communist and national elements because of the narrow base and indoctrination of the Soviet elite.

Is Soviet expansionism due to Communist or nationalist influences? Is communism merely a tool of a long-standing, pre-Bolshevik expansionist tradition? Edward Crankshaw, a British observer of Soviet affairs, has argued that "Russia has been an expanding power since the foundation of the Muscovite state in the fourteenth century" [45] because of strategic, economic, and missionary factors. Like Louis Halle, Crankshaw has suggested that Russia has been expansionist for essentially defensive reasons, because it is not protected as are Britain and the United States by oceans or as are Italy and Spain by mountain barriers. "The Russians voyaged across the [Russian] plain, much as Tudor seamen explored the oceans. It is hard to know where to stop. If the Muscovites themselves had not expanded outwards from their centre and deep into the plain, their neighbors would have done so in their place." [46] Russian leaders have thus become obsessed with security and have expanded along lines of least resistance to keep "the enemy at the gates" as far away as possible.[47] Economic reasons, especially the search for maritime outlets, plus visions of Moscow as the third Rome (the true heir to Christian leadership and exponent of the Christian faith after the fall of Constantinople), reinforced this expansionist tradition and even gave it a strong missionary or messianic flavor. Experience in the state system, geographical position, and strategic and economic considerations are all concrete. In contrast, ideology tends to be abstract and subject to many different, usually conflicting interpretations; indeed, the practical relevance of ideology to foreign policy decisions is questionable. Is ideology not invoked more often to rationalize decisions than to influence them? What, then, is Soviet in Soviet Russian foreign policy? What is Russian? What in American policy is American and what is unique to the policy-making elite? Indeed—if we wish to be even more empirical and careful in our analysis—we can ask: What is unique to liberal policy makers like Truman and Kennedy as distinct from more conservative ones like Eisenhower, Nixon, and Reagan?

Are National and Elite Styles Constant?

The third question is whether the concept of national style suggests that characteristics are carried from one generation to the next. Common sense tells us that even if there is such a thing as national style, some of its characteristics will change over time. The Vietnam War, it has been suggested, was the product of a crusading style, but other critics have suggested that this costly tragedy may at least have had the beneficial result of sobering up the United States, of changing its style so that in the future American policy makers will take longer and harder looks at American vital interests, will not define an adversary by ideology alone, but by who that adversary is and the extent to which its policies threaten American interests. The American missionary style will, it is hoped, be tempered, and the United States, having finally been socialized into the state system, will behave more as other nations do. This point, of course, raises the question: What will be American about the United States' international conduct? Did Nixon's and Kissinger's emphasis on the balance of power—for example, using China against the Soviet Union—mean that the old crusading style has already been largely abandoned? All succeeding presidents have played this "divide and rule" policy.

Elite style is also subject to change as perceptions change. Soviet commentators and ideologues have shown an increasing awareness that the American government, rather than acting simply as an instrument of Wall Street, has a high degree of autonomy on foreign policy issues.[48] The bourgeoisie may share common interests and attitudes, but it is divided over which foreign policy to pursue. The idea of a united and cohesive group of monopoly capitalists with a single policy, enacted on their behalf by an "executive committee," has been replaced by a focus on Washington, D.C., as at least semi-independent of Wall Street. And in Washington itself the government is now divided between different sets of policy makers with varying interests and points of view on the conduct of foreign policy. Instead of an organized "power elite," there is a pluralistic decision-making system. The Soviets view American policy makers as divided into two groups, reflecting a division within the bourgeoisie itself: the "realists" and the "madmen," or "maniacs."[49] The former wish to avoid a war, are cautious while seeking reduction of international tensions, and recognize American power and influence as limited; the latter prefer military solutions to international problems, are militantly anti-Communist, and seek a *pax americana*. They also recognize nonbourgeois groups such as trade unions and churches as seeking to influence policy.

By and large, then, American foreign policy, as conducted by the realists, is aimed not at destroying the Soviet Union and risking nuclear warfare but at preserving the state system and peaceful coexistence with the Soviets. In terms of our own previous analysis of the changed nature of American-Soviet relations, the leaders in Moscow view the contemporary pattern as a relationship incorporating both conflict *and* cooperation. Although the Soviets are still committed to the vision of a Communist world, they appear to perceive it as more distant. In the early 1960s Khrushchev believed that there would be significant advances toward that goal during the next two decades; within a few years his successors were stressing the several centuries that it had taken capitalism to supplant feudalism. In short, the leaders of the Soviet Communist party—like the leaders of the British Labour party after World War II—have become increasingly "socialized" by the state system. Indeed, "it is to structural changes in the Soviet Union's position in the international system that one might primarily look for an explanation of the evolution of Soviet perspectives on the international system."[50] As one of the two superpowers, the Soviet Union has increasingly acted as other great powers have always done—that is, it has shown a keener concern for its place in the existing system than for the conversion of this system into a new order. As it has become a "have" power, an equal of the United States, the Soviet Union's interest in managing the state system, in the survival of which it has acquired a vested interest, has risen. And this reason has been reinforced by nuclear weapons, which have made it necessary to think of "peaceful coexistence" in more than tactical terms.[51] Revolutionary ambitions have had to be adjusted to the realities of the existing system.

Or Is Style Confused with the Distribution of Power?

These results of the confrontation between style and reality raise the fourth question: How can the outside observer distinguish between national style and responses to the distribution of power in the state system? We noted earlier that, when Britain, France, and Germany collapsed after World War II, the United States emerged as the only power capable of counterbalancing the Soviet Union in Eurasia. Emerging bipolarity generated the containment policy. To be sure, the ability of American policy makers to mobilize popular support for this policy in terms of the traditional dichotomy between Old World and New World, authoritarianism and democracy, was very helpful in these circumstances. But can it be claimed that the United States would not have reacted as it did in the context of external bipolar pressures except for its national style?

Is Style a Product of What Is Said or Done?

This question in turn raises the fifth and final question about national style as an analytical tool: Is style, to the extent that it exists, to be defined by what policy makers say, by what they do, or by particular patterns of behavior that they and their predecessors have exhibited before? Does the United States really act according to its style, or does it merely verbalize in a certain way in order to disguise a policy dictated pretty much by power politics and first-level considerations? When Secretary of State John Foster Dulles spoke of a "moral crusade against communism," was he really sincere, or was he trying to mobilize congressional and public opinion according to a rather old but successful formula? When presidential candidate Carter spoke of replacing balance-of-power politics with "world-order politics," was he suggesting a different kind of foreign policy or merely setting himself and the Democrats off from the Republican administration and Secretary of State Kissinger's "realist" philosophy? Is the Soviet Union's "adversary partnership" with the United States consistent with its ideological outlook, or is ideology invoked merely to justify a policy dictated by the necessity of coexistence in a nuclear state system? The leaders in Beijing certainly left no doubt that they believe the Soviet Union has betrayed the faith in establishing its relationship with the United States. But, then, have not the Chinese done the same thing because of balance-of-power calculations?

Notes

1. Arnold Wolfers and Laurence W. Martin, eds., *The Anglo-American Tradition in Foreign Affairs* (New Haven, Conn.: Yale University Press, 1956), ix-xxvii.
2. Louis Hartz, *The Liberal Tradition in America* (New York: Harvest Books, 1955).
3. Zbigniew Brzezinski, "The Soviet Union: Her Aims, Problems and Challenges to the West," in *The Conduct of East-West Relations in the 1980s*, Part I (London: The Institute of Strategic Studies, 1984), 4; and Richard Pipes, *Survival Is Not Enough* (New York: Simon & Schuster, 1984), 37-44.
4. Alexander L. George, "The 'Operational Code': A Neglected Approach to the Study of Political Leaders and Decision-Making," *International Studies Quarterly* (June 1969): 190ff.
5. An exhaustive analysis of the American "style" may be found in *Gulliver's Troubles, or The Setting of American Foreign Policy*, by Stanley Hoffmann, (New York: McGraw-Hill, 1968), 87-213. See also Hans J. Morgenthau, *In Defense of the National Interest* (New York: Alfred A. Knopf, 1951); Robert E. Osgood, *Ideals and Self-Interest in America's Foreign Relations* (Chicago: University of Chicago Press, 1953); George F. Kennan, *American Diplomacy 1900-1950* (Chicago: University of Chicago Press, 1951); and John W. Spanier, *American Foreign Policy Since World War II*, 10th ed. (New York: Holt, Rinehart & Winston, 1985).
6. The hypothesis about democratic behavior offered by Klaus Knorr and others and discussed in Chapter 2 is generally supported by Gabriel A. Almond, who, in *The American People and Foreign Policy* (New York: Holt, Rinehart & Winston, 1960), strongly emphasizes the "extraordinary pull of domestic and private affairs even in periods of international crises." See particularly Chapter 3, with Almond's summation of the American value orientation.
7. Paul Seabury, *The Rise and Decline of Cold War* (New York: Basic Books, 1967), 39-45, offers some fitting quotations, especially a poem by Archibald MacLeish celebrating the *pax americana* as a preamble to the *pax humana* during World War II. The moralism of Secretary of State John Foster Dulles is discussed by William L. Miller, "The 'Moral Force' Behind Dulles' Diplomacy," *Reporter*, Aug. 9, 1956.
8. Quoted by Arthur S. Link, *Wilson the Diplomatist* (Baltimore: Johns Hopkins University Press, 1957), 89.
9. Quoted in Joseph M. Jones, *The Fifteen Weeks* (New York: Viking, 1955), 272.
10. Robert E. Osgood, *Limited War* (Chicago: University of Chicago Press, 1957), 28-45, focuses on this point in explaining the difficulties that the nation experiences in conducting limited wars.
11. John W. Spanier, *The Truman-MacArthur Controversy and the Korean War* (Cambridge, Mass.: Harvard University Press, 1959), 221-238.
12. Denis W. Brogan, "The Illusion of Omnipotence," *Harper's*, Dec. 1952, 21-28.
13. Robert C. Tucker, *The Soviet Political Mind* (New York: Holt, Rinehart & Winston, 1963), 181-182.
14. There is, in fact, a very important eighth characteristic: the belief that political problems can be solved through economic means. For an elaboration of this characteristic, see Chapter 20.
15. Tang Tsou, *America's Failure in China* (Chicago: University of Chicago Press, 1963), 538-541. For a study of the accusation of a leading State Department figure by Senator Joseph McCarthy, see McGeorge Bundy, *The Pattern of Responsibility* (Boston: Houghton Mifflin, 1952), 201-220.

16. The repetitious pattern of charges of conspiracy in American political life has been explored by Richard Hofstadter, *The Paranoid Style in American Politics* (New York: Vintage, 1967).

17. Leslie H. Gelb, *The Irony of Vietnam* (Washington, D.C.: The Brookings Institution, 1979), 220-226.

18. Daniel Ellsberg, *Papers on the War* (New York: Simon & Schuster, 1972), 101-102.

19. Bill Moyers, President Johnson's special assistant from 1963 to 1966, reports this comment in an interview with the *Atlantic Monthly* reprinted in *Who We Are*, ed. Robert Manning and Michael Janeway (Boston: Little, Brown, 1969), 262.

20. For details, see the inside account revealed in *The Pentagon Papers*, ed. Mike Gravel, 5 vols. (Boston: Beacon Press, 1971); a shorter account may be found in *Vietnam* by Stanley Karnow (New York: Viking, 1983). Also see the careful reconstruction of the beginning of the 1965 bombing campaign in *The Limits of Coercive Diplomacy* by Alexander L. George (Boston: Little, Brown, 1971), 144-200.

21. Larry Elowitz and John W. Spanier, "Korea and Vietnam: Limited War and the American Political System," *Orbis*, Summer 1974, 510-534; and John E. Mueller, *War, Presidents and Public Opinion* (New York: John Wiley & Son, 1973). Mueller comes to the startling conclusion that the war had no *independent* impact on President Lyndon B. Johnson's declining popularity, though the rate of the decline was the same as that for Truman during the Korean War. See also Milton J. Rosenberg et al., *Vietnam and the Silent Majority* (New York: Harper & Row, 1970).

22. J. William Fulbright, *Arrogance of Power* (New York: Vintage, 1967), 256-258.

23. Ronald Steel, *Pax Americana* (New York: Viking, 1967), 353-354.

24. John Lewis Gaddis, *Strategies of Containment* (New York: Oxford University Press, 1982), 320.

25. Zbigniew K. Brzezinski, *The Soviet Bloc* (Cambridge, Mass.: Harvard University Press, 1967), 388ff.

26. Herbert J. Spiro, *Government by Constitution* (New York: Random House, 1959), 180.

27. George F. Kennan, *Russia and the West Under Lenin and Stalin* (Boston: Little, Brown, 1961), 179-183, emphasis in original. Used by permission of the publisher.

28. Tucker, *Soviet Political Mind*, 185-189.

29. Ibid., 190

30. Ibid., 190-191.

31. Nathan Leites, *A Study of Bolshevism* (New York: Free Press, 1953), 27-63; and Robert Strausz-Hupé et al., *Protracted Conflict* (New York: Harper & Row, 1959), 21-22.

32. Kennan, *American Diplomacy 1900-1950*, 118.

33. *New York Times*, Nov. 15, 1985.

34. Adam B. Ulam, *Expansion and Coexistence* (New York: Holt, Rinehart & Winston, 1968), 410; and Paul E. Zinner, "The Ideological Bases of Soviet Foreign Policy," *World Politics*, July 1952, 497-498.

35. Winston S. Churchill, *Closing the Ring*, vol. 5 of *The Second World War* (Boston: Houghton Mifflin, 1948), 363, 382.

36. Ulam, *Expansion and Coexistence*, 398-402.

37. *New York Times*, May 3, 1970.

38. Ibid.

39. *New York Times*, Nov. 13, 1985.

40. Kennan, *American Diplomacy 1900-1950*, 118.

41. Dexter Perkins, "American Wars and Critical History," *Yale Review* (Summer 1951): 682-695.

42. For some of the revisionist histories that place the responsibility for beginning the cold war upon the United States, see D. F. Fleming, *The Cold War and Its Origins*, 2 vols. (Garden City, N.Y.: Doubleday, 1961); Gar Alperovitz, *Atomic Diplomacy: Hiroshima and Potsdam* (New York: Vintage, 1967); William A. Williams, *The Tragedy of American Diplomacy* (Cleveland: World, 1959); Gabriel Kolko, *The Politics of War: The World and United States Foreign Policy, 1943-1945* (New York: Random House, 1968); and Thomas G. Paterson, *Soviet American Confrontation* (Baltimore: Johns Hopkins University Press, 1973).

   Evaluations of the Fleming-Alperovitz thesis, in which American anticommunism is blamed directly, may be found in Arthur Schlesinger, Jr., "The Origins of the Cold War," *Foreign Affairs* (October 1967): 22-52; J. L. Richardson, "Cold War Revisionism: A Critique," *World Politics*, July 1972, 579ff.; and John W. Spanier, "The Choices We Did Not Have: In Defense of Containment," in *Caging the Bear*, ed. Charles Gati (New York: Bobbs-Merrill, 1974), 128ff. The Gati book provides a discussion of Kennan's analysis and the policy of containment twenty-five years after the latter's anonymous article "The Sources of Soviet Conduct" in *Foreign Affairs* (July 1947): 566-582, later republished in *American Diplomacy 1900-1950*, 107-128. In that article Kennan had provided the Truman administration with a rationale for its containment policy. Finally, for an assessment of economic interpretations of American policy, see Robert W. Tucker, *The Radical Left and American Foreign Policy* (Baltimore: Johns Hopkins University Press, 1971). For an analysis that suggests either poor scholarship or deliberate distortion of the documents, see Robert J. Maddox, *The New Left and the Origins of the Cold War* (Princeton, N.J.: Princeton University Press, 1973).

43. J. H. Huizinga, "America's Lost Innocence," *New York Times Magazine*, Jan. 26, 1969, 82.

44. Fred Iklé, *How Nations Negotiate* (New York: Harper & Row, 1964), 238-253.

45. Edward Crankshaw, *Cracks in the Kremlin Wall* (New York: Viking, 1951), 58.

46. Ibid., 59.

47. Ibid., 60.

48. William Zimmerman, *Soviet Perspectives on International Relations, 1956-67* (Princeton, N.J.: Princeton University Press, 1969), 214-218. For Kennan's own reassessment of his original view of Soviet foreign policy, see Charles Gati, "Mr. X Revisited: An Interview wth George Kennan," and "Mr. X Reassessed: The Meaning of Containment," *Caging the Bear*, 27, 40.

49. Zimmerman, *Soviet Perspectives*, 221-225.

50. Ibid., 282.

51. Jan F. Triska and David D. Finley, *Soviet Foreign Policy* (New York: The Macmillan Co., 1968); and Hannes Adomeit, *Soviet Risk-Taking and Crisis Behavior* (London: Allen & Unwin, 1982).

CHAPTER 14

The Less-Developed Countries: The Primacy of Domestic Concerns

FOREIGN POLICY AS THE CONTINUATION OF DOMESTIC POLITICS

During the cold war years, the term *Third World* was used to describe the former colonial, mostly non-Western, largely nonwhite, less-developed countries (LDCs). These nations did not, of course, constitute the unitary bloc implied by the label. There was considerable diversity among them: in history and experience, in religion and culture, in population and resources, and in ideology and political and economic systems. Some nations were more developed than others. Some had very large populations; many had small populations. Some possessed sizable resources; others were not well endowed. Some were governed by religious tradition (especially in the Islamic world), but most were secular. What united them was their past colonial history, a determination to modernize, and a desire to fulfill the "revolution of rising expectations." In these respects, they were distinct from the First World (Western industrial) and the Second World (Soviet-led Communist). In their foreign policies, the Third World states generally preferred nonalignment.

Since 1970 there has been increasing emphasis on the conflict between the First and Third Worlds, also called the North-South, or rich-poor, conflict. The term *South*, like Third World, claims more than it should. Indonesia and India are *South*, but Australia and New Zealand are *North*. Geographically erroneous as the term may sometimes be, the phrase North-South does have the advantage of emphasizing the frustration of most LDCs over the continued division of the world between rich and poor nations (see Figure 14-1). What united the poor nations is a set of common attitudes: anger against the

Western industrial nations and a sense that the LDCs do not control their own political and economic destinies.

The 1973 embargo of the Organization of Petroleum Exporting Countries (OPEC) against the United States and the quadrupling of oil prices dramatically united the LDCs, even though the higher oil prices hurt most of them more than it did the West. But the LDCs supported OPEC because, for the first time, they sensed that the industrial nations were vulnerable and could be pressured by means of producer cartels. Their firm belief that they were the victims of the Western-dominated international economic system and that they must stand together to regain control over their fates led the Third World nations to move from nonalignment closer to confrontation with the

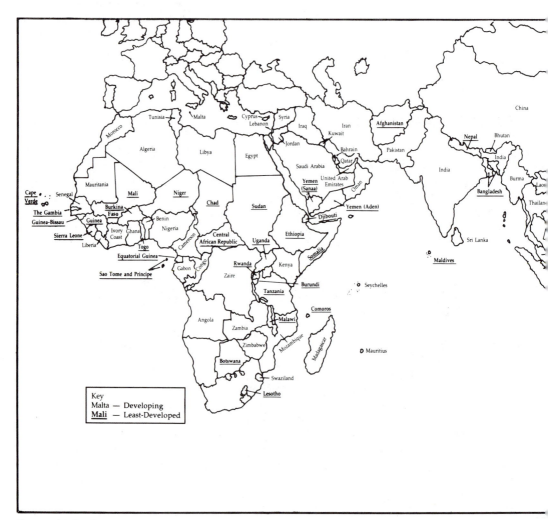

Figure 14-1 Developing and Least-Developed Countries

West. This division between rich and poor nations may in fact be somewhat oversimplified; a continuum between very rich and very poor is probably a more accurate image. While the distance between the extremes is growing, that between the developed countries and the top rank of the LDCs (those with more than $2,000 per capita annual income) is narrowing. Nevertheless, the policy of nonalignment has increasingly shifted to that of alignment against the West.

The desire to modernize molds the LDCs' perceptions of the world. Their foreign policies reflect this preoccupation with nation building. It has been said that, for a "new state, foreign policy is domestic policy pursued by other means; it is domestic policy carried on beyond the boundaries of the state." [1]

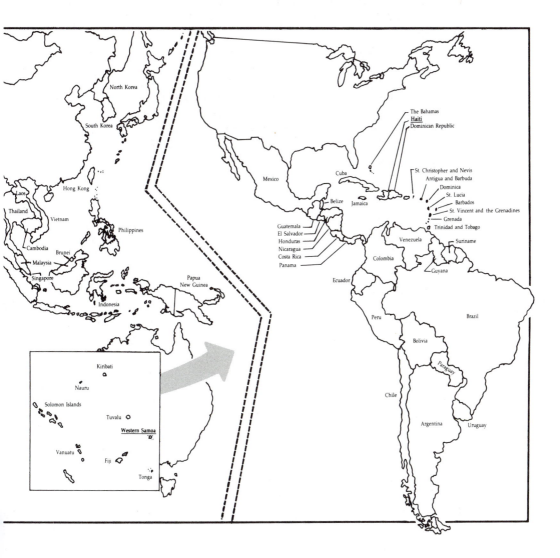

DEPRIVATION, DESPERATION, AND DEGRADATION

The right to national self-determination, conceived in the West but denied by Western industrial powers to their overseas territories, became a key issue after World War II. Throughout Asia and Africa, former colonies sought national independence and most gained it. The common denominator of this global nationalist revolution has been a fundamental urge to be free from the control of former colonial powers. From the beginning, colonialism contained the seeds of its own destruction. Humiliation and resentment of foreign domination stirred a "reactive nationalism" that asserted itself in terms of the very values by which the Westerners justified their rule—national self-determination, dignity, and equality. A nation must be master of its own destiny; no one must ever dominate it again or treat it condescendingly.

Accompanying this drive for national independence has been the determination to achieve a higher standard of living and to abolish the abject poverty and misery of past centuries. In the economically less-developed countries, people have continued to live on subsistence agriculture because they have not possessed modern tools—factories, machinery, dams, and so forth—with which to increase productivity. Even more important, they have lacked the cultural values, social structure, and political order necessary for industrialization. Less-developed nations do not necessarily lack natural resources, however. They can in fact be divided between those that possess plentiful supplies of resources (for example, the oil states) and those that control either less desirable raw materials or very little of nature's wealth at all. Many of the latter are, like the industrialized countries, victims of higher oil prices. But the hallmark of an LDC is its inability to attain *continued* economic growth. The dividing line between developed and less-developed societies is usually pegged at an average annual income per person of $500. For the 70 percent of the world's population living in the new nations, the per capita income figure is far lower—about $380 a year, or 87 cents a day.

In contrast, the annual average per capita incomes in Western Europe, Japan, and the United States were astronomical by the beginning of the 1980s. The American figure stood just over $11,000, and West Germany, Sweden, and Switzerland were even higher. But OPEC members, until the recent decline in oil prices, had some of the highest figures; for example, Kuwait reached $23,000 a year. Further, these Western incomes continue to rise, while those in the non-OPEC LDCs have been at a virtual standstill. The industrial West has had the capital for further growth; the new nations have suffered from lack of capital. But the dividing line between developed and less-developed countries is not purely economic; it is also reflected in differences in infant mortality, life expectancy, general health, availability of consumer goods and housing (especially, bathing facilities and living space), calorie intake per person, and sources of energy.

For the affluent middle-class American who has never known what it is to be poor, it is impossible to conceive of the life led by a typical family in a developing nation. In the early 1960s Robert Heilbroner graphically conveyed what such an existence would mean to an American suburban family then living on $9,000-$10,000 a year:

> We begin by invading the house of our imaginary American family to strip it of its furniture. Everything goes: beds, chairs, tables, television set, lamps. We leave the family with a few old blankets, a kitchen table, a wooden chair. Along with the bureaus go the clothes. Each member of the family may keep in his "wardrobe" his oldest suit or dress, a shirt or blouse. We will permit a pair of shoes to the head of the family, but none for the wife or the children.
>
> We move into the kitchen. The appliances have already been taken out, as we turn to the cupboards and larder. The box of matches may stay, a small bag of flour, some sugar and salt. A few moldy potatoes, already in the garbage can, must be hastily rescued, for they will provide much of tonight's meal. We will leave a handful of onions, and a dish of dried beans. All the rest we take away: the meat, the fresh vegetables, the canned goods, the crackers, the candy.
>
> Now we have stripped the house: the bathroom has been dismantled, the running water shut off, the electric wires taken out. Next we take away the house. The family can move to the toolshed. It is crowded, but much better than the situation in Hong Kong, where (a United Nations report tells us) "it is not uncommon for a family of four or more to live in a bedspace, that is, on a bunk bed and the space it occupies—sometimes in two or three tiers—their only privacy provided by curtains."
>
> But we have only begun. All the other houses in the neighborhood have also been removed; our suburb has become a shantytown. Still, our family is fortunate to have a shelter; 250,000 people in Calcutta have none at all and simply live in the streets. Our family is now about on a par with the city of Cali, Colombia, where, an official of the World Bank writes: "on one hillside alone, the slum population is estimated at 40,000—without water, sanitation, or electric lights. And not all the poor of Cali are as fortunate as that. Others have built their shacks near the city on land which lies beneath the flood mark. To these people, the immediate environment is the open sewer of the city, a sewer which flows through their huts when the river rises."
>
> And still we have not reduced our American family to the level at which life is lived in the greatest part of the globe. Communication must go next. No more newspapers, magazines, books—not that they are missed, since we must take away our family's literacy as well. Instead, in our shantytown we will allow one radio. In India the national average of radio ownership is one per 250 people, but since the majority of radios is owned by city dwellers, our allowance is fairly generous.
>
> Now government services must go. No more postman, no more fireman. There is a school, but it is three miles away and consists of two classrooms. They are not too overcrowded since only half the children in the neighborhood go to school. There are, of course, no hospitals or doctors nearby. The nearest clinic is ten miles away and is tended by a midwife. It can be reached by bicycle, provided that the family has a bicycle, which is unlikely. Or one can go by bus—not always inside, but there is usually room on top.
>
> Finally, money. We will allow our family a cash hoard of five dollars. This will prevent our breadwinner from experiencing the tragedy of an Iranian peasant who went blind because he could not raise the $3.94 which he mistakenly thought he needed to secure admission to a hospital where he could have been cured.

Then the head of our family must earn his keep. As a peasant cultivator with three acres to tend, he may raise the equivalent of $100 to $300 worth of crops a year. If he is a tenant farmer, which is more than likely, a third or so of his crop will go to his landlord, and probably another 10 percent to the local money lender. But there will be enough to eat. Or almost enough. The human body requires an input of at least 2,000 calories to replenish the energy consumed by its living cells. If our displaced American fares no better than an Indian peasant, he will average a replenishment of no more than 1,700-1,900 calories. His body, like any insufficiently fueled machine, will run down. That is one reason why life expectancy at birth in India today averages less than forty years.

But the children may help. If they are fortunate, they may find work and thus earn some cash to supplement the family's income. For example, they may be employed as are children in Hyderbad, Pakistan, sealing the ends of bangles over a small kerosene flame, a simple task which can be done at home. To be sure the pay is small; eight annas—about ten cents—for sealing bangles. That is, eight annas per gross of bangles. And if they cannot find work? Well, they can scavenge, as do the children of Iran who in times of hunger search for the undigested oats in the droppings of horses.[2]

A quarter of a century later, things are not much better for the average person in the Third World, and certainly not in Africa where in 1985-86 millions faced outright starvation. The average income for an African is less than one-thirtieth of the average American income. The gross national product (GNP) of all forty-six sub-Saharan African states is less than 6 percent that of the United States. Africa supports 400 million people on an economy that is about as productive as that of Illinois; and Africa has the highest birthrate of all the regions in the world.[3] It is not surprising that, as a former Pakistan finance minister once said, for the children who survive the age of five years in the less-developed countries, life is a matter of "deprivation, desperation, and degradation. It is an intense, but mercifully a short struggle, as their life expectancy is no more than thirty years."

Although life expectancy has risen in the LDCs, as has the standard of living in some, there remains a huge disparity of wealth between a minority of people who live in the West and the vast majority of those who live in the Third World. The widening gulf between the First World's wealth and the poverty of the less-developed countries can only result in an unstable world that is ripe for exploitation by anti-Western movements, be it Soviet communism or Islamic fundamentalism, to the detriment of Western security interests.

THE 'WESTERNIZATION' OF THE LESS-DEVELOPED COUNTRIES

Although the LDCs generally tend to blame Western capitalism for these conditions, the role played by the Western industrial nations in forging the nationhood of these countries cannot be ignored.

Territorialization

Usually it has been "territorialization" by the colonial powers that has defined the present frontiers of the developing countries. The Western powers drew arbitrary lines on the map, often straight through tribal or ethnic boundaries, and then imposed administrative and legal structures upon the resulting territories. All who lived within a particular structure were treated as if they belonged to a single nation. A graphic example of the impact of such actions on the new nations is provided by Indonesia. When Indonesia received its freedom, it did not receive the territory of Dutch New Guinea or West Irian. The Dutch claimed that the people of New Guinea were ethnically, racially, and culturally distinct from the Indonesians. Nevertheless, Indonesia persisted in claiming the region until, in 1963, it acquired West Irian. The territory had been part of the old Dutch East Indies empire, and Indonesia defined its territorial limits by the former imperial frontiers. Similarly, India, in its quarrel with China over precisely where the Sino-India boundary lies in the Himalayas, has defined its claim by the line drawn by British colonizers.

Infrastructure

Another by-product of colonialism has been the construction of harbors, roads, railroads, airports, telephone and telegraph lines, and factories, as well as the development of natural resources. These facilities have provided what economists call the infrastructure, or capital overhead, the prerequisite for any major industrialization.[4] To be sure, Europeans did not undertake such projects for the benefit of the natives. The roads and railroads were to carry resources or crops from the interior to the harbors; they were also used for troop movements to quell uprisings and riots. Nevertheless, their impact upon the traditional native economy and society was disruptive. The traditional patterns of life and expectations of the vast majority of peasants who had migrated from the land were altered in the cities. European-built centers of government, business, and communications offered the peasants who came there to work a new way of life and values. Urban life provided the "demonstration effect."[5] The Europeans lived better and longer. Why, the natives wondered, could they not live as well and as long? They could hardly avoid awareness of the technical and scientific knowledge, tools, and skills that had given the Europeans their higher material standards, as well as their power. Why, the natives asked themselves, could they not learn these secrets? One point was especially noteworthy: Europeans believed that life could be improved here on earth and that poverty need not be accepted as one's fate.

Education

The urge to transform backward societies into modern societies thus began with the European introduction of urbanization, industry, wage-labor forces, and exchange economies. But the most significant contribution of Western colonialism was education of the social groups determined to lead their shackled nations into freedom and modernity. A relatively small and youthful group, this secular nationalist intelligentsia produced the leadership of revolutionary movements in the less-developed countries. Its members were doctors, journalists, civil servants, lawyers, and so forth; what they had in common was their "Westernization." Educated in Europe or the United States—or in Western schools in their own countries—they had learned Western ways. Even more significant, in the course of their professional training they had learned to think in characteristically Western rational and secular terms. This "scientific" and "material" pattern of thought has revolutionary implications; for the LDCs' intelligentsia, it provided an escape from the traditions, customs, and privileges that had held their societies in the tight grip of economic, social, and political backwardness. Materialism, with its simple but powerful message that human beings can be the masters of their own destinies, was exhilarating, a promise of intellectual liberation from religious superstition; it substituted rationalism for obsolete traditions and institutions. It had been the absence of just such a material attitude that had been responsible for these nations' economic underdevelopment.

Education, then, was the chief means by which Western political and social thought was diffused to non-Western peoples. As one political analyst had observed, "The future will look back upon the overseas imperialism of recent centuries, less in terms of its sins of oppression, exploitation, and discrimination, than as the instrument by which the spiritual, scientific, and material revolution which began in Western Europe with the Renaissance was spread to the rest of the world." [6] It was this Westernization that transformed members of the intelligentsia into leaders of the nationalist and modernist movements of their own countries.[7]

But, as intensely aware as the first generation of leaders and their successors were of the underdeveloped condition of their countries and as determined as they have been to initiate development, they have faced almost insuperable obstacles to the necessary economic "takeoff" and self-sustaining economic growth. Lack of national cohesion, far too rapidly growing populations, dearth of capital, inability to feed their people, and traditional social structures and values all have impeded the modernization of their societies, with grave foreign policy implications.

OBSTACLES TO DEVELOPMENT

Absence of National Unity

The first obstacle to transforming the LDCs into nations is the lack of national unity. The Westernized intellectuals have become rulers of new nations, but few of their subjects share their nationalism. Concepts of nation, of national loyalty, of national governments making decisions for the benefit of the entire community, and of national laws and regulations taking precedence over local rules and tradition are new and strange to most of the peoples of the less-developed areas. The first requirement of leaders of the new nations has been to construct the very nations in whose names they have revolted against colonial domination. They must be "nation builders." The masses' lives have been rooted in smaller communities, and their first loyalties are to tribes, regions, or to religious, racial or linguistic groups.[8] Loyalties are parochial, and attitudes are particularistic. They stand as formidable barriers to the formation of national consciousness and devotion to national symbols and may, in fact, reach such intensity as to cause civil war. People from other regions are regarded not as fellow nationals but as strangers, foreigners, outsiders. Disunity, rather than unity, is the spirit of most new nations. The communities created by the colonial powers may have become "national" in the sense that the people living in them have rid themselves of foreign rulers. But their common resentment and aspiration to be free has not developed into shared allegiance to nations with artificial frontiers previously drawn by Europeans.

Indeed, once the colonial ruler that united them had gone, the new nations have tended to fall apart. When the British kept order and public security in India, the Muslims, Hindus, and Sikhs could coexist; once Britain withdrew, their mutual fear and hatred of one another led to disintegration and bloodshed. The various groups that compose a new nation realize how little they have in common, indeed how many things divide them. The issue facing the new nations, then, is not whether they will develop economically, but whether they will survive as national entities. For when people obey racial, religious, or tribal authority instead of legitimate national authority, secession and civil war may result. Ironically, the new nations face the task of nation building at a time when some Western states are once more confronting similar demands for independence and greater self-government. In Canada the French-speaking population has been pressing for independence, and in the United Kingdom the Scots have been making similar demands; in other societies, such as Belgium, Spain, and Ireland, communal conflicts, even hatreds, keep these countries deeply divided. But no advanced industrial nation has yet fallen apart as have new states such as India, Pakistan, Nigeria, and Zaire; of those new nations that have managed to remain united, many have had to cope with demands for greater autonomy, if not independence. Civil wars continue presently in the Sudan, Ethiopia, and Angola.

Race. Integrating diverse masses into a new nation, forming a national consensus, is therefore crucial. Race is one element impeding this "integrative revolution." For example, many of the countries of Southeast Asia, such as Thailand, Malaya, and Singapore, contain numerous and sizable minority groups, chief among them the ethnic (overseas) Chinese. Almost everywhere in Southeast Asia the Chinese function as middlemen. They are distributors of consumer goods, bankers, investors, shopkeepers. And while dominating Southeast Asian economic life, they have retained their language and customs, tending to isolate themselves; they remain foreigners in the nations where they live. But centuries of Chinese invasion and conquest have left a residue of suspicion that is only intensified by this culture separatism. The result is fear, jealousy, discrimination, accusations of "alien exploitation," and occasionally, as after the abortive Indonesian Communist party coup in 1965, the slaughter of the Chinese population. Another example is the cruel expulsion of the Chinese from Vietnam in the late 1970s. The majority were forced out on unsafe boats after most of their money had been taken from them, and many drowned on the high seas. Most of these "boat people" found refuge in other Southeast Asian countries. Vietnam's anti-Chinese sentiment was one of the factors contributing to the short Vietnamese-Chinese war in 1979.

It is not just the inhumanity of such behavior that is notable, but the fact that it is counterproductive. In non-Communist states, these minorities play a critical role in the process of development. In some traditional societies, such as in Southeast Asia, the Chinese minority are the entrepreneurs. In Africa, this role is often played by the Indian-Pakistani community. Hostile or discriminatory actions, such as expelling this minority, as happened in Uganda, or rioting and attacking their shops, as in Kenya, are likely to hurt economic growth.

Religion.   A second element is religious animosity. When this sparks wars and leads to massive dislocation of millions and slaughter of hundreds of thousands, it seems incomprehensible—at least to Westerners, unless they have studied the Thirty Years' War of the early seventeenth century. When India gained its independence in 1949, it was partitioned into Hindu India and Muslim Pakistan because the Muslim minority wanted its own nation. The division was accompanied by a great bloodbath. More than half a million people died.[9] In the middle of all this were the Sikhs. The Sikhs' prosperity as a result of India's agricultural revolution had led Sikhs to forget their religious background. This, in turn, resulted in a counterrevolution as young radicals, often from well-to-do families, were attracted to religious fundamentalism and the idea of a Sikh nation in the Punjab, India's breadbasket. This spilled over into violence during the 1980s as the Sikhs' conviction grew that they were being discriminated against by the Hindu-dominated national government. One victim was Indira Ghandi, India's prime minister, who was assassinated by her Sikh bodyguards after she had ordered Indian troops to attack the Sikhs' sacred Golden Temple where militants had fortified themselves.

Religious divisions have tended to be disastrous. Internal religious differences have hampered nation building in Lebanon, where religious and political hostilities among Maronite Christians and other Christian sects, as well as Druse, Shi'ite, and Sunni Muslims, have destroyed the country. While the impact has not been as devastating as in Lebanon, other countries too have suffered from religious conflicts. In Nigeria, for instance, the religious differences between the Muslim Hausas and the Christian Ibos fueled a conflict that also reflected tribal, regional, and economic divisions. In the Sudan, conflict erupted between the black Christian South and the Arab Muslim North when the government tried to enforce the Islamic laws on the Christians. This conflict, combined with millions of refugees from Ethiopia and rioting as a result of government removal of food subsidies, led to the overthrow of the government. But the fighting continued.

Regionalism.   Regional differences are a third divisive element, particularly when they are accompanied by the uneven distribution of resources and wealth. An example is Indonesia, a nation of islands. The main islands are Java (on which the capital, Jakarta, is located), Sumatra, the Celebes, most of Borneo, and about half of New Guinea (West Irian). Sumatra is the source of Indonesia's oil and rubber wealth, and the Sumatrans have little use for the Javanese, whom they believe they are subsidizing. The inhabitants of the Celebes, on the other hand, are suspicious of both the Javanese and the Sumatrans. Finally, the people of West Irian have little, if anything, in common with the people of the other islands. In Indonesia, as well as in new African countries such as Zaire and Nigeria, "Regionalism is understandable because ethnic loyalties can usually find expression in geographical terms. Inevitably, some regions will be richer than others, and if the ethnic claim to power combines with relative wealth, the case for secession is strong." [10] In India, this is the basis for the Sikhs' demands for greater autonomy, if not independence.

Tribalism.   As if these three elements contributing to disunity were not sufficient, there is yet a fourth—tribalism. Particularly in Africa, the tribe is still the psychological, economic, and political touchstone for many, for it is the social organization closest and most familiar to them. The colonial powers—particularly Britain, which ruled its colonies "indirectly" (through traditional chiefs)—helped to preserve this tribalism. The African tribes generally are not small groups of a few hundred or a few thousand members. The larger tribes would be considered ethnic or national minority groups in any Western state. The problem is not the large numbers of tribes but rather the large sizes of some tribes. The cohesion of new nations may be weakened by the desires of tribal chieftains to invoke the same claim of national self-determination that the intelligentsia previously invoked on behalf of their nations. Additionally, because Europeans often split up tribal groups when they drew their artificial boundary lines in the conference rooms of Berlin, London, and Paris, the new nations' frontiers tend to be unstable. Tribes freely cross frontiers in search of water and grazing lands; one part of a tribe may try to break away from its "nation" to join the rest of the tribe in the neighboring nation.

   The result may be a frontier war such as that between Ethiopia and Somalia in 1977, when Somalia tried to unite with its ethnics in Ethiopia who sought to secede and join Somalia. One consequence was that the Soviets were forced to choose between two friends, Ethiopia and Somalia; together with the Cubans, the Soviets intervened on the side of Ethiopia, the larger nation. Tribalism obviously also affects domestic politics. In Uganda in 1985, for example, a military coup occurred as a result of a mutiny by soldiers of the Acholi tribe who were upset by the promotion of officers from the Langi tribe, which was the president's tribe. The two tribes had a long history of conflict. By 1986 the president had been overthrown by the military, and the country was in the midst of a civil war between the government, long dominated by the northern tribes, and a resistance composed mainly of people from the southern tribes who had long been oppressed by a succession of tyrannical and murderous Ugandan leaders. Rebel forces finally won but not before the economy collapsed, education ground to a halt, and law and order broke down in the capital. In Kenya, generally regarded as one of the few stable African states, President Daniel arap Moi is from a small tribe. He came to office with the support of the majority Kikuyi, the tribe of Jomo Kenyatta, who led the country to independence. Kenyatta had wanted to unite the country by letting other tribes hold the presidency, but Moi began to consolidate his power and declared Kenya a one-party state, raising tribal rivalry.

Language.   The new nations' lack of political and cultural cohesiveness is clear in the language problem, the fifth element in their disunity. Language is one of the most important factors in forming and preserving a sense of nationality, and uniformity of language not only helps people to communicate with one another but also promotes common attitudes and values. Group consciousness and common interests are stimulated in turn; people learn to think in terms of "we," as opposed to "they." Yet in many LDCs several languages are spoken, and any attempt to impose a single language is resisted. The prospects for national cohesion in these circumstances are not promising.

In India's small neighbor, the island of Sri Lanka (formerly Ceylon), the Tamil minority has long feuded with the Sinhalese majority. This conflict erupted into violence when the Tamil protested government policy to make Sinhalese the official language. The result has been to widen the ethnic split of the population with the Tamils claiming that the eclipse of their language causes them to suffer greater discrimination at school and work. In India itself, the government has tried to make Hindi the official language in a nation with fifty major regional languages, fourteen of which are officially recognized.[11] The fact is that English, the colonizer's language, has become the preferred language of many urban Indians, especially India's educated, rapidly expanding middle class. English is the language of commerce, computers, finance, science, and social sciences, as well as of the leading newspapers, advertising, and the growing television network. Even though it is emerging as the nation's first language, English is spoken by only about 150 million Indians, reflecting what may well be a schism between modern India and traditional India. Since the key decisions that affect most Indians' lives and the important discussions that are carried on in the news media are in English, most Indians may increasingly be cut off from public life.

Overpopulation and the Malthusian Problem

The second problem in modernizing the LDCs is overpopulation. Not all LDCs have this problem, but where it exists, overpopulation casts doubt on whether a country can make any economic progress at all. World population has already passed the 4 billion mark and is increasing at an annual rate of just over 2 percent. On the average, 207,000 children are born each day, almost 1.5 million a week. The annual rate of population growth in the developed world for 1980-85 was 0.64 percent; that of the less-developed countries in the same period was 2.02 percent. Africa had the highest rate (3.01 percent), Latin America was next (2.30), South Asia, with India, was just behind (2.20), and East Asia, excluding Japan, was last (1.20). All these rates, except Africa's, were down from earlier periods, suggesting a slow deceleration of population growth. Having peaked at 2.11 percent in the second half of the 1960s, the estimated annual rate for the 1980s is 1.67 percent. It should, however, be noted that this figure is largely the result of China's sharp drop; in much of Africa and South Asia and in some Latin America countries there has not been a significant reduction in fertility. Indeed, in Africa, it has continued to rise.[12] Mexico's population in 1950 was 27 million; thirty-five years later it was almost 70 million. China's population of 547 million in 1950 grew each year by a sum greater than the total population of Canada; the Chinese population has since passed the billion mark. Kenya has the highest population growth in the world: 6 million people in 1950 had almost tripled by 1980. In 1900 there was one European for every two Asians; in 2000, the ratio will probably be one to four. It is also estimated that by 2000 there will be two Latin Americans for each North American—and this is based on a 300 million population in the United States.

There is, then, a population explosion. World population first reached 1 billion in 1830. By 1930 it had doubled; in 1960 the total was 3 billion people, and nearly half the world's population was under twenty years old; and the fourth billion took only another 15 years (see Figure 7-1, page 175). By the year 2000 the current population of 4.7 billion is expected to be between 6.2 and 6.7 billion. Although the people of the Third World (including China) constitute 70 percent of the world's total population, by the turn of the twenty-first century they will constitute more than 80 percent. Fewer than 20 percent—perhaps only 15 percent—of the rest of the people will live in North America, Europe, the Soviet Union, and Japan. Can our "crowded earth" continue to sustain such enormous increases of population, despite the recent decrease in population growth in the Third World? (See Table 14-1.)

Table 14-1 Population Projections: 1980-2100 (in millions)

	1950	1980	2000	2025	2050	2100	Total Fertility Rate 1980[a]	Year in which NRR = 1[b]
Selected Countries								
China	547	980	1,198	1,397	1,414	1,426	2.3	2005
India	350	675	1,001	1,361	1,605	1,778	4.7	2020
Indonesia	80	146	216	297	351	388	4.4	2020
Brazil	53	118	177	239	274	297	3.9	2015
Bangladesh	42	89	156	259	342	412	6.3	2035
Nigeria	32	85	169	329	472	600	6.9	2040
Pakistan	40	82	148	249	329	394	6.4	2035
Mexico	27	69	115	166	197	214	4.8	2015
Egypt	20	42	64	88	104	115	4.6	2020
Kenya	6	17	40	84	122	153	8.0	2030
Regions								
Developing countries								
Africa	223	479	903	1,646	2,297	2,873	6.4	2050
East Asia	587	1,061	1,312	1,542	1,573	1,596	2.3	2020
South Asia	695	1,387	2,164	3,125	3,810	4,328	4.9	2045
Latin America	165	357	543	748	868	944	4.1	2035
Subtotal	1,670	3,284	4,922	7,061	8,548	9,741	4.2	2050
Developed countries	835	1,140	1,284	1,393	1,425	1,454	1.9	2005
Total world	2,504	4,424	6,206	8,454	9,973	11,195	3.6	

[a] Total fertility rate is the number of children an average woman would have during her lifetime.

[b] NRR (Net reproduction rate) refers to a level of childbearing in which each couple on average replaces itself in the next generation. This column thus projects a decline of the level of fertility to just a replacement level.

SOURCE: Robert S. McNamara, "The Population Problem," *Foreign Affairs* (Summer 1984): 1113. Reprinted with permission.

Disturbance of Malthusian Checks.　The less-developed countries have come face to face with the realities of the Malthusian problem: the constant hunger and grinding poverty that result when the population grows faster than do the means of subsistence. More than 150 years ago the Reverend Thomas Malthus, a British cleric who was also an economist, predicted this fate for the Western world—unless population growth was limited by "positive checks" (such as wars and epidemics) or "preventive checks" (such as sterilization and contraception). The great economic progress of the West— despite the huge population increase since 1800—had seemed to refute the Malthusian prediction. Agricultural production increased to provide a plentiful supply of food, and industrial production raised the standard of living to new heights. For years, therefore, Malthus's dire warning was ignored by all save diehard pessimists.

Unfortunately, the conditions that confront the less-developed nations are quite dissimilar to those experienced in the West. First, the Western industrial countries had far smaller populations when they began industrializing, and their subsequent population increases did not outdistance their economic gains. Ironically, the pattern in the LDCs to a significant degree has been brought about by the colonial powers. In the precolonial period the Malthusian "positive checks" had, in their own cruel way, contributed to some sort of balance between population and resources. The typical pattern was simple: once a tribe had eaten most of the available food in the area it inhabited and had overfarmed the land so that soil erosion had begun, it would invade the preserve of neighboring tribes. In warfare, members of both tribes would be killed, thus decreasing the number left to be fed. Periodic famine and pestilence also helped to maintain a balance between births and deaths. This seemingly eternal cycle of peace and population growth succeeded by violence and population decline was broken by the entry of the colonial powers.

The Western colonial states, by preserving peace in the areas they ruled and introducing modern medicine, upset the balance: more of the newborn survived, people lived longer, and populations began to increase at much greater rates. In 1950 the average life expectancy of a child born in the LDCs was approximately forty years; by 1965 it had reached fifty-five years; in other words, the gain in life expectancy was one year for each intervening year. In Africa, life expectancy increased from thirty-seven years in 1950 to forty-seven years by the mid-1970s, and in Asia, the corresponding figures were forty-three and fifty-seven. In Latin America, where life expectancy was fifty-two years in 1950, by 1975, the figure was sixty-two.[13] While life expectancy has increased rapidly for more than a quarter of a century, fertility has only just begun to decrease in most of the Third World, with the significant exception of sub-Sahara Africa.

Hindrances to Birth Control.

Hindrances to Birth Control. Children in many of these countries are a religious, social, and even economic necessity. In India, for instance, Muslims believe that children are a "gift of Allah," and the childless couple is pitied or despised; a woman does not even establish herself with her husband or his family until she has borne a son. A Hindu man needs a son to perform certain rituals after his death, and during life he needs sons to fight in village feuds or in tribal warfare. Furthermore, there is a fear of having *too few* children, for they may be needed to work in the fields and support their parents as—and if—the latter grow older. Children are in this sense a substitute for the Social Security payments or endowment policies common in the West. People, in short, are not poor because they have large families; they have large families because they are poor. Birth controls can be economically disastrous in these circumstances. The family is also the hub of life for Indian villagers. Weddings and births are festive social occasions, important village events. A woman's prestige may even be measured by the number of children, especially sons, that she bears. A voluntary reduction in the size of her family would in these circumstances strike at the very basis of her life.

At the 1974 UN World Food Conference, the LDCs were hardly willing to recognize that their growth, which is doubling their population every twenty years, is a problem. They shifted the focus of attention from birth control, which they saw as an infringement of their sovereignty, to economic and social development. Arguing that fuller exploitation of the world's resources could comfortably support ten times the then global population of 4 billion, they placed responsibility principally upon the industrialized nations to waste fewer resources in support of their already very high standards of living and to accelerate development in the LDCs. They emphasized that a declining birth rate would come as modernization occurred. "Development is the best contraceptive" seemed to be the slogan. Despite this public position, many LDCs have begun birth control programs. But the central question remains: Can these countries develop rapidly enough to keep ahead of the growing populations?

For the LDCs, the following maxim may be painfully true: *Industrial revolutions may be defeated by Malthusian counter-revolutions.*[14] In countries that have achieved economic growth, as many LDCs have done, population increases may cancel most, if not all, of the hoped-for increase in living standards or savings for capital investment. How can the LDCs possibly provide housing, education, and jobs for all these people? The Aswan dam, planned in 1955 and completed in 1970, added 25 percent to Egypt's arable land, but in those fifteen years, Egypt's population increased by 50 percent to more than 30 million. By the year 2000 the Egyptian population will double to more than 65 million if the present rate of growth continues. Mexico, with a population in 1980 of 69 million people and projected to add 50 million by the year 2000, must create 700,000 new jobs per year in order not to increase its already high unemployment rate even more, but the prediction is for only 350,000 jobs a year.

Mexico City by the year 2000 will have the distinction of being the world's largest city with a population of 31 million. Like other future huge Third World cities or megalopolises—most big cities will then be in the LDCs—the masses of people will probably strain, if not collapse, the already inadequate social services and facilities such as transportation, sanitation, education, and housing. Such cities may well come to resemble huge slums outside of the small inner-city enclaves of middle-class dwellers.

In any event, the continued LDC "population bomb" with its critical growth rate in the age group of twenty to forty years—between 1980 and 2000, young adults will increase by 630 million, compared to 20 million in the developed countries—has dire consequences for the political and social stability of Third World countries. In the words of a former president of the World Bank: "Rapid population growth, in sum, translates into rising numbers of labor force entrants, faster-expanding urban populations, pressure on food supplies, ecological degradation, and increasing numbers of 'absolute poor.' All are rightly viewed by governments as threats to social stability and orderly change. Even under vigorous economic growth, managing the demographic expansion is difficult; with a faltering economy it is all but impossible." [15] And there will obviously be a spillover into the international arena of LDC instability, poverty, unemployment, and malnutrition.

During the nineteenth century, Europe's population rose by approximately 0.5 percent per year; today, the poorer countries grow at more than 2 percent per year, or about 200,000 each day. Yet more than 60 million Europeans emigrated from the mid-seventeenth century to 1940; from 1820 to 1940, 33 million went to the United States. During the 1970s, 7.5 million foreign workers plus 5.5 million dependents from southeastern Europe (Greece, Turkey) and North Africa (Algeria, Morocco, and Tunisia) went to Western Europe. Before West Germany's economic downturn in the late 1970s, there were more than 1 million Turks in Germany; in Britain, the majority of immigrants were "colored" people from British Commonwealth countries. By the late 1970s, immigration to the United States stood near or at an all-time high; the country was the world's largest receiver of refugees and immigrants, the latter very largely Spanish-speaking people from the Caribbean and Mexico. In the first decade of this century, legal immigration to the United States averaged 880,000 annually; by the end of the 1970s, the estimated legal plus illegal immigration averaged more than 1 million (of whom more than 50 percent were Spanish-speaking). Even were economic conditions better in the West, can this influx of populations long continue?

Fertility, once the key to survival, seems to have become the curse of humankind. Yet at the 1984 UN International Conference on Population, despite a World Bank study that predicted that even with the declining birth rate the world's population will double by 2050, the United States took a strong stand against abortion and family planning. Since 1974, U.S. law has prohibited the use of foreign aid for abortion, reflecting the domestic controversy over family planning. President Ronald Reagan's administration, strongly influenced by prolife groups, strictly administered the law, withdrew its contribution to the UN Fund for Population Activities in 1986, and cut off all funds for nongovernmental organizations (NGOs) working in family planning if they supported abortions. Planned Parenthood, for example, had to cancel programs in eighteen African countries. Remarkably, Reagan's secretary of state could still say, "Rampant population growth underlies the third world's poverty, and poses a major long-term threat to political stability and our planet's resource base." [16] This was an accurate assessment. But U.S. policy was guaranteed to ensure a more crowded planet.

The Problem of Food

The third problem impeding modernization is inadequate food supplies. The paradox of the LDCs is that, although the overwhelming majority of their populations live on the land, the peasants have great difficulty producing enough food. The emphasis was on industrialization and visible projects such as steel factories and automobile plants. The aim was to replicate at least the outward symbols of industrial society and, hopefully, to raise living standards. This usually led to the neglect of agriculture, which required costly long-term investment in land reclamation, irrigation, fertilizer plants, and extension services. Furthermore, to the leaders of these countries, agriculture meant poverty; it was a constant reminder of colonial subjugation and of their continued status as suppliers of raw materials. Industry symbolized freedom and national dignity. Given the continued swings in the prices of agricultural commodities, investing more money in food is, not surprisingly, viewed without enthusiasm.

Yet food production must be raised dramatically not only to feed the rapidly growing populations, both rural and urban-industrial, but ideally also to earn foreign exchange with which to buy required goods and services. *An industrial revolution requires a prior or simultaneous agrarian revolution.* Instead of being separate and distinct processes, agricultural development and industrial development are intertwined. An industrial revolution cannot occur without the provision of extra food to feed the urban population, and to raise food production above the subsistence level requires the application of machinery and science to farming. Britain, the first nation to industrialize, also had the highest agricultural productivity at the time. By contrast, most LDCs have to spend their hard-earned currency to import food.

The Issue of Land Reform.

Such productivity is difficult to achieve in traditional societies, where peasants have for centuries tilled the soil by the same methods. Western farmers produce cash crops for market and are therefore alert to technical innovations that may increase production, enabling them to buy other goods, including food items they do not grow. But the peasants in LDCs are all too often subsistence farmers, producing primarily for their own families, exchanging with village neighbors any surplus for necessities. Usually, peasants are the last to be touched by the currents of modernization. Poorly educated and physically isolated from the growing urban centers, they have no contact with the latest trends in politics or the new intellectual and technical currents that sweep the cities. Peasants are subject mainly to conservative influences: to religion, which tells them that they must bear their lot patiently, and to landowners, who are the local political leaders and to whom the peasants traditionally pay deference as well as portions of their crops. Not surprisingly, it is usually city dwellers who are the activists and organizers of revolutionary movements; peasants tend to be politically passive.

Not that peasants have no grievances that can be manipulated by revolutionary leaders in their attempts to break the power of the landowners and to undermine existing society. For peasants have an intense "land hunger." They want to own the land they till. In both Russia and China it was this land hunger that finally brought down the czarist and Nationalist Chinese governments, both dominated by landowners. Today there are still areas where most of the land that peasants work is owned by a few wealthy landlords. In Latin America in the 1960s, years after Fidel Castro had taken power in Havana, 90 percent of all land was still owned by 10 percent of the population. Furthermore, land-tenure systems were frequently subject to abuses such as excessive payments in crops (generally from 10 percent to more than 50 percent, sometimes even 90 percent) or in work to be done on the landlord's estate. On the other hand, peasants who own their own land are handicapped by the small size of their holdings, as well as by their crude methods of cultivation. Even if backward and impoverished peasants own land, they are compelled to borrow money to survive. Usually they can do so only by paying a money-lender—usually a local landowner—extremely high interest rates (ranging from 20 to 40 percent or even more). The peasants are thus condemned to live in a state of continued indebtedness if they are to buy fertilizer and other things they need.

Increasing Agricultural Productivity. The technical backwardness of peasants, their small holdings of land, and the concentration of ownership all stand as formidable obstacles to agricultural development. Consequently, the dispossession of the old landowning class where it is still in control is not simply a matter of social justice. It is a political and economic prerequisite for modernization that a nation destroy the traditional social structure, which is founded upon a grossly uneven distribution of wealth, channel investments into industrialization, and encourage increases in food production by investing in agriculture as well. Such changes involve not simply reform but revolution. Ownership of land in traditional society is bound up with social status, wealth, and political power; land reform therefore involves complete and profound alteration of the very basis on which society allocates these benefits. Those who have them do not surrender them voluntarily. Growing more food in societies in which the modernizers are not yet in power requires wholesale rearrangement of the social order, a more complex matter than simply sowing more seeds.

Fundamentally, the peasants must be granted land. Crop production may, however, still be insufficient because of the small farms and rapidly increasing populations. Small farms are simply too unproductive. Mechanical equipment is too costly and too inefficient for use on small farms. Collectivization of the land has not been very successful where it has been tried, largely because of bitter peasant opposition; after almost half a century, agriculture remains the weakest area in the Soviet economy. More land must also be brought into cultivation. Of the potentially arable land, only 22 percent in Africa, 11 percent in South America, and approximately 45 percent worldwide was being cultivated at the end of the 1970s.[17]

In addition, whatever the size of the farm, if peasants are to till the soil and produce a surplus that can be siphoned off to feed the city population, it is absolutely essential that a good part of the population be moved off the land. Population growth has crowded the land with small, inefficient subsistence farms. With fewer peasants on the land, it would be possible to form larger farming units and thus to raise overall output. At the same time, such a shift of population could provide the necessary labor force for a growing industrial sector. But this possibility raises another dilemma: cheap food for urban workers means keeping prices down, but low prices provide little incentive for farmers to raise production. Higher prices for farmers may, however, bring trouble, even rioting or a *coup d'état*. Governments in the LDCs have therefore failed to provide farmers with the necessary economic incentives to provide more food. Cheap food is used to curb economic and political unrest; higher food prices are dangerous when wages are low and many unemployed or underemployed. Few governments have had the courage to stake their own survival on this issue. Government policy is, in short, a principal block to food production. Several former "bread baskets" have become just empty baskets, no longer able to feed themselves and forced to import food.

Furthermore, the threat that population will outstrip food supplies remains. The Green Revolution, so-called because of its use of high-yield strains of grain and rice to increase production per acre, has been remarkably successful in several countries. Between 1954 and 1973 the food supply increased sufficiently to feed an extra 1.3 billion mouths. India, once the recipient of American food aid, became self-sufficient in food and has even begun to export wheat. While malnutrition remained during this period, starvation did not occur except in the Sahel or Central West Africa. Still, if the population continues to grow at present or near-present rates in the LDCs, the Green Revolution may have only postponed the global food crisis. Africa, according to the UN World Food Council, may be facing a permanent food crisis. Some 440 million Africans, a tenth of the world's population, had less to eat in 1980 than in 1970.[18] And food production continues to decline while Africa's population growth is the highest in the continent's history. The result was very visible in Ethiopia, the Sudan, and other East African nations in the mid-1980s as millions faced starvation. Food production had already been declining before the sustained drought of the early 1980s.

Estimates of how many people in the Third World suffer from daily chronic hunger range from 500 million to 1 billion people, although some experts, such as Nick Eberstadt of the Harvard Center for Population Studies, have pegged this figure at most about 100 million, "a lower fraction, in all likelihood, than for any previous generation in man's recorded history." [19] Regardless of what the overall figure might be, 7 million people faced starvation in 1984-85 in Ethiopia. The UN Food and Agriculture Organization stated that at least twenty-four African countries had serious food shortages and that 150 million of Africa's 450 million people might confront the prospect of starvation. The reasons for this situation are the ones already mentioned: overpopulation, misguided government policies, and drought; but in Ethiopia's case, two other factors were present, a civil war and government callousness.

Ethiopia's Soviet-style collectivization of land by its Marxist rulers had created hunger and malnutrition before 1985 and the drought; the fact is that despite its people's starvation, Ethiopia spent $100 million on the tenth anniversary celebration of the revolution. Had it not been for a foreign photographer, who sold his film to Western television, the widespread starvation would not have become known outside of Ethiopia. The government had suppressed the news in favor of glorifying "Ethiopian socialism." Even after trucks and food had been shipped to Ethiopia, the regime gave priority to unloading Soviet arms to Western food, and used the trucks for military purposes rather than take food to the people in need. The government, moreover, would not allow food distribution to rebel areas. In any event, the outcry in the West was the only reason that compelled the Ethiopian regime to pay some attention to its starving people and it was largely private Western relief agencies that transported the food, often in the face of government obstruction and incompetence.

Ethiopian indifferences to the suffering of its people unfortunately is not unique.[20] LDC governments, aware of food crises, can today call upon reserve food that Western governments put aside each year; if LDC governments do not possess the administrative skills and organization for emergency relief, international relief organizations are available to help. The fact is that governments for various reasons, including the desire not to publicize failures that reflect poorly on them, may not care about the feeding of their peoples; for example, in China from 1959-62 in the wake of the Great Leap Forward, a disastrous economic experiment in which several millions are believed to have starved; in Nigeria, where the government encouraged starvation to bring a rebel province back into the national fold, at the cost of perhaps 1 million ethnic Ibos who lived there; in East Pakistan in 1970, when the government in West Pakistan responded slowly to the distress caused by a typhoon with the result of not only about 100,000 deaths, but also a secession by those living in what was to become the new state of Bangladesh; in Ethiopia, where the emperor, before he was overthrown, tried to conceal news of a famine; in Afghanistan, where Soviet forces have deliberately destroyed crops to force hungry peasants either into the Soviet-controlled towns and cities or to flee the country; or in Cambodia in the early 1980s, where the regime was indifferent to the suffering of the population, killing altogether 2-3 million out of a population of 8 million.

Some writers, while not condoning the behavior of governments in these instances, have favored a policy about starvation that has been called *triage*.[21] This term was adopted from the French army's World War I policy of sorting its wounded into three groupings: those who would probably recover even without medical assistance, those who would die regardless of medical treatment, and those who would recover if cared for right away. Because of the limited availability of medical personnel, medicine, and facilities, priority was given to the last group. The analogy suggests that in countries that outgrow their food supplies, starvation will be nature's way of correcting this imbalance and reducing the numbers of people. To intervene by sending relief supplies for humanitarian reasons would simply worsen the problem by creating even greater food crises and needs in the future until eventually even relief would not suffice. It is hoped that this awful choice—a moral choice—will be avoidable. At the beginning of the twentieth century the world population was 1.5 billion; three quarters of a century later it was 4 billion. A Malthusian pessimist would have predicted an inability to feed so many mouths. Will contemporary pessimists be equally wrong?

There is a sign of hope. More and more LDCs have begun to realize that the rush to industrialize and the neglect of agriculture was wrong. Agricultural development is beginning to receive the emphasis reserved in the late 1950s, 1960s, and 1970s for industrialization. China's impressive increases in food production, like India's, are a symptom of a change that holds up the farmer rather than the industrialist as the key figure in pulling the LDCs up out of poverty and hunger. If successful, this will not be without cost for the United States, which together with Canada (and, to a lesser extent, Australia, Argentina, and, more recently, France and Britain), has been the breadbasket of the world. Highly efficient American farms have produced large quantities of surplus food with which to feed not only LDCs but also the Soviet Union, whose agricultural system consistently falls short in meat, vegetable, and fruit production even in years of good weather. Agricultural export has been a mainstay of the American farmer and helped earn foreign exchange in international trade—especially during the 1970s when the country needed to earn as much as possible to pay its oil bills. As more Third World countries, in addition to Western European states, will be able to feed themselves, and even to export food, the market for American farmers will be cut; and the large U.S. surpluses of food may only succeed in driving food prices down, forcing more farmers into bankruptcy. The prospects, in short, are of a growing number of exporters, declining numbers of importers, and growing global surpluses.[22]

Still, that day has not yet arrived. One final point needs to be mentioned: affordability is the real problem with food in the Third World.[23] Even if sufficient food were available because farmers are provided with the incentive of higher prices, many people in the LDCs cannot afford to buy food, especially if prices rise. During the 1974 world food crisis, for example, there was enough to go around. The cause of hunger was simple: poverty and poor income distribution in the affected areas. The higher the price of different food items, the more widespread the hunger will be because the poor already spend 60 to 80 percent of their income on food. Even in those countries where the Green Revolution increased food production—India, Pakistan, Bangladesh, and Mexico—malnutrition remains. The Sub-Saharan region will continue to be a chronic food deficit area, with a limited supply and too many people. The key to reducing malnutrition and eliminating starvation is therefore the ability of the LDCs to raise themselves by their sandal-straps out of poverty. This requires an agricultural *and* industrial revolution.[24]

Accumulating Capital for Modernization

Besides problems caused by the lack of national unity, overpopulation, and inadequate food supplies is the fourth, overwhelming problem of backward, even stagnant, economies. It is upon such bases that the new nations must build industrial economies to banish poverty, end economic dependence on the former colonial powers, and achieve international standing. Industrialization, as a symbol of modernity, was also a means of escaping a past as "raw-materials appendages" to the industrial powers. Eager for economic development, the LDCs must somehow accumulate the requisite capital.

They are, as we already know, exporters of raw materials. Many of them rely on single commodities for export; others have two or three resources each. Figure 14-2 shows some examples of exports from LDCs. Theoretically, these countries should be able to earn sufficient capital from their exports to carry out large-scale industrialization, for, ideally, as Western industrial nations continue to consume more, their demand for raw materials should rise. In practice, however, it usually has not worked out that way. The LDCs' dependence on exports of raw materials has limited their earning capacities. One reason is that their exports reflect every fluctuation of the Western business cycle. As Western industrial economies approach full employment, the demand for raw materials rises, and so do prices; when these economies turn downward, demand declines, and so do prices. A drop of just one cent in copper or coffee prices can result in the loss of millions of dollars, sometimes tens of millions of dollars. As the Mexicans used to say, "A sneeze in the American economy could lead to pneumonia in Mexico." A second reason is that advanced Western industrial technology has, in many instances, made it both possible and profitable to develop synthetics and other substitutes. The demand for resources by industries, no longer dependent on certain natural raw materials, then decreases and prices drop. A final reason for the LDCs' difficulty in earning money through their exports is their practice of producing more to compensate for low prices. The result is a glut on the international market, which drives prices even lower. For Chile or Zambia, dependent solely on copper exports, the drop in price from $1.34 per pound in 1980 to 65 cents in 1985 was a disaster; the same is true for Ghana with cocoa, Uganda with coffee, Cuba with sugar, or Chad with cotton.

The dilemma of the LDCs is agonizing. They desperately need capital, and they rely on their raw-material exports to earn it. But the harder they work to enlarge their volume of exports to enhance their earnings, the more prices may fall. At the same time, because of their difficulties in producing enough food for their rapidly growing populations, they must buy food. They also must import the machinery required to stoke their industrialization—Western machinery, the prices of which are usually rising. The "terms of trade," the LDCs' earnings form their exports versus the cost of their imports, are thus against them. Exports of raw materials, then, do not seem a likely route of escape from poverty for the LDCs.

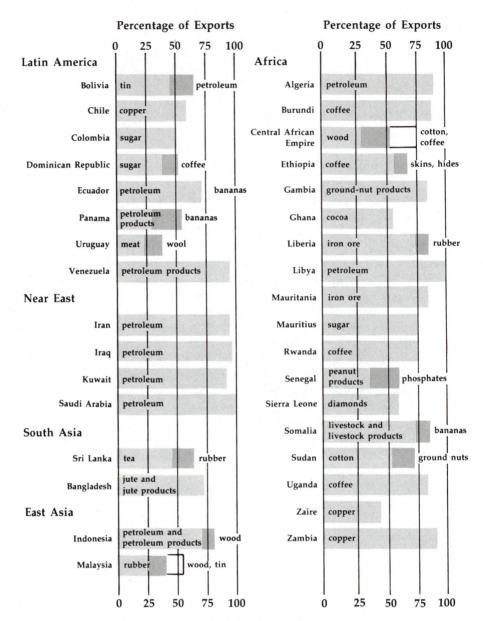

Figure 14-2 Developing-Country Dependence on Primary Products for Foreign-
Exchange Earnings

The Newly Industrialized Countries

The international economy is, however, in the process of major change. While
in the past the developed states imported raw materials and agricultural

products from the LDCs, they are now increasingly importing finished goods. This change results partly from a vast increase in the activities of multinational corporations (MNCs). During the 1960s the international economy began to be turned on its head as rich nations invested in the poor nations to produce manufactures for export. As of 1985 more than half the LDCs' exports were manufactured goods. The industrial nations now export agricultural goods to the poor states, a startling change from the previous pattern. In discussing the United States, Richard Barnet and Ronald Müller have called this phenomenon the "Latinamericanization of the United States."

> Production of the traditional industrial goods that have been the mainstay of the U.S. economy is being transferred from $4-an-hour factories in New England to 30 cents-an-hour factories in the "export platforms" of Hong Kong and Taiwan. Increasingly, as the cars, televisions, computers, cameras, clothes, and furniture are being produced abroad, the United States is becoming a service economy and a producer of plans, programs, and ideas for others to execute . . .
>
> The United States trading pattern is beginning to resemble that of underdeveloped countries as the number one nation becomes increasingly dependent on the export of agricultural products and timber to maintain its balance of payments and increasingly dependent on imports of finished goods to maintain its standard of living. . . . (Unlike poor countries, however, the U.S. also exports "software"—i.e. technical knowledge.) [25]

Of course, this situation involves only a few LDCs, the newly industrialized countries (NICs) or export platforms: Hong Kong, South Korea, Singapore, Taiwan, and Brazil. Most LDCs unfortunately remain dependent on raw-materials exports. For 110 Third World nations, 75 percent of their total exports are still raw materials, which are processed and consumed elsewhere. Half the LDCs depend on single commodities for their earnings on the international market.

Cultural Transformation

It should be obvious by now that the term *economic development* suggests a one-dimensional picture of the actual process of transition from a traditional rural society to an advanced modern nation. Economic development implies that the only requirement is industry, that industrialization follows automatically from the formation of capital, and that mobilizing capital is therefore the crucial problem. Even when agricultural growth is included, as it must be, the term *economic development* is an oversimplification—indeed, a distortion—of the complex realities of modernizing a traditional society. Modernization is more than simply building steel mills and constructing dams. It means, above all else, changes in values, aspirations, and expectations. The necessary changes are not simply economic, but political, social, and cultural. Modernization is multidimensional; it aims at the complete transformation of society, including revolutionary changes in class structures and the centralization of political authority.

Traditional societies have not usually regarded economic activity as a prime concern of life. Surprising as it may seem, even in Western history, money making was not always the chief pursuit. In the Middle Ages religion was the principal concern. Earthly existence was considered merely a short prelude to eternal life, for which people prepared themselves through adherence to the moral code of the Roman Catholic church. Every aspect of behavior was subject to the spiritual authority of the church; in the economic sphere, the church condemned the charging of interest—a basic necessity in a monetary economy—as usury. The desire for profit was equated with greed, and economic competition was simply not part of the accepted way of life. This attitude toward interest and profits was, of course, inimical to business. Economic competition, profits, savings, investments, and the whole concept of economic growth were alien ideas in the Middle Ages.

To modernize, Europe had to shift its emphasis from the spiritual world to the temporal world of secular concerns. It also had to replace the landowning nobility with a class eager for capital accumulation; achieve a more fluid social structure to permit upward mobility on the basis of achievement; and finally, create a larger political, social, and economic framework. None of these changes came quickly. A major break with the medieval attitude came with the introduction of the Protestantism of John Calvin in the sixteenth century. In contrast to Catholicism, it gave priority to earthly works. Industriousness, profits, savings, and investments were in this way legitimated by religion. Thrift, character, and hard work represented the earthly trinity. A person's energy had to be focused on the work to which God had called him or her. Luxury, leisure, entertainment, and sexual enjoyment were to be shunned. In order not to succumb to temptation and become morally corrupted, each person had to exercise stringent discipline over his or her weaknesses and emotions.

It is hardly surprising that this "Protestant ethic" and capitalism became closely identified.[26] It was but a short way from Calvin to the eighteenth-century British economist Adam Smith, whose theory of capitalism was based upon recognition of the acquisitive passion that the Roman Catholic church had earlier condemned. Smith accepted the desire for gain as a fact of life, calling it "enlightened self-interest." *Laissez faire* capitalism was merely to harness this acquisitive instinct to the public welfare.

In the contemporary world, such a process of secularization is also critical. But it has not gone unchallenged. Islamic fundamentalism, spreading throughout much of the Middle East and West Asia from the late 1970s on, is essentially a reaction against "Westernization" and an attempt to uphold traditional society and values—and the status of the mullahs or religious leaders.[27] The process of modernization uproots the traditional society and historic social relationship, causing great personal insecurity while eroding customary and religious norms. It brings with it a "foreign" way of life, whose external manifestations such as rock music, dancing, public displays of affection between couples, and pornography are often as shocking for old societies as are the ostentatious displays of wealth by the new rich, the striking contrast to the lifestyles of the ordinary persons, and the omnipresence of foreigners doing business.

We must realize what modernization means psychologically: a recognition of the inferiority of the old ways and old society, and the superiority of the foreigner's—the Westerner's—way. It is worth reemphasizing that it was colonialism that first began to erode traditional society. Westerners may have been able to colonize the non-Western world because they had the guns, but the gun to the natives was an indicator of a more advanced society. It was the inferiority of the traditional society and its way of life that had made it possible for Western states to conquer. And the natives could see the evidence everywhere: the Western soldier, as well as Christian missionary, businessman, doctor, engineer, and agronomist. Westerners lived better, longer, healthier, and more of their children survived.

The West not unnaturally considered itself to be the model of what an advanced, modern society should be; where it led, the others would follow. It was not a matter of coercion, but preference. Islamic fundamentalism is the most profound, widespread, and angry reaction to this phenomenon; it is also the most violently anti-American because the United States represents the most advanced secular Western society and is the most powerful Western state. Islamic fundamentalism asserts the dignity and worth of the ways of Islam, and it provides the mass of people untouched by the prosperity of Westernization—indeed, often displaced by it as, for example, the people driven off the land into urban shantytowns—a sense of belonging and spiritual and emotional comfort. In Iran, this movement was led by the mullahs, the traditional religious leaders whose property had been confiscated by the shah and whose role in a modern secular society would be much less important than that of other groups. Islam not only has gained a firm grip in Iran, but rulers in other states from Pakistan to the Sudan and Egypt have either adopted Islamic laws or become sensitive to it. Its potential to spread among Muslims in other Arab countries, the Israeli-occupied West Bank, and potentially even the Soviet Union north of Afghanistan, is a matter of concern to many. As cultural transformation is a necessary part of modernization, it appears that the process will be delayed in some areas or not take place at all. But in Asia, this cultural change has advanced spectacularly, including in Communist China.

NATION BUILDING AND CIVILIAN AND MILITARY AUTHORITARIANISM

The Tasks of Nation Building

To build a nation is thus enormously difficult and complex. A number of tasks must be accomplished.

Creation of a Nation.   First, a new state must create a nation within boundaries probably inherited from colonial days. The secular intelligentsia may be intensely nationalistic, but the mass of the population may not share this sentiment. There are, of course, exceptions. Algeria and Vietnam had to struggle for their independence in wars against colonial powers and their allies, but most LDCs have been "given" their independence; they have not had to win it in wars that might have aroused popular feelings of nationalism. For this largest category of LDCs, after independence the first task is to achieve national cohesion. Citizens of the new nation have shared only the experience of colonial rule, and only the desire to gain national freedom has enabled various internal groups to cooperate. Once the colonial power has been ejected, these groups have little sense of belonging to a distinct cultural entity with certain shared expectations about the future. When the opponent against which they united is gone, there is little else to hold them together in a political, economic, and administrative entity; centrifugal forces then begin to exert themselves. Ironically, the resulting disintegration is given impetus by the very principle of national self-determination in the name of which the anticolonial revolution was carried out.

Creation of Legitimate Political Institutions.   The second task under these circumstances is not only to centralize power and counter the tendency toward political and social fragmentation but also to create a set of political institutions to keep order and to represent the many factions and interests in society, mediate conflicting views and aspirations, and empower the government to act on behalf of society as a whole. This means the creation of legitimate governmental institutions through which conflict can be channeled peacefully and compromise achieved. Otherwise, *coups d'état,* rioting, revolutions, assassinations, and civil wars will remain the methods of resolving differences. Without a government to exercise effective authority, as well as a common political culture or values widely shared by the people in the society, the domestic politics of a nation begins to resemble international politics, in which there is a high expectation of violence as a means of conflict resolution.

The term *less developed* refers not only to economies but also to political institutions. As Samuel Huntington has put it, "The most important political distinction among countries concerns not their form of government but their degree of government." [28] The United States, Britain, and the Soviet Union have different forms of government, but they all do govern. Many, perhaps most, of the LDCs are characterized not only by problems in health, education, food, productivity, and income but also by an even greater "shortage of political community and of effective, authoritative, legitimate government." [29]

Economic Development.   A third task is economic development. For new nations, the response to the "revolution of rising expectations" is important for humanitarian reasons as well as for political reasons and the cause of nation building. The degree to which expectations are satisfied will be proof of the effectiveness of the new national government. Economic development produces a better life for the citizen; its significance is its *political* payoff. To the people of a new nation not yet solidly knitted together, the nationalist intelligentsia must prove that what it is seeking to establish will be beneficial to them. Otherwise, why should they transfer their loyalty to the nation? Economic development can in this way strengthen the fragile bonds of national unity and give the new nation legitimacy. It can also contribute to this goal in other ways. An industrial economy, because of specialization and division of labor, links different sectors of a country together; people of diverse ethnic backgrounds and religious beliefs work together because of the imperatives of economic interdependence. As these people interact economically, travel to other sections of the country, and communicate with people in different areas, they become more aware that they are all part of one nation and that unity is essential if their common hopes for the future are to be realized. An advancing economy also creates a new pattern of interests. The old farming interests are supplemented by a host of new economic and professional interests. In this context, individuals define their roles less in terms of ethnic or religious allegiances than in terms of "interests." The rise of new social classes (the urban, middle, and working classes) is of key significance, for such classes are national, rather than regional. Human beings thus become nationally self-conscious.

Moderating the Effects of Modernization.

A fourth task is moderating the effects of modernization, specifically the enormous social ferment that accompanies the collapse of tradition and customs, a ferment that can lead to political discontinuity and instability. Because the old ways of doing things no longer suffice, new ways must be adopted. The result for most people is bewilderment and intense frustration. They find it difficult to adjust lifelong behavior and attitudes to the changing environment. The peasants' sense of belonging (which results from being part of an old way of life) collapses—particularly if they are forced off the land and herded into the city and a new factory, where they must learn the values and habits of industrial civilization. They resent the factory, with its discipline and monotony, long hours, and low pay, and they hate the vast slums where they live in filth, poverty, and disease, with tens of thousands of other uprooted peasants. They feel degraded. As peasants, poor as they are, they at least have status and a role in society; as peasant workers, torn loose from their traditional and religious moorings and submerged in the anonymity of the labor force, they feel their individuality denied.[30] They become isolated atoms in a secular mass society.

Peasants who stay on the land are also subject to frustration, hostility, and impatience. The transformation from subsistence peasants producing for the family to commercial farmers producing for a market is difficult. They must learn to operate new farm machinery and to try new methods. If herded into a collectivized farm, they feel deprived of "their" piece of land and their personality. Furthermore, even if they are not collectivized, they are resentful if the state takes away their surplus crops at low prices in order to feed the workers in the cities, and to earn foreign exchange. Their consumption, like that of the factory laborer, then, does not materially improve.

Before independence, the masses were constantly told by the leaders of the independence movement that life would improve, once the colonial rulers had been ousted. But this better life cannot come for a long time, for capital formation requires postponement of consumption. The greater the gap between expectation and satisfaction, the greater each person's frustration. Only gradual closing of this gap, providing each person with some improvement in life and some personal security, can relieve the dissatisfaction.

Dealing with the Tasks of Nation Building

How does the nationalist intelligentsia deal with these tasks? One way is to "nationalize" the people—to inculcate in them national consciousness and loyalty, recognition of the national government as *their* government, of its laws as reflecting *their* adherence. The majority must acknowledge that they are citizens of one nation and that the national government has the legitimate authority to make decisions on behalf of the entire population. Such popular consciousness cannot be developed overnight. An entire people must, in a sense, go to school—to learn their nation's language and history (much of it mythical, devised for the purpose of fostering national identification) and to be brought into the mainstream of national life. Only then will the national symbols stimulate deep emotion, and only then will a truly national community emerge.

The Hero.   In the meantime, if the nation is to be held together, the leader must be a "hero," the single person who more than anyone else symbolizes the new nation.[31] If he led the nationalist movement before independence, he may have agitated for freedom for years, propagated national mythology, and served time in jail as a result. He and the nation are thus in a very real sense identical. As "the founder of the nation," he provides a kind of symbolic presence without which the unity of the new nation would erode. Loyalty can usually be felt more keenly toward an individual who incorporates an idea—like the "nation"—than toward the idea itself. The hero in a new nation is a transitional figure in a transitional society. He serves the indispensable function of encouraging a shift from traditional, parochial loyalties to tribe or region to broader loyalties to the impersonal nation-state. The hero usually has charisma—"a quality of extraordinary spiritual power attributed to a person ... capable of eliciting popular support in the direction of human affairs."[32] He is, in fact, a *substitute* for the nation and for the national institutions that have yet to be built; he also confers legitimacy upon the new nation and its government.

One-Party Rule. Such a hero is usually supported by a single party as the principal instrument of national integration. Unlike Western political parties, the primary function of which is to represent the various interests within the nation, the single party in a developing country has a double rationale. First, the party is an effective means of socializing the traditionally "tribalized" people on a national basis. Once the masses in the towns and countryside have been organized in provincial and local cells, the party, by drawing them into national life, tries to instill in them a sense of identification as citizens of a distinct national community. Just as the charismatic hero replaces the traditional chieftain, the nation is supposed to replace the tribe. The party claims to represent the nation. National elections, in this context, may not have much meaning as rituals of democratic choice among different parties and potential rulers. But the ritual of elections is not without meaning, theoretically at least. Elections are supposed to reflect involvement in the affairs of the nation and to establish meaningful links to national leaders. One effect is that, to the degree that political participation mobilizes the masses, their desire for greater economic payoffs or welfare greatly increases the pressures on the rulers to succeed.

The second rationale of one-party rule is its alleged efficiency in mobilizing the economic and human resources of a nation for the purpose of modernization. As one African leader said:

> Once the first free government is formed, its supreme task lies ahead—the building up of the country's economy, so as to raise the standards of the people, to eradicate disease, to banish ignorance and superstition. This, no less than the struggle against colonialism, calls for the maximum united effort by the whole country if it is to succeed. *There can be no room for difference or division.* In Western democracies, it is an accepted practice in times of emergency for opposition parties to sink their differences and join together in forming a national government. *This is our time of emergency,* and until our war against poverty, ignorance, and disease has been won, we should not let our unity be destroyed by a desire to follow somebody else's "book of rules." [33]

By American standards, such a one-party system is, of course, undemocratic. In the United States the opposition is a loyal opposition whose allegiance is to the same nation and values as the governing party. But in a new African nation the opposition's allegiance is often regional and tribal, and it thus represents the centrifugal forces in society. In these circumstances, a change in the form of government favoring greater democracy could result in disintegration of the state. The choice is *not* between democracy and dictatorship but between nationhood and disintegration. The problem is not one of restraining power to ensure individual freedoms, but one of accumulating sufficient power to ensure that the government will be obeyed.[34]

Military Rule. Because of the tenuous nature of the bonds holding the nation together and the immense difficulties inherent in modernization, civilian one-party governments often give way to military governments. In LDCs the trend toward military control of government is widely established. In Africa, more than half the nations were governed by the military in the middle 1970s. More than two-thirds of the countries of Asia, Africa, the Middle East, and Latin America have experienced varying levels of military intervention since 1945. The trends away from or toward military governments vary by region and circumstance. In the late 1970s, thirteen of Latin America's twenty republics were governed by generals, Haiti by a family dictatorship, and Cuba by a Communist dictator. That changed again in the 1980s. Eleven of the thirteen states elected civilian governments; only Chile and Paraguay remained right-wing regimes. In several of the new civilian governments, however, the army remains visible in the background. The reason, as in other Third World areas, is that several conditions in the contemporary world favor military intervention in politics.[35]

The first is the low level of political culture and legitimacy in the new states. In a modern nation with developed and accepted political institutions, which contain and mediate conflict in society, the military would find it difficult to justify seizing power and demanding public obedience (or proving it possessed legitimate authority). In a new country, however, in which political obligation still follows largely along ethnic, religious, and racial lines and there is little agreement about the rules of the game, the military can seize power. Instead of being regarded as a usurpation, such a seizure can be claimed as legitimate if embryonic political institutions and politicians appear to the public to have failed. Military rule may even be welcomed in situations where civilian leaders, overwhelmed by the massive problems confronting them, have proved themselves inept and indecisive.

In addition, the one-party system may not have provided the necessary organizational cohesiveness and discipline to mobilize the population for the difficult tasks of modernization. More frequently, in the absence of any opposition, single-party governments have grown lax, self-indulgent, and corrupt. Political instability, deteriorating or stagnant economic conditions, and national humiliation in international conflicts, tend to undermine popular faith in politicians, political institutions, and politics. The people turn instead toward the army, another symbol of the nation and sworn to defend it. The army, opposed to a lack of discipline and widespread dishonesty in government and usually somewhat contemptuous of politicians (particularly self-enriching, incompetent, and squabbling ones), often interprets public opinion in this way, for it tends to perceive itself as the true protector and guardian of the public, even though its interventions are motivated primarily by its own corporate interests. Having the coercive means to seize power, it has an advantage over other institutions.

A second condition favoring domestic military intervention is the low level of economic development. In contrast, a Western army, regardless of its organization and technical sophistication, could not run a society as complex as Britain or the United States—probably not even New York City. When, after 1945, the U.S. Army ran the occupation of a part of Germany, for example, it did so only with the help of leaders from American business and professional life. But, in a far less developed society, the military has an advantage over its civilian competitors. Armies are, by and large, microcosms of modern industrial societies. They are technically and rationally oriented to their occupational activities. They cannot function without engineers, mechanics, communications specialists, and so forth; even the operation of jeeps, tanks, guns, and other military equipment by the ordinary soldier demands elementary "industrial" skills. Military units have, in fact, on occasion been used for tasks such as the construction of roads, bridges, and harbors (we may recall the role of the U.S. Army Corps of Engineers in the development of the American West).

A third condition is that the army in a new nation is often said to be in a good position to organize the nation for its economic "takeoff" and to surmount the turbulent transition from the traditional agrarian to modern urban society. An army is founded on centralized command, hierarchy, and discipline, the very characteristics that Communist parties have claimed will allow them, and only them, to modernize an underdeveloped nation successfully and rapidly.

Finally, as a fourth condition, it is claimed that the real power in many of the new armies lies with the younger, highly nationalistic officers, who are dedicated personally and institutionally to the modernization of their nations. In the past, the senior officers usually came from the landed upper class, which had a vested interest in preserving traditional society. Today it is not the generals but the captains who play the key role in control of the army. As sons of small landowners and low-grade civil servants, they consider themselves the true "sons of the land" and despise the traditional ruling class where it still governs. They are aware of the comparative weakness of their armies, a weakness reflecting not only the absence of modern weapons but also the preindustrial nature of their societies. They also know from experience that, whereas in a traditional society a man's status is decided at birth, in the Westernized or modern army, personal advancement is possible. For this reason, these young and ambitious individuals, whose prospects of social advancement and economic reward are cut off as long as civilian society is highly stratified, have entered the armies, where their status in many instances is determined not by birth and family but by ability and hard work. The fact that there is a relationship between effort and reward in the military highlights the injustice of the surrounding civilian society and the need for reform. The younger military leaders thus tend to share the nationalistic and modernizing desires of the Westernized secular intelligentsia; indeed, they are usually called the "military intelligentsia" or the "intelligentsia in uniform." [36]

Yet, the performance of military governments falls far short of the expectations arising from conditions in the country and the organizational and social characteristics of the military.[37] Soldiers overthrow governments basically because they see the corporate interests of the armed forces threatened, whether from channeling of funds elsewhere or from attempts to deprive them of their autonomy and to politicize them. To be sure, the military, given its traditional perception of itself as the servant and protector of the state, finds it easy to justify political intervention in patriotic and selfless terms and, undoubtedly, believes that what it is doing is in the national interest. Furthermore, the fortunes of many countries with low levels of development and single-resource economies are, of course, affected by external economic forces beyond their control. Military regimes have all too often demonstrated little success in promoting economic growth.

Not unnaturally, given the armed forces' organizational interests, the share of the national budget going to the military goes up quite dramatically in most instances of takeover (usually 50 to 75 percent of the previous budget), thus eating up whatever small increases in productivity may have been gained. Although economic growth is viewed as desirable, the military's interests come first—even at the cost of modernization. Furthermore, however apt soldiers are at managing barracks and infantry regiments and flying airplanes, they do not necessarily have the skills of economists and business owners in assessing alternative economic-growth strategies, understanding fiscal policies, and directing large sectors of the economy. The economic record of military governments is hardly an enviable one, certainly no better than that of civilian governments.

Even the reputation of military regimes as reformers, is, on the whole, undeserved. Although nationalistic military governments frequently claim to be progressive, determined to bring about redistribution of land and wealth and to enhance the people's welfare, their often militant rhetoric is in direct conflict with their corporate aggrandizement. In economies of scarcity, in which a gain for one group means a loss for other groups, increased military spending leaves less to redistribute. In addition, armies more often than not represent one or two tribal or ethnic groups, rather than a mixture of all the different groups in the nation. Attempts to favor the communities from which much of the military leadership comes serve only to deepen the already existing social divisions.

Yet the image of many military regimes as progressive persist, largely because in areas where the traditional landed elite still governs, as in much of Africa, Asia, and the Middle East, the military does, upon coming to power, redistribute land and wealth. The breakup of landed oligarchies, which does provide greater social mobility and economic opportunities, clearly favors the rural and urban middle classes with which the officers identify themselves. But where, as in Latin America, there already exists a relatively high level of modernization and where the lower class of peasants and especially workers is more poltically self-conscious and mobilizable, military regimes will crack down if challenged. As a contender for sharing the power and wealth in society, a mobilized lower class is viewed as a threat to the military's corporate interests and to middle-class interests in general. The result is that the military government is transformed into a defender of the social and economic status quo.

The military thus plays different roles in different societies. In traditional society, the middle-class military becomes radical, and its coups are "breakthrough" coups; in middle-class society, the military becomes a participant and arbiter; in mass society, the military becomes the conservative guardian of the prevailing order, and its coups are "veto" coups. In other words, the less developed the society, the more progressive the military's role; the more developed that society, the more conservative and reactionary that role.[38]

Still, however poorly or well what S. E. Finer has called the "armed modernizers" govern and advance their nation's economic growth and welfare, military regimes are likely to be common throughout the less-developed areas for some time to come. Civilian governments' inability to handle communal strife and advance economic development, plus their propensity for self-indulgence and corruption, will continue to weaken or destroy their legitimacy and incite the military to *coups d'état* while much of the population cheers and welcomes the new governors in uniform. It is the presence or absence of legitimacy that, in the final analysis, permits translation of motives to intervene into action. "Where public attachment to civilian institutions is strong, military intervention in politics will be weak. . . . By the same token, where public attachment to civilian institutions is weak or nonexistent, military intervention will find wide scope"[39] and will not be regarded as a usurpation of power. *Coups d'état* are symptoms of the failing of civilian rulers, especially to modernize their nations. In these circumstances, the new nations' domestic problems will continue to affect profoundly the conduct of their foreign policies.

FOREIGN POLICY IN THE BIPOLAR ERA

The leaders of the new states clearly confront problems that are vast and seemingly insoluble so that, rather than concentrating on their nations' domestic needs, they are tempted to play dramatic and popular roles on the international stage. Indeed, foreign policy may help them accomplish their various internal aims.

Nationalizing Their Peoples

First, foreign policy may help them to "nationalize" their peoples. As often the only force that united the people was hatred of the former colonial power—and this "reactive nationalism" tends to lose its force as a socially cohesive factor soon after independence—the only way to arouse people and keep them united is to continue the struggle against European colonialism or "imperialism" in general. The more tenuous the bonds uniting the members of a society, the more ardent will be the campaign against the "vestiges of imperialism." By asserting that the nation is once more the victim of the West, the leaders seek to arouse their peoples and unite them against a common external danger. Anticolonialism thus does not end with the achievement of national independence. The struggle against "neocolonialism" must be continued until a measure of national unity and economic progress has occurred. "[A]nti-colonialism is a cement that holds together otherwise incompatible domestic factions. The cohesive function of the 'common enemy' must be perpetuated even when the foreign 'enemy' is no longer a real threat.... This, perhaps, is the reason why opposition to colonialism frequently grows more intense *after* independence." [40] Foreign policy thus serves as *a continuation of the revolution against colonial rule to preserve the unity of the new nation.*

Search for Identity

Second, and closely related, the foreign policy of the LDCs involves a search for identity, status, and dignity. Many of these countries are new nations, former colonies, with no national history, no commonly accepted political institutions, no domestic unity, and almost no strong national commitment among their populations. Even if they have had a glorious past and are at present independent, the feeling that they are still subject to Western influence may lead to an assertive foreign policy.

> In short, the state's legitimacy is more easily asserted through its foreign policy than through its domestic policies and it is more apparent when performing on the international than on the national stage. Domestic issues divide the nation and disclose how little developed is its consciousness of itself; foreign issues unite the nation and mark it as a going concern. [41]

Foreign policy, therefore, is also an effort to *discover and establish the new state's personality and to affirm its identity as a nation separate from the former colonial power.*

Assertion of Equality

The new states are very self-conscious that the history of the international system is the history of inequality. By and large, as less-developed states, they are aware of their lower places in the hierarchy of states dominated by the superpowers and the Western industrial states (including Japan). While the leaders of the LDCs have vigorously asserted their equality as legally equal sovereign states in the United Nations, they bristle at being excluded from conferences and institutions that deal with issues that affect their countries, particularly economic and financial issues. The LDCs tend to see themselves as the West's "dependencies" who do not control their own destiny. Thus, a third aim of foreign policy is to *secure greater participation in decisions that have an impact upon their societies, and, more generally, play a more influential role in the state system.*

Maximization of Foreign Aid

Fourth, foreign policy is aimed at gaining the most foreign aid. By the late 1970s, the Third World accounted for 75 percent of the world's population but received only 10 percent of the world's revenues. Unable to earn sufficient funds to support their people, many LDCs have no choice but to seek external assistance. Indeed, it was widely believed in the industrial West during the 1950s and 1960s that the LDCs would need considerable foreign aid until they achieved self-sustaining economic growth. More specifically, on the assumption that communism thrives on misery, Western leaders believed that they ought to supply more of that aid so that the LDCs could modernize. For the LDCs, one aim of foreign policy has been to *attract the external funds necessary for their domestic transformation from rural, economically backward societies to urban-industrial societies with high standards of living.*

Preserving Power

Fifth, nationalist leaders want to stay in power and, therefore, frequently seek to divert popular attention from domestic problems. At home only painfully slow progress can be made, the task of development is bound to be long and arduous, and the masses will tend to become increasingly restless and dissatisfied. The gap between their rising material expectations and satisfaction seems unbridgeable as increasing numbers of people become politically conscious and demand that their needs be met. In addition, increased movement from the country to the impersonal and unfamiliar cities disrupts the traditional loyalties and ties of the people; unable to find substitutes, they live isolated in a mass society. And the tendency to political fragmentation remains ever present.

The pressure on national leaders to improve living conditions and build the new nation is unrelenting. If these demands remain unsatisfied, however, the revolution of rising expectations may turn into a revolution of rising frustration, and the leaders and their governments suffer declining prestige and support.

To preserve or recapture the people's support, stay in power, and stabilize the government, they are tempted irresistably to assert themselves in foreign policy. In circumstances of economic stagnation, cultural alienation, and governmental insecurity, political leaders will be tempted to preserve their power by externalizing domestic dissatisfaction; foreign scapegoats will be required to relieve internal stresses and strains. It is easier for leaders to play prominent and highly visible international roles—at the United Nations, at meetings of the nonaligned states, during visits to Moscow or Western capitals—than to undertake the difficult work of modernizing their nation. Foreign policy, therefore, may serve the *purpose of exporting domestic dissatisfaction and mobilizing popular support for the government.*

CHARACTERISTICS OF NONALIGNMENT

A foreign policy of nonalignment favors the implementation of all these aims. Bipolarity made nonalignment feasible. By taking an in-between position, a new state could maximize its appeal to both the Soviet Union and the United States, as well as to their respective allies. The two superpowers would act as if they were suitors seeking to win the same woman. By occasionally hinting at a commitment, the new nation could gain leverage, despite its lack of power. For each suitor was compelled to demonstrate its serious intentions, usually with large amounts of foreign aid. The further a new state moved away from the West, the more eagerly the Communists would offer it assistance; the nearer it moved to the West, the greater the number of Western loans or grants that were offered.

Although bipolarity favors nonalignment, not all non-Marxist nonaligned countries practice this approach in the same way. The Yugoslavs consider themselves nonaligned; so do the Egyptians, Indians, Ethiopians, Malaysians, and Tunisians. Yet the dispositions of these countries range from sentiments that might be described as pro-Soviet to those that might be called pro-American. In a way, the problem of classifying the varieties of nonalignment is one of *time*. A regime may be looking eastward one moment yet normalize its relations with the West the next. Ethiopia is pro-American one year; then the new Marxist regime shifts toward the East. But in Somalia, the Marxist government, once close to Moscow, shifted toward the United States when the Soviet Union switched its support from Somalia to Ethiopia with which Somalia was in conflict. Egypt for many years seemed to be a Soviet pawn— indeed, in 1971 it formalized its association with a treaty of friendship and cooperation—but a year later it threw out its Soviet advisers and within two more years its president had reestablished diplomatic relations with the United States, called Secretary of State Henry Kissinger (who is Jewish) his "good friend and miracle worker," and denounced the treaty of friendship with the Soviet Union. Similarly, in the early 1970s India under Indira Gandhi signed a friendship treaty with the Soviet Union. But a few years later, after she had been defeated in a general election, her successor declared that his government would adopt a foreign policy of "proper nonalignment" and that the Indian-Soviet friendship treaty would not be allowed to interfere with India's relations with other countries—presumably the Western states. Upon reelection, Gandhi shifted again somewhat toward the Soviet Union, and, after she died, her son continued to stress the Indian-Soviet link.

Nonalignment is even more a matter of *issue areas*.[42] One such area is military. Egypt and India received vast amounts of military equipment from the Soviet Union; on the other hand, Singapore was willing to make its naval base available to the West in the event of hostilities, and Tanzania once relied upon the former mother country's (Britain's) military forces to restore domestic order. Yet all these countries consider themselves nonaligned. Some seek and gain military aid from both sides. The same is true for other issue areas such as economic assistance and trade, diplomacy, and ideology. Country A may be leaning to the West because it places a high priority on democratic values, receives most of its military hardware from the West, receives about equal amounts of economic aid from both sides, and gravitates more toward Western than Soviet diplomatic positions. An exception is India, which, democratic tradition notwithstanding, has often gravitated toward the Soviets. Country B, in contrast, is politically sympathetic to the East, a source of its military hardware; obtains much of its economic aid and trade from the West; and leans notably to the East on diplomatic issues. In this example, Egypt is an exception. A one-party state, Egypt, with its "Arab socialism," has switched from a pro-Soviet stance toward rapprochement with the United States. It has also dismantled much of its brand of socialism in order to stimulate private initiative and attract foreign investments while retaining some public ownership over certain sectors of the economy.

Even when a nonaligned country seems to lean more toward the Soviet Union or the United States, however, one must be careful about classifying it one way or another. The term *pro-Soviet* may reflect a general attitude and preference on the part of national leaders, but it may also indicate positions that those leaders would have taken even in the absence of a cold war—anticolonial or antiapartheid, for example—and with which the Soviets seek to identify themselves. The same is true of a country that seems pro-American. Anwar Sadat was an Egyptian nationalist first, and when he made overtures to the West, it was because he knew U.S. leaders could better help him achieve his goal of recovering Egyptian lands lost in 1967 because they had influence in Israel and the Soviets did not. On balance, however, nonalignment more often than not has seemed—and may continue to seem—to be pro-Soviet because of continuing anti-Western feelings.

The LDCs still attribute all sorts of ills, from their continued role as raw-material suppliers for Western industries to conditions in South Africa, to the West's neocolonial control by economic means. The conviction that the distribution of power between the First and Third Worlds is still stacked against them and that the West thereby keeps them poor and dependent has led the nonaligned countries to take increasingly anti-Western stands. If the many countries of Asia, Africa, and Latin America can be thought of as a cohesive bloc, it is because they share this set of attitudes.[43]

FROM NONALIGNMENT TO THE NEW INTERNATIONAL ECONOMIC ORDER

The Failure of Western Development Models

Forty years after World War II, much of the Third World remains poor, illiterate, hungry, and unhealthy, despite an economic growth rate higher than that of the First World. The difficulty is that, because these countries started so far behind in per capita income, it was virtually impossible for them to catch up. A person earning $300 whose income rises by 10 percent increases the yearly income to $330; another earning $3,000 whose income rises by 5 percent has $3,150. Indeed, from 1955 to 1980 per capita income in the United States, in constant dollars, grew from $7,000 to $11,500. In India, during the same time, it grew from $170 to $260. A gap of $6,830 in 1955 had almost doubled to $11,240! In short, the income gap between rich and poor states widens, even if the poorer nation has a faster rate of economic growth. Some of the LDCs, to be sure, managed surprisingly well—the resource-rich, especially oil-rich countries, and the export platforms.

Nevertheless, many of the LDCs remained just that, less developed. This result was contrary to the early models of development drawn up by Western social scientists as more and more colonial countries achieved independence. Essentially, it was said, nations went through certain stages of development. In this process, as in the development of individuals as they progress from childhood to old age, nations passed, according to the economists, through several "stages of economic growth," and, according to the political scientists, through a number of "stages of political growth." [44] At the end of their growth, the new nations would look like Western states: industrialized, with high standards of living and income relatively equitably distributed, politically pluralistic, democratic, and stable. Peaceful was another characteristic often added, although sometimes it was left implicit. Development, thought of mainly as an economic transformation of a traditional rural society into a modern urban-industrial one, was, therefore, also called *Westernization*. Having no models of global development to work with, Western social scientists not surprisingly looked back at their own societies and then generalized about their evolution into modern societies. The paths the European states had trodden, therefore, seemed likely to be the ones the new states of Asia and Africa would walk along. The West, then, held itself up as the model for the rest of the world. [45] This ethnocentric view focused basically upon accumulating the capital necessary for the task of Westernization.

It was in this context that the United States and other Western states began to provide the LDCs with economic aid. Nations living at the poverty level, it was pointed out, could not squeeze the required capital out of their low-paid work force; foreign funds were, therefore, necessary to stoke the fires of development. But aid did not help the vast majority of LDCs to realize a self-sustaining growth. Finding their status as recipients of Western "charity" rather humiliating, the LDCs' slogan became "Trade, Not Aid." In an industrial world, they expected orders for their natural resources to earn the funds they needed for capital investment. This would enable them to diversify their economies and make them less dependent upon single commodities for exports. This too failed.

Increasingly, therefore, the First and Third Worlds took opposite views of why the LDCs have not been able to modernize. The Western industrial countries argued that the LDCs' problems are primarily internal. They arise from overpopulation; ethnic, religious, and racial divisions; lack of natural resources; lack of professional training; government corruption and mismanagement; low priority given to agriculture; the hostile attitude toward private capital investment; and expulsion or mistreatment of productive minorities. The LDCs have argued that they cannot modernize because they are the victims of an international economy dominated by the industrial West. The causes and cures of their underdevelopment, they claim, were not internal but external. Specifically, they assert that the reason for their economic backwardness is international capitalism.[46]

LDC Dependency and World Capitalism

We have already noted the difficulties that most LDCs face in earning money on the international market. They are too dependent on single resources, and the prices of these resources fluctuate with the Western industrial economies. Competition among resource producers tends to lead to oversupplies, forcing prices downward, and, when Western industries substitute other resources or synthetics, prices are further depressed. In the meantime, the manufactured goods bought in the West tend to rise in price. The terms of trade do not favor the LDCs.

It is in this context that the LDCs have generally claimed that their relations with the industrial West have not changed much since colonial days. Formerly the colonies were governed directly from London, Paris, or other Western capitals. Since independence, the former colonies have achieved self-government but, they insist, their independence is only formal, rather than meaningful. Indeed, this formal independence masks the fact that *real* self-government does not exist. The LDCs remain tied to their former masters by the same economic chains that characterized the colonial era. These chains keep them dependent on the capitalist West. Politically independent in name only, they remain in neocolonial bondage as raw material suppliers for Western industry.

As a result, they claim, their economies are not oriented toward their national needs, toward improving the lives of their own peoples. Their resources were originally developed by the West and then used by Western industry for the production of goods that have raised the *Western* standard of living to the highest in the world. That is why the West grew rich while the LDCs remained poor. The relationship of mother country to the colony was one of exploitation. The LDCs were poor because they had been robbed; the Western states were rich because they had been exploiters. Even today, the former colonies still provide cheap raw materials—except for oil—to Western industry. The United States, Western Europe, and Japan are said to benefit enormously from the international economy. They are the *core countries* of world capitalism. (The Soviet-bloc economies are by and large not a part of the world trading system.) The LDCs constitute the *peripheries*. Thus the free market, which in theory benefits all nations, actually favors the strong and keeps the LDCs in a subordinate position.

Dependency is a relationship characterized by asymmetry, in which the LDCs' economic growth is conditioned by events in the industrialized nations' economies. (Interdependence, on the other hand, is characterized by symmetry.) More specifically, the LDCs' dependency takes several forms. One is trade dependency; the LDCs depend on the industrial states for markets in which to sell their commodities and are obviously both sensitive and vulnerable to levels of demand. Another form is investment dependency. Western investors control key sectors of the LDCs' economies: production of natural resources and any manufacturing that may have been developed. Foreign aid creates yet a third form of dependence.

A more radical viewpoint asserts that these economic chains are supplemented by Western political alliances and by military and police links to the LDCs' ruling elites, which have a vested interest in preserving this dependency relationship. The reason is that these governing elites owe their social status, political power, and wealth to this exploitive arrangement. They are the Western capitalists' "front men"; they are dependent for their survival on the preservation of the status quo. By the same token, these elites have no strong ties to their own people. Ruling on behalf of foreigners, they are domestically unpopular and, as a result, resort to authoritarian regimes. If their power is threatened, covert or overt foreign intervention—usually by the United States since it is the world's most powerful capitalist state—may occur. U.S. foreign policy is, therefore, a counterrevolutionary one. Despite its verbal commitment to democracy, the United States in fact suppresses democracy abroad. In this way, the LDCs are "managed" by the United States and its Western partners, the real beneficiaries of the free market.

To sum up the general LDC case: (1) the current old international economic order favors the states who organized it, the Western capitalist states; (2) ex-colonial, now neocolonial states, occupy permanent subordinate status and will always be underdeveloped, and this underdevelopment is caused by capitalism and is not the result of internal problems; and (3) a new international economic order is needed to right past injustices and bring about a more equitable distribution of wealth, status, and power between the nations of the First and Third Worlds.

CHANGING THE INTERNATIONAL ECONOMY: REVOLUTION OR REFORM?

At the heart of the dependency theory is the assertion that capitalist states—and in the post-World War II age, especially the United States—are dependent upon the Third World for cheap raw materials, investment opportunities, and export markets. In fact, as we shall see in a critical analysis of the

Marxist interpretation of history and international politics (Chapter 15), the U.S. economy has not been dependent on dominating the Third World for its prosperity. Nevertheless, those who believe that the old international economic order is not only unfair but permanent, and that this global inequality of wealth is directly attributable to an inherently exploitive capitalism, advocate a strategy of revolution as a prescription.

Because the United States and its Western allies are the preeminent capitalist states, and their domination of the international economy is the prerequisite for the continued exploitation of the peripheral states, a strategy of liberation must seek to destroy this link and America's role in the world economy. Theoretically, the best solution would be a revolution in the United States that would replace capitalism with a socialist economy. By definition, a socialist United States would not exploit the LDCs and would allow them to live in political *and* economic freedom; under socialism, people no longer exploit each other, domestically or internationally, for profit. Practically, this is an unlikely solution. A more feasible course, it is suggested, would deprive the United States and its capitalist associates of the Third World markets and resources. Cutting the economic links that bind the LDCs with the core states is an alternative strategy that can be achieved by revolutions that overthrow the capitalist puppet regimes in the LDCs. Such revolutions may well involve guerrilla war, as in China and Vietnam. However the revolution is brought about, violence is the only way of gaining true national liberation.

The reformist approach agrees that an exploitive relationship exists between the Western industrial states and the raw-material producing LDCs, but explains it differently. Instead of attributing the cause to capitalism and advocating a revolutionary solution, the reformers blame the structure of the system; in other words, the inequality of power between states with advanced and less-developed economies. Their solution is to reduce this inequality of wealth and power. Initially, the prescription was "import substitution." The LDCs had to develop their own industries. They should not import the industrial and consumer goods they needed, but produce them. This would require the temporary protection of their "baby industries" until they were able to compete internationally. Unfortunately, this solution, which tended to make industries uncompetitive behind their protective barriers, did not prove to be correct. It was in this context that in 1974 the new international economic order was offered as a solution.

The political objective of the LDCs was to change the international economy so that wealth would be more equitably distributed. The LDCs sought several concrete goals: (1) They wanted higher and more stable commodity prices (to provide steady income "decoupled" from Western economic fluctuations) so that they can plan for several years ahead, diversify their economies, and become less dependent on the sale of single resources. (2) They wanted the protection of their purchasing power through "indexing," linking the sale of resources to Western inflation rates and rising prices for Western machinery, weapons, and food. (3) They wanted the doubling or tripling of foreign aid and capital contributions from institutions such as the International Monetary Fund, the International Bank for Reconstruction and Development, and the World Bank, and they wanted more influence in these organizations. (4) They wanted preferential Western tariffs for LDC exports, which would give them a competitive edge and enhance their earning capacity. (5) They wanted a voice in controlling the levels of production and prices of alternative sources of minerals, such as those found on the sea beds. (6) In addition, they wanted to defer their debt, which had stood at $142 billion in 1974, but was $970 billion by 1985 for the non-OPEC LDCs—which meant postponing the costs of servicing the debt. (7) Finally, they wanted greater control over the multinational corporations. Although satisfaction of these demands would not constitute a revolutionary transformation of the international economy, it would constitute a new international economic order in which the Western states' perceived control of the economic rules of the game would be reduced.[47] The LDCs' demands reflected their struggle to end past humiliations and their determination to participate actively in shaping their futures.

The less-developed countries are deeply resentful of their past treatment and present lot in the system. It may be said that the poor and plentiful people of the southern half of this planet are no longer willing to be the "hewers of wood and drawers of water" for the rich states of the northern half. It is worth repeating that this attitude is the main reason why the poorer LDCs, though the hardest hit by OPEC policies, continued to support OPEC during the 1970s. The louder the rich Western countries squealed, the greater the delight of all the LDCs. As William Wordsworth wrote of the French Revolution, "Bliss was it in that dawn to be alive/But to be young was very heaven." A Third World poet might have written those lines in the winter of 1973-74. Throwing off the alleged chains of economic dependence was the critical task for the LDCs. Clearly, though economics can be discussed rationally, the issues being negotiated are only partly economic. The discussion of the terms of trade was deeply symptomatic of a general assertion of non-Western nationalism against the West. The economic bargaining took place, therefore, between parties who were all too frequently and too deeply separated by wide psychological and cultural barriers.

Insisting that their poverty was the result of Western exploitation, the LDCs were really claiming that the West owed them a moral debt for past colonial sins, which it must pay off in more earthly coin. Charging that the West had plundered them in the past and continues to do so today, they repeated over and over that such "imperialistic exploitation"—the slogan of the LDCs—was wrong. Presumably, in their view, Western political organization, economic ideas, scientific inventiveness, and technological skills have had little to do with creating Western prosperity.[48] The attempt to induce a sense of Western guilt for past behavior was a shrewd tactic, however, because many Westerners feel ashamed and morally culpable for what their forefathers did, even though the political standards and moral codes were quite different in the colonial age. Making reparation for past errors seemed the right thing to do; helping the poor by narrowing the gap between them and the rich constituted, for those Westerners, a morally worthy cause, a way of gaining national redemption and of living up to the promise of a democratic way of life. The LDCs have little leverage, but, by charging Western exploitation, they hoped to place the West on the defensive. Morality, no less than arms, can be an effective weapon.

The Latest Prescription: The Magic of the Marketplace

Indeed, the public discussions of a new international economic order often became diatribes. But the era of confrontation in the 1970s has given way to a more reflective attitude in the Third World. The key problem to development is still capital accumulation. Economists, including those in the Third World, have found that considerable capital resources exist in the LDCs, especially in the more developed states in Latin America. But that capital is wasted by governments whose leaders indulge themselves with Rolls Royces and Mercedes cars or villas on the French Riviera or in Miami, whose bureaucracies are so oversized that they are a drain on the economy, and whose military forces spend too much on weapons for wars that they will never fight. (Many of them are nothing but gendarmeries or police forces, particularly in Latin America.) The solution returns to a standard capitalist prescription: emphasize internal savings, austerity, and investment in economic growth. Government, while taxing consumption heavily, would encourage industrial and agricultural development.

Critical to this shift in position was an increasing endorsement of the private market (since the alternative of state-controlled industries was more and more perceived as dangerous to the development of democracy). President Reagan's view of the "magic of the marketplace," which initially met with skepticism, seems to have gained support and placed on the defensive the more traditional view that free-market economies were inappropriate and that state-directed economies were the answer. Even more surprising is that the LDCs were not alone in recognizing the importance of the market; even Communist China was experimenting with the profit motive and greater political decentralization.

While more governments in all areas were showing a new interest in private enterprise, in large part because their state-controlled economies were going broke, it was Asia that was the model. Japan, of course, and South Korea, Taiwan, Hong Kong, and Singapore, but also Malaysia and Thailand, were all growing rapidly and doing so on the basis of market-oriented policies. Unlike so many LDCs who denounced American imperialism and American multinational corporations and demanded a new deal, these countries were asking only for a fair deal: access to the U.S. market for their export-driven economies. Japan and its East Asian neighbors are, interestingly enough, "neo-Confucian" societies: they are relatively homogeneous in population, with a strong belief in the work ethic and a commitment to education. Thus reform, composed of some of the measures included in the new international economic order plus domestic measures and efforts in the LDCs, appears more likely than revolution to be the path many countries will take.

The Vanishing Soviet Model

While the early Western development models appeared increasingly irrelevant, the American system of a mixed economy, with its emphasis on private enterprise and competition, drew more attention. Simultaneously, fewer and fewer LDCs were attracted to the Soviet model. The Soviet Union's continuous problems in providing its citizens with a balanced diet, its failure to produce a sufficient number and variety of quality consumer goods, and its lagging behind Japan and the United States in the new industrial revolution made the Soviet economy more and more inappropriate as a model. Those nations outside the Soviet bloc that followed this model—such as Ethiopia, Cuba, and Nicaragua—themselves became examples of mismanaged economies. Soviet-style communism's main attraction for Marxist leaders and groups remained its ability to seize power by helping to ideologically attract supporters and organize them for revolutionary warfare (China, Vietnam, Nicaragua), as well as assist its friends engaged in civil wars with Soviet and Soviet-bloc advisers, weapons, and troops (largely Cuban). But as an economic model for tilling the land or industrial productivity of nonmilitary goods, it was increasingly useless. In short, the Soviet Union can help its friends in the seizure and consolidation of power, but not to modernize and manage their economies.

Even Communist China has turned away from what a Chinese leader called the "radical leftist nonsense" of Mao Zedong and turned toward a more flexible economic system that has encouraged some private enterprise and property ownership.[49] Largely abandoning the collective farm, China has experienced a "great leap forward" in food production, and the Chinese are now introducing capitalist ideas to urban industries and services. The widespread slogan, "To get rich is glorious," appeals to the Chinese. "Marx died 100 years ago," says Beijing's *People's Daily*. "There have been tremendous changes since his ideas were formed.... So we cannot use Marxist and Leninist works to solve our present-day problems."[50] Still, Marxism-Leninism may not have lost all of its appeal in a world divided between rich and poor nations whose population will soon compose the vast majority of mankind.

THE RICH AND THE POOR: INTERNATIONAL CLASS WAR?

In the original Western rationale for economic aid to countries of the Third World, it is clear that, besides simple humanitarian sentiments, security considerations were uppermost. Perhaps the basic reason for such concern sprang from a logic frequently articulated by government spokesmen, academicians, and journalists and thus often implicit in policy: that a world divided between rich and poor nations is an explosive world in which the majority, which is poor, is set against the privileged minority. Such a gap is no more acceptable internationally than it was within each of the Western nations a hundred years ago.

Social Justice in Western Nations

The two situations are believed to be so similar that the "lesson" of earlier domestic experience is thought to apply to the international division of wealth. As the Industrial Revolution gathered momentum in nineteenth-century Europe and the United States, it created a privileged minority that owned most of the wealth. The distribution of income was, to say the least, unequal. Laborers, including many children and women, worked fourteen to sixteen hours a day six or seven days a week, earned little beyond subsistence, and lived in overcrowded slums. The rich became richer, and the poor became poorer. This trend was so obvious that the British stateman Benjamin Disraeli spoke of England as not one nation but two.

But, according to the prevailing free-market, or *laissez faire*, philosophy, nothing could be done to alleviate this situation. Government intervention, whether to end the grosser forms of exploitation or to redistribute income to help the poor lead more decent and dignified lives, was rejected as contrary to the "laws of economics." Any outside interference with the workings of the market, it was said, would stifle the private incentive and initiative that stoked the competitive capitalist system. These "laws," which condemned a large section of the population to hopeless and miserable existence, received even further support from the biologist Charles Darwin's theory of evolution, with its emphasis on the "struggle for survival" and the "survival of the fittest." The philosophy of Social Darwinism was based on the very simple proposition that the rich are rich because they are the most fit; conversely, the poor are destitute because they are unfit. It never occurred to Social Darwinists to ask whether everyone had an equal start or opportunity in this struggle.

These philosophical justifications for permitting abject poverty were ultimately rejected in all Western societies. The long working hours, unsanitary and unsafe working conditions, and teeming slums were blots on the national conscience. Permitting them to continue would also have been politically shortsighted and economically foolish. Politically, the permanent division of people into haves and have-nots could end only in revolution, with the industrial middle class, or bourgeoisie, being overthrown by the working class, or proletariat. The bourgeoisie could, perhaps, retain its power by surrendering democratic beliefs and values and establishing authoritarian governments to crush proletarian protests and uprisings. Neither of these alternatives seemed attractive to the ruling middle classes. Nor did the policy of squeezing the workers for maximum profit make sense economically, for, the less money people have, the fewer things they can buy. Industry needs consumers. Social justice thus made sense—morally, politically, and economically.

In the late nineteenth century, governments in every Western society began to intervene increasingly in the economy. Growing public awareness of social problems and ills eventually led to the regulation of business: passage of minimum-wage and maximum-hours legislation; abolition of child labor and "sweatshop" working conditions; recognition of trade unions; measures to counteract the swings of the business cycle; implementation of a progressive income tax; and the initiation of unemployment insurance, public-works programs, and other "pump priming" projects to increase the purchasing power of the people during depressions and thus to stimulate renewed demand and production. These measures helped to create the twentieth-century mass market and gave the working class a vested interest in the existing social and economic order.

Social Justice Among the Nations of the World

It is the same problem of inequitable distribution of income that is now plaguing the world. But this time the problem exists not within nations but among nations. The rich countries are becoming richer, most poor countries poorer. Currently, three-quarters of the world's population uses 25 percent of its resources, the other one-quarter in the industrial Western world consumes 75 percent.[51] Such a maldistribution of wealth has to be as dangerous to the stability of the international system as it was in the nineteenth century to the domestic system. The Marxist prophesy that the exploited proletariat will overthrow the bourgeoisie may have been incorrect as far as Western industrial societies are concerned, but will it be fulfilled on the global plane? Will the poverty-stricken nations of the world, the international proletariat, rise up in revolution against the privileged and wealthy Western countries, the international bourgeoisie?

Indeed this question hovers ominously over the international system. There is no world government to do globally what Western governments did domestically. One need but examine the fundamental reason for the failure of the new international economic order. In its aim of redistributing wealth through agreements on higher and stable commodity prices, economic aid, and preferential access to Western markets, the missing ingredient was the lack of a feeling of community between the core and peripheral states. The program for "structural reform in the global economy depends upon a sense of community *between* rich and poor states that is every bit as strong as that existing *within* advanced industrial states with a long tradition of national unity."[52] This sense of community between the rich and poor states, however, does not exist at present.

Thus, a key question is whether the rich states will define their national interests in a way that helps the LDCs solve their principal problems. Will they, for example, encourage the LDCs to develop agriculture? Will they forgo financing spectacular dams and power stations and focus more aid on smaller-scale health programs, including family planning? Will they permit entry of LDC industrial and consumer goods or will they protect inefficient American and European industries? Above all, will they encourage the LDCs to do more for themselves? Clearly, avoiding an intensification of the confrontation between the haves and have-nots is a task that will require the understanding, efforts, and cooperation of both the less-developed nations as well as the industrial states. For the LDCs enhancing their welfare is a possession goal, for the economically advanced states it is a milieu goal. Both are critical to the stability of the international system.

Notes

1. Robert C. Good, "Changing Patterns of African International Relations," *American Political Science Review* (September 1964): 638.
2. Robert L. Heilbroner, *The Great Ascent* (New York: Harper & Row, 1963), 23-26. Used by permission of the publisher and A. D. Peters & Co.
3. Lawrence S. Eagleburger and Donald F. McHenry, "How the U.S. Can Help," *New York Times*, Nov. 29, 1985.
4. The disruption of traditional colonial society by Western industrial nations' economic behavior is analyzed in *The Emerging Nations*, ed. Max F. Millikan and Donald L. M. Blackmer (Boston: Little, Brown & Co., 1961), 3-17; and Immanuel Wallerstein, *Africa: The Politics of Independence* (New York: Vintage, 1961), 29-43.
5. Barbara Ward, *The Rich Nations and the Poor Nations* (New York: W. W. Norton, 1962), 54.
6. Rupert Emerson, *From Empire to Nation* (Cambridge, Mass.: Harvard University Press, 1960), 6.
7. "The term 'intelligentsia' used to denote specifically those intellectuals who are experiencing internal conflict between allegiance to traditional cultures and the influence of the modern West. Within these terms of reference it is not the amount of knowledge or education that determines membership in the intelligentsia.... No man, no matter how learned, is classified as a member of the intelligentsia if he has retained his identity with his national background. As long as he remains integrated in his society and accepts the values of that society as his own, he is likely to remain essentially a conservative without that revolutionary spark which ... would class him as a member of the intelligentsia. If, on the other hand, he is an intellectual who has felt the impact of Western civilization and has been drawn into the vortex of conflicting ideas, he enters the ranks of the intelligentsia.... Within the intelligentsia, however, rebelliousness is a common characteristic. Beset with doubts about traditional cultural values, its members have felt a driving need to search for something new." Klaus Mehnert, "The Social and Political Role of the Intelligentsia in the New Countries," in *New Nations in a Divided World*, ed. Kurt London (New York: Holt, Rinehart & Winston, 1964), 121-122.

8. See particularly Emerson, *From Empire to Nation*, 89-187, 295-359; Clifford Geertz, "The Integrative Revolution," in *Old Societies and New States*, ed. Clifford Geertz (New York: Free Press, 1963), 105-157; and Walter Connor, "Nation-Building or Nation-Destroying?" *World Politics*, April 1972, 219ff.

9. Michael Brecher, *Nehru: A Political Biography* (New York: Oxford University Press, 1959), 362-363.

10. Wallerstein, *Africa*, 88.

11. *New York Times*, May 19, 1983.

12. Robert S. McNamara, "The Population Problem," *Foreign Affairs* (Summer 1984): 1111-1112.

13. Davidson R. Gwatkin and Sarah K. Brandel, "Life Expectancy and Population Growth in the Third World," *Scientific American*, May 1982, 57-65.

14. Alexander Gerschenkron, *Economic Backwardness in Historical Perspective* (New York: Holt, Rinehart & Winston, 1965), 28.

15. McNamara, "The Population Problem," 1119. Also Lester R. Brown, *In the Human Interest* (New York: W. W. Norton, 1974).

16. *New York Times*, July 25, 1985.

17. *Gainesville Sun*, Dec. 2, 1979. These estimates were reported from a study by Earl O. Heady, a well-known agricultural economist at Iowa State University.

18. *Gainesville Sun*, July 10, 1980.

19. Nick Eberstadt, "Hunger and Ideology," *Commentary*, July 1981, 43.

20. Nick Eberstadt, "Famine, Development & Foreign Aid," *Commentary*, March 1985, 25-31; and Arch Paddington, "Ethiopia: The Communist Use of Famine," *Commentary*, April 1986, 30-39.

21. William Paddock and Paul Paddock, *Famine—1975!* (Boston: Little, Brown & Co., 1967).

22. Barbara Insel, "A World Awash in Grain," *Foreign Affairs* (Spring 1985): 892-911.

23. Francis Moore Lappé and Joseph Collins, *Food First* (Boston: Houghton Mifflin, 1977).

24. W. Arthur Lewis, *The Evaluation of the International Economic Order* (Princeton, N.J.: Princeton University Press, 1978).

25. Richard J. Barnet and Ronald E. Müller, *Global Reach* (New York: Simon & Schuster, 1974), 216-217; Lewis, *Evaluation of the International Economic Order*, 34-37.

26. See R. H. Tawney, *Religion and the Rise of Capitalism* (Baltimore: Penguin, 1947).

27. Robin Wright, *Sacred Rage* (New York: Linden Press, 1985.)

28. Samuel P. Huntington, *Political Order in Changing Societies* (New Haven, Conn.: Yale University Press, 1968), 1.

29. Ibid., 2.

30. Karl Marx, who confused capitalism as a mature economic system with the early phase of capital accumulation under any economic and political system, caught the essence of these peasant-laborers' protests. The bourgeoisie, he said, "has pitilessly torn asunder the motley feudal ties that bound man to his 'natural superiors,' and has left remaining no other nexus between man and man than naked self-interest, than callous 'cash payment.' . . . It has resolved personal worth into exchange value." Marx might more appropriately have used the words "Industrial Revolution" for "bourgeoisie." Indeed, he did say: "Owing to the extensive use of machinery and to division of labor, work of the proletarians has lost all individual character, and, consequently, all charm for the workman. He becomes an appendage of the machine. . . . Modern industry has converted the little workshop of the

patriarchal master into the great factory of the industrial capitalist. Masses of laborers, crowded into the factory, are organized like soldiers.... Not only are they slaves of the bourgeois class, and of the bourgeois state; they are daily and hourly enslaved by the machine, by the supervisor, and, above all, by the individual bourgeois manufacturer himself. The more openly this despotism proclaims gain to be its end and aim, the more petty, the more hateful, and the more embittering it is." Quoted in *The Essential Works of Marxism*, ed. Arthur P. Mendel (New York: Bantam, 1961), 15, 19-20; see also Adam B. Ulam, *The New Face of Soviet Totalitarianism* (Cambridge, Mass.: Harvard University Press, 1963), 19-20.

31. Wallerstein, *Africa*, 98.

32. Ibid., 99.

33. Julius Nyerere, quoted in *The Ideologies of the Developing Nations*, by Paul E. Sigmund, Jr. (New York: Holt, Rinehart & Winston, 1963), 199 (emphasis in original).

34. Wallerstein, *Africa*, 96.

35. General analyses of the role of the military in new nations are Morris Janowitz, *The Military in the Political Development of New Nations* (Chicago: University of Chicago Press, 1964); S. E. Finer, *The Man on Horseback*, rev. ed. (Baltimore: Penguin, 1976); John J. Johnson, ed., *The Role of the Military in Underdeveloped Countries* (Princeton, N.J.: Princeton University Press, 1962); Huntington, *Political Order*, 192-263; Edward Feit, "Pen, Sword and People: Military Regimes in the Formation of Political Institutions," *World Politics*, January 1973, 251ff; and Feit, *The Armed Bureaucrat* (Boston: Houghton Mifflin, 1973).

36. The degree to which the military leaders' perception of their role is influenced by the values they have learned in Western military academies is analyzed by Robert M. Price, "A Theoretical Approach to Military Rule in the New States," *World Politics*, April 1971, 399-430.

37. See Eric A. Nordlinger, "Soldiers in Mufti," *American Political Science Review* (December 1970): 1131ff; and Nordlinger, *Soldiers in Politics* (Englewood Cliffs, N.J.: Prentice-Hall, 1977) for the best overall evaluation of the military in power. Our analysis has been heavily influenced by Nordlinger's judgments.

38. Huntington, *Political Order*, 192-263. The Huntington-Nordlinger view of the different roles the military plays in different societies is questioned by Robert W. Jackman, "Politicians in Uniform," *American Political Science Review* (December 1976): 1078-1097.

39. Finer, *Man on Horseback*, 21.

40. Robert C. Good, "State-Building as a Determinant of Foreign Policy in the New States," in *Neutralism and Nonalignment*, ed. Lawrence W. Martin (New York: Holt, Rinehart & Winston, 1962).

41. Ibid., 8-9.

42. Cecil V. Crabb, *The Elephants and the Grass* (New York: Holt, Rinehart & Winston, 1965), 20-38.

43. For the evolution of nonalignment from 1955 to 1983, see Robert A. Mortimer, *The Third World Coalition in International Politics* (Boulder, Colo.: Westview Press, 1984).

44. W. W. Rostow, *Stages of Economic Growth* (New York: Cambridge University Press, 1960) and A. F. K. Organski, *The Stages of Political Development* (New York: Alfred A. Knopf, 1965).

45. Tony Smith, "Requiem or New Agenda for Third World Studies?" *World Politics*, July 1985, 533-544.

46. Ibid., 544-558; Brandt Commission, *North-South: A Programme for Survival* (Cambridge, Mass.: MIT Press, 1980); Barbara Ward, Lenore D'Anjou, and J. D. Runnalls, eds., *The Widening Gap* (New York: Columbia University Press, 1971); Karl P. Sauvant and Hajo Hasenplug, eds., *The New Inter-National Economic Order* (Boulder, Colo.: Westview Press, 1977); Jagdish Bhagwati, ed., *The New International Economic Order* (Cambridge, Mass.: MIT Press, 1977); and Mitchell A. Seligson, ed., *The Gap Between Rich and Poor* (Boulder, Colo.: Westview Press, 1984).

47. Stephen D. Krasner, *Structural Conflict* (Berkeley, Calif.: University of California Press, 1985).

48. For a rebuttal of this view, see Nathan Rosenberg and L. E. Birdzell, Jr., *How the West Grew Rich* (New York: Basic Books, 1985).

49. *New York Times*, Feb. 21, 1985.

50. Orville Schell, *To Get Rich Is Glorious* (New York: Pantheon, 1985).

51. Pranay Gupte, *The Crowded Earth* (New York: W. W. Norton, 1984).

52. David H. Blake and Robert S. Walters, *The Politics of Global Economic Relations*, 2d ed. (Englewood Cliffs, N.J.: Prentice-Hall, 1982), 35.

CHAPTER 15

The Economic Interpretation of International Politics

THE MARXIST—LENINIST INTERPRETATION OF POLITICS

Marxism-Leninism is an analytical framework in which the domestic system is the principal basis for explaining and predicting national foreign policy. Specifically, Marxism-Leninism suggests only one responsible factor: the economy. The basic thesis is that a nation's foreign policy reflects the nature of its economic system and the corresponding class structure. This explanation, unlike those based on national and elite styles, is not intended to account for all nations' foreign policies. It claims a special insight into the foreign policies of a few states—the developed or industrial states with capitalist economies. It argues that a capitalist state, because of its economy, is compelled to be expansionist, militaristic, interventionist, and reactionary; the capitalist search for profit leaves no choice but to extend control beyond national frontiers. (By definition, a socialist state, one that does not have an economy based on profit, is not expansionist and is concerned only with guarding itself against the capitalist enemy.) How was this framework arrived at and why do Soviet leaders believe it? And why is it so persuasive to many leaders and others in the less-developed countries (LDCs)?

THE MARXIST BACKGROUND: THE CLASS STRUGGLE AND THE GRAVEDIGGERS

Moral Protest Against Industrialization

Marxism arose as part of a general protest movement—which ranged from revolutionary anarchism to utopian socialism, from the Luddites to the Christian Socialists—against nineteenth-century industrial capitalism in western Europe. Although industrialization eventually led to rapidly rising standards of living for the masses, the principal goal in its early stages was sustained economic growth. The reason was inherent in the process of industrialization itself: basic to the process is the accumulation of capital, or what economists call capital goods—factories, machinery, and other durable equipment. This, of course, is an oversimplification. Industrialization is essentially a process of economic growth, but it is also vastly more than that; without an accompanying cultural, political, and social revolution in which the old rural and static society is uprooted, no industrial revolution can occur. The industrialization of a society is thus more than a "technical" problem. Nevertheless, the essence of industrialization remains the increase of a society's industrial capital, for it is that capital, combined with human labor, that will permit an increase in productivity. The machine allows the worker to raise his or her industrial output, producing in a day what he or she might otherwise have produced in a week. This higher productivity can more adequately meet consumer demands for whatever goods are required. The result is better living conditions.

Ironically, capital can be accumulated only if consumption is postponed. To build a factory, expand an already existing factory, or buy more machinery, a business owner must invest money. But where does the investor obtain this money? The answer is that the sum invested comes primarily out of profits. Although the business proprietor could simply save this money, the desire for more profit leads him or her to reinvest it. And to acquire maximum profits, workers are paid as little as possible for the longest possible hours. Otherwise, the profit margin will be lower, and money for investment will accumulate more slowly—which, in turn, will slow the rate of industrialization. The industrial working class, therefore, pays a large part of the price for the process. The farmer, too, pays a price because the cost of food must also be kept low. The process of industrialization is essentially the same, regardless of the nature of the economic system. Even a Communist society accumulates capital in this manner; there, however, it is the state, rather than the private entrepreneur, that accumulates the capital and squeezes it out of the general population.

The terrible effects of industrialization on workers in the nineteenth century have been vividly described in many works, including Karl Marx's *Das Kapital*. Edmund Wilson, in his recreation of the arrival of Friedrich Engels in Manchester, described it thus:

> He saw the working people living like rats in the wretched little dens of their dwellings, whole families, sometimes more than one family, swarming in a single room, well and diseased, adults and children, close relations sleeping together, sometimes even without beds to sleep on when all the furniture had been sold for firewood, sometimes in damp, underground cellars which had to be bailed out when the weather was wet, sometimes living in the same room with pigs; ill nourished on flour mixed with gypsum and cocoa mixed with dirt, and their wailing

children with laudanum; spending their lives, without a sewage system, among the piles of their excrement and garbage; spreading epidemics of typhus and cholera which even made inroads into the well-to-do sections.

The increasing demand for women and children in the factories was throwing the fathers of families permanently out of work, arresting the physical development of girls, letting the women in for illegitimate motherhood and yet compelling them to come to work when they were pregnant or before they had recovered from having their babies, and ultimately turning a good many of them into prostitutes; while the children, fed into the factories at the age of five or six, receiving little care from mothers who were themselves at the factory all day and no education at all from a community which wanted them only to perform mechanical operations, would drop exhausted when they were let out of their prisons, too tired to wash or eat, let alone study or play, sometimes too tired to get home at all. In the iron and coal mines, also, women and children as well as men spent the better part of their lives crawling underground in narrow tunnels, and emerging, found themselves caught in the meshes of the company's cottage and the company store and of the two-week postponement of wages. They were being killed off at the rate of fourteen hundred a year through the breaking of rotten ropes, the caving-in of workings due to overexcavated seams and the explosions due to bad ventilation and to the negligence of tired children; if they escaped catastrophic accidents, the lung diseases eventually got them. The agricultural population, for its part, deprived by the industrial development of their old status of handicraftsmen and yeomen who either owned their own land and homes or were taken care of with more or less certainty by a landlord on whose estate they were tenants, had been transformed into wandering day laborers, for whom nobody took responsibility and who were punished by jail or transportation if they ventured in times of need to steal and eat the landlord's game.

It seems to Engels that the medieval serf, who had at least been attached to the land and had a definite position in society, had had an advantage over the factory worker. At that period when legislation for the protection of labor had hardly seriously gotten under way, the old peasantry and hand-workers of England, and even old petty middle class, were being shoveled into the mines and the mills like so much raw material for the prices their finished products would bring, with no attempt even to dispose of the waste. In years of depression the surplus people, so useful in years of good business, were turned out upon the town to become peddlers, crossing-sweepers, scavengers or simply beggars—sometimes whole families were seen begging in the streets—and, almost as frequently, whores and thieves.[1]

Marxism was a legacy of the Industrial Revolution. Specifically, it was one of many *moral* protests against the cruelties and miseries suffered by the worker. Such exploitation of human beings by human beings had to be ended, for it violated the whole Western humanitarian tradition from its Judeo-Christian beginnings to the French Revolution. Professed equality of human beings had become meaningless in a society so deeply divided between the privileged few and the underprivileged many. The dignity and freedom of the individual had little reality, for the majority of men and women were paid only subsistence wages if they found any employment at all. Capitalism had enslaved people economically.

A system based on production for the "profit of the few" had to be changed to one based on production for the "use of many." To be sure, capitalism had brought mankind great benefits. And no one praised its success more openly than its greatest critic. Marx wrote in *The Communist Manifesto:* "The bourgeoisie, during its rule of scarce one hundred years, has created more massive and more colossal productive forces than have all preceding generations together. Subjection of nature's forces to man, machinery, application of chemistry to industry, and agriculture, steam-navigation, railways, electric telegraphs, clearing of whole continents for cultivation, canalization of rivers, whole populations conjured out of the ground—what earlier century had even a presentiment that such productive forces slumbered in the lap of social labour?" [2]

But, although the bourgeoisie had created the industrial machinery, it was itself the greatest obstacle to mass production for the benefit of society. Marx believed that capitalism could never abolish poverty by providing human beings only with basic necessities because an economic system based upon the profit motive could result only in inequitable distribution of income. It was the desire for profit that itself caused workers' poverty and degradation, and profit was the outcome of private control over means of production. Capitalism therefore had to be replaced by a more just system—socialism—if the "acquisitive society" was to be transformed into a society concerned with social justice for the underprivileged. In a socialist society the working class would own the means of production and would therefore receive a fair share of the national income.

Scientific Theory and the Proletarian Revolution

But Marxian socialism was more than a moral protest; it was also *scientific.* Indeed, *Marxism can be defined as that school of socialism that seeks to prove that the coming of socialism is inevitable.* [3] In that respect, it is a natural outgrowth of the general Western belief in the inevitability of progress and the widespread equation of progress with improvement. This optimism was itself an offspring of the eighteenth-century Age of Reason. The Age of Reason—the Enlightenment—was a reaction to medieval society and philosophy. It stood in direct contradiction to the religion-dominated and tradition-bound ethos of feudal Europe. The Enlightenment substituted reason for God, and the material world became the chief human concern; the creation of a better life was the chief goal. The perfect society was to be created here and now. The human condition, the result not of sin but of ignorance, was to be altered through reason, not grace. As controllers of their own fate, human beings could create the kind of world they wanted because God had given them reason with which to build paradise on earth; secular, rather than spiritual, activities were to be the chief focus of human strivings. The thinkers of the Enlightenment posited a rational universe, which could be mastered through knowledge. Knowledge would reveal comprehensible laws. Once those laws had been discovered, all problems of human existence could be solved. The Age of Enlightenment thus stressed "materialism," defined simply as "realism," the rational inquiry into the secular universe, composed of matter, in order to discover its laws.

Capitalist Market.   Marx inherited this "mind set," and it was in this context he claimed that the capitalist system is historically doomed. Capitalist thinkers asserted that the individual responds to economic self-interest in the same way that an individual atom responds to gravity. Given self-interest as the basic human motivation, the "economic laws" that supposedly will maximize society's economic benefits are the laws of supply and demand operating through the free market. The capitalist argument is simple. The individual wishes to augment his wealth; the desire for profit therefore leads him to produce whatever product consumers demand. Naturally, he will try to charge as much as possible. But the price must be competitive because others, in their search for profit, may produce the same item. If he charges more for the same item, no one will buy it. And what price can he charge? Each producer, hoping for increased sales, will try to undersell competitors. But no producer can sell at less than cost and stay in business. And, if costs are higher than those of the competitors, the producer must go out of business or find a more efficient method of production. Free competition thus has four results: (1) supplies of products that consumers demand, (2) sale of goods at minimal cost to consumers, (3) profit for producers, and (4) the continuation of only efficient operations in business. The economic laws supposedly channel each individual's self-interest in socially beneficial directions, and the competitive mechanism of the market is said to provide for the "greatest good of the greatest number." The free market as a way of organizing an economy for production and distribution theoretically guarantees harmony of interest between producers and consumers.

Theory of Surplus Value.   Marx accepted this description of the capitalist market and the assumption that economics is the primary motivation for human behavior. He, however, focused his criticism on what he considered the central feature of the market: the transformation of all relations among individuals into exchange or monetary relations. In a market society, it seemed to Marx, such relations were the only meaningful bonds among individuals. The consumer, to obtain the goods he wants, offers a cash incentive; the producer, to sell his goods, responds to the consumer's demands. Human beings are thus linked to one another as buyers and sellers through money. But they are also linked as employers and employees, and again the relation is a monetary one. For, in fact, the employer *buys* labor power, which the workers sell to obtain money with which to buy the goods necessary to sustain themselves. For Marx, the distinguishing feature of capitalism was the fact that not only goods but also *people* were sold on the market. Indeed, human labor was sold as was any other product. The bourgeoisie, as Marx bitterly remarked, "has left no other bond between man and man than naked self-interest, than callous 'cash payment.' . . . It has resolved personal worth into exchange value, and in place of the numberless indefeasible chartered freedoms, has set up that single, unconscionable freedom—Free Trade." [4]

In the end, the exploitation of the workers is the result of this treatment of human beings as commodities. Marx, like *laissez faire* economists, maintained that the value of a product is equivalent to the amount of labor expended in its production. How then, he asked, is profit derived? If the exchange value, or cost, of a product equals its labor cost, then profit can be gained only by raising the price above market value or by paying the worker less. The latter option, he claimed, was the one chosen. The workers received only a subsistence wage—enough to keep them alive and able to work and reproduce; to the employer, the workers' labor was worth no more than it took to keep them alive. The difference between what the workers should have been paid in terms of the cash *value* of their labor invested in the product and what they were actually paid represented the profit or "surplus value."

The significance of Marx's theory of surplus value lies in its sociological implications. His analysis of the free market emphasizes not only the production and exchange of commodities, but also the *social organization* for production. Capitalists and the proletariat need each other; both classes are compelled to cooperate. Each contributes a specific function: one the capital goods (what Marx called the "means of production"), the other the labor power. But, although the two classes are functionally interdependent, they are also mutually antagonistic. The capitalists exploit the proletariat because the market transforms human relations—whether between buyer and seller or between employer and employee—into exchange, or monetary, relations. The capitalists, to maximize their profits, will squeeze as much surplus value out of labor as possible. And, although they constitute only a minority of the population, they can continue their exploitation of the majority because they own and control the means of production and thus the power of the state.

Political philosophers since Aristotle have analyzed the interaction between private power and control of the state. It has long been understood that groups organize to protect their interests and to extend their reach into the political arena. In some ways, Marx was furthering this interpretation when he noted that the bourgeoisie controls not only economic but also political power. But for Marx capitalism was more than an attempt to manipulate the apparatus of the state by private interests: the state is, in his words, nothing but the "executive committee of the bourgeoisie," a superstructure that reflects and reinforces the economic arrangements (capitalism) of the substructure. The state accordingly perpetuates capitalist exploitation of the proletariat. The result can be no less than a class struggle between the exploiters and the exploited.

Class Struggle. The class struggle, according to Marx, is not unique to capitalism. In every economic system, the "forces of production" create corresponding "relations of production," or social structure. In the Greek and Roman slave system, which succeeded the stage of "primitive communism" (in which all production and distribution had been communal), there were slaveowners and slaves. In the medieval manorial system there were landowners and serfs. And in industrial capitalism there are capitalists and proletarians. In each system the "superstructure"—the state and the law, the moral and religious code, even art and family life—have reflected the economic substructure. Every economic system has been divided between haves and have-nots, and consequently all have been racked by class struggle.[5] Because the political system has been controlled, a political solution to the class struggle has been foreclosed; political reforms are meaningless, for the haves will never willingly relinquish control. Will the workers ever achieve abundance and freedom from their "economic slavery"? Not by means of reforms, according to Marx. The "laws of economics," he argued, will, however, assure such liberation.

The bourgeoisie and the proletariat, then, are not fated to face each other eternally. "Judgment day" for the capitalist class will come, Marx predicted, for the proletarian revolution is *historically inevitable.* The economic forces that caused the death of the slave and manorial systems will do the same for capitalism. From the theory of surplus value, which for him was the axle around which the capitalist wheel revolved, Marx derived three economic laws to explain the behavior of the system—and predict its doom.

The first was the *law of capitalist accumulation.* Each capitalist, seeking to maximize profits, expands output in order to sell more than competitors sell. To do so, the capitalist must hire more workers, but, as the labor supply is bought up, labor costs will rise and, in turn, cut into profits. Each employer must therefore install labor-saving machinery to reduce costs and preserve profit margins. In this way, employers accumulate capital. But they are simultaneously working against themselves. The source of surplus value is the worker who must be replaced by the labor-saving device. The increasing proportion of machinery to labor therefore produces the very thing that the introduction of machinery was supposed to prevent: a decline in profits.

The second law—*the concentration of capital*—follows logically. The competitive process arising from the struggle for profits drives weaker capitalists into bankruptcy, thus concentrating capital in fewer and fewer hands. Eventually, this process ends in the establishment of monopolies.

Together, these two laws produce the third, the law of *increasing misery.* As the capitalists are driven out of business and the workers are displaced by machinery, there will be large-scale unemployment. Simultaneously, the size of the proletariat will increase as former capitalists join it. The capitalists, compelled to compensate for falling profits, must intensify exploitation of the workers by further decreasing their subsistence wages. Because the unemployed—Marx called them the "industrial reserve army"—have no other means of existence, they have little choice but to accept work at any price. The wage level is then driven down for all workers. Surplus value increases but only for a time. The competitive process begins again, further decreasing profits, concentrating capital, and increasing the size and misery of the proletariat. And, through a series of recurring crises, each more severe than the preceding one, capitalism arrives at the final stage of its development—the proletarian revolution.

Capitalism, Marx held, would be its own gravedigger—for through industrialization it has fathered the very class that will overthrow it when it reaches economic maturity. The laws of the free market, ironically, will result in the overthrow of its main advocates. The forces of production will then no longer be privately owned. The exploitation of human beings by human beings will be ended forever, for society will no longer be divided between haves and have-nots. Industry, publicly owned by the "dictatorship of the proletariat," is to be used for the benefit of the proletariat. The dictatorship, however, is to be only temporary. Once its principal purpose—the liquidation of the bourgeoisie—has been accomplished and private property (the source of class formation and the class struggle) eliminated, the state is to "wither away," and a new period of history is to begin. Human beings will then be able to live in harmony, and the classless society will finally fulfill the ideals of fraternity, liberty, equality—and affluence—for the vast majority.

LENIN, IMPERIALISM, AND GLOBAL REVOLUTION

Failure of the Marxist Prediction

The fundamental error committed by Marx was confusing capitalism with democracy. Because the state is the "executive committee" of the bourgeoisie, he said, capitalism cannot reform itself; the parliamentary institutions of capitalist states are merely facades for the "dictatorship of the bourgeoisie." According to Marx, the bourgeois minority will continue to use the power of the state to preserve its dominance over, and exploitation of, the proletariat and to quell any workers' disturbances or riots. This state of affairs will end only on the day the proletariat rises up to overthrow its exploiters; revolution is the only means of changing the system because reform from within is impossible. This conclusion was perhaps natural at the time Marx wrote, for the bourgeoisie was politically very powerful and the reform movement very weak. Certainly ruling groups or classes in the past have not willingly surrendered their power. The French Revolution, a bourgeois revolution against the traditional order, offers good evidence to support this conclusion.

Democracy, however, has helped to avoid the violent revolution that Marx forecast. Capitalism might well have precipitated such a revolution had it been left unreformed. If a democratic reform movement had not responded to workers' grievances and needs, there would have been no alternative but to seek satisfaction outside the system by nondemocratic and violent means. Capitalism, if it was to survive, had no choice but to accept democratic reforms. By accepting them, it won popular allegiance and actually consolidated its position. By meeting the aspirations of the workers through the creation of the welfare or social-service state, it "derevolutionized" them. As a result, the labor parties in central and western Europe abandoned the proletarian revolution. Revolution was replaced by democratic gradualism and peaceful change through the ballot box, and revolutionary Marxism became evolutionary socialism.

Marxists then had to ask themselves why the proletarian revolution had failed to occur. Democratic reform was the one answer they would not accept. Something that is evil cannot be made less evil by means of reform. Perhaps its outward appearance can be altered, but it will remain basically unchanged. If capitalism is still evil and if it remains an exploitative order, why has it not collapsed, as Marx predicted? The usual explanation for the failure of the revolution is that the workers' rising living standards have given them a vested interest in the capitalist system and have been the principal reason why democratic socialists have given up their plans to overthrow it. In V. I. Lenin's view, however, a movement to abandon the revolution and to acquire a larger share of the capitalist pie was no longer Marxist. Lenin recognized that higher wages for workers had undermined their proletarian consciousness and had made them reform-minded: to improve their material standards, they had developed what he called a "trade-union consciousness." The crucial question posed by this development was: What had made it possible for capitalists to raise paychecks, rather than, as had been predicted, being forced to decrease them further?

Lenin's Resurrection and Internationalization of the Revolution

As the ability of capitalism to reform itself had already been excluded, the answer had to be found in external circumstances. Colonialism, or imperialism, provided the key.[6] The "internal contradiction" of capitalism—the class struggle between the bourgeoisie and the proletariat—had been resolved by means of the capitalist indulgence in imperialism. It was imperialism that had changed the first and third laws of capitalism. The second law remained in force: capital *was* concentrated in fewer and fewer hands. The era of imperialism was, indeed, the era of monopoly capitalism. But the law of capital accumulation, which had forecast declining profits, had been reversed. Imperialism was the source of huge profits—so huge, in fact, that Lenin called them "superprofits." Colonies provided inexpensive raw materials and cheap labor. They provided investment opportunities for surplus capital and markets in which goods produced in the metropolitan countries could be sold.

It was now clear why the European workers' living standards had risen, despite the law of increasing misery. For the proletariat had shared in the society's enormous increase of wealth. In the age of imperialism, capitalists could afford to make economic concessions to their laboring classes to gain their support. They could permit political concessions. Once the workers' allegiance to the capitalist system had been won, they could be allowed to vote, as voting would be meaningless when the choice involved only two parties, both representing the capitalist class; the choice was which group of capitalists should exploit workers, not whether to abolish exploitation. The working class became increasingly "embourgeoisied," losing its revolutionary drive and spirit and acquiring a vested interest in the preservation of capitalism. This commitment to capitalism was reinforced by new and intense nationalistic feelings among the proletariat. Although it had been hostile to the capitalist class in the preimperialist phase, the proletariat acquired nationalistic feelings as it came to identify its interests with capitalist imperialism.

Lenin's explanation for the failure of the proletarian revolution implied pessimism about the future. While imperialism continued, the capitalists would reap sufficient superprofits with which to "buy" the support of the working classes. Only if those profits were eliminated would the capitalists have to resume their preimperialist domestic exploitation. Then the class struggle would resume and bring about the revolution. This end was exactly what Lenin predicted, for, through imperialism, the "inner contradiction" of capitalism had been projected onto a global plane. Just as the capitalist class had exploited the proletariat for profit, so the capitalist countries came to exploit the proletarian (colonial) countries for "surplus value." *Imperialism had, through its conquest of most non-Western areas, transformed the fight against capitalism into a global conflict.* The domestic class struggle had become an international class struggle. Indeed, because the uprising of workers in developed capitalist nations had come to depend upon elimination of colonial holdings, the prerequisite for the proletarian revolution had become the anti-imperialist revolution of the precapitalist colonial countries. "National liberation" thus became the most immediate task of communism.

Lenin had turned Marx upside down. The proletarian revolution was to begin in nonproletarian societies. The workers' revolution would arise in lands with economies that were basically agrarian, where peasants (not workers) constituted the vast majority of the populations. Marx had said that the proletarian revolution would occur spontaneously when the capitalist economy matured. Lenin observed that, when the economy had matured, the capitalists had avoided revolution by means of imperialism. In those circumstances the consciousness of the proletariat was transformed from a revolutionary to a reformist cast. Conversely, the proletarian mood—the awareness of people that they are exploited—had become most intense in the colonial countries. Marx had declared that economic maturity and political consciousness are parallel developments that will precipitate the proletarian revolution, but Lenin recognized that in the age of imperialism they are *inversely* related. The contrast was stark: Marx had stressed *economic maturity* as the prerequisite for the revolution; Lenin emphasized *political consciousness.* Joseph Stalin later said, in his lectures on Leninism:

Where will the revolution begin? Where, in what country, can the front of capital be pierced first?

Where industry is more developed, where the proletariat constitutes the majority, where there is more culture, where there is more democracy—that was the reply usually given formerly.

No, objects the Leninist theory of revolution: *not necessarily where industry is more developed*, and so forth. The front of capital will be pierced where the chain of imperialism is weakest, for the proletarian revolution is the result of the breaking of the chain of the world imperialist at its weakest link; and it may turn out that the country which has started the revolution, which has made a breach in the front of capital, is less developed in a capitalist sense than other, more developed, countries, which have, however, remained within the framework of capitalism.[7]

AMERICAN CAPITALISM, THE COLD WAR, AND IMPERIALISM

Marxism-Leninism, as we have already analyzed (Chapter 13), has given the Soviet believers a way of viewing the world in terms of adversary relationships; continuing and long-term conflict; total distrust of capitalist states, including professions of goodwill; and a keen appreciation of "power politics." Given this intellectual framework, it is not surprising that in the interwar period they saw Western—French and British—foreign policies as hostile, and, that during World War II, as the United States emerged as the most powerful Western state, the Soviets assumed its intentions were hostile as well. All three Western countries were viewed as capitalist states. With this perspective, Moscow could find plenty of what it considered evidence to confirm its initial judgment.

Among these were: (1) the Western intervention in the civil war following the Bolshevik Revolution in 1917 was seen as a capitalist attempt to overthrow the new regime; (2) the anti-German French alliances with Poland, Czechoslovakia, Romania, and Yugoslavia were seen as a barrier to keep the Soviet Union out of central and western Europe; and (3) the British appeasement policy toward Hitler was perceived as an effort to redirect German power from west to east, specifically, toward the Soviet Union. During World War II, after France's defeat in 1940, the decline of British power, and the emergence of the United States as the strongest of all Western states, it became quite natural and logical, in Soviet eyes, to see American capitalism as its next enemy. The Soviets attributed the cold war to "American imperialism," and saw itself as the victim of an expansionist U.S. policy. The Soviets felt their very existence was sufficient cause for this "war." The Soviet Union represented the wave of the future, an anticapitalist state that would be the nucleus of a postimperialist, socialist world order. It was necessary, therefore, while the United States was still strong for it to try to destroy the Soviet Union. Failure to do so would doom the United States to defeat, along with the socioeconomic system it represented. Thus Stalin is absolved of all responsibility for the eruption of the cold war. Stalin was merely a nationalist representing limited Russian and historic security interests in the area just west of the Soviet Union. It was the United States—pursuing an expansionist anti-Soviet policy which was not motivated by a legitimate concern for its own safety—that was the aggressor. The United States, after all, had "the bomb"; the Soviet Union did not. How could one believe that Moscow threatened America? [8]

In the resulting cold war with the Soviet Union, anticommunism was invoked by the United States to justify American imperialism. The striving for political and economic independence by the LDCs, upon whose continued exploitation the prosperity of the United States depended, was condemned. As a result, the United States became the citadel of the *ancien régime,* the supporter of reactionary dictatorships and military cliques throughout the Third World as part of its effort to prevent the rise of nationalist and revolutionary regimes. U.S. policy, not unnaturally under these circumstances, was virtually global in scope; it was also militaristic and interventionist. Interpreted in this context, the war in Vietnam was unavoidable, despite its costs and despite the fact that South Vietnam was of so little economic value to the United States. The stake was nothing less than American control of the economies of the LDCs. Should Vietnam demonstrate that a genuinely nationalist, revolutionary movement could throw off imperialist shackles, it would set an example for all the other colonial countries. American leaders therefore had to intervene to crush the Viet Cong. The subsequent Viet Cong victory, followed by national liberation campaigns in Angola, Ethiopia, Yemen, Nicaragua, and the ongoing struggle in El Salvador, means that the domino effect from Vietnam has been to weaken American imperialism.

A CRITIQUE OF THE IMPERIALIST INTERPRETATION

How valid is this economic theory of imperialism as a general explanation of a nation's foreign policy, especially American foreign policy?

War Is Older than Capitalism

One fundamental criticism is that conflict and war were occurring among independent political units—empires, city-states, dynasties—long before industrial capitalism developed. How then can we attribute wars in general to fundamental economic causes and especially to the profit motive? Once it is admitted that perhaps not all wars are caused by capitalism, the basic thesis is gravely weakened and can no longer stand as a broad explanation. Although specific wars may have been profitable, can we say that profits are the *motivation* for those wars? And even if we could, would we be justified in raising these instances to the level of a universal historical law? Most Western colonial expansion, in fact, occurred in the period from the sixteenth to the eighteenth century, the period before the rise of industrial capitalism. Most of the strife and hostilities in the nineteenth and early twentieth centuries—the three Prussian wars against Denmark, Austria, and France; the Russo-Turkish and Russo-Japanese wars; and World War I—can hardly be attributed to capitalist rivalries. Moreover, Russia and Italy, active imperialist states in the sense that they were expansionist and used their superior power to exploit the weak, were not capitalistic at all. Soviet behavior after World War II throws even more doubt on the presumed relation between industrial capitalism and war.

Imperialism's Political Purposes

A second criticism is that other students of Western imperialism have claimed that

> international friction over private investments has been a good deal more frequent and dangerous where private investments have been pressed into service as instruments, tools, of a larger political purpose which the investments themselves did not originate. Investments used in the quest for national glory, and the like, have been more productive of international friction in the past than investments actuated solely by private profit motives.[9]

Specifically, acquisition of colonies often served the state's political, rather than its economic, purpose. In a system in which states felt insecure and were constantly concerned with relative power, colonies represented more than profits: they enhanced the master nation's prestige. For Germany, which was nationally unified only in 1870, far later than the other great powers, colonies represented a means of gaining a "place in the sun." Some German colonies in the South Pacific were far from profitable; the Germans actually had to spend money to maintain them. But this money was considered well spent because colonies had the same importance that atomic bombs have had since 1945 as signs of rank and power. On the other hand, for France, defeated by Germany in 1870, colonial expansion in Africa was a way of regaining lost status and disguising national humiliation. Germany had a far larger population, but the manpower of the colonies meant that France had more soldiers to balance its neighbor's army. Tunisia may thus have "paid off" economically, but the colonies in equatorial Africa generally did not; the French government had other purposes in mind in acquiring them.

Although economics should not therefore be discounted as a motive for nineteenth-century Western imperialism, it should also not be exaggerated as the driving force behind political expansion; very clearly, the state system and power considerations were then—as before—fundamental in explaining state expansion. Indeed, Benjamin Cohen, in a detailed analysis of imperialist theory and Western colonialism, finds the taproot of imperialism in the anarchical organization of the international system: "Nations yield to the temptations to domination because they are driven to maximize their individual power position" by their uncertainty and insecurity.[10] Imperialism, which Cohen defines as "any relationship of effective domination or control, political or economic, direct or indirect, of one nation over another," is the offspring of competing national sovereignties.[11] The "logic of dominion" is a rational operational strategy for a nation to adopt in these circumstances. It was also logical that governments would use corporations to advance their political purposes and bring pressures to bear on them if they were reluctant to comply.

An interesting postwar instance was the 1953 CIA overthrow of the nationalist government of Mohammed Mossadegh in Iran and the restoration of the shah who had fled his country earlier. Rather than testifying to the dominance of big business—notably the large oil companies—over foreign policy in America, this CIA operation was undertaken in support of broader national-security goals, not to rescue private investments or enhance corporate profits. Mossadegh, who had received medical treatment at the U.S. Army's Walter Reed Hospital in Washington, D.C., had nationalized the Anglo-Iranian Oil Company in 1951. This act in itself did not alienate the United States, which in both 1951 and 1952 gave sizable foreign aid funds to Iran. What led the United States to reconsider its support of Mossadegh was his quarrel with Britain and the virtual cutoff of Iranian oil shipments.

It should be noted that at the time the United States was an oil exporter and that U.S. oil companies were not present in Iran. Oil for the United States or private investments were not, therefore, considerations affecting Washington's policy. And the loss of Iranian oil had been made up by production elsewhere. The U.S. government did not even become involved until it became clear that Iran would not accept an exclusively British-owned operation. Hence the proposal for an international consortium, including American, French, and British companies, to produce and ship Iranian oil. The American oil companies were unenthusiastic but finally acceded to governmental pressure after receiving relief from a criminal antitrust suit that had been brought against the oil companies by the Justice Department. The United States wanted to see Iran's oil flowing again so that Iran could maintain a stable, non-Communist regime. Short of cash, Iran appeared increasingly unstable and on a leftward path. (For the U.S. oil companies, the resumption of Iranian production meant a cutback in their production—and profits— to prevent an oil glut.) Street riots had already burst out in 1951 and 1952, and in 1952 Mossadegh had concluded oil sale agreements with Eastern Europe. It was in this context that the CIA restored the shah and ended the weak, increasingly radical nationalist Mossadegh regime. The impetus for action came from the government in Washington, not the oil companies, which in the absence of political pressure would have stayed out of Iran. And the CIA coup was the result of fears of growing Communist influence in Iran.[12] The 1950s were a time when anticommunism was U.S. policy; the Eisenhower administration, therefore, resorted to covert intervention.

Imperialism Is Not the Cause of the Cold War and LDC Exploitation

A third criticism centers on the question whether, even though capitalism cannot generally be held responsible for interstate conflicts and wars, and even though power and prestige were important factors in the colonialism of the late nineteenth century, *American capitalism after World War II* cannot be held to blame for the outbreak of the cold war. More important in this radical perception of American foreign policy is the question of whether it cannot be blamed for the alleged subjugation of the Third World?

On the origins of the cold war, we can be brief for we have already found the causes of American-Soviet rivalry in the state system and emerging bipolarity after the defeat of Germany. The United States, still unsocialized by the state system, during the war had sought to overcome the Soviet leaders' suspicions of the West to lay the foundations for postwar cooperation and peace. Also, as the war drew to a conclusion, its principal concern had been not to eliminate the self-proclaimed bastion of world revolution and enemy of Western capitalism or to push the Soviet Union out of Eastern Europe and convert that area into a market for American corporations (poverty-stricken Eastern Europe would not in fact have been a very profitable market for American goods), but to forestall a complete return to historic isolationism. The public mood was all too apparent in the hasty military demobilization. For the United States to have pursued an assertive foreign policy complete with atomic threats, as the revisionists have claimed it did, would have required a dictatorial disregard for widespread public demands, which set limits on what the administration could do.

It was not until a year and a half after World War II had ended that the Truman Doctrine was enunciated. The policy of containment was launched only after further attempts to reconcile differences with the leaders in Moscow had failed and after continued Soviet pressure, denunciations, and vilifications. Hostile Soviet behavior was the reason for the gradual shift of American policy and public opinion from amity to emnity; American policy was not the product of a virulent and preexisting anti-Communist ideology. Indeed, it was Soviet policy that had reflected an anticapitalist animus predating both the Bolshevik Revolution of 1917 and subsequent Western anti-Soviet behavior. Even before the Bolshevik leaders had seized power, they had judged capitalist states hostile simply because they were capitalist.[13]

But what about the charge of American domination of the Third World as the cause of its permanent poverty and misery? What about the military interventions in the Dominican Republic and Vietnam or the more subtle economic and political interventions in countless other countries such as El Salvador and Nicaragua, where U.S. imperialism supports or in the past has supported what Gabriel Kolko has picturesquely called the "local *compradors* [sharks] and oligarchies"?[14] Is it really true that the relationship between the United States and the Third World is one of dependency and exploitation? Are the LDCs really locked into a subordinated status by a global division of labor between the core capitalist states, of whom the United States is the leading power, and the peripheral states whose decisions on what to produce, how to produce it, and for whom to produce are all determined by an American-dominated international economy? Specifically, is the U.S. economy so dependent on the LDCs' natural resources that it must control them or face the loss of their resources, lowering the rates of U.S. economic growth, employment, and prosperity? Is the likely result of the loss of the Third World really large-scale unemployment, an end to the economic "trickle-down" from the corporations' "superprofits," and massive social and political unrest as a prelude to the proletarian revolution?

Clearly, the United States, with more than half the world's productive capacity, until fairly recently has not needed to import extensive natural resources. Kolko has argued that the cause of American imperialism in the Third World is not the total volume of resources that the United States imports. But rather, it is the critical resources it needs. The economies of industrial societies like the United States are "so intricate that the removal of even a small part, as in a watch, can stop the mechanism." [15] Each ton of steel, he points out, requires the addition of about thirteen pounds of manganese; the steel industry cannot do without the manganese. "The same analogy is true of the entire relationship between the industrial and so-called developing nations: the nations of the Third World may be poor, but in the last analysis the industrial world needs their resources more than these nations need the West." [16]

In fact, there is simply no evidence that any Communist country or nationalist regime of the Third World will not sell its resources to the West—although, as the Organization of Petroleum Exporting Countries (OPEC) has shown, the LDCs do want higher prices and what they consider a fairer return for the resources that keep Western industry running. In addition, the sources of these raw materials are numerous and frequently in politically safe areas. In Kolko's example of manganese, he notes that it is available from Brazil, India, Gabon, and South Africa and that more than half the world's known reserves are in the Soviet Union and China. In any event, it is unlikely that all these sources will cut off their supplies to the West or to the United States at the same time. As Robert Tucker has caustically noted, "Radical intellectuals may harbor such romantic notions but governments, revolutionary governments included, do not"—because they need the capital. [17]

Finally, as we know, the United States—while increasingly importing key resources such as oil, bauxite, tin, and natural rubber from the LDCs—possesses many of the raw materials it needs. We need only look at recent attempts to exploit more fully domestic oil deposits and to clean up an old source, coal, of which the United States has a vast supply. Indeed, most raw material production in the world occurs in the West, whereas the poorer and more populated of the LDCs remain net importers of natural resources. The need for the LDCs' resources, therefore, was hardly a cause for American policies toward the Third World during the cold war days, an era in which the United States was an oil exporter and more self-sufficient in resources than it is today.

There is thus a major theoretical weakness in the imperialist thesis, the claim that the capitalist state must exercise imperial domination over the Third World. The theory is that either it controls these raw material sources, or it has no access to raw materials at all. Clearly, this either-or proposition is false. As Jerome Slater noted, an inverse relationship between "imperialism" and prosperity in the postwar period has been demonstrated. It has been the least imperial countries, countries that have had to buy more of their raw materials on the international market than the United States, that have exhibited the highest rates of economic growth (West Germany, Japan, Canada, Norway, and Denmark). Those countries that have shed their former colonies more slowly (France and Britain until the 1950s and Portugal in the 1970s) have done far less well.[18]

What has been true of the United States' alleged dependence on Third World natural resources has been equally true of its alleged need of the LDCs' markets and investment opportunities. American exports in the past have found their principal markets in the rich Western states. Only in the 1970s, as the Vietnam War was winding down, did the United States start selling more manufactured goods to the LDCs than to Western Europe and Japan; similarly, the LDCs became an important market for American wheat, cotton, and rice exports. But in 1968, at the height of the Vietnam War, American exports represented 4 percent of the gross national product (GNP); 67 percent went to Western Europe, Canada, and Japan, whereas exports to the LDCs had actually decreased between 1955 and 1968.[19] American investments also went primarily to Western industrial countries, even though the U.S. government attempted to control the outflow of dollars because of its negative impact on the balance of trade. By the beginning of the 1970s, 60 to 70 percent of American direct investments were in Europe and Canada; Latin America and the rest of the less-developed world were far behind. Direct investments abroad as a percentage of total investments were only 6 percent, although the return on foreign investment was 9.3 percent, a figure higher than domestic corporate profits (and explainable largely by the high concentration of investments in petroleum).[20] These export and investment figures, therefore, do not explain why the United States should seek control over the LDCs.

This analysis suggests, contrary to the imperialist thesis, that the industrial countries are not structurally dependent on the Third World. One additional point is certainly clear: although all the societies mentioned are capitalist—and they all do exhibit certain common economic structures such as the free market and private property—they handle their socioeconomic problems in quite different ways. The United States may be the archetype of capitalism and imperialism, but Norway is hardly imperialist, Denmark's society is not divided between rich and poor, West Germany before 1973 had not suffered from the recurrent unemployment problems common in the United States, and Switzerland hardly has a foreign policy, let alone an expansionist one.

Noneconomic factors, therefore, seem critical to the manner in which capitalist states manage their domestic and foreign problems. But for a Marxist to stress social and political forces and to abandon the Marxist faith in the determining drive of economic forces would be to surrender the belief that the future course of capitalist states can be predicted on the basis of their economic structures.

American Business Support of Détente

A fourth criticism of the Marxist-Leninist interpretation of imperialism, and perhaps its greatest irony, is that, after the administration of Richard Nixon moved toward détente with the Soviet Union, the business community became one of its strongest supporters—just as it had looked forward to close American-Soviet relations after 1945. There seemed to be money in this approach. It was not the capitalists who had precipitated the cold war, nor did they oppose détente. Businesses are interested in making profits, and, in the same way that the church wants to reach people the world over, whether in democratic or nondemocratic societies, multinational corporations (MNCs) prefer cold cash to cold war. MNCs have no political preferences; they focus on what Marx, in another connection, called the *cash nexus*. They seem anxious to prove correct Lenin's famous dictum that the capitalists would sell him the rope with which he would hang them. And so the corporations have sought contracts, and farmers, who grow the wheat that the Soviets want, usually have opposed using economic boycotts to advance American political purposes.

Indeed, as we saw in our discussion of MNCs, business owners have been as frequently portrayed as pacifists as they have been seen as exploiters and warmongers. The pacifist attitude results from the belief that "war does not pay" and that peace does pay because it permits international trade and therefore enables businesses to earn profits. Whether this interpretation is correct or incorrect, American industrial and agrarian capitalists have demonstrated that they tend to act as a constraining force on the U.S. government when the latter on occasion decides to take a hard line against the Soviet Union on some specific issue. If the capitalists sought to destroy the bastion of world revolution, they had chosen a strange way of "making the world safe for capitalism."

U.S. Support of Israel

A fifth criticism, and the real blow to the theory of imperialism, surely comes from the Middle East. There the oil companies, which according to the theory, should have determined U.S. policy in the area, clearly have had almost no influence at all. American policy has been consistently favorable to Israel; the oil companies obviously have favored the Arabs. U.S. policy became more even-handed after 1973, when Richard Nixon's administration was heavily influenced by the desire to avoid yet another Arab-Israeli war that might lead to Soviet-American confrontation and possible nuclear war. In 1973 the two superpowers almost clashed after the Soviets apparently threatened to send in their troops unilaterally when the Israelis were about to defeat the Egyptians. Hence, there have been sustained American efforts to find a basis for peace in the area. Western oil needs admittedly reinforced this determination to seek accommodation between the Arabs and Israel. In any event, U.S. policy until recently has reflected economic concerns less than cold war concerns. Indeed, had anticommunism been the overwhelming American motivation, the national interest would have been identical with that of the oil companies. It was U.S. support of Israel that alienated the Arabs and provided Soviet leaders with the opportunity to exert influence in the Middle East.

Imperialism Without Empiricism

In the final analysis, as this example has shown, the best argument against the imperialist interpretation of American policy is the lack of empirical evidence for it.[21] If the United States is an imperialist power and if economic power confers political control, as the theory of imperialism maintains, then where is the American empire? We would certainly expect that, at the very least, the United States could protect MNCs abroad. Yet, since the 1960s, almost everywhere in the Third World, American corporations have been nationalized while Washington's leaders have been helpless to prevent it, only going through the ritual of protest whenever sufficient compensation has not been offered. Especially in Latin America, where the United States has presumably most effectively extended its imperialist tentacles, nationalist regimes have expropriated billions of dollars worth of American corporate property in Argentina, Peru, Bolivia, Ecuador, even Chile. Seventy, or even fifty, years ago the marines would have been sent in.

To be sure, the United States has intervened in Guatemala, Cuba, the Dominican Republic, Chile, Grenada, and Nicaragua, but these interventions have been intended not to rescue corporate or private investments but to destroy governments that American leaders have perceived—rightly or wrongly—as aligning themselves with the Communist world. The motives have been political, related to security. Even in the Caribbean area and Central America, where anti-Americanism and a high degree of nationalism have characterized events, the United States has agreed that at the end of this century it will turn over control of the Panama Canal to the the Panamanians.

On the other hand, the United States did not intervene when OPEC quadrupled prices in 1973, inflicting more damage on the United States than the Soviets had in the thirty years since World War II. The Western industrial powers, including the United States, accepted this change and did not resort to force—strange behavior indeed for so-called imperialists! Similarly, American, European, and Japanese MNCs have increasingly accommodated themselves to host countries' gradually requiring foreign corporations to contribute more to the countries' economics plans. Corresponding to this growing MNC-host country alliance has been an increasing estrangement between MNCs and their home country. As a result, when MNCs are subjected to more stringent host controls, they do not normally appeal for help to their home governments. Take the oil companies: once the masters of the little oil kingdoms, the MNCs have become their servants as majority control was transferred to the Persian Gulf states; in the process, the companies learned that what benefited their hosts benefited them, even though it did not benefit their home countries. A significant shift of power between the MNCs and the host countries' governments, which control the MNCs' access to and prices of the resources they extract, has occurred.

If only the so-called imperialist powers did control the Third World! If the proponents of the imperialist theory were logically consistent, they would have changed their tune after 1973, for Saudi Arabia should, according to that theory, have been the world's leading imperialist power in the 1970s and the Western countries, especially Japan, its dependencies, or "neocolonies."

> The growing acceptance of the "imperial" model or metaphor to the contrary notwithstanding, we may boldly but confidently conclude that the United States today does not "control" any country anywhere, and in only a slightly more qualified manner we may also reject the notion of United States "domination." That the United States has varying degrees of influence in the Third World is of course undeniable, but is a declining influence, and limited in scope and effectiveness to only certain matters. The United States has been all but powerless to stop rising nationalism and radicalism, as well as attacks on its interests and policies around the world. How does the United States today typically react to the nationalization of property, to dramatic increases in the prices of critical raw materials, to demands that it remove its military bases, to anti-American riots, to insults and contempt? On increasingly rare occasions with suspension of economic assistance to the offending state, more typically with mere diplomatic protest, and, increasingly, simply with silence—a sullen silence born of futility, perhaps, but significant precisely for that reason. "Imperialism" should be made of sterner stuff—and certainly it used to be.[22]

As already noted, a more accurate description of American relations with the LDCs would be one of *"mutual* dependence, *mutual* power, and *mutual* vulnerability."[23]

One interesting point about dependency analysis is that it attributes dependency to capitalism. Cuba and Nicaragua are considered independent; all other Latin American states are dependent. The fact is that socialist Cuba is as dependent on the Soviet Union as presocialist Cuba ever was on the United States. One reason is simply that Cuba is a small country that must rely on exports for its economic welfare. Cuban and Soviet foreign policy are closely aligned. By contrast, only one Latin American country sent troops to Korea, none to Vietnam, and the majority opposed U.S. efforts to establish an Inter-American peace force after the United States intervened in the Dominican Republic in 1965. Dependency analysts strongly condemn U.S. interventions in Guatamala, Cuba (1961), the Dominican Republic, and Grenada—ironic in itself since, in terms of their analysis, the United States could not do otherwise because of its capitalist system. Yet, these same analysts ignore the repeated Soviet interventions in Eastern Europe and Afghanistan. But that is because the Soviet Union, like Cuba, is a socialist state, and, by definition, cannot therefore be an aggressor.

Clearly, analysts who use the capitalist-imperialist model as a total explanation for the plight of the LDCs are guilty of vast oversimplification. One cannot simply posit an economic motivation because it seems persuasive and because whatever situation one seeks to explain seems clear in the light of such analysis. Although it is true that economic factors may contribute to interstate conflict and war, so do other factors. The real question, then, is whether a specific conflict can be explained primarily or exclusively in economic terms. To do that, the analyst must show that economic motives have actually been converted into aggressive and expansionist policies, including the outbreak of hostilities. Vernon Van Dyke has argued:

> Those who approach the question of the causes of imperialism and war through a study of the formulation and execution of foreign policies in concrete situations rarely emerge with an answer that is exclusively economic. Almost always non-economic factors are found to be heavily involved, and very often they appear to play a decisive role.[24]

THE 'DEVIL' THEORY OF THE MILITARY-INDUSTRIAL COMPLEX

Whereas in Marxism-Leninism the conduct of a capitalist states' foreign policy is attributed to the nature of its economic system, a "devil" theory is focused upon a presumed conspiracy, which is said to explain capitalist state's external behavior. The Marxist-Leninist theory is based upon an elaborate intellectual structure; the devil theory is based on the assumption that certain people and groups—the so-called military-industrial complex (MIC)—profit from war and therefore are responsible for international tensions and interventionist policies.[25] It is not the system that is viewed as the cause of capitalist expansionism, but rather a group of "war profiteers." In contrast to the Marxist-Leninist interpretation, the devil theory recognizes that capitalism may be quite compatible with the status quo and a peaceful policy—if it can restrain the MIC.

Members of the MIC

Who are the members of the MIC? They include, first of all, the professional military, whose roles, status, and shares of the budget all depend on "peace not breaking out," and, second, the managers of industrial corporations that serve the military and gain handsomely by it. The relationship is one of mutual need. Some U.S. companies are extremely dependent on the armed services: Lockheed Aircraft, General Dynamics, McDonnell-Douglas, and Boeing would not survive without military orders. They employ large numbers of retired officers to help solicit contracts and to find out what kinds of weapons are wanted. Others, such as General Motors, IBM, and Exxon also make great profits, though they are not strictly dependent for their economic well-being on the production of arms. The military, in turn, needs the corporations, especially those that are virtually public corporations, for they have the managerial talent, technological ability, and production lines to function as military arsenals.

A third category of groups, however, also supposedly possesses vested interests in the continuation of the cold war. These groups include those whom Richard Barnet has labeled "national security managers," including not only military leaders but also the more influential "militarized civilians." [26] These men and women come from the world of corporations, high finance, and corporate law, and they keep the United States at "permanent war" both because their economic goals are necessarily expansionist and because they perceive and operate in much the same ways as do professional military leaders. "The principal militarists in America wear three-button suits." [27] Having embraced military "realism," these officials and their subordinates supposedly gained a sense of accomplishment and public stature, as well as contacts for their later professional lives. They therefore did not favor relaxation of international tensions or resolution of conflicting interests, which were their *raison d'être.*

There is a fourth segment as well: the labor unions, whose members find employment and paychecks in defense industries; the universities, where physical and biological scientists are engaged in government research and development and social scientists have contracts for policy-oriented studies; and the various states where economic growth is spurred by military installations and defense plants. Indeed, few segments of society seem to be exempt: even local real estate dealers, contractors, and retail merchants all profit from the population influx that defense installations bring to their communities.

Defense is thus good business. Vested interests pervade American life, which is reflected in Congress, the fifth element of the MIC. Mobilizing support for arms production and a tough international stand is easy. Until the 1970s, anticommunism was the means for arousing the evangelistic spirit and enthusiasm of the American people; their crusading behavior served the national-security managers well. Few members of Congress asked questions about the defense budget or argued for reduced levels of force, different strategies, or fewer weapons. To do so was to risk being accused of neglecting the nation's defenses against communism; perhaps to risk one's constituents' welfare; certainly to risk the disapproval of colleagues, many of them with bases and defense industries in their districts, where the voters controlled members' careers in Congress. It was also to risk the ultimate accusation, that of being "un-American." [28] Yet defense spending has benefited the entire U.S. economy. It has constituted a huge subsidy for stability and growth. Without it, the United States could have expected sizable unemployment and a decline in profits. According to the devil theory, the United States cannot afford peace, for too many powerful participants in the policy process have a stake in the system as it now operates. The world's first democracy, dedicated to human life, is now committed to an "economy of death." Private enterprise has been replaced by "Pentagon capitalism" and a "weapons culture," and the efficiency of the private sector has been replaced by highly inefficient "military socialism." Weapons are produced years after their target dates and all too frequently they turn out to be unreliable and very expensive. The cost "overruns" on the originally submitted price to the Pentagon often mount into the billions.

MIC Interpretation of Foreign Policy

This interpretation of American foreign policy—like the earlier imperialist interpretation—provides a very satisfactory explanation for its advocates. It furnishes them with a key that appears to unlock the mysteries and problems of the world, for it constitutes a complete analysis of all domestic and foreign events. Economics seems such an obviously fundamental force. For an American especially, the striving for monetary success and material abundance (even for one who deliberately rejects such pursuit) is ever present. Explanations of American domestic politics often have been based upon assumptions about economic competition among business, labor, agriculture, and the military. Americans have been viewed as the "people of plenty," and American politics as largely a question of dividing that plenty. An analysis of U.S. foreign policy in terms of the quest for profits by big corporations thus suggests a tangible and demonstrable underlying motivation for the continuing arms race and large-scale investment in the military.

As with the imperialist theory, the MIC thesis omits any analysis of the state system; the thesis rests in a vacuum. It takes on the conspiratorial tone of the virtually identical "merchants of death" interpretation of the United States' entry into World War I in 1917.[29] The financiers, the munitions manufacturers, and the Eastern political and economic elite with its anti-German and pro-British sentiments, were said to be responsible for American entry into that war. Had it not been for those groups, the United States would supposedly have stayed neutral and spared "the people" from war. German hegemony in Europe and the threat to American security that it constituted were ignored.

The contemporary version of this thesis also defines those forces with a vested interest in the cold war. It is again suggested that, if political control were exerted over them, the American people could once more live in peace, cut the defense budget, reduce military influence in government, and rearrange priorities between foreign and domestic policies. In both instances it is asserted that, if the United States but wills abstinence, it can abstain. And, arising from this peculiar version of "the illusion of omnipotence" is the claim that no threat, or certainly no great threat, to American vital interests exists. The perceived threat is largely imaginary, deliberately created and manipulated to arouse fear and hysteria. This tension meets the needs of the MIC, which has established itself as a very expensive and dangerous kind of Frankenstein's monster, escaping from traditional democratic controls.

It is hard to understand, however, how this conclusion can be arrived at if there are in fact so many millions of both influential and working Americans who benefit from the continuation of the arms race. Indeed, there is a contradiction at the heart of the theory of the MIC. On the one hand, it is suggested that American foreign policy is too interventionist, too involved, and too expensive and that it distorts national priorities. The emotional appeal of the MIC explanation lies in the belief that the United States' allegedly overextended and dangerous policy is contrary to the interests of the vast majority of Americans, who would benefit from a cutback in external commitments and concentration on domestic affairs. The MIC is presented as a conspiracy blocking the "real interests" of the majority. On the other hand, almost every group in the United States seems to have a cash interest in international tension, including the growers who supply flowers for battle monuments; if so, the nation must have an interest in the continuation of cold war policies.

Changes in Policy

If the MIC thesis is correct, it is impossible to comprehend how such policies can be changed. Yet they have been changed. The percentage of GNP spent on defense during the 1970s declined to the lowest levels since the Korean War in 1950. Defense-related employment was half the 10 percent it reached during the 1950s. A number of large aerospace firms were in serious financial trouble (Lockheed had to be rescued from bankruptcy by the government), and defense profits were down in relation to nondefense earnings.[30] How can this be explained? Or, how do we understand the elimination of 1,500 Strategic Air Command (SAC) bombers in the late 1950s and early 1960s with hardly a whimper, or the virtual elimination of the antiballistic missile (ABM) in the first strategic arms limitation treaty? It goes without saying that defense spending is profitable for some industries, labor unions, and even states (for example, California and Texas). But this admission is certainly not tantamount to a theory of arms races that explains the start or resumption, conduct, and termination of such races. If the MIC thesis has any validity, arms races would be never ending. To attribute war to industries seeking profit is a bit like saying that doctors and pharmaceutical companies deliberately encourage disease in order to earn higher salaries and profits.

Similarly, whether defense spending is a crutch for the economy is at least debatable; if the skilled personnel and technology devoted to weaponry had been devoted instead to the growth of the nonmilitary sector of the economy (assuming no external threat), would not the economy have grown more rapidly? Seymour Melman has argued that the "permanent war economy" has resulted in technical stagnation in many principal productive sectors of the economy, such as manufacturing, transportation, and energy. He has estimated that the total investment in military hardware since World War II has exceeded industrial investment in plants and machinery in the same period! The U.S. military establishment's demands for capital have left only 10 percent of the national income to be plowed back into productive investments, whereas Japan, by contrast, has plowed back 30 percent and West Germany almost 20 percent. Despite the widely accepted radical wisdom that war production is necessary for a capitalist economy to maintain high employment, a war economy in reality slows economic growth and reduces the capacity to generate prosperity and jobs. Production of arms shifts human resources, such as scientists and engineers, as well as raw materials, factories, and finances from civilian production. With the reduction of innovation and investments, various nonmilitary industries suffer. Melman seems to have focused on one of the key causes for the declining U.S. industrial competitiveness in the world economy.

In addition, defense expenditures create fewer jobs than the same amounts of money spent in civilian fields. In January 1975, the U.S. Bureau of Labor Statistics estimated that $1 billion spent on defense had created 51,000 jobs. The same $1 billion would have created 61,000 jobs in public housing, or 88,000 jobs in Veterans Administration health care, or 136,000 jobs if spent on manpower training.[31] And because military jobs pay money to workers without also expanding the supply of available goods—few individuals buy tanks or missiles—military spending results in inflation. More money chases fewer goods, driving prices up on the items people do buy. During the Vietnam War the sudden sizable increase in military spending following President Lyndon Johnson's intervention resulted in a sharp increase in inflation because the government did not raise taxes to soak up the additional purchasing power. During the administration of Ronald Reagan, as already noted at some length (Chapter 4), the simultaneous military buildup costing more than $1 trillion and a tax cut resulted in an enormous budget deficit, an overvalued dollar, and a growing trade deficit because American products were too high-priced and imports were cheaper. The rapid military growth, in short, took its toll economically.

The MIC in the State System

A better perspective on the military-industrial complex can be gained in the context of the state system. In a bipolar system in which both powers, regardless of their domestic structures or values, confronted one another continuously, policy makers were naturally concerned with their nations' military strength and had to respond to rapidly changing technology. The possibility of a technological breakthrough by the opponent was bound to worry those whose main concern was deterrence of an enemy believed to be expansionist. As ever newer delivery systems were invented, a series of qualitative arms races was understandable. For deterrence to remain effective, the offense had to stay ahead of the defense; the deterrer could never leave its adversary in doubt that second-strike forces could eradicate it. President Reagan has complicated this equation by trying to reverse this offensive-defensive priority. His plan for a Strategic Defense Initiative (SDI) was bound to keenly stimulate not only research into a new generation of defensive weapons but also new offensive ones.

Perceptions of the deterrent balance and technology are the principal factors affecting the decisions of every U.S. president. Even when Soviet military strength rises, it takes some *action* by the Soviet Union or its friends to bring about an American buildup. It took a Korean attack or a threat to Berlin to raise the executive and legislative branches' perceptions of external threat and to make it politically feasible to propose the postponement of new domestic programs or raise new taxes for more weapons. Before the Korean War, Harry Truman refused to enhance the nation's military capability; Dwight Eisenhower, even after the launching of the Soviet satellite Sputnik in 1957, did little, despite grave warnings about a potential missile gap and SAC's new vulnerability. It was the liberal administration of John Kennedy that launched a large missile production program to counter the threats implicit in Soviet premier Nikita Khrushchev's tough behavior at the Vienna summit meeting in 1961 and the renewed Soviet challenge in Berlin. The Nixon administration was the first among postwar American administrations to decide upon a major arms production and deployment in the *absence* of an obvious and visible security threat—and this decision aroused vigorous criticism. In response, the president could only assert the possibility of grave future danger, but in the absence of aggressive Soviet behavior there was no proof. He was therefore unable to rally widespread political support and to still the critics of his plans for the deployment of anti-ballistic missiles (ABMs)—which Nixon then traded in SALT I. Nor do the American people seem particularly persuaded that SDI is a necessity required by an over-whelming Soviet threat to launch a first strike. In the years in which the Reagan administration cut social services because of enormous budget deficits, Congress has also cut SDI funding despite the president's repeated objections.

Even the military has not generally lived up to its popular warlike image. Adolf Hitler once remarked of the German military that, before he became the führer, he had thought he would have to put a leash on his soldiers to hold them back; instead he had constantly to push them forward. An army, navy, or air force is a bureaucracy. It is obviously interested in the expansion of its capabilities and influence in decision making, but, like any bureaucracy, it has a tendency to play safe. War is a gamble; it is risky and can spell defeat for a country and loss of influence, if not collapse, for the military bureaucracy. It is, in a real sense, easier to play soldier in peacetime. For example, the U.S. Army perceived its prime role in the post-1945 period to be the defense of Europe. Believing that it never received sufficient resources, the army was always aware that national commitments could exceed its capabilities; generally, therefore, it has not been particularly enthusiastic about taking on new commitments. Army leaders preferred to concentrate on what they believed to be their primary responsibility.

For another example, the army (and other services) did not favor intervention in Korea; it was the civilian leaders who thought it necessary to intervene. After China's entry into the war, when pressure to retaliate against it became intense—from General Douglas MacArthur in the field and from the Republican party in Congress—it was the military as a whole that took a leading role in opposing this move. The Soviet Union was the primary enemy; the United States should not invest excessive resources against a secondary opponent and weaken itself in such a struggle. The services have hardly been war dogs straining at the leash and seeking to promote further commitments and interventions.

The Korean War was not the only example of this attitude. The military was not the prime force in the Bay of Pigs operation in Cuba, the American blockade of Cuba a year later, or the intervention in the Dominican Republic. Nor was the military enthusiastic about intervening in Vietnam. After the disillusioning experience in Korea—a limited war in which the military leaders believed that they had been improperly restrained politically—a clique called the "Never-Again Club" had been organized in the military. Nevertheless, once the civilians had decided to intervene *with* limits, the military went in and, hardly unexpectedly, sought to increase its strength and to relax the political restraints to increase the pressure on the enemy. One study of military advice on the use of force has concluded that the Joint Chiefs have exercised the greatest influence on issues of intervention when they vetoed it.[32] During the Reagan administration, the Department of Defense reportedly opposed American intervention in Grenada, Lebanon, and Nicaragua.

Theorizing and Faith

On the whole, it is probably correct to say that the MIC thesis is primarily a devil theory, a polemical tool rather than an analytical one. The writings of the MIC theorists reveal a pattern: they decry both the nature and methods of American foreign policy, what the United States has done to the world, how it has done it, and the price it has paid in terms of delaying the fight against poverty and injustice at home. They hold the military and business interests and their "servants" in Congress responsible for starting the cold war, continuing hardline policies, and escalating the arms race; in brief, the MIC is invoked to discredit the policies and institutions responsible for these policies. Someone must be to blame for the mess; clearly international tension and domestic injustice are not in the majority's interests. Logically, according to these theorists, it follows that this minority of privileged people act as conspirators. Note also that the logic of this argument is backwards: the substance of the policies is condemned first; the MIC analyst then reasons from that back to those allegedly to blame. The whole argument rests on guilt by association: if someone has an interest in arms, bureaucratically or economically, this must be the cause of arms races and increased international tensions.

Arms, of course, do acquire vested domestic interests, but does that mean that arms races are initiated by those interests, or that they will stoke such a race and prevent its slowing down or cessation? The 1972 ABM treaty, for example, set levels which were further reduced by the 1974 protocol agreed to at the Brezhnev-Nixon summit meeting that year; a lot of jobs and some vested interests lost out in those agreements. The same was true for the B-1 bomber, which the U.S. Air Force wanted as a replacement for the aging B-52. Despite intensive lobbying by its contractor and by other groups, such as labor, with a vested interest in building the B-1, and despite support for the bomber in Congress, President Jimmy Carter decided not to go ahead with the construction and deployment of a B-1 bomber fleet of 224 planes. (President Reagan revived 100 B-1s.) Thus, the MIC's influence on defense spending was more a symptom of presidential perceptions of dangers and judgments on what is needed to maintain the deterrent than the result of illegitimate pressures brought to bear on the government. The same might be said of President Reagan's SDI. Until his proposal, the MIC had shown little interest in strategic defense. But, as the president pushed the program along, it began to acquire constituencies within the military-industrial complex.

It is this emphasis on illegitimate policy processes that is the common thread that runs through both the Marxist-Leninist and MIC views of American policy. As John Sloan has suggested about dependency theory, the advocates of these approaches or theories have "dealt with their conclusions more as true believers than as social scientists." Accepting these models with something akin to "religious fervor," such scholars "have resembled self-flagellating monks atoning for the sins of their nation in Vietnam, Cuba, Guatemala, and the Dominican Republic." Unlike most scholars, they appear to "enjoy the luxury of having their social theory perfectly congruent with their normative beliefs" and continue to believe with great conviction that one key explains virtually any nation's foreign and domestic policies.[33] Or, as E. H. Carr said several decades ago about the realist approach to international politics, "It lacked an ultimate goal and vision which gave it both a strong emotional appeal and grounds for moral judgment, especially for condemning current policies."[34] The imperialist and merchants-of-death theories lack none of these characteristics. Hence their appeal regardless of the evidence which may or may not support them; truth with a capital T is a matter of faith, even if it is poor social science. Empirical study of the policy process suggests a quite different model, one that is pluralistic, competitive, and open, exactly what the Marxist-Leninist and MIC explanation deny.

Notes

1. Edmund Wilson, *To the Finland Station* (Garden City, N.Y.: Anchor, 1953), 134-136. Used by permission. For revealing documents of the period, see E. Royston Pike, *"Hard Times": Human Documents of the Industrial Revolution* (New York: Holt, Rinehart & Winston, 1966); and Albert Fried and Richard M. Elman, eds., *Charles Booth's London* (New York: Pantheon, 1968).
2. Arthur P. Mendel, *The Essential Works of Marxism* (New York: Bantam, 1961), 17-18.
3. Alfred G. Meyer, *Communism*, rev. ed. (New York: Random House, 1967), 12.
4. Quoted in ibid., 15.
5. Ibid., 13-14.
6. V. I. Lenin, *Imperialism, the Highest Stage of Capitalism*, rev. ed. (New York: International Publishers, 1939).
7. Joseph Stalin, *The Foundations of Leninism*, quoted in Mendel, *Essential Works of Marxism*, 228-229 (emphasis in original).
8. Ibid., 49. See, for example, David Horowitz, *The Free World Colossus* (New York: Hill & Wang, 1965); William Appleman Williams, *The Tragedy of American Diplomacy*, rev. ed. (New York: Delta, 1962); Lloyd C. Gardner, *Architects of Illusion* (Chicago: Quadrangle, 1970); Joyce and Gabriel Kolko, *The Limits of Power* (New York: Vintage, 1968); Walter La Feber, *America, Russia and the Cold War* (New York: John Wiley & Sons, 1967); Gar Alperovitz, *Atomic Diplomacy* (New York: Vintage, 1965); and Harry Magdoff, *The Age of Imperialism* (New York: Monthly Review Press, 1969). For evaluations of this thesis, see Arthur Schlesinger Jr., "Origins of the Cold War," *Foreign Affairs* (October 1967): 22-52; and John Lewis Gaddis, *The United States and the Origins of the Cold War, 1941-1947* (New York: Columbia University Press, 1972). For criticism of some of the imperialist school's scholarship, see Robert James Maddox, *The New Left and the Origins of the Cold War* (Princeton, N.J.: Princeton University Press, 1973); and Raymond Aaron, *The Imperial Republic* (Cambridge, Mass.: Winthrop, 1974).
9. Eugene Staley, *War and the Private Investor* (Garden City, N.Y.: Doubleday, 1935), xv-xvi.
10. Benjamin J. Cohen, *The Question of Imperialism* (New York: Basic Books, 1973), 67.
11. Ibid., 16.
12. Stephen D. Krasner, *Defending the National Interest* (Princeton, N.J.: Princeton University Press, 1978), 119-128.
13. An interesting characteristic of the imperialist interpretation of post-World War II American foreign policy is that it is based on examination in depth of the American economic system and social structure, in which every nook and cranny of the White House, the State Department, and the Pentagon have been searched for evidence of anti-Soviet motivation. Yet there has been hardly a look at the Soviet system and the dynamics of Soviet foreign policy since 1917; the latter is portrayed as primarily a reaction to American policy. Soviet policy apparently has no inherent purpose apart from the limited security interests in Eastern Europe. Anything that does not fit the view of Soviet policy as legitimate and defensive is omitted by revisionist critics; first-level analysis in which the American-Soviet conflict is viewed as a product of bipolarity is conveniently rejected because it would preclude the possibility of blaming the cold war solely or primarily on Washington's leaders and absolving Moscow's leaders of at least half the responsibility.

14. Gabriel Kolko, *Roots of American Foreign Policy* (Boston: Beacon Press, 1967), 86.
15. Ibid., 50.
16. Ibid.
17. Robert W. Tucker, *The Radical Left and American Foreign Policy* (Baltimore: Johns Hopkins University Press, 1971), 126.
18. Jerome Slater, "Is United States Foreign Policy 'Imperialistic' or 'Imperial'?" *Political Science Quarterly* (Spring 1976): 185-186.
19. Tucker, *The Radical Left*, 134-136.
20. Ibid., 126-131.
21. See Aaron, *Imperial Republic*, Part II, for a general evaluation of American postwar "imperialistic" policy.
22. Slater, "Is United States Foreign Policy 'Imperialistic'?" 86.
23. Ibid.
24. Vernon Van Dyke, *International Politics*, 2d ed. (New York: Appleton, 1966), 110.
25. Sidney Lens, *The Military-Industrial Complex* (Philadelphia: Pilgrim, 1970); Richard J. Barnet, *The Economy of Death* (New York: Atheneum, 1969); Ralph Lapp, *The Weapons Culture* (Baltimore: Penguin, 1968); William Proxmire, *Report from Wasteland* (New York: Holt, Rinehart & Winston, 1970); Seymour Melman, *Pentagon Capitalism* (New York: McGraw-Hill, 1970); Melman, *The Permanent War Economy* (New York: Simon & Schuster, 1974); Adam Yarmolinsky, *The Military Establishment* (New York: Harper & Row, 1971); Steven Rosen, ed., *Testing the Theory of the Military-Industrial Complex* (Lexington, Mass.: Lexington Books, 1973); and Anthony Sampson, *The Arms Bazaar* (New York: Viking, 1977).
26. Richard J. Barnet, *The Roots of War* (Baltimore: Penguin, 1973), 13-22.
27. Barnet, *Economy of Death*, 79.
28. The correctness of these assumptions by believers in the power of the "military-industrial complex," as well as congressional voting behavior in relation to defense issues, is analyzed in Bruce M. Russett, *What Price Vigilance?* (New Haven, Conn.: Yale University Press, 1970).
29. A characteristic description of the role of the military was "the alliance of the military with powerful economic groups to secure appropriations on the one hand for a constantly increasing military and naval establishment, and on the other hand, the constant threat of the use of that swollen military establishment, in behalf of the economic interests at home and abroad of the industrialists supporting it. It means that subjugation of the people of the various countries to the uniform, the self-interested identification of patriotism with commercialism, and the removal of the military from the control of civil law." This statement, which could have been spoken by a liberal senator or a representative of Students for a Democratic Society in the 1970s, is from conservative senator Gerald P. Nye's investigations, held during the 1930s, attributing U.S. involvement in World War I to the military-industrial complex of its time. "Munitions Industry," *Report on Existing Legislation*, Senate Report No. 944, Part 5, 74th Cong., 2d sess. (Washington, D.C.: Government Printing Office, 1936), 8-9, quoted in *Principles and Problems of International Politics*, ed. Hans Morgenthau and Kenneth Thompson (New York: Alfred A. Knopf, 1950), 62-63.
30. Philip Odeen, "In Defense of the Defense Budget," *Foreign Policy*, Fall 1974, 94-95.
31. Seymour Melman, "Go Civilian or Go Broke," *New York Times*, Dec. 14, 1976.
32. Richard K. Betts, *Soldiers, Statesmen and Cold War Crises* (Cambridge, Mass.: Harvard University Press, 1977).

33. John W. Sloan, "Dependency Theory and Latin American Development: Another Key Fails To Open the Door," *Inter-American Economic Affairs*, Winter 1977, 30. Also fn. 46, ch. 14.

34. Edward H. Carr, *The Twenty Years' Crisis, 1919-1939* (New York: Harper Torchbooks), 89-94.

CHAPTER 16

The Games
Policy Makers Play

THE ROLE OF PERCEPTION AND GOVERNMENTAL POSITION

The decision-making approach to understanding the foreign policy of a country is based on the assumption that we should look at the specific personnel officially responsible for making the policy and the positions they occupy.[1] When we speak of a state's doing this or that, we are really speaking of those officials, the policy decisions they make, and how they implement them. The state, in short, equals the official policy makers whose decisions and actions constitute its policies. Decisions are the "outputs" of the domestic political system. By focusing on the decision makers, this approach emphasizes, first, how they *see* the world. What is important is not what the international system is objectively like, but how the policy makers perceive it. For it is on their perceptions that these officials act or, for that matter, do not act; reality does not exist independent of the policy makers' definitions of it.

As we noted earlier, a balance-of-power analysis can explain what British prime minister Neville Chamberlain should have done to counter Adolf Hitler in the 1930s, but not what he did. Without studying the prime minister and his advisers, and without analyzing their perceptions of Hitler, the goals of Nazi Germany, and the Versailles peace treaty, first-level analysts could not tell why the British did not choose another course of action, or why they bungled and brought on the war they had hoped to avoid. Such an analysis was thus not very helpful. A useful analysis would have included Chamberlain's misperception of Hitler as simply a German nationalist who, while seeking some territorial adjustments, had otherwise only limited ambitions. Such an analysis would also have been focused on the pacifist nature of British public opinion, still guided by memories of horrible losses during

514

World War I. The strength of this opinion acted as a constraint upon British political leaders, even had they wished to contain Germany.

Similarly, while another concept may properly explain some particular event, as the concept of national style can account for U.S. intervention in Vietnam, such an explanation may be rejected as too broad and vague. How can we attribute the war to national style without scrutinizing the officials who have made the decision to fight it, the departments in which they have served, organizational pressures to intervene or not to intervene, and legislative and public pressures? As national style presumably affects all policy makers, did it make intervention in Vietnam inevitable? Whatever the answer, there is much to be learned from a look at the personnel, sometimes described as "the best and the brightest," who made the decision. Had the United States not intervened in Vietnam, would that abstention also have been attributed to national style? If whatever a nation does arises from its style, then style is too encompassing a concept; by explaining everything, it explains nothing. The same can be said of economic explanations, especially Marxist-Leninist determinism. An event is ordained by history, or it is not ordained. A skeptic rightfully chooses to study the specific officials who make the specific decisions.

The Rational-Actor Model

One model of decision making—the *rational-actor model*—has been central to first-level analysis. Each state is viewed as a unitary actor, making foreign policy changes in four clearly separate steps: selecting objectives and values, considering alternative means of achieving them, calculating the likely consequences of each alternative, and selecting the one that is most promising. Henry Kissinger wrote in 1957 that if American policy is to seek security and peace, it cannot be based on a strategy of massive retaliation against the Soviet Union when confronted with limited challenges. To respond in this manner would only ensure American suicide; not to respond at all would be tantamount to surrender. Both courses are therefore irrational. The only rational option in these circumstances is "limited war." [2] This rational model, as ought to be clear, underlies not only analyses of international politics and specific foreign policies but also other spheres of decision making. In the competitive "games nations play," with their informal rules, but also in other games, such as courtship and politics, each player creates a strategy designed to lead to "victory." There are usually several options, and players must decide at each point in the game which play is the best in terms of the ultimate goals.

The Governmental Politics Model

The other model is that of *governmental politics*. It focuses on the executive branch of government and especially on the bureaucracies whose official responsibility is to formulate and execute foreign policy. The model is, indeed, usually referred to as *bureaucratic politics*. We use the term *governmental politics* because it also focuses on the legislature, at least in free countries, and on many interest groups, the mass media, and the various publics that together constitute public opinion. The bureaucracy, in short, is viewed in its broader governmental and societal setting. The emphasis is on the *pluralistic nature of decision making* in which, in general, the actors' views reflect their positions and interests. As one saying puts it, *"Where you stand depends on where you sit."* Policy in these circumstances is formulated through conflicts among many actors with different perceptions, perspectives, and interests, but also through reconciling these differences. These two elements of the policy struggle will determine who receives what and when. Such a political way of making policy generally applies to noncrisis security policies, which express continuing goals and involve continuing sets of actors, including Congress (if only because security policies usually need funding).

Graham Allison has illustrated aptly the difference between rational and bureaucratic policy making.[3] When in the late 1950s, the Soviet Union tested its first intercontinental ballistic missile (ICBM), American leaders became very concerned about a possible "missile gap" favoring the Soviets. Following the rational model, they concluded that the Soviet Union would exploit this technological breakthrough, mass-produce ICBMs, and use them to pressure the United States to concede territorial changes in central Europe, specifically in the symbolically significant western half of Berlin. In terms of the balance of power, the Soviets had achieved a major technological breakthrough, which, if fully exploited before the United States could test and deploy an ICBM, could give them superior power. Rationally, in terms of the rules of the game of the international system, that is what the Kremlin leaders should have done—at least, that is what American policy makers expected them to do. Had the United States been the nation to test the first ICBM, it would have gone into large-scale production, which would have strengthened the American hand in relation to the Soviet Union. It would have seemed the logical thing to do.

If the same American policy makers had used the pluralistic policy-making model, however, they would have been more cautious in drawing this conclusion. The Red Army controlled the missiles, and it was unlikely to abandon suddenly the traditional definition of its role on the ground in favor of intercontinental strategic deterrence with ICBMs. The very thought would be alien to an organization preoccupied with land defense and a role limited to Eurasia. A dramatic shift of deterrence from within the army to another service certainly would have been accompanied by an observable policy struggle. The development of a large ICBM force would have required a vast transfer of funds to that other service, creating interservice rivalries and quarrels. The different models, then, offered grounds for quite different assessments of what the Soviets would do and implied quite different American defense and foreign policies. The incoming administration of John Kennedy, acting upon the rational model, initiated a more numerous missile deployment than it might otherwise have done; the Soviets' reaction, after the Cuban missile crisis in 1962, was an extensive buildup that resulted in the achievement of strategic parity.

We shall now examine these two models in more detail. But first it must be noted that, although the decision-making models can be used in explaining other countries' foreign policies, we shall use American examples and focus on American policy process because of more readily available materials, the many decisions that have been made in Washington since World War II, and the greater familiarity of American readers with recent history in which the United States has been actively involved. Later we shall return to the comparative usefulness of the models in decision making and, indeed, to their analytical limitations as well.

CRISIS DECISION

The rational-actor model is probably the most relevant to explaining and understanding crisis decisions. A crisis is characterized by a number of features, including that the decision makers are taken by surprise, feel that they must make decisions rapidly, and that vital interests are at stake.[4] In these circumstances, decisions cannot be made in the day-to-day routine manner that is the way of bureaucracy. The element of surprise is likely to reduce the possibility that the crisis will elicit standard operating procedures in its management. The need for quick decisions requires that the number of officials be limited. Above all, the perception that vital interests are involved means that decision making quickly becomes centralized and goes to the top: the president and his chief advisers in the United States, equivalent officials in other governments.

These characteristics of crises, then, tend to be highly functional. The usual long haggling over differences in policies between different bureaucracies, the separation of powers between the executive and Congress, and all the efforts of interest groups to influence policy, if not undermine it, are, so to speak, short-circuited. The different way crises are managed in the government means that the policy process works speedily and efficiently, free of the traditional domestic pressures, for the short duration of crises. And the fact that crisis decisions flow upward to the top officials has another important consequence—the careful and cautious management of superpower crises. A crisis obviously results in stress and anxiety and there is always the possibility of rash or impetuous actions. Another possibility is that the policy makers may not examine all the alternative options and may choose the wrong one because some officials are reluctant to express doubts about the policy being adopted. But these tendencies are likely to be reduced, if not minimized, by the risks and costs involved when the two nuclear powers face each other. The consequences of mismanaging the crisis are so awesome that they provide the best antidote to being reckless, complacent, and not considering all possible options.

The Rise of Decision Making to the Top

One characteristic of the decision-making process, then, is that decision making rises to the top of the governmental hierarchy, specifically, to the president and the president's closest advisers. Some will be statutory advisers, such as the secretaries of the chief foreign policy agencies; others will be people both in and out of government whose judgment the president particularly trusts. During the potentially explosive Cuban missile crisis of 1962, the executive committee that managed the crisis included the president and vice president; the secretaries of state and defense; their seconds in command; the director of the Central Intelligence Agency (CIA); the chairman of the Joint Chiefs of Staff; the president's special assistant for national security affairs; and certain other individuals such as the secretary of the Treasury, the attorney general (the president's brother), the president's special counsel (perhaps his closest friend after his brother), an ambassador just returned from Moscow, and President Harry Truman's former secretary of state.[5] During the 1972 spring offensive of North Vietnamese troops, when the defeat of the South Vietnamese army seemed imminent, the decision-making process was more narrowly confined. There were several reasons for this: the concentration of foreign policy decision making in the White House under Kissinger, President Richard Nixon's style as a "loner," and the president's tactic of confronting a Senate increasingly critical of the war with *faits accomplis* (which would not have been possible if there were leaks before the action). As a result, decision making seems to have been confined largely to these two men, although the members of the National Security Council were consulted formally.[6]

The Central Role of the President

A second characteristic of making crisis decisions is the central role of the president, who interprets events and evaluates the stakes in the crisis. Kennedy's and Nixon's "readings" of the situations they confronted, the consequences these situations might have for American security, and their own political futures and abilities to lead the nation were responsible for their actions. (The latter two factors can hardly be separated, for the external challenges, as the president sees them, do not really leave a choice of accepting a loss of personal prestige without a loss of national prestige. For the president of the United States, personal and national cost calculations tend to be identical.)

Kennedy saw the installation of Soviet missiles in Cuba as a personal challenge, with potentially damaging national effects. In response to earlier congressional and public clamor about possible Soviet offensive missiles in

Cuba—as distinct from ground-to-air or ground-to-ship defensive missiles—Kennedy had publicly declared that the United States would not tolerate offensive missiles on the island ninety miles off the Florida coast. Intended primarily as a declaration to cool domestic criticism that had come largely from Republicans, Kennedy's statement had also led Soviet leaders to respond that they had no intention of placing missiles in Cuba; the Soviet Union had, they said, more than enough missiles at home. In this way, the president publicly discounted the possibility that the Soviets would install such weapons in Cuba, and the Soviets then signaled their understanding of his declaration. Privately they further reassured him that they had no intention of installing missiles anywhere outside the Soviet Union. Kennedy thus was pledged to act if the Soviets lied—as it turned out they had—unless he wished to be publicly humiliated. If he did not act, the Soviet leaders would not believe other pledges and commitments the president had made or inherited from his predecessors. At least, that is how Kennedy perceived the situation.

He saw the consequences as very dangerous because he feared that Soviet premier Nikita Khrushchev had interpreted previous acts—the abortive Bay of Pigs invasion of Cuba and the inaction of U.S. troops when the Berlin Wall went up—as signaling a lack of will, an absence of sufficient resolution and determination to defend American vital interests. Khrushchev spoke openly of an American failure of nerve. The United States, in his view, spoke loudly but carried a small stick. It was not so much the effect of the Soviet missiles upon the military equation between the two powers that mattered, though that was important; it was the political consequences of the *appearance* of a change in the balance of power that were deemed critical by Kennedy. The Soviet Union was supposed to be on the short end of the missile gap, but Kennedy feared that American inaction would persuade the world that Soviet claims of missile superiority were accurate. This would lead allied governments to fear that, in the new situation in which the United States would be vulnerable to nuclear devastation, they could no longer count on this country to defend them. Above all, it might tempt the Soviets to exploit the situation and to seek to disrupt American alliances—especially the North Atlantic Treaty Organization (NATO), since Khrushchev already had restated his determination to eject the Western allies from West Berlin. If Khrushchev succeeded in Cuba, why should he take seriously Kennedy's pledge to defend West Berlin? And, if he did not, would not Soviet and American troops soon be clashing in an area where they would be hard to separate?

The real irony of the Cuban missile crisis is that Kennedy was also determined to try to seek a more stable and restrained basis of coexistence with the Soviet Union during his years in office. This long-range goal, which hardly had the massive support it would have later, could not be realized if Khrushchev did not take Kennedy seriously and tried to push him around. Then serious negotiations, in which each party recognized the other's legitimate interests, would be impossible. A major change in the cold war atmosphere was at stake, in addition to the United States' reputation for power and willingness to keep commitments. Domestically, of course, another "defeat" in Cuba, discrediting Kennedy's foreign policy, was bound to affect his personal standing with his party, Congress, and the public. It also would lead to strong right-wing Republican pressures to be more forcible in foreign policy and give less priority to the president's liberal domestic reform program.

Nixon also saw the United States' reputation for power, its prestige, as the central issue in Vietnam.[7] When he came into office, there was little question that Americans were weary of the war's high costs, especially in casualties. These costs seemed totally disproportionate, particularly since the war promised no successful end in the near future. For Nixon, the crux of the problem was not whether the United States should leave Vietnam but, as he repeatedly stressed, *how* it should leave. If its chief adversaries, the Soviet Union and China, were to be deterred and contained, if fruitful negotiations with the Soviets over arms control were to occur, if relations were to be established with the Beijing government, and if a more stable and peaceful "structure of peace" were to be worked out with those nations, then the United States' reputation in the two major Communist countries was the crucial factor. If it were humiliated in Vietnam, it would be viewed as a "pitiful, helpless giant," one that could be pressured, was not to be negotiated with seriously, and offered few attractions as a potential partner for either the Soviet Union or China against the other.

Nixon's strategy was therefore to "Vietnamize" the war. The South Vietnamese army was increasingly to take over the fighting and receive large-scale U.S. air support to help preserve a non-Communist government in South Vietnam. If American public opinion would support a strategy that would result in casualties for the United States, and if the pressure to leave Vietnam completely could be reduced at home, then the Hanoi regime would have an incentive to negotiate a compromise settlement. Confronted by the continued use of U.S. air power and a better-trained South Vietnamese army equipped by the United States, Hanoi's leaders would find their hopes for all-out victory in the South dimming and would prefer to end hostilities with a political settlement.

This strategy, however, brought the United States to the brink of disaster in spring 1972. Just after Nixon's dramatic visit to Beijing and just before his extremely important visit to Moscow to negotiate limitations on defensive and offensive missiles and other key topics, the North Vietnamese launched a spring offensive into South Vietnam. Nixon, like Kennedy, rejected the possibility of inaction, even though the Moscow summit meeting might be jeopardized if he took strong action against the Soviet Union's fraternal socialist state. The president believed that the Soviet government, having supplied the government of Hanoi with much of its modern military paraphernalia, including ground-to-air missiles and tanks for conventional offensives, should have restrained the North Vietnamese leaders just before the summit meeting. As Nixon perceived the situation, whether Moscow had been aware of the timing of the North Vietnamese offensive or not, the fact that it took place seriously endangered his Vietnamization policy and humiliated him on the eve of vital negotiations. The president did not intend to enter these negotiations under the cloud of defeat and failure.

The failure of Vietnamization also, of course, would undermine his prestige and leadership at home. He had already ordered the bombing of North Vietnam; now he ordered that its harbors be mined to stop incoming Soviet and Chinese supplies. President Lyndon Johnson had always refused to take this step because of the risk of a confrontation with the Soviets. Nixon accepted that risk and re-Americanized the war. The Soviets did not call off the Moscow summit meeting.

Nixon apparently did not consider other courses of action; he rejected inaction as the price for the Moscow summit. Kennedy had considered alternative responses to the Soviet missiles in Cuba, everything from diplomatic pressures and a secret approach to Fidel Castro to precision air strikes at the missiles, invasion, and blockade. Feeling strongly that he had to act to impress Khrushchev, Kennedy chose the blockade as the option most likely to attain the removal of the Soviet missiles. Although the blockade could not by itself achieve this objective, it was a sign of American determination. It permitted the United States the option of increasing the pressure on the Soviet regime later if the missiles were not removed. It also provided a relatively safe middle course between inaction and invasion (or an air strike), which might provoke the Soviets. Finally, it placed on Khrushchev the responsibility for deciding whether to escalate or deescalate the crisis. It is significant that, thanks to information provided by a U-2 "spy plane," the administration had a whole week to debate the meaning and significance of the Soviet move, its likely military and political effects on American security interests, the different courses of action open to the United States, and which course was most likely to achieve removal of the Soviet missiles without precipitating nuclear war. Many crises simply do not afford such time for preparation and the careful consideration of alternatives. Even during the missile crisis, the initial reaction of most of the president's advisers had been to bomb the missile sites. Slowing down the momentum of events is crucial if impulsive actions are to be avoided.

The Role of the Bureaucracy

The third characteristic of crises is the subordination of bureaucratic interests to the need to make a decision to safeguard the "national interest." The crisis is accompanied by a sense of urgency, as well as by the policy makers' perception that the nation's security is at stake and that war looms. Thus, although decision making has risen to the top levels of the government, and the men and women in those positions reflect their departmental points of view, they do not necessarily feel themselves limited to representing those points of view. Organizational affiliation is not *per se* a good predictor of those points of view. Senior participants in crises behave more as "players" than as "organizational participants." Secretary of Defense Robert McNamara did not reflect the Joint Chiefs' readiness to bomb and invade during the Cuban missile crisis (just as late in the Vietnam War he was to disagree increasingly with their views and recommendations); he became the leading proponent of the blockade. Other players in that crisis did not even represent foreign policy bureaucracies—the two men closest to the president, the attorney general and the president's special counsel, along with the secretary of the Treasury and a former secretary of state, for example, represented only themselves. The bureaucratic axiom that "you stand where you sit" is thus not necessarily correct, at least during a crisis.

The Role of Congress

Finally, decision making in a crisis is characterized by congressional noninvolvement. Congressional leaders usually are called in and informed of the president's decision just before he announces it publicly. This form is followed as a matter of courtesy. But their advice is not requested. Presidents consider themselves more representative than any senator or House member and as representative as Congress as a whole. Interestingly enough, Kennedy, after informing a congressional delegation of his decision to blockade Cuba, did ask for its opinions. When the response was to question the utility of the blockade and to propose an air strike instead, Kennedy reacted angrily. After the members left, he consoled himself by saying that, had they had more time to think it over, they also would have decided on the blockade. If presidents assure themselves like this, why indeed consult members of the legislative branch? In any event, in crises what choice do they have but to support the only president the country has at the moment?

DECISION MAKING AS A PLURALISTIC POWER STRUGGLE

Multiple Actors

The governmental politics model of decision making is characterized first by multiple institutional actors: the three branches of the federal government. In foreign policy matters, the principal participants are the executive and legislative branches. Within these institutions there are a multitude of departments, organizations, staffs, committees, and individuals concerned with foreign policy. Within the executive branch, there are (1) the president, the assistant for national-security affairs, and the assistant's staff; (2) the senior foreign policy departments—the State and Defense Departments and the CIA; (3) the junior departments—Agency for International Development (AID), U.S. Information Agency (USIA), and Arms Control and Disarmament Agency

(ACDA); and (4) departments with domestic jurisdictions that occasionally deal with foreign policy issues falling within their areas of expertise—Departments of the Treasury, Commerce, and Agriculture. On the legislative side, both the Senate and the House are divided into many different party groupings and committees—the latter being subdivided even further into subcommittees. Currently, there are 37 standing committees in Congress—22 in the House, 15 in the Senate—and 250 subcommittees.[8] Often several committees and subcommittees hold hearings and issue reports on the same policy.

This institutional pluralism is supplemented by organized groups representing many economic, ethnic, racial, religious, and public interests. As for foreign policy, however, "it is questionable, in fact, whether we are really entitled to talk about group influence on 'foreign policy'; with very rare exceptions, the influence of nongovernmental groups is on particular, discrete, rather highly specialized matters, which, even if they may be deemed to be within the foreign policy field, are very far from constituting or defining that field."[9] Business groups and labor may be interested in particular tariff issues when certain industries and their employees are exposed to foreign competition; an ethnic group may be stimulated by disputes involving a specific country, such as Israel or Greece. Yet continuing concern with foreign policy as a whole usually is lacking; mainly, it is intermittent and tied to special issues.

The reason why there is less interest in security policy than in domestic affairs is easy to understand. Interest groups have abundant knowledge and experience of internal affairs, but on foreign policy issues they rarely show comparable information and skill; they must rely on foreign policy experts, who do not encourage lay involvement. In addition, interest groups are consulted regularly by the respective executive departments while domestic legislation is being drawn up—they, after all, constitute the departments' clientele—but in foreign policy the departments tend to be their own constituencies and spokesmen. Institutional interests (within the government) therefore predominate over associational interests (outside it). The responsible agencies have their own experts and are in contact with other experts, be they at the RAND Corporation or at Harvard University. Although there is a fairly stable structure of societal interest groups concerned with domestic policies, the comparable structure in the traditional area of foreign policy concerned with security issues is weak and at times even ephemeral.

In short, the main differences between foreign and domestic policy making are that the latter involves more participants in both the executive and legislative branches and that interest groups and public opinion are more active. The larger the number of actors, the more important the stakes that key legislators, committees, and lobbyists perceive at issue, the more difficult it will be to arrive at policy decisions (see Table 16-1). Negotiations will be long and very difficult, and compromises acceptable to so many involved parties will not be reached without immense effort, if they can be arranged at

Table 16-1 Policy Characteristics

Type of Policy	Chief Characteristics	Primary Actors	Principal Decision Maker	Role of Congress	Role of Interest Groups	Relations Among Actors
Crisis	Short run; bureaucracy and Congress short-circuited	President, responsible officials, and individuals from in and out of government	Executive (presidential preeminence)	Postcrisis legitimation	None	Cooperation
Noncrisis (security)	Long run; bureaucratic-legislative participation	President; executive agencies; Congress; interest groups; public opinion	Executive bureaucracy	Congressional participation	Low to moderate	Competition and bargaining
Domestic (welfare)	Long run; bureaucratic-legislative participation	President; executive agencies; Congress; interest groups; public opinion	Executive-congressional sharing	High	High	Competition and bargaining

SOURCE: This table is modeled on one in *Congress, the Bureaucracy, and Public Policy*, by Randall B. Ripley and Grace A. Franklin (Homewood, Ill.: Dorsey 1976), 17.

all. In these circumstances, the president's ability to initiate, lead, and maneuver will be seriously circumscribed. In many foreign policy issues no immediate tangible interests are perceived to be at stake and in which the president is generally—although not always—acknowledged to have greater expertise. In contrast, domestic issues involve many concerns, especially material ones, that arouse many actors who believe they are just as expert and experienced as the executive.

Presidential involvement, therefore, does not guarantee successful domestic negotiations. On key issues, the president, lacking votes, may be reluctant to enter the policy arena at all, lest he fail and his reputation for "getting things done" be impaired. The contrast to most foreign policy issues is striking; there he can normally count on achieving his aims, building a successful record, benefiting his party, and presumably helping the nation.

Conflict

A second characteristic of the governmental politics model of decision making is conflict among actors. Because the president is both the nation's chief diplomat and the commander in chief of its armed forces, this conflict occurs primarily within the executive branch, among executive departments that are responsible for foreign policy—both formulation and implementation.[10] We can speak, for example, of the State Department versus the Defense Department, though conflict between the executive and legislative branches of government also occurs. Actually, as must be clear, the executive departments and the two houses of Congress rarely speak with a single voice. At the State Department, the head of the bureau for European and Canadian affairs may express a view quite different from those of the heads of the Inter-American or African bureaus. In the Defense Department, the position of the air force may differ from those of the army and navy. Indeed, within each service there are differences, as between the Strategic Air Command and Tactical Air Command, the surface navy and strategic submarine navy and aircraft-carrier navy. In the Senate, the Foreign Relations Committee may be in conflict on a specific issue with the Armed Services Committee, and subcommittees of each committee may disagree with one another. This situation must be multiplied by the other committees and subcommittees in both houses. Each of these institutions, bureaucracies, committees, and interest groups develops intense organizational identifications, and all are determined not only to survive but also to expand their influence in the policy-making process. Furthermore, each, viewing a problem from a special perspective, is likely to develop strong convictions about the content of policy, especially when "national interests" are involved and the organization or department thinks that it has a vital contribution to make. Institutional struggles between the executive and legislative branches, as well as within each branch and within executive departments, are consequently the norm.

This kind of policy-making process is often condemned as "parochial," on the assumption that more comprehensive—more "correct"—solutions to all policy problems could be found were it not for the selfish and narrow points of view of the various participants in the policy process. Adherents of this view ignore the fact that, in any pluralistic institution, diverse convictions compete. Different policy recommendations are offered as solutions to the problems being considered, and these recommendations represent a fairly broad spectrum of choice. Just as in a democracy different groups and individuals have the right to articulate their values and interests, so the various parts of the executive and legislative branches articulate their own policy views and seek to protect their own interests. The issue is not which policy position and recommendations are correct; clearly there is not a single correct policy. *The issue is how to reconcile conflicting interpretations of what the correct policy ought to be.* This reconciliation of the policy preferences of the various "players" is complicated by the many players outside the executive branch.

Consensus Building

The third characteristic of the governmental politics model of decision making, resulting from the first two, is a reconciliation of these different points of view to build a "consensus" or majority "coalition" from these so that decisions can be made. Negotiating thus occurs throughout the executive branch as officials and agencies in one department seek support in another or attempt to enlist the aid of the president or his advisers to achieve their goals. The process is one of widening the base of support within the executive branch and then seeking further support in the two houses of Congress, gaining allies through continual modification of the proposed policy. The official policy "output" that emerges represents the victory of one coalition formed across institutional lines over an opposing coalition of the same kind.

More specifically, a coalition across institutional lines, for example, can be an alliance among the personnel of a particular desk in the State Department, of a specific service in the Defense Department, and of various bureaus in the Departments of the Treasury and Commerce, as well as of several committees in Congress. It may be opposed by personnel of other desks, services, bureaus, and committees in the same or other departments and the legislative branch. Such a coalition, furthermore, usually holds together only for the specific issue being considered. A different issue requires mobilization of a different coalition. The reason is that in the United States political parties are undisciplined and party loyalty cannot be counted upon automatically for any given presidential policy. Great energy must be expended on this task.

Roger Hilsman has compared this process of making policy through conflict and cooperation with the behavior of states in the international system.[11] Politics, as we noted earlier, is distinguished by three features: the existence of multiple groups or organizations (including nation-states); an accompanying set of conflicting perspectives, values, and interests; and different amounts of power. *Policy is therefore not only a matter of which point of view seems to have the most merit and pertinence; it is also a matter of who has power and exercises it the most effectively.* The resulting intragovernmental policy struggle is every bit as intense and persistent as intergovernmental conflicts.

Incrementalism and Crisis

A fourth characteristic of the governmental politics model of decision making is the effect of conflict and coalition building on policy output. One of the most important results of continuous bargaining within the "policy machine" is that policy in any area moves forward one step at a time and tends to focus on fleeting concerns and short-range aims.[12] This is usually called *incrementalism*. Another word is "satisficing." Policy makers, this word suggests, do not sit down each time they have to make a decision and go through the rational procedure of decision making. They do not try to isolate which values and interests they wish to enhance, examine all the means that might achieve these goals, calculate the consequences of each, and then select the one most likely to be successful. Policy makers have neither the time nor resources to go through this process. Instead, they pick the policy that is likely to be the most satisfactory, and they judge this point by whether the policy has been successful in the past. If so, why not take another step forward on the same path?

The presumption is that what has worked in the past will work now, as well as in the future. In addition, once a majority has been forged, after hard struggle and probably much "bloodletting," the "winning" coalition will normally prefer modification of existing policy to another major fight. The assumption is, of course, that a policy will result, which is not necessarily true. Negotiations among different groups with conflicting perspectives and vested interests can produce a stalemate and a paralysis of policy.

As a result, policy tends to vacillate between incrementalism and crisis, either because incrementalism is not adequate to a developing situation or because stalemate produces no policy at all. It may be said with reasonable correctness that, during "normal" periods, low external pressure on the policy machine favors continuation of existing policies; during crises, high pressure tends to produce innovative reaction, perhaps because a stalemated policy machine must have an *external "trigger"* in order to undermine the coalition supporting the status quo. A crisis may break up coalitions, may awaken a sufficiently great sense of danger to dampen the pluralistic struggle, even if only for a short time, and may create a feeling of urgency—and therefore a common purpose—among the various participants in policy making. Additionally, as already suggested, crisis policy is decided in an inner circle, composed of the president and a few top officials and trusted advisers; at a time of perceived danger these officials function relatively free of departmental points of view and interests. The usual process of consensus or coalition building is thus short-circuited.[13] There are, then, two policy processes: the pluralisic advocacy system and the crisis-management system, the latter involving top officials (assistant secretaries and up), the former a broader mix of interests.

It took the bombing of Pearl Harbor in 1941 to harness the strength of the United States and direct it toward warding off German and Japanese threats to the nation's security. Symbolically, after December 7, 1941, Franklin Roosevelt, who had called himself "Dr. New Deal"—the physician called in to cure a sick economy—became "Dr. Win the War." Similarly, after World War II, it was the overwhelming Soviet threat that allowed Truman to mobilize the country for containment; before the threat became so obvious that it could no longer be ignored, Truman had been unable to take the necessary countermeasures. Again, it was Castro and his attempts to stir anti-American revolutions in Latin American countries that allowed President Kennedy to mobilize support for the Alliance for Progress, which was intended to help relieve some of the potentially revolutionary problems in the Southern Hemisphere.

Need for Time

A fifth characteristic of the policy-making process, implicit in our analysis so far, is its time-consuming nature. Incrementalism suggests a policy machine in low gear, moving along a well-defined road rather slowly in response to specific short-run stimuli. A proposed policy is normally discussed first within the executive branch. It passes through official channels, where it receives "clearances" and modifications as it gathers a broader base of support on its way "up" the executive hierarchy to the president. Constant conferences and negotiations among departments clearly slow the pace. The process takes even longer when the policy requires extensive congressional participation and approval. On domestic policy particularly, potential opponents can occupy many "veto points" to block legislation within Congress; such veto points are the numerous House and Senate committees and subcommittees that hold hearings on legislation, and the floor debate and votes in both chambers. Should both houses of Congress pass the legislation, the differences between the two versions must be compromised and resubmitted to both for final approval. Only then does the legislation go to the president for his signature. Should he veto it, it will go back to Congress, which can override his veto, but only by a two-thirds vote. The advantage of this slow process lies with those who oppose specific pieces of legislation, for it is difficult to jump all the hurdles along the route to final approval and enactment. This process, admittedly, is more common in domestic than in foreign policy because of the president's greater responsibility and freedom to make policy in the latter area.

Given this slow negotiating process, the formidable obstacles, and the great effort needed to pass a major new policy, old policies and the assumptions upon which they are based tend to survive longer than they should. For example, policy based on the assumption that the Communist world is cohesive continued even after the Sino-Soviet conflict had surfaced in the late

1950s, and preoccupation with strategic deterrence persisted long after the need for a limited war capacity had been painfully demonstrated in the Korean War.

Appealing Packaging and Shared Images

Sixth, the competition among various groups involved in the policy-making process is also likely to place a premium on attractive and appealing packaging and advertising. This means that, rather than presenting complex and sophisticated reasons for a particular policy position, proponents will try to make it more acceptable by oversimplifying the issues, tying their "product" up with a pretty moral ribbon, and overselling it by insisting that it will definitely solve the buyer's problems. The sellers may indeed exaggerate these problems in order to enhance the buyer's feeling that he or she absolutely needs the policy "product" being offered.[14] In foreign policy, the presentation of issues in terms of anticommunism versus communism, good against evil, hardly promoted understanding of the real issues involved and made it difficult to adjust policies to a changing international environment and a changing Communist world. The threat of Russia, simply as a great power, was real enough; that it was Soviet Russia constituted an even greater threat. Nevertheless, the menace of "international communism" was exaggerated, partly because it was an effective device for persuading various governmental agencies to accept certain policies, and partly because it helped mobilize majority support in Congress and the country for those policies.

More specifically, the commonly shared assumptions upon which the decision makers operate—their biases, or images—help to determine which decisions are made. If anticommunism is the bias—the belief that communism is expansionistic and aggressive, that it must be contained rather than appeased, that military force is to be used to prevent its expansion wherever and whenever necessary—those who try to "sell" their preferences in terms of these "shared images" have a good chance of putting together a majority coalition. On the other hand, those whose preferences are not in line with these assumptions lose out. Other writers have said the same thing more crudely: they have suggested that the toughest anti-Communists, posing as the most vigorous "operators," have won the bureaucratic and wider governmental struggle. Bureaucratic *machismo* is the easiest policy to sell. Those who question the shared images lose influence.

All proponents of specific policy preferences especially seek to sell their "products" to their potentially best customer—the president. His approval and support are obviously decisive. The competition is therefore intense. All important policies are likely to come to the president's attention and to require decisions. The president, as the sole nationally elected official, holds the only position in which all the many considerations bearing on policy can be balanced against one another. There is no other point at which conflicting views and interests so converge; in his office, nonmilitary and military programs, foreign policy and domestic claims conflict, are weighed, and are compromised. Yet the very fact that the president is central to the policy-making process and that demands upon his time are pressing means that he cannot give many issues the time they deserve. He may have little time for them until a crisis erupts. A remote problem will usually be ignored or receive scant attention until it reaches a crisis level, and then it will be managed.

Public Debate

Seventh, one further characteristic of American foreign policy decision making is that it is usually public. In a democracy, public involvement is inevitable. Although policy may be made primarily by the executive, its limits are established by public opinion. No British government before 1939 could have pursued a deterrent policy toward Hitler, and no American government before the fall of France in 1940 could have intervened in Europe to preserve the balance of power. In general, however, public opinion tends to be permissive and supportive as far as presidential conduct of foreign policy is concerned.[15] The public is aware that it lacks information and competence in this area, which is remote from its everyday involvement, and it looks to the president for leadership. Only when setbacks arise or painful experiences pinch the voters will public opinion on foreign policy be expressed, the limits of public tolerance broadly clarified, and perhaps the party in power punished. Even though most of the time public opinion does not function as a restraining factor, policy makers are always aware of its existence, however amorphous it may be. Because mass opinion does not tend to take shape until *after* some foreign event has occurred, it can hardly serve as a guide for those who must make policy; nonetheless, the latter will take into account what they think "the traffic will bear," because they know that if a decision is significant enough, there is likely to be some crystallization of opinion and possibly retribution at the polls.

Reflecting public opinion, Congress was, until the Vietnam War, usually *supportive* of the president's foreign policy. Throughout most of the post-World War II period, Congress had followed the president's lead, and its role had been essentially reactive and peripheral. The executive initiated and devised foreign policies, which Congress rarely rejected; primarily, its role was to legitimate those policies in either the original or amended form.[16] The record of American foreign policy since 1945 shows clearly that all major presidential initiatives, from the Truman Doctrine and the Marshall Plan to the Alliance for Progress and the Treaty on the Nonproliferation of Nuclear Weapons, have been accepted and supported by Congress.[17]

This situation has changed since the Vietnam War, however, as Congress became both more skeptical of presidential wisdom in foreign policy and more assertive on the many issues facing the United States with the Soviet Union, its allies, and Third World countries. Several presidents were condemned as being "imperial"; they were said to have abused the powers of their office, especially the war powers in going to war in Korea (Truman) and Vietnam (Kennedy, Johnson, and Nixon). Congress passed legislation to restrict the president's use of force and subversion. Above all, Vietnam raised Congress' sense of confidence and competence in foreign policy. It surely could do no worse than the executive branch. Issues were more thoroughly debated, executive judgments were less readily accepted and more critically evaluated, and restraints were imposed on the president's ability to use the armed forces and overt intervention without legislative knowledge and consent. Nevertheless, presidential leadership, while more constrained than before Vietnam, still exists. President Ronald Reagan has been especially skillful in setting the overall foreign policy agenda, even when many in Congress have disagreed with specific policies and tried to constrain his conduct of foreign affairs.

THE ANTIBALLISTIC MISSILE AND 'STAR WARS'

The seven characteristics discussed in the preceding section by no means exhaust the characteristics of the foreign policy process in the federal government, but they are the most obvious. In 1983 President Reagan proposed a strategic defense of the United States, known as the Strategic Defense Initiative or "Star Wars," as his critics dubbed SDI. To place SDI in some perspective, we will look back at the original antiballistic missile decision made by President Johnson during the 1960s. That decision provides a keen insight into governmental decision making and is especially important because the ABM treaty, incorporated into SALT I, became part of the controversy over SDI. The United States' deterrent policy, as we know, was based upon a second-strike or retaliatory capability (see Chapter 8). It was generally assumed that a defense of either the missiles or U.S. population was unnecessary. The deterrent forces were supposed to be invulnerable to a first strike and, if they were, the assumption was that the people in the cities were also protected; no enemy would be foolish enough to attack America's cities if the United States could retaliate in kind. A first strike made sense only if U.S. retaliatory capability could be destroyed; therefore, as long as this force was invulnerable, the enemy would be deterred.

From time to time, however, the defense of either the population and/or America's land-based deterrent forces has been proposed and debated publicly. The first time was in 1967 when Secretary of Defense Robert McNamara made a speech that seemed to make no sense because it included contradictory themes. On the one hand, he denounced the ABM as an expensive venture that would stimulate another round of the arms race and leave the United States less secure in the end; on the other hand, he proposed building a "small" ABM system against the Chinese (who were verbally more radical and militant than the Soviets but had few ICBMs)! To say the least, it was a strange speech, but it reflected the opposing views on defense within the government.[18]

Principal Contestants and Arguments

On the anti-ABM side were McNamara and Secretary of State Dean Rusk, plus the ACDA. All believed that the decision to deploy an ABM would mean a spiraling and costly arms race and would destroy all chances for a stabilization of the American-Soviet deterrent balance. McNamara believed that a U.S. decision to deploy the ABM would virtually preclude any possibility of initiating arms-limitations talks with the Soviets. He was also skeptical of the technical feasibility of the proposed ABM. The secretary, however, was in the minority within his own department on this question. The Pentagon's Office of Defense Research and Engineering, concerned with development of modern weapons, and its Office of Systems Analysis both supported deployment of ABMs. Within the Defense Department only the Office of International Security Affairs agreed with McNamara.

The principal bureaucratic supporters of the ABM were the armed services, which, in contrast to the situation on most defense issues, were united in their support. Although the army, navy, and air force each "saw a different face of ABM and reached different conclusions," [19] the very fact of this interservice agreement is worth noting. Earlier, McNamara had exploited divisions among the services to prevail on issues of defense spending. Their united front, however, compelled him to go above the services and to appeal directly to the president. Different departments and, indeed, different bureaus within the various departments thus all saw different "faces" of the same ABM problems and had different stakes in the issue.

Congress, too, had interests and stakes in the ABM debate. Supporting the services were several senior members of the Senate Armed Services Committee, including Chairman Richard Russell, John Stennis, and Henry Jackson. These senators were supporters of Johnson's Vietnam policy and had been friends of the president when he served as the Democratic majority leader in the Senate during the administration of Dwight Eisenhower. Indeed, Johnson had served with them on the Armed Services Committee and trusted their judgment. He was particularly close to Russell.

In arguing their case, proponents and adversaries often emphasized different factors. Supporters stressed the fact that the Soviets had already developed such a system, that it threatened the U.S. deterrent capacity, and that the ABM would save American lives. They argued that an ABM would provide Americans with an extra bargaining chip in any negotiations on a mutual defensive-weapons limitation. Opponents, on the other hand, were less concerned about the Soviet deployment of ABMs than about the potential for a new arms race. Another factor that concerned them was the price tag. Estimates of the cost of an ABM system ranged from $30 billion to $40 billion.

The View from the Presidency

In the presence of these opposing pressures, no decision was possible at a level below that of the president. But a president's stake in any given issue is always greater than that of anyone else, and the White House perspective is different from that of any other player. For one thing, unity in the administration is a primary goal, and, therefore, Johnson sought to avoid, if at all possible, a direct break with McNamara. They were already at odds over the war in Vietnam, but the president still valued his secretary of defense too highly to reject his advice out of hand. McNamara viewed the ABM choice as a direct confrontation between himself and the Joint Chiefs of Staff, and he would have seen a decision to deploy the system as a rejection. In addition, a president also needs congressional support for foreign and domestic policies. A negative decision on the ABM would have alienated key senators who were also long-time friends and colleagues whose opinions and convictions Johnson respected. But presidents are also more than the chief officers of their administrations and chief architects of legislation to be submitted to Congress. They are also the head of their parties and concerned with reelection and their parties' fortunes at the polls. The Republicans were already talking of an ABM gap, threatening to do to the Democrats what Kennedy and Johnson had done to Nixon in 1960—to use the potentially powerful charge of neglecting the nation's defenses. Johnson, who had not yet decided not to seek reelection, had to be worried about the possible impact of such an accusation.

But there are still other considerations and pressures that presidents must take into account. They know that in the final analysis they are responsible for the country's security and protection; others can advise them, but only presidents can make the required decisions, and it will be they who will be judged not only by the people but also by history.[20] And that judgment is their ultimate stake. They will be compared to others: George Washington, Thomas Jefferson, Abraham Lincoln, Theodore Roosevelt, Franklin Roosevelt, Harry Truman; no one who occupies the White House (or its equivalent in other countries) can possibly ignore his or her future historical reputation. Johnson, whose involvement in Vietnam was already arousing popular and congressional criticism and casting doubt on his place in history, was keenly interested in a major arms-limitation agreement with the Soviet Union to help his standing at that time and in the future; he needed a major breakthrough in the area of international reconciliation.

Minimal Decision Making

In this situation, given the "pitfalls" he saw in the ABM issue and the stakes he had in it, yet buffeted by conflicting pressures, the president would have preferred to make no decision at all and to allow the proponents and opponents of ABM to reach some kind of compromise among themselves. The problem of gaining presidents' support for one side or another thus is not limited to reaching them, but also includes persuading them to make decisions. Their tendency is to procrastinate or to make only a "minimal decision." Warner Schilling's apt phrase, in connection with another important presidential decision, is "how to decide without actually choosing":

> The President did make choices, but a comparison of the choices that he made with those that he did not make reveals clearly the minimal character of his decision. It bears all the aspects of a conscious search for the course of action which would close off the least number of future alternatives, one which would avoid the most choice.

> One of the major necessities of the American political process [is] the need to avert conflict by avoiding choice. The distribution of power and responsibility among government elites is normally so dispersed that a rather widespread agreement among them is necessary if any given policy is to be adopted and later implemented. Among the quasi-sovereign bodies that make up the Executive the opportunities to compel this agreement are limited.[21]

Truman put this need for gaining support to decide policy in fewer and more picturesque words: "They talk about the power of the president, how I can push a button and get things done. Why, I spent most of my time kissing somebody's ass." [22]

The critical question thus became: What would be the nature of the ABM compromise? At least part of the answer became clear in a meeting between Johnson and McNamara and Soviet premier A. N. Kosygin at Glassboro, New Jersey, in June 1967. Johnson pressed the Soviets for a date for the opening of arms limitation talks. This declaration would allow him to postpone the decision on the ABM. But Johnson did not receive an answer. Kosygin described the Soviet ABM system as defensive and therefore unobjectionable. As a weapon that would save lives, it was, in the Soviet premier's judgment, a good weapon that would not destabilize the arms balance and was not a proper subject for strategic arms limitation talks. McNamara's principal objection to the ABM had been refuted by the Soviets. Consequently, Johnson no longer saw the ABM as a possible stumbling block to beginning arms limitations talks.

Johnson then made his minimal decision: to adopt a small anti-Chinese ABM system. McNamara announced the decision in his contradictory speech: on one hand, he said that the most effective way to overcome a Soviet ABM was to saturate the defense with offensive missiles, suggesting that the Soviets could do that to the United States as well. On the other hand, should the Chinese be as irrational as their militant revolutionary rhetoric suggested, a small ABM system might help to deter a strike. In one sense, McNamara had won a victory against the Joint Chiefs of Staff and ABM supporters in Congress, who favored a nationwide anti-Soviet (and more expensive) ABM system. The very fact that he made the speech showed that he had by no means suffered a major defeat on this issue. He could view the president's decision as leaving open the possibility that the system would never be deployed at all if the Soviets would later agree to limitation of mutual defensive weapons. The administration had come out *not* in support of deployment but only in support of increased funding for the procurement of certain ABM parts that would require a long lead time. But the administration had publicly changed its position, and that represented a victory for ABM supporters in Congress and the Joint Chiefs. Proponents of the more extensive system viewed the change in the administration's position as a hopeful sign and expected that they could accomplish their goal later. There were as yet no "winners" or "losers." Compromises had prevented that.

The fight over ABM continued into the Nixon administration. At the time, the large Soviet missile buildup, which overtook the United States in the number of ICBMs and to which there seemed no end in sight, was perceived as an increasing threat to U.S. ICBMs. The fear was that the number of missiles plus the numbers of warheads the Soviets would place on them over the coming years, would give the Soviet Union a first-strike capability. President Nixon, therefore, switched the ABM from defending cities to defending ICBMs. This would counter the possibility of a successful Soviet strike and help keep the mutual deterrent balance stable.

Nixon also wanted a bargaining chip for the Strategic Arms Limitation Talks (SALT). There had been no U.S. missile buildup, so he could not trade some of them against the larger number of Soviet missiles. The ABM might be the only thing the United States could trade. As it turned out, the strategic arms limitation treaty placed a low level on ABMs (the Soviets had already deployed about sixty around Moscow), so low that the United States abandoned it. At the same time, as noted earlier, the two powers agreed to freeze all offensive systems for a five-year period during which they would negotiate mutually acceptable ceilings on all strategic systems.

Note that neither Johnson nor Nixon were strongly committed to a strategic defense. Johnson was concerned that the Republicans would make the lack of an ABM defense a key issue in the next presidential election, and he was also worried about his relations with his own secretary of defense and several senators whose friendship and support he needed for his Great Society domestic reform program. Nixon, in his turn, wanted a bargaining chip in an attempt to slow the Soviet strategic buildup at a time the public and Congress were in an antimilitary mood and the defense budget had reached its lowest percentage of the gross national product since 1950, *before* Korea.

President Reagan, by contrast, was committed to a strategic defense and did not think of SDI as a bargaining chip.[23] More than that, Reagan's advice on some sort of defensive system had come from outside the government, primarily from Edward Teller, the "father" of the hydrogen bomb. There was no pressure within the executive branch or Congress for SDI. Indeed, at the time of the president's speech proposing it, the Defense Department's assessment of a strategic defense was that it was not feasible. Many in the administration were surprised by the president's speech. Unlike McNamara's speech, which reflected the various bureaucratic pulls, the SDI conclusion to Reagan's speech apparently had been added by the president at the last moment. The idea had not been submitted to the relevant departments for their examination, analysis, and recommendations. The president surprised most members of his administration.

This is not to say that SDI reflected a momentary whim. Reagan had expressed concern both before and immediately after he became president that the U.S. population was not being defended. The strategic balance when he assumed the office of presidency was, in his judgment (although not that of most experts), shifting in the Soviet Union's favor. Whether it was, the president worried about the long-term consequences of a deterrent balance that depended upon the threat of wiping out millions of Russians. Would it not be better to build deterrence upon a defense that would shoot down incoming missiles and protect, rather than incinerate, the civilian population of *both* countries? And, if the Soviets were behind us technologically, he offered to share SDI technology with them.

The security of the United States was not Reagan's only reason for advancing SDI. The president was seen by many as a militant anti-Communist crusader; he and other members of his administration had made a number of careless comments about nuclear war. Moreover, members of the administration had talked of *nuclear war fighting, limited nuclear war,* and of *prevailing* in a nuclear exchange, not of deterrence. Partly because of all this talk, partly because détente had ended and the United States was embarking on a major modernization of its strategic forces, many people feared a possible nuclear war. There was a striking emphasis on "the day after" by the media, physicians, Catholic and Methodist bishops, and other groups; the nuclear freeze movement gained a large public following. In these circumstances, the president was on the defensive, especially against the bishops who denounced the immorality of using, if not possessing, nuclear weapons—which, in effect, was tantamount to saying that nuclear deterrence was immoral. SDI placed the president back in charge and gave him the initiative in the nuclear debate. If nuclear war was bad for the nation's health and bad for Americans' souls, why not propose a nuclear shield that would protect the population? Instead of mutual assured destruction—that is, the mass destruction of America's and Russia's people—why not seek mutual assured survival?

With the president its principal advocate, a constituency for SDI began to build, especially among the civilians in the Defense Department, led by Secretary Caspar Weinberger. The question then became which SDI? Was it the president's SDI, which looked forward to the day when offensive nuclear forces would be eliminated, or the SDI that would defend ICBMs, thus not eliminating deterrent forces but providing them with greater protection against a hostile first strike? The difference remained unresolved, the issue being ignored with the comment that the former was the long-range goal, the latter merely the intermediate one. There was also a contrary view that was skeptical of SDI's feasibility but, because the Soviets appeared very concerned that it might work, wished to trade SDI deployment—as distinct from research—for a radical cut in Soviet ICBMs. The administration had long professed that this was its goal in the Strategic Arms Reduction Talks (START) because U.S. ICBMs were vulnerable to a Soviet first strike. Whether SDI would remain nonnegotiable or, like the ABM before it, become a bargaining chip to achieve such a cut remains to be seen. President Reagan's meeting with Soviet leader Mikhail Gorbachev in Iceland in 1986 did not resolve this issue. The Soviets offered a 50 percent cut in strategic forces for a postponement of SDI deployment; only research in laboratories would be allowed. Reagan turned the deal down because the Soviets demanded strict adherence to the ABM treaty.

ABMs had already become a source of controversy in the United States because the Reagan administration had given the treaty a "broad" interpretation so that SDI testing could go forward. The treaty in fact bans the development and testing of space-based or mobile defenses. The administration called that the "narrow" interpretation, but felt compelled to stick to it because of widespread congressional and popular support for the treaty. Since 1972 the treaty has become a symbol of superpower arms control cooperation, as well as a restraint on defensive weapons. If the treaty were violated, an offensive arms race could be needed to overcome such defenses. Nevertheless, the administration seemed bent on getting rid of the treaty to perfect its missile defenses. Or was the administration's hostility toward the ABM treaty, like its denunciation of SALT II in 1986, part of a strategy to pressure Moscow to trade a deep reduction in Soviet strategic forces for some yet unknown concessions on SDI?

THE VIETNAM WAR: INTERVENTION AND DE-ESCALATION

The analysis of the formulation of ABM and SDI policies furnishes a good illustration of how decisions emerge from the interactions of multiple actors with conflicting perspectives. The Vietnam War, that traumatic conflict that tore the United States apart at home and resulted in its first defeat abroad, provides an excellent example of the incremental nature of policy making.

Early Aid

A commitment of sorts to Vietnam had begun during the period when the French were still engaged in establishing their colonial control after World War II. After an initial period of nonsupport for this colonial effort, the United States during the Truman presidency began to supply economic and military assistance to the French, in return for French support of American policy in Europe, an area of vital interest to the United States. This aid was stepped up after the outbreak of the Korean War in 1950 and the subsequent Chinese military intervention in Korea. It was during this period, just after the birth of Communist China, its alliance with the Soviet Union, and the outbreak of war in Asia, that the bipolar image of the world held by American policy makers seemed most valid (it was certainly shared by leaders in Moscow and Peking). As the expansion of any Communist country's power was viewed in Washington as an expansion of Soviet power and as a gain of power and security for the Soviet Union was equated with a loss of power and security for the United States, it is not surprising that the possible loss of Vietnam was viewed in terms of a domino image. If Vietnam fell, the rest of the dominoes in Southeast Asia were expected to fall. The other countries of the area would turn toward pro-Communist neutralism or would themselves be taken over because of Communist revolutions or Communist pressures from outside.

Gradual Intervention

The second Indochinese war, which began in the late 1950s, was to be a problem for the Kennedy administration. But Kennedy, during his years in office, never really had time for Vietnam. He was swamped by other foreign policy crises, as well as by an increasingly troubled domestic racial situation. Cuba, Berlin, Laos, Vienna (where he had a tense confrontation with Khrushchev), and the Alliance for Progress preoccupied him. Vietnam was not then in crisis, though the situation was deteriorating. Because of Kennedy's essentially bipolar view of the international conflict, his perception of "wars of national liberation" as instigated by Moscow's leaders, and his desire to avoid further foreign policy setbacks and accusations of being soft on communism, he committed military advisers to help shore up the Saigon government and avoided making a clear-cut decision about what to do next.

After Kennedy's assassination in 1963, Johnson also sought to procrastinate, hoping for the best even while planning escalation. His time was devoted primarily to restoring domestic calm and unity in the wake of national tragedy, to persuading Congress to pass the largest volume of progressive domestic legislation in a single term in the century, and to the forthcoming election campaign.[24] The president's experience, expertise, and interests were domestic. His attempt to win time and to convince Hanoi's leaders of the futility of persisting in the struggle may have been understandable, but in the meantime South Vietnam was nearing total collapse. By early 1965 procrastination was no longer feasible. The choice had become one of either withdrawing from the war or expanding and escalating it. Johnson at that point decided to follow what he and his advisers saw as a continuing American commitment to the Saigon government begun by Truman, continued by Eisenhower, escalated by Kennedy (who sent 16,500 American military personnel), and expanded further by himself when he ordered air strikes against the North after an alleged attack on two American destroyers in the Gulf of Tonkin in August 1964.[25]

Johnson had inherited a situation in which only ad hoc decisions had been taken in response to immediate problems. Only piecemeal economic and military commitments had been made; each constituted the minimally necessary step to prevent a Communist victory.[26] At no point were the fundamental questions and long-range implications of increasing involvement in Vietnam analyzed: Was South Vietnam vital to American security? Would its fall simply lead to consolidation of one country under a nationalist leader, or would it be the first step in the communization of all of Southeast Asia? Did the political situation in South Vietnam warrant or preclude American intervention? Were political conditions both in the United States and in South Vietnam conducive to effective military action? How large a commitment would the United States be required to make, and what costs should be expected? What role should the Saigon government and its forces play? If these questions were even asked by President Kennedy and other responsible foreign policy officials as they sent military advisers into South Vietnam— thus creating a powerful military bureaucracy in Saigon that had a vested interest in succeeding and that fed deliberately overoptimistic reports to the Washington government in order to acquire more arms, men, and money— the answers did not provide guidelines for the policies that ultimately were followed. The assumption was that South Vietnam was vital, a test of the credibility of American commitments and power. Policy was built upon that assumption. The approach was incremental, and, as the overall situation deteriorated badly, Johnson, like Kennedy before him, continued to react to the symptoms of the problem and to apply short-range solutions: covert operations, followed by increasingly frequent "retaliatory" air strikes against North Vietnam, followed again by round-the-clock bombing, and, when none of these measures had compelled Hanoi's leaders to "cease and desist" in the South, finally the use of American ground forces in South Vietnam.

Yet counterrevolutionary warfare is political first and military second; its success depends upon the development of relations of trust and support between the government and its citizens. The failure of Vietnam's president, Ngo Dinh Diem, followed by the American agreement to depose him and tacit acceptance of his murder, convincingly demonstrated that the political situation in South Vietnam was not conducive to success. Indeed, intervention frequently was advocated to boost the South Vietnamese government's morale! But how American intervention could infuse that government with the will and determination to fight was never discussed: Should morale in Saigon not have been a prerequisite for American help? In any event, a sizable contingent of American advisers was already involved, and American prestige had been committed. The war had already become "Americanized."

Military Pressures and Escalation

Up to that point incrementalism had occurred within the broader context of cold war perceptions of American policy makers, from Truman to Johnson; then the pressure from the military intensified the general pressures and escalated the conflict. Indeed, it may well be that the tendency to oversell—

along with Johnson's obvious political interest in ending the war as quickly as possible, certainly by 1968—placed military considerations uppermost. Despite much evidence to the contrary, the military considered the war a modified, limited form of conventional warfare. For example, in 1962, General Earle Wheeler, then army chief of staff and later chairman of the Joint Chiefs of Staff, said:

> Despite the fact that the conflict is conducted as a guerrilla warfare, it is nonetheless a military action.... It is fashionable in some quarters to say that the problems of Southeast Asia are primarily political and economic rather than military. I do not agree. The essence of the problem in Vietnam is military.[27]

American commanders in Vietnam agreed. Vietnam would not be much different from Korea, they claimed. It was just a matter of Americanizing the war a little more than it already had been. The Joint Chiefs of Staff assured Johnson that a couple of years and 200,000 troops should do it. (This sloppy evaluation by the JCS and its advice to Johnson contrasted strongly with the approach of Matthew B. Ridgway, former army chief of staff, who in 1954 had sent teams to Vietnam to calculate what would be required if the United States should intervene. His report to President Eisenhower, a former general himself, was a principal reason why the United States had stayed out of the war at that time.)[28]

There were few opposing arguments from other senior officials or organizations. Secretary of State Rusk largely concurred in the conclusion that a war in Vietnam would be essentially conventional and that, because it would be a military affair, he should stay out of it. Walt Rostow, the presidential assistant for national security affairs, was particularly concerned with the problem of supplies infiltrated from external "sanctuaries" and therefore suggested that only attacks on the "ultimate source of aggression" would bring such a war to an end. What opposition there was came from the CIA (whose predictions were remarkably accurate), the State Department Bureau of Intelligence and Research, Assistant Secretary for Far Eastern Affairs Averell Harriman, and some of the bright "young turks" he had recruited, as well as certain Pentagon military officers working on counterrevolutionary strategy and tactics. But their efforts were in vain, and gradually most of them, especially in the State Department, lost their jobs, were replaced, or simply lost much of their influence, as did the CIA.[29]

In these circumstances, it is not surprising that the air force managed to oversell the benefits of bombing North Vietnam. The U.S. Air Force was essentially fighting for its identity. In World War II strategic bombing had had limited effects until the late stages; during the Korean War, the tactical bombing of the Communist supply lines also had had only limited impact. The air force regarded Vietnam as a test. In the words of a former assistant secretary of defense for public affairs, "the bombing of North Vietnam became the symbol of the importance of air power."[30] Even though Vietnam, an unindustrialized country with external sources of military supplies and supply routes often hidden by jungles, was a poor place for such a test, the air force was determined to prove itself at least capable of tactical interdiction. Rivalry with the navy, which was trying to demonstrate the capability of its carrier-based air power, only intensified the resolution of the air force to prove itself and to demonstrate its superiority over the navy. Both services thought future missions, morale, and budgets to be at stake. Indeed, the navy had supported the air force bombing campaign in its initial stages in order to participate in it and demonstrate *its* competence in its rivalry with the air force. But why did the army support the air force? The answer appears to be "so that the air force could fail"! General Wheeler and General William Westmoreland probably knew that air power could hardly accomplish the goal of compelling North Vietnam's leaders to desist in the South or cutting off the supplies flowing to the South.[31] But the very failure of the air force would mean greater subsequent military commitment so that the United States would be successful, and this commitment was bound to mean the involvement of the army. The president, on the other hand, hoped that bombing would frighten the North Vietnamese into desisting and that the conflict could be won "on the cheap" without the heavy losses that would be involved if ground forces were committed. Diverse actors with different interests thus formed a coalition in support of the bombing. If air power then failed, as the navy and army expected, they would be sent in; if it succeeded, as the president hoped, the ground war with its heavy casualties would be unnecessary. For all, however, the

> bombs were dropped as a necessary political prerequisite to the engagement of American troops. . . . [F]or those who had to concern themselves with the bounds of public opinion, the function of air power was to fail openly so that large scale losses of American lives on the ground in Asia could be justified.[32]

Public Opinion, Congress, and Deescalation

The role of public opinion in decision making was also apparent in the Vietnam War, certainly more so than in connection with the ABM. But, apart from Johnson's general knowledge from the Korean War that a long war would not be popular, public opinion was not much of a guide at the beginning of the escalation of U.S. involvement in Vietnam. What was important throughout 1964 and the first months of 1965 was how the president perceived public, as well as congressional, opinion: Johnson's conclusion was that neither the general public nor its representatives in Washington wanted the United States "to lose South Vietnam to communism." This view placed an especially powerful pressure on Democratic presidents, as they saw it; as a party they were sensitive to charges of having "lost" China. The president did not want to be placed on the defensive by such a charge and to jeopardize the rest of his foreign policy and perhaps his Great Society program as well. Johnson certainly received widespread popular approval for his action during the Gulf of Tonkin episode, and, by and large, he continued to receive majority approval during the initial period of open intervention.

Nonetheless, Johnson never went to the public or to Congress to explain either the seriousness of the situation in South Vietnam or the necessity of large-scale American intervention, which probably would mean a long war. Increasing intervention thus was not accompanied by much public debate, nor was there much public criticism. But the longer the war lasted, the greater the dissatisfaction with American policy became, and the more extensive and intensive were the criticism and dissent expressed both in Washington and in the country as a whole. Administration officials frequently sought to justify their policy; officials who disagreed sometimes resigned but, more often, leaked their points of view or expressed them to newspaper correspondents. Members of Congress also articulated their views. Well-known Democratic and Republican liberals voiced their increasing opposition. Senator J. William Fulbright, chairman of the Senate Foreign Relations Committee, held hearings to give a forum to critics, frequently former government officials and concerned and informed scholars.[33] The senator also offered his own wide-ranging critique of American foreign policy in two books.[34] In addition, Robert Kennedy, President Johnson's principal rival in the party, as well as a powerful critic of the war, had entered the primaries to contest Johnson's renomination. The Republican leadership, on the other hand, increasingly attacked the administration for its military restraint and favored the full unleashing of American air power; in these attacks, they were joined by a number of powerful conservative Democrats, especially in the Senate.

Criticism and dissent, of course, were not limited to Washington. Support, but more often opposition, spread to many college campuses and cities. Demonstrations, teach-ins, marches, vigils, and, on occasion, riots accompanied this widening opposition. The administration, of course, counterattacked.[35] General Westmoreland and Ambassador Henry Cabot Lodge, for example, were called home and appeared before Congress and the public—on shows such as *Meet the Press*—where they presented optimistic forecasts and belittled Viet Cong achievements. The president gave speeches defending his policies and denouncing his critics as "nervous Nellies." After the Viet Cong's Tet offensive had revealed the fallaciousness of official optimism about victory, the criticisms grew even more widespread and pointed. The press was by then very hostile, and congressional opposition to mobilizing larger reserves and an even more costly war was clear.

The immediate issue around which much of the debate revolved was the bombing of North Vietnam. It had been initiated to bring Hanoi leaders to the negotiating table, but its cessation became the precondition for holding talks about ending hostilities. On March 31, 1968, the president announced a halt to bombing, which, most significantly, signaled an end to the previously open-ended commitment to South Vietnam, implicitly acknowledged repudiation of military victory as the objective, and began the shifting of ultimate responsibility for the conduct of the war to the Saigon government. He also announced that he would not run for a second term. This example leaves little doubt that, the longer an issue persists, the more congressional and public opinion will become involved. In contrast to a crisis that can be managed by the president and a few of his most trusted advisers and is over quickly, in a limited war legislative and mass opinion pressure policy makers to end the war either by escalation or withdrawal once the conflict becomes protracted and appears to show "no light at the end of the tunnel." President Nixon, succeeding Johnson in 1969, had no choice about continuing the war as an "American war" with U.S. ground troops. He had to get out; the only questions were when, how, and on what terms. It took four years to get the answers.

A CRITIQUE OF THE DECISION-MAKING APPROACH

'Where You Stand Depends on Where You Sit'

The slogan sums up the decision-making approach. In contrast to first-level analysis in which each state is considered as a unitary actor, in the decision-making literature each government is viewed as composed of multiple actors. Instead of regarding foreign policy as a product of a rational choice among several options that maximize a chosen value such as security, analysts focus on the many conflicting values, perspectives, and interests that result in a specific policy. Two scholars have gone so far as to suggest that

> a focus on the international objectives of a state is essentially misleading, in that the participants' attention primarily is focused on domestic objectives. . . . [T]he scholar requires an understanding of a nation's domestic political structure and of its national security bureaucracy in order to explain or predict the foreign policy actions it will take.[36]

The "games nations play" are the result of the "games bureaucrats play" to enhance their personal influence, as well as that of their own agencies; the same can be said of nonbureaucratic players.

For example, a noncrisis decision like the one President Johnson made to go ahead with the anti-Chinese ABM system is not easily explained in terms of the rational-actor model. The decision might not have been made had it not been for congressional and bureaucratic pressures, for the president really was primarily interested in starting the SALT talks and avoiding an expensive and possibly destabilizing arms race. But, even for a president, there are constraints. Specifically, Johnson wanted to avoid a break with influential senators, as well as with his own secretary of defense, over the ABM. The political costs of such breaks were greater than he was willing to pay. He also had to consider the probable electoral costs if he decided to avoid any ABM decision. So he compromised, he made a minimum decision, satisfactory to all the chief actors, who all thought that they had "won" the president over to their position. In fact he had kept his options open for a more definitive decision in the future.

The president was merely one of many players. To be sure, he may be "first among equals," but his ability to impose his decisions is limited by the other players. Johnson did not want an ABM but was pushed into taking the first minimal step toward acceptance of it. He could not ignore the Joint Chiefs' coalition with powerful leaders in the Senate. A president, according to the organizational charts of the executive branch, may be "the boss" and presumably can order the Joint Chiefs, for example, to do or not to do what he chooses. In reality, the relationship is more equal, and the participants bargain with one another. The close relation between military leaders and a powerful congressional committee and ranking legislative leaders or the threat of resignation by military leaders (which reportedly occurred during the Vietnam War) makes it necessary for the president and the secretary of defense to persuade their subordinates.

It must often seem to presidents that statements about their enormous power are exaggerated; they are very sensitive to its limits. President Jimmy Carter, it has been reported, could not even get rid of the mice in the Oval Office! When a couple of mice ran across the carpet one evening, a call went out to the General Services Administration (GSA), the official housekeeper for federal buildings. A few weeks later, however, another mouse apparently died in the wall of the Oval Office. The resulting odor became quite noticeable just as the president was preparing to receive a foreign dignitary. An emergency call was made to the GSA, but it refused to come back. It insisted that it had already exterminated all the "inside" mice in the White House! The mouse that had died must have come from the outside and was therefore a matter for the Department of the Interior. The department, however, refused jurisdiction because the mouse had died *in* the White House. President Carter exploded: "I can't even get a damn mouse out of my office." [37]

Thus the "foreign policy" decision that emerges from this bureaucratic system, which in turn is set in the broader governmental system,

> is not necessarily "policy" in the rational sense of embodying the decisions made and actions ordered by a controlling intelligence focusing primarily on our foreign policy problems. Instead it is the "outcome" of the political process, the government actions resulting from all the arguments, the building of coalitions and countercoalitions, and the decisions by high officials and compromises among them. Often it may be a "policy" that no participant fully favors [for the system is] more responsive to the internal dynamics of our decision-making process than to the external problems.[38]

This point certainly raises a key issue: How can one judge the substance of policy—its wisdom and its potential contribution to the security of the country—by the fact that a consensus has been reached among multiple actors? As Robert L. Gallucci has aptly observed, "A wretched policy for the United States may be perfectly understandable as a superb compromise among competing interests, but it must ultimately be evaluated as undesirable by some criteria of what is in fact good for the nation." [39] But what is the point of making such a judgment if policy is not made rationally?

Overemphasis on Constraints on the President.   Three criticisms may be made of the governmental politics model. The first is that it overemphasizes the constraints, especially within the executive branch, on presidential leadership and initiative in foreign policy.[40] Rational policy making, as we have noted, is the key to crisis decision making, but it can also occur in other areas of policy, especially when policy makers strike out in new directions. The reasons why the presidential perspective is preeminent in what Robert Art calls "innovative policy" were exemplified in the first Nixon administration. First, the president can seize for himself certain specific policy areas, such as SALT, negotiating the end of the Vietnam War, and rapprochement with China. "The ability of bureaucracies to independently establish policies is a function of Presidential attention. Presidential attention is a function of Presidential values. The Chief Executive involves himself in those areas which he determines to be important." [41] In contrast to the emphasis in the bureaucratic model, it is more correct to say that, to a large degree, bureaucratic influence is a function of presidential—and, it ought to be added, congressional and public—inattention. The bureaucracy plays its largest role in routine daily affairs, its smallest during crises.

A president can also structure the organization for making foreign policy decisions. Nixon did so by making Kissinger his special assistant for national security affairs, a kind of supersecretary of foreign affairs, giving him a fairly sizable staff, and clearly ignoring the established bureaucracy or subordinating it to the White House. Kissinger's staff asked the established bureaucracy for policy papers on certain areas or policies, gathered them together, evaluated the alternatives, and, once the president had selected the best policy, sent the decision back to the bureaucracy for implementation.[42] The Nixon experiment was an attempt to institutionalize rational policy making. As he said, "I refuse to be confronted with a bureaucratic consensus that leaves me no options but acceptance or rejection and that gives me no way of knowing what alternatives exist." [43] Foreign policy decisions that are primarily the result of bureaucratic infighting and compromise, rather than of rational responses to perceived external challenges and problems, were to be avoided. Bureaucratic interests, though not totally eliminated, were greatly limited and subjected to presidential perspectives and interests—at least, until the Watergate scandal in 1973.

A president also chooses cabinet officials. And, although they do represent the various bureaucracies and agencies in government, they also normally reflect the president's general views and values, for they owe their places in the history books to the person who appointed them and they are likely to feel some gratitude. They know too that the president, if displeased, can fire them and that most of them are expendable. Moreover, the president can ignore them; the president decides to whom to listen and whom to exile from the policy-making circle. Kennedy chose to heed McNamara, rather than Rusk. Nixon, during his first term, listened to his national security assistant and paid little attention to his secretary of state. During the Vietnam War,

Johnson eliminated powerful and respected men such as McNamara from his administration when they increasingly opposed his bombing policy, and he simply did not listen to others. He appointed Rostow as his national security assistant, because Rostow reportedly filtered out dissenting views before they could reach him. An observer who has stressed the constraints on Johnson admits: "Lyndon Johnson was surrounded, or more accurately, *surrounded himself with loyal advisors who supported him in what he thought he had to do. . . . The President himself was clearly setting the tone and choosing isolation.*" [44] In other words, the president was structuring his decision-making environment. The limits on presidential initiatives and preferences in crises and other key policy areas probably have been overstated in much of the literature on decision making. For confirmation, one need but look at President Reagan's SDI initiative to realize the presidential freedom to initiate new policies. Examples of policies employing force include American involvement in Nicaragua, Grenada, and Lebanon.

Exaggeration of Conflict.   A second criticism of the governmental politics model is that it also exaggerates the degree of conflict among the multiple actors. Throughout the cold war the policy makers, both senior political appointees and bureaucrats, tended to be united, despite their varying institutional responsibilities, by a set of commonly shared assumptions or "shared images" of the external world. These shared images minimized conflict and indeed usually made the executive branch and government appear similar to the unitary actor that the government-politics model had rejected. Among these images were the central conflict in the international system between the United States and the Soviet Union (or the "free world" versus the "Communist world"); the expansionism of the Soviet Union; that an increment to Soviet power meant a loss to American power whenever a country "fell"; and because of its great economic and military strength, the United States had the responsibility for defending the free world (*free* meaning non-Communist, not necessarily democratic); and preserving the balance of power against the Soviet Union (and after 1949 a potentially strong China as well). These images were held throughout the long cold war period and were reassessed only after the disaster in Vietnam had left the country no choice but to reexamine the assumptions that had led it into war. These assumptions, amounting to a virtual consensus among policy makers, help to account for the tenacious continuity of American foreign policy over two decades, and they set outer boundaries to the conflicts within the government. Those who did not fully share this set of images and thus did not take a tough anti-Soviet stand were generally unable to influence policy.

Psychologist Irving Janis argued that conformity has been especially common within the relatively small circle of leading officials because there is a great deal of pressure to conform to "groupthink." [45] "Dovish" views were suppressed among a group whose members were trying to impress one another with their toughness. The more cohesive the group, the greater is the inclination of its members to reject a nonconformist; the greater the desire to remain in the group, the more likely an individual with doubts about a proposed policy will supress them and go along with the majority. If others too suppress their reservations, there will exist a consensus on policy, but clearly it is a superficial one. More serious, however, is the possibility that, because searching questions about the policy are not asked, the nation may be embarking on a course reflecting poor collective judgment and greater risk taking.

Although a broad scope of agreement may exist on an overall policy such as the containment policy toward the Soviet Union, more often than not specific policies are debated. And while there are notable exceptions, such as the attempt to overthrow Fidel Castro at the Bay of Pigs and the incremental involvement in Vietnam, this is less true of Soviet-American crisis situations. In other words, U.S. policy makers have sometimes felt very confident of success when they were confronting what they believed to be a second- or third-rate opponent. But when facing the Soviet Union directly, they have been very cautious and keenly aware of the dangers of a miscalculation. The risks and costs of not examining all alternatives, not scrutinizing the assumptions upon which they were acting, were all too clear—and a clear antidote to groupthink. But it is true that, during the period from the declaration of the Truman Doctrine to the Vietnam War, top government officials argued for an expanded American role far more frequently than their organizational or bureaucratic interests dictated.

Indeed, it is questionable whether, for "senior players," the axiom "where you stand depends on where you sit" indicates what positions they will take in a policy debate. Rather, as Art has stressed, institutionally motivated policies are primarily reflected in decisions

> which we may call the "bread and butter choices" that determine the long-term competitive position of an institution, decisions regarding career advancement in the foreign service or in the uniformed military, budgetary allocation decisions, or those regulating the instruments by which institutions will carry out the tasks assigned to them (like weapon systems for the services).[46]

Downplaying Executive-Legislative Relations.

Third, and perhaps most important, the governmental politics model may also have downplayed domestic politics. Although it has been generally true that in foreign policy Congress has supported presidential policy, largely because of a shared set of images, electoral politics particularly has intruded. In 1960 Kennedy ran on the issue of the "missile gap"; in 1968 Johnson (though he did not run) did not wish to hand the Republicans the "ABM gap" issue. Summit meetings and major diplomatic achievements may be necessary in themselves, but they are also related to important—especially presidential—elections, as the timing of such announcements or events frequently demonstrates.

The critical foreign policy conflicts induced by domestic political considerations have, as noted, come in the area where general executive-legislative collaboration has broken down: for example, Far East policy in the wake of Nationalist China's collapse and the birth of Communist China. Subsequent Republican efforts to exploit this issue electorally led to vicious attacks on the Democrats for deliberately selling out China, continued indictments for the "fall of China," and widespread hunts for alleged traitors in government, universities, and the media, who had "sold China down the river." Two-party competition and the natural temptation to exploit the in-party's setbacks paralyzed U.S. policy in Asia for two and a half decades. Later presidents— even Eisenhower, the moderate Republican, but particularly Democratic presidents—remained fearful of improving relations with Communist China and, more broadly, of any "appeasement of communism." Knowing the great difficulties that they would have with Congress if they defied it, they were afraid to take any but strong positions against Communist China. Johnson, informed within hours of becoming president that South Vietnam was collapsing, responded that he was not going to be the president who saw Southeast Asia go the way of China. Congressional and public pressures—or the anticipation of such pressures—have repeatedly affected the content of American foreign policy.

The price in this instance obviously has been very high. Had China been recognized in early 1950, the Truman administration might have made a more accurate assessment of how the Chinese would react to U.S. intervention in Korea. Had American observers been stationed in Beijing, the Kennedy and Johnson administrations would have known that the war in South Vietnam was not part of "Asian communism's expansionism," and U.S. involvement might have been avoided. More broadly, better relations with China could have been established earlier in order to exploit the increasing Sino-Soviet conflict and help bring about a parallel reduction in American-Soviet tensions.

Instead, it took a long and costly war and a new president, a Republican, to open the door to the People's Republic of China. The years of fighting in Vietnam, with no victory in sight, had made the country weary of inflexible anticommunism. President Nixon himself believed that the problems of Asia could not be solved without Communist China; certainly the Vietnam War could not be ended unless Beijing's leaders would help. As an old-time "hardliner," Nixon could hardly be accused of coddling or appeasing Communists. But he still was concerned about the possibility of strong opposition from within his own party (Vice President Spiro Agnew, for example, was opposed) and from the powerful China lobby, which had long been organizing support in this country and in Congress against Communist China and mobilizing support for the Nationalists. He, therefore, made the decision alone and confronted the bureaucracy, Congress, and public opinion with a *fait accompli*, announcing that he would visit the People's Republic. The subsequent trip symbolized a basic and irreversible change of direction in American foreign policy. In terms of enhancing American security, this rapprochement was highly rational and a long-overdue adjustment to the changing international distribution of power. For far too long, U.S. policy toward China had been hostage to domestic and congressional politics.

With the erosion of the cold war's anticommunism, executive-legislative conflict has affected virtually the whole range of American foreign policy. Congressional questioning and criticism of presidential policy grew during the 1970s and 1980s.[47] The Vietnam War discredited the leadership of the executive branch and its expertise in foreign policy; the Watergate scandal and other revelations of CIA and FBI added to congressional determination to be more assertive in foreign policy in a period in which there was no new consensus on which to base policy. In the early days of détente, when Kissinger wanted to supplement the military stick with economic carrots to induce more restrained Soviet behavior, the Senate added the Jackson-Vanik amendment on Jewish emigration from the Soviet Union to a commercial treaty. Because of this attempt at interference with its domestic affairs, Moscow rejected the treaty, thus reducing the economic leverage the United States might have gained. The Senate also almost undermined the Panama Canal treaties and failed to vote on SALT II, which effectively killed it. Congress as a whole imposed an arms embargo against Turkey to punish it for its 1974 invasion of Cyprus, which had been intended to protect the Turkish minority there from a Greek attempt to unite Cyprus with Greece. But Congress as an institution is more splintered than ever before: party loyalty has further declined; the authority of committee chairmen has been reduced; and subcommittees have become more numerous and influential. Given this high degree of decentralization, pressure groups have gained increased access to congressional policy makers. Especially active are ethnic groups, such as Greek-Americans, who favor the Turkish embargo, and American Jews, who have dissuaded American governments from pressing Israel to be more conciliatory in the Middle East peace negotiations. It has become much more difficult for a president to mobilize Congress on foreign policy issues; obstructing, delaying, changing, and even emasculating policy have become considerably easier.

Congress is especially sensitive to any presidential use of force. It was frequently charged that Vietnam had been the result of the United States having becoming the "world's policeman." After the war, Congress was anxious to cut back on the nation's role in the world; the United States had become overextended and it should reduce its commitments. Although a powerful country, the United States was not omnipotent and its obligations around the world needed to be brought into line with its "limited power." Because the global role of the United States was identified with the growth of presidential power, the president after all being the nation's chief diplomat, as well as commander in chief, Congress needed to exercise its check and balance role more assertively. Indeed, a popular theme in the 1970s was that presidents had acted like "imperial presidents" and ignored or deceived Congress, and this had to be ended.

The War Powers Resolution played a key role. This resolution, which required the president to consult with Congress before using American forces, and required Congress to approve presidential use of force after sixty days (or the troops would have to be withdrawn), was intended to avoid future wars like Korea and Vietnam. While Congress generally has gone along when presidents have used force in a quick, effective, and successful manner as in the invasion of Grenada or attacks on Libya as reprisals for terrorism, Congress has been far more reluctant to support the president if the actions appeared to involve the United States in "another Vietnam." Thus President Reagan's support for the government of El Salvador and, even more so, his support for the "contras" in their war with the Sandinista government in Nicaragua, have not always received the backing he wanted. Congress was far more willing to question presidential wisdom than in the pre-Vietnam days, especially when it feared that if the assistance did not work, U.S. troops might have to be sent in to do the job. Thus the focus of policy-making studies today is less "bureaucratic politics" than "governmental politics," encompassing both the executive and legislative branches.

Conclusion

It therefore appears that the decision-making approach requires three major modifications. First, analysts must distinguish between different kinds of foreign policies. Second, the approach should be more focused on presidential preferences, the shared images among the principal executive and legislative officials, and especially domestic politics, including public opinion, party competition and executive-legislative relations (or similar officials and institutions in other countries). Third, while not denying the relevance of governmental politics, decision making must be viewed within the broader context of the state system. The making of foreign policy decisions occurs within this international context, which places limits upon what countries can do, regardless of their power, their leaders' ideological commitments, public opinion, and the conflict among the many actors involved in the decision-making process.

OTHER SYSTEMS, DIFFERENT DECISION MAKING

Although we chose the U.S. government as an example of pluralistic decision making, the same type of analysis can be applied to other goverments, such as the Soviet or British. In the Soviet Union, too, there are multiple bureaucratic interests behind the totalitarian facade: party, army, policy, and industrial and agricultural interests, all of which have representatives to voice their needs and grievances. Conflict among these actors occurs within the Soviet government, but, in contrast to the U.S. government, these bureaucracies are unable to mobilize interest groups or legislative and popular support for their policy preferences. Outside the government, groups such as the trade unions do not have autonomous existence; the Communist party controls all appointments, promotions, and demotions. Obviously, the party also commands the legislature; the Supreme Soviet has no independent role. And there is no freely expressed public opinion in the Soviet Union. Within overall party control and the context of "shared images," however, bargaining and coalition building presumably occur in the making of foreign policy.[48] In the succession struggle for leadership in the Soviet Union, a new leader seeking to consolidate power, needs the support of the several bureaucracies, especially that of the military; support is not likely to be given to a leader contemplating major reductions in the military budget or steep cuts in arms. If Gorbachev follows precedent, there will be no major arms reductions until he feels he can no longer be challenged by other contenders. Indeed, until then he cannot afford to be too conciliatory in foreign policy, not just in arms control, although he may well appear so in his speeches and proposals. It is critical that his fellow citizens believe he is "tough." Only when he is firmly established in office and has appointed enough of his own people to high places can he find compromise solutions with the United States if he wishes and impose these on his colleagues. No Soviet leader since Joseph Stalin, whose tyrannical rule is remembered vividly, has been more than a first among equals. He may be very much the first but he rules by consensus.

But once leaders like Nikita Khrushchev, Leonid Brezhnev, or Gorbachev have consolidated power, they have the ability to lead. However, they cannot make too many mistakes. Khrushchev, after succeeding Stalin, was too innovative for his colleagues. His attempts to stir up the Soviet economy led to a number of different proposals which, quite apart from their merit, met strong opposition. Among other things, Khrushchev wanted to cut the bureaucracy in Moscow and send officials out to the provinces. The bureaucrats, however, preferred life in the Soviet capital. Other programs aroused opposition because they were seen to weaken the bureaucracies' central control and preeminence. Khrushchev's humiliation in the Cuban missile crisis—which his colleagues blamed on his "adventurism," a dirty word in the Soviet political lexicon—plus what were called his "harebrained" domestic schemes led to Brezhnev's *coup d'état* in 1964.

Still, a comparison between the American and Soviet political systems suggests that making a decision in the Soviet Union is considerably easier than in the United States, and, once a decision is made, it is easier to execute. One need but note how, despite illness and old age, the doddering Brezhnev hung on to power for five years until his death, even though critical decisions, especially with regard to the economy, needed to be made. Once in power, if they do not arouse too much opposition from colleagues and the many bureaucracies, Soviet leaders are hard to dislodge. Khrushchev may be the exception rather than the rule, although he served as a warning to his successors not to be too innovative or upset vested interests.

In the British government many of the same types of players are involved in the policy process as in the United States. A prime minister's cabinet colleagues represent different institutional and socioeconomic interests, and he or she cannot neglect the members of the party in the House of Commons because the party cannot be led where it does not want to go. (And the Labour party in Commons has in recent years been greatly influenced by militant constituencies outside of Parliament.) Kenneth Waltz has argued that a prime minister tends to avoid innovations in policy unless he or she has gained support from cabinet colleagues and the rank and file.

> Seldom will a prime minister try to force a decision widely and genuinely unpopular in his party. The prime minister must preserve the unity of the party, for it is not possible for him to perpetuate his rule by constructing a series of majorities whose composition varies from issue to issue [as in the United States]. He is, therefore, constrained to crawl along cautiously, to let situations develop until the necessity of decision blunts inclinations to quarrel about just what the decision should be.[49]

Incrementalism thus seems to be as much a feature of British as of American government. Continuity of policy, slow adjustment to changing circumstances, policy deadlocks, and evasion of issues until they become crises are features in common. Innovations in policies are few and far between.

Nevertheless, unlike the U.S. government, the British government is not characterized by a separation of powers or, more accurately, separate institutions sharing powers; rather, the executive and legislative branches are unified. And because, unlike American political parties, British parties are disciplined, the prime minister has much greater control over his or her members in the House of Commons than a president has over party members in Congress. It would be inconceivable for a British prime minister to sign a SALT II treaty and then not see it gain Parliament's approval. When a prime minister and the cabinet decide to adopt a policy, they can mobilize the necessary party support and carry out that policy. A president can never be sure.

DECISION MAKING AND INTERNATIONAL NEGOTIATIONS

Finally, the decision-making model holds several important implications for international negotiations. One is how difficult they are likely to be, quite apart from the substantive complexity of the problems being negotiated. For misunderstandings, failures of communication, disappointed expectations, and even failure of the negotiations between two countries may easily result when each set of national policy makers for foreign affairs is so deeply engaged in its own bureaucratic and governmental "games" that it does not pay sufficiently close attention to the other side. Even between countries as close as Britain and the United States, negotiations can break down because the Londoners are negotiating with other Londoners and Washingtonians with other Washingtonians in trying to formulate policy. "Their self-absorption is a day-and-night affair; it never flags. They calculate accordingly and act to suit. So do their counterparts inside the other government. ... Comprehension of the other's actual behavior is a function of their own concerns."[50]

Another implication is that in negotiations between two highly bureaucratized governments, the international negotiations are only one of *three* simultaneous sets of negotiations—including those between the governments and those among the various participants within each government. Kissinger used to complain that it was easier to negotiate with the Soviet leaders than to negotiate an agreed-upon policy in Washington; this complaint may be common in many capital cities.[51]

Notes

1. See Roger Hilsman, *To Move a Nation* (Garden City, N.Y.: Doubleday, 1967); Graham Allison, *The Essence of Decision* (Boston: Little, Brown & Co., 1971); Morton H. Halperin, *Bureaucratic Politics and Foreign Policy* (Washington, D.C.: The Brookings Institution, 1974); and Morton H. Halperin and Arnold Kanter, eds., *Readings in American Foreign Policy* (Boston: Little, Brown & Co., 1973).

2. Henry A. Kissinger, *Nuclear Weapons and Foreign Policy* (New York: Harper & Row, 1957).

3. Graham Allison, "Conceptual Models and the Cuban Missile Crisis," *American Political Science Review* (September 1969): 716.

4. Oran Young, *The Politics of Force* (Princeton, N.J.: Princeton University Press, 1968), 6-15; Charles F. Hermann, ed., *International Crises* (New York: Free Press, 1972); and Phil Williams, *Crisis Management* (New York: John Wiley & Sons, 1976).

5. For the Cuban missile crisis, see Elie Abel, *The Missile Crisis* (New York: Bantam Books, 1966); Alexander L. George et al., eds., *The Limits of Coercive Diplomacy* (Boston: Little, Brown & Co., 1971); and Robert F. Kennedy, *Thirteen Days* (New York: W. W. Norton, 1967).

6. Tad Szulc, "Behind the Vietnam Cease-Fire Agreements," *Foreign Policy*, Summer 1974, 39-40.

7. Henry Kissinger, *White House Years* (Boston: Little, Brown & Co., 1979), 1097-1123, 1165-1200; and Richard Nixon, *RN* (New York: Grosset & Dunlap, 1978), 363.

8. For elaboration, see John Spanier and Eric M. Uslaner, *How American Foreign Policy Is Made*, 4th ed. (New York: Holt, Rinehart & Winston, 1985).

9. Bernard C. Cohen, "The Influence of Non-Governmental Groups in Foreign Policy-Making," in *Readings in the Making of American Foreign Policy*, eds. Andrew Scott and Raymond Dawson (New York: Macmillan, 1965), 96-116.

10. See Samuel P. Huntington, *The Common Defense* (New York: Columbia University Press, 1961), 123ff., for formulation of defense policy.

11. Hilsman, *To Move a Nation*, 552-555.

12. Charles E. Lindblom, "The Science of Muddling Through," *Public Administration Review*, Winter 1959, 79-88.

13. Theodore J. Lowi, *The End of Liberalism* (New York: W. W. Norton, 1969), 160-161.

14. Ibid.

15. Francis E. Rourke, "The Domestic Scene," in *America and the World: From the Truman Doctrine to Vietnam*, ed. Robert E. Osgood (Baltimore: Johns Hopkins University Press, 1970), 147-188; William R. Caspary, "The 'Mood Theory': A Study of Public Opinion and Foreign Policy," *American Political Science Review* (June 1970): 536-547; and James N. Rosenau, "Foreign Policy as an Issue Area," in Conference on Public Opinion and Foreign Policy, *Domestic Sources of Foreign Policy* (New York: Free Press, 1965).

16. Former secretary of state Dean Acheson offers some amusing and somewhat sarcastic comments on the way Senator Arthur Vandenberg helped to legitimate presidential policy during the crucial days after 1945. *Present at the Creation* (New York: W. W. Norton, 1969), 223.

17. James A. Robinson, *Congress and Foreign Policy-Making*, rev. ed. (Homewood, Ill.: Dorsey Press, 1967). For the early postwar period, see Daniel S. Cheever and H. Field Haviland, Jr., *American Foreign Policy and the Separation of Powers* (Cambridge, Mass.: Harvard University Press, 1952), 106ff. For the post-Vietnam days, see John Spanier and Joseph Nogee, eds. *Congress, the Presidency and American Foreign Policy* (New York: Pergamon Press, 1981).

18. This section relies heavily on the account by Morton H. Halperin, "The Decision to Deploy the ABM: Bureaucratic and Domestic Politics in the Johnson Administration," *World Politics*, October 1972, 62ff. For the development of the ICBM, see Edmund Beard, *Developing the ICBM* (New York: Columbia University Press, 1976).

19. Halperin, "Decision to Deploy the ABM," 67-69.

20. Halperin, *Bureaucratic Politics and Foreign Policy*, 81-82.

21. Warner R. Schilling, "The H-Bomb: How to Decide Without Actually Choosing," in Halperin and Kanter, *Readings*, 253, 255.

22. Quoted in *Time*, Jan. 25, 1968.

23. *New York Times*, March 4, 1985.

24. Tom Wicker, *JFK and LBJ: The Influence of Personality upon Politics* (Baltimore: Penguin, 1969), 151-182.

25. See *New York Times*, June 13 and 14, 1971; and Joseph C. Goulden, *Truth Is the First Casualty: The Gulf of Tonkin Affair—Illusion and Reality* (Chicago: Rand-McNally, 1969).

26. Chester L. Cooper, *The Lost Crusade* (New York: Dodd, Mead, 1970); Hilsman, *To Move a Nation*, 413ff.; and, especially, David Halberstam, *The Best and the Brightest* (New York: Random House, 1972), a good though not unbiased account of the incremental nature of the American commitment. See also Daniel Ellsberg, *Papers on the War* (New York: Simon & Schuster, 1972); and Paul M. Kattenburg, *The Vietnam Trauma in American Foreign Policy, 1945-75* (Brunswick, N.J.: Transaction Books, 1980); Larry Berman, *Planning a Tragedy* (New York: W. W. Norton, 1983); and Wallace J. Thies, *When Governments Collide* (Berkeley: University of California Press, 1980).

27. Hilsman, *To Move a Nation*, 426.

28. Melvin Gurtov, *The First Vietnam Crisis* (New York: Columbia University Press, 1967).

29. Halberstam, *The Best and the Brightest*, 361-378.

30. Quoted by Robert L. Gallucci, *Neither Peace Nor Honor* (Baltimore: Johns Hopkins University Press, 1974), 72.

31. Ibid., 49.

32. Ibid., 53.

33. *The Vietnam Hearings* (New York: Vintage, 1966).

34. J. William Fulbright, *Old Myths and New Realities* (New York: Vintage, 1964); and Fulbright, *The Arrogance of Power* (New York: Vintage, 1967).

35. The battle within the executive branch over Vietnam, and especially over halting the bombing of North Vietnam, is told in some detail by Townsend Hoopes in *The Limits of Intervention* (New York: McKay, 1969).

36. Halperin and Kanter, *Readings*, 3.

37. *New York Times*, Jan. 15, 1978.

38. I. M. Destler, *Presidents, Bureaucrats, and Foreign Policy* (Princeton, N.J.: Princeton University Press, 1972), 64, 74.

39. Gallucci, *Neither Peace Nor Honor*, 142.

40. For the critique that follows I am indebted to Robert J. Art, "Bureaucratic Politics and American Foreign Policy: A Critique," *Policy Sciences* 4 (1973): 467-490; and Stephen D. Krasner, "Are Bureaucracies Important?" *Foreign Policy*, Summer 1972, 159-179.

41. Krasner, "Are Bureaucracies Important?" 168. Krasner's emphasis on the state as a unified actor pursuing its "national interest" is elaborated in his *Defending the National Interest* (Princeton, N.J.: Princeton University Press, 1978).

42. Destler, *Presidents, Bureaucrats, and Foreign Policy*, 118-152; for a more recent and favorable assessment, see Robert J. Strong, *Bureaucracy and Statesmanship* (New York: University Press of America, 1986).

43. Ibid., 100. Also see Alexander L. George, "The Case for Multiple Advocacy in Making Foreign Policy," *American Political Science Review* (September 1972): 751ff.

44. Gallucci, *Neither Peace Nor Honor*, 99, 105 (emphasis added).

45. Irving Janis, *Victims of Groupthink* (Boston: Houghton Mifflin, 1972).

46. Art, "Bureaucratic Politics and American Foreign Policy," 484.

47. Spanier and Nogee, eds., *Congress, the Presidency and American Foreign Policy*; John Rourke, *Congress and the Presidency in U.S. Foreign Policymaking*; and William P. Quandt, *Camp David* (Washington, D.C.: The Brookings Institution, 1986).

48. Zbigniew K. Brzezinski and Samuel P. Huntington, *Political Power: USA/USSR* (New York: Viking, 1964), 196-197; and Darrel P. Hammer, *The Politics of Oligarchy*, 2d ed. (Boulder, Colo.: Westview Press, 1986). Also see Arnold L. Horelick, A. Ross Johnson, and John D. Steinbruner, *The Study of Soviet Foreign Policy: Decision-Theory-Related Approaches* (Beverly Hills, Calif.: Sage, 1975), for an evaluation of decision-making models as they have been used in studying Soviet politics.

49. Kenneth N. Waltz, *Foreign Policy and Democratic Politics* (Boston: Little, Brown & Co., 1967), 59-62.

50. Richard E. Neustadt, *Alliance Politics* (New York: Columbia University Press, 1970), 66.

51. For the Reagan administration's internal fights on arms control, see Strobe Talbott, *Deadly Gambits* (New York: Alfred A. Knopf, 1984).

CHAPTER 17

Foreign Policy: A Conclusion

THE FOCUS ON PERCEPTION

The single thread that runs through the preceding chapters is *perception:* the way nations, political elites, specific bureaucracies, and individual leaders see the world, the way they define vital issues and the international role their countries should play. It quickly becomes clear that although states see the same "reality," they view it differently. The United States and the Soviet Union see their conflict with each other as the primary one; the threat each poses to the other is the key to their foreign policies. National security is their critical concern. The less-developed countries (LDCs) view the struggle for modernization and a more equitable distribution of status and wealth in the state system as the chief issue. Their focus is on the North-South tensions; the East-West competition is of secondary interest to them, although they are not reluctant to use it to advance their goals. The resulting emphasis on conflict of interests in international politics should not, therefore, be surprising. Individual policy makers view the world through the lenses of the organizations of which they are members, and their policy recommendations tend to reflect their organizations' interests. The result is a conflict of interest within government and competition among multiple versions of what is truly in the national interest.

Policy makers, whether their views are filtered through national, elite, or bureaucratic lenses, will be persuaded that the way *they* see the world is correct. It is the *other* policy makers in the other states who see the world incorrectly. Each nation can justify its perceptions and policies and marshal an impressive array of facts and historical analyses. How can that be? Do the facts not speak for themselves? We can, after all, neither ignore them nor mistake

556

them. Facts are facts. Or are they? The truth is that a fact as such does not possess any meaning. What gives it meaning is the perceptual framework of an observer influenced by personal experiences, beliefs, and interpretations of history. It is this image of the world that leads the observer to select that specific fact from the thousands available. The question is why that particular fact was chosen. The answer is our selective vision, which not only allows us to pick out some facts and ignore others—those picked are consistent with our way of viewing the world—but also gives meaning to those we select, thereby allowing us to understand the world better. Policy makers too, influenced by national values and experience, elite ideologies, or bureaucratic interests, have their *Weltanschauung,* or world view. A common perception of "reality," therefore, is unlikely.

The emphasis on national, elite, and bureaucratic perceptions minimizes the role of individuals. If the Marxist-Leninist ideology of Soviet leaders focuses on underlying economic forces and class conflict, then the resulting stress on the competition between socialist and capitalist states—a competition that is long term, irreconcilable, and can end only when communism triumphs worldwide—means that a change of leaders is not therefore the critical issue Americans often believe it is. The American hope that the Soviet succession will yield a more moderate and reasonable leader who will end the cold war, or at least greatly reduce tensions, is bound to be disappointed. Although new leaders may change the emphasis on this or that policy, the critical issue will be the set of perceptions they share with their predecessors. For all Soviet leaders, this means a focus on power, struggle, unceasing competition, military strength, and expansion of Soviet influence to advance the new postcapitalist international order of which the Soviet Union will be the nucleus.

Thus, the personality of Mikhail Gorbachev, who ultimately succeeded Leonid Brezhnev, is less important than his views, which will continue to emphasize the rivalry with the United States. He may seek a respite from this rivalry to deal with other problems, such as the poor performance of the Soviet economy or the continuing problems of Eastern Europe. But whether the tensions of the postdétente "cold war II" at times decline or rise, the conflict and competition between the superpowers will not end. Gorbachev may have a personal style different from his predecessors' and be more adept at public relations, but that is likely only to make him a shrewder opponent. He has unprecedented military power at his command, greater than that of any previous ruler in Russian history. But, in addition to domestic problems, Gorbachev faces difficulties over the cohesion of the Soviet bloc. The problem is that Soviet policy has transformed all of the Soviet Union's Eurasian neighbors into adversaries: China, Japan, Western Europe, and even Eastern Europe, if it could free itself of Soviet control. Finally, Gorbachev confronts a reinvigorated United States, and what he especially fears is that the United States, already industrially more advanced, may be on the verge of a techno-logical quantum leap as a result of President Ronald Reagan's Strategic

Defense Initiative. For SDI's implications go far beyond the military to affect the political, economic, and scientific statuses of both superpowers as they enter the twenty-first century.

Similarly, as one American administration has succeeded another, the continuity of policies and approach has been striking. With the partial exception of the administration of Richard Nixon, they all have exhibited in varying degrees the characteristics of the American national style, especially the need to moralize power. Was it not characteristically American to delay recognition of Communist China for more than twenty years, as earlier it took fifteen years to recognize the Soviet Union? Was it not typical that, in crusading against communism, Americans too often overlooked the differences between individual Communist states, especially between China and the Soviet Union? Is it really surprising that the United States soon became disillusioned with détente, which it thought meant the end of the cold war, while to the Kremlin it meant a safer environment in which to wage the struggle against world capitalism by supporting movements of "national liberation"? Or that President Reagan, seeking to refocus public and congressional attention on the American-Soviet conflict, would call the Soviet Union an "evil empire" and invoke the Scriptures to present the conflict as one of morality versus sin?

Thinking in terms of *perception* to understand a state's foreign policy is thus very useful. As Walt Rostow once put it, "If the study of national character is an effort to establish a collective personality, the examination of the national style seeks to define how that collective personality reacts to and acts upon its environment." [1] The adoption of a particular foreign policy or role in the world may therefore be easier to understand. Nevertheless, a more detailed analysis of a decision may be required at other levels of analysis. For example, the moralism so characteristic of the American style may partly explain the U.S. decision to delay recognition of Communist China, but it is not a complete explanation. After all, the United States had recognized and dealt with other Communist countries. Therefore, national style analysis needs to be supplemented with a focus on the policy makers themselves and the policy process. In the case of recognizing Communist China, such an analysis would take into account the decline of bipartisanship in U.S. foreign policy, the struggle within the Republican party between the liberal internationalists and conservative nationalists, the lack of appeal of Republican domestic programs to the voters who remembered Herbert Hoover and the Great Depression, the search for a dramatic foreign policy issue to exploit in the upcoming presidential election, and the five consecutive losses the Republicans had suffered at the polls since 1932—the last three under the leadership of liberal internationalists.

The collapse of Nationalist China was a godsend. It could be labeled a Democratic failure and provide the basis for a Republican appeal to the electorate for the stewardship of the nation. In short, a more detailed analysis, focusing on leading executive policy makers, the bureaucracies, Congress, and American electoral politics, is needed to explain the timing of the attacks on the China issue and the hostility and inflexibility of American policy toward Communist China for more than twenty years.

Decision making lends itself well to in-depth case studies and to understanding the decision-making process for specific types of decisions. But focusing on the perceptions of the policy makers allows us to gain a broader perspective of a country's conduct of its foreign affairs.

MISPERCEPTIONS AS THE CAUSE OF WAR

One conclusion frequently drawn from studies that emphasize policy makers' perceptions is that these perceptions are incorrect and therefore are a principal cause for conflict and war. The reason for this is obvious: policy makers act on the basis of subjective images of the world, regardless of what objective reality is. The more distorted their view is, the more likely they are to stumble into trouble.[2]

Nicaragua provides a contemporary example. President Reagan, it is said, is a "cold warrior." He thinks of the United States as leading a crusade against Soviet communism. The Soviet Union was "the focus of evil" in the world and hostile to the West. In Central America, Nicaragua, a self-proclaimed Marxist state, had aligned itself with the Soviet Union and Cuba. The containment of the Communist threat in Central America was the logical extension of the containment policy. According to Reagan, the new regime in Nicaragua had proclaimed its belief in "revolution without frontiers" and, therefore, constituted a threat to American interests in a strategically vital area. The United States was already helping the guerrillas in neighboring El Salvador.

Critics charged that Reagan was seeing the world through a distorted lens and pursuing unsuitable and dangerous policies. The reality was that the Sandinistas had come to power in Nicaragua as a result of political oppression and social injustices committed by the earlier U.S.-supported regime. To attempt their overthrow would drive the Sandinistas, who are not only Marxist but also nationalist and independent, into the arms of the Soviets and Cubans. In short, if the president only had the correct perception of the Sandinistas and stopped his campaign to overthrow them, he could avoid conflict in Central America and another possible Vietnam, as well as attract the regime away from Moscow and Havana.

It is one thing to argue that misperceptions lead to errors of policy, even grave errors on occasion; it is quite another, however, to claim that they are *the* cause of international conflicts and tensions. The latter strongly suggests that *conflicts among states have no real causes and would be resolvable if policy makers would only correct their misperceptions.* Much of this thinking betrays a strong normative bias; namely, if only policy makers perceived each other correctly, there would be peace and relative harmony in the world.

The thinking of Ralph K. White is typical of this school: "Misperceptions might explain how normally sane human beings can unwittingly, without intending the consequences, involve themselves step by step in actions that lead to war."[3] War is thought to erupt only as the result of mistakes. Misperceptions or distorted "cognitive maps" provide the only sensible explanation of why states continue to resort to warfare when the world "desperately wants to avoid it" and where "only a madman could start a war." White, indeed, entitled the opening chapter of his 1968 book "Misperceptions as a Cause of Two World Wars," stating that the two most significant twentieth-century wars resulted from mistakes and that the world would have been better off had they not occurred. (But E. H: Carr wrote that this characteristically Anglo-Saxon view was considered incorrect by the Czechs and Poles, who owed their national existence to World War I; by the French, who had regained Alsace-Lorraine in 1918; and by the Germans, who had regretted only that they had lost the war, not that they had entered it.)[4] Misperceptions of reality, White stresses, can result from any of six kinds of distorted thinking: the image of a diabolical enemy, a virile self-image, a moral self-image, selective inattention, absence of empathy, and military overconfidence.[5]

These six distortions involve black-and-white thinking in which, consciously or unconsciously, evidence is distorted, facts are selected to fit preconceived images, and the interpretation of events is slanted. Such "irrational" thinking is supposedly what creates "unnecessary wars." White admits that not all wars do result from irrationality and that not all devils are imaginary; some "semimad semidevils" are dangerous and must be restrained. And analysts may sometimes, by means of "realistic, evidence-oriented thinking," rather than "biased thinking," arrive at a genuine black-and-white picture.

As all perception is selective, how can we tell when our perceptions are correct and when they are distorted? Winston Churchill was accurate in his perception of Nazi Germany in the 1930s, but few in Britain shared his views; the logical conclusion to his thinking, after all, meant risking another war with Germany. Neville Chamberlain's views seemed far more reasonable: satisfying Adolf Hitler's legitimate nationalistic aims would make it possible to avoid war. Had White been writing during the period just prior to World War II, one suspects that he would have found Churchill's thinking irrational and Chamberlain's realistic and reasonable. In any event, hindsight has made it clear that Chamberlain was grievously wrong. Despite such actual historical experiences, the literature on misperception maintains that it is the cause of conflict and war; correct perception, it seems, prevents strife and preserves peace.

Misperceptions of Secretaries of State

For further confirmation, one need but look at two studies of two prominent U.S. secretaries of state during the early cold war years: Dean Acheson, who served President Harry Truman, and John Foster Dulles, who served President Dwight Eisenhower. Both were key figures in the development and evolution of the containment policy. In a biography of Acheson, Gaddis Smith argued that underlying Acheson's thought and policy advice was "an extraordinarily articulate expression of thoughts which guided American foreign policy for a third of a century after outbreak of the Second World War. An appraisal of Acheson must therefore be an appraisal of the nation's behavior in world affairs for an entire generation." [6] In Smith's interpretation, Acheson's general image of the world and what ought to be the American role in it was shared by his successor Dulles, as well as by Presidents Truman, Eisenhower, John Kennedy, Lyndon Johnson, and Nixon. All were heavily influenced by their generation's experiences and perceptions. Postwar U.S. leaders had been tempered in the crucible of the 1930s; the career of Hitler and the appeasement at Munich, as well as the Nazi-Soviet pact, had made deep impressions on them.

More specifically, this generation had learned from the interwar period that the American isolationist stance had helped to bring on World War II and that American participation in the defense of western Europe after World War I would have helped to deter Hitler. Isolationism no longer seemed a feasible policy; expansionistic totalitarian movements, whether Nazi or Soviet, had to be contained. A second lesson was that appeasement only whets a dictator's appetite—it seemed better to stand firm against demands and "present arms." Soviet policy was expansionist and aggressive and had to be resisted, by force if necessary. "Driven by the ghost of Hitler," [7] of concessions made from a position of weakness, and of failure to match the adversary's military strength, this generation had learned that peace cannot be preserved solely by good intentions and military force.

Acheson approached American-Soviet relations as a deadly contest in which a gain in power for the United States was good and a gain for the Soviet Union bad. Negotiations with the devil were to be avoided. Soviet totalitarianism had to be contained and its expansionist attempts dammed, until some day it mellowed. Inflexible American policies, distrust of all Soviet and other Communist states' aims and interests, and an inability to recognize the diversity within the Communist world were purportedly the results, as was the unnecessary continuation of the cold war.[8]

Whereas analysts such as Smith have attributed misperceptions to drawing the wrong lessons from history, political scientist Ole Holsti has attributed them to other factors. In focusing on Acheson's successor, Secretary of State Dulles, Holsti emphasized his rigid personality and his equally inflexible anti-Communist view. Holsti argued that Dulles drew a distinction between the Soviet state and the governing Communist party, between Soviet national interests and Marxist-Leninist ideology with its universal revolutionary goals, and between the Soviet people and Soviet leaders. The consequence of these distinctions, Holsti claims, was that in Dulles's mind the American quarrel was with the Soviet leaders, whose aims reached beyond legitimate and limited Soviet interests. The United States was not in conflict with the Soviet people, who, had they been represented by a democratic rather than a totalitarian government, would have followed only limited national interests and not global expansionism. Soviet expansionism, in Dulles's view, was the cause of the cold war. The United States had to prevent the spread of "atheistic communism" and be constantly on guard against Communist attempts to lull the West.

Given Dulles's black-and-white image of the world—and this is of central importance to the misperception approach—all incoming information had to be filtered through his particular perceptions: what fitted his preconceived image was accepted, and what did not fit was filtered out. The image thus remained intact. *Psychologic* is the term sometimes used to describe this tendency to see what we want to see and to reject contrary evidence; psychologists call it a "reduction of cognitive dissonance." On the basis of Dulles's public statements, Holsti argues that various Soviet pronouncements and moves, including a major reduction in the size of the Soviet army during Dulles's tenure as secretary of state, were not recognized as possible concessions and attempts to relax tensions. They served only to reinforce his preexisting views of the Soviet Union and were interpreted as signs of Soviet weakness and attempts to win a respite in order to recoup strength for a more effective and successful struggle with capitalism. A more flexible, less suspicious personality, Holsti has suggested, might have been more receptive to new and conflicting information; presumably, this kind of person might also have made a more serious and sustained effort to test Soviet intentions and perhaps to bring about what is now popularly known as détente.

Misperceptions of Nations

Sometimes, instead of attributing misperceptions to individual leaders' images or personalities, analysts attribute them to nations as a whole. Nations, claims John Stoessinger, "live in darkness." Great gaps appear between image and reality as they respond not to realities but to fictions—what former senator William Fulbright called myths—that they themselves have created. "[G]reat nations struggle not only with each other, but also with their perceptions of each other." [9] These misperceptions are not easily changed. As in pluralistic decision making, with its incremental development of policy, change comes mainly after disasters like the Vietnam War; only at such moments are old perceptions and policies reexamined. In the absence of disaster, however, Chinese, American, and Soviet self-images and images of one another and other states remain intact. Clearly, nations are in need of "light."

One popular version of this theme is that of the "mirror image": [10] two adversaries find it impossible to resolve an arms race, for example, because they bring to the negotiating table the distrust and fear that they have acquired as opponents. Each believes that it represents wisdom, virtue, and morality and that the other is the embodiment of evil seeking its destruction. The United States views the Soviet Union as a Communist dictatorship that exploits the masses at home and is bent on a global crusade for communism. The Soviet Union is equally convinced that the United States is a dictatorship of the bourgeoisie that has enslaved the proletarian majority and seeks to export capitalism by force. Americans, of course, know how false this image of the United States is. At the same time, the Soviets claim that they do not exploit their masses, that the austerity of the period of intensive industrialization is being replaced by increased attention to the welfare of Soviet citizens, and that in international politics they seek only to be left alone to complete their industrialization. Their large armies and powerful rockets are needed only because of the threat of American attack (paralleling the American claim that military forces are needed only to deter Soviet attack). On the basis of these distorted images, both act belligerently, thus bringing the world to the precipice of utter destruction.

As Erich Fromm has said, each side views the other "pathologically"—in terms of paranoia, projection, fanaticism, and Orwellian doublethink.[11] Fromm and others think of war and peace in terms of individual psychology and see war as a deviation comparable to personal psychotic behavior. In such a framework, there is no objective reason for conflict, which exists only because of distorted perceptions, unhealthy attitudes, and outmoded ways of thinking.[12] If only political leaders would abandon such "dysfunctional" thinking, nations would no longer misperceive one another; they would then see one another as defensively oriented, harboring no expansionist aims, possessing only peaceful intentions.

Why Are Policy Makers Not Smarter?

How do we know whether policy makers are being misled by their perceptions? One difficulty in analyses like those applied to Acheson and Dulles is that they involve reconstructions from public statements of how individual policy makers saw reality in general and certain situations in particular. A more serious problem is that of knowing whether a policy maker's image of an adversary can be attributed to a rigid personality, religious attitudes, false historical analogy, or thinking based on experience in the state system. Was Acheson's historical analogy between Joseph Stalin and Hitler really that far-fetched in the years between 1945 and 1950? Was it based on false perceptions or correct perceptions of Stalin's behavior? Did not Stalin's brutal takeover of Eastern Europe; the show trials, executions, and disappearances of non-Communist leaders; and his unending vilification of the West create the widely held perception of him as cruel and inhuman, seeking to expand Soviet power westward? If, in fact, Stalin had only limited security aims, then was he himself not responsible for Western misperceptions?

Were Dulles's moralizing and anticommunism really determined by his personality and religious views or were they simply means of mobilizing congressional and public backing for a foreign policy that historically has received such support when it has drawn moral distinctions and crusaded against evil? Even if one were to grant that Dulles was unduly rigid in his foreign policy, was he not also responding to constant attacks upon the softness of American foreign policy from the dominant right wing of the Republican party in Congress and to the Republican administration's desire to unify the party and avoid the kinds of attacks that had paralyzed the Truman administration's ability to conduct foreign policy after 1950? [13]

How much of the strongly anti-Soviet, anti-Communist stance of Acheson and Dulles should be attributed to personality or domestic politics and how much of it to external conditions—to a system characterized by a high degree of mistrust? One gains the sense from the literature that many of the analysts who stress misperception are merely *substituting their own judgments for those of the policy makers.* As critics of official policy, they tend to attribute that policy to the distorted views of the decision makers and therefore conclude that the remedy is to correct these distortions. Each analyst could paraphrase Professor Higgins of the musical comedy *My Fair Lady:* "Why can't the policy makers be as smart as I?" If those who formulate policy were more flexible, continuously testing reality and adjusting their perceptions to that reality (as defined by the critics), there would presumably be less and possibly no reason at all for conflict.[14] It cannot be denied that decision makers, like most individuals, see the world through distorted lenses and by and large select the facts that confirm their preconceptions. But it is also true that, "if we consider only the evidence available to a decision-maker at the time of decision, the view later proved incorrect may be supported by as much evidence as the correct one— or even by more." [15] The evidence is often ambiguous and subject to more than one interpretation. Alexander George noted:

> For example, when the investigator disagrees with the policy a leader continues to pursue despite evidence of its mounting costs, he is more likely to judge that leader as rigid and stubborn than when he supports that policy. Similarly, a leader who takes a firm stand and draws the line in disputes with political opponents may be judged to be engaged in highly adaptive behavior by an investigator who believes that such behavior is required by the situation; but the same behavior may be judged to be irrationally aggressive by a different investigator whose system of values leads to a different perception of the requirements and dangers implicit in the same situation.[16]

CORRECT PERCEPTIONS AND WAR

Instead of claiming that false images cause or greatly magnify conflict, it might be more correct to conclude the opposite hypothesis: *conflict among states usually demonstrates not that the adversaries misunderstand one another but that they understand one another only too well.* While Neville Chamberlain misperceived the nature of Hitler's aims, Britain tried to appease Hitler; once the prime minister's perceptions had been proved erroneous by events, however, and he saw Hitler for what he really was, Britain declared war on Germany. The British prime minister's incorrect perception of Hitler and his attempts to come to an understanding thus avoided conflict for several years, giving Nazi Germany time to build up its armed forces and expand its strategic position. Had Chamberlain understood Hitler's aims earlier, and risked war before Germany strengthened its military and expanded its territory, the world might have been spared a war—or, at least, a long war.

During World War II President Franklin Roosevelt, in characteristic American wartime fashion, focused U.S. policy on Germany's defeat. Military considerations received priority because the U.S. aim was a total victory. No precautions were taken for a possible postwar conflict with the Soviet Union. Despite numerous examples throughout history of victorious coalitions breaking up, the American expectation was one of friendly postwar relations. Once the war would be over, "normalcy" would be restored.

Roosevelt was confident he could win the Russian leader's cooperation. Stalin became "Uncle Joe," a genial member of the wartime family. Typical of the American approach that to win a friend one had to be a friend, the president simply projected his domestic experience. At home he dealt constantly with other politicians; as a democratic politician, socialized in the arts of negotiation and compromise, he believed that all problems were solvable. Stalin was just another politician, and, as reasonable men, he and Stalin could compromise differences and avoid conflict. But Stalin was a product of a different political culture. While Roosevelt was optimistic about the future, as were the majority of Americans, Stalin's policy was based upon the assumption of the inherent antagonism between capitalism and Soviet socialism.

The irony was terrific. While Roosevelt viewed Stalin as basically a Russian Roosevelt, Stalin saw Roosevelt as a kind of capitalist Stalin! There were no mirror images present. To Stalin, the president was the leader of an imperialist state, a tool of Wall Street. To Stalin, there was no fundamental difference between Roosevelt and Hitler, also a leader of a capitalist state. No distinctions between Nazi fascism and American democracy existed. All capitalist states were believed to be hostile; Nazi Germany was simply the most extreme capitalist state. After Germany's defeat, the United States would take its place. Thus, Stalin dismissed all of the president's professions of peace and good will. Capitalist statesmen, he *knew*, possessed no such feelings for the Soviet Union. They were merely using words of good intentions to lull the Soviets into relaxing their guard. Roosevelt—and Churchill—were "adversaries who would do unto him approximately what he would do unto them, assuming they got the opportunity." [17]

Had Roosevelt understood that he and Stalin held opposite conceptions of what the postwar world would be like, he might have advocated different policies opposing Stalin, and Truman might have resisted demobilizing U.S. military strength once the war was over. Its enormous conventional power—it did not need to use the threat of the atom bomb—could have provided political leverage that Stalin would have understood. Protest over Stalin's brutal "satellization" of eastern Europe was disregarded as the Soviets, after Germany's defeat, established themselves in the center of Europe and then attempted to expand into Iran and Turkey. It was President Truman's accurate perception of Soviet behavior, as exhibited in these events, that led to the Truman Doctrine and the containment policy.

Thus neither World War II nor the cold war was the result of mirror images. Misperceptions certainly ensured both conflicts; probably neither war was avoidable. *Correct perceptions by the two democracies finally led each to recognize the stakes at issue and take a firm stand.* Had they done so earlier, they would have been in a stronger position for their respective conflicts. Democracies appear reluctant to acknowledge that there are states that wish them ill. Rather than face the unpleasant fact that they confront enemies and that vital interests may be at stake, it is more comforting to explain away enemies as unfortunate victims of past history (invasions, mistreatments), or to believe that no critical interests are threatened. In the process of this explanation, formerly perceived vital interests become secondary, not worth the cost of any lives.

American democracy seems particularly unwilling to admit the existence of genuine threats. In both world wars, the United States stayed out until its enemies attacked. The United States would not have declared war had the Germans in 1917 not launched their unrestricted submarine campaign to starve Britain into submission and, in the process, sunk American ships. Had Hitler not stupidly declared war on the United States after the Japanese attack on Pearl Harbor, the American war effort would have been directed only at Japan, and Germany, the greater threat, might have defeated Russia and Britain. In fact, it is questionable whether the United States, with a divided public, would have declared war on either Germany or Japan, had it not been for Pearl Harbor. One historian has perceptively noted that, during the 1930s,

> [a]lthough it was the single most powerful nation on the globe, the United States abdicated its responsibilities and became a creature of history rather than its molder. By surrendering the initiative to Germany and Japan, the nation imperiled its security and very nearly permitted the Axis powers to win the war. In the last analysis the United States was saved only by the Japanese miscalculation in attacking Pearl Harbor.[18]

The ultimate decisions to go to war were made by Germany and Japan. The United States did not take the initiative even though the balance of power in Europe and Asia was at stake. Unable to act wisely, the United States was saved by its enemies from the consequences of its behavior. In both cases, the nation was slow to react to external dangers, and this was the result of its belief that threats to American interests did not exist. The U.S. reaction to Germany, as to the Soviet Union later, were all part of the same syndrome: the reluctance to admit that the nation has enemies.

Changing Circumstances and Changing Perceptions

Given the thesis that misperceptions are likely to cause conflicts and possibly wars, the examples just given suggest that misperceptions may prevent great powers from recognizing an emerging threat and acting either to forestall an opponent or to place themselves in a better situation in anticipation of that conflict. Therefore, it is nonsense to suggest that major struggles, such as the two world wars and the cold war, are the products of black-and-white thinking and other forms of distorted perceptions. That mistakes in policy making may occur in a changing international environment is obvious, but not necessary.

One need look only at U.S. cold war containment policy. Despite its general anti-Communist crusade, the United States offered to aid Yugoslavia in 1948 after its break with the Soviet Union and a few years later made several attempts to "build bridges" to Eastern Europe. Such efforts began in earnest in 1956 with the Polish and Hungarian upheavals. Similarly, after Nationalist China's collapse in 1949, the allegedly indiscriminately anti-Communist Acheson recognized the potential for differences between the two Communist giants and planned to recognize the new Chinese regime, once Chiang Kai-shek on Taiwan had been eliminated by Mao Zedong. Even during the Korean War, Acheson believed that crossing the thirty-eighth parallel would be safe because the Beijing government was already too absorbed with the Soviet threat in the North to pay much attention to events in Korea. It was U.S. *domestic* politics that for the next two decades prevented Washington from seeking to exploit the increasing Sino-Soviet friction that had begun in the late 1950s.

Other changes occurred too. The United States and the Soviet Union began to cooperate with each other on arms control; they shifted from a total adversary relationship to a more limited adversary relationship. Perhaps one of the best proofs that perceptions change with external circumstances is President Nixon's pursuit of détente with the Soviet Union and rapprochement with China. During the 1950s Nixon had been a militant anti-Communist. No so-called psychohistorical analysis has yet satisfactorily explained how a man allegedly so loaded with misperceptions, character defects, and inner anguish could have conducted such a flexible, nonideological, pragmatic balance-of-power foreign policy.[19] In addition, China's revolutionary and anticapitalist posture and rhetoric did not stand in the way of improving relations with the United States when the Soviet Union seemed a growing threat. Nor did they inhibit China from supporting capitalist European integration and a strong capitalist North Atlantic Treaty Organization (NATO) to balance Soviet power in the West. The philosophies of Karl Marx and of Mao had become subordinate to the balance of power.

As Hans Morgenthau has commented more generally, "the assumption that the issues of international conflict, born as they are of misunderstandings, are but imaginary and that actually no issue worth fighting about stands between nation and nation" is wrong.

> Nothing could be farther from the truth. All the great wars which decided the course of history and changed the political face of the earth were fought for real stakes, not for imaginary ones. The issue in these great convulsions was invariably: who shall rule and who shall be ruled? Who shall be free, and who, slave? [20]

'Deep Down, We're All Alike'

Yet the penchant for wishing to believe that conflict and war are the products of misperceptions must in part be attributed to the American belief, which nothing seems to shake, that conflict is not normal and that war is a malfunction from "normal," that is, peaceful and rational behavior. Conflict must be the result of misunderstandings and misperceptions which, given good will and reason, can be corrected. The mirror-image emphasis, so characteristic of this belief, suggests not only that there is no objective basis for conflict but also that "deep down, we're all alike." [21] As human beings, who share many of the same hopes, needs, and fears, our common humanity should prevail over our differences. We all want to support our families, care for our children, and love and be loved. We should, therefore, get along and not allow ideologies and national concerns to stand in the way of peaceful and harmonious relations. If we do not get along, it must be due to a failure of communication.

This American approach to international politics has been perceptively referred to as "the broken telephone theory of international conflict." It accounts for the recurring emphasis on the "repair service by the expert": the professor skilled in negotiations who also believes that all conflicts are susceptible to compromise; [22] the vogue for peace research and peace academies, such as the congressionally funded Institute of Peace whose task it will be to educate "practitioners, policymakers, policy implementers, and citizens and noncitizens directed to developing their skills in international peace and conflict resolution"; [23] the search for mediators and envoys who can be sent to areas of trouble and find a fair and equitable solution; and on the need for people-to-people contact and exchanges so that we can all learn that we are all basically alike.

But it is not the absence of telephones and telephone lines that stand in the way of the peaceful resolution of conflicts. Washington and Moscow; Jerusalem, Damascus, and wherever the Palestine Liberation Organization is headquartered; Iran and Iraq all have telephone communication. "They need only an operator to make the connection. Their problem is that they have very little to say to each other." [24] *The key problem is not the question of misperceptions; it is the question of conflicting intentions.* Human beings may well be alike, in spite of their different languages, clothing, and manners. But politics starts where the commonalities of humanity stop, and it starts here because of the different interests, values, ideologies, and histories of the many collectives of people we call nation-states. All want peace—but only on their terms. Any state can preserve peace when faced with demands from another state; it has only to accede to the demands made even if these endanger its security and way of life. Few states have followed this course. Those who emphasize humanity's common characteristics and conclude that there is no necessity for conflict and war fail to distinguish between people as private individuals concerned with their personal values and people as citizens who identify with their nations—entities for which they may sacrifice their own welfare and even their lives. The belief that people-to-people contact will lead nations to understand one another better and that this will reduce the dangers of conflict and war is called into question by the fact that many neighboring nations have detested each other (the Germans and the French, the Russians and the Poles, the Greeks and Turks, the Israelis and Arabs). While human beings may be alike, familiarity often breeds contempt rather than friendship. Thus, we cannot separate our second- and third-level analyses from the state system with its emphasis on nations' intentions and objectives.

Back to the Levels of Analysis

It is all too easy to see the misperceptions of leaders divorced from the larger context. Before World War II British public opinion was pacifist, and the prime minister accurately reflected this feeling. Britain's desire for peace was indicated by the fact that Churchill's warnings were ignored, that he was not a member of the government, that he did not become so until the war broke out, and that he did not become prime minister until after the initial disasters of the war.

President Roosevelt's hopes and attitudes represented U.S. opinion. Most Americans wanted to believe that there were no basic conflicts between the United States and Russia. Said General Eisenhower: "[T]he ordinary Russian seems to me to bear a marked similarity to what we call an 'average American.' " [25] How, given such views, could the United States have started an anti-Soviet policy against an ally who had borne the brunt of the fighting and whose wartime courage and endurance were much admired? And how could it have been done when, characteristically, the United States was still preoccupied with the military conduct of the war and the total defeat of Germany, and when, after the war, again typically, it demobilized militarily and psychologically? The democratic nature of England in the late 1930s and the United States in 1945-46 prevented them from formulating policies that contained their enemies more effectively. In short, the misperceptions of Chamberlain and Roosevelt have to be explained in the larger social setting.

The resulting cold war often has been attributed to American anticommunism or Soviet anticapitalism. But this ignores the dilemmas of power and security confronting all members of the state system and the environment in which states exist. The result is not only a restricted understanding of state behavior but also a misreading of history that could, if extended, result in a misreading of the future as well. To suggest, as American revisionist writers do, that without an alleged American anti-Communist animus predating Soviet postwar behavior there would have been no cold war is to ignore the anarchical character of the state system. In the absence of a first-level perspective, the cold war is bound to be misunderstood, for it will then be viewed solely as the result of American anticommunism or Soviet anticapitalism, of Truman's toughness or Stalin's paranoia, rather than as the result of the age-old game of "power politics," which members of the state system are compelled to play. And, if the reasons for this conflict are perceived incorrectly, the lessons drawn—lessons that may influence future policy—will also be incorrect. We should thus guard against an overemphasis on misperception as the cause of conflict and war. The key conflicts in international politics are the result of neither accident nor misunderstanding.

Notes

1. Walt W. Rostow in *The American Style,* ed. Elting E. Morrison (New York: Harper & Brothers, 1958), 147.
2. J. William Fulbright, *The Arrogance of Power* (New York: Vintage Books, 1967) 3-46.
3. Ralph K. White, *Nobody Wanted War* (Garden City, N.Y.: Doubleday, 1968), 3.
4. E. H. Carr, *The Twenty Years' Crisis 1919-1939* (New York: Macmillan, 1961), 51-52.
5. White, *Nobody Wanted War,* 6.
6. Gaddis Smith, *Dean Acheson* (New York: Cooper Square, 1972), 414.
7. Ibid., 423.
8. Gaddis Smith, "The Shadow of John Foster Dulles," *Foreign Affairs* (January 1974): 403-408; see also Townsend Hoopes, *The Devil and John Foster Dulles* (Boston: Atlantic/Little, Brown & Co., 1973).
9. John Stoessinger, *Nations in Darkness* (New York: Random House, 1971), 5; and Stoessinger, *Why Nations Go to War* (New York: St. Martin's, 1974).
10. Ralph K. White, "Images in the Context of International Conflict," in *International Behavior: A Social-Psychological Analysis,* ed. Herbert C. Kelman et al. (New York: Holt, Rinehart & Winston, 1965), 238-275.
11. Erich Fromm, *May Man Prevail?* (New York: Doubleday, 1961).
12. For an analysis of alleged distorted American perceptions of the Soviet Union and an attack upon the foundations of "realist" thinking, see Anatol Rapoport, *The Big Two: Soviet-American Perceptions of Foreign Policy* (New York: Pegasus, 1971).
13. Michael A. Guhin, *John Foster Dulles* (New York: Columbia University Press, 1972), 3-10.
14 For example, see Ross Stagner, *Psychological Aspects of International Conflict* (Belmont, Calif.: Brooks-Cole, 1967), 1-16; and Otto Klineberg, *The Human Dimension in International Relations* (New York: Holt, Rinehart & Winston, 1964).
15. Robert Jervis, "Hypothesis on Misperception," *World Politics,* April 1968, 460. For a more detailed analysis of the effects of perception where institutional and political constraints are underestimated, see Jervis, *Perceptions and Misperception in International Politics* (Princeton, N.J.: Princeton University Press, 1976).
16. Alexander L. George, "Assessing Presidential Character," *World Politics,* January 1974, 235-236.

17. William Taubman, *Stalin's American Policy* (New York: W. W. Norton, 1982), 39.

18. Robert A. Divine, *The Illusion of Neutrality* (Chicago: University of Chicago Press, 1962), 280-281.

19. Bruce Mazlish, *In Search of Nixon* (New York: Basic Books, 1972).

20. Hans J. Morgenthau, *Politics among Nations*, 5th ed. (New York: Alfred A. Knopf, 1972), 504. Also see Arthur A. Stein, "When Misperception Matters," *World Politics*, July 1982, 505-526.

21. Charles Krauthammer, "Deep Down, We're All Alike, Right? Wrong," *Time*, Aug. 15, 1983, 30-31.

22. Roger Fisher and William Ury, *Getting to Yes* (New York: Penguin Books, 1983).

23. Donald Kagan, "The Pseudo-Science of 'Peace,' " *Public Interest*, Winter 1985, 43-61.

24. Krauthammer, "Deep Down," 30.

25. Dwight D. Eisenhower, *Crusade in Europe* (New York: Doubleday, 1952), 457, 473-474.

Part Five

FROM STATE SYSTEM TO INTERDEPENDENCE

CHAPTER 18

Preserving Peace
in the State System

RESTRAINING STATE BEHAVIOR

The outlook for peace in a system of almost 170 states certainly does not appear bright. The hierarchy of great powers that historically maintained the international version of "law and order" has been eroded through the birth of so many states; the assertiveness of many of them, especially those with ambitions for regional leadership; the diffusion of modern conventional arms and possibly also nuclear weapons; the instability of many Third World regimes; the likelihood of conflict—even violent conflict—among the states because of ethnic, racial, and religious differences; the possibility that the superpowers may be drawn into these quarrels; the increasing reluctance of Western industrial states to use force in their disputes with smaller, non-Western nations; and the spread of terrorism. This weakening of the hierarchy that has served as a stabilizing influence is bound to be disruptive. But, whatever the future may hold, the past has taught us that no previous balance in history has in the long run prevented war permanently; no deterrent strategy has been proof against failure. Two world wars and a cold war in little more than thirty years are evidence enough; and, although the possibility of Armageddon is ever-present, will it be sufficient to guarantee peace in a world characterized by more states, more civil strife, more international conflicts, more conventional arms, more nuclear weapons, and more terrorism?

How, in short, can the basic problem of peace be approached *within* the existing state system? How can state behavior be restrained and made more responsible? Can peace be achieved through cooperation among states in an international organization such as the United Nations, through disarmament agreements, and through international legal and moral norms? For many of its advocates the United Nations symbolizes the expectation that war will be abolished, for, ideally at least, it represents the embodiment of a new spirit of internationalism that is supposed to replace national egotism. In the words of former senator and chairman of the Senate Foreign Relations Committee J. William Fulbright, the United Nations is an institution intended to protect "humanity from the destructiveness of unrestrained nationalism" and therefore to be strengthened by subordination of short-run national needs to long-run needs.[1]

A second approach, in contrast to the first, is disarmament. Disarmament agreements are not addressed to the problem of conflict resolution; their purpose is the extermination of the weapons with which conflicts may be waged. Whereas the United Nations approach stresses a spirit of accommodation and the peaceful settlement of disputes, the disarmament approach is based on the assumption that differences in interests will continue but that, if nations no longer possess the vast quantity and variety of arms that industry has provided, wars will not occur.

A third approach stresses the self-restraint that states would have to exercise if they obeyed international law or behaved more morally. How realistic are these three approaches to making the state system safe for humanity? If they offer practical solutions, the abolition of the state system may not be necessary; if they do not, the case for the creation of a new world order may be stronger.

THE UNITED NATIONS: THREE PHASES

To understand the United Nations, it is necessary to understand what it is *not.* It is not the "great peacemaker" and solver of all problems. It is not a superstate, usurping members' sovereignty and imposing its will on them. Nor is its behavior independent of states' national interests and political considerations. United Nations decisions are not made according to some impartial, nonpolitical, and therefore purportedly superior standard of justice. The organization is not above politics because it cannot exist or act independently of its members' politics. Rather, it reflects the political interests, attitudes, and problems of its member states. It is only the channel through which the power and purposes of its members are expressed. The United Nations is not a substitute for power politics; it only registers the power politics of the state system. It is a mirror, not a panacea; there is no magic wand by which it can resolve all international problems. It cannot transcend the cold war or anticolonial struggles. It must function in the world as it exists, and it cannot solve any problems that its members, because of conflicting interests, are not prepared to solve. Its failures demonstrate only its members' inability to reach agreement.

First Phase

Because the United Nations is not a superstate but a body registering its members' political interests, attitudes, and problems, its functions can best be understood in terms of the changing conditions of the state system. After its birth in 1945, in its first phase the United Nations reflected the hope that, once victory over Germany had been won, cooperation among great powers would continue and peace would be maintained. Primary authority for the preservation of peace and security in the United Nations was vested in the Security Council (originally composed of eleven members, six of them on two-year rotation; the total membership has since been raised to fifteen). Real authority, however, was to be exercised by the five permanent members: the United States, the Soviet Union, Britain, France, and China (at first Nationalist China and subsequently Communist China). With the votes of seven members of the Security Council, including all the permanent members, the council could take enforcement action against aggression, and its decision was then supposed to be obeyed by all members of the United Nations; each permanent member of the council could veto such action. Through an oligarchical structure that reflected the global distribution of power, the great powers were able to become the masters of the United Nations. Indeed, the United States and the Soviet Union, actually the only two great powers remaining in 1945, were the real masters. As long as the two superpowers could maintain harmony, peace would be preserved.

The security system was thus directed only against the smaller nations; if they disturbed the peace, they could be squashed if the great powers could agree to take punitive action. The United Nations was, in the words of one delegate to its first conference, "engaged in establishing a world in which the mice could be stamped out but in which the lions would not be restrained." [2] The purpose of the veto was to prevent one of the great powers from mobilizing the United Nations against another great power. Because a decision to punish a great power for aggression would precipitate global war, the

> insertion of the veto provision in the decision-making circuit of the Security Council reflected the clear conviction that in cases of sharp conflict among the great powers the Council ought, for safety's sake, to be incapacitated—to be rendered incapable of being used to precipitate a showdown, or to mobilize collective action against the recalcitrant power. The philosophy of the veto is that it is better to have the Security Council stalemated than to have that body used by a majority to take action so strongly opposed by a dissident great power that a world war is likely to ensue. [3]

Conflicts among great powers were to be handled *outside* the United Nations under collective self-defense arrangements, which did not require prior Security Council authorization for individual or joint military action in response to an attack.

Second Phase

As the two superpowers took opposite sides at the beginning of the cold war, the United States sought to mobilize the support of the United Nations for the containment of the Soviet Union and thus to associate its own policies with the humanitarian, peaceful, and democratic values underlying the organization. The transition from the first to the second phase was most dramatically illustrated in the Korean War. The United States had no choice but to oppose the Soviet Union, but acted under UN auspices. Soviet absence from the Security Council on the day of the vote to intervene enabled it to do so. But such an absence was not likely to occur a second time. The United States therefore introduced the "Uniting for Peace" resolution in November 1950, the purpose of which was to transfer primary responsibility for the preservation of peace and security to the General Assembly should the Security Council be paralyzed by the veto. Constitutionally, this transfer of authority should not have been possible. The General Assembly had authority only to debate, investigate, and make recommendations on issues of international peace and security. Even then, it could offer no recommendations affecting matters on the Security Council's agenda; by placing an issue on the agenda, then, the council could supposedly reduce the assembly to a debating society.

The Americans argued, however, that the United Nations' responsibility for the preservation of international peace and security could not be abandoned just because the Security Council was paralyzed. If the council could not fulfill its "primary responsibility" for this function, the assembly would have to assume the task. It need hardly be added that in the assembly, as it was then constituted, the United States could easily muster the two-thirds majorities needed for important resolutions from among members of the North Atlantic Treaty Organization (NATO) countries, the older British dominions, the Latin American republics, and one or two Asian states. The Soviet Union, with no veto in the assembly, was of course consistently outvoted, though it was still able to use the body as a forum for its own point of view. American policies were, therefore, legitimated by world public opinion.

American use of the assembly to support anti-Communist policies did not last long. Just as the configuration of power underlying the original Security Council—the wartime alliance—had changed shortly after the establishment of the United Nations, so the political alignment at the outbreak of the Korean War was not destined to survive even that war, despite the "Uniting for Peace" resolution. The United States had received UN support at first for two reasons. First, an overwhelming number of member nations, including the nonaligned states,[4] saw in the North Korean aggression a test of the United Nations itself. If the organization failed to respond, it would follow the League of Nations into the dustbin of history. Second, the smaller powers saw in the transfer of authority on security matters to the assembly an opportunity to play a larger role than assigned to them in the original UN charter. But Communist Chinese intervention in late 1950 made American-sponsored use of the United Nations as an instrument of collective enforce-ment against the Communist bloc more difficult. The involvement of a major Communist power and the possibility that the American government might accede to strong domestic pressures to extend the war to China by air bombardment, naval blockade, and the landing of Nationalist Chinese forces on the mainland, dramatized the wisdom of the UN architects' original effort to prevent the organization's involvement in military conflicts among great powers. The danger of a large war, which might even bring in the Soviet Union, was simply too great.

In addition, the twelve Arab-Asian members of the General Assembly were determined to remain nonaligned in the cold war. Their earlier support for American intervention in Korea had been motivated by their concern for the United Nations as an institution. It was essential that North Korean aggres-sion be met, and, because the United States had the strength to take appropri-ate measures, the Arab-Asian members had approved of the original Ameri-can reaction. But they had no desire to participate in collective measures against one side or the other, which would in effect have forced them to become allied to one of the cold war blocs through the mechanism of the UN voting procedure. The problem was to prevent a military clash between the great powers and, simultaneously, to avoid becoming aligned in the cold war themselves. The answer was to shift the function of the United Nations from enforcement to conciliation.[5] The United Nations was to serve as an instru-ment of mediation in conflict between the great powers. The original assump-tion that peace could be preserved by having five lions, led by the two biggest lions, act as world guardians was replaced with recognition of the imperative need to keep the lions from mauling one another to death—and trampling the mice while they were at it.

Third Phase

A third phase of the United Nations thus began. In the first phase the members had been dedicated to preserving the wartime Grand Alliance; in the second, the United Nations had become an American instrument for prosecuting the cold war. This phase had begun to fade during the Korean War. By exerting great pressure, the United States could still, in the spring of 1951, obtain the two-thirds majority needed in the General Assembly for a condemnation of Communist China. Already, though, it had to make conces-sions to muster these votes—the price being that it not follow the condemna-tion with additional military or economic measures. Instead, the United States was to give primary emphasis to conciliatory efforts of the Arab-Asian bloc—supported by most of the NATO allies, which were also concerned about possible escalation of the conflict—to end the war. By 1955 the United Nations had reached adolescence and it matured quickly as the number of newly independent members, especially African, grew rapidly after 1955. In 1955 six new Asian and North African states were admitted; the next year four

Table 18-1 Growth of United Nations
                  Membership

Year	Members
1946	55
1950	60
1955	76
1960	99
1965	107
1970	127
1975	144
1985	159

SOURCE: These figures are taken from successive issues of
the *United Nations Yearbook* (New York: United Nations,
1946-1985).

more were added. In 1960 the number of new states admitted was seventeen,
mainly from sub-Saharan Africa. By 1974 Asian, African, and Latin American
states made up three-quarters of the 138 members (see Table 18-1). Both the
American and the Soviet blocs previously had used the United Nations for
their own cold war purposes, but the neutral bloc soon learned how to use the
organization to erase the vestiges of Western colonialism as quickly as possible. The General Assembly was a particularly good forum in which to voice
anticolonial sentiments and state demands for the new international economic order, the global redistribution of wealth and power between rich and
poor countries.

In this third phase, the United Nations could not help becoming involved
in the cold war. The United States and the Soviet Union, to be sure, did not allow the organization to interfere in *their* clashes. The Soviets had no intention
of permitting the United Nations to intervene in Hungary or Czechoslovakia.
Nor would the United States permit it to become involved in negotiations
over the post-1958 Berlin crises, Cuban problems,[6] and the war in Vietnam.
East-West issues were debated only; no action was taken. The superpowers
handled their own direct confrontations. But, on the periphery of the cold
war, the United States and the Soviet Union were constantly tempted to
interfere in the conflicts arising from the end of colonialism. Such interference, by threatening the peace and involving neutrals in the cold war, was
bound to lead the nonaligned nations to take protective action. The United
Nations was for them more than a political platform. It was also a shelter in
which they sought refuge from great-power pressure. In this third phase, they
thought of the United Nations as *theirs*, and they were determined to use it to
remain nonaligned.

The chief function of the United Nations thus became "preventive diplomacy"[7]—that is, the stabilization of local conflicts *before* either of the super-

powers could become involved and provoke its antagonist's intervention. To state this point negatively, preventive diplomacy was intended to keep American-Soviet clashes from extending beyond the cold war zone. At the same time, by containing the cold war, the small nations could safeguard their independence and control their own future to some extent. The mice were to keep the lions apart so that they could not grapple with each other and trample them. The chief means of stabilization was establishment of a "United Nations presence" in these peripheral quarrels; the organization thus functioned as a fire brigade, devoted to minimizing potential hazards. It could not douse a fire, but its presence could signal that fire was imminent or had already broken out and should be controlled quickly.

PREVENTIVE DIPLOMACY IN THE THIRD PHASE

In a real sense, the United Nations has performed a crucial function in a highly combustible world. But to perform this role, it has needed not only support, or at least acquiescence, from the superpowers but also active support and participation of the Third World countries. The contribution of the latter to the stability of the state system was in response to two conditions. The first is the tendency of their problems to spill over into the international arena. One example is the disintegration of a state, as happened in the Congo after it attained independence in 1960; in the resulting attempts to reunify it, competing factions sought outside help. Another example is a clash between states in a region when each party has friends in the superpower camps. This kind of clash occurred during the Israeli-Egyptian war in 1956, when France and Britain intervened militarily on Israel's side and the Soviet Union supported Egypt diplomatically—and even talked of firing missiles at Paris and London.

The second condition is that these types of problems tend to attract the attention of the Soviet Union and the United States, leading to possible confrontations, with all the attendant dangers of military conflict. The two superpowers are attracted, of course, because these problems may bring to power groups favorable to one side and thus inimical to the other, or they may lead to a regional expansion that would benefit one side and hurt the other. If one of the two superpowers is unwilling to tolerate what it may consider a local or regional setback, it will intervene; if it fears that its opponent may intervene, it may make the first move. In either instance, it risks counterintervention. The conflicts that have arisen on the periphery of the American-Soviet rivalry thus have tended to feed the major confrontation between the two superpowers.

Conflict in the Middle East

Further analysis of the Suez crisis of 1956 can be instructive in this connection. Egypt had been a British protectorate from 1881 to 1936, when it was granted independence. Britain retained control of the Suez Canal, however, and in effect maintained a dominant position. But mounting Egyptian nationalism and a corresponding rise in anti-British feeling eventually led Britain in 1954 to relinquish its Suez military base, though not control of the canal. The moment that British troops had withdrawn, President Gamal Abdel Nasser launched an energetic anti-Western campaign to eliminate all "colonial" governments from the Middle East and North Africa. Success would, of course, have made him the leader of all Arabs and given him control of most Arabian oil. If successful, Nasser would have tremendous bargaining power, for Europe, especially Britain, was dependent on Middle Eastern oil. The United States and Britain were alarmed by these attempts to eliminate Western influence in the economically and strategically vital Middle East, particularly as Nasser was leaning more and more toward the Soviet Union, for which the Middle East offered a means of outflanking NATO without a shot being fired. Shortly after Nasser extended diplomatic recognition to Communist China, therefore, the United States withdrew its offer to finance the Aswan High Dam, which was to provide irrigation for much of Egypt's weather-beaten soil and thus to promote its economic development. Nasser's response was to nationalize the Suez Canal, claiming that he would use income from it to build the dam.

Britain then felt compelled to act. If Nasser were allowed to seize the Suez Canal with impunity, the British believed, then other Arab governments would also expropriate Western property—particularly oil property. Furthermore, no pro-Western Arab government would be safe from overthrow by pro-Nasser elements within its own country. Britain was joined by France, which sought to stop Egyptian shipments of arms to Algerian nationalists to be used against France. They found their opportunity when Israel attacked Egypt. This moment occurred after Nasser's well-publicized arms deal with the Soviet Union, the stated purpose of which was to drive Israel into the sea. The consequent hostilities threatened to develop into major war, as the Soviet Union, which shared Egypt's interest in expelling the West from the region, threatened to send volunteers to Egypt and even to rain atomic rockets on London and Paris.

The possibility of Soviet intervention naturally elicited an American response. The United States disapproved of its allies' attack on Egypt, which smacked of nineteenth-century colonialism and risked alienating the new nations. American support for the British and French action would have allowed the Soviet Union to pose as the friend and defender of those new nations. The United States therefore voted with the Soviet Union in the Security Council to condemn Britain and France's aggression and to call upon them to desist. At the same time, it could not stand by and let the Soviet Union send military "volunteers" into the Middle East, let alone attack Britain and France; a warning note was therefore sent to Moscow. Yet the Soviet Union, posing as Egypt's protector, could hardly have remained inactive in the event of American intervention without endangering its good relations with the other nonaligned states. At the very least, then, the situation was dangerous.

In 1973 there was almost a replay of this crisis. In October Egypt and Syria attacked Israel during the highest Jewish holiday, Yom Kippur, the Day of Atonement. Egypt was then governed by Anwar Sadat, an Egyptian national-ist but a more moderate figure than Nasser, who had been an Arab nationalist, or pan-Arabist. The country had become increasingly frustrated by Israel's continued occupation of Egyptian territory on the east bank of the Suez Canal. This territory, captured during the 1967 Six Day War, seemed likely to remain in Israeli hands for a long time because Israel had no incentive to surrender it. After the war in which it had gained its independence, Israel had fought for survival in 1956 and 1967. The Arab states continued to be hostile toward it, and Nasser, the only Arab leader of stature who could have mobilized popular support throughout the Arab world for a compromise settlement that included recognition of Israel's existence, refused to play the role of peacemaker. Instead, allying himself with the rulers of Jordan and Syria, he proclaimed in 1967 that Egypt was ready for the "final struggle." Even after losing yet another war, he refused to sit down with Israeli leaders and negotiate a settlement; Egyptian defeat therefore had brought not peace but only another cease-fire.

For Israel, however, that was a peace of sorts. It thought itself militarily superior and therefore not likely to be attacked. The American-Soviet détente also benefited Israel, for the United States did not press it to give up the captured Egyptian and Syrian territories. The Soviet Union, needing Ameri-can technology, investments, and trade goods to bolster its own sagging economy and also wanting strategic arms limitation talks, was in no position to press Israel or to give active political and military support to the Arab states. The territorial status quo became frozen.

But Sadat was unwilling to live with that status quo. As the new leader of the most important Arab country, he felt the need to prove to the Egyptians and Arabs in general that he was a worthy successor to the charismatic Nasser as the defender of the Arab cause. He therefore launched the Yom Kippur War, taking Israel by surprise and achieving initial success in crossing the Suez Canal and driving into the Sinai desert. But, once Israel had recovered from the shock and had driven Egypt's Syrian allies back from the Golan Heights, its forces concentrated on Egypt; the Israelis crossed the Suez Canal to the west bank, cutting off supplies to the Egyptian forces on the east bank and encircling them. At that point, the United States and the Soviet Union agreed upon a cease-fire resolution in the UN Security Council. The United States agreed because it thought that no peace could be arranged if Egypt was again humiliated in war—indeed the psychological boost derived from its initial successes had to be preserved if it was to be expected to make any concessions in a peace settlement—and the Soviet Union agreed in order to avoid an Egyptian defeat that might compel the Soviets to enter the war to rescue what it still regarded as a client state.

Indeed, the Soviets almost did enter as the shooting continued and the Israelis tried to encircle and destroy the Egyptian army on the eastern side of the Suez Canal. Sadat then requested the United States and the Soviet Union to use their own forces to impose a cease-fire. When the United States declined to intervene with its forces and the Soviet Union threatened to do so unilaterally, the two superpowers found themselves in confrontation. American military forces were placed on a worldwide alert, and another highly inflammable situation had suddenly arisen.

Conflict in Africa

The Republic of Congo (now Zaire) became an independent state in 1960. But the Belgians, unlike the British and the French in most of their colonies, had not trained native leaders to take over. Complete disorder soon broke out, and the native army rioted. The Belgian settlers fled, and to protect them Belgium flew in troops. The Congolese prime minister, Patrice Lumumba, interpreted the Belgian action as an attempt to restore colonial rule and appealed to the United Nations to compel the Belgians to withdraw. The Soviets immediately supported his appeal and condemned Belgium, accusing it of acting as a front for "NATO imperialism." An even more serious situation developed when the province of Katanga (now Shaba) seceded. Katanga's rich copper mines were the Congo's main source of revenue, and secession threatened the survival of the entire nation. Lumumba demanded that the United Nations crush Katanga president Moïse Tshombe's mercenary army and help to restore Congolese unity. When his demand went unheeded, Lumumba appealed to the Soviet Union for help against the "colonialists." He received both Soviet diplomatic support and military supplies, and it looked as if the Soviet government was about to establish an important base in Africa. Lumumba thereupon was dismissed from office by Congolese president Joseph Mobutu, whom the United States supported in order to prevent the establishment of a Soviet foothold in central Africa. The Soviets, however, refused to recognize Lumumba's successor, insisting that only Parliament had the right to dismiss Lumumba and that, as it had not done so, he was still the legitimate Congolese prime minister and must be restored to his office. The subsequent murder of Lumumba exacerbated the situation.

The national coalition government of the Congo, formed in early 1961, faced a major crisis from the beginning, a crisis that could only benefit the Soviet Union unless a solution was found. The government, committed to a policy of nonalignment, had national reunification as its first objective. Failure to achieve this goal would undermine its authority and lead to collapse from political and financial weakness. The transfer of power to a more radical pro-Communist government would then be a real possibility. The central government, to head off its own collapse, might even turn toward the Soviet Union, just as Lumumba had done. In either instance there would be a Soviet-American confrontation in the Congo.

Role of the United Nations

It is in such situations—in which the two superpowers are drawn into confrontations that threaten the peace of the world—that the United Nations in its third phase can play its most important role. Just as the Security Council had been intended as the focus of authority in the first phase and the General Assembly had become the focus in the second phase, the secretary-general was to be the principal actor in the third phase. No longer merely the prime administrative officer of the organization, the secretary-general, largely through partnership with the nonaligned nations, had become its leading political officer. It was Dag Hammarskjöld who, by establishing the precedent of UN presence in troubled areas, first assumed the role of "custodian of brushfire peace." The most dramatic expression of this custodianship has been the "nonfighting international force," the purpose of which is not military but political. The size of the force, drawn primarily from states not involved in the particular dispute, and its firepower are not as significant as its political presence, which forestalls the use of Soviet or American forces.

During the Suez crisis in 1956 a UN Emergency Force (UNEF I) supervised the withdrawal of British, French, and Israeli troops from Egypt. It did not seek to *compel* withdrawal through combat. The cease-fire agreement was the prerequisite for its use, yet the mere fact that it was available made it easier to obtain British, French, and Israeli agreement to withdraw. Once withdrawal had been completed, fewer than five thousand UN soldiers were left to guard the Israeli-Egyptian frontier and to maintain peace in that area. Symbolically, it was Nasser's demand that these forces be withdrawn in 1967, leaving Egypt and Israel to confront each other directly, that led to the Six Day War. Similarly, the interposition of UN forces between Israeli and Egyptian troops after the 1973 war helped keep the peace. It was these forces that stood between the hostile troops on both the Egyptian front (UNEF II) and the Syrian front (UN Disengagement Observer Force, or UNDOF) as American secretary of state Henry Kissinger patiently negotiated disengagements of the combatants as a prelude to more comprehensive peace negotiations.

Conditions for Peace-Keeping Forces

At least three conditions are imposed on such an international force. First, as already mentioned, it must be neutral and must therefore exclude permanent members of the Security Council. Second, the nation upon whose territory the force is to show its "presence" must grant permission for such entry. In this way, the host nation, as a sovereign state, exercises some control over the composition of the international force and can exclude troops from nations it considers unfriendly or undesirable. It can also demand the withdrawal of these troops, as Egypt did in 1967. Even had the secretary-general not agreed to their withdrawal, he would have had no option; UNEF I was a small force and not fit for fighting. (Israel had refused to accept United Nations forces on its side of the frontier with Egypt; had it done so, it would have been protected against an Egyptian strike by their very presence.) UNEF II, however, was placed under the jurisdiction of the Security Council and thus differed in this respect from UNEF I, which had been created by the General Assembly. Since the presence of the UN forces had to be approved every six months, they could not be terminated during that period except with the unanimous consent of the five permanent members. A veto by any one of them at the semiannual meeting could end a mission.

The third condition is that the UN force may not intervene in any purely internal conflict and become party to the dispute. In Egypt in 1956 and 1973, the force was not used to impose a specific settlement on Nasser or Sadat; it merely disentangled the combatants. The UN presence was not intended to deal with the causes of the two wars, but with their effects. The same was true in the Congo, though with a special twist. It was precisely the United Nations' refusal to interfere in the domestic politics of the Congo that created most of the difficulties. After the Congo had disintegrated, the head of the "national" government insisted that the UN Operations in the Congo (UNOC) crush the secession of Katanga. In the end, the international organization could not isolate itself from the Congolese civil war. The effect of United Nations *non*intervention was to freeze the schism and to ensure the collapse of the Congolese government because Katanga's rich copper mines were the major source of national revenue. United Nations forces eventually did fight to crush the secession of Katanga. The third condition of domestic nonintervention is thus a qualified one.

The nations of the Third World, it must be noted, can use this preventive diplomacy function *only* if the superpowers permit them to do so. The assumption underlying the pacifying role of the nonaligned states is that both the United States and the Soviet Union wish to avoid new areas of conflict in the cold war because of the high risk. Their desire to avoid nuclear war gives them a vested interest in keeping peripheral conflicts under control. They will thus at least acquiesce in the establishment of a United Nations presence: "It cannot be done *against* the major parties; it cannot be done *by* them; it can only be done *for* them and by their leave." [8]

Four alternative kinds of action are possible in conflicts not involving direct American-Soviet confrontations, especially to achieve preventive diplomacy. The United Nations may take a pro-Western action, an impartial action, no action at all, or a pro-Soviet action. Obviously, the American preference is in that order; the Soviets prefer the exact reverse. Neither extreme is really feasible, but the difficulty is that between the remaining alternatives the United States prefers impartial, neutralizing action, whereas the Soviet Union prefers inactivity. The reasons are obvious. The United States fears that inactivity will lead either to a Soviet advantage or a collapse requiring American intervention—and Soviet counterintervention. It also hopes that impartial action will accomplish pro-American results. Conversely, the Soviets hope that inaction will produce pro-Soviet results and prevent American intervention. The Soviets fear that the course preferred by the United States may indeed yield results detrimental to Soviet interests.

Assessment of Preventive Diplomacy

By limiting the scope of marginal conflicts and seeking to stabilize tense situations, preventive diplomacy has on the whole served U.S. purposes better than Soviet ends. In Egypt in 1956 and 1973 UN forces helped to preempt possible Soviet intervention. In the Congo in 1961 United Nations intervention eliminated the bridgehead the Soviets had established. The Soviet Union was therefore frustrated; from its perspective, the moving force in both crises, but especially in the Congo, had been the secretary-general, and the results demonstrated the need for a Soviet veto over his actions. The Soviets proposed a "troika" plan, calling for the appointment of three secretaries-general, each of whom would represent one of the major blocs in the world. The Soviets sought to supplement their actual veto in the Security Council and their virtual veto in the General Assembly (where the Soviets usually find enough votes among the nonaligned states to prevent a two-thirds majority vote against them) with a hidden veto at the top of the Secretariat. This veto would ensure that the United Nations could not do anything that was in any way detrimental to Soviet interests.

The Soviet leaders' reaction to UN intervention in the Congo was growing disenchantment with the international organization, as far as its peace-keeping operations were concerned; in fact, the Soviet Union refused to contribute any funds for those operations. The nonaligned states, to be sure, have shown no such disenchantment. They unanimously opposed the troika plan to hamstring the secretary-general, for they value the organization as the bastion of their independence and "neutralist" positions in the cold war. Because of Soviet refusal to pay for UN peace-keeping operations and American insistence that the Soviet Union must pay if it was not to lose its voting rights in the General Assembly, the international body became deadlocked and remained so until American leaders saw that they would receive little support for stripping the Soviet Union of its voting rights in the assembly. They were then willing to recognize instead the principle that no great power must pay for operations that it regards as detrimental to its interests.

It is inconceivable that the United States would be any more likely than the Soviet Union to give financial support to operations that were injurious to its national interests. Indeed, when the United States abandoned its position, it declared that it too reserved the right not to pay for future peace-keeping operations of which it disapproved. Although this move at the time may have been a face-saving way out of an awkward situation, the United States went further than the Soviets and reduced its contribution to the United Nations as a whole in 1971 when Beijing was seated in the international organization. At a time when President Richard Nixon was seeking rapprochement with Beijing's leaders, the U.S. House of Representatives decided unilaterally to cut the American share of the United Nations budget to 25 percent from 31 percent. The Senate eventually restored the cut, but the American government did notify the General Assembly, which assesses member states, that the United States wished to negotiate such a reduction.

Another interesting result of the clash of the superpowers over the Congo was the revival of the Security Council as the main UN organ concerned with security issues. If the Soviet Union could not be assured of majority support in the General Assembly and if it could not control the secretary-general, then it seemed better to retain peace-keeping operations in the Security Council, where, with judicious use of the veto, the Soviet government could keep some degree of control and influence over whatever is decided. The United States also cannot be certain of controlling the Security Council, as it was able to do in the first phase, because in 1966 the nonpermanent membership of the council was expanded. Events in 1974 suggested a similar loss of American influence in the General Assembly. It is thus not surprising that during the Yom Kippur War of 1973 the two superpowers cooperated in the council to pass a cease-fire resolution, to sponsor jointly under UN auspices the Geneva peace conference between Arabs and Israelis, and to follow a similar procedure when Greece and Turkey almost came to war over Cyprus in 1974.

Can the United Nations Prevent Wars?

Although the United Nations has managed to prevent the continuation and escalation of fighting in which one or both of the superpowers have not been participants themselves, it should be emphasized that this success is not to be confused with the prevention of war. That is one lesson of the war in 1967, when Egypt exercised its sovereign right to expel UN forces. Sometimes wars do not even come under the jurisdiction of the United Nations. In 1971 Pakistan brutally crushed an attempt by East Pakistan to secede and become independent. Claiming that the proposed secession was a domestic matter, the Pakistani government rejected UN intervention. Three million people were subsequently killed. India, burdened by 10 million refugees from East Pakistan and eager to eliminate its only rival on the subcontinent, went to war with Pakistan, helped to establish the state of Bangladesh, and sent the refugees back there. India too rejected UN intervention. When the Vietnamese invaded Cambodia to overthrow the pro-Chinese Pol Pot government and impose a pro-Vietnamese government, after which Chinese forces crossed the frontier with Vietnam to teach the Vietnamese a lesson, none of these Communist states wanted a debate on aggression in Indochina. It would have been too embarrassing. Nor have all conflicts in Africa received attention in the halls of the United Nations. In 1977 Somalia actively supported, perhaps even sponsored, an uprising in the Ogaden area of Ethiopia; later the Ethiopians, with Soviet-Cuban support, moved toward Somalia's border, but no debate occurred. Nor was there debate when Idi Amin of Uganda provoked Tanzania and, in the subsequent war, Tanzanian troops deposed him. Similarly, the

Iraqi attack upon Iran in 1980 was never placed on the Security Council's agenda; nor was Libya's invasion of Chad in 1980.

Civil wars, with their potential for spilling over into interstate conflict, or the barbarous treatment of people by their own governments usually are not placed on the international agenda. While the Nigerian government was engaged in civil war against the Ibos in the secessionist state of Biafra from 1967 to 1970, approximately half a million people died, but the issue was not debated in the United Nations because many LDCs did not wish to legitimate Biafra and encourage secession in their own countries. After its victory in Cambodia, the Communist government of Pol Pot adopted a barbarous policy of genocide against its own people, yet this problem never appeared on the United Nations agenda; 2 million to 3 million of Cambodia's 8 million people reportedly died as a result of these policies before the regime was forcibly replaced in 1979 by a Vietnamese puppet regime. The United Nations consists of sovereign states, which means that each has the right to exclude any intervention aimed at protecting the rights of individuals among its citizens. But the increasing number of wars that are *not* brought before the Security Council raises a serious question about the continued relevance of the United Nations on peace and security issues.

THE FOURTH PHASE: DECLINING U.S. COMMITMENT TO THE UNITED NATIONS

Limitations of the United Nations

Several points about the limits on UN power are worth restating.

Subject to Power Politics. First, the organization is *not* a substitute for power politics. To idealize the United Nations, to expect it to rise "above that sort of thing" and to be superior in morals and general demeanor to the nation-states that are its members is not only unwarranted but also likely to breed disillusionment and cynicism. Unrealistically high expectations, when disappointed, result in declining support for its highly important "preventive diplomacy." The United Nations is not simply a debating society. Speeches there serve the purpose of articulating conflicting views and making the world more aware of key issues that are likely to be troublesome. United Nations representatives from various nations are also able to gather informally, to try to reconcile differing interests, and to arrange compromises out of the limelight.

No Authority over the Superpowers. Second, although the United Nations is neither a world government nor totally impotent, it is not very powerful in dealing with the superpowers. In 1979 the General Assembly demanded that Vietnam withdraw its troops from Cambodia after two attempts to censure Vietnam in the Security Council had been vetoed by the Soviet Union. The assembly resolution, sponsored by Vietnam's non-Communist neighbors and supported by many LDCs, was ignored by Vietnam. And all this came after the Security Council had briefly discussed the Vietnamese invasion of Cambodia, only quickly to drop it. In 1979-80, the Security Council agreed that Iran ought to release the American hostages held in the embassy in Tehran. Because seizure of diplomatic personnel threatened to make diplomacy itself impossible, such unanimity was to be expected. If the United Nations could not speak for the safety of diplomats, what could it speak for? But, when Iran continued to hold the hostages, economic sanctions were vetoed by the Soviets in the Security Council. (The United States did not take the issue to the General Assembly, allegedly because a supportive vote there would have no legal force, but actually because a majority could not be obtained. Domestic support for U.S. military action against Iran was also lacking.) When the Security Council called for Soviet military withdrawal from Afghanistan after its 1979 invasion, it was vetoed by the Soviets. The assembly did vote 104-18 (with 30 states not voting) to condemn the Soviet move, a rare occurrence in the United Nations. The Soviet-inspired establishment of martial law in Poland in 1981 did not even come before the United Nations, although this "occupation of Poland by its own army" eliminated the hard-won freedoms of the previous months and represented a gross violation of human rights.

Influenced by National Interests.   Third, because the United Nations reflects the real world and not the ideal world, it should not be surprising that all member nations continue to follow their national interests, regardless of how moralistic and altruistic their rhetoric. When the Soviet Union was in a minority in the first phase of the United Nations, it could counter majority resolutions in the Security Council only through its veto power as one of the five permanent members. It did indeed cast many vetoes, partly because the United States, using diplomacy as a tool of propaganda, repeatedly introduced resolutions to which it knew the Soviet Union would object. Precisely because the United Nations is associated in the popular mind with idealism, the United States was able to place the Soviet Union in a position of seeming to obstruct the peaceful work of the organization, and to align itself with the majority in the pursuit of all that is good and true. Conversely, the United States did not have to cast a single veto; it had majority support in the Security Council. In using majority votes to reject Soviet proposals, the United States was exercising what has been called a "hidden veto"—a negative vote hidden beneath a democratic cloak.

Not until 1966, when enough nonpermanent members had been added to the Security Council to jeopardize American control of that body, did the United States begin to cast vetoes itself. Because national interests dictate how members vote, American voting behavior in the council, despite fewer vetoes, is not fundamentally different from that of the Soviets. And, faced with the fact that many LDCs participate with the Soviet Union in an anti-Western coalition, the United States also began to cast vetoes in the Security Council. Moreover, the United States withdrew from the United Nations Educational, Scientific, and Cultural Organization (UNESCO) in 1985 because of UNESCO's politicization of issues before it and its anti-Western orientation, reduced its contribution for the United Nations' upkeep from 40 percent to 25 percent, refused to sign the 1982 Law of the Sea Treaty, and rejected the jurisdiction of the International Court of Justice when Nicaragua brought charges of U.S. aggression before the Court.

Double Standards.   Fourth, as the United Nations does represent its constituents and as these nations pursue their national interests through the organization, it follows that the United Nations will reflect double standards of judgment. When Israel retaliates against one of its Arab neighbors for brutal guerrilla attacks and outright murder, it is likely to find itself condemned by a majority of members, for the Arab states, both as LDCs and as Muslim nations, have lots of friends. The guerrillas and the Arab states harboring them will not be similarly condemned. The United States cast its second veto when Israel, having exacted reprisals for the murder by Palestinian terrorists of several members of the Israeli Olympic team in Munich in 1972, was about to be condemned in the Security Council. And, although South Africa is frequently condemned, the LDCs never censured Amin for as many as 300,000 murders or the persecution and expulsion of 60,000 Asians from Uganda, or Burundi for over 100,000 Hutus reported killed within its borders; or Cambodia for its genocide. "The countries of the Third World are not subject to criticism or attack, even by each other, while any part of the rest of the world which can be labelled racist or imperialist must be held accountable."[9] An early, and blatant, example was India's invasion of the Portuguese colony Goa in 1961. India argued that the colony represented "imperialism," which automatically constituted "aggression." The Indian invasion was justified as a completely legitimate act of liberation. A majority of UN members supported India's claim. That set the precedent for supporting later "national liberation" movements. But American-supported resistance against the Soviet-Cuban-backed government in Angola did not qualify for the label of national liberation. Not even the clear-cut case of Afghan resistance to Soviet occupation has qualified it as a national liberation movement! And in the Iran-Iraq war, a war between Third World states, Iraq was not condemned for invading its neighbor in 1980; nor has either side been condemned for their brutal treatment of each other's prisoners of war.

Not Representative of World Opinion.   Fifth, the United Nations does not represent "world public opinion," which allegedly restrains state behavior. Most states cannot be considered democratic, although many of them claim to be. Many are authoritarian, whether civilians or military officers are in charge; public opinion has no means of expression on national issues in such countries. Nor do they allow competing parties or a free press and other mass media; the masses hear only what their governments wish them to hear. In addition, a government's public statements may not reflect its private views.

In any event, the absence of a world public opinion reflects the existence of many nations with varied historical traditions, philosophies, ideologies, and political and moral standards. There is little consensus among countries on what is moral and what are acceptable standards of behavior. Certainly there is nothing equivalent to those that exist in modern Western political systems. What does exist is a set of *governmental* views and opinions, which are often mistaken for "world public opinion." When a government solemnly declares in the United Nations that "our people wish to express their outrage" or whatever else, it is presenting its own opinion as the *vox populi.*

A state is admittedly sensitive to what other states think of its actions, and it may take prospective reactions into account in deciding on its aims, how they are to be achieved, and how publicly to explain them. Concern for other states' opinions is an everyday affair of which extensive public relations and propaganda efforts are the symptom. And no state relishes a UN vote against it, for the popular image of the United Nations as a "good" organization, symbolic of humanity's desire for peace, is deeply rooted. Nevertheless, when governments feel genuinely strong about an issue, they will pursue their aims, regardless of the *national* opinions expressed in the General Assembly and Security Council. The Soviet invasions of Hungary, Czechoslovakia, and Afghanistan are examples. Iran continued to hold American hostages, despite a disapproving vote in the Security Council.

Adaptability.   Sixth, the United Nations has been very adaptable in the world in flux. Like the American Constitution, it has proved flexible and pragmatic. It was originally established on the assumption that the great powers would cooperate, with the added safeguard that, if they could not cooperate, it was better to cast a veto than to attempt to ride roughshod over a great power. It seemed preferable to paralyze the Security Council and to prevent action, for that would reflect the genuine stalemate outside the United Nations; to have abolished the veto might have cured the Security Council's impotence, but it would also probably have meant war. When one great power opposes another, it is the better part of wisdom to attempt to negotiate differences, rather than to outvote one of the parties and then to try to enforce the majority decision. In any event, the United Nations was not permanently paralyzed in its area of primary responsibility, keeping the peace. This function was first shifted to the General Assembly, then to the secretary-general, and then back—or so it seems—to the Security Council. Thanks to this flexibility, the United Nations has demonstrated a vitality that its predecessor, the League of Nations, never exhibited during the period between the two world wars. It has survived and performed some vital functions during four decades of changing American-Soviet relations, the appearance of many new states, and the subsequent division between rich and poor countries. Presumably it will continue to survive in the rapidly changing world of the future.

Arena of Confrontation or Conflict Resolution?

Yet the key question is whether in being so adaptable the United Nations may not have made itself irrelevant. Its current problems arise from the fact that it is the forum in which the LDCs publicize their causes. It is there that they voice their demands for the new international economic order and raise various specific issues related to this demand: management of food reserves, setting of commodity prices, ownership of ocean mineral resources, curbing population growth, meeting minimum human needs, and the fulfillment of women's rights. The years after the 1973 war in the Middle East were years of confrontation between Western industrial countries and the Third World, in which rhetoric often became strident and the double standard plain. The Western countries were continually criticized for past and present exploitation even while they were being called upon for assistance. The Communist countries, which offered virtually no material help, suffered no rebuke and even enjoyed acclaim for their view that poor countries are poor because they have been exploited by the rich. The temper of the LDCs, most of which had in the past prided themselves on nonalignment, was symbolized by their 1979 meeting in Cuba. Vietnam and North Korea, which, like Cuba, were not nonaligned at all, attended this meeting and tried to influence the assembly to support Soviet policy. Although the subsequent Soviet invasion of Afghanistan aroused overwhelming disapproval, later nonaligned meetings have not hesitated to criticize American policies while abstaining from mentioning Soviet policies. Even in calling for the withdrawal of Soviet forces in Afghanistan, the reference was to "foreign forces"; the nonaligned refused to mention the Soviet Union by name. Later meetings were no different. The 101-nation 1986 meeting in Zimbabwe condemned the United States by name fifty-four times—including for "state terrorism" against Libya—the Soviet Union not once.

An Anti-Western Phase

The main danger to the visibility of the United Nations arises from its failure to observe its own charter and decisions. The dangerous Middle Eastern situation first suggested the possibility that the United Nations is entering a fourth, anti-Western phase. The assembly in 1974 invited the head of the Palestine Liberation Organization (PLO), a nonstate actor whose acts of terrorism and hijacking it had debated only a few years earlier, to address it. It treated PLO leader Yasir Arafat as a head of government and greeted him with sustained applause while limiting the time for an Israeli reply, which was delivered to a virtually empty auditorium. Simultaneously, the Arab-

African-Asian majority, supported by the Communist states, barred Israeli participation in the previously nonpolitical UNESCO. In addition, the assembly ousted South Africa from its sessions because of that nation's racial practices after the Security Council, which exercises ultimate suspension power, had refused to do so. Israel and the United States have been attacked repeatedly for trading with South Africa, even though the countries of Western Europe, the Soviet bloc, the Arab states, and many black African nations also trade with South Africa. The PLO, as well as SWAPO (South West African People's Organization in Namibia), have "permanent observer" status at the United Nations and receive UN funds—all in the name of national liberation and becoming future states.

It was in 1979, however, that the most dramatic confrontation in the General Assembly occurred. That was the year Amin, then president of Uganda and chairman of the Organization for African Unity (OAU), a man who had voiced approval of the slaughter of Israeli athletes at the Munich Olympics and had said that Adolf Hitler's only error had been not killing more Jews, claimed to speak on behalf of forty-six African members when he charged that the United States had been colonized by Zionists and that Israel had no right to exist. The coalition of African, Asian, Arab, and Communist nations also was able to pass a General Assembly resolution equating Zionism with racism. A similar resolution was passed almost unnoticed in the closing weeks of the 1979 session. The earlier resolution, sponsored by the Arab states, also proclaimed the Palestinians' right to independence and sovereignty but failed to recognize the same right for Israel. The resolution thus represented acceptance by the majority in the General Assembly of the rights of Palestinians, as defined by leaders who refused to accept the rights of the nation of Israel, over the birth of which the United Nations had presided.

Concern for human rights has also become very selective, especially during the 1980s. Israel and South Africa remain the perennial targets. No human rights violations by Castro's Cuba have ever been discussed and condemned. El Salvador's government may be criticized but not the rebels, who have refused to participate in or accept the decisions of the majority of the Salvadoran people at the polls and continue the insurrection. Nor has the Sandinista government been condemned for the gradual strangulation of the Nicaraguan people's civil and political rights, despite its original commitment to political democracy, mixed economy, and nonalignment in foreign policy. Instead, the attacks are on United States' allies, and most of those attacking those policies are themselves authoritarian regimes whose human rights records are very poor.

Is the United Nations Still Relevant?

The relevance of future Security Council resolutions may be reduced; this possibility is even greater for General Assembly resolutions, which are of an advisory nature only. The authority of a majority composed of many small nondemocratic states, whose financial contribution to the United Nations' upkeep is minimal, will be widely questioned—at least in the West. Former U.S. ambassador Jeane Kirkpatrick in the early 1980s voiced an additional complaint. Not only did the LDCs frequently vent their anti-American sentiments, but the United Nations, by repeatedly debating the same issue and sometimes calling for sanctions (usually against Israel and South Africa), generated "a process of conflict extension, polarization, and exacerbation." Rather than facilitating the resolution of disputes, the United Nations debates hardened positions, embittering the contending nations.[10] American successes, she said, increasingly amounted to little more than blocking anti-American resolutions. U.S. policy thus added up to little more than "damage control," warding off attacks ranging from attacks on Israel to calling for the independence of Puerto Rico.

Besides lamenting this outcome, Kirkpatrick pointed out that the reason for this was the increase in bloc voting. The General Assembly has grown to 159 members in which every state has one vote, whether it is Communist China with more than 1 billion people or St. Kitts-Nevis, a microstate with a population of less than 100,000. Thus the thirty-eight microstates with populations of fewer than 1 million have an influence in the United Nations totally disproportionate to their size, population, wealth, and financial contribution to the UN budget. By organizing into blocs, such as the East European bloc, the 20-member Arab grouping, the 12 members of the European Economic Community plus Japan, the 42 Islamic Conference countries, and the more than 100 countries that call themselves the nonaligned group (of which approximately one-third are African states and which includes the above members of other LDC groupings), the LDC-Soviet bloc coalition can easily muster anti-Western majorities in the General Assembly and most of the specialized agencies, such as UNESCO, while often ignoring other critical peace and human rights issues (especially those they do not want aired).[11] (See Table 18-2.)

The upshot, Kirkpatrick said, has been twofold: the United Nations has become increasingly less relevant to many of the world's problems, and its capacity for conflict resolution has decreased as repeated condemnations have made it even more difficult to find a compromise solution. Reasoned debate has more and more fallen prey to ritualistic and repetitive slogans whose aim is, directly or implicitly, to condemn the United States, and which only serve to aggravate conflicts rather than resolve them. The "all-too-familiar scenario," Kirkpatrick said,

> features one victim, many attackers, a great deal of verbal violence and a large number of indifferent and/or intimidated onlookers.
>
> In these carefully staged productions, the Security Council serves as the stage, the presence of the world press ensures an audience, the solidarity of the "blocs" provides a long procession of speakers to echo, elaborate and expand on the original accusations. The goal is isolation and humiliation of the victim—creation of an impression that "world opinion" is united in condemnation of the targeted nation.

Table 18-2 UN Member Countries, 1945-1985

	Americas		*Europe*	

1945 Original Members	Argentina
	Bolivia
	Brazil
	Canada
	Chile
	Colombia
	Costa Rica
	Cuba
	Dominican
	    Republic
	Ecuador
	El Salvador
		Guatemala
		Haiti
		Honduras
		Mexico
		Nicaragua
		Panama
		Paraguay
		Peru
		United States
		Uruguay
		Venezuela
			Belgium
			Belorussia
			Czechoslovakia
			Denmark
			France
			Greece
			Luxembourg
			Netherlands
			Norway
			Poland
			Turkey
				Ukraine
				USSR
				United
				    Kingdom
				Yugoslavia

1945-1965	Jamaica Trinidad and Tobago		Albania Austria Bulgaria Finland Hungary Iceland Ireland Italy Malta Portugal Romania Spain Sweden	

1965-1985	Antigua and
	    Barbuda
	The Bahamas
	Barbados
	Belize
	Dominica
	Grenada
	Guyana
		St. Christopher
		    and Nevis
		St. Lucia
		St. Vincent
		    and the
		    Grenadines
		Suriname
			East Germany
			West Germany	

SOURCE: U.S. Department of State, *Atlas of United States Foreign Relations,* 2d ed. (Washington, D.C.: Government Printing Office, 1985), 18.

The enterprise more closely resembles a mugging than either a political debate or an effort at problem solving.[12]

Solutions to difficult problems may increasingly have to be found outside of the United Nations, if solutions exist at all. Because of the blocs, UN voting

Asia/Oceania		Africa	
Australia		Egypt	
China		Ethiopia	
India		Liberia	
Iran		South Africa	
Iraq			
Lebanon			
New Zealand			
Philippines			
Saudi Arabia			
Syria			
Afghanistan	Pakistan	Algeria	Mali
Burma	Singapore	Benin	Mauritania
Cambodia	Sri Lanka	Burkina Faso	Morocco
Cyprus	Thailand	Burundi	Niger
Indonesia	Yemen (Sanaa)	Cameroon	Nigeria
Israel		Central African	Rwanda
Japan		Republic	Senegal
Jordan		Chad	Sierra Leone
Kuwait		Congo	Somalia
Laos		Gabon	Sudan
Malaysia		The Gambia	Tanzania
Maldives		Ghana	Togo
Mongolia		Guinea	Tunisia
Nepal		Ivory Coast	Uganda
		Libya	Zaire
		Madagascar	Zambia
		Malawi	
Bahrain	Solomon Islands	Angola	Mauritius
Bangladesh	United Arab	Botswana	Mozambique
Bhutan	Emirates	Cape Verde	Sao Tome and
Brunei	Vanuatu	Comoros	Principe
Fiji	Vietnam	Djibouti	Seychelles
Oman	Western Samoa	Equatorial Guinea	Swaziland
Papua New Guinea	Yemen (Aden)	Guinea-Bissau	Zimbabwe
Qatar		Lesotho	

patterns are unlikely to change in the near future, regardless of changes in policy in Washington. At present the United Nations is unfriendly to American values and interests (as during its second phase, it was unfriendly toward the Soviet Union). The best the United States can do is to play "hard ball" to ensure that those who repeatedly vote against U.S. positions know that the votes they cast will have consequences outside of the United Nations, for example, in loss of aid. In fact, the U.S. Senate passed a resolution reducing the American contribution to the United Nations' annual budget from 25 percent to 20 percent by October 1986 unless the UN voting formula of one state, one vote is changed. This resolution calls for the United Nations to shift to a system under which voting strength on budget matters is proportional to each member state's financial contribution. The four largest contributors—the United States, Japan, West Germany, and France—would then have slightly more than 50 percent of the vote and control of the budget. The current formula, it is charged, is "taxation without representation." Obviously, a majority that would lose much of its influence in the General Assembly would oppose such a change in the voting formula (and probably point out that the U.S. Senate's own equal representation formula might itself constitute taxation without representation for the larger and wealthier of the fifty states). Even if the United States takes no action, the Senate's mandated cut— later relaxed by the Reagan administration in return for budgetary and secretarial staff reforms—demonstrates U.S. frustration at the United Nations and serves as a warning to the LDCs.

The new secretary-general, Javier Pérez de Cuéllar, called attention to the increased inability of the United Nations to prevent or halt wars. His efforts to mediate the 1982 Argentinian-British dispute over the Falkland Islands failed. The Security Council was ignored, if not defied when it called repeatedly and unanimously in 1982 for a cease-fire in Lebanon and for Israel to withdraw its troops. In earlier years the United Nations was unable to get the Soviet Union to withdraw its troops from Afghanistan, to get Vietnam to pull out of Cambodia, to end the Iran-Iraq war, or to resolve the conflicts in Nicaragua and El Salvador. An editorial in the *New York Times* summed up the situation:

> The problem is that an assembly of nations called "sovereign," or subject to no higher authority, can never be more than the sum of its members. Nations can behave inside the U.N. only as they behave outside, bartering interests, including their interest in peace. But the Charter notwithstanding, they insist on the right to redress grievance by force, which is what distinguishes a nation from province, county, town or individual.
>
> To yield that right, nations would need a common parliament to write laws, courts to interpret them and police to enforce them. They would have to disarm and pay taxes to a protecting authority instead. The United Nations cannot evolve into such a higher authority; it was designed to foreclose it, to let peoples relate only *internationally*, through the prism of their armies.
>
> That does not mean the U.N. is useless as mediator when any parties want to avoid war. But it does mean that anarchy—the absence of higher authority—is the desired, if undesirable condition.[13]

In short, the sovereignty of the member states will continue to limit its contribution to resolving nations' security and welfare problems.

DISARMAMENT AMONG STATES

Arms as a Cause of War

From the moment the first atomic bomb was exploded, the central question has been whether "absolute" weapons can be compatible with the continued existence of humanity organized in nation-states. If nations are unwilling to relinquish their sovereign rights or at least to adopt a new spirit of accommodation within the United Nations, might not some future quarrel spark a global conflagration that will leave the world in ruins, its smoldering ashes a monument to human scientific genius and human malevolence? The Spanish philosopher José Ortega y Gasset once wrote that man is "lord of all things, but he is not lord of himself." The devil in George Bernard Shaw's *Man and Superman* put the point even more poignantly, long before the bombing of Hiroshima in 1945:

> And is man any less destroying himself for all this boasted brain of his? Have you walked up and down upon the earth lately? I have; and I have examined Man's wonderful inventions. And I tell you that in the arts of life man invents nothing but in the arts of death he outdoes Nature herself, and produces by chemistry and machinery all the slaughtered, of plague, pestilence, and famine . . . when he goes out to slay, he carries a marvel of mechanism that lets loose at the touch of his finger all the hidden molecular energies, and leaves the javelin, the arrow, the blowpipe of his fathers far behind. In the arts of peace Man is a bungler. . . . I know his clumsy typewriters and bungling locomotives and tedious bicycles; they are toys compared to the Maxim gun, the submarine, torpedo boat. There is nothing in Man's industrial machinery but his greed and sloth: his heart is in his weapons. This marvelous force of life which you boast is a force of Death: Man measures his strength by his destructiveness.[14]

If Shaw is correct, our first level of analysis may lead us only to a rather gloomy prediction for the future. Given the conflict inherent in the state system, nuclear war is only a matter of time. But we can logically draw several other conclusions from our model that may help us to deal with the power and security dilemma inherent in the state system and to avoid ultimate catastrophe. One recommended solution is general and complete disarmament. Even before the bombing of Hiroshima, it was apparent that, in a competitive system, political conflict is accompanied by arms buildups; these arms races tend to erupt in warfare. The question has been whether it would be safer for all nations to disarm. If nations continue to accumulate arms, is their use not inevitable? Have not all previous arms races ended in wars? The answer seems obvious, and disarmament seems an obvious solution, particularly in the nuclear age. Armaments are no longer a means of protecting nations, and only disarmament could guarantee national security. Merely controlling arms cannot prevent war; it cannot save the world from destruction. The goal, therefore, according to some analysts, must be total or quantitative disarmament; even partial or qualitative disarmament, aimed at specific types of weapon, like nuclear arms, will not suffice.

However *theoretically* feasible disarmament may seem, it is unlikely to provide the answer to the problem of nuclear weapons in political conflict. In the first place, there can be no such thing as *total* disarmament. The problem is not just semantic. In assessing a nation's strength and capacity to wage war, as we know, we must take into account—along with the number of people under arms and the weapons they possess—geographical position, population, natural resources, productive capacity, and scientific ability, which are all equally important. Military power is only one aspect of a nation's overall strength, and that strength cannot be artificially eliminated. Even total disarmament would leave a "war potential" that could be mobilized after a declaration of war. International quarrels would not cease with the abolition of armaments. Second, no disarmament treaty can eradicate knowledge of nuclear physics and the ability to construct atomic or hydrogen bombs. In any event, even elimination of nuclear weapons would leave the countries that possess vast resources and skills, such as the United States and the Soviet Union, with more than enough potential conventional military power to conduct a long and very destructive war.

The belief that disarmament is the solution to war in the state system is based on the assumption that arms races cause wars. To protect itself, a nation increases its military strength; another nation then builds up its military power to guard against possible attack from the first nation. The ensuing arms race develops its own momentum and creates a war psychology; at a favorable moment, when one country believes that it is stronger than the other—or that the other side is beginning to pull ahead—it will attack. Interaction between the contestants is considered to produce an arms spiral that, when it reaches a critical point, automatically precipitates hostilities through a sort of "spontaneous combustion." But, because in the state system arms accompany competition, the critical question is why wars sometimes occur and sometimes do not. The answer requires an examination of political causes.

To attribute wars to the simple existence of arms is to confuse cause and effect. An arms race does not follow a logic of its own. It is not an autonomous process divorced from the political context in which it occurs. Capabilities cannot be artificially separated from intentions. Military power serves the political ends of the state.[15] An arms race reflects political tensions between nations; it does not cause those tensions. States need armaments to protect what they consider to be their interests; they do not fight simply because they possess arms. Rather, they possess arms because they believe it may someday be necessary to fight. Prime Minister Margaret Thatcher of Britain said at the 1982 United Nations disarmament session:

> The springs of war lie in the readiness to resort to force against other nations, and not in "arms races," whether real or imagined. Aggressors do not start wars because an adversary has built up strength. They start wars because they believe they can gain more by going to war than by remaining at peace.[16]

Disarmament and good intentions, she explained, do not therefore ensure peace. Indeed, it may be added that when nations involved in political quarrels fail to arm, they invite aggression. Although it is true that, when power confronts power, there may be danger, it is certain that, when power meets weakness, there will be far greater danger. It is all too easy to attribute conflicts to arms races. It is much more difficult to mention wars that have been prevented because nations have armed themselves.

As arms are a *symptom* of interstate political conflict, it is illusory to expect nations to disarm while conflict persists. *The prerequisite for disarmament is political agreement on issues separating the nations involved in the arms race.*[17] How can nations be expected to agree to total elimination or major reduction of the instruments with which they seek to protect themselves and gain their ends? In the absence of reliable substitutes with which states can defend and seek their objectives, states need arms. This need is bound to influence their disarmament proposals. If a nation is already stronger than its opponent, it will want to preserve and even enhance this superiority, and its disarmament proposals will contain that built-in bias. If it is weaker, it will want to catch up with and, if possible, surpass its opponent, and its proposals will reflect those objectives. An attempt to freeze the status quo will arouse anger and frustration in a revisionist state; efforts to erode the status quo will be a source of annoyance and worry to a state that benefits from it. Disarmament negotiations in these circumstances are merely another form of the arms race itself, in which each nation aims to increase its relative power position.

The lack of mutual trust in these circumstances becomes an impediment to agreement on disarmament. The United States since 1945 has been proposing inspection as a substitute for trust. States are not going to rely on good faith for the implementation of whatever accords may be reached, especially in the nuclear era. Any form of disarmament, whether involving strategic nuclear arms or conventional weapons, is in itself an incentive to cheat, for gaining an advantage over the adversary may result in a significant political "payoff." But all states, including the Soviet Union for most of the postwar period, have rejected calls for inspection and have denounced them as attempts at espionage. (It is doubtful, for instance, that Washington's leaders would have been any more willing to tolerate inspection by Soviet personnel of American industrial plants and military installations than the other way around.) Although the Soviets in recent years have appeared more willing to allow inspections, the difficulties of negotiating such verification of agreements continues to reflect basic U.S.-Soviet distrust. The consequence was that both superpowers were compelled to rely primarily on remote means of inspection, which became increasingly feasible with newer technology; but aerial survey cannot do some things that inspections on the ground and under the ground can do.

Mutual confidence is the necessary prerequisite for inspection to work; it is precisely the absence of confidence that makes leaders believe it imperative to possess arms. And that is exactly where the problem lies: in an essentially anarchical state system, arms serve useful functions; without reliable alternative means of achieving the same purposes, potential adversaries are unlikely to surrender or accept significant restriction on their arms. It is perhaps symbolic that the very first disarmament conference, in 1898, was called by the Russian czar to discuss "the most effective means of assuring to all peoples the blessing of real and lasting peace, and above all of limiting the progressive development of existing armaments." [18] The conference was born out of fear that Russia was falling behind Germany in the European arms competition because it was unable to afford to keep up. Underneath the noble words about a "real and lasting peace," the conference was actually called to keep Russia *in* the arms race.

Aims of Disarmament Negotiations

Why, then, do states pursue disarmament at all? Are states merely hypocritical, pretending that they wish to eliminate weapons, when it is clear that few agreements can be reached unless real political differences are first resolved? Clearly, disarmament negotiations serve a number of other purposes.

Arms Competition.   The fundamental purpose is that disarmament *negotiations* are, as already suggested, a form of arms competition. It could not be otherwise. In the state system, each nation must defend itself against attack. As the possibility of war is inherent in the conflict of national wills, each state must pay attention to its armed strength. Salvador de Madariaga wrote:

> All disarmament conferences are bound to degenerate into armament conferences. In all of them discussion is based on the assumption of war, and they all reveal the inevitable conflict between the ardent endeavors of the delegations present, each of which has for its main aim to secure the highest possible increase of its relative armaments in a general reduction of absolute forces, if such a reduction there must be.[19]

A fable illustrates this point. A group of animals, having decided to disarm, convene to discuss the matter. The eagle, looking at the bull, suggests that all horns be cut off. The bull, looking at the tiger, says that all claws should be clipped. The tiger, looking at the elephant, is of the opinion that tusks should be either pulled out or shortened. The elephant, looking at the eagle, thinks that all wings should be clipped. Then the bear, glancing around at all his brethren, says in tones of sweet reason: "Comrades, why all these halfway measures? Let us abolish everything—everything but a fraternal, all-embracing hug." All countries need arms, but, because of their importance, they usually cannot agree on the ratio of power that ought to exist among them.

Remember that the first disarmament conference was called by the czar. Was it to advance international peace and lift the burden of armaments from humanity? The answer is absolutely not. At the 1986 summit conference in Iceland Soviet leader Mikhail Gorbachev and U.S. president Ronald Reagan discussed the elimination of all strategic nuclear weapons, stressing their hopes for a nuclear-free world. In a world without nuclear weapons, the Soviet Union, because of its huge conventional forces, would become the dominant Eurasian power unless the West responded with a large, expensive military buildup. Such a buildup would require the United States to revive the draft and to raise taxes; conventional forces are more expensive to maintain than nuclear weapons. Nevertheless, to focus on eliminating nuclear arms was good public relations. Whether it is wise for the United States and its allies to abolish their nuclear arms if they wish to avoid a bear hug is another matter. What Russia was after in the first disarmament conference was a freeze so that it would not fall even further behind in producing arms. Despite this reality, the 1898 conference—like its 1986 counterpart in Iceland—gave the Russians a peace-seeking image.

Propaganda. A second reason for pursuing disarmament is propaganda. Disarmament is like motherhood, the flag, and apple pie: Who can be against it? Disarmament conjures up an image of peace and harmony among states, a willingness to coexist amicably and to resolve disputes with reason, to act with restraint, to radiate good will, and to show concern for all people, not just those of one's own nation. Disarmament is good, moral, clean, and virtuous; to be against it is to be in favor of war, conflict, and national egotism and against humanity. Disarmament is thus an issue on which diplomacy is concerned to a very large extent with propaganda. Because disarmament is a popular goal, no nation is willing to reject an invitation to discuss it. The disarmament "deck," however, frequently contains a "joker" that the opponent cannot possibly accept.[20] The joker serves a dual function: compelling rejection of the entire plan (while placing the onus for the resulting diplomatic deadlock on the other side) and protecting the vital interests of the proposing side. In fact, Gorbachev appears to have indulged in this in Iceland. He offered a major series of arms concessions, above all, a 50 percent reduction of Soviet ICBMs, but contingent on the United States' restricting research on the Strategic Defense Initiative and no deployment for at least ten years. He may have guessed that the president would continue to consider SDI nonnegotiable as he has done since 1983 when he proposed it. In that case he would reap a great propaganda coup and put the United States on the defensive diplomatically, as indeed did occur; if the president were willing to confine SDI to the research laboratory, the Western alliance would have been deprived of the strategic nuclear weapons that remain the ultimate deterrent. In either event, Gorbachev could not lose.

Economics. A third reason for disarmament negotiations is economic. Earlier we spoke of the choices between guns and butter that governments, especially governments of great powers, must make. The arms bill for the superpowers is enormous and continuous. Furthermore, it rises with increasing technical complexity—at least in industrialized Western economies. Since World War II the United States and the Soviet Union have produced nearly $20 trillion in gross national product (GNP), approximately $15 trillion in the

United States alone. "Of this amount more than $2 trillion had been spent on arms by the end of the Vietnam era, about $1.3 trillion by the United States and an estimated $1 trillion by the Soviet Union."[21] Costs remain high. Soviet spending has been calculated at between 12 percent and 14 percent of its GNP during the 1970s and early 1980s. It was estimated that Soviet leaders outspent the United States by more than $100 billion during the 1970s. While these estimated figures have been lowered somewhat by U.S. intelligence agencies recently, the Soviet figures remain impressive nevertheless, given the considerably lower Soviet GNP. And, after declining to below 5 percent of GNP for several years (the lowest since before the Korean War), U.S. defense spending started going up again during the late years of the administration of Jimmy Carter. The administration of Ronald Reagan, claiming that it intended to make up for this neglect of American military strength during most of the 1970s, proposed a five-year $1.6 trillion rearmament program, enlarging the Navy by 30 percent to six hundred ships, increasing tactical air power from thirty-six to forty units, and filling out army divisions, on top of a major revitalization of the nation's nuclear armory.

The costs of weapons are enormous and going up. A single nuclear-propelled aircraft carrier costs $3 billion. One M-1 tank costs almost $3 million, an attack helicopter $30 million, an attack submarine $500 million, an F-16 fighter more than $15 million, and an F-18 more than $32 million. An air-launched cruise missile costs $14 million; the one hundred MX missiles and one hundred B-1 bombers the Reagan administration proposed building are estimated to cost more than $27 billion and $40 billion respectively; SDI has been estimated at $50 billion and upward.

But it is not only the superpowers and their allies that spend large sums on arms. The developing countries, too, are buying arms, including the most advanced conventional arms, on a large scale, for both protection and prestige.[22] Ironically the poor countries are growing poorer—in part, at least—because they are buying more weapons. In 1974, for example, India exploded a nuclear device and, despite its claim that it had no intention of building a nuclear force, starkly raised the issue of national priorities in an LDC. Ten years earlier India had had a population of 580 million, growing at a rate of 13 million a year. Approximately 30 percent was illiterate. The nation's industrial production was stagnant. Three-fourths of its university graduates could not find employment. After India's nuclear explosion an editorial in the *New York Times* was very blunt. It stated that India had placed "considerations of national power and prestige above the needs of its people," that the Indian explosion was "another monument to human folly" in general, and that the appropriate reaction was "one of despair that such great talent and resources have been squandered on the vanity of power, while 600 million Indians slip deeper into poverty. The sixth member of the nuclear club may be passing the begging bowl before the year is out because Indian science and technology so far have failed to solve the country's fundamental problems of food and population."[23]

Perhaps these words smack a little too much of the moral outrage of a nation that already had the bomb, yet they address a basic dilemma: the cause of disarmament is very often advanced not only to increase spending on domestic welfare but also with the idea that the rich countries will be able to allocate more money to the poorer nations for economic development. A prominent economist has indeed claimed precisely that: "The only tangible 'reserves' that could be used to break decisively the grip of poverty throughout the world are the huge amounts of labor, capital and natural resources that are being devoted year in and year out to the maintenance and gradual expansion of military establishments." [24] Whether these resources would be devoted to raising standards of living is, of course, unknown. But there can be no question of the huge amounts of money devoted to arms. In both the developed and developing states the figure was up to $800 billion by 1985 and still rising (Figure 18-1).

In the final analysis, however persuasive the economic reason for disarmament is, considerations of security are greater. Symptomatic of the failure to solve the problems of interstate conflict is the fact that disarmament negotiations do not even occur until nations are locked in political struggle, and by then they are too late. Settlement of differences, political agreement, and the existence of some degree of mutual confidence are the ingredients necessary to achieve a successful disarmament agreement among states that believe that otherwise they may have to go to war with one another. In the absence of these ingredients, disarmament negotiations are bound to fail, for the conflicting nations will insist that, in the absence of reliable substitutes,

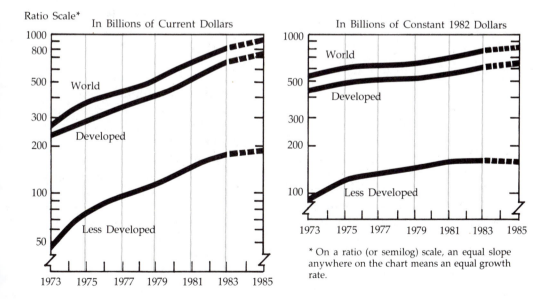

Figure 18-1   World Military Expenditures, 1973-1985

they need arms for defense and realization of their goals.

> States will not disarm so long as they insist upon maintaining their national
> sovereignty intact.... A sovereign state invariably asserts the power to be the
> ultimate judge in its own controversies, to enforce its own conception of rights....
> Moreover, sovereignty necessarily implies the right to make war in the national
> interest.[25]

INTERNATIONAL LAW AND MORALITY

In our earlier presentation of the model of the state system, international
politics was called "politics without government" because in the system there
are none of the institutions of government—legislative, executive, or judicial—that in domestic systems perform the functions of regulating society and
distributing goods. Even more fundamentally, there is no shared set of values
and no common political culture in the international community. In this
decentralized, even anarchical, state system, the principal restraint on states is
the balance of power. Power unmet is power abused; power must therefore
restrain power. If this model of the state system is essentially correct—as our
analysis has shown in detail—then it becomes easy to understand why state
behavior is so little tempered by international law and morality when vital
interests are at stake. These elements may on occasion reinforce restraints
imposed by calculations of power and prudence, but usually they are secondary and supplementary. The limited impact of international legal and moral
considerations is symptomatic not of inherent lack of merit but of the primitive nature of the state system.

Sources of International Law

This conclusion may appear surprising in connection with international law,
for states are themselves the principal source of that law. Most international
law is customary. Certain norms of conduct that have evolved over a long
period of time at some point become accepted as binding by the states that
have followed them; new states then tend automatically to accept them. One
other principal kind of international law is treaty law. Unlike customary law,
which is applicable to all states, treaty law binds only the parties that sign and
ratify the treaties. As two states alone can hardly establish a rule of conduct,
treaty law can be created only by a large number of states. In 1982, for
instance, 117 nations, mainly Third World nations, voted for a new treaty
governing the use and exploitation of the seas. The United States voted
against the new Law of the Sea, as did West Germany and Britain, and 46
nations abstained.

Despite widespread opinion to the contrary, states usually obey international law because they need it. The rise of states as independent political

units made the development of law necessary. Each sovereign state enjoyed complete jurisdiction and authority over its own territory and people, but it enjoyed neither beyond its boundaries. As states are compelled to coexist, however, they have to regulate their relations. If they are to stay in official contact, they must exchange representatives, which means that the rights and immunities of diplomats have had to be defined so that they can be protected on foreign soil. Other matters that have had to be covered include how title to territory is acquired (a matter that retains some importance because of continuing frontier disputes), ceded, and recognized. Also to be dealt with are a state's jurisdiction over territorial waters, air spaces, and aliens on its soil; conditions under which treaties come into effect and are terminated; legal methods for resolving disputes; and conduct of warfare and determination of the rights of neutrals.

The 1982 Law of the Sea, for example, covers issues such as territorial waters (12 nautical miles from the coastline); the right of "innocent passage" through territorial waters for all ships, including military; the right of ships to pass through international straits (for example, Gibralter or Hormuz) that do not become territorial waters; a 200-mile economic zone in which coastal states have the exclusive right to fish and other marine life; a 350-mile zone for the exploitation of oil, gas, and other resources; and arrangements for the mining of seabed nodules of copper, nickel, cobalt, and zinc. The United States, as well as West Germany and other Common Market countries, did not sign, largely because of fear that the organization in charge of the mining would be controlled by the LDCs. Still, coexistence requires rules.

Obedience and Disobedience of International Law

It should be obvious now why states do not normally violate international law—indeed, why it is virtually self-enforcing, except in the area of warfare. The legal norms provide a degree of order and predictability in an all too uncertain and chaotic environment. States expect to benefit from the reciprocal observance of obligations; if a particular state gains a reputation for not keeping its agreements, other states will be reluctant to sign further agreements with it, and reprisals may also occur.

This rule is as true for Western states, among which customary international law originated, as for non-Western states. It has sometimes been held that Western-derived international law is unacceptable to the Third World and that, therefore, the law must be developed further to reflect the values and interests of the latter. But this view has led to confusion: on the one hand, the non-Western states are attempting to articulate their economic and political interests, shaped mainly by their desire for modernization, so that they can play a more influential role in the state system; on the other, they seek to express their resentment of a legal order that mirrors primarily the interests of the rich and powerful Western states. The new countries have thus accepted the prevailing law, invoking it when it favors them in disputes with other states, while seeking certain changes—for example, in the areas of foreign investments and property and the settlement of claims after expropriation and nationalization of such holdings. Yet, even on the latter issue, we suspect that, if some of the newer states gain greater stakes in the international system and become exporters of capital, their views will move closer to those held by the more industrialized Western states.

Because of the anarchical nature of the state system, however, international law has shortcomings. The international legal system, unlike a national or municipal one, exists in the absence of a supranational legislature. Customary law and treaty law are substitutes for legislated rules. The difficulties inherent in a decentralized system are clear: states may disagree about when a custom becomes a legal norm; they may differ in defining their obligations because even well-established customary law may be unclear on specific details; and there is no accepted authority to impose a uniform interpretation. Law that evolves over time is also, of course, slow to adapt to rapidly changing conditions; as a result, it may become obsolete. Treaty law may not be subject to such obsolescence, but it does not apply to nonsignatories. Few treaties are signed by even a majority of states, let alone all states. This may mean that while parties to a treaty are bound by its terms with regard to each other, their relationship to nonparties continues to be based on customary law. Treaty law, like customary law, may also suffer from a lack of specificity. Nor is there a supranational executive to impose sanctions when international law is violated, as in domestic systems, although, as one noted British international legal expert noted:

> The weakness of international law lies deeper than any mere question of sanctions. It is not the existence of a police force that makes a system of law strong and respected, but the strength of the law that makes it possible for a police force to be effectively organized. The imperative character of law is felt so strongly within a highly civilized state that national law has developed a machinery of enforcement which generally works smoothly, though never so smoothly as to make breaches impossible. If the imperative character of international law were equally strongly felt, the institution of definite international sanctions would easily follow.[26]

In a sense, the word *law* is a misnomer in this context. A proper designation would be *norm*, a prescribed rule of conduct that one *ought* to follow; not to follow it may bring a bad conscience, disgrace, or even social ostracism. A law is similar, except that violation also leads to legal sanctions (fines, jail sentences, or executions). But there is no international government with superior force to apply to those states that break the law. The principal shortcoming of international law, in these circumstances, is that its subjects decide when it applies! No state is indicted, tried, and punished. States normally obey international law and accept their obligations under it because it applies to everyday relations; on the whole, the routine business of coexistence makes light demands on states and does not have major political significance. When the law is violated, it is because of issues that involve high political stakes, and the offended party usually applies its own sanctions.

International Law and the 'National Interest'

Such violations are relatively few in number but tend to be dramatic and sensational when they occur, thus giving rise to the impression that international law is weak. For example, during the 1950s the United States sent U-2 intelligence planes over the Soviet Union in the name of national security, even though the Soviet Union has legal jurisdiction over its own air space and had given no permission for such flights. Cuba, as a sovereign state, has a perfect right to welcome the strategic missiles of the Soviet Union on its soil, and the United States has no legal right to demand their withdrawal. Yet American security interests and the balance of power with the Soviet Union were perceived to require such withdrawal in 1962. The United States therefore blockaded Cuba; but, as a blockade is legally a *casus belli*, a reason for war, this action was called a quarantine. In these and similar instances, it would be more correct to say that international law is *restricted* in the range of its application, rather than that it is weak; this limited range of application is the reverse of the broad freedom of independent action that states claim for themselves.[27]

The great powers thus ignore international law when it would restrain them from doing what they believe they must do in their interest. When Italy invaded Ethiopia in 1935, international lawyers thought that Italy had violated the League of Nations Covenant and that sanctions ought to be invoked. Yet Britain and especially France wished Italy to remain a friend and potential ally against the new Germany of Hitler. To apply sanctions would be to alienate Italy and to make it more difficult to keep the European balance. International law is also a problem for smaller states concerned with their security. Israel, surrounded in the 1950s and 1960s by states that were clearly hostile and refused to recognize its right to exist, struck preemptively in 1956 and 1967, when it believed that its enemies were about to attack. Yet such a war is generally considered illegal.[28]

In 1979 Iran seized the U.S. Embassy in Tehran, even though, according to international law, embassies are to be regarded as parts of the nation they represent and diplomats are legally immune to seizure and captivity. The new militant Islamic regime insisted that it was the United States that had violated international law since World War II by interfering in Iran's domestic affairs by supporting the shah. It demanded his return for trial (and presumably execution) for what it condemned as his cruel tyranny and alleged subservience to the United States. In short, Iran claimed that the United States had violated international law and that seizure of the embassy and its personnel—labeled spies, rather than diplomats—was retribution for past injustices and therefore legitimate. The United States took the case to the International Court of Justice, which found that the hostage-taking was illegal and the hostages should be freed. Iran ignored the ruling. The United States then took the matter to the UN Security Council where the Soviet Union cast a veto. In these circumstances, the United States fell back on self-help and attempted the ill-fated hostage rescue attempt. In this instance, self-help was the only course left to protect America's legal rights.

Disputes can be categorized in two types: those that are amenable to settlement on a legal basis or *justiciable* and those that are political or *nonjusticiable*.[29] Political disputes are usually nonjusticiable not because there is no law that can be invoked but because they involve vital interests. If a state is dissatisfied with the status quo—for example, the settlement imposed upon it at the end of a war—it does not appeal to the law for a remedy because the law upholds the status quo. On the basis of existing law, an appeal for legal revision would have to be disallowed. But the question of change is not a judicial one; consequently, adopting judicial methods would be of no avail. The question of revision is political. Germany in the 1930s knew that it was violating the Versailles peace treaty and that international law would support the territorial status quo. Since it rejected the status quo, Germany would not submit its claims to an international court. This kind of dispute could be resolved peacefully by negotiations and compromise, but not by appeal to the law. The distinction between a legal and political problem is therefore somewhat arbitrary, reflecting a state's attitude toward the status quo. Nevertheless, it is a critical distinction, as became clear in 1984 when Nicaragua took the United States to the International Court of Justice, accusing the United States of supporting revolutionary actions against its government and of mining and blockading its ports. The court ruled unanimously for the United States to halt such actions and by a 14-1 vote that Nicaragua's political independence "should be fully respected and should not be jeopardized by any military or paramilitary activities."[30]

When Nicaragua took the case to court, however, the United States announced that it would not accept the court's judgments in matters relating to Central America for a period of two years. The United States accused Nicaragua of misusing the court for political and propaganda purposes and of hiding efforts to export revolution to its neighbors, which, the United States claimed, provoked the U.S. assistance to the contras.[31] Calling the court's findings "clearly erroneous," the U.S. State Department claimed that the issues "represented political questions that are not susceptible to resolution by any court" under the UN Charter. The implication of this statement was that if the court proceeded to hear Nicaragua's arguments and evidence and ordered the United States to stop supporting the contras, the United States would defy the court, which, of course, could not compel compliance. The United States also stated a broader rule: in the future it would refuse to participate in "cases of this nature." After October 1985, the United States announced, it would formally cease to recognize the authority of the World Court except in nonpolitical cases.

The U.S. decision to flout the court was widely criticized. The United States was supposed to stand for the law, be a law-abiding country, but it refused to participate in the court and accept its verdict. "It's like Al Capone saying he refuses to recognize the jurisdiction of the criminal court. It's the most compelling admission of guilt one can imagine," said one of the American lawyers arguing Nicaragua's case. The Reagan administration's defense was summed up by a quote from Winston Churchill, made in reference to the democracies' observance of the international law during the 1930s: "[I]t would not be right or rational," Churchill reportedly said, "that the aggressor powers should gain one set of advantages by tearing up all laws and another set by sheltering behind the innate respect for the law of their opponents." [32] The fact remains that the United States, like the majority of the 159 UN member nations, including the Soviet Union, is technically subject to the court's jurisdiction, but placed limits on the court's authority. These had been cases essentially within U.S. domestic jurisdiction as determined by the United States; probably the United States, like India or Kenya, should also have excluded disputes involving armed conflict.

States create the law, interpret it, and decide when to obey it. The International Court of Justice has no compulsory jurisdiction. Refusing to submit a dispute to it is the legitimate right of sovereign states. And no state will submit a case on an important issue if it feels it may lose; it will therefore submit only issues that do not involve vital interests. The United States, knowing it would probably lose the Nicaraguan case, did what might have been expected. By the same token, Nicaragua, a weak state, took the case to court to help strengthen its political and psychological position relative to the United States. The reverse was true in Iran. Iran knew the law and did not show up to argue its case; the United States did, also not so much because it expected Iran to obey the court's ruling, but to strengthen its political and moral case.

The Morality of Nations

The anarchical nature of the state system also limits the impact of moral norms on the competition and rivalry of states. Indeed, probably in no sphere of human endeavor is there a greater gap between actual behavior and professions of moral principles and declaration of noble intentions than in international politics. A frequent definition of a diplomat is "an honest man sent abroad to lie for his country." A man or woman who slays another human being is normally called a killer; if apprehended, tried, and, convicted, the killer is isolated from society in prison or, in many countries, put to death. But a person who kills other people called enemies on behalf of his or her country is hailed as a hero, presented with medals, and sometimes even immortalized in a statue or on a postage stamp. Ordinary soldiers receive veterans' benefits from a grateful country. A leader of the Italian unification movement once said, "If we did for ourselves what we are doing for Italy we should be real scoundrels."

The usual explanation for the alleged immorality of states is that their concern for their security requires them to do "whatever must be done." In a domestic system of law and order, the resulting sense of security allows individuals and groups to act with at least some degree of morality; but, in the international system, the absence of law and order means that all states, like the cowboys in a lawless western town, must figuratively go armed and must be prepared to shoot when their lives are endangered. In Thomas Hobbes's philosophy the war of every man against every other man in a state of nature arose not from fear of death but from fear of *violent* death at the hands of another; in the resulting state of perpetual war nothing was unjust. The idea of right and wrong, justice and injustice, simply had no place. The present state system is essentially a Hobbesian jungle; in a jungle one must behave appropriately. The "nice guy" is devoured.

In such a system it is perhaps the better part of wisdom to adapt and to play the game of nations, however rough that game is at times. For a national leader, being a good person and possessing moral intentions are not enough. Prime Minister Neville Chamberlain of Great Britain was such a person. More than anything, he wanted to avoid another war with Germany and to spare his people another awful bloodletting. Surely preserving the peace was a moral goal. Peace is precious, not to be lightly sacrificed, to be forfeited only if absolutely unavoidable. Had Chamberlain been a less noble individual, had he been more willing to take up arms and risk surrendering peace, he might have saved the peace he so treasured.

This line of thinking suggests that power and morality are antithetical. If a state is concerned with security and power, it must throw off morality as so much excess baggage. If, on the other hand, it seeks to act morally, it will suffer badly in the international struggle. This position, however, is false. Acts by individuals and groups, subnational or national, all involve moral considerations: decisions involve choices, and the choice of one course over another is influenced by moral predispositions, which are inherent in larger social values. In an international context, it is more accurate to say that *the closer relations among states move toward enmity, the more likely the states are to adopt policies normally considered immoral; the closer relations move toward friendship and the more secure the states feel, the more moral will be the conduct of their foreign policies.*[33]

Whatever the degree of morality that influences states in different situations, the source of this morality lies within the states themselves. A number of points are worth mentioning in this connection.

Nationalism and Morality.
First, states identify their interests with morality. Clearly, no state is going to admit publicly that its actions are unethical. President Julius Nyerere of Tanzania once said on behalf of his country and the "poor nations" of the world:

> I am saying it is not right that the vast majority of the world's people should be forced into the position of beggars, without dignity. In one world, as in one state, when I am rich because you are poor, and I am poor because you are rich, the transfer of wealth from the rich to the poor is a matter of right; it is not an appropriate matter for charity.... If the rich nations go on getting richer and richer

at the expense of the poor, the poor of the world must demand a change, in the same way as the proletariat in the rich countries demanded change in the past.[34]

The LDCs believe they are poor because the Western industrial states are rich; the LDCs therefore have a legitimate grievance based on the West's plunder of their resources and continued "capitalist" exploitation. The Western countries owe them reparations and help as a moral obligation and historic duty. This formulation is the essence of the claim for a new international economic order. The definition of what is moral and what is immoral is egocentric—and obviously very practical if it induces guilt feelings among the former colonial powers so that they seek to relieve those feelings by means of "alms for the poor."

Different Definitions of Morality. Second, states define morality differently, as President Nyerere's words illustrate, according to whether they are satisfied with their position in the state system. A status quo state, which benefits from the current power distribution, will espouse a morality identified with the interests of the larger state system and will emphasize peace. If its interests coincide with those of most other members of the system, there is no occasion for challenges from the latter: upholding peace will give the state a political and psychological advantage against challengers, which must threaten war or actually go to war to effect change and can therefore be denounced as aggressors and warmongers. The status quo state stresses the need for diplomacy, claiming that no problem is insuperable, that all can be settled by patient and sincere negotiations, rather than by unjustified intimidation or force. The peace of a region—of the world—should be everyone's prime consideration; no injustice or wrong, however strongly felt, is worth the even greater injustice of war and the sacrifice of peace.

In contrast, a revisionist state that seeks to transform the status quo to its own advantage will attempt to avoid being morally discredited by claiming that it is underprivileged, a have-not state, and that it seeks only equality or national self-determination. A good example occurred at the November 1976 UN General Assembly meeting, when a resolution was passed linking South African apartheid with Western governments and especially with the government of Israel. This resolution called the South African government "illegitimate," having "no right to represent the people of South Africa." It declared support for "the legitimacy of the struggle of the oppressed people of South Africa and their liberation movement, by all possible means, for the seizure of power by the people."[35] This resolution was an open call for the use of violence, justified in this instance by the morality of the goal—the end of discrimination and the equality of all people, black and white. The challenger must convince other states that the status quo demands alteration because it is no longer morally justifiable.

Note again what a very practical instrument morality can be. The weak usually have few other weapons, and appeals to morality in states where public opinion is accessible to foreign persuasion can be effective. If the international system could be made to function according to moral principles, the inequality of power among states would not matter. It would even work to the advantage of the weak. Note also that the moral issues raised publicly in international forums and those not raised reflect political circumstances and votes taken in international organizations. The issue of the human rights of blacks in South Africa has been made an international issue by black African states in the United Nations, but the issue of the human rights of black Africans in some black African states, whose rulers abuse the political and civil rights of their subjects, has not been raised in the same forum. Black leaders do not want to raise the issue of human rights in their own states, and they have enough votes to prevent it.

Moral Restraints on National Behavior.   Third, although we should not be surprised that states try to justify themselves, it would be a mistake to assume that "anything goes" just because officials who decide specific policies stamp them "morally approved." The domestic principles of a state can and do act as restraints on its behavior. For example, many Britons, as well as many people throughout the English-speaking world, disapproved of the British intervention at the Suez Canal in 1956 because they believed colonialism was no longer legitimate and the invasion of Egypt unjustifiable in an age of nationalism.

Similarly, many people in the United States—and in much of the rest of the world—found American support of the Saigon government in Vietnam illegitimate; in that "civil war" Hanoi's leaders were widely identified with the principle of national self-determination. How could the democratic United States support an autocratic regime that denied every democratic principle to which the United States professed commitment, in a war against those who were fighting for national unity and independence? In addition, the often massive use of force against a small unindustrialized country—on which the United States dropped more bombs than it had dropped on Germany and Japan combined during World War II—seemed outrageous. The means used to wage the war and the destruction wrought appeared excessive to many in the light of the proclaimed moral purposes of the intervention. Both the ends and the means of U.S. policy in Vietnam were widely questioned.

These two examples are part of a growing normative restraint, anchored in the values of Western democratic societies, in military confrontations between the First and Third Worlds. The use of force in such conflicts, short of a clear threat to national security or prestige, is now widely regarded as illegitimate in the West. In 1974, after the Organization of Petroleum Exporting Countries quadrupled oil prices and caused a surge in Western inflation and unemployment, no Western power thought of using force; OPEC's right to set prices, even to withhold oil, was recognized.

Arthur Schlesinger, Jr., rather picturesquely remarked once that a nation's foreign policy is the face that it wears to the world, and, if this policy embodies values that appear incompatible with the nation's ideals, either the policy will lose public support and have to be abandoned, or the nation will have to toss its ideals overboard. A nation, like an individual, must in the final analysis be true to itself, or the "consequent moral schizophrenia is bound to convulse the homeland." [36] During the Cuban missile crisis in 1962, to cite only one example, when President John Kennedy and his advisers were debating whether to attack or blockade the island, Robert Kennedy argued strongly against attack on the grounds of American tradition. A surprise attack, which would kill thousands of Cuban civilians, seemed inconsistent with that tradition. The United States was not like Japan, and his brother, the president, was not like Tojo Hideki, who had launched the surprise attack on Pearl Harbor. There were, of course, other reasons— "practical" reasons—that helped the government to decide in favor of the blockade, but morality unquestioningly contributed to the decision. Note that the moral factor was also perceived by Robert Kennedy as politically beneficial. A surprise attack, he declared, "could not be undertaken by the United States if we were to maintain our moral position at home and around the globe. Our struggle against Communism throughout the world was far more than physical survival—it had as its essence our heritage and our ideals and these we must not destroy." [37]

One of the more interesting recent moral phenomena in the United States has been the rejection of nuclear arms by American Catholic and Methodist bishops.[38] Up to the 1980s the emphasis had always been that nuclear war was bad for one's health. This was hardly news; the threat to biological survival was the main reason for effective deterrence. But groups such as the Physicians for Social Responsibility began to reemphasize this message as if it were new. Presumably, the intent was to counter widespread mass complacency about the dangers of the arms race and the use of nuclear weapons. It was the context within which this message was promulgated that was new. The point was not to reinforce support for deterrence but to point to its failure; the focus of the message was on "the day after." The only solution to this terrible nuclear problem was nuclear disarmament.

If the physicians pointed to the danger that nuclear arms posed for people's bodies—a nuclear war would be "the last epidemic"—the bishops pointed to the consequences that their possession posed for people's souls. The use of nuclear weapons was condemned as immoral, even in retaliation against an enemy's first use. Nuclear war was opposed to the churches' teachings and could not, therefore, receive its blessings; the defense of a free society was not a sufficient cause for having such weapons. Because deterrence is the result of the possession of nuclear weapons *plus* the will to use them if the enemy strikes, and is *not* just the product of the possession of these weapons, the denunciation of the determination to use them—for moral or other reasons— means that deterrence no longer exists; at best, it becomes a sheer bluff. Besides, if the use of nuclear weapons is immoral, then deterrence has to be immoral, too. One cannot have a morally acceptable deterrent strategy without an operational doctrine governing its use. Basically, the moral position points to a unilateral nuclear disarmament. One need but note that the only time the bomb was used was at the end of a war against a fanatical enemy who did not possess the bomb and therefore could not retaliate in kind.

The bishops' position is an interesting offspring of the increasing Western reluctance to use any kind of force except in strictly defensive circumstances to ward off "aggression." Deterrence had not been questioned on moral grounds until the 1980s, and not everyone agreed with this point of view. Was the purpose of deterrence not to prevent war? Was preventing a nuclear attack not moral, even if the way this goal was achieved was by producing nuclear weapons? Were the latter not the lesser evil and the prevention of nuclear war the greater moral good? (The French Catholic bishops thought so.) Can the threat of using nuclear weapons be morally equated to their actual use? In short, can one jump from the condemnation of nuclear war to the rejection of a deterrent strategy? Would the two churches' positions not also lead to policies, if they were adopted, that would result in the greatest of all evils, a nuclear attack or the submission to a foreign, antireligious, dictatorial power? [39] Is survival the highest moral good of both churches' teachings? Or is it justice? Should a moral nuclear strategy not only deter nuclear war but also help contain the expansion of a system of government which all Western states agree is tyrannical? And have nuclear weapons not achieved *both* objectives since World War II? Have the moral attacks on deterrence not ignored the forty-year history of deterrence?

Morality in an Insecure World

A nation, particularly a democratic nation, thus can find itself in a dilemma, caught between its values and its security interests, at least in terms of its immediate foreign policy. It is, after all, always easier to justify short-term deviations from the nation's values if it can be maintained that in the long run the deviations protect the values. We noted earlier the tensions inherent in any U.S. policy that calls for alliance with undemocratic states to enhance U.S. security. Similar, but more shocking to many Americans, is the tension between the democratic ethos and security that has been revealed in a number of other ways: assassination plots by the Central Intelligence Agency (CIA) against foreign leaders, especially Fidel Castro; the overthrow of a legitimately elected government in Chile; and the "secret" bombing of Cambodia. The dilemma of making foreign policy in the face of conflicting pressures and values is finding a way to *achieve some of the principal objectives with minimum sacrifice of other equally important objectives*. In our analysis of competition among objectives, we asked how a state balances security and welfare; security, democracy, and individual liberty; and security and peace? The problem is *not* simply to choose between one element and another, but how to achieve the best combination of all the elements.

There is no more dramatic or tragic illustration of this dilemma than the events leading up to the seizure of the U.S. Embassy in Tehran in 1979. The shah, admittedly both dictatorial and ruthless, was also strongly pro-American. He had supported President Anwar Sadat of Egypt in his search for peace after 1973, and he had long supplied oil to Israel, even during the 1973 war. There is no question about the firm support that the United States had given the shah over the years; in the early 1950s the CIA had restored him to power after he had been forced to flee his country. Nor is there much doubt that the shah's secret police used torture or that his relatives and aides made millions of dollars. It was always clear that the shah was quite unpopular. American interests, however, were equally clear; control of the strategic Persian Gulf and plentiful supplies of oil. In 1979 Iranian oil constituted only 4 percent of American consumption, but U.S. allies in Europe and Japan were very dependent on it.

Could there have been a greater disaster for the United States and its allies than the shah's collapse? Oil prices shot up virtually 100 percent in one year because of reductions in Iranian oil supplies and the resulting tight world market. Egypt lost a staunch friend and had to buy its oil elsewhere; so did Israel, which felt even more insecure now that Iran was also militantly anti-Israel. Furthermore, the security of the Persian Gulf, which the United States had counted on the shah to guard, was now endangered by a zealous religious regime bent on fomenting an Islamic rebellion against the United States and overthrowing pro-Western Arab Muslim leaders in the oil kingdoms along the Persian Gulf. It is also questionable that the Iranians themselves are better off under this regime, which is bent upon restoring traditional customs. It banned Western music, dance, and drink; tried to crush all opposition; and killed its enemies in ways all too reminiscent of the shah's own dictatorial rule. Modernization fell by the wayside, the economy declined, and large-scale unemployment and inflation grew worse. Furthermore, the government had to devote a large part of its energies to resisting forces of disintegration, as represented by the Kurds and other ethnic groups that sought autonomy. In view of these complexities, was American support for the shah "criminal"? [40] Indeed, given the subsequent actions of Iranian-supported terrorist groups against the United States in the Middle East, including twice blowing up the American Embassy in Beirut and killing 241 marines in a suicide attack (see Chapter 12), this question is all the more pertinent.

Morality as an Incentive to Crusades

If morality generally serves as a constraint on state behavior, despite the frequent dilemmas involved in moral choices, it can also result in "unrestraining" or unleashing foreign policy. For, as noted earlier, an attempt to impose moral values on another state means that conflicts among states become transformed from conflicts of interest, which may be resolvable through hard bargaining, to conflicts of moral philosophies, between good and evil, which tend not to be peacefully resolvable. Viewing the international arena as one in which St. George must always be slaying dragons leads to a complete misunderstanding of the nature of international politics. Instead of a method by which to analyze the behavior of states in terms of their sense of insecurity, their legitimate interests and aspirations, the great difficulties involved in coexisting, and their common and conflicting interests, politics among nations becomes a matter of virtue and vice, in which purity is to vanquish villainy. And, if the struggle among states is viewed as a struggle between right and wrong, those who *know* they are right all too often become zealots and crusaders. Like a religious fanatic, a state convinced that it represents morality easily and rapidly strikes poses of absolutism and self-righteousness.

Translated into foreign policy—as postwar American foreign policy has amply demonstrated—such moralism has several undesirable results, two of which are failure to recognize other governments because of moral disapproval and unwillingness to meet with adversaries to reconcile conflicting interests. "One does not compromise with the devil"—to do so would be to become tainted. In addition, states that view themselves as moral arbiters also exhibit a crusading spirit in peace and war, which makes it difficult for their governments to distinguish between vital and secondary interests and may even entice them into disputes that involve only peripheral interests (as in the American intervention in Vietnam). Finally, a nation imbued with the crusading spirit is likely to transform war into total war, to seek the unconditional surrender of the infidel. Crusaders remain oblivious to the fact that total military victory may make a postwar balance of power much more difficult to attain. Thus, moralism not only results in misunderstanding of international politics but, when applied to policy, also guides it on a course that in most instances will be detrimental to the state's own interests. Countries in which fanaticism has led to rigidity and self-righteousness are intolerant of other countries; coexistence with them then becomes very difficult, if not impossible. Zeal and peace are mutually exclusive, for zeal gives rise to intervention in order to reshape and reform other states. Do democratic states have a moral mandate to remake other states in their own images? Indeed, can any state really expect—should it have the right to expect—to do more than influence the foreign policy behavior of another state when the latter impinges on its interests? Is foreign policy also to concern itself with reforming another state domestically and to make for virtuous a lay criteria for its foreign policy?

In international politics, the moral thing to do may be to avoid "the histrionics of moralism," to restrain the tendency to self-righteousness and moralizing. It may be morally satisfying "to appear noble and altruistic in the mirror of our vanity," but its impact on international politics has generally been to make national positions more rigid, render diplomacy less able to reconcile conflicting positions, and transform wars into total wars. In the words of George Kennan, "In a less than perfect world, where the idea so obviously lies beyond human reach, it is natural that the avoidance of the worst should often be a more practical undertaking than the achievement of the best, and that some of the strongest imperatives of moral conduct should be ones of a negative rather than a positive nature"—as in the strictures of the Ten Commandments.[41]

Conflicting Moral Claims

In a world composed of many nations, then, there are many different historical traditions, philosophies, ideologies, and political and moral standards. There is little consensus among countries on which is moral and immoral, good and bad. Let us refer again to the LDCs' claim that the industrialized West has a moral duty to help them eliminate the inequalities and injustices of international life that keep them poor. To limit ourselves to only one aspect of this issue, we can ask the following question: Are the non-Western states poor *because* of past colonial rule and the extraction of their natural resources at low cost? If that is true, perhaps the former colonial countries do owe reparations to their former colonies. But the fact is that some states, Tanzania, for example, were not only not states but were also poor before Western colonialism. Whatever economic progress they have made—indeed, their very search for modernization—is because of the impact of Western ideas, capital, technology, and enterprise. The colonial states extracted copper or tea, but they also founded the mines and plantations, and it was Western industrialization and demand that gave economic value to their products. The non-Western states now stress nationalism and the right to self-determination, economic development and the welfare society, all values reflecting those of the Western colonial states that brought these values with them. There is no reason to believe the LDCs' claim that they would have improved their standard of living on their own but for the exploitation of colonialism; the very idea of progress has been inherited from colonial days.

The least advanced Third World countries are those that have not had any or much contact with the industrial West. The most advanced—whether the standard of measurement be literacy, life expectancy, economic wealth, or the presence of modern industry—are former colonies with extensive economic links to the West. Not that poverty does not continue to exist throughout the less-developed areas. What is questionable is that poverty exists solely or mainly *because* of past colonialism.[42] Many Western industrial states therefore reject the idea that the LDCs have a moral claim on their treasuries. Richard Cooper, undersecretary of state for economic affairs in the Carter administration, has complicated this question of exploitation even further. In those instances in which living standards have declined, rather than risen, as a result of Western contacts, he has argued, the decline has resulted principally from rapid population growth. This growth directly reflects the introduction of Western medicine and standards of sanitation (Cooper cites the population of the Indonesian island of Java, which increased from 4.5 million to 63 million between 1815 and 1960, an increase of fourteen times, while the population of Britain increased only five or six times).[43] Is the West therefore responsible for poverty resulting from larger populations? Should it not have introduced modern medicine? And, we may ask, next time there is a food shortage in the underdeveloped world, should the industrial West allow starvation in order to bring population, food, and other resources back into balance? Or would that course be immoral, even though the additional population will hamper efforts at modernization even further?

Indeed, the question is even more complex because the governments of less-developed countries often pursue policies *after* independence that are highly inefficient. President Nyerere, who has claimed that Tanzania—like other Third World countries—is poor because the West is rich, has forgotten that Tanzania was always poor and probably would be poorer still today had it not been for British colonial rule; furthermore, his government, unlike that of his better-off neighbor, Kenya, has chosen to pursue a policy hostile to private enterprise. Although drought and higher oil prices are partially responsible, governmental policy also has played a role in reducing the per capita agricultural yield. In Uganda, former president Amin's policy of driving out the Asians, who had lived in the country for generations and constituted its business community, helped shatter that nation's economy. Algeria, one of the Third World's more radical states and an OPEC member that annually sought higher oil prices during the 1970s, was once an exporter of wheat. Seventeen years after independence, it imports more than two-thirds of its domestically consumed cereals, paying for them with two-thirds of its earnings from oil and natural gas.[44] When Nigeria became independent in 1960, its agricultural products were the prime source of export earning, and subsistence farming fed many. In 1981 when 80 million of Nigeria's 100 million people still lived on the land, the country could not feed itself and had to import food, much of it from the United States. Governments, in short, are not always blameless for their countries' poverty; the domestic policies they pursue frequently contribute to continued lack of economic progress.

Moral questions and claims, then, may be simple to put forth, but they are not simple to answer. Moral judgments that seem easy at first glance often turn out not to be so clear-cut. Furthermore, what one party calls moral is not necessarily moral to another. There are no universal standards of morality or of justice. This lack of agreement in turn reflects the decentralized nature of the state system. There do not, then, appear to be solutions to security problems in the state system.

ON TO MACROPOLITICS: FROM DOOM TO SALVATION

We therefore turn from the state system to "world order." In the final analysis, it is the claim that today's problems—the superpowers' arms race, nuclear (and indeed, nonnuclear) arms proliferation, as well as poverty, overpopulation, lack of food, finite resources, disturbances to the ecology—

affect all nations that is the fundamental argument for shifting our attention away from the state system. If these problems are transnational, affecting all humanity, more attention ought to be focused on the global system. The logic of the arms race provides a good example. The overriding issue, it is asserted, is preventing the death of the earth. When the problem of the arms race is stated in these apocalyptic terms, there can be no choice: because the problem *must* be resolved, it must be *resolvable.* To admit that it may not be possible to disarm is to discourage further efforts to seek agreement and to encourage complacency that can end only in disaster. In this view, obstacles blocking the way to disarmament should not be considered insurmountable; they are seen merely as difficulties to be overcome. If the problem of nuclear fission could be solved, why cannot human ingenuity—applied to the abolition of weapons rather than to the production of ever-more destructive ones—solve the problem of disarmament? Why should human beings not for once apply their reason to constructive, rather than destructive, purposes?

Because disarmament is so desirable, its advocates conclude that it is technically and politically possible.[45] Disarmament may not be the usual way to resolve conflicts, and politicians may reject it outright as "impractical and impossible," but our unique times demand bold solutions. However impossible disarmament may have been in the past, these observers argue, there is no alternative to it today. The search for disarmament is therefore not idealistic; it is highly realistic. The admonition to "love thy neighbor" becomes "Love thy neighbor *if* you love yourself." [46] No great power can afford *not* to love its neighbor if it values its own life. Note these words from the respected British physicist and novelist C. P. Snow:

> We are faced with an either/or and we haven't much time. The *either* is acceptance of restriction of nuclear armaments. . . . The *or* is . . . a certainty . . . [If the American-Soviet arms race is not halted] other countries join in. Within, at the most, six years, China and six other states have a stock of nuclear bombs. Within, at the most, 10 years, some of these bombs are going off. . . . *That* is a certainty.[47]

In short, disaster was a certainty if the superpowers did not initiate a reversal of the arms race by taking some risks with their security. These words were spoken by Snow in 1969. China has since joined the nuclear club; so has India. But the ten-year deadline on a nuclear explosion has long since passed.

Still, the logic of this line of reasoning leads to an obvious conclusion: the world must not destroy itself simply because the leaders of the great powers still think in outdated terms of "national interests," rather than in realistic terms of the "common interest of mankind" in preserving peace. What the world needs is not more old-fashioned "power politics," which in the past has always led to war; rather it needs imaginative and radical solutions. Nuclear bombs made it mandatory for national leaders to change habits and ways of thinking inherited from the prenuclear age. If the world is not to be engulfed in flames, political leaders must be concerned about the needs of humanity, regardless of their own subjective prejudices and national ideologies, which pale into insignificance beside the overwhelming central issue of survival.

The alternative to such a common sense solution is thus labeled disaster. The abolition of all weapons and the weakening of sovereignty may involve risks, but disaster from nuclear warfare is unthinkable. And no "sane" person would hesitate between such risks and the certainty of catastrophe. For these observers, it is a simple either/or problem, and the solution is just as simple. All people have to do is to recognize the peril to their existence, the stark alternatives, and the urgency of the remedy.

Implicit in this line of thinking is a clear-cut division between those who have vested interests in the preservation of the nation-state—after all, what jobs would there be for soldiers, diplomats, and "merchants of death," for example, if the nation-state and arms were abolished?—and the vast mass of "humanity." The former obviously oppose disarmament and cannot success-fully participate in negotiations, for their patterns of thought are rooted in the state system. But the future of the world demands that leaders think as if the state system had *already* been transcended.

It is argued, in short, that *our concepts of state behavior are outdated.* Reflecting the experiences of the historical state system, our thinking has not yet caught up with the "necessities" of a rapidly changing world. The central point is that we cannot afford any longer to focus on the states in the system, their objectives, and their interactions. The focus of international politics must be enlarged from the individual nation-state—the "micropolitics" that we have been studying up to this point—to world politics, or "macropolitics," in which the fate of each nation is tied to the fates of all other nations. According to Richard Sterling, macropolitics

> is the understanding that the world is becoming too small and vulnerable to survive unless global needs are recognized and acted upon with the same commitment and energy that have traditionally characterized responses to national needs . . . [for] the survival and prosperity of the globe is the necessary condition for the survival and prosperity of its parts. The negative corollary is easily deduced: unconcern for the whole will jeopardize its continuing existence, with the parts suffering the neces-sary consequences.
>
> Macropolitical analysis must therefore begin with the questions central to its global concerns: What is the *international* interest? What policies and institutions appear to benefit all men, and what appear to benefit some but not others? What is likely to disadvantage them all? It must ask what any given nation-state contributes to the international interest and judge the value of any particular national interest in terms of the answer to that question.[48]

Notes

1. J. William Fulbright, "In Thrall to Fear," *New Yorker*, Jan. 8, 1972, 59.
2. Quoted in *Power and International Relations*, by Inis L. Claude, Jr. (New York: Random House, 1964), 59.

3. Ibid., 160; and Inis L. Claude, Jr., *Swords into Plowshares*, rev. ed (New York: Random House, 1964), 80-86.

4. Egypt, because of its complaint that the United Nations had not supported it in the war against Israel in 1947-48, was an exception.

5. Ernst Haas, "Types of Collective Security: An Examination of Operational Concepts," *American Political Science Review* (March 1955): 40-62, examines this transition from "permissive enforcement" to "balancing."

6. In Cuba, only after the Cuban missile crisis of 1962 had already been resolved was the organization to be used—and then it was to check that all Soviet missiles had been removed from Cuba. But, because Fidel Castro refused to submit to international inspection and the United States was certain that all the missiles had been shipped back to the Soviet Union, the United Nations remained uninvolved.

7. Andrew Boyd, *United Nations: Piety, Myth and Truth* (Baltimore: Penguin, 1962), 85ff; Inis L. Claude, Jr., *The Changing United Nations* (New York: Random House, 1967), 23ff; Arthur L. Burns and Nina Heathcote, *Peace-Keeping by U.N. Forces: From Suez to Congo* (New York: Holt, Rinehart & Winston, 1963); and Linda B. Miller, *World Order and Local Disorder* (Princeton, N.J.: Princeton University Press, 1967).

8. Inis L. Claude, Jr., "Containment and Resolution of Disputes," in *The U.S. and the U.N.*, ed. Francis O. Wilcox and H. Field Haviland, Jr. (Baltimore: Johns Hopkins University Press, 1961), 101-128 (emphasis in original).

9. Rupert Emerson, "The Fate of Human Rights in the Third World," *World Politics*, January 1975, 224.

10. *New York Times*, Jan. 30, 1982.

11. *New York Times*, Sept. 22, 1985.

12. *New York Times*, March 31, 1983.

13. *New York Times*, Sept. 11, 1982 (emphasis in original). Also former UN secretary-general Kurt Waldheim, "The United Nations: The Tarnished Image," *Foreign Affairs* (Fall 1984): 93-107.

14. George Bernard Shaw, *Man and Superman* (Baltimore: Penguin, 1952), 145.

15. On the nature of the arms race, see Samuel P. Huntington, "Arms Races: Prerequisites and Results," in *Public Policy: A Yearbook of the Graduate School of Public Administration, Harvard University 7*, ed. Carl J. Friedrich and Seymour E. Harris (Cambridge, Mass.: Harvard University Press, 1956), 41-86; George H. Quester, *Nuclear Diplomacy* (New York: Dunellen, 1971); Colin S. Gray, "The Arms Race Phenomenon," *World Politics*, October 1971, 39ff.; Gray, "The Urge to Compete: Rationales for Arms Racing," *World Politics*, January 1974, 207ff; Gray, *The Soviet-American Arms Race* (Lexington, Mass.: D. C. Heath, 1976); Albert Wohlstetter, "Is There a Strategic Arms Race?" *Foreign Policy*, Summer 1974, 3-20; and Wohlstetter, "Rivals, But No Race," *Foreign Policy*, Fall 1974, 48-81.

16. *New York Times*, June 24, 1982.

17. Merze Tate, *The United States and Armaments* (Cambridge, Mass.: Harvard University Press, 1948) makes this point very well in analyzing the only reasonably successful disarmament agreement in history, the Washington Naval Conference of 1921-22.

18. Ibid., 35-36.

19. Salvador de Madariaga, *Disarmament* (New York: Coward-McCann, 1929), 62-63. For an account of the disarmament negotiations as part of the postwar arms race, see John W. Spanier and Joseph L. Nogee, *The Politics of Disarmament* (New York: Holt, Rinehart & Winston, 1962).

20. Spanier and Nogee, *Politics of Disarmament.*
21. U.S. Department of State News Release, August 1972.
22. See, for example, "Poor Nations Spend Fortune on Arms Purchases," *New York Times*, Aug. 2, 1974, 1, 14, for the situation as these nations entered the 1970s.
23. *New York Times*, May 20, 1974.
24. Wassily Leontief, "Cutting U.S. and Soviet Military Outlays," *New York Times*, March 24, 1977.
25. Tate, *The United States and Armaments*, 3. For a contrary view, see Burns H. Weston and Thomas A. Hawbaker, eds., *Toward Nuclear Disarmament and Global Security* (Boulder, Colo.: Westview Press, 1984).
26. J. L. Brierly, *The Law of Nations*, 6th ed., (New York: Oxford University Press, 1949), 73. Also see Werner Levi, *Law and Politics in the International Society* (Beverly Hills, Calif.: Sage, 1976).
27. Brierly, *Law of Nations*, 74.
28. Hedley Bull, *The Anarchical Society* (New York: Columbia University Press, 1977), 108-109, 143-144.
29. P. E. Corbett, *Law & Society in the Relations of States* (New York: Harcourt, Brace & Co., 1951), 77-79.
30. *New York Times*, Nov. 15, 1984.
31. *New York Times*, Jan. 19, 1985.
32. Quoted by Michael A. Ledeen, "When Security Preempts the Rule of Law," *New York Times*, April 16, 1984.
33. Arnold Wolfers, *Discord and Collaboration* (Baltimore: Johns Hopkins University Press, 1965), 54.
34. Quoted by P. T. Bauer and B. S. Yamey, "Against the New Economic Order," *Commentary*, April 1977, 27.
35. *New York Times*, Nov. 10, 1976.
36. Arthur Schlesinger, Jr., "National Interests and Moral Absolutes," in *Ethics and World Politics* by Ernest W. Lefever (Baltimore: Johns Hopkins University Press, 1972), 35.
37. Robert F. Kennedy, *Thirteen Days* (New York: New American Library, 1968).
38. National Conference of Catholic Bishops, *The Challenge of Peace* (Washington, D.C.: United States Catholic Conference, 1983); and *New York Times*, Dec. 26, 1985. For the final draft see *New York Times*, April 27, 1986. For a critical evaluation see James E. Dougherty, *The Bishops and Nuclear Weapons* (Hamden, Conn.: Archon Books, 1984).
39. Charles Krauthammer, "On Nuclear Morality," *Commentary*, October 1983, 48-52. Also Robert W. Tucker, *The Nuclear Debate* (New York: Holmes & Meier, 1985); and Joseph S. Nye, Jr., *Nuclear Ethics* (New York: Free Press, 1986).
40. If so, most of the world's leaders can be called "criminal," for few have not supported regimes that have jailed domestic opponents and violated human rights. Indeed, many rule their own countries in this manner.
41. George F. Kennan, "Morality and Foreign Policy," *Foreign Affairs* (Winter 1985/86): 213.
42. Richard N. Cooper, "A New International Economic Order for Mutual Gain," *Foreign Policy*, Spring 1977, 81-86.
43. Ibid., 86-87.
44. John P. Entelis, "Algeria, Myth and Reality," *New York Times*, Dec. 1, 1979, 21.
45. Robert Gilpin, *American Scientists and Nuclear Weapons Policy* (Princeton, N.J.:

Princeton University Press, 1962). Also see Jonathan Schell, *The Fate of the Earth* (New York: Avon Books, 1982).

46. John H. Herz, *International Politics in the Atomic Age* (New York: Columbia University Press, 1952), 333.

47. C. P. Snow, "Risk of Disaster or a Certainty?" *New York Times*, Aug. 17, 1981.

48. Richard W. Sterling, *Macropolitics* (New York: Alfred A. Knopf, 1974), 5-6. Also see Schell, *Fate of the Earth*, 218-231.

CHAPTER 19

Peace Through the Transformation of the State System

WORLD GOVERNMENT AND THE ABOLITION OF CONFLICT

If conflict cannot be eliminated in the state system, the *abolition* of the system may be the only hope for the future existence of mankind. Many observers believe that the anarchy of the state system must be replaced by *world government*. Governments preserve peace and maintain law and order on the domestic scene. If a government could be created that would supersede the governments of sovereign nations, could it not, like national governments in their own spheres, ensure global peace once and for all?

The American Example

It is often argued, by analogy, that under the American Articles of Confederation, the states retained their sovereignty and continued their quarrels. But, under the Constitution, the states were reduced in status to nonsovereign members of a new federal system in which the government could apply national law directly to individuals and had the responsibility and the authority to ensure domestic tranquility. Can we not argue, then, as advocates of world government do, that the American Constitutional Convention was the "great rehearsal" [1] for a global convention that will transfer the sovereignty of all nations to a world government, the purpose of which will be to ensure global peace through establishment of the "rule of law"? Such partisans seem to believe that, wherever a "legal order" is established—that is, wherever government applies law directly to its citizens—government functions as a peace-keeping institution. What leads them to this conclusion? Inis Claude has suggested that one factor is the attractiveness of certain terms and the

626

images that they produce in people's minds—terms such as *government* and *law and order:*

> A clue may perhaps be found in the intimate association between the idea of world government and the fashionable theme of world rule of law. *Law* is a key word in the vocabulary of world government. One reacts against anarchy—disorder, insecurity, violence, injustice visited by the strong upon the weak. In contrast, one postulates law—the symbol of the happy opposites to those distasteful and dangerous evils. Law suggests properly constituted authority and effectively implemented control: it symbolizes the supreme will of the community, the will to maintain justice and public order. This abstract concept is all too readily transformed, by worshipful contemplation, from one of the devices by which societies seek to order internal relationships, into a symbolic key to the good society. As this transformation takes place, law becomes a magic word for those who advocate world government and those who share with them the ideological bond of dedication to the rule of law—not necessarily in the sense that they expect it to produce magical effects upon the world, but at least in the sense that it works its magic upon them. Most significantly, it leads them to forget about politics, to play down the role of the political process in the management of human affairs, and to imagine that somehow law, in all its purity, can displace the soiled devices of politics. Inexorably, the emphasis upon law which is characteristic of advocates of world government carries with it a tendency to focus upon the relationship of individuals to government: thinking in legal terms, one visualizes the individual apprehended by the police and brought before the judge.[2]

Apart from the seductive quality of certain terms and the favorable images they create, the key argument of proponents of world government is that peace depends primarily upon the creation of a government that, because of its superior power, will be able to enforce the law upon individuals. This argument, however, shows that these proponents misunderstand the function of government and exaggerate the coercion necessary to maintain law and order. Admittedly, government power does play a role in preserving peace. A peaceful society is—at least to a degree—a policeful society. At the same time, however, as we have seen in our own analysis (see Chapter 5), this power is not the principal factor in achieving peace, particularly in democratic societies. There have simply been too many civil wars, *coups d'état*, revolutions, and secessions to justify as much trust as world federalists place in the establishment of government as a solution for the disorder inherent in the international system. If government fails to produce law and order and is unable to keep the nation united, as we have seen often in the last few decades, then what confidence can we have that world government is the answer to anarchy and war?

The fact is that domestic peace results from political negotiations and compromises required by the constantly changing distribution of power among conflicting, usually organized interests with a common political culture. It is not the application of law to individual violators and their imprisonment for disobeying the law that are primarily responsible for domestic peace. Neither is it the policeman swinging a club or the judge hearing a case and sentencing citizens who broke the law. Most citizens obey laws not out of fear but out of habit, respect, and recognition of their legitimacy. Peace is essentially the result of constant political adjustment and accommodation, accomplished through the efforts of the much-maligned politicians. When groups and classes have what they consider genuine grievances and unfulfilled aspirations for which they seek—but are unable to find—redress, then disorder, rioting, and civil war are likely. Applying a law that sanctifies the status quo becomes an incitement to conflict, not a solution. The issue then is not what the law is but what it should be. The analogy of catching the individual lawbreaker and applying sanctions is hardly appropriate; indeed, it is irrelevant.

The example of American nation building—from confederation to federation—in fact offers evidence that the belief that the mere creation of government as an answer to conflict is mistaken. Those who argue for world government consistently underrate the difficulties in forming the United States of America. They want to show that if the will to organize a world government is present, it can be done. This falsifies history. More than will is required; a common political culture or sense of community is necessary. Such a sense of community is apparent in the Preamble to the U.S. Constitution, in which it is declared that the purpose was to establish a "more perfect union." There was already a union, formed during the long colonial period and tested in the war for independence; it had only to be made "more perfect." By 1787 Americans already shared a language, a common cultural tradition, and a democratic heritage.

> The thirteen colonies formed a moral and political community under the British Crown, they tested it and became fully aware of it in their common struggle against Britain and they retained that community after they had won their independence.... The community of the American people antedated the American state, as a world community must antedate a world state.[3]

The final test of this union came during the Civil War, in which the issues of slavery and the country's values had to be settled before the United States could become a durable political community. And it is precisely the absence of an equivalent sense of global community or political culture that makes it impossible to establish a world government—along with, it ought to be added, a historical amnesia in which the civil wars and political disorders of the West have been forgotten and the past romanticized, especially that of the United States and Britain.

The Lack of International Community

Ironically, in an essentially anarchical or Hobbesian state system that exists in a state of potential war, a world government, if it could be established at all, would have to be a dictatorship. When a sense of community is absent, the only government capable of restraining the various nations would have to wield immense power, creating what Thomas Hobbes called a Leviathan. This kind of government is not what world federalists want, however; they want a democratic world state. But a constitutional or limited government based upon the consent of the governed is dependent—as shown by the American experience—on a preexisting community. Proponents of world government are caught in an insoluble dilemma: to emphasize the urgency of transforming the existing state system, they describe the system in Hobbesian terms, but then they reject the logical consequences of their own analysis by seeking a democratic result. World government may be not only impossible to create but also may be undesirable—at least for democrats.

This contradiction has not discouraged some analysts of world affairs, however. Indeed, their goals have become more ambitious. Given the "endangered planet" on which we are said to live, they claim that even if a world government is impossible a new *world order* is more than ever necessary.[4] Specifically, four values are emphasized in this new thinking about world order. The first is peace. The superpowers, to be sure, are already concerned about peace and the stability of the state system, as is shown by their avoidance of nuclear war and their various attempts to reduce tensions. But the present definition of peace as the absence of a destructive total war, although it allows for high levels of interstate conflict (as during the cold war) or lower levels of tension (as in détente), is no longer sufficient for many proponents of a world order, because it is quite compatible with continued tolerance of poverty and social injustice in the world.

As Richard Falk has presented them, after peace the other values to be embodied in a world order are: second, economic well-being, the antithesis of the large-scale poverty in the less-developed nations and the lower social classes of the rich nations; third, social and political justice, the recognition of "inalienable rights" to freedom, self-expression, and human dignity, as well as the collective claim to self-determination and self-government; and fourth, ecological balance to prevent the pollution of "spaceship earth" and the depletion and waste of the globe's finite resources.

Given the critical importance of preventing war and building a more decent and humane world without poverty and social injustice, many people believe that it is more important today than ever before to think of world order as the best alternative to the present state system. Even if it remains practically a utopian solution—attainable only in the distant future, if at all—it still can serve as a goal toward which we can build. The growth of nationalism in the real world, however, indicates that the prospects for laying the foundation for a future world order are not bright—at least, they have not been bright so far. But the new interdependence presumably increases the prospects for it. Creating a new world order is, then, no longer entirely a matter of wishful thinking and naïveté. Human beings cannot afford to indulge in old patterns of thinking and behaving. Balance-of-power statecraft is outmoded, and to cling to it is only "romantic adherence." Says Falk boldly, "the new utopians are the old realists and vice versa."[5] Even a former UN secretary-general commented in 1970:

> I do not wish to seem overdramatic but I can only conclude from the information that is available to me as Secretary General that the members of the United Nations have perhaps ten years left in which to subordinate their ancient quarrels and launch a global partnership to curb the arms race, to improve the human environment, to defuse the population explosion and to supply the required momentum to development efforts.
>
> If such a global partnership is not forged within the next decade, then I very much fear that the problems I have mentioned will have reached such staggering proportions that they will be beyond our capacity to control.[6]

Unfortunately, the mere fact that a goal is necessary and desirable does not render it attainable, no matter how fragile the world's security, how much its population burgeons, how rapidly its resources diminish, how vast the gap between rich and poor countries grows, and how calamitous the future may appear. There is no evidence that states have begun to place international interests ahead of national interests.

In the final analysis, a deep pessimism is common among proponents of world order. But there is a veneer of optimism; Falk, for example, views the 1970s, 1980s, and 1990s, as decades of consciousness raising, mobilization, and transformation, respectively, so that on January 1, 2000, the new order is to be born. But, apart from such marvelous timing, we sense a deep gloom. If spaceship earth does in fact confront military, economic, and environmental self-destruction, talk of raising consciousness of future dangers and of "world-order modeling" and exhorting nations to think of "international interests" seems rather futile and desperate, given the scope and nature of the transformation in attitudes and structures required.[7]

SUPRANATIONAL COMMUNITY BUILDING THROUGH FUNCTIONALISM

The establishment of a world government by means of federation, on the model of American nation building, is hardly likely to occur in the near future. Is there another way, then, to overcome the divisiveness of present-day nationalism and to establish on an international basis the sense of community that is the basis of government? And could such a government be democratic rather than dictatorial? Several political scientists have studied this issue empirically. How have political units in the past been integrated into larger political organizations, the authority of which then superseded their own? How relevant are these historical examples to the contemporary problem of integrating nation-states into a supranational political community?

Definition of Terms

Note three terms that we have just used: *integrating, supranational,* and *political community.* Karl Deutsch and several associates who analyzed various instances of integration of political units in the preindustrial era defined *integration* as "the attainment, within a territory, of a 'sense of community' and of institutions and practices strong enough and widespread enough to assure, for a 'long' time, dependable expectations of 'peaceful change' among its population." [8] Closely related is the term *supranational,* which refers to the formation of a community and institutions above those of the integrating states; this community would have the authority to make political decisions on behalf of the states that would require their obedience (as the American federal government has authority superior to that of the individual states). *Supranational,* then, is not to be confused with the word *international.* An international or intergovernmental organization is an organization composed of states. Its decisions are reached through negotiation and compromise among the states, not imposed from above. Finally, according to Amitai Etzioni, a *political community* is

> a community that possesses three kinds of integration: (a) it has an effective control over the use of the means of violence (though it may "delegate" some of this control to member-units); (b) it has a center of decision-making that is able to affect significantly the allocation of resources and rewards throughout the community; and (c) it is the dominant focus of political identification for the large majority of politically aware citizens. [9]

Among states the threat of violence remains a key element in the resolution of differences, but the chief characteristic of a supranational organization is the absence of intimidation and war from bargaining over important issues. *The anarchical model of the state system,* with its frequent focus on negotiations through threat and counterthreat—or force and counterforce—is no longer applicable. Deutsch and his colleagues have therefore called such an enlarged supranational organization a "security community." [10] Historically they distinguish between two kinds: the *pluralistic* security community, composed of states that retain their national autonomy while forming certain specific and subordinate agencies of cooperation on particular matters (as do the United States and Canada or Norway, Denmark, and Sweden), and the *amalgamated* security community, in which states surrender autonomy to new set of political institutions, as did the provinces of Italy and Germany at the time of unification in the nineteenth century. Deutsch found that pluralistic security communities are easier to achieve and more durable; amalgamated security communities are more difficult to establish and more likely to fail.

The movement toward a united Europe after World War II has been the principal historical experiment by industrialized states in supranation building. Deutsch and his colleagues had been interested in the conditions essential to produce a successful amalgamated security community. Not surprisingly, some of the conditions that had been present in preindustrial amalgamations were also present in the experiment that began in 1950 with the formation of the European Coal and Steel Community (ECSC) and produced eight years later the European Economic Community (EEC), or Common Market (see Figure 19-1). And it is on this important—perhaps revolutionary—experiment that we shall concentrate here. The European experience provides the sole modern example of a nation-state seeking to integrate itself into a larger political unit by shedding sovereignty and nationalism. It also, if successful, would be the first of perhaps several regional building blocs upon which a globally integrated world order could be based.

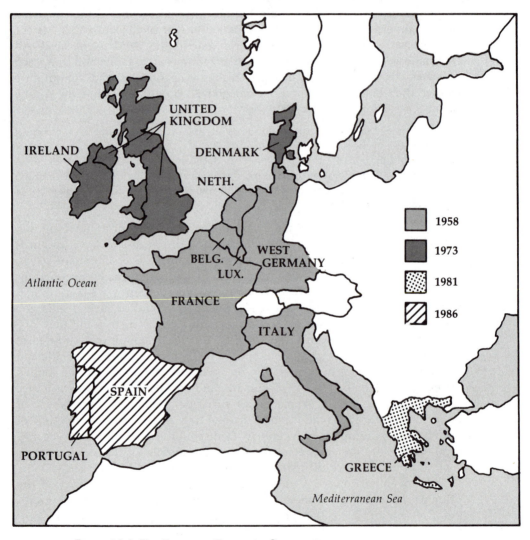

Figure 19-1 The European Economic Community

Conditions for Supranation Building

One condition for building a United States of Europe was a *compatibility of values and expectations* among the amalgamating states. The six original members, sometimes called the Inner Six, certainly had such a compatibility; all were pluralistic societies (although Germany and Italy recently had been fascist states), and each had representative political institutions. In the larger countries, West Germany, France, and Italy, as well as in smaller Belgium, the governing Christian Democrats shared a European outlook and held similar views on social welfare, the free market, and other issues. A second condition was that the political elites of the integrating countries believed their way of life to be distinctive. The Iron Curtain was to them more than an ordinary political division; it separated the "West" from the "East," thus forming two distinct geographical and cultural entities. Christian Democrats were particularly disposed to think of the East-West conflict in terms of the historic struggle between Christendom and the "barbarian" invaders from the East, such as the Mongols and the Turks. Russia, usually regarded as non-European, now fitted this role. For the Christian Democrats, the defense of "civilization" once again required Western countries to subordinate their own differences and unite in the struggle against the Communist Soviet Union.

A third condition of particular significance in amalgamation was the expectation of mutual economic benefit. For the Inner Six this benefit was to be realized in two ways: through the mutual elimination of trade barriers, import quotas, and other restrictions, and through establishment of a common tariff to protect this market. European industry would then enjoy an enormous potential market, and efficient enterprises would presumably expand and modernize their plants to take advantage of this enlarged market. By the same token, inefficient plants unable to compete—and unwilling to make the effort—would be closed. Business in general would profit from European integration. Labor would acquire a similar stake in the new Europe as production rose and the level of employment and real wages followed. To be sure, workers in less efficient industries would lose their jobs, and they might have to move to other areas in search of new employment. But in general the Common Market would produce more jobs. Consumers also would benefit from the expanding economy. As they saw national economic barriers tumbling and industry converting to techniques of mass production—large-scale production at reasonable cost and with wages sufficient to enable consumers to buy in quantity—they, too, would recognize the advantages of the Common Market.

These conditions, then, are among those necessary for the existence of a supranational community. Others include superior economic growth, high political and administrative capabilities in the participating units, unbroken links of social communication, broadening of the political elite, mobility of individuals, and multiple ranges of communication and transaction.[11]

The Process of Supranation Building

But how about the *process* of integration? How does it occur? Functionalists think they know. David Mitrany, the father of this school of thinking, assumed that the *vertical* divisions between states, which produce conflict and war, can be overcome by tying the various functional areas of the economies of different countries together *horizontally*, to resolve their common social, economic, and humanitarian needs.[12] He regarded these needs as essentially nonpolitical and noncontroversial for they involve values such as welfare and social justice, rather than national security and prestige. As each area of need is tackled, a transfer of state authority to supranational institutions will occur; as the satisfaction of more needs is undertaken, more and more authority will be transferred to supranational institutions. Sovereignty is to be whittled away until at some point, nations find themselves brought very close together in this ever-expanding web of activity. They will then have a greater stake in maintaining peace and transferring national authority to new supranational organs. In Frederick Schuman's apt phrase, integration of the various functional areas could bring "peace by pieces." [13] Mitrany called it a "working peace system," distinct from peace safeguarded by the balance of power. In Mitrany's words, "the problem of our time is not how to keep nations peacefully apart but how to bring them actively together." [14]

Ernst Haas was the first to study this process of integration in great detail after the start of the movement toward a more unified Europe. Like Mitrany and Jean Monnet, the French master planner of the New Europe, Haas found the driving force behind integration to be economic self-interest. There had to be "something in it for everyone." Haas also emphasized, as did the French government when it launched ECSC, the importance of step by step economic integration. In 1950 Foreign Minister Robert Schuman of France proposed that the Six pool their coal and steel industries in the ECSC. The choice of coal and steel, the backbone of industry, was deliberate, for it would tie together German and French heavy industry to such an extent that it would become impossible to separate them. Germany would never again be able to use its coal and steel industries for nationalistic and militaristic purposes.

Economic Spillover.   Because the coal and steel sector forms the basis of the entire industrial structure, Haas suggests it was chosen for its economic "spillover." ECSC would exert pressure on the unintegrated sectors of the economy, and, as the benefits of the pooling of heavy industry became obvious, these other sectors would follow suit. ECSC was thus the first stage in an attempt to create a wider market. It was expected that this approach would be gradually extended to other functional areas of the economy, such as agriculture, transportation, and electricity, with the eventual creation of a federal European state enjoying a huge market and a highly developed mass-production system. Once integration had been set in motion, it would pick up momentum on its own.

The first economic spillover occurred in 1958, when the Six established the Common Market. Their aim was the formation of an economic union. All tariffs, quotas, and other restrictions hampering trade among themselves would be completely eliminated; in turn, they would establish a common tariff to reduce imports and to keep as much of the market for themselves as possible. Furthermore, they gradually would abolish restrictions on the movement of labor, capital, and services within the community. Finally, the Six established a third community, Euratom, for the generation of industrial energy. Together, ECSC, EEC, and Euratom, would constitute a European political community.

Political Spillover.   Apart from economic spillover, the most important effect Haas stressed was the political spillover. If there was to be a Common Market and if it was to be more than just a customs union, there had to be a uniform set of rules to govern the economic and social policies of the member countries.[15] For example, if one nation should adopt a deflationary policy, its industries would be able to undersell those of its partners and capture their markets. Clearly, this kind of development had to guarded against. Or, if a nation, after abolishing its tariffs for a specific industry, then subsidized that industry's production or imposed an internal tax on competitive foreign goods, it would gain an obvious advantage for its own industry. Such discrimination by a single government had to be forbidden. Uniform rules could not be established, however, simply for preventing deviant behavior; affirmative action was also required. Because prices reflect production costs, which in turn partly reflect national regulation of wages, hours, working conditions, and social welfare programs, the industries of a nation with lower standards have an advantage over competitors in neighboring states. A single set of standards in areas such as minimum wages, maximum hours, and welfare programs was therefore considered necessary. In addition, as workers would be able to move from one country to another in search of employment and better jobs, there had to be a single social security program for all six nations. This increasing need to harmonize the social and economic policies of the Six would demand a single governmental center for policy formulation in Europe. Common policies would require common institutions with supranational authority.

In real terms, such supranational authority, one observer has noted, "starts to come into play when a state agrees . . . to carry out decisions to which it is itself opposed. Most obviously, such a situation arises when it has agreed to be outvoted if necessary by other states—either by a simple or by some weighted or qualified majority." [16] Common institutions with supranational authority extending beyond trade and tariff matters play a central role in furthering the larger political community.

> If economic integration merely implied the removal of barriers to trade and fails to be accompanied by new centrally made fiscal, labor, welfare, and investment measures, the relation to political integration is not established. If, however, the

integration of a specific section (e.g., coal and steel), or of economics generally (e.g., the "General Common Market") goes hand in hand with the gradual extension of the scope of central decision-making to take in economic pursuits not initially "federated," the relation to the growth of political community is clear.[17]

The development of a political community is demonstrated most readily by interest group activity. In a developed supranational economy those whose interests are affected by the decision-making institutions, adversely or otherwise, will organize to lobby at the supranational level to influence particular decisions. One is reminded of the United States, where various interest groups lobby at the state and the federal levels. In an open, pluralistic society interest groups and political parties (as aggregates of interest groups) normally act at whatever level of government important political policies are decided; this pattern has indeed been the aim of the EEC's founders. Interaction between decision-making institutions and the multitude of interest groups was considered of vital importance to the political integration of the Six.[18]

Social Spillover. In the long run, however, the self-interest of various groups will not suffice. A truly federal Europe must have popular support as well. Eventually, the political spillover leads to social spillover: the transfer of national loyalty to the supranational community.

> As the process of integration proceeds, it is assumed that values will undergo changes, that interests will be redefined in terms of a regional rather than a purely national orientation and that the erstwhile set of separate national group values will gradually be superseded by a new and geographically larger set of beliefs. . . .
> As the beliefs and aspirations of groups undergo change due to the necessity of working in a transnational institutional framework, mergers in values and doctrines are expected to come about, uniting groups across former frontiers. The overlapping of these group aspirations is finally thought to result in an accepted body of "national" doctrine, in effect heralding the advent of a new nationalism. Implied in this development, of course, is a proportional diminution of loyalty to and expectations from the former separate national governments. Shifts in the focus of loyalty need not necessarily imply the immediate repudiation of the national state or government. Multiple loyalties have been empirically demonstrated to exist.[19]

Based upon the logic of the integration of economic, political, and social functions, the EEC was designed to develop into a United States of Europe through three stages: a *customs union,* an *economic union,* and a *political and social union.*

Limits of Functional Logic

Three fundamental assumptions underlay this logic: (1) that economic and social, or low-politics, problems could be separated from political and security, or high-politics, issues; (2) that the ever-widening vested interests and habits of cooperation formed in the low-politics area would spill over into high politics; and (3) that there would be a massive shift of loyalty from the nation to the new supranational community, as citizens—producers, laborers, farmers, and consumers—came to recognize the economic benefits from the new and larger community.

Inseparability of Economics and Politics. The ups and downs of the European unification movement reflect on the validity of these assumptions. It should not have come as too much of a surprise to discover that in practice, even if not in theory, social and economic affairs are not neatly separable from political considerations. The modern industrial welfare state testifies to that. Virtually no social or economic issue, be it farmers' subsidies, corporate survival, women's rights, or abortion, is outside of the realm of political controversy and action. The same is just as true in international politics. Years ago, Inis Claude asked:

> Is it in fact possible to segregate a group of problems and subject them to treatment in an international workshop where the nations shed their conflicts at the door and busy themselves only with the cooperative tools of mutual interests? Does not this assumption fly in the face of the evidence that a trend toward the politicization of all issues is operative in the twentieth century? [20]

States have remained jealous guardians of their sovereignty, national identities, and military strength; the more an economic policy has seemed to infringe on security issues, the greater the difficulties in achieving a united policy. France and the other five countries may pool their coal- and steel-producing facilities to increase their standards of living, but it is quite another story when it comes to coordinating their foreign and defense policies. France and Britain (which joined the EEC, together with Ireland and Denmark, in 1973) each possess small nuclear forces; despite the advantages that combining these forces might have for the two countries and the other Common Market countries, they have been unable to do so. The basic reason for this failure is that the EEC members could not agree on a common foreign policy that such a nuclear force would serve.

Indeed, the original impetus for the formation of a United Europe was political, not economic. The French sought to ensure themselves against any future danger from German rearmament and aggressive policies, as well as to gain equality of status and influence with the "Anglo-Saxons" in the Western alliance. More broadly, France and its partners in the ECSC viewed it as the initial step toward a United States of Europe. Europe was not to be merely a Europe of butchers and candlestick makers, as implied by the later term "Common Market," but a third world power ranking with the United States and the Soviet Union. For otherwise, how could Europe stand on its own feet and play a role again in world affairs? A divided and weak Europe would remain subordinate and subservient to the United States. High politics also motivated French president Charles de Gaulle's later efforts to slow down the European integration movement.

Success an Obstacle to Political Unity. Nor did the economic spillover have quite the results it was supposed to have had. Economically, of course, there can be no doubt that the Common Market has been successful. The ten members with 270 million consumers constitute the largest market in the world, buying a quarter of all its imported goods and selling a fifth of its exports. As a single unit, the EEC possesses great bargaining strength on economic issues, and it has been responsible for tariff reductions among all the industrial countries and easier access to one another's markets. Trade among the six founding members has grown even faster, and this growth has probably been a major factor contributing to the industrialization of France and northern Italy. In 1958 the EEC countries' per capita income was $1,200, compared to $2,800 in the United States. By 1981 the figures were $9,000 and $11,000 respectively.[21]

Ironically, the very success of the Common Market may prove to be one of the greatest obstacles to the political spillover. As the national wealth of EEC members rose, the urgency for further integration declined. The functional analysts had emphasized that fulfillment of some needs would result in growing support for the integration of other sectors of the economy and further development of new supranational attitudes. But contrary to these expectations, economic gains through the customs union seem to have led to protection of the status quo and reduced support for further integration.[22] The citizens and interest groups who gained the most economically from the European unification movement attributed those benefits largely to their own governments. Thus once more the confidence in nation-states, supposedly lost as a result of defeat in World War II and the postwar economic collapse, was enhanced.

Even more ironically, the post-1973 recession lasting into the 1980s also has strengthened the concern with national interests. Member states have tried to protect industries and jobs by keeping out imports from other EEC states. This policy has, in turn, made EEC decisions more difficult to reach as governments, facing voter wrath, have been less able to make the necessary compromises. France and Italy, for example, waged a "wine war" when French growers tried to keep out cheaper Italian wine. Thus, the increasing national resistance to free trade is accompanied by growing government support for troubled industries.

At a time when cooperation is not always present in the low-politics area, one should not be too optimistic about its transfer to the high-politics area. Admittedly, there were indications of new life in the European unification movement. Greece joined the EEC in 1981, and Spain and Portugal joined in 1986. Also, in 1979, the member states for the first time held elections for the European Parliament, a move that was at least symbolic and may some day augment that body's rather limited authority. Although the Common Market countries were prosperous and at peace, the United States of Europe remained a distant objective. The automatic spillover from the economic to the political arena had not been automatic enough. More than thirty years after the launching of the ECSC and more than twenty years after the EEC began its life, nationalism and the nation-state was alive and well in Western Europe.

National loyalties remain. Only in the long run may generational changes result in greater attraction to a new Europe for those born after World War II, whose values are said to be largely "postbourgeois." [23] (Bourgeois values are largely based on individual material and physical security, whereas post-bourgeois values are based more on community values and intellectual and esthetic satisfaction. Adherents of the latter tend to be more cosmopolitan than parochial in their identifications.)

External Conditions for Integration. The functionalists' belief in "the victory of economics over politics," in short, may have been exaggerated, as has the emphasis on the domestic conditions for integration. The neglect of external conditions as a motivation for integration is particularly ironic given the bipolar environment, which stimulated the drive for a United States of Europe. Indeed, just as the Soviet threat had spurred the movement, so its momentum has slowed down as the perceived Soviet threat has diminished. As the defeated and discouraged Continental states recovered and the unique circumstances in which integration was launched changed, the larger vision seems to have dimmed.

During the 1973 oil crisis, each nation scrambled for oil and attempted to make its own deals, raising questions about the cohesion of the Common Market. In a surprisingly frank declaration on the state of the EEC in February 1974, EEC officials declared:

> Europe is being put to the test. It is faced with a new situation which is pitilessly highlighting its weakness and its dependence, but which is also revealing how badly it is in need of unity.
>
> It is facing this situation in a state of crisis: A crisis of confidence, a crisis of will and a crisis of lucidity. . . .
>
> Now that it is put to the test, Europe must show the world its common resolve. Over the last few weeks, setbacks and failures have . . . disturbed us and have raised doubts as to the will of the governments to make progress and as to the ability of our institutions to fulfill their tasks. . . .
>
> At a time when international relations are undergoing a far-reaching transformation, with vital consequences for us all, is there a single European country which can exercise real influence and carry weight comparable to that of a united Europe? [24]

The years following this statement have underlined the importance of these questions. In 1984 a special committee, convened to address the problem of declining confidence in the EEC, stated that Europe is in a state of crisis and counseled that "Europe must recover faith, faith in its own greatness and launch itself on new ventures—the setting-up of a political entity." [25] But the committee was very cautious in offering recommendations. The fact was that the nations of Europe no longer thought of themselves as partners in the great enterprise of "building Europe." Each concentrated on how to get the best deal for itself. The focus was on trading off oranges and lemons, Riesling and Chianti. With its mind still on the grocery list, it was not surprising that the Common Market countries attached thirty footnotes in twenty-three pages of text listing their reservations.[26] Britain, Denmark, and West Germany expressed reservations about the committee's insistence on moving toward greater integration. Iceland, a neutral, objected to defense aspects of the plan, but without a common defense policy, a European political community was meaningless. As it was, Western Europe's reaction to the steady increase and modernization of Soviet forces in Central and Eastern Europe, was modest.

Despite a North Atlantic Treaty Organization (NATO) commitment in 1978 to raise defense spending by 3.5 percent over the level of inflation, few European member states followed through. And in the early 1980s, large crowds marched through the streets of many European cities (except in France) protesting the emplacement of American missiles, although European governments had asked the United States to do so in response to the Soviet deployment of intermediate-range missiles aimed at Western Europe. These popular demonstrations against the ally upon whom Western Europe's defense rested—as if it were the United States that was creating the "arms race"—suggested a strong sense of neutralism and pacifism in Europe. The "peace marches" certainly raised fundamental questions about Western Europe's will as the Common Market countries struggled to maintain their separate détentes with Moscow.

The one thing that the Common Market countries did, however, was to expand from ten to twelve by including Portugal and Spain, two fascist dictatorships that had turned to democracy. Like Greece, which had been admitted after it shed its right-wing regime, Spain and Portugal were rather fragile democracies. The rationale for their admission was obviously the extension and stabilization of democracy in these countries, making democracy more secure throughout Europe. The EEC admitted them even though all three were less-developed industrially, and the larger number of members made efforts to integrate more difficult.

The addition of Portugal and Spain increased the population of the Common Market countries from 280 to 325 million, the West's largest market (with a combined GNP of $2,361 billion and a per capita income of $7,341). It had taken six years to negotiate their admission. France and Greece had opposed the admission for fear of agricultural competition. Their votes were bought with a $4.4 billion agricultural subsidy. Although tariffs had been reduced, free trade was still hampered by these subsidies and protectionist measures. The Common Market was swimming in lakes of wine and building mountains of butter, dumping surplus food on the international market, competing with U.S. farmers, and undermining the competition of the poorer nations of Asia and Latin America. West Germany amd Britain protested, largely in vain, at the money being used to subsidize Europe's farmers who, like U.S. farmers, had considerable political power as voters; they wanted to invest in high technology and industries for future growth. Western Europe remained largely the Europe of butchers and candlestick makers, and its countries remained nationalistic.

THE MULTINATIONAL CORPORATION AND THE NEW GLOBALISM

The Global Business Organization

In contrast to international and supranational organizations, transnational actors can be defined as organizations that carry on "significant centrally directed operations in the territory of two or more nation-states." One of the most potent of these actors (as we saw in Chapter 3) is the gigantic business enterprise or multinational corporation (MNC) such as General Motors, an American-controlled and directed MNC that carries on activities in many different countries. Such a corporation pursues its purposes *across* international boundaries in many different markets. Business organizations, banks, churches (notably the Roman Catholic church), and revolutionary groups certainly are not new to the international scene. But, in the years since World War II, there has been a vast proliferation and growth in the size of transnational actors and in the expansion of their operations to a virtually global scale.

Lester Brown, in comparing the size of multinational corporations with the sizes of nation-states at the beginning of the 1970s, ranked them according to gross annual sales and gross national product respectively. He found that of the top fifty, forty-one were nations and nine were MNCs; of the second fifty, eighteen were nations and thirty-two were MNCs. In the top one hundred, countries barely outnumbered corporations, fifty-nine to forty-one.[27] As another indicator of size, Standard Oil of New Jersey at that time had three times as many employees overseas than the United States State Department and a tanker fleet larger than that of the Soviet Union. Clearly, many MNCs' resources are much greater than those of most members of the United Nations, and many operate on a geographical scale exceeding that of the great empires of the past. Oil has enhanced these trends. After the 1973 oil crisis, Exxon overtook General Motors as the world's largest corporation. The oil companies all profited enormously; so, of course, did the oil-producing states, raising them in the rankings. Banks, too, have done well, as a result of "petrodollars," the internationalization of business, the flow of money across frontiers, and consumer financial services. The Bank American Corporation (which issues VISA cards) and Citicorp (which issues MasterCards) each have achieved resources of $100 billion, equivalent to the total 1978 output of Belgium, a prosperous country. No more than two dozen states in the world have such output. With the collapse of oil prices, General Motors is again the largest MNC.

What has made it possible to speak of a "transnational organizational revolution in world politics."?[28] Modern means of rapid transportation and communication are one factor, and another is technical and organizational capabilities to operate across long distances. This revolution has become very visible in business in particular, because of the emergence of strong consumer-oriented economics in the industrialized First World and because of high-technology industries such as electronics. Exporting may also have become increasingly disadvantageous for many industrial concerns. Because of lower local labor costs and transportation costs in the importing country, a corporation may decide that it can remain competitive only if it establishes production facilities there. Pepsi-Cola, for example, has 512 plants in 114 countries, and in 1973 it was the 119th largest MNC. The extension of production facilities has been especially important in Western Europe, where the Common Market has provided a dynamic market but where non-Market goods are subject to import duties. The purpose of the tariffs was to restrict the market to industries of the member countries, among which tariffs had been eliminated as an incentive to growth. Yet it is behind this common tariff wall that extensive American capital investment and business growth have taken place in Europe, a growth so large that we can speak of *two* American economies, one in the United States and the other in Europe; in the trans-Atlantic world the latter is second only to the former.

American corporations, accustomed to coping with the different regulations of various states, have adapted better than many of their European competitors to operating within the Common Market. European firms, which historically have confined themselves to protected national markets, consequently have lagged behind U.S. corporations. The transnational business organization operating in multiple markets shifts its resources from one country to another as needed: its aim is to maximize profits, and the various national markets function as parts of a single larger one, in which capital, technology, and other resources can be shifted at will. American firms, thinking in continental terms, thus have become more "European" than European firms; the largest corporations in Europe are American.[29] This overseas investment pattern suggests that the growth of the MNC is a rational response to new business opportunities, as well as a defensive move to protect overseas markets to which these firms had previously exported. Given the kind of managerial talent, financial resources, and technical skills that American MNCs possess, the tools of modern business—telexes, telephones, and jet liners— have enabled them to coordinate operations and pursue a virtually global business strategy. We should note, however, that some European and Japanese MNCs have responded in the same manner in other markets; some makes of European and Japanese cars, for example, are now manufactured in the United States.

The vast reach of the MNC has aroused a great deal of speculation about the impact of such transnational actors on the state system. There are three major interpretations of the role of the MNCs: Marxist-Leninist, mercantilist, and liberal (see Table 19-1).

Table 19-1   A Comparison of Marxist, Mercantilist, and Liberal Ideas About the Multinational Corporation and the International Economy

	Marxist	*Mercantilist*	*Liberal*
Actor	Capitalist class	State	Multinational corporation
Nature of economic relations	Clashing interests and conflict	Clashing interests and conflict	Clashing interests and harmony
Goal of economic activity	Maximization of class interest	Maximization of national welfare	Maximation of global welfare
Economic-political assumption	That economics does determine politics	That politics determines economics	That economics should determine politics

SOURCE: Adapted from Table 6, "Comparison of the Three Conceptions of Political Economy," in Robert Gilpin, *U.S. Power and the Multinational Corporation* (New York: Basic Books, 1975).

The Marxist-Leninist Interpretation.   The first is the *Marxist-Leninist,* or imperialist, interpretation. It claims that the capitalist class, having long exploited the domestic proletariat and squeezed all possible profits out of the Third World, has now found a larger, better-organized, and more effective vehicle to continue its exploitation. The MNCs thus represent a further stage of corporate capitalism. They serve as an instrument of an expansionist foreign policy based on resources and cheap labor from the Third World and dependent upon investment opportunities for "surplus capital." The state, controlled by the capitalist class, is the chief actor, the MNC its tool, the best means in an age of rapid transportation and instant communication for the "monopolists" to exploit the vast majority of the world's population and to keep it in poverty. The basic determining force, as in all Marxist theory, is economics. The capitalist state is by nature imperialist. The MNCs are merely the latest instruments of exploitation.

The Mercantilist Interpretation.   The second interpretation of the role of MNCs is mercantilism. It is the reverse of Marxism-Leninism: politics precedes economics. The growth of transnational corporations basically reflects American political influence in most regions of the world. During the cold war the United States used political alliances in every region to contain the Soviet Union and China. American military and political organizations, as well as private economic ones, followed in the wake of political commitments in Western Europe, the Middle East, South Asia, East Asia, and Latin America. Trade, so to speak, followed the flag. Historically, this process has been called *mercantilism.* The state encourages the activities of its businessmen—whether in trade with foreign countries or in overseas investment—in order to create greater wealth at home (see Chapter 11). Robert Gilpin has argued strongly that "political values and security interests are the crucial determinants of international economic relations. . . . Throughout history each successive hegemonic power has organized economic space in terms of its own interests and purposes." [30] Although it is true that transnational actors are the products of modern technology, it is American power that has created the conditions for their expansion. Most MNCs are controlled by Americans. The implication is that a reduction in the American political role in the world will bring about a decline in American MNCs' activities, though European and Japanese MNCs will be more active, reflecting their economic strength.

The Liberal Interpretation. The third interpretation is the *liberal* one, which states that if there is no interference with free international movement of capital, technology, and goods, MNCs will create a new world of plenty for all and conflict for none, a view popular with the MNCs' own managements and supporters. Each MNC is viewed as an independent actor, not as a tool of the state. With its managerial skills and technology it can stoke the fires of economic development, eventually abolishing poverty throughout the less-developed areas. In its search for profits, it neither blocks economic development nor perpetuates destitution. Indeed, its corporate selfishness leads to maximum global·welfare as long as there is no political interference. Furthermore, it is argued that, in a world divided by nationalism, the MNCs can provide the impetus for creation of a world community. George Ball, a former undersecretary of state, has argued that the MNC, which he calls "Cosmocorp," has outgrown the state; national boundaries are anachronistic, for they confine its activities.[31] Unlike traditional imperialism, which presumably encouraged the state to open up new lands for business to exploit, the new business corporation seeks not territorial and political control but access to different markets. In this multinational context, the Cosmocorps' managers are the new "globalists," the "advance men" of "economic one-worldism," who view the globe as a single market—or, in Peter Drucker's phrase, "a global shopping center."

Dependent upon foreign states for permission to produce and sell within their frontiers, these managers regard states, national egotism, and assertively militarist foreign policies as contrary to their own interests. Their primary loyalty is to the corporation, rather than to the nation, and global corporate interests take precedence over national interests. MNCs need peace; national rivalries are economically too costly from their perspective. MNCs, the devils of anti-imperialist theory, are the angels of the liberal theory, for they provide a major restraint on foreign adventures as peace and profits become interdependent.[32] The MNCs are thus regarded as likely to replace nation-states as the most visible and potent actors on the world scene, and welfare will then replace power politics. The MNCs have burst through the confining jurisdictions of national sovereignty and will bring a better life to all peoples. Unable to fulfill their citizens' expectations, nation-states, have become anachronisms. The managers of International Business Machines, General Motors, Exxon, General Electric, Coca-Cola, Lever Brothers, and other large MNCs make decisions daily that appear to have a more immediate and visible impact on consumers' lives than governments do.

Multinational Corporations or Nation-States?

Do MNCs threaten the viability of nation-states and the future of the state system? It is easy to understand why states are anxious and concerned about the MNCs in their territories. Even advanced industrial states are wary. Multinational corporations represent high technology. Will other industrial economies become their "technological colonies," that is, dependencies of the country whose MNCs possess the most advanced technology and skills? A French observer wrote in the late 1960s:

> Electronics is not an ordinary industry; it is the base upon which the next stage of industrial—and cultural—development depends. In the nineteenth century the first industrial revolution replaced manual labor by machines. We are now living in the second industrial revolution, and every year we are replacing the labor of human brains by a new kind of machine—computers.
>
> A country which has to buy most of its electronic equipment abroad will be in a condition of inferiority similar to that of nations in the last century which were incapable of industrializing. Despite their brilliant past, these nations remained outside the mainstream of civilization. If Europe continues to lag behind in electronics, she could cease to be included among the advanced areas of civilization within a single generation.[33]

By the early 1970s, just after these words were written, American MNCs already controlled 80 percent of Europe's computer business, 90 percent of its microcircuit industry, 50 percent of its transistor industry, and 65 percent of its telecommunications. In addition, they controlled sizable portions of more traditional industries, such as automobiles (40 percent), synthetic rubber (45 percent), and petrochemicals. Concern that the MNCs would come to control the technologically most advanced, most rapidly growing, and most profitable sectors of industrial economies was understandable, even though at the time American firms owned only 5 percent of overall European corporate assets. This European fear of falling behind the United States (and now, Japan as well) has not changed. It is the reason that Britain, West Germany, and other U.S. allies wanted to participate in the Strategic Defense Initiative (SDI) research. These governments were profoundly skeptical about SDI, but understood that the research, for example, in laser beams, could have peacetime application in areas such as basic science, industry, and health.

Another concern about MNCs is their huge size and assets compared with the GNPs of the host states. This issue is particularly sensitive in the LDCs, which fear that MNCs will dominate their economies, "repatriating" their excessive profits and draining capital from states that need it. Additional complaints are that they fail to produce the goods needed for modernization. For example, Coca-Cola attracts money that could be spent on necessities such as milk, meat, vegetables, and educational materials. MNCs are also said to impose Western culture and consumer-oriented values (the term "cultural imperialism" is often used).[34] These fears about the MNCs, however, have changed significantly as the LDCs, since the 1960s, have gained a sense of confidence in dealing with them. The LDCs also need the cash generated by the MNCs because of the decline of foreign aid and the drop in commodity prices. The generally poor economic performances of many LDCs committed to publicly run economies have led their governments to reassess the value of private enterprise and capital.

But whether an MNC operates a manufacturing plant in Europe or an extractive industry in the Third World—and it is the former that has attracted most American investment capital[35]—the common fear in the host country is that the MNC will exploit its power in a way that will hurt national interests. For example, if an MNC finds the investment climate no longer suitable in one country, it can pick up its chips and move to another country, leaving behind unemployment and ill-feeling. Because other states seek to attract the MNC, it can play off one state against the other. During the cold war, U.S. law forbade shipment of certain products to designated countries. This restriction applied to all U.S. corporations, domestic as well as multinational. A foreign country, wishing to pursue a more friendly policy toward a U.S. adversary or simply to improve its balance of payments, could have been prevented from trading these restricted products if they had been manufactured by a subsidiary of an American MNC. The apprehensions of nations about their control over their own economies have been strengthened by the MNCs' political interference, such as International Telephone and Telegraph's efforts at subversion in Chile and bribes offered and subsidies paid by Lockheed and other firms to governmental and political leaders in many countries for orders or the right to sell their products. Host governments are understandably sensitive to infringements of their right to maintain control over their economies.

Nevertheless, states will survive the challenge of the new transnational business actor. The reason is that while some conflict between the two is unavoidable, they need each other. Their conflict is complementary.

> It is conflict not between likes but between unlikes, each of which has its own primary set of functions to perform. It is, consequently, conflict which, like labor-management conflict, involves the structuring of relations and the distribution of benefits to entities which need each other even as they conflict with each other. The balance of influence may shift back and forth from one to the other, but neither can displace the other.[36]

Indeed, the MNC appears to strengthen, rather than weaken the state, for it needs the latter's permission for access to its territory. The multinational corporation may well be one of the leading reasons for the increasing role of the state in economic affairs and the extension of state power into the economic realm. In Europe, for example, governments intervene in the economic sphere in order to create domestic competitors to counterbalance the size and influence of American corporations. Governments remain sensitive to retaining national control over their economies and are concerned that their goals not be upset by corporate decision made on a multinational basis. As John Fayerweather has noted, "At critical points every nation-state finds that its objectives of national military security, domestic economic stability, protection of particular national groups, and even national pride become more important than potential economic increments from full participation in global economic optimization."[37]

Host countries therefore increasingly have set the terms of access and established relations in which they benefit from the presence of MNCs in terms of employment, taxes, balance of payments, transfer of technology, and managerial skills, while simultaneously permitting the MNCs to earn enough to provide an incentive to stay. Some hosts establish employment quotas for nationals, require MNCs to establish themselves in so-called depressed areas (for which they may, however, receive tax incentives), forbid layoffs, and demand the training of whatever local workers are required (which may, however, be subsidized). Almost all host countries set dates for achieving complete or majority ownership; they may also set export figures for the MNCs (which some may be reluctant to comply with to avoid competing with their own brands in other countries). In return for access to markets, MNCs in recent years have increasingly complied with these types of demands by the host countries. The result has been greater cooperation between host states and MNCs. Indeed, the host country's strength in setting the terms of MNCs' access has been increased by the fact that American management, finance, and technology now face increasing competition from the Europeans and Japanese.

> In short, sovereignty is no longer at bay in most countries. To be sure the degree of this shift in power differs from country to country, and from industry to industry. It is virtually complete in most industrial host countries and some developing countries as well, and is well underway in many other developing countries.[38]

The "state-centric" model of international politics is thus likely to remain the principal explanation of what occurs in the international environment. The MNC continues to operate in a system in which the peace so necessary to business operations is preserved by states. It is the states that control the terms of access—if there is access—and remain the focus of citizens' loyalties; it is they who will determine the future of the MNC and not the reverse.

In turn, corporations essentially want to be left alone to do their business, although fear remains that the large MNCs will interfere in national politics. They are interested in politics in order to gain access to a nation's market and gain a hospitable environment in which they can make money. MNCs are very flexible. They will work with a democratic government in a democratic society and with despotic and even racist governments in other countries (just as the Roman Catholic church historically has come to terms with all types of governments to have access to their people).[39] In the short run, the MNCs may well reinforce the status quo in the societies in which they operate. In the long run, however, they may help to undermine the status quo—in non-Communist societies, at least—by making visible new technology, ideas, social and cultural values, and ways of life that challenge especially the LDCs' more traditional cultures, as Western colonialism once did.

> There is little evidence to substantiate the argument that the multinational corporation as an independent actor has had a significant impact on international politics.
>
> While the evidence is indisputable that the multinational corporation is profoundly important in the realm of international economic relations, its political significance is largely confined to its impact on domestic politics where it is an irritant to nationalistic sentiments. . . .
>
> Where these business enterprises have influenced international political relations, they have done so, like interest groups, by influencing the policies of their home governments. . . .
>
> Contrary to the argument that the multinational corporation will somehow supplant the nation-state . . . it is closer to the truth to argue that the role of the nation-state in economic as well as in political life is increasing and that the multinational corporation is actually a stimulant to the further extension of state power in the economic realm.[40]

This point is well illustrated by the relationship between the MNC and its home country. As relations with host nations become closer, the relationship with the home nations grows more and more distant. Such MNC-host nation negotiations are having an increasingly significant impact on the national interest of the United States. In these negotiations the MNC represents itself and the host country is represented by its government; but the U.S. economy and the American public, both of which will be affected by the outcome, are underrepresented. Labor particularly has become protectionist, opposing what the unions call the "export of jobs" to LDCs, especially Taiwan, Hong Kong, South Korea, and Singapore. The home government increasingly may seek to restrict the outflow of investment capital when it is suffering high unemployment and balance-of-trade deficits (more money going out to pay for imports than coming in from exports). Ironically, the relations may well worsen, for the "stake is nothing less than the international division of production and the fruits thereof."[41] As the American government more and more experiences the shift of benefits to other countries—and the same is true for other home countries of MNCs—domestic political pressures to restrict the MNCs will increase. The American government, like other Western governments, may find itself compelled to intervene at some point to protect U.S. prosperity. According to Fred Bergsten, such intervention may then be the only way to avoid "the threat of investment wars."[42] Note that states will be interfering and negotiating with one another to resolve this and other issues; that is, it will be the states that will seek to avoid conflicts resulting from the very economic forces that some proponents of MNCs believe will bring the world together in prosperity and render national divisions essentially meaningless.

Notes

1. Emery Reves, *The Anatomy of Peace* (New York: Harper & Row, 1945), 253-270. See also Carl Van Doren, *The Great Rehearsal* (New York: Viking, 1948), for a discussion of American constitutional nation building as an example for the world.
2. Inis L. Claude, Jr., *Power and International Relations* (New York: Random House, 1964), 260-261.
3. Hans J. Morgenthau, *Politics among Nations*, 4th ed. (New York: Alfred A. Knopf, 1967), 498, 499. See also Crane Brinton, *From Many One* (Cambridge, Mass.: Harvard University Press, 1948).
4. Saul H. Mendlovitz, *On the Creation of a Just World Order* (New York: Free Press, 1976); Richard A. Falk, *A Global Approach to National Policy* (Cambridge, Mass.: Harvard University Press, 1975); and Falk, "Future Worlds," *Headline Series* no. 229 (New York: Foreign Policy Association, February 1976); and Richard L. Rubenstein, *The Age of Triage* (Boston: Beacon Press, 1983).
5. Falk, "Future Worlds," 47.
6. These words of U Thant were reported by James Reston, *New York Times*, Oct. 22, 1970.
7. See, for instance, Harold D. Lasswell, "The Promise of World Order Modelling Movement," *World Politics*, April 1977, 425-437.
8. Karl Deutsch et al., *Political Community and the North Atlantic Area* (Princeton, N.J.: Princeton University Press, 1957), 5.
9. Amitai Etzioni, *Political Unification* (New York: Holt, Rinehart & Winston, 1965), 4.
10. Deutsch et al., *Political Community*, 3-21.
11. Ibid., 46-58.
12. David Mitrany, *A Working Peace System* (London: National Peace Council, 1946).
13. Quoted by Inis L. Claude, Jr., *Swords into Plowshares* (New York: Random House, 1964), 376.
14. Mitrany, *A Working Peace System*, 7.
15. Two of the better early discussions of the expected harmonizing of national policies are Michael Shanks and John Lambert, *The Common Market Today—and Tomorrow* (New York: Holt, Rinehart & Winston, 1962), 56-105; and U. W. Kitzinger, *The Politics and Economics of European Integration* (New York: Holt, Rinehart & Winston, 1963), 21-59. See also Emile Benoit, *Europe at Sixes and Sevens: The Common Market, the Free Trade Association, and the United States* (New York: Columbia University Press, 1961).
16. Kitzinger, *Politics and Economics of European Integration*, 60-61.
17. Ernst B. Haas, *The Uniting of Europe* (Stanford, Calif.: Stanford University Press, 1958), 12-13.
18. Ibid., xiii.
19. Ibid., 13-14.
20. Claude, *Swords into Plowshares*, 4th ed. (New York: Random House, 1971), 385.
21. *New York Times*, March 23, 1982.
22. This result is explained by the concept of "equilibrium": see Leon N. Lindberg and Stuart A. Scheingold, *Europe's Would-Be Polity* (Englewood Cliffs, N.J.: Prentice-Hall, 1970). See also Joseph S. Nye, Jr., *Peace in Parts* (Boston: Little, Brown & Co., 1972).
23. Ron Inglehart, "An End to European Integration?" *American Political Science Review*

(March 1967): 91-105; and Inglehart, "The Silent Revolution in Europe: Intergenerational Change in Post-Industrial Societies," *American Political Science Review* (December 1971): 991-1017.

24. "State of the Community," *European Community*, April 1974, 12-14. On elite and mass attitudes toward European unification, generally showing the softness of support for a united Europe, see Werner J. Feld and John K. Widgen, eds., *Domestic Political Realities of European Unification* (Boulder, Colo.: Westview Press, 1977). On the future of the European community and its impact on economic and political relations in the world, see Werner J. Feld, *The European Community in World Affairs* (Port Washington, N.Y.: Alfred, 1977).

25. *New York Times*, Dec. 4, 1984.

26. *New York Times*, Dec. 9, 1984.

27. Lester R. Brown, *World Without Borders* (New York: Vintage Books, 1973), 213-215, 216.

28. Samuel P. Huntington, "Transnational Organization in World Politics," *World Politics*, April 1973, 333ff. See also Luiz Simmons and Abdul Said, eds., *The New Sovereigns* (Englewood Cliffs, N.J.: Spectrum, 1974); and Charles P. Kindleberger, ed., *The International Corporation* (Cambridge, Mass.: M.I.T. Press, 1970).

29. Robert L. Pfaltzgraff, *The Atlantic Community* (New York: Van Nostrand Reinhold, 1969), 80, 108-110.

30. Robert L. Gilpin, "The Politics of Transnational Economic Relations," in *Transnational Relations and World Politics*, ed. Robert O. Keohane and Joseph S. Nye, Jr. (Cambridge, Mass.: Harvard University Press, 1972).

31. George W. Ball, "Cosmocorp: The Importance of Being Stateless," *Atlantic Community Quarterly*, Summer 1968, 168.

32. Richard J. Barnet, *The Roots of War* (Baltimore: Penguin, 1973), 229-238.

33. J. J. Servan-Schreiber, *The American Challenge* (New York: Avon, 1969), 42.

34. A strong indictment of the MNCs may be found in *Global Research* by Richard J. Barnet and Ronald E. Müller (New York: Simon & Schuster, 1974).

35. David H. Blake and Robert S. Walters, *The Politics of Global Economic Relations* (Englewood Cliffs, N.J.: Prentice-Hall, 1976), 78-80; and Joseph S. Nye, Jr., "Multinational Corporations in World Politics," *Foreign Affairs* (October 1974): 162.

36. Huntington, "Transnational Organization," 366.

37. John Fayerweather, "The Internalization of Business," *Annals of the American Academy of Political Social Science* (September 1972): 6-7.

38. C. Fred Bergsten, "The Coming Investment Wars?" *Foreign Affairs* (October 1974): 135ff.; and C. Fred Bergsten, Thomas Horst, and Theodore Moran, *American Multinationals and American Interests* (Washington, D.C.: The Brookings Institution, 1978).

39. Ivan Vallier, "The Roman Catholic Church: A Transnational Actor," in Keohane and Nye, *Transnational Relations*, 135-140.

40. Gilpin, "Politics of Transnational Economic Relations," 68-69.

41. Bergsten, "The Coming Investment Wars?" 148.

42. Ibid.

CHAPTER 20

Interdependence as a Substitute for Power Politics

THE HALFWAY HOUSE

State behavior is restrained primarily by the balance of power. International organization and legal and moral norms may strengthen this restraint to some degree, but the essentially anarchical nature of the state system appears likely to continue; so does the existence of national self-help and national egotism. Perhaps these consequences of the state system could be eliminated if the anarchical structure was transformed and replaced by a world government and order that allowed for peaceful change, provided for the security of member states, and engendered a more prosperous world with a decent standard of living and justice for all people. But this possibility does not seem feasible either; the outlook for the world appears bleak.

Interdependence is a sort of halfway house between the anarchy of the contemporary state system and the promise of a world-state in the future.[1] Believers in the promise expect the state system to continue but with the fangs of national interest drawn; even before world government comes into existence, they expect some of its benefits—greater cooperation, less emphasis on violent resolution of conflict, more emphasis on joint solutions peacefully arrived at—to become common. States may even remain the principal actors and a world-state only the ultimate objective, but interdependence increasingly will bind all states together, catch them in its web, and make their individual security, especially their economic fortunes, dependent on one another. Whatever the problems confronting a single state, solutions will no longer be national solutions achieved at the cost of other states. Instead, they will be reached collectively and will benefit all. The maxim of the historic state system, "Your gain is my loss," is to be replaced by the maxim "We shall all lose or gain together" in the new interdependent state system.

There is, in this view, nothing idealistic about relying on interdependence. It already exists to a degree, and every day people become increasingly aware of it, regardless of where they live. Simultaneously, historic concern with security issues and the old ways of conducting international politics, "power politics," are becoming outmoded. Except for nuclear proliferation, the new international agenda is focused on issues such as resources (especially energy resources), population and poverty in the LDCs, the growing gap between rich and poor nations, the environment, and human rights. Such issues are economic, technological, social, and even moral, to the extent that the gap between rich and poor is seen as a moral question.

This kind of interdependence will be discussed and analyzed here in three parts: first, an example to illustrate what is meant by interdependence; second, a more detailed analysis of the character of interdependence and exactly how behavior in the old state system is said to differ from that under interdependence; and third, an evaluation of the validity of the interdependence thesis.

AN EXAMPLE OF INTERDEPENDENCE

The Impact of the Oil Price Rise

The idea of interdependence came into vogue with the 1973-74 oil price rise. The reason was the serious effects on the economies of the First World during the 1970s caused by the actions of the Organization of Petroleum Exporting Countries (OPEC):

Inflation. OPEC's continual price rises were not the only cause of inflation, but they were a major stimulus. Pumping oil out of the ground costs $0.25 a barrel, but OPEC's official price at the beginning of the 1980s was $34 a barrel.

Recession and substantial unemployment. Economic growth rates were at their lowest since the Great Depression of 1929-30. Millions lost their jobs. In 1982 this figure was more than 30 million in the twenty-four industrial democracies.

Stagflation. Inflation and recession occurred simultaneously. Policies to reduce inflation raised unemployment, and policies aimed at reducing unemployment heightened inflation. There seemed no way out, and economists were baffled. They knew how to "cure" inflation or recession but not both at the same time, and their inability to solve this problem was intensified by the political pressures to lower the rate of inflation and to raise employment.

Reduction in the standard of living. The cost of living exceeded wage settlements; less could be bought with wages; and powerful union attempts to keep up with or stay ahead of inflation stimulated inflation. Nonunionized workers, the white-collar middle class, the elderly, and the poor all suffered lower living standards.

Inability to forecast national economic growth, employment levels, and inflation rates. A government could do all the planning it wished, but if foreign states had a major, perhaps a decisive, influence on its economy, accurate predictions became impossible.

Threats to the welfare state. Rapid economic growth after World War II provided the wealth and the taxes to fund the many social services of modern democratic countries. As more and more groups in society gained bigger slices of the ever-expanding "economic pie," social conflicts were eliminated or kept to acceptable levels. In a shrinking, stagnant, or slowly growing economy, one sector could gain only at the expense of another. Such a situation intensifies social conflicts and sets class against class, region against region, and union workers against nonunion workers.

Changing ways of life. Perhaps the most immediate impact was visible in smaller cars, lower speed limits, adjustments in heating and air conditioning, and the curtailing of trips and vacations.

Vulnerability to events. Prices of oil shot up more than 100 percent after the fall of the shah of Iran in 1979. Gas lines appeared in many places in the United States, and prices for heating oil rose sharply. That the collapse of a monarchy halfway around the world should have such a dramatic impact conveys inescapably the meaning of interdependence and its profound impact on each one of us.

Threats to Western unity. Paying for oil year in and year out strained the financial ability of some nations and incited "trade wars" among Western states. Each sought to maximize exports and reduce imports to earn sufficient money to pay oil bills that at times seemed to bring some of them to the brink of bankruptcy. They also tried to gain advantages over their allies in the scramble for oil. This placed strains on the North Atlantic Treaty Organization (NATO) and displaced attention from the containment of Soviet influences.

Reduction of Western defense capabilities. The Western democracies (even the United States and West Germany) experienced difficulties increasing the size of their forces and equipping them with modern arms in response to the Soviet buildup. The days of affording both guns and butter appeared over. A strong defense might have to be paid for by money taken from domestic welfare programs. Conversely, any increase in social services was likely to mean less money for defense.

Effects on international currency stability. During the 1970s, as more dollars flowed to OPEC to pay for oil, the flood of oil dollars—"petrodollars"—reduced the value of the dollar. There were simply too many dollars in the world market.

Rising cost of imports. As dollars flowed outward and declined in value, the cost of imported goods rose. American manufacturers, instead of undercutting the competition, also raised prices, partly to compensate for their higher costs, and partly to increase profits. The spiral of inflation was thus pushed even higher, while the dollar continued to decline.

There appeared to be no quick "miracle cures." Discovery of more oil requires periods of exploration and the investment of enormous amounts of capital. Even if plentiful supplies are found, they are not immediately available. In the meantime, drilling and transportation of oil in ships continued to pose major environmental hazards. Nor were other alternatives—coal, shale oil, and nuclear energy—available. Furthermore, all posed environmental problems.[2]

The impact of the increases in oil prices was also severe in those less-developed countries (LDCs) that did not themselves produce oil:

Reduction in ability to "earn their way." As demand in the industrial West for the commodities of the LDCs decreased, the prices of those commodities also declined. Yet the LDCs needed foreign exchange and earnings to buy machinery and food. Their solution, as noted, was to borrow money and go into debt.

Less foreign aid. The Western economies sent less assistance to the poorer nations.

Threat of Western tariffs. Western nations raised tariffs to keep out the few products young industries exported. Western labor, suffering from unemployment, was not committed to the free flow of trade when domestic jobs were at stake.

Increased costs of Western exports. Western machinery, food, and consumer items were less available to the LDCs as their foreign earnings shrank in amount and value.

Social and political turmoil. The economic lot of the poorer LDCs, especially in Africa, worsened, and this sometimes resulted in political instability. The countries that went deeply into debt found that the Western demands to repay these debts meant cutting the few social services they had, causing riots in some countries.

Clearly, then, not only did OPEC's activities affect Western economies and the LDCs' prospects, but also the Western response had a further impact on the LDCs.

Even the OPEC countries themselves learned some lessons. They had to export their oil. They needed Western technology and trade to modernize their societies. Some of them needed Western—especially American—political support to protect their governments from external attack, subversion, and *coups d'état.* They wanted to buy modern arms for their defense, increasing their dpendence on Western technicians to maintain the equipment and train people in its use. They presumably had an interest in Western economic

Table 20-1 Cheaper Oil: Its Impact on the United States

Favorable	*Unfavorable*
Major savings, lower trade imbalance	Curtailment of new oil and gas exploration, slowing production of energy, dropping domestic production
Stimulation of economic growth	Reduced need for conservation, raising consumption
Reduced inflationary pressures	Loss of revenue, causing recessions in energy-producing areas and industries
Lower interest rates	Increased oil imports, which will increase vulnerability to higher oil prices and/or cut-offs
Lower consumer bills for gasoline and heating	Danger to banks due to difficulties debtor countries have repaying loans

stability and prosperity because of the heavy investment of OPEC earnings in the West. To sum up, then, every state's actions had an impact on all other states.

The Impact of the Oil Price Decline

The plummeting of oil prices in 1985-86 obviously reversed some of the above effects, although it also raised other problems. The price decline presumably will benefit other First World economies the same way it benefits the United States (see Table 20-1). If the United States, as the world's largest economy and market, is the "engine" that pulls the other economies behind it, the overall benefits are obvious. For one thing, lower U.S. interest rates should keep more investment capital in Europe. Those LDCs that produce no oil also should reap benefits: fewer precious dollars spent on oil, greater demand for their resources, and fewer restrictions on their imports to the West as industrial employment and consumer demands pick up. Obviously, some countries will benefit less, if at all. All OPEC countries will be hit hard, some more than others. Nigeria will have severe problems making ends meet, and Mexico even greater difficulties paying off its debts to several large American banks (which, should they fail, will have a fallout on the economy as a whole). Even Saudi Arabia, needing more money to complete its modernization, committed itself at the end of 1986 to raising oil prices again.

For Egypt, a small oil producer, the most important effects will be political. With its current population of almost 50 million, about half of which is under fifteen years of age, Egypt will have a difficult time providing social services or adequate food, which will have to be imported. But the reduction in the nation's income is due not only to lower oil prices, but also to the hundreds of thousands of Egyptians who worked in the Gulf states, lost their jobs, and returned home. As domestic dissatisfaction rises, political instability may also grow, and this could be exploited by the Islamic fundamentalists. How long can the current government maintain the peace with Israel and remain isolated from the Arab world? To get help from the oil-producing Arab states and appease the opposition at home, will the government have to freeze the peace process? With the Islamization of Sudan to the south, an Iranian victory over Iraq (if that were to occur), plus Egypt's domestic troubles, the future of this pro-Western government is not assured. If another regime were to replace it and return Egypt to the Arab fold, the entire political-military situation for the United States, as well as for Israel, would change for the worse. The multilayered effects of the oil price drop throughout the international system is surely sufficient testimony to the new interdependence.

A MODEL OF INTERDEPENDENCE

The Meaning of Interdependence

What is the point made by the preceding examples of interdependence? It is first and most important, according to its proponents, that interdependence means mutual vulnerability. OPEC's actions since 1973 have affected the economies of all non-Communist states. Developed or less developed, they have all been seriously dislocated, as plans for economic growth have been transformed into efforts to prevent further stagnation and to regain economic momentum. Both their industrial and agricultural sectors have been affected; inflation and recession have left no nation untouched. Yet the OPEC nations, which need to sell their oil and choose to invest their capital in the West, cannot afford to hurt the industrial states too much without hurting themselves. Economic growth, then, apparently can no longer be carried out on a national basis but requires coordination with other economies. No state remains immune to events elsewhere; national economic autonomy is a thing of the past. The nations of the First and Third Worlds are clearly and irrevocably tied together.

Each is sensitive to the other's needs and actions and can hurt the other. What A does will quickly affect B; for example, an oil-price increase by A results in further inflation and unemployment in B. How seriously A's decisions will affect B depends upon alternative available oil supplies, other energy sources, and whether the increases in inflation and unemployment occur in small steps or in a single big jump. If alternative oil is available, A's action may not hurt much. B may be sensitive to A but not too vulnerable. If B, on the other hand, has no other sources of energy and must pay large price increases, B will be very vulnerable. Interdependence means both sensitivity and vulnerability.[3]

Second, interdependence focuses on essentially economic and social issues, even moral issues. For example, in the industrial nations, high prices for oil and natural gas are obviously a major problem for low-income people, who may have to give up food to heat their homes or suffer the cold if there is not enough money left after the rent has been paid. Whether people should be hungry or cold or both for reasons beyond their control or whether they should be assisted with government subsidies is a social and moral issue. On a much broader scale, do human beings *as* human beings have a fundamental right to a decent standard of living? Is it acceptable that in the United States so many people overeat that the control of obesity is a booming business, while in the LDCs millions suffer from hunger and malnutrition? In the final analysis, is not the sizable gap in wealth between the First and Third worlds a moral issue?

There can now be no doubt of the importance of these socioeconomic, or low-politics, issues; since 1973, OPEC has erased any doubt that may have existed. But the proponents of interdependence are arguing something far more important. Most pre-1973 international politics analysts neglected economic issues, relegating trade and financial matters to a subordinate place in the scheme of things. Economic problems were regarded as basically technical and resolvable by experts who understood such matters. The proponents of interdependence argue that interdependence among states is the principal characteristic of the contemporary international system; indeed, as other actors, such as multinational corporations (MNCs), are prominently featured, the words *global system*, rather than *state system*, are usually used. This interdependence supposedly will lead to more peaceful and collaborative behavior among states; at the very least, the penchant for conflict and resolving disputes with violence will be curbed. Above all, the new interdependent system will be characterized by cooperation. States that are mutually vulnerable *have* to work together; they cannot, as in power politics, seek advantage at the cost of potential adversaries.

The Building Blocks of World Politics

Let us look in more detail at the building blocks of this interdependence model to understand more fully why "the logic of interdependence" supposedly will lead to a more peaceful and harmonious world.

The Assumption of Security. The first block consists of nuclear arms, which, precisely because of their suicidal nature, have engendered a greater sense of security. This sense, although not absolute, has diminished the importance of the security issue. Deterrence works, and threats of violence have taken the place of unrestrained violence. When force is used, it is circumscribed so that escalation of tension between the superpowers will not occur. The awesome nature of nuclear weapons has led to an increasing reluctance to use force. Furthermore, in both limited conventional and guerrilla warfare, a superpower has no advantage just *because* it is a superpower; indeed, the increasingly high costs of using force against Third World states inhibit the great powers even more. Never before in history, then, have the old symbols of great-power status been so useless, aside from defending the status quo.

The Priority of Low-Politics Goals.

The second building block is the change in the principal aim of national foreign policies. The single best word to describe this change is *modernization.* The harnessing of labor to machinery to enhance productivity and to increase standards of living began in western Europe in the nineteenth century, spread to North America, and has now been extended to the Third World. For citizens of most lands, low-politics issues are more important than high-politics issues. These citizens want to improve their material way of life. In democratic countries, where the "revolution of rising expectations" began, electoral pressures guided governmental concern about improving peoples' lives. But their very example has led even nondemocratic nations to seek the same goals. Initially the presence of the colonial power, with its superior standard of living, longer average life expectancy, lower infant mortality, greater literacy, and technological and scientific prowess, offered vivid demonstrations of alternatives to the colonies' way of life; the conquering foreigners' guns were symbols of a superior way of life and technology. The West was therefore to be emulated.

Governments have therefore had to be increasingly responsive to low-politics issues. Their choices have had to satisfy people's economic needs and desires; their success has been judged by their provisions of social services and the growth of the gross national product (GNP). The management of the economy—even a free-enterprise economy—by government is politically necessary to ensure high employment, rapid economic growth, economic stability, and the equitable distribution of income. Governmental incompetence in economic management is not easily forgotten or forgiven at election time.

End of National Self-Sufficiency.

Because low politics, or domestic welfare, has assumed priority over traditional security concerns, the third building block is the recognition that states are no longer self-sufficient. The days of autonomy, when at least the great powers had most of the resources they needed and controlled their own economic destinies, are gone. If governments are to satisfy their people's demands for greater prosperity, they increasingly will have to enter into the international economy. To fail to do so will be too costly politically because economic growth will be slow. Governments thus are drawn further and further into interdependence. Note that implicit in this line of reasoning is the virtual elimination of the line between foreign policy and domestic policy. The two become almost indistinguishable. To provide their citizen-consumers with the services and goods they want, governments pursue domestic economic policies that depend for their success on events beyond their own borders. Foreign policy becomes thoroughly enmeshed with issues of trade, aid, development, monetary stability, exchange rates, and debt problems.

The "socioeconomic game" reflects a new awareness that states have become economically interdependent and that each society's economic viability and prosperity depend on those of all other societies. Highly industrialized states and developing nations all must cope with limited supplies of raw materials, depletion of resources, overpopulation, food shortages, and environmental damage. To paraphrase the seventeenth-century poet John Donne, no nation is any longer, "an island unto itself." The economic futures of all are inextricably intertwined, and the many economic links among nations constitute a web of interdependence. All states become "trading states" as they gain access to each other's resources and markets.[4]

The Necessity for Cooperation.   The fourth block follows logically: low politics involves cooperation, whereas high politics involves conflict. Nations have become so interdependent on bread-and-butter issues that a given nation has no choice but to cooperate if it wishes to promote its own prosperity. On security issues, states still operate as separate political units. A single nation's increase in power and security is still usually seen by a potential adversary as a loss of power and security for itself and as something to be opposed. But an increase in welfare for the same nation depends on increases in welfare for other nations as well. In the new "socioeconomic game" states gain or lose together. An interdependent world is a world of exchange and sharing; war would disrupt this mutually beneficial relationship.

The Irrelevance of Force.   Building block five is the fundamental irrelevance of force to low-politics issues. Interdependent states must cooperate over a long period; the use or threat of force, effective as it may once have been in managing conflict, is inefficient and counterproductive in a game of coordination. Coercion or violence may perhaps pay off on a single issue, but, given the need for long-term collaboration, anger and resentment following such tactics may lead to some sort of economic revenge. If another nation possesses a much-needed commodity, it is hardly helpless, even if it is militarily inferior. The gains from force would therefore be few, if any, and the costs probably quite high.

Force, in short, is a clumsy weapon, not very cost-effective on socioeconomic issues, on which even the militarily weak have bargaining power that traditional means of calculating power hardly reveal. "Imagine, for example, one state threatening a resort to force if another did not comply with its demand for a currency devaluation. Or consider the likelihood of two neighboring states going to war over a question of pollutants that flow downstream or downwind across their common borders."[5] These issues call for a kind of bargaining in which force plays no role. Trading states recognize that their own economic development and standards of living depend on the worldwide market for their goods and services. War in this context is counterproductive.

Changing Concept of Power.   Sixth, the very meaning of power has changed, given the uselessness of force, the need for cooperative behavior if common problems are to be solved, and the complexity of such issues as population control, increased food production, development of alternative energy sources, monetary stability, and economic growth, all of which demand great technical expertise.

> Bargaining over differences, trading issues off against each other, promises of future support, threats of future opposition, persuasion through appeals to common values, persuasion through the presentation of scientific proof—these are the prime control techniques through which the problems of interdependence must be addressed. They are, of course, as old as diplomacy itself, but they have taken on new meaning in the light of the decline of force as a viable technique and in view of the complex nature of the interdependence issues.... The inclination to rely on appeals to common values, with a corresponding diminution in the tendency to threaten reprisals, appears especially likely to emerge as central to the conduct of foreign affairs.[6]

Egalitarianism. The seventh building block is this bargaining relationship, which, in contrast to the cold war and détente relationships, is not bipolar but multipolar. Whether the issue is resources, the environment, population, food, foreign investments, or the MNCs, many nations are involved, usually different nations on different issues. In Stanley Hoffmann's phrase, there are many "chessboards"; different players with different power resources negotiate on each issue.

This point may not seem particularly novel. Yet, when many nations participate on many issues, and force is not a viable bargaining instrument, it seems that the historical power hierarchy based on security issues has been eroded and that all states are essentially equal on welfare issues. Surely this claim is audacious, if not revolutionary. The dominance of the superpowers and traditional power politics are said to have disappeared; security is now basically a "given," and the primary objective of states is welfare.

Interdependence and Regimes

The envisioned interdependent world, then, is one in which states will still exist, but they will not be the kinds of states we have been studying so far. Interdependence will have "tamed" them, drawing the "sharp teeth of sovereignty": it will also have dissolved selfish national interests and bonds of national loyalty.[7] Genuinely equal states will live together in greater harmony and mutual understanding; at the very least, they will be disposed to resolve conflicts peacefully. Economic and technological forces will bind them together, and national frontiers will become increasingly irrelevant, for economic cooperation will cross borders. Geopolitics and security conflicts will become anachronistic. Interdependence may not engender world government, but it can make the nation-state and power politics irrelevant in a "world without frontiers." Nations can no longer adequately solve their own problems and serve their people's desire for better lives. Global problems such as insufficient natural resources and energy, overpopulation, poverty, and shortages of food, as well as the potential revolutionary situations created by the division between rich and poor nations, can be solved only at the global level. National solutions are no longer possible.

This view embodies an international system that is radically different from the one we described earlier. While the structure of the state system remains, the power hierarchy has been replaced by a new egalitarianism; force is no longer "thinkable," and the key values of national security, prestige, and power have been replaced by economic welfare, consumerism, social justice, and environmental concerns. If there is one word that sums up the distinction, it is *cooperation*. Cooperation replaces conflict, the hallmark of the old system. This cooperation has been institutionalized in what are called *regimes*.[8] The term can be defined as a set of rules or decision-making procedures in a particular issue area used to resolve disputes and encourage cooperation. In a world in which population growth, pollution, poverty, and nuclear proliferation all have transnational consequences; in which social and economic forces, be they oil prices or the "debt bomb," affect many, if not all nations, international regimes became the new focus of studies. Regime members were not only individual states but also international governmental organizations (IGOs) and nongovernmental organizations (NGOs). Regimes spanned everything from high-politics issues such as U.S.-Soviet arms control and nuclear diffusion to the more usual type of low-politics issues, such as international trade, monetary systems, the law of the seas, population, and health. These are all areas in which states find it to their own benefit to have a set of rules to guide them and inform them about the multilateral problem-solving procedures. Table 20-2 sums up the basic distinction between the old security game and the new socioeconomic game.

EVALUATION OF INTERDEPENDENCE: 'NEW' COOPERATION OR 'OLD' STRIFE?

Priority of National Solutions over Global Solutions

In evaluating interdependence, Robert Paarlberg raised a fundamental issue when he questioned the emphasis on managing national welfare at the global level. He stressed instead that the prerequisite for prosperity is improvement in domestic policy leadership. It may sound convincing to say that global problems require global solutions, but fertility, for example, is hardly amenable to agreement among states. The problem of rapidly growing populations is still primarily a national responsibility. What can foreign governments do in the absence of a domestic will to manage this issue? Similarly, emergency food shipments or worldwide food reserves are no substitute for national policies emphasizing agricultural development. These problems require greater national commitments and shifts of internal priorities and resources than most LDCs have been willing to make in the past; for many, painful and

Table 20-2 Claimed Distinctions Between Power Politics and Interdependence

	Power Politics	*Interdependence*
Issues	High politics: security, balance of power, spheres of influence	Low politics: natural resources, energy, food and population, environment
Actors	States (primarily in the First and Second Worlds)	States (primarily in the First and Third Worlds), multinational corporations
State relationships	Conflicting "national interests"	Interdependence, common interests, and transnational cooperation
Rule	Conflict: "What you gain I lose" (balance of power)	Cooperation: "We gain or lose together" (community building)
Management	Bilateral	Multilateral
Role of power	Coercion	Rewards
Role of force	High	Low, if not obsolete
Organization	Hierarchical (bipolar or multipolar)	More nearly egalitarian
Future	Basic continuity	Radical change

difficult structural reforms in landowning patterns also will be necessary. "[G]lobal welfare cannot be properly managed abroad until it has been tolerably managed at home. Without a prior exercise of domestic political authority, the global welfare crisis will not admit to efficient interstate control." [9] States remain the most effective means for resolving nations' internal problems. Like charity, global welfare management must begin at home.

Indeed, we may add to Paarlberg's comment that, when the distinction between foreign and domestic policies has been blurred, weak domestic efforts to encourage economic growth and promote prosperity may lead to corresponding tendencies to pin the blame for domestic problems on other nations. This appeal to nationalism and the search for foreign devil figures increase tensions among the states whose alleged interdependence is supposed to create more harmonious relations. The incentive to externalize domestic failure will surely be very strong if the LDCs do not modernize fairly rapidly. And such failure is very likely to produce more activist, radical, authoritarian governments that will be more disposed to confrontation than to conciliation. Beleaguered governments, struggling with massive domestic dissatisfaction, may well adopt intensely nationalistic and aggressive policies out of desperation.

Continuing Emphasis on Security

Another issue is that, although there can be little doubt that welfare concerns have become prominent on the international agenda, it is an overstatement to assert that they have achieved priority because security can be taken virtually for granted. The threat of global war has not vanished just because the nuclear balance has so far guaranteed the peace. Both superpowers still use the threat of force and from time to time have confronted one another in crises that could have escalated. Miscalculation in future crises remains a distinct possibility. And there is always the possibility that a limited war might escalate. But most of all, technological innovations in offensive or defensive weapons that lead to asymmetry might yet undermine the strategic balance, which is the main reason interdependence theorists argue that security can be taken for granted and primary attention paid to economic issues. Projecting mutual deterrence into the distant future and assuming that the issue of security is no longer relevant, or at least no longer of principal importance, may be a bit premature.

More fundamental, however, is that the security game is not some antique remnant from the Dark Ages, which is now best forgotten; the socioeconomic game may be more worthwhile, but it is not the only game being played. The superpowers still give priority to their relations with one another. China pays a great deal of attention to the Soviet Union and to Asian security in general. Western Europe must focus on its relations with the Soviet Union and the question of Atlantic security. Even in the Third World's preoccupation with regional security, competition for leadership, maintenance of military strength, and alignments with extraregional powers typify international politics. The socioeconomic game is, in fact, played within the larger framework of the security game. Instead of economic interdependence generating a new kind of international order that weakens traditional reliance on forcible means of conflict resolution, the historical and ever-present security problems are more likely to continue conditioning the character of interdependence.

For example, it was American postwar security policy, with its focus on alliances with Europe and Japan, that established the conditions for the high degree of interdependence that exists today within the European Economic Community (EEC) and between its members and the United States and Japan. Multiple public and private links in trade, investment, and currency bind these highly industrialized states together. But for the U.S.-Soviet security conflict, U.S. protection of Europe, and the European integration movement, the present measure of interdependence would probably not have come to exist. Symbolically, the chiefs of governments of the major nations of the Atlantic community (which includes Japan) have met regularly at economic summit conferences for years. It may well be, therefore, that

> [i]f major conflagration between the superpowers is avoided, if lesser conflicts are kept from spreading, if indeed governments are able to devote their energies to solving those planet-wide economic, social, and ecological problems which undeni-

ably call for universal cooperation, it will be *because* of successful management of the strategic relationships between the superpowers.[10]

Varying Degrees of Interdependence

A third issue is that the degree of interdependence among states varies. The United States is in some ways the least vulnerable of the Western states. Militarily, it provides security for its allies around the world: thus, they are dependent upon the United States. On economic issues, the United States is comparatively invulnerable, except for oil. It produces abundant food and feeds much of the world. The United States also remains a major producer of raw materials and, thanks to superior technology, has a significant capacity for making substitutions for those raw materials it lacks. Even in energy, it has enormous coal reserves and the technology to develop other sources. But Europe and Japan are less secure in regard to resources. In short, some states are more vulnerable than other states. There is nothing new about that; some states have always been able to use another state's vulnerabilities to influence its behavior. Even if it were granted that military power is less useful today than in the past, the substitution of economic means to achieve the same purpose is surely not an argument that the fundamental nature of international politics has been transformed.

A Choice of Policies

A fourth issue is that states, while interdependent, may not be equally vulnerable. This means that states have a choice of policies to pursue. During the 1970s the United States pursued a deliberate strategy of *increasing* interdependence with the Soviet Union on trade and arms control. The United States also sought to strengthen its ties with Saudi Arabia by helping it to modernize and by supplying it with arms. Conversely, states can also pursue a policy of *decreasing* interdependence, such as the various programs proposed by the administrations of Richard Nixon, Gerald Ford, Jimmy Carter, and Ronald Reagan to make the United States more self-reliant in energy. During the 1970s also many LDCs became increasingly concerned about their dependence on the United States for food and began to emphasize their agricultural development programs, which previously had been regarded as less important than industrialization.

The prospects of too much interdependence may provide the incentive for a state to make itself *less* dependent! Few states, if any, seem ready to accept any radical infringement of their freedom of choice and action. There is no available evidence, for instance, that Soviet leaders have given much thought to the problem of interdependence and the allegedly obvious conclusion that their stake in a peaceful and orderly international system is growing. Indeed, the Soviet economy, rich in resources, is less dependent on the rest of the world than are most Western economies. Given the nature of the Soviet

regime, it will undoubtedly try to limit the political consequences of importing Western technology and food. Nor did countries like Iran, Libya, Algeria,
or Iraq during the 1970s appear very concerned about the effects of their
constant push for higher oil prices on the world economy.

The Primacy of Politics

A fifth issue, as the above examples show, is that political considerations
remain primary in international politics. Events in Iran since the shah's
overthrow suggest that interdependence among nations is more than simply a
matter of mutually beneficial exchanges and the internationalization of production and services. It is also a matter of compatible political regimes.
Ayatollah Ruhollah Khomeini of Iran clearly considers his regime less "interdependent" with the West, especially with the United States, than did the
pro-Western shah. Khomeini was convinced that the United States, and even
more Western Europe and Japan, were *dependent* on Iranian oil. American
actions confirmed this conviction. Before the Iranians seized the American
hostages in late 1979, the United States did everything it could to avoid
arousing the ayatollah's wrath and causing a break in oil shipments. For
example, Washington refused to let the shah settle in the United States after
he left Iran. These efforts notwithstanding, Khomeini encouraged the fanatical Muslim "students" in their invasion of the American Embassy and their
holding of its personnel as hostages. Only as Iran's war with Iraq continued
did Khomeini become concerned with markets for his oil because he needed
the money to pay for the war.

Is it accidental that the highest degree of interdependence is among the
Common Market countries and between them and the United States and
Canada—that is, among primarily industrialized and democratic countries
with closely linked political and security interests? Is it surprising that interdependence between the United States and the Soviet Union is much less
likely to occur except on arms control issues? The Soviet Union has rejected
all U.S. attempts to create economic links that would make it more dependent
on the United States. And is it really amazing that governments in conflict
with the United States and the West should reject claims of interdependence
as attempts to prevent them from advancing their national purpose? Was
interdependence in the 1970s not actually the cry of the vulnerable?

Interdependence as a Western Construct

Indeed, interdependence, a Western and especially American intellectual
construct, holds little appeal in the Third World, even though those nations
presumably would be the principal beneficiaries of a global redistribution of
wealth. Indeed, the LDCs are very suspicious of Western ideas about interdependence. When it is suggested that a major problem is overpopulation in the
LDCs, the latter reply that birth control is tantamount to genocide. Allegedly

the West is seeking to maintain a favorable ratio of white to nonwhite peoples and to preserve its own high standard of living, which is purportedly based on the exploitation of the LDCs' resources. More people in the Third World would mean the LDCs would keep these resources for themselves, thus interfering with Western patterns of consumption. Or when it is proposed that all nations show more concern for the environment, the LDCs reply that such concern would prevent them from industrializing. After decades of polluting the land, sea, and air freely, the hypocritical West now seeks to persuade the LDCs to remain simply raw-material suppliers. In addition, suggestions that nuclear diffusion is dangerous to all states are countered with arguments that efforts to limit proliferation of nuclear arms hinder the LDCs' development of nuclear energy for peaceful purposes—even while the nuclear powers continue to build up their arsenals. In short, these arguments show that Western suggestions as to how the LDCs might develop more quickly are not viewed by the LDCs as well-intended, helpful proposals, but as a means of holding them down.

Economics an Encouragement to Conflict

A seventh point is that not only is the issue of security far from old-fashioned and outdated, but also that it is likely that economic issues will underscore and reemphasize the essentially Hobbesian character of international politics. The reaction to the oil crisis of the 1970s vividly demonstrated the continued stress on national interest, even if close allies and friends were hurt. The United States sought greater energy independence; Canada decided to keep more of its oil and not send it to the United States; and the various European states scrambled to make their own oil deals with OPEC countries, including offers of trading technical expertise in nuclear engineering for oil. Cooperation fell victim to a me-first policy among the Western industrial countries.

Other nations were hardly wiser or more virtuous, least of all the OPEC countries, which regularly raised oil prices. Indeed, OPEC's more radical anti-Western members—whose declarations of policy were generally filled with denunciations of "imperialism" and sympathy for the lot of the poor deprived masses in the underdeveloped world—were frequently in the vanguard of the price hawks seeking to maximize their earnings. They "beggared" all their neighbors, Western and non-Western; when oil supplies exceeded demand (which should have lowered oil prices), they cut supplies to keep prices high. In both security and economic terms, nations, by and large, continued to fear that another state's advantage was their disadvantage; one state's increase in security and/or wealth was perceived as a loss of security and/or wealth for themselves.

The downfall of OPEC in the 1980s is further testimony to the priority nations give to their specific national interests. Had each OPEC member accepted the production quotas allotted, all would have earned far more than at present. But to enhance earnings, individual countries ignored their quotas, produced more oil, and created an oil glut. The collapse of oil prices was the result. OPEC's experience is not unique. Economic conflicts are severe even among the Western industrial countries, where a genuine interdependence exists. The growth of the new mercantilism is but one symptom of this trend.

Prescription Rather than Description

An eighth point is that much of the discussion in favor of interdependence is *prescriptive*. The emphasis is on a strategy of increasing the degree of interdependence among nation-states; the more links there are, the more cooperation will be required, and the greater will be the restraints on states' freedom of action. This point is really the crux of interdependence thesis: that by *placing constraints on the national egotism and assertiveness of states by catching them in a "web of interdependence" in which they will become so deeply enmeshed, states will be unable to extricate themselves without suffering great harm and will be compelled therefore to cooperate for the "good of humanity."* An argument supposedly based on description of the facts of interdependence, whether in security or in economics, thus shifts almost imperceptibly to advocacy of a course of policy intended to suppress conflict in the state system in favor of a focus on the welfare of all people. Says Lester Brown, "At issue is whether we can grasp the nature and dimensions of the emerging threats to our well-being, whether we can create an integrated world economy and a workable world order, and whether we can render global priorities so that the quality of life will improve rather than deteriorate." [11]

For those who are not optimistic about the feasibility of supranational integration and a possible new world order, but who despair of the ability of states to solve their security problems in the nuclear age and achieve the welfare of their people in an age of overpopulation, scarcity of food, and environmental pollution, interdependence becomes an argument for a world without borders, a unified global society, a halfway house. In short, the advocacy of interdependence frequently tends to become a plea for a world beyond the contemporary nation-state. It is a plea for changing international behavior and building a better, more cooperative, and more harmonious world order, for subordinating power politics to welfare politics and national interests to planetary interests, for recognizing before it is too late that humanity shares a common destiny. *Advocacy of interdependence is essentially a normative, rather than a functional, argument for a revolutionary shift to a new world order from the current state system in which asymmetrical interdependence equals the capacity to coerce.*

It may be that appeals to global solidarity, moral imperatives, and humanitarian motives are more favorably received today than in the past and that images of a "global village" and "planetary humanism" have been increasingly reflected in world conferences on the environment, population, food, the new international economic order, and women's rights. But this receptivity does not constitute an

effective consensus on global redistribution of income or wealth, or global guarantees of minimum human needs, or on global equality of opportunity. Those precepts
have scarcely achieved a solid footing domestically, even in the most advanced
societies, where democratic voting pushes governmental policies toward egalitarianism. At the international level, no corresponding political structure is either in hand
or in prospect.[12]

Today there may be more interaction in more areas linking humanity than
ever before, but it is questionable whether these will create the necessary
international consensus or community upon which common institutions and
rules can be built.

It is probably for this reason that the facts of interdependence so often, and
almost unnoticed, become a plea for a better and less conflict-prone
"world politics" which, while acknowledging the continued existence of
states, will produce a behavior among them as if they had already been
abolished. In short, the *process* of collective cooperation and problem solving
will overcome the defects of the state system's decentralized *structure*—a
dubious proposition.

And Beware of Regimes

It is for this reason, among others, that the word *regime* is so inappropriate to
describe the cooperation of states in specific issue areas. Why was the term
introduced at all? After all, state cooperation on issues of common interest is
not a new phenomenon. Admittedly, there are more states today and low-
politics issues have gained a new prominence. But is that reason enough for
labelling such interstate cooperation *regimes*? And why was that particular
word chosen? Not only is it commonly used to describe left- or right-wing
dictatorships of which most people disapprove, but the word clearly denotes
government and authority. Yet, as Susan Strange in her devastating critique
of regimes has noted, the state system is basically characterized

> not by discipline and authority, but by the absence of government, by the precari-
> ousness of peace and order, by the dispersion not the concentration of authority, by
> the weakness of law, and by the large number of unresolved conflicts over what
> should be done, how it should be done, and who should do it.
>
> Above all, a single, recognized focus of power over time is the one attribute that
> the international system conspicuously lacks.[13]

That the word *regime* is used in these circumstances suggests the special
meaning with which the term has been invested: the collective management
by the "international community" in the absence of world government of
what is now commonly called the transnational or global agenda (population,
food, resources, ocean management, and so forth). Regimes composed
of the agreements, treaties plus associated international machinery, are
viewed as an essential ingredient of a spreading "global political process" or
expanding "politics of global problem solving."[14] Susan Strange comments
as follows:

All these international arrangements dignified by the label *regimes* are only too easily upset when either the balance of bargaining power or the perception of national interests (or both together) change among those states who negotiated them. In general, moreover, *all the areas in which regimes in a national context exercise the central attributes of political discipline are precisely those in which corresponding international arrangements that might conceivably be dignified with the title are conspicuous by their absence.* (Emphasis added.) [16]

INTERDEPENDENCE, ECONOMICS, AMERICAN NORMS, AND ESCAPISM

The fundamental assumption underlying arguments for interdependence is that technological, economic, and social forces operating transnationally are "inevitably" driving all nations toward greater cooperation. With a faith in the determinism of economic forces reminiscent of Marxism, proponents of this view are ready to abandon the troublesome world of politics. Perhaps their emphasis on economic necessities should not be surprising. Americans are especially prone to see economics as the universal palliative for the human condition. The basic assumption of *laissez faire* capitalism is that people are economically motivated; the laws of supply and demand will thus transform individual economic selfishness into social benefits, "the greatest good for the greatest number." The role of the government, according to the principle of *laissez faire,* is to stay out of the market; the best government is the one that governs least, for political interference with economic laws will upset the results those laws are said to produce.

Not surprisingly, when the logic of the free market is projected internationally, it is possible to conclude that a peaceful international society will be created by free trade. People all over the world will gain a vested interest in peace if they carry on their economic relations. War and trade are supposedly incompatible. War impoverishes and destroys, creating ill will among nations, whereas commerce benefits all participating states. Commerce is thus nationally and individually profitable and creates a vested interest in the preservation of peace. War, by contrast, is economically unprofitable and therefore obsolete. Free trade and peace are one and the same cause. This version of the argument for interdependence was already quite common at the time of the United States' birth.

> This feeling that one civilization now encompassed the whole world was reinforced by the astounding growth of economic interdependence. The [national political] barriers that existed seemed artificial and ephemeral in comparison with the fine net by which the merchants tied the individuals of the different nations together like "threads of silk." . . . [T]he merchants—whether they are English, Dutch, Russian, or Chinese—do not serve a single nation; they serve everyone and are citizens of the whole world. Commerce was believed to bind the nations together and to create not only a community of interests but also a distribution of labor among them—a new

comprehensive principle placing the isolated sovereign nations in a higher political unit. In the eighteenth century, writers were likely to say that the various nations belonged to "one society"; it was stated that all states together formed "a family of nations," and the whole globe a "general and unbreakable confederation." [16]

During the late years of the cold war, another variant surfaced. The thesis was that the economic development of the LDCs would create affluence and political democracy, which, given the peaceful nature of democracies, ensured a peaceful world. Helping the LDCs to modernize with foreign aid seemed essential. Economic development was even expected to transform the Communist Soviet Union; as that country became more industrialized and modern, Soviet ideology was expected to erode, its foreign policy would become "derevolutionized" and the country changed into a status-quo state willing to live and let live. The United States had only to continue its containment policy while waiting for the results of the Soviet Union's own efforts to develop economically. A peaceful world was inevitable as the result of beneficial economic forces.

Just as the failure of free trade to bring about lasting peace had led people to pin their hopes on economic development, so the failure of economic development to narrow the gap between rich and poor nations and to generate a more stable and peaceful world gave rise to the thesis of functional integration. When that failed, it gave way to the "businessman's peace"; and disappointment in the ability of MNCs to do what governments had failed to do finally gave rise to interdependence. The goal of a peaceful system of more harmonious states has remained constant; so has the focus on the economic forces that will purportedly bring it about. "Economics good, politics bad" appears to be the motto. Economics caters to people's needs and brings benefits; politics brings destruction and misery. Economics binds people together; politics drives them apart. Yet trade and economic development have each in turn failed to achieve this goal. The current degree of interdependence has neither replaced the "security game" inherent in the structure of the state system nor passed beyond the stage of an asymmetrical interdependence that makes some states vulnerable and confers upon others the capacity to coerce. The "trading" state has not yet replaced the "warrior" state, however lamentable that may be.

The argument for interdependence reflects an attempt to escape from power politics into a calmer, more decent and humane world.[17] The Vietnam War intensified this urge to escape from the wicked world of power politics among many disillusioned supporters of U.S. cold war policies. Having previously supported a policy that they believed was a crusade in defense of democracy against totalitarianism, they now both sought forgiveness for past error and a new way to achieve the same goal of a more just and peaceful world. However, it would not be power—which was bad and divisive—but economics—which was good and healing—that would achieve this objective.

Characteristically American, they argued that it was the United States' responsibility to lead the world into the new era. They remained crusaders for the moral cause. It is ironic that only a few years after the United States was widely criticized—often by the current proponents of interdependence—for pursuing a global foreign policy and extending American commitments beyond the nation's alleged capacities, including the costly "adventure" in Vietnam, globalism reappeared in a new form. Only the agenda has changed. Because the new welfare issues could not be managed by single nations, it was asserted, "foreign policy leaders schooled in the old arithmetic of national security will have to learn the formula of economic interdependence, the advanced calculus of planetary bargains and global welfare." [18] More than just a reaction to Vietnam, interdependence represents a deeply felt utopian streak—usually left implicit—in American thinking on international politics. The state system, conflict, and war remained unacceptable. If the United States could no longer abstain from power politics by isolating itself, or abolish it by democratizing its wicked practitioners, then it would dissolve the nature of international politics in the *bonhommie* of interdependence.

Notes

1. For some of the basic books and articles on the nature of interdependence and the role of power, see Seyom Brown, *New Forces in World Politics* (Washington, D.C.: The Brookings Institution, 1974); Robert O. Keohane and Joseph S. Nye, *Power and Interdependence* (Boston: Little, Brown & Co., 1977); Andrew M. Scott, *The Dynamics of Interdependence* (Chapel Hill: University of North Carolina Press, 1982); and Stanley Hoffmann, "Choices," *Foreign Policy*, Fall 1973, 3-42. More popular treatments can be found in *World Without Borders* by Lester R. Brown (New York: Vintage, 1972); and *Global Ecopolitics* by Dennis Pirages (North Scituate, Mass.: Duxbury, 1978). Excellent critiques may be found in Kal J. Holsti, "A New International Politics? Diplomacy in Complex Interdependence," *International Organization*, Spring 1978, 513-531; and Stanley J. Michalck, Jr., "Theoretical Perspective for Understanding International Interdependence," *World Politics*, October 1979, 136-150.
2. Robert Stobaugh and Daniel Yergin, eds., *Energy Future* (New York: Random House, 1979).
3. Keohane and Nye, *Power and Interdependence*, 12-16.
4. Richard Rosecrance, *The Rise of Trading States* (New York: Basic Books, 1986).
5. James N. Rosenau, "Capabilities and Control in an Interdependent World," *International Security*, Fall 1976, 39.
6. Ibid., 44.
7. For a critique of the theory of interdependence as applied to relations between the First and Third Worlds, see Robert W. Tucker, *The Inequality of Nations* (New York: Basic Books, 1977). For a suggestion that the United States make a world order, rather than the balance of power, the focus of its policy, see Stanley Hoffmann, *Primacy or World Order* (New York: McGraw-Hill, 1978).
8. Keohane and Nye, *Power and Interdependence*; and the Spring 1982 issue of *International Organization*, which was completely devoted to regimes.

9. Robert L. Paarlberg, "Domesticating Global Management," *Foreign Affairs* (April 1976): 571.

10. John J. Weltman, "On the Obsolescence of War," *International Studies Quarterly* (December 1974): 413-414. It needs to be noted that even among these interdependent states, the recession has produced increasing economic nationalism and political quarrels.

11. Brown, *New Forces in World Politics*, 12.

12. David H. Blake and Robert S. Walters, *The Politics of Global Economic Relations*, 2d ed. (Englewood Cliffs, N.J.: Prentice-Hall, 1982), 35.

13. Susan Strange, "Cave! hic dragones: a critique of regime analysis," *International Organization*, Spring 1982, 487.

14. Frederic S. Pearson and J. Martin Rochester, *International Relations* (Reading, Mass.: Addison-Wesley, 1984), part IV, 395.

15. Strange, "Cave! hic dragones," 487.

16. Felix Gilbert, *To the Farewell Address* (Princeton, N.J.: Princeton University Press, 1961), 57.

17. For the contrasting and conflicting views on whether interdependence is utopian or not, see Ray Maghoori and Bennett Ramsberg, eds., *Globalism vs. Realism* (Boulder, Colo.: Westview Press, 1982).

18. Paarlsberg, "Domesticating Global Management," 576.

CHAPTER 21

The Primacy
of Realism

It is hardly surprising that theories about international politics have centered on the problem of war, the most traumatic event a nation can experience.[1] The causes and consequences of war, its possible elimination, or at least the reduction of its frequency have dominated theorizing about international politics. The increasing horrors and costs of war in the twentieth century have accentuated this trend, although it began in the nineteenth century with greater citizen participation in politics, the growth of nationalism and industrialization, and the invention of ever more efficient and destructive weapons. The birth of the nuclear age in 1945 intensified the search for solutions to the problem of war; without such a solution, the human race faces the very real possibility that it may not survive.

THE FIRST LEVEL REVISITED

At the first, or state-system, level war is explained by the anarchical environment in which states live. In the absence of a world government to settle disputes, each state must rely on its own capabilities to protect its national interests and remain secure. States seek to enhance their security by increasing their power, or, more accurately, they try to reduce their sense of vulnerability to the potential actions of other states. They may not succeed in this enterprise because other states are also seeking security in the same ways. The result is a "security dilemma" in which one state's activities give the others no choice but to follow suit, perhaps leaving all of them less secure. The security dilemma describes succinctly the trap created by the anarchical structure of the state system. War is embedded in this structure.

Some scholars of international politics attempt to resolve the problem of war by transcending the state system and creating a world government. Others, who recognize that this prescription may be theoretically correct but unachievable in the real world, try to find cures within the framework of the state system. Among these cures are declawing states through disarmament, denationalizing them through cooperation within a universal organization, and—currently fashionable—taming states "from which the sharp teeth of sovereignty have at last been drawn" and "the parochial interests of the past have been replaced by the planetary interests"; the logic of interdependence necessitates this.[2]

As states moved from functionalism, with its expectation of an automatic process of political integration of separate countries into larger security communities (first on a regional level, then on a global level), to interdependence, the expectation was that economic and technological forces would override political, cultural, and national differences. Instead the state system persists, and state behavior has not essentially changed. So far, none of the various political or economic prescriptions has proved capable of providing a solution to the recurring problem of war. In the anarchical environment that persists, the truth is that conflict and the possibility of war can never be abolished. *The best that can be achieved is to manage the system in order to minimize the possibilities of an outbreak of the most violent forms of war.* This management is an ongoing process that promises no end to the problem of war.

This conclusion has never been accepted by liberal intellectuals. Michael Howard, a renowned British military historian, has commented that since the eighteenth century, liberal intellectuals have blamed war either upon the stupidity or self-interest of governing elites. War was obviously "a pathological aberration from the norm, at best a ghastly mistake, at worst a crime."[3] Inherent in this view is that if sensible people controlled governments, war could be abolished. This idea implied a shift in emphasis from the environment in which states exist to the character of the states themselves and of the people who govern them; that is, to second- and third-level analyses. A reluctance to accept the inevitability of war, or that the best states can do is to manage the system skillfully enough to prevent all-out war, led to the countereffort to eliminate war by thinking about it at the second or third levels. Bad states and bad leaders were to blame. Eliminate them and the problem of war would go away; reason and peace would prevail. Kenneth Waltz has called this method of resolving problems *reductionism.*[4]

There has been no shortage of states whose internal organization has been considered the cause of war. During the eighteenth century, kings and the aristocracy were responsible, and war benefited only them. The French Revolution posed a solution: eliminate the warmongers, and reason, not force, would resolve interstate conflicts. The rule of monarchs and aristocrats was to be replaced by democracy in which the people would elect their rulers and then hold them accountable. Because ordinary people pay for wars with their lives and their tax money, they would be interested in preserving the peace. Democracy was by nature peaceful.

Liberal thought also recommended that all nationalities should live within their own natural boundaries because, they asserted, it is unnatural for human beings to be organized on any basis except national identity. The map would have to be redrawn so that people would live in political units based on the principle of nationality. If the nature of the internal political system was the cause for war, then democracy and national self-determination would abolish war.

Marxist thinkers did not agree with these remedies. War could not be eradicated by establishing so-called democratic government, for behind democracy's facade ruled a small class of capitalists or bourgeoisie who exploited their fellow citizens. For true democracy to bloom, according to the Marxists, the proletariat must gain control of the state, and this could be achieved only through revolution. Many non-Marxist thinkers, not sharing the belief that capitalism is inherently warlike, focused on political control of the "merchants of death."

THE AMERICAN EXPERIENCE AND THE ELIMINATION OF WAR

Marxist thinking on the elimination of war has not had much appeal for Americans, but liberal thought has found a congenial reception. The belief that war was a permanent feature of existence was simply unacceptable; most Americans considered conflict and war abnormal, temporary, and avoidable. Balance-of-power thinking was generally considered "un-American," when it was not ignored altogether. This was not surprising. The United States had long been isolated from Europe, and its own domestic experiences and values shaped American thinking about international politics. The United States was a liberal society that placed value on individualism, private enterprise, and political democracy. This contrasted strongly to Europe, which had not only a liberal tradition but also conservative and socialist traditions. Liberalism therefore never established its supremacy; balance-of-power thinking retained its influence, especially among policy makers.[5]

Furthermore, once the United States was forced to give up its isolationism, the American experience in international politics confirmed the nation's liberal assumption about war. The countries that provoked or attacked the United States were led by authoritarian and antidemocratic men: the kaiser in World War I, Hitler and Tojo in World War II, and Stalin during the cold war. In war the goal of the United States was first the total defeat of the enemy and then the establishment of democratic governments, trusting the good sense of the citizens to avoid future wars. "Power politics" was to be banished once and for all; the world would be made peaceful by democratizing it.

Indeed, the Treaty of Versailles, drawn at the close of World War I, embodied liberal thinking on international politics. National self-determination and the establishment of democracy were the basic principles underlying the treaty. The result was a redrawing of the map of central and southeastern Europe, leading to the rise of a number of new nations from the ruins of Austria-Hungary. Moreover, because the Allies insisted that they would deal only with a democratic Germany, the kaiser abdicated and a new democratic government was formed. Many Germans believed that democracy itself, in the form of the Allies, was responsible for imposing upon them a punitive peace treaty and a new form of government, which they were forced to accept.

National self-determination and democracy came together in the establishment of the League of Nations. "Open covenants, openly arrived at," was President Woodrow Wilson's slogan. The peoples of all nations could watch their governments at work on the world stage and would hold them accountable. They would know what their leaders and diplomats were doing and have all the necessary information to determine who was the aggressor in any situation; the days of irresponsible elites and secret diplomacy were over. Democracy and peace were to be the wave of the future as a pacific and informed world public opinion would prevail. The league, and later the United Nations, would deter aggression, punish the transgressor if it occurred, and maintain law and order among the community of nations.

All the liberal assumptions about how to preserve the peace proved to be wrong. Indeed, experiences prior to World War I already had shown how flimsy these assumptions were. From 1815 to 1914 Europe had not suffered a total war; wars in the nineteenth century were limited in objectives, casualties, and duration. Diplomacy, largely secret, minimized the effects of public opinion; negotiations were conducted by an aristocratic elite, which, because it spoke a common language, shared a code of conduct, mixed socially and intermarried, also avoided misunderstandings. The assumption underlying the nineteenth-century European system was that the great powers were reponsible for maintaining peace because they had the power to do so.[6] No single great power tried to conquer or destroy another; the overall pattern was one of cooperation and restraint. For most of the century, the memory of Napoleon and his unleashing of a total war that had lasted twenty-five years cautioned all the principal European powers to compromise and to limit the purposes and intensity of force, if force was used.

Starting in the late nineteenth century, however, public opinion increasingly affected the conduct of foreign policy. Popular involvement in foreign policy encouraged jingoism and bellicosity, not pacifism, and, once aroused, nationalistic enthusiasm made it more difficult for governments to practice restraint. This was as true for the European democracies as for the great autocracies of Russia, Austria-Hungary, and Germany. Moreover, the rise in popularity of a moderate social democratic party in Germany aroused the fear of revolution in the aristocracy as well as among the industrialists and bankers, whose answer was a "strong" foreign policy in Europe and colonialism overseas. By encouraging nationalism, the upper classes sought to avoid what they regarded as a dangerous domestic situation. The fear of revolution had a similar effect on the rulers of Russia and Austria-Hungary. Even in the United States at the turn of the century, jingoism, aroused by the Hearst newspaper chain, was basically responsible for the Spanish-American War. President William McKinley had tried to avoid war with Spain, but an aroused public and Congress forced his hand.

Nor did national self-determination play the peace-keeping role envisaged for it. Although World War I had been precipitated by the nationalist aspirations of many of the ethnic groups in the Balkans and was fought in part to remedy these boundaries and unite nationalities, the wisdom of this solution was soon subject to doubt. The unification of Germany proved to be a disaster for all of Europe. Nationalism in Germany, as well as the nationalism of its neighbors, confounded even the Marxists. Having claimed that the working classes had no interest in supporting the nationalist causes of the capitalists and that working-class loyalty was to the workers of other lands, the Marxists were shocked when the social democratic parties everywhere voted funds for a war.

Once World War I was over, it was public opinion in the democracies that destroyed any chance of a lasting peace. French and British public opinion insisted on a punitive peace treaty that included a German "war guilt" clause and the imposition of astronomic economic reparations. By imposing this treaty on the new and fragile German democracy, the Allies ensured that Germans would associate democracy with defeat, and they provided Hitler with a means to condemn German democracy and to keep alive hostile feelings toward the Allies. Having exacted revenge, Allied opinion then turned pacifist. It was the hideousness of the war that transformed the democracies' attitude. Germany, a fascist state, did not share its neighbors' doubts about the continued legitimacy of modern warfare; it exploited their fears and doubts. Hitler, too, had a popular following.

Postwar Realism

The failure of the democracies to maintain peace was the main reason that realism gained intellectual respectability in the United States. World War II offered proof that the dream of subordinating national conflicts to the broader interests of humanity was not shared by all states. The power struggle among nations was all too evident, and democracies, if they wished to defend themselves, had to play power politics too. The wartime dream that the United Nations, the embodiment of hopes for a world community, would preserve the peace better than had the League of Nations faded quickly as the cold war began.

The United States, however, could tell itself that it was not behaving as states historically have behaved and thus keep its conscience clear. The postwar bipolar struggle involved both power and ideology, and the United

States could practice *Realpolitik* while disguising it as another moral crusade. This was also the period of liberal Democratic administrations, "cold war liberals" as they were called. Liberals in the executive and legislative branches were quite willing to assert U.S. power and to use force, precisely because they were liberals. Committed to the freedom and dignity of the individual and social justice at home, they were equally committed to the defense of liberty against totalitarianism overseas. To be a "hardliner" and support the containment of Soviet or Chinese power was not considered a betrayal but an affirmation of liberal values. Only after the Vietnam War did domestic liberalism disassociate itself from a strong anti-Soviet interventionist stance. But it did not take long for the American penchant to crusade, to moralize international politics, to find a new outlet in interdependence and the building of a new world order beyond the balance of power.

In academic circles, the reaction to realism came earlier, in part because Hans Morgenthau, who had presented the realist position so articulately in his 1948 book, *Politics among Nations,* was an easy target. His critics charged, among other things, that to Morgenthau power appeared to be an end, not just a means, and that his use of the term *national interest* suggested that there was always an objective, discoverable, and "correct" policy. He was said to subordinate morality to power, and his prescription of the balance of power, diplomacy, and prudence was said to hold no greater promise of avoiding a future war than it had in the past. Only the next war would be a nuclear war. In part, the criticism also reflected the desire to try new approaches as older ones became familiar and perhaps boring, but in large part it was normative. Realism's tolerance of continued conflict and war was simply unacceptable. Postrealism's multiple perspectives once more reflected liberal ideas of the causes and cures for war.

In a liberal society, it is not really surprising that liberal assumptions should be *implicit* in the study of politics, whether domestic or international, even if researchers appear unaware of their influence and believe that they are carrying on objective and scientific work.[7] To be sure, studies of international politics claim to be scientific. But no matter how carefully researchers assemble and quantify the data, the researchers' purposes will affect their conclusions. Purpose and analysis are inseparable. Data can be explained in a number of different ways; in themselves they have no meaning. But how they are selected, the importance assigned to them, and how they are organized and interpreted depend on the perspectives brought to a particular study.

The Reaction to Realism

Two of the postrealist approaches were the examination of leaders' decision making and the effort to understand their perceptions. Both were concerned with states' domestic policy processes, and in both the state system played a very subordinate role. Decision making, or bureaucratic politics, was essentially a resurrection of the group approach to explain American domestic politics and a reflection of the American pluralist tradition. Translated into the foreign policy arena, this meant that policy was seen as evolving from the interactions among the various institutions, each with its own policy preferences. This shift of focus in the study of international politics from the external arena to the policy process within the state meant that if a policy were judged "defective," the necessary changes in organization or procedure could be introduced. For example, if there were a tendency among top policy makers to "groupthink," a devil's advocate might be brought in to challenge the assumptions underlying official policy. Policy problems could be resolved by organizational reforms.[8] The second reaction to realism, the emphasis on perception, meant that "wrong" policies could be attributed to misperceptions and, therefore, to misunderstandings. Policy must not be dominated by "diabolical enemy images," mirror images, or other forms of distortion. Rational—that is, correct—perceptions should govern policy makers if conflict is to be avoided. A solution to the problem of war would be found in domestic politics, psychology, and classical economies in their contemporary form—interdependence.

After its brief fling with *Realpolitik*, then, the American study of international politics once more embraced the reductionist orientation embodied in the traditional perceptions we earlier labeled "national style." As John Weltman has perceptively remarked about some of the contemporary debate:

> Great contemporary controversy revolves around that complex of questions relating to: the survival and viability of the nation-state; the interdependence of nations; the role of force; the importance of the "high political" or strategic, as opposed to "low-political" or welfare concepts and issues; the significance of economic matters; the dominance of "North-South" concerns as opposed to "East-West" issues. *Empirical investigation is only superficially useful in answering this complex of questions.* When examined carefully the positions of the participants in these controversies resolve themselves into modern versions of ancient outlooks.[9] (Emphasis added.)

Those who emphasize the obsolescence of high politics represent basically the old utopian or idealist side in its continuing quarrel with realism.

The fact that all the questions Weltman lists are often debated suggests that realism is still under siege. For many American scholars international politics has become the politics of world order. The primacy of the state is rapidly disappearing in a welter of transnational nongovernmental organizations and intergovernmental organizations; the national interest, with its egotism and selfishness, has been (or must be) restrained by the new interdependence; and the self-help of states has been replaced by the search for a more moral and just world through disarmament, the abolition of world poverty, and the fulfillment of universal human rights. Military power has lost its crucial role as security issues have become subordinated to welfare issues and conflict between states has given way to cooperation for the collective interests of all mankind. Indeed, to many scholars and commentators, emphasizing the crucial role of military power in international politics in any context other than arms control, especially in East-West relations, is a mark not only of a lack of sophistication but also a misunderstanding of international politics.

Economic Peace or Pax Atomici?

That power politics and war are obsolete is hardly a novel conclusion in the age of economic interdependence. In 1910 Norman Angell's best seller, *The Great Illusion,* argued that war between modern industrial states had become an anachronism because it would be economically ruinous. Four years later, Germany was at war with two of its most important trading partners, Russia and Britain. The war proved Angell correct about the enormous cost in lives and economic resources. But the thesis that war and industrial society are incompatible is more than a mere reflection of this cost; the thesis rests on the conviction that uninterrupted commerce and war are incompatible and that the true interest of all states is the peaceful enjoyment of material progress. The eighteenth-century French philosophers (whose views were reflected in the institutions of the young United States) and the nineteenth-century British utilitarians had argued that modernization was playing the role that war had played in preindustrial society.[10] This same faith in man's reason and the common interest of mankind persists today.

How ironic it is, then, that "the bomb" is the foundation for the contemporary abstinence of war among the great powers. Because Americans regard war as an aberration, once provoked they fight to eliminate war itself, as in the two world wars. Aggressors must be punished so severely that they would never dare attack the United States again. Deterrence fits this approach exactly. Its purpose was to prevent war, but, should that fail, the United States was prepared to retaliate so that the enemy's industries and population would be utterly destroyed. The bomb carried the American concept of war to its logical conclusion: total elimination of the enemy. The irony is all the greater because the bomb may be the means *par excellence* to finally realize the American dream of abolishing war for all time.

THE CONTINUING NEED FOR REALISM

Reductionist approaches to international politics are very appealing for one reason; namely, they allow proponents to project their own solutions upon a rather intractable world. Systemic explanations offer far more understanding. This is not to belittle explanations at the second and third levels, merely to place them in context. The behavior of states—as well as of nonstate actors—can be analyzed and understood only in terms of the system or environment in which they live. A focus on the nature of states obviously concentrates on the individual member of the system, not on the system as a whole. Factors such as political systems, national and elite styles, class structures, and the process of decision making should not be neglected in any analysis of how states behave. *But any theory of international politics will be inadequate if it ignores the dominant influence of the state system and the security dilemma.* States have no choice about their concern for security and, indeed, survival. The system may not determine their behavior, but it does condition it. And from the anarchical nature of the state system everything else flows: the need for states to pay attention to their power, to maintain an equilibrium, and to be aware of the ever-present dangers of conflict and war. It is easy to understand why all this is condemned as immoral power politics, a denial of all civilized values, but it does not eliminate the need for states to "play the game."

Power politics is not some passing phase of international politics, a relic left over from the 1940s and 1950s. It is not a concept brought to American shores by refugee scholars from Europe. (Hans Morganthau and Henry Kissinger, both from Germany, are the the best-known proponents from the academic and diplomatic worlds, respectively. Kissinger once said that when he hears the phrase "balance of power" in the United States, it is usually preceded by words such as *old-fashioned* and *former*, as if the balance were irrelevant, of historic interest only.) To be sure, these scholars emphasized the role of power, including military power, in international politics, and such an emphasis was alien to an American tradition rooted in legal and moral concepts of law, human rights, and justice. But the end of its long isolationism and its deep involvement in the post-World War II world meant that the United States would have learned to play power politics, even if reluctantly. Many American scholars, however, have refused to accept the role of force and sought with mathematical techniques and other social science methods to eliminate it through peace research, conflict resolution studies, and world order modeling.

Earlier we compared the levels of analysis to psychological analysis. The focus on individual states, it was suggested, was comparable to the analysis of an individual's behavior in terms of personality and character. Clearly, this by itself does not suffice. An analysis of a person's behavior requires an understanding of the environment in which that person lives and what has conditioned his or her personality: family background, especially relations with parents; various peer groups; even society as a whole, for a person's "socialization" has been influenced by all of these. What is true for individual human beings is true for states.

Obviously, the primacy of the state system does not lead us to pleasant conclusions about the future abolition of violence and war. Nevertheless, the emphasis on the importance of contemporary economic interdependence should not blind us to the real limits to any possible reforms of the system and behavior of states. The proponents of interdependence are not so much wrong about its existence as they are wrong in concluding that its existence implies that security issues and the use of force no longer count. The fact is that economic interdependence and war coexist; one is not incompatible with the other. Drawing unsound conclusions about a gradual but fundamental transformation of the state system in which international harmony and peace will reign reminds one of Rudyard Kipling's words that

> Thinking of beautiful things we know,
> Dreaming of deeds that we meant to do,
> All complete, in a minute or two—
> Something noble, and grand and good,
> Done by merely wishing we could.

It is no contribution to any theory of international politics to forget what is fundamental to the subject: survival, security, and influence.[11] Or, to put it more frankly, international politics is about power, however ambiguous, imprecise, or unfashionable that concept may be. But power itself is about more than physical survival and physical security. It is also about the survival and security of different states' values. For Americans, the strength of American power and the willingness to assert that power is organically related to the political, social, and economic freedoms that American society cherishes. Power remains a means to an end. The purpose of power politics is to preserve the security of a democratic America. The relative power and influence of states is of critical importance to the United States, as it is to other states equally determined to defend their "way of life."

Thus, while there are numerous approaches to understanding international politics, many more than we have included in this text, the only approach that permits us to appreciate the *essence* of the field is *realism* or the state system, our first level of analysis. Decision making, transnational relations, class structures, and all the other approaches contribute to the understanding of international politics, and each is valuable in its own right. But this does not mean that all approaches are equally valuable. Realism reveals the critical features of international politics. Without it, an understanding of the subject is impossible.

Notes

1. This chapter is strongly indebted to the writings of John Weltman, especially "The American Tradition in International Thought: Science as Therapy" (Paper delivered at a Colorado College symposium, April 9, 1981; Weltman, "Interpretation of International Thought," *Review of Politics* (January 1982: 27-41; and Weltman, "On the Obsolescence of War," *International Studies Quarterly* (December 1974): 395-416.
2. Robert W. Tucker, "Egalitarianism and International Politics," *Commentary*, September 1975, 35.
3. Michael Howard, *The Causes of War* (Cambridge, Mass.: Harvard University Press, 1983), 10-11.
4. Kenneth N. Waltz, *Theory of International Politics* (Reading, Mass.: Addison-Wesley, 1979), 18ff.
5. Louis Hartz, *The Liberal Tradition* (New York: Harvest Books, 1955).
6. W. W. Rostow, *Commentary*, November 1985, 86.

7. Bernard Crick, *The American Science of Politics* (London: Routledge & Kegan Paul, 1959).

8. See Alexander L. George, *Presidential Decisionmaking in Foreign Policy* (Boulder, Colo.: Westview Press, 1980), especially 169-174, 191-208; and· "The Case for Multiple Advocacy in Making Foreign Policy," *American Political Science Review* (September 1972): 751-785; Robert Jervis, *Perception and Misperception in International Politics* (Princeton, N.J.: Princeton University Press 1976), 415-418; and for a variation on this theme—that policy makers must not use historical analogies carelessly, but should examine their relevance, if any—see Richard E. Neustadt and Ernest R. May, *Thinking in Time* (New York: Free Press, 1986).

9. Weltman, "Interpretation of International Thought," 34.

10. Robert E. Osgood and Robert W. Tucker, *Force, Order, and Justice* (Baltimore: Johns Hopkins University Press, 1967), 16-18.

11. Colin Gray, *The Geopolitics of the Nuclear Era* (New York: Crane, Russak & Co., 1977), 2-5. For different perspectives on the future, see Dennis Pirages, *Global Ecopolitics* (North Scituate, Mass.: Duxbury Press, 1978); Barry B. Hughes, *World Futures* (Baltimore: Johns Hopkins University Press, 1985); the pessimistic *The Global 2000 Report to the President*, vols. I and II (Washington, D.C.: Government Printing Office, 1980); and the optimistic Julian L. Simon, *The Ultimate Resource* (Princeton, N.J.: Princeton University Press, 1981); and Herman Kahn, *The Next 200 Years* (New York: Morrow, 1976).

A Selective Glossary

ABM An antiballistic missile, which is designed to "knock down" incoming missiles and/or their warheads (nuclear bombs) before designated targets are struck.

alliances Agreements among states to support each other militarily in case of attack and/or to enhance their mutual interests. Alliances supplement national power and clarify spheres of interest. Examples: the North Atlantic Treaty Organization and the Warsaw Pact.

anticolonialism The rejection of the former "father" or "mother" country by a Third World state.

appeasement In contemporary usage, a term of shame meaning one-sided concessions to an adversary. Prior to the Munich Conference of 1938, the term was respectable because it referred to the settlement of legitimate grievances and the consequent avoidance of war.

arms control The process of securing agreements that place restrictions upon numbers, types, and performance characteristics of strategic weapons. In the U.S.-Soviet context, the process has aimed at stabilizing mutual deterrence and avoiding nuclear war by eliminating the incentive to strike first at the other side.

arms race Competitive arms acquisitions by a nation or alliance against its adversaries through increases in the production of weapons and/or technological breakthroughs. Arms races often are characterized by an action-reaction pattern among nations that are either trying to stay ahead of, or at least not fall behind, their adversaries.

balance of capability and balance of resolve The two mutually supportive components of the balance of power. Although quantifiable military strength is important, the perception of a nation's willingness to use its power to defend its vital interests has assumed great significance in both nuclear deterrence and crisis management.

balance of power A relationship in which nations strive to achieve security through the establishment of an approximate power equilibrium in the state system, thus reducing the probability of warfare or domination. In short, power checks power.

balance of trade The difference between the value of a nation's exports and its imports. The balance can be either a surplus or deficit.

behavioral approach A school of thought that developed in reaction to idealism and realism; behaviorism claimed to have no *a priori* assumptions about state behavior

I

and emphasized the need for empirical research. How to study, especially by means of value-free quantitative methods, often appeared to be its preoccupation rather than the key substantive issues in the "real world."

bilateral Between two states.

bipolar system An international system dominated by *two* superpowers and/or coalitions. This system is characterized by a high degree of insecurity, clear distinctions between friend and foe, sensitivity to power shifts, arms races, and cohesiveness of each coalition.

bipolycentrism A state system characterized by the loosening of rival bipolar blocs into less cohesive alliances and the simultaneous rise of influential Third World actors. Although the dominant military powers remain the United States and the Soviet Union (bi), the growing influence from other (poly) centers of influence marks the possible transition to future multipolarity.

boycott An economic weapon used to pressure another nation by cutting off imports from it.

bureaucratic politics See **governmental politics model.**

capitalism An economic system based on the private ownership of property, a free market based on the laws of supply and demand, a general absence of governmental interference, and the pursuit of individual profit.

charismatic hero In a developing country, the leader whose striking personality and oratory, often displayed in the struggle for its independence, symbolizes national unity and confers legitimacy upon the new nation and its government.

cold war The relationship characterized by conflict and competition, often accompanied by tension and hostility, that evolved between the United States (the West) and the Soviet Union (Communist bloc) after World War II.

Comecon The Council for Mutual Economic Assistance, founded in 1949 by the Soviet Union as a means of integrating the economies of the East European states and asserting Soviet control over them. Mongolia, Cuba, and Vietnam were allowed to join later.

Common Market The European Economic Community (EEC), founded in 1958, the purpose of which was to create unified national economic policies (uniform external tariff wall, mobile labor and capital, and so forth) among its original members (Belgium, France, West Germany, Italy, Netherlands, and Luxembourg). Eventually, their economic unity was to lead to a political federation of Europe. Added six more members (Britain, Denmark, Ireland, Greece, Spain, and Portugal).

communism A revolutionary ideology and political movement that seeks the destruction of capitalism and its replacement by a collectivist society in which private ownership of property is no longer necessary. Subsequently, both social/economic classes and the state will cease to exist.

compensation A balance-of-power technique dividing a strategically located country in order to preserve the balance among the neighboring great powers (example, the Soviet-German division of Poland in 1939).

containment The fundamental post-World War II American foreign policy aimed at blocking Soviet expansion through countervailing American economic/military power. It was expected that the Soviet leadership would eventually mellow, abandon its expansionist drive, and accept the international status quo.

counterforce strategy Strategic weapons targeted at the adversary's military capabilities such as bomber bases, ICBM silos, air defense installations, and so on.

countervalue (countercity) strategy Strategic weapons targeted at the adversary's population centers and industries, targets which it presumably values and does not want to lose.

credible commitment A nation's stated obligation to defend an ally or friendly state that is *believed* by adversaries.

crises Intense, relatively brief superpower confrontations that have become substitutes for war in the nuclear era. Crises involve threats to vital national interests, an increased perception of the possible use of force, and each party's reputation for power.

cruise missile A nuclear missile, resembling a pilotless aircraft, that operates entirely within the earth's atmosphere and is launched from the air or sea.

crusade Policy characterized by an unshakable missionary zeal to eliminate evil from the world. Tends to be transformed into total wars to utterly destroy adversaries.

Cuban missile crisis The thirteen tense days in October 1962 when the United States and the Soviet Union clashed over the issue of Soviet missiles emplaced in Cuba. The crisis ended with Khrushchev's promise to remove the missiles in exchange for Kennedy's pledge not to invade Cuba.

decision-making approach The level of analysis that focuses primarily on the specific policy makers and the bureaucracy officially responsible for the conduct and implementation of foreign policy.

dependency An analytical perspective that views the state system and international economy as divided between the *core* First World (industrial capitalist states) which is rich because it dominates the global economy, and the *peripheral* Third World, which is poor because it is exploited.

détente In general, a relaxation of previously more tense relations between two or more countries. Specifically, in the United States détente meant that U.S.-Soviet global conflict and competition could be moderated and "restrained" by cooperation in arms control, trade, technology, and so forth.

deterrence (nuclear) In bipolar nuclear context, the assumption that total war is synonymous with mutual destruction because both superpowers possess effective second-strike capabilities. The resulting standoff, if perceived as credible by rational policy makers on both sides, prevents the outbreak of war.

diplomacy International negotiations and/or bargaining to compromise conflicts among states over issues such as territorial division, arms ratios, or trade imbalances.

disarmament Agreement to reduce (or abolish) existing military force and/or weapons.

divide-and-rule A balance-of-power technique in which Nation A attempts to exploit existing differences among Nation B and its allies to gain an advantage.

domino theory The belief that if one country on your "side" falls to the enemy, that country's neighboring nations will also fall, upsetting the balance of power.

East A term encompassing the Communist states of Eastern Europe plus the Soviet Union.

East-West conflict Another term for cold war or the American-Soviet conflict and competition for influence in the world.

economic fat In cases where a nation's economy is blessed with great productivity and wealth, a significant amount of "butter" can be converted into "guns" and still leave the population with enough butter.

economic flexibility A nation's ability to convert its economy quickly from the production of peacetime goods to military hardware.

economic slack The amount of unused productivity in a nation's economy.

EEC European Economic Community or Common Market.

embargo An economic weapon used by one nation to prevent its goods from being sold to the targeted nation.

first strike See **counterforce strategy.**

First World Refers to the advanced urban-industrial economies and political democracies of Western Europe, North America (Canada and the United States), and Japan.

foreign policy A nation's efforts to realize its objectives or national interests in the state system.

functionalism The theory that envisions economic and social cooperation among nations in various fields and eventually a new international political community.

games nations play The games analogy is used in this book to refer to the need for states in the international system to pursue a strategy—a set of moves to be made in a competitive and conflictual situation—to advance their interests.

General Assembly The body of the United Nations in which all its members are represented. Intended originally to be an advisory organ to the Security Council, its influence has grown with the addition of many Third World nations, which now constitute the majority.

GNP Gross national product or the sum market value of all consumer and capital goods and services produced in a year. It is one indicator or index used in calculating power rankings among nations.

governmental politics model A pluralistic decision-making approach that stresses the bargaining between the executive/legislative branches, nongovernmental interest groups, and the executive agencies participating in the making of foreign policy.

graduated escalation A wartime strategy of increasing incrementally the scope and intensity of force in the expectation that the enemy will at some point agree to negotiate an end to the war.

groupthink A term coined by Irving L. Janis to indicate the tendency of small decision-making groups to conform to the group's apparent views, rather than ask awkward questions. Policy is therefore made on the basis of insufficient information and the failure to consider all available options.

guerrilla warfare See **revolutionary warfare.**

guns versus butter A competition of objectives, which many states confront, involving spending on security (military-defense) needs or welfare (schools, hospitals, education, housing, and so forth).

human rights policy A moral dedication to individual freedoms and opposition to governments that flagrantly violate these principles.

ICBM Intercontinental ballistic missile, which can be launched over a range of 3,000 to 4,000 (or more) miles (example: U.S. Minuteman III).

idealist approach A school of thinking that focuses on how nations *ought* to behave in order to eliminate international conflict and create greater international cooperation and peace.

ideology A comprehensive set of beliefs that critically describe and explain contemporary reality while prescribing a better state of affairs in the future.

IGOs Intergovernmental organizations, which may be classified as global (United Nations) or regional (Organization of American States, League of Arab States). Political, military, social, and economic functions can also distinguish IGOs (examples: North Atlantic Treaty Organization, World Health Organization).

imperialism (general) A relationship in which one nation dominates or controls, politically or economically, directly or indirectly, another nation.

imperialism (Lenin) Lenin's theory that argues that the revolution of the proletariat (workers) did not occur as expected in Western capitalistic states because they engaged in colonial expansion to earn high profits, invest surplus capital, and exploit cheap native labor. These profits increased the workers' living standards and "derevolutionized" them.

incrementalism The tendency of policy makers to move forward step-by-step on a specific course of policy while concentrating upon momentary, short-run aims rather than comprehensive long-range planning.

intangible components of power Components that do not lend themselves to accurate calculations or quantifications, such as a state's national morale, quality of leadership, or the effectiveness of its political system.

integration The creation within a territory, of a "sense of community" and of legitimate institutions and practices creating an expectation of "peaceful change" among its population.

intentions versus capabilities The former refers to a state's goals or objectives, the latter to its power to achieve them.

interdependence The argument that the nations of the world have become *mutually sensitive and vulnerable* through an interrelationship of socioeconomic and technological issues and that their future behavior will be oriented toward long-term collaboration rather than toward conflict over security issues.

international system See **state system.**

intervention Either overt or covert involvement in the affairs of a state by another state or alliance to influence policy and events.

irredentism The desire of state A to annex territory of state B that contains people who possess linguistic, racial, or ethnic backgrounds similar to state A's citizenry.

isolationism In general, the noninvolvement of a state in the affairs of the international system, although the degree of disinterest can vary considerably.

kiloton weapon A nuclear weapon, the yield of which is measured in thousands of tons of TNT. A 10-kiloton weapon is equal to the explosive power of 10,000 tons of TNT.

Kto-kovo In Soviet ideological parlance, "Who will destroy whom?" Signifies the belief in the irreconcilable struggle between capitalism and communism.

LDCs The less-developed countries of the international system, usually categorized as belonging to the Third World. Economic backwardness and/or ineffective, weak political institutions are typical of these states.

levels of analysis Explanatory levels, such as the state system (balance of power), the nation-state (its internal nature), and decision making (leadership elites), to collectively explain and describe how and why nations play the games they do. Each level of analysis derives its analytical power from selective variables and data, thus stressing *different* cause-and-effect relationships behind *similar* international events and behavior.

limited war An armed conflict fought for limited political objectives and with definite restrictions upon the use of force.

macropolitics The view that the *international interest* of mankind should be given priority over the traditional national interests of states in an increasingly interdependent world.

MAD Mutual assured destruction, a doctrine that is at the heart of strategic deterrence aimed at preventing all-out war between the United States and the Soviet Union. Because both sides would be destroyed, nuclear war is prevented.

Marshall Plan A massive program of American economic aid ($15 billion) aimed at rebuilding war-torn Western Europe during the 1948-52 period.

Marxism The doctrine developed during the nineteenth century by Karl Marx and Friedrich Engels, which explained historical developments as a series of economic class struggles. Capitalism would eventually be overthrown by a proletarian revolution (workers) against the bourgeoisie (propertied, exploiting class), ushering in a classless, nonpropertied, nonexploitive utopia.

megaton weapon A nuclear weapon whose yield is explosively equivalent to 1 million tons of TNT. For example, a 5-megaton missile warhead would equal the explosive power of 5 million tons of TNT.

mercantilism A political philosophy that proposes the use of economic means to increase the welfare and power of the state.

microstates — States with tiny populations (such as Grenada or the Seychelles).

military industrial complex (MIC) The alleged conspiratorial alliance of the professional military, defense-corporation executives, national security managers, labor union members, university researchers, and prodefense members of Congress, which benefits economically and politically from sustained international tension and the resulting high levels of defense spending on strategic and conventional arms.

mirror image An explanation of international violence resulting from misperception. Each nation sees itself as good and its opponents as bad.

MIRV A multiple independently targeted reentry vehicle; a single ballistic missile that carries a cluster of warheads with each warhead capable of hitting a separate target.

misperception The belief that wars occur because decision makers have good and evil or black-and-white images of the world that filter out any incoming information that conflicts with their preconceived cognitive maps. But for these maps, international harmony and peace would prevail.

modernization The long, complex, and often painful transformation of a state from an agrarian, politically fragmented entity to a politically unified, urban-industrialized society. Modernization involves fundamental changes in the population's values and expectations.

motivational power A nation's political will in actively employing its power and/or persuasive capabilities in the international system.

multilateral Between more than two states.

multinational corporations (MNCs) Business enterprises that conduct their operations across international boundaries and in multiple markets, in effect creating a global shopping center. American MNCs include Exxon, Pepsi-Cola, and General Motors.

multipolar system A system that has at least four approximately equal powers. In contrast to simple and rigid bipolarity, multipolarity is considered complex and flexible. Frequent alliance realignment and lowered sensitivities to changes in the balance of power are characteristic of this international structure.

national interests An ordering of priorities in accordance with national goals.

national morale An intangible component of power that refers to a population's patriotism, national loyalty, and willingness to sacrifice during times of war and/or international tension.

national style Each state's particular approach to foreign policy based on its historical experience, political and social values, economic status, and cultural perspective.

NATO North Atlantic Treaty Organization, the alliance between the United States and Western Europe.

neutralization A balance-of-power technique or hands-off policy toward a strategically important country lying between two major powers.

NGO Nongovernmental organization, such as a multinational corporation, national liberation, terrorist, religious, humanitarian, and other groups such as the Catholic church and the Red Cross.

NIEO (new international economic order) A demand made by the LDCs for a more equitable distribution of the world's wealth because the present order favors the rich Western industrial nations who allegedly exploited them in the past and continue to do so.

nonalignment A policy of not aligning formally (particularly evident in the Third World) to either the Communist or free world alliances, mainly during the bipolar cold war period.

North A term usually referring to the Western democratic industrialized states (including Japan).

nuclear proliferation The acquisition of nuclear capabilities by a significant number of middle- and smaller-rank states.

OPEC The Organization of Petroleum Exporting Countries (Saudi Arabia, Algeria, Quatar, Kuwait, Libya, Iraq, United Arab Emirates, Iran, Nigeria, Gabon, Indonesia, Venezuela, and Ecuador), a producer cartel whose purpose is collectively to fix the levels of production and the price of crude oil on the world market.

peace A complex, multifaceted concept which, in its most general sense, refers to the absence of major warfare in the international system.

peaceful coexistence A Soviet term which, acknowledging the dangers of nuclear war, asserts that the Communist-capitalist struggle can be channeled into nonmilitary areas of competition.

petrodollars The money paid to OPEC by the industrialized states for oil.

PGMs Precision guided munitions, more often known as smart bombs, which can hit their intended targets with great accuracy.

pole A major actor or state in the international system, more often referred to as a great power.

political community A community that effectively controls the means of violence, possesses a set of political institutions that peacefully allocates resources, and whose population shares a common political identification.

political idealism See *idealist approach.*

population explosion The rapid increase of the world's population.

power (among states) The capacity of one state to influence others in accordance with its own objectives; that is, to change the behavior of the others or prevent them from taking a particular action.

preemptive strike A defensive attack to forestall what is believed to be an imminent first strike by the opponent. Differs from preventive strike, which is motivated by the offensive aim of eliminating the enemy and is independent of a perception that he is about to strike.

prestige A nation's reputation for power among its fellow states and the degree of respect that it is subsequently accorded.

preventive diplomacy A UN peace-keeping function whereby multinational forces are injected into a conflict to separate the combatants and prevent the escalation of that conflict by the possible intervention of the superpowers.

preventive strike An aggressor's unprovoked, carefully calculated attack upon an opponent with the expectation of defeating it.

quota Numerical limit on imports.

rational actor A decision-making approach that stresses a clear definition of policy goals and an examination of the alternative means of attaining those goals.

realist approach A school of thinking that focuses on the conflicts and rivalries among nations in an anarchical system. The balance of power plays a central role in this analysis, and war remains a continuing characteristic of international politics, to be avoided or limited through prudent management. But war cannot be erased.

relinquishing the initiative The deterrer makes it known that he will stand firm and that the responsibility for starting any conflict rests on the other side.

revolutionary state A state whose leadership condemns the existing order as oppressive and exploitive and seeks to liberate mankind, bringing it freedom, justice, and peace. Examples are late eighteenth-century France and the twentieth-century Soviet Union.

revolutionary warfare (guerrilla warfare) Lengthy conflicts fought by a band of insurgents (or self-proclaimed liberators) whose primary goal is to capture state power as a means of transforming the nation's sociopolitical structure and economy.

SALT The Strategic Arms Limitation Talks, negotiations between the United States and the Soviet Union, which began in 1969.

search and destroy   The primary U.S. ground strategy in the Vietnam War in which American forces in helicopters searched for Communist guerrillas in the countryside to destroy them.

second-strike capability   The ability, after absorbing a nuclear first strike from the enemy, to deliver a retaliatory blow with sufficient remaining force (missiles and bombers) to destroy the enemy.

Second World   The Soviet Union and the Communist states of Eastern Europe.

Security Council   The primary organ in the United Nations responsible for the preservation of peace and security. The fifteen-member council can take enforcement action against international aggression provided one of the five great powers (permanent members) does not veto it.

security dilemma   In an anarchical state system, the security dilemma follows from a state's attempt to ensure its security by increasing its power; as its potential adversary does the same, the first state's sense of insecurity recurs, leading it to increase its power once more, and so forth.

security policy   Basic policy of a noncrisis nature. Examples: the defense budget, foreign aid, and arms control policy.

Sino-Soviet split   The conflict between Communist China (People's Republic of China) and the Soviet Union over ideological interpretations, leadership of the international Communist movement, disputed territories, and major policy issues.

SLBM   A submarine-launched (long-range) ballistic missile (such as the U.S. Poseidon or Trident).

South   A term encompassing the LDCs.

sovereign state   The primary political actor in the international system. Each of almost 170 states is characterized by a territorial base, jurisdiction over its internal and external affairs, and, to varying degrees, a conception of self-identity (nationalism) and unity.

spheres of influence   Areas under the influence or domination of a great power (example: Eastern Europe for the Soviet Union.)

stable deterrence   The strategic nuclear American-Soviet balance in which the deterrent forces of both sides are invulnerable to the opponent's first strike.

stable state system   A system characterized by minimal violence and generally by the peaceful settlement of national differences.

stagflation   The simultaneous occurrence of recession and inflation.

stalemate   A form of conflict resolution in which victory for either side is rejected as a result of *mutual* battlefield exhaustion, reluctance to invest further resources, or unwillingness to escalate due to the risks involved.

state-centric   An analysis focusing on the behavior of nation-states as the principal actors in international politics.

state system   The regular and observable interactions of political actors (primarily nations) within a basically anarchical global context.

substructure   In Marxist-Leninist theory, the fundamental economic forces of a society (the ownership of property and wealth).

superpowers   Nations that possess an extraordinary amount of power (military, economic, diplomatic) allowing them to pursue an independent role in global affairs and/or states whose actions have a substantial effect upon the policies of other political actors throughout the entire state system.

superstructure   In Marxist-Leninist theory, the political, social, and cultural institutions/beliefs that are creations or reflections of the underlying economic forces or substructure.

supranational actor   Best exemplified by the European Economic Community (EEC), or Common Market, in which twelve sovereign states—Belgium, France, Greece, West Germany, Italy, Luxembourg, Netherlands, Britain, Denmark, Ireland, Portugal, and Spain—have transferred a degree of their sovereign authority on economic issues to a superior decision-making body.

surplus value In Marxist theory, the difference between what workers should be paid in terms of the cash value of their labor in the product and what they are actually paid (profit).

tacit negotiations Informal, indirect bargaining activity among states as opposed to traditional face-to-face diplomacy.

tangible components of power Usually, components that can be measured or quantified, such as a nation's population, size, military strength, and economic productivity.

tariff A tax imposed on imports.

terrorism The use of political violence by nonstate actors (although some are state-supported) to intimidate their enemies and gain publicity for their causes.

Third World The world of the non-Western, largely economically underdeveloped countries.

total war A war in which political objectives of complete victory over the enemy are matched by the full mobilization of a nation's military, economic, and social resources (example: World War II).

totalitarianism A political system that attempts to control every aspect of a citizen's life.

transnational actor A nongovernmental organization that is characterized by headquarters in one country but that also conducts its centrally directed operations in two or more countries. A prominent example is the multinational corporation.

triad Strategic deterrent composed of bombers, submarines, and ICBMs.

tripolarity An international system in which three major power centers exist. Tripolarity is considered more stable than bipolarity by some analysts, but less stable by others.

Truman Doctrine The 1947 presidential pronouncement that "it must be the policy of the United States to support free peoples who are resisting subjugation by armed minorities or outside pressures." Originally directed at Greece and Turkey, the doctrine actually marked the beginning of the containment era and the United States' role in preserving the balance of power in a bipolar world.

UNCTAD The United Nations Conference on Trade and Development, sometimes equated with Third World coalition strategy.

unilateral One-sided.

Uniting for Peace resolution A U.S.-sponsored resolution in November 1950, which transferred the authority to preserve peace from the Security Council to the General Assembly so that support for American anti-Communist policies in Korea would not be blocked by Soviet vetoes.

unstable deterrence The U.S.-Soviet nuclear balance, in which one or both of the deterrent forces has become vulnerable, thereby tempting the other side to strike preemptively, especially during a crisis.

unstable state system A system prone to the outbreak of major wars.

utopianism See *idealist approach.*

war Hostilities between states that are conducted by armed force.

warhead The part of a missile that contains the explosive material.

West Same as *North.*

world government The idealistic concept of a supreme global authority that would make wars among states impossible.

yield The explosive force of a warhead.

zero-sum What one nation gains (for example, security), another loses. International politics is often said to be a zero-sum game, underlining its conflictual character.

Brief Selective Bibliography of Books

International Politics and the State System

Aron, Raymond. *Peace and War.** Garden City, N.Y.: Doubleday, 1966; London: Weidenfeld and Nicolson, 1966. Paperback ed., Holt, Rinehart & Winston.

Bull, Hedley. *The Anarchical Society.** New York: Columbia University Press, 1977.

Carr, Edward H. *The Twenty Years' Crisis 1919-1939.** New York and Basingstoke: Macmillan, 1961. Paperback ed., Harper Torchbooks.

Dougherty, James E., and Robert L. Pfaltzgraff, Jr. *Contending Theories of International Relations.** Philadelphia: Lippincott, 1971.

Duchacek, Ivo D. *The Territorial Dimension of Politics.* Boulder, Colo.: Westview Press, 1986.

Fromkin, David. *The Independence of Nations.** New York: Praeger Publishers, 1981.

Gilpin, Robert. *War and Change in World Politics.* New York: Cambridge University Press, 1982.

Herz, John. *Political Realism and Political Idealism.* Chicago: University of Chicago Press, 1951.

Knorr, Klaus, and James N. Rosenau, eds. *Contending Approaches to International Politics.** Princeton, N.J.: Princeton University Press, 1969.

Krasner, Stephen D. *Defending the National Interest.** Princeton, N.J.: Princeton University Press, 1978.

Morgan, Patrick M. *Theories and Approaches to International Politics.** 3d ed. New Brunswick, N.J.: Transaction Books, 1981.

Morgenthau, Hans J. *Politics among Nations.* 5th ed. New York: Alfred A. Knopf, 1972.

Rosenau, James N., ed. *International Politics and Foreign Policy.* 2d ed. New York: Free Press, 1969.

Singer, J. David. *Quantitative International Politics.* New York: Free Press, 1968.

Waltz, Kenneth N. *Man, the State, and War.** New York: Columbia University Press, 1959.

_____. *Theory of International Politics.** Reading, Mass.: Addison-Wesley, 1979.

Wight, Martin. *Power Politics.* Edited by Hedley Bull and Carsten Holbraad. New York: Holmes & Meier, 1978.

Wolfers, Arnold. *Discord and Collaboration: Essays on International Politics.** Baltimore: Johns Hopkins University Press, 1965.

---

* Indicates paperback.

Peace and War

Beer, Francis A. *Peace Against War.** San Francisco: W. H. Freeman, 1981.

Blainey, Geoffrey. *The Causes of War.** New York: Free Press, 1973.

Bueno de Mesquita, Bruce. *The War Trap.* New Haven, Conn.: Yale University Press, 1981.

Clausewitz, Carl von. *On War.* Edited and translated by Michael Howard and Peter Paret. Princeton, N.J.: Princeton University Press, 1976.

Harvard Nuclear Study Group. *Living With Nuclear Weapons.** New York: Bantam Books, 1983.

Howard, Michael. *The Causes of War.** Cambridge, Mass.: Harvard University Press, 1983.

Preston, Richard A., Sidney F. Wise, and Herman O. Werner. *Men in Arms.* Rev. ed. New York: Praeger Publishers, 1962.

Ropp, Theodore. *War in the Modern World.* 2d ed. New York: Collier, 1962.

Small, Melvin, and J. David Singer. *Resort to Arms.* Beverly Hills, Calif.: Sage Publications, 1982.

Wright, Quincy. *A Study of War.* Abridged ed. Chicago: University of Chicago Press, 1964.

Deterrence and Arms Control

Allison, Graham T., Albert Carnsdale, and Joseph Nye, Jr. *Hawks, Doves, and Owls.** New York: W. W. Norton, 1985.

Brodie, Bernard. *Strategy in the Missile Age.** Princeton, N.J.: Princeton University Press, 1959.

Bull, Hedley. *The Control of the Arms Race.** 2d ed. New York: Holt, Rinehart & Winston, 1965.

Collins, John M. *American and Soviet Military Trends Since the Cuban Missile Crisis.** Washington, D.C.: Georgetown University, Center for Strategic and International Studies, 1978.

Freedman, Lawrence. *The Evolution of Nuclear Strategy.* New York: St. Martin's Press, 1981.

George, Alexander L., et al. *The Limits of Coercive Diplomacy.** Boston: Little, Brown & Co., 1971.

____ and Richard Smoke. *Deterrence in American Foreign Policy.** New York: Columbia University Press, 1974.

International Institute for Strategic Studies. *World Military Balance.** Published annually.

Jervis, Robert. *The Illogic of American Nuclear Strategy.** Ithaca, N.Y.: Cornell University Press, 1984.

Kahan, Jerome H. *Security in the Nuclear Age.** Washington, D.C.: The Brookings Institution, 1975.

Kahn, Herman. *Thinking About the Unthinkable.** New York: Horizon, 1962. Paperback ed., Avon Books.

Katz, Arthur M. *Life After Nuclear War.** Cambridge, Mass.: Ballinger, 1981.

Krepon, Michael. *Strategic Stalemate.* New York: St. Martin's Press, 1985.

Levine, Robert A. *The Arms Debate.* Cambridge, Mass.: Harvard University Press, 1962.

Mandelbaum, Michael. *The Nuclear Revolution.* Cambridge, Mass.: Cambridge University Press, 1979.

Martin, Laurence, ed. *Strategic Thought in the Nuclear Age.* Baltimore: Johns Hopkins University Press, 1980.

Morgan, Patrick M. *Deterrence.* * Beverly Hils, Calif.: Sage Publications, 1977.

Nacht, Michael. *The Age of Vulnerability.* * Washington, D.C.: The Brookings Institution, 1985.

Newhouse, John. *Cold Dawn.* New York: Holt, Rinehart & Winston, 1973.

Office of Technology Assessment. *The Effects of Nuclear War.* * Washington. D.C.: Government Printing Office, 1980.

Osgood, Robert E., and Robert W. Tucker. *Force, Order, and Justice.* * Baltimore: Johns Hopkins University Press, 1967.

Payne, Keith B., and Colin S. Gray. *Nuclear Deterrence in U.S.-Soviet Relations.* Boulder, Colo.: Westview Press, 1982.

_____. *Strategic Defense.* * Lanham, Md.: Hamilton Press, 1986.

Quester, George H. *The Future of Nuclear Deterrence.* Lexington, Mass.: Lexington Books, 1986.

Ranger, Robin. *Arms and Politics 1958-1978.* Boulder, Colo.: Westview Press, 1982.

Schell, Jonathan. *The Fate of the Earth.* * New York: Avon Books, 1982.

Schelling, Thomas C. *Strategy of Conflict.* * Cambridge, Mass.: Harvard University Press, 1960. Paperback ed., Oxford (London).

_____, and Morton H. Halperin. *Strategy and Arms Control.* * New York: Twentieth Century Fund, 1961.

Scoville, Herbert, Jr. *MX.* * Cambridge, Mass.: M.I.T. Press, 1981.

Talbott, Strobe. *Endgame.* * New York: Harper & Row, 1979.

Tucker, Robert W. *The Nuclear Debate.* * New York: Holmes & Meier, 1985.

Wolfe, Thomas W. *The SALT Experience.* Cambridge, Mass.: Ballinger, 1979.

Crisis and Limited War (Conventional and Revolutionary)

Abel, Elie. *The Missile Crisis.* * Philadelphia: Lippincott, 1966. Paperback ed., Bantam Books.

Adomeit, Hannes. *Soviet Risk-Taking and Crisis Behavior.* Winchester, Mass.: Allen & Unwin, 1982.

Blaufarb, Douglas S. *The Counterinsurgency Era.* New York: Free Press, 1977.

Blechman, Barry M., and Stephen S. Kaplan. *Force Without War.* Washington, D.C.: The Brookings Institution, 1978.

Galula, David. *Counterinsurgency Warfare.* New York: Holt, Rinehart & Winston, 1964.

Greene, T. N., ed. *The Guerrilla—and How to Fight Him.* * New York: Holt, Rinehart & Winston, 1962.

Heilbrunn, Otto. *Partisan Warfare.* New York: Holt, Rinehart & Winston, 1962.

Kennedy, Robert F. *Thirteen Days.* * New York: W. W. Norton, 1969. Paperback ed., Signet.

Kissinger, Henry A. *Nuclear Weapons and Foreign Policy.* * New York: Harper & Row, 1957. Abridged paperback ed., W. W. Norton.

Lebow, Richard L. *Between Peace and War.* Baltimore: Johns Hopkins University Press, 1981.

Mao Tse-tung on Guerrilla Warfare. Translated and with an Introduction by Samuel B. Griffith. New York: Holt, Rinehart & Winston, 1961.

Osgood, Robert E. *Limited War.* Chicago: University of Chicago Press, 1957.

Paret, Peter, and John W. Shy. *Guerrillas in the 1960's.* * Rev. ed. New York: Holt, Rinehart & Winston, 1962.

Shoemaker, Christopher C., and John W. Spanier. *Patron-Client State Relationships.* New York: Praeger Publishers, 1984.

Smoke, Richard. *War: Controlling Escalation.* Cambridge, Mass.: Harvard University Press, 1978.

Snyder, Glenn H., and Paul Diesing. *Conflict Among Nations.** Princeton, N.J.: Princeton University Press, 1978.

Spanier, John W. *The Truman-MacArthur Controversy and the Korean War.** Cambridge, Mass.: Harvard University Press, 1959. Rev. paperback ed., W. W Norton, 1965.

Speier, Hans. *Divided Berlin.* New York: Holt, Rinehart & Winston, 1961.

Stern, Ellen P., ed. *The Limits of Intervention.* Beverly Hills, Calif.: Sage Publications, 1977.

Thayer, Charles W. *Guerrilla.** New York: Harper & Row, 1963.

Williams, Phil. *Crisis Management.* New York: John Wiley & Sons, 1976.

The Vietnam War

Draper, Theodore. *Abuse of Power.** New York: Viking, 1967.

Fall, Bernard B. *The Two Viet-Nams.* 2d rev. ed. New York: Holt, Rinehart & Winston, 1967.

_____. *Viet-Nam Witness, 1953-66.* New York: Holt, Rinehart & Winston, 1966.

Herring, George C. *America's Longest War.** New York: John Wiley & Sons, 1979.

Hoopes, Townsend. *The Limits of Intervention.** New York: McKay, 1969.

Kattenburg, Paul M. *The Vietnam Trauma in American Foreign Policy, 1945-75.* New Brunswick, N.J.: Transaction Books, 1980.

Lewy, Guenter. *America in Vietnam.** New York: Oxford University Press, 1978.

Lomperis, Timothy J. *The War Everyone Lost—And Won.** Baton Rouge, La.: Louisiana State University Press, 1984. Paperback ed., Congressional Quarterly.

Oberdorfer, Don. *Tet.* Garden City, N.Y.: Doubleday, 1971.

Palmer, Bruce, Jr. *The 25-Year War.** New York: Touchstone Paperbacks, 1985.

*The Pentagon Papers.** Chicago: Quadrangle, 1971. Paperback ed., Bantam Books.

Pike, Douglas. *Viet Cong.** Cambridge, Mass.: M.I.T. Press, 1966.

Summers, Harry G. *On Strategy.** New York: Dell, 1984.

Thompson, Sir Robert. *No Exit from Vietnam.* New York: McKay, 1969.

Nuclear and Nonnuclear Proliferation

Dunn, Lewis A. *Controlling the Bomb.** New Haven, Conn.: Yale University Press, 1981.

Gompert, David C., Michael Mandelbaum, Richard L. Garwin, and John H. Barton. *Nuclear Weapons and World Politics.** New York: McGraw-Hill (for the Council on Foreign Relations/1980s Project), 1977.

Greenwood, Ted, Harold A. Feiveson, and Theodore B. Taylor. *Nuclear Proliferation.** New York: McGraw-Hill (for the Council on Foreign Relations/1980s Project), 1977.

Lefever, Ernest W. *Nuclear Arms in the Third World.** Washington, D.C.: The Brookings Institution, 1979.

Pierre, Andrew J. *The Global Politics of Arms Sales.** Princeton, N.J.: Princeton University Press, 1982.

Economics

Hofheinz, Roy, Jr., and Kent E. Calder. *The East Asia Edge.* New York: Basic Books, 1982.

Hsiung, James C., et al., eds. *The Taiwan Experience.* New York: Praeger Publishers, 1981.

Knorr, Klause, and Frank Trager, eds. *Economic Issues and National Security.* Lawrence, Kans.: Allen Press, 1977.

Nove, Alec. *East-West Trade.* Beverly Hills, Calif.: Sage Publications, 1978.

Phillips, Kevin T. *Staying on Top.* New York: Random House, 1985.
Rustow, Dankwart A. *Oil and Turmoil.* New York: W. W. Norton, 1982.

American Foreign Policy

Alexander, George L., ed. *Managing U.S.-Soviet Rivalry.** Boulder, Colo.: Westview Press, 1983.
Almond, Gabriel. *The American People and Foreign Policy.** New York: Holt, Rinehart & Winston, 1960.
Gaddis, John Lewis. *Russia, the Soviet Union, and the United States.* New York: John Wiley & Sons, 1978.
_____. *Strategies of Containment.** New York: Oxford University Press, 1982.
Gati, Charles, ed. *Caging the Bear.** New York: Bobbs-Merrill, 1973.
Gilbert, Felix. *To the Farewell Address.** Princeton, N.J.: Princeton University Press, 1961.
Halle, Louis J. *The Cold War as History.** New York: Harper & Row, 1967.
Hoffmann, Stanley. *Primacy or World Order.** New York: McGraw-Hill, 1978.
Jones, Joseph M. *The Fifteen Weeks.** New York: Viking, 1955. Paperback ed., Harcourt.
Kennan, George F. *American Diplomacy 1900-1950.** Chicago: University of Chicago Press, 1951. Paperback ed., Mentor.
Morgenthau, Hans J. *In Defense of the National Interest.* New York: Alfred A. Knopf, 1951.
_____. *A New Foreign Policy for the United States.** New York: Holt, Rinehart & Winston, 1969.
Mueller, John E. *War, Presidents, and Public Opinion.** New York: John Wiley & Sons, 1973.
Osgood, Robert E. *Ideals and Self-Interest in America's Foreign Relations.** Chicago: University of Chicago Press, 1953.
Quester, George. *American Foreign Policy.** New York: Praeger Publishers, 1982.
Smith, Gaddis. *American Diplomacy During the Second World War.** New York: John Wiley & Sons, 1966.
Spanier, John W. *American Foreign Policy Since World War II.** 10th ed. New York: Holt, Rinehart & Winston, 1985.
Tsou, Tang. *America's Failure in China.** Chicago: University of Chicago Press, 1963.
Tucker, Robert W. *The Radical Left and American Foreign Policy.** Baltimore: Johns Hopkins University Press, 1971.
_____. *The Purposes of American Power.** New York: Praeger Publishers, 1981.
Weintraub, Sidney, ed. *Economic Coercion and U.S. Foreign Policy.* Boulder, Colo.: Westview Press, 1982.

Memoirs and Biographies of American Statesmen and Administrations

Acheson, Dean. *Present at the Creation.** New York: W. W. Norton, 1969. Paperback ed., Signet.
Brown, Seyom. *The Crises of Power: Foreign Policy in the Kissinger Years.* New York: Columbia University Press, 1979.
Brzezinski, Zbigniew. *Power and Principle.* New York: Farrar, Straus, Giroux, 1983.
Byrnes, James F. *Speaking Frankly.* New York: Harper & Brothers, 1947.
Eisenhower, Dwight D. *White House Years: Mandate for Change.** Garden City, N.Y.: Doubleday, 1963. Paperback ed., New American Library.
_____. *White House Years: Waging Peace.* Garden City, N.Y.: Doubleday, 1965.
Gerson, Louis L. *John Foster Dulles.* New York: Cooper Square, 1967.
Haig, Alexander M., Jr. *Caveat.* New York: Macmillan, 1984.

Hoopes, Townsend. *The Devil and John Foster Dulles.* Boston: Little, Brown & Co., 1973.

Kissinger, Henry. *White House Years.* Boston: Little, Brown & Co., 1979.

———. *Years of Upheaval.* Boston: Little, Brown & Co., 1982.

Nixon, Richard. *RN.** New York: Grosset & Dunlap, 1978.

Truman, Harry S. *Memoirs.** 2 vols. Garden City, N.Y.: Doubleday, 1958. Paperback ed., Signet.

Soviet Foreign and Military Policy

Aspaturian, Vernon V., ed. *Process and Power on Soviet Foreign Policy.* Boston: Little, Brown & Co., 1971.

Berman, Robert P., and John C. Baker. *Soviet Strategic Forces.** Washington, D.C.: The Brookings Institution, 1982.

Bialer, Seweryn, ed. *The Domestic Context of Soviet Foreign Policy.* Boulder, Colo.: Westview Press, 1981.

———. *The Soviet Paradox.* New York: Alfred A. Knopf, 1986.

Brzezinski, Zbigniew K. *Ideology and Power in Soviet Politics.** Rev. ed. New York: Holt, Rinehart & Winston, 1967.

———. *Game Plan.* Boston: The Atlantic Monthly Press, 1986.

Dallin, David J. *Soviet Foreign Policy After Stalin.* Philadelphia: Lippincott, 1961.

Dinerstein, Herbert S. *War and Soviet Union.** Rev. ed. New York: Holt, Rinehart & Winston, 1962.

Donaldson, Robert H., ed. *The Soviet Union in the Third World.* Boulder, Colo.: Westview Press, 1980.

Douglas, Joseph D., Jr., and Amoretta M. Hoeber. *Soviet Strategy for Nuclear War.** Stanford, Calif.: Hoover Press, 1979.

Garthoff, Raymond L. *Soviet Strategy in the Nuclear Age.** Rev. ed. New York: Holt, Rinehart & Winston, 1962.

———. *Detente and Confrontation.** Washington, D.C.: The Brookings Institution, 1985.

Hammond, Thomas T. *Red Star Over Afghanistan.** Boulder, Colo.: Westview Press, 1983.

Holloway, David. *The Soviet Union and the Arms Race.** 2d ed. New Haven, Conn.: Yale University Press, 1984.

Horelick, Arnold L., and Myron Rush. *Strategic Power and Soviet Foreign Policy.* Chicago: University of Chicago Press, 1966.

Kanet, Roger, ed. *Soviet Foreign Policy in the 1980s.** New York: Praeger Publishers, 1982.

Kennan, George F. *Russia and the West under Lenin and Stalin.** Boston: Little, Brown & Co., 1961. Paperback ed., New American Library.

Leites, Nathan. *The Operational Code of the Politburo.* New York: McGraw-Hill, 1951.

———. *A Study of Bolshevism.* New York: Free Press, 1953.

Mackintosh, J. M. *Strategy and Tactics of Soviet Foreign Policy.* London and New York: Oxford University Press, 1962.

Nogee, Joseph L., and Robert H. Donaldson. *Soviet Foreign Policy Since World War II.** 2d ed. New York: Pergamon Press, 1984.

Pipes, Richard. *Survival Is Not Enough.** New York: Touchstone Paperbacks, 1986.

Scott, Harriet F., and William F. Scott. *The Armed Forces of the USSR.* Boulder, Colo.: Westview Press, 1978.

Shulman, Marshall D. *Stalin's Foreign Policy Reappraised.** Cambridge, Mass.: Harvard University Press, 1963. Paperback ed., Atheneum.

Taubman, William. *Stalin's American Policy.* New York: W. W. Norton, 1982.

Triska, Jan F., and David D. Finley. *Soviet Foreign Policy.* New York: Macmillan, 1968.

Ulam, Adam B. *Expansion and Coexistence.** 2d ed. New York: Holt, Rinehart & Winston, 1974.

———. *Dangerous Relations.** New York: Oxford University Press, 1983.

Valkenier, Elizabeth Kridl. *The Soviet Union and the Third World.* New York: Praeger Publishers, 1983.

Von Laue, Theodore. *Why Lenin, Why Stalin?** Philadelphia: Lippincott, 1964.

Whetten, Lawrence L., ed. *The Future of Soviet Military Power.* New York: Crane, Russak & Co., 1976.

Wolfe, Thomas W. *Soviet Power and Europe, 1945-1970.** Baltimore: Johns Hopkins University Press, 1970.

———. *Soviet Strategy at the Crossroads.* Cambridge, Mass.: Harvard University Press, 1964.

Zimmerman, William. *Soviet Perspectives on International Relations, 1956-1967.* Princeton, N.J.: Princeton University Press, 1969.

Communist China

Barnett, A. Doak. *China and the Major Powers in East Asia.** Washington, D.C.: The Brookings Institution, 1977.

Hinton, Harold C. *Communist China in World Politics.* Boston: Houghton Mifflin, 1966.

Kim, Samuel S., ed. *China and the World.* Boulder, Colo.: Westview Press, 1984.

Low, Alfred D. *The Sino-Soviet Dispute.* Madison, N.J.: Fairleigh Dickinson University Press, 1978.

Oksenberg, Michel, and Robert D. Oxnam. *Dragon and Eagle.* New York: Basic Books, 1978.

Salisbury, Harrison E. *War Between Russia and China.** New York: W. W. Norton, 1969. Paperback ed., Bantam Books.

Wint, Guy. *Communist China's Crusade.** New York: Holt, Rinehart & Winston, 1970.

Zacoria, Donald S. *The Sino-Soviet Conflict, 1956-1961.* Princeton, N.J.: Princeton University Press, 1962.

Less-Developed Countries and Modernization

Berliner, Joseph S. *Soviet Economic Aid.* New York: Holt, Rinehart & Winston, 1958.

Black, C. E. *The Dynamics of Modernization.** New York: Harper & Row, 1966.

Black, Eugene R. *The Diplomacy of Economic Development.** New York: Atheneum, 1963.

Bodenheimer, Susanne J. *The Ideology of Developmentalism.* Beverly Hills, Calif.: Sage Publications, 1971.

Brandt Commission. *North-South.* Cambridge, Mass.: M.I.T. Press, 1980.

Crabb, Cecil V., Jr. *The Elephants and the Grass.** New York: Holt, Rinehart & Winston, 1965.

Ehrlich, Paul. *The Population Bomb.** New York: Ballantine, 1968.

Emerson, Rupert. *From Empire to Nation.** Cambridge, Mass.: Harvard University Press, 1960. Paperback ed., Beacon Press.

Gupte, Pranay. *The Crowded Earth.* New York: W. W. Norton, 1984.

Hansen, Roger D. *Beyond the North-South Stalemate.* New York: McGraw-Hill (for the Council on Foreign Relations/1980s Project), 1979.

Heilbroner, Robert L. *The Great Ascent.* New York: Harper & Row, 1963.

Higgins, Benjamin, and Jean Downing Higgins. *Economic Development of a Small Planet.* New York: W. W. Norton, 1979.

Hunter, Robert E., and John E. Rielly, eds. *Development Today.* New York: Holt, Rinehart & Winston, 1972.

Huntington, Samuel P. *Political Order in Changing Societies.** New Haven, Conn.: Yale University Press, 1968.

Janowitz, Morris. *The Military in the Political Development of New Nations.** Chicago: University of Chicago Press, 1964.

Johnson, John J., ed. *The Role of the Military in Underdeveloped Countries*. Princeton, N.J.: Princeton University Press, 1962.

Krasner, Stephen D. *Structural Conflict*. Berkeley, Calif.: University of California Press, 1985.

Lewis, W. Arthur. *The Evolution of the International Economic Order.** Princeton, N.J.: Princeton University Press, 1977.

Martin, Laurence W., ed. *Neutralism and Nonalignment.** New York: Holt, Rinehart & Winston, 1962.

Millikan, Max F., and Donald L. M. Blackmer, eds. *The Emerging Nations.** Boston: Little, Brown & Co., 1961.

Moran, Theodore H. *Multinational Corporation and the Politics of Dependence.** Princeton, N.J.: Princeton University Press, 1974.

Mortimer, Robert. *The Third World Coalition in International Politics*. 2d ed. Boulder, Colo.: Westview Press, 1984.

Myrdal, Gunnar. *Rich Lands and Poor*. New York: Harper & Row, 1957.

———. *The Challenge of World Poverty*. New York: Pantheon, 1970.

Nordlinger, Eric A. *Soldiers in Politics.** Englewood Cliffs, N.J.: Prentice-Hall, 1977.

Organski, A. F. K. *The Stages of Political Development*. New York: Alfred A. Knopf, 1965.

Rostow, W. W. *Stages of Economic Growth.** New York: Cambridge University Press, 1960.

Rothstein, Robert L. *The Weak in the World of the Strong*. New York: Columbia University Press, 1977.

———. *Global Bargaining*. Princeton, N.J.: Princeton University Press, 1979.

———. *The Third World and U.S. Foreign Policy*. Boulder, Colo.: Westview Press, 1981.

Salas, Rafael. *Reflections on Population*. 2d ed. New York: Pergamon Press, 1985.

Singer, Hans, and Jared Ansan. *Rich and Poor Countries*. London: Allen & Unwin, 1982.

Staley, Eugene. *The Future of Underdeveloped Countries.** Rev. ed. New York: Holt, Rinehart & Winston, 1961.

Tapines, Georges, and Phyllis T. Piotrow. *Six Billion People*. New York: McGraw-Hill (for the Council on Foreign Relations/1980s Project), 1978.

Tinbergen, Jan. *Reshaping the International Order*. New York: Dutton, 1976.

Tucker, Robert W. *The Inequality of Nations*. New York: Basic Books, 1977.

Ward, Barbara. *The Rich Nations and the Poor Nations.** New York: W. W. Norton, 1962.

Wriggins, Howard W., and Gunnar Adler-Karlsson. *Reducing Global Inequities*. New York: McGraw-Hill (for the Council on Foreign Relations/1980s Project), 1978.

Foreign Policy Decision Making (Including Military-Industrial Complex)

Allison, Graham T. *Essence of Decision.** Boston: Little, Brown & Co., 1971.

Barnet, Richard J. *The Economy of Death.** New York: Atheneum, 1969.

———. *The Roots of War.** Baltimore: Penguin, 1973.

Betts, Richard K. *Soldiers, Statesmen, and Cold War Crises*. Cambridge, Mass.: Harvard University Press, 1977.

Destler, I. M. *Making Foreign Economic Policy*. Washington, D.C.: The Brookings Institution, 1980.

Gelb, Leslie H., and Richard K. Betts. *The Irony of Vietnam.** Washington, D.C.: The Brookings Institution, 1979.

George, Alexander L. *Presidential Decision Making in Foreign Policy.** Boulder, Colo.: Westview Press, 1980.

Graber, Doris. *Public Opinion, the President, and Foreign Policy.** New York: Holt, Rinehart & Winston, 1968.

Halperin, Morton. *Bureaucratic Politics and Foreign Policy.** Washington, D.C.: The Brookings Institution, 1974.

Head, Richard G., Frisco W. Short, and Robert C. McFarlane. *Crisis Resolution.* Boulder, Colo.: Westview Press, 1978.

Hilsman, Roger. *The Politics of Policy Making in Defense and Foreign Affairs.** New York: Harper & Row, 1971.

Janis, Irving L. *Victims of Groupthink.** 2d ed. Boston: Houghton Mifflin, 1982.

Krasner, Stephen D. *Defending the National Interest.** Princeton, N.J.: Princeton University Press, 1978.

Levering, Ralph B. *The Public and American Foreign Policy, 1918-1978.* New York: William Morrow, 1978.

Purvis, Hoyt, and Steven J. Baker, eds. *Legislating Foreign Policy.* Boulder, Colo.: Westview Press, 1984.

Rourke, John. *Congress and the Presidency in U.S. Foreign Policymaking.* Boulder, Colo.: Westview Press, 1983.

Spanier, John W., and Eric M. Uslaner. *American Foreign Policy Making and the Democratic Dilemma.** 4th ed. New York: Holt, Rinehart & Winston, 1985.

Spanier, John W., and Joseph L. Nogee, eds. *Congress, the Presidency and Foreign Policy.** Elmsford, N.Y.: Pergamon, 1981.

Yarmolinsky, Adam. *The Military Establishment.** New York: Harper & Row, 1971.

Perception and Psychology

De Rivera, Joseph H. *The Psychological Dimension of Foreign Policy.* Columbus: Merrill, 1968.

Frank, Jerome D. *Sanity and Survival.** New York: Random House, 1968.

Jervis, Robert. *Perception and Misperception in International Politics.** Princeton, N.J.: Princeton University Press, 1976.

Kelman, Herbert C., ed. *International Behavior.* New York: Holt, Rinehart & Winston, 1965.

Klineberg, Otto. *The Human Dimension in International Relations.** New York: Holt, Rinehart & Winston, 1964.

Stagner, Ross. *Psychological Aspects of International Conflict.** Belmont, Calif.: Brooks-Cole, 1967.

Stoessinger, John G. *Nations in Darkness.** 3d ed. New York: Random House, 1982.

_____. *Why Nations Go to War.* New York: St. Martin's Press, 1974.

White, Ralph K. *Nobody Wanted War.** Garden City, N.Y.: Doubleday, 1968.

United Nations

Bailey, Sidney D. *The United Nations.** New York: Holt, Rinehart & Winston, 1963.

Bloomfield, Lincoln P., et al. *International Military Forces.* Boston: Little, Brown & Co., 1964.

Boyd, Andrew. *United Nations.** Baltimore: Penguin, 1963.

Burns, Arthur Lee, and Nina Heathcote. *Peace-keeping by U.N. Forces.* New York: Holt, Rinehart & Winston, 1963.

Calvocoressi, Peter. *World Order and New States.* New York: Holt, Rinehart & Winston, 1962.

Claude, Inis L., Jr. *The Changing United Nations.** New York: Random House, 1967.

_____. *Power and International Relations.* New York: Random House, 1964.

_____. *Swords into Plowshares.* 4th ed. New York: Random House, 1971.

Dallin, Alexander. *The Soviet Union at the United Nations.** New York: Holt, Rinehart & Winston, 1962.

Franck, Thomas M. *Nation Against Nation.* New York: Oxford University Press, 1985.
Goodrich, Leland M. *The United Nations in a Changing World.* New York: Columbia University Press, 1974.
Miller, Linda B. *World Order and Local Disorder.* Princeton, N.J.: Princeton University Press, 1967.
Miller, Lynn H. *Organizing Mankind.** Boston: Holbrook Press, 1972.
Nye, Joseph S., Jr. *Peace in Parts.** Boston: Little, Brown & Co., 1971.
Stoessinger, John G. *The United Nations and the Superpowers.** New York: Random House, 1966.

Disarmament

Barnet, Richard. *Who Wants Disarmament?** Boston: Beacon Press, 1960.
Bull, Hedley. *The Control of the Arms Race.** 2d ed. New York: Holt, Rinehart & Winston, 1965.
Dougherty, James E. *How to Think about Arms Control and Disarmament.** New York: Crane, Russak & Co., 1973.
Noel-Baker, Phillip. *The Arms Race.** Dobbs Ferry, N.Y.: Oceana Publications, 1958.
Spanier, John W., and Joseph L. Nogee. *The Politics of Disarmament.** New York: Holt, Rinehart & Winston, 1962.
Tate, Merze. *The Disarmament Illusion.* New York: Macmillan, 1942.
_____. *The United States and Armaments.* Cambridge, Mass.: Harvard University Press, 1948.

International Law

Bozeman, Adda. *The Future of Law in a Multicultural World.* Princeton, N.J.: Princeton University Press, 1971.
Brierly, J. L. *The Law of Nations.* 6th ed. New York: Oxford University Press, 1963.
Corbett, Percy E. *Law and Society in the Relation of States.* New York: Harcourt, 1951.
Deutsch, Karl W., and Stanley Hoffman, eds. *The Relevance of International Law.* Garden City, N.Y.: Doubleday, 1971.
Henkin, Louis. *How Nations Behave.** New York: Holt, Rinehart & Winston, 1968.
Kaplan, Morton A., and Nicholas DeB. Katzenbach. *The Political Foundations of International Law.* New York: John Wiley & Sons, 1961.

International Morality

Butterfield, Herbert. *International Conflict in the Twentieth Century: A Christian View.* New York: Harper & Row, 1960.
Davidson, Donald L. *Nuclear War and the American Churches.* Boulder, Colo.: Westview Press, 1983.
Dougherty, James E. *The Bishops and Nuclear Weapons.* Hamden, Conn.: Archon Books, 1984.
Herz, John H. *Political Realism and Political Idealism.* Chicago: University of Chicago Press, 1951.
Johnson, James Turner. *Just War Tradition and the Restraint of War.* Princeton, N.J.: Princeton University Press, 1981.
Lefever, Ernest W., ed. *Ethics and World Politics.** Baltimore: Johns Hopkins University Press, 1972.
National Conference of Catholic Bishops. *The Challenge of Peace.* Washington, D.C.: United States Catholic Conference, 1983.

Niebuhr, Reinhold. *Moral Man and Immoral Society.** New York: Scribner, 1932.
———. *The Children of Light and the Children of Darkness.* New York: Scribner, 1944.
———. *The Irony of American History.** New York: Scribner, 1952.
Thompson, Kenneth W. *Political Realism and the Crisis of World Politics.* Princeton, N.J.: Princeton University Press, 1960.
Wolfers, Arnold. *The Anglo-American Tradition in Foreign Affairs.* New Haven, Conn.: Yale University Press, 1956.

Functionalism and Community Building

Deutsch, Karl, et al. *Political Community and the North Atlantic Area.* Princeton, N.J.: Princeton University Press, 1957.
Etzioni, Amitai. *Political Unification.** New York: Holt, Rinehart & Winston, 1965.
Haas, Ernst B. *The Uniting of Europe.* Stanford, Calif.: Stanford University Press, 1958.
Lieber, Robert J. *British Politics and European Unity.* Berkeley, Calif.: University of California Press, 1970.
Lindberg, Leon N., and Stuart A. Scheingold. *Europe's Would-Be Polity.** Englewood Cliffs, N.J.: Prentice-Hall, 1970.

Transnationalism, World Order, and Socioeconomic Issues

Barnet, Richard J., and Ronald Müller. *Global Reach: The Power of the Multinational Corporation.** New York: Simon & Schuster, 1975.
Beres, Louis R., and Harry R. Targ. *Planning Alternative World Futures.** New York: Holt, Rinehart & Winston, 1975.
Bergsten, Fred, Thomas Holst, and Theodore H. Moran. *American Multinationals and American Interest.** Washington, D.C.: The Brookings Institution, 1978.
Blake, David H., and Robert S. Walters. 2d ed. *The Politics of Global Economic Relations.** Englewood Cliffs. N.J.: Prentice-Hall, 1982.
Brown, Lester R. *World Without Borders.** New York: Vintage, 1973.
———. *In the Human Interest.** New York: W. W. Norton, 1974.
Falk, Richard A. *A Study of Future Worlds.* New York: Free Press, 1975.
Gilpin, Robert. *U.S. Power and the Multinational Corporation.* New York: Basic Books, 1975.
Hopkins, Raymond F., Robert L. Paarlberg, and Mitchel B. Wallerstein. *Food in the Global Arena.* New York: Holt, Rinehart & Winston, 1982.
Johansen, Robert. *The National Interest and the Human Interest.** Princeton, N.J.: Princeton University Press, 1980.
Keohane, Robert O., and Joseph S. Nye. *Power and Interdependence.** Boston: Little, Brown & Co., 1977.
———, eds. *Transnational Relations and World Politics.* Cambridge, Mass.: Harvard University Press, 1972.
Keohane, Robert O. *After Hegemony.* Princeton, N.J.: Princeton University Press, 1984.
Kim, Samuel S. *The Quest for a Just World Order.* Boulder, Colo.: Westview Press, 1984.
Kindleberger, Charles P., ed. *The International Corporation.* Cambridge, Mass.: M.I.T. Press, 1970.
Laqueur, Walter. *Terrorism.* Boston: Little, Brown & Co., 1977.
Maghoori, Ray, and Bennett Ramberg, eds. *Globalism vs. Realism.** Boulder, Colo.: Westview Press, 1982.
Mansbach, Richard W., Yale H. Ferguson, and Donald E. Lampert. *The Web of World Politics.** Englewood Cliffs, N.J.: Prentice-Hall, 1976.
Marden, Parker G., Dennis G. Hodgson, and Terry L. McCoy. *Population in the Global Arena.* New York: Holt, Rinehart & Winston, 1982.

Mendlovitz, Saul H. *On the Creation of a Just World Order.** New York: Free Press, 1975.

Miller, Lynn H. *Global Order.* Boulder, Colo.: Westview Press, 1985.

Phillips, Kevin T. *Staying on Top.* New York: Random House, 1985.

Pirages, Dennis. *Global Ecopolitics.** North Scituate, Mass.: Duxbury, 1978.

Rosecrance, Richard. *The Rise of the Trading State.* New York: Basic Books, 1986.

Said, Abdul, and Lutz R. Simons, eds. *The New Sovereigns.** Englewood Cliffs, N.J.: Prentice-Hall, 1975.

Spero, Joan E. *The Politics of International Economic Relations.** 2d ed. New York: St. Martin's Press, 1981.

Stanley, C. Maxwell. *Managing Global Problems.** Iowa City: University of Iowa (for the Stanley Foundation), 1979.

Sterling, Claire. *The Terror Network.** New York: Holt, Rinehart & Winston, 1981.

Taylor, Philip. *Nonstate Actors in International Politics.* Boulder, Colo.: Westview Press, 1982.

Tucker, Robert W. *The Inequality of Nations.* New York: Basic Books, 1977.

Vernon, Raymond. *Sovereignty at Bay.* New York: Basic Books, 1971.

____, ed. *The Oil Crisis.** New York: W. W. Norton, 1976.

Willetts, Peter, ed. *Pressure Groups in the International System.* New York: St. Martin's Press, 1982.

Wu, Yuan-li. *Raw Material Supply in a Multipolar World.** 2d ed. New York: Crane, Russak & Co. (for the National Strategy Information Center), 1979.

Index